ONE FINE DAY

Also by Matthew Parker

The Battle of Britain
Monte Cassino
Panama Fever (UK paperback: Hell's Gorge)
The Sugar Barons
Goldeneye
Willoughbyland

ONE FINE DAY

29 SEPTEMBER 1923

BRITAIN'S EMPIRE
ON THE BRINK

MATTHEW PARKER

abacus
books

ABACUS

First published in Great Britain in 2023 by Abacus

1 3 5 7 9 10 8 6 4 2

Copyright © Matthew Parker
Maps by Martin Brown

A CIP catalogue record for this book
is available from the British Library.

Hardback ISBN 978-1-4087-0858-3
Trade paperback ISBN 978-1-4087-0859-0

Typeset in Garamond by M Rules
Printed and bound in Great Britain by
Clays Ltd, Elcograf S.p.A.

Papers used by Abacus are from well-managed forests
and other responsible sources.

Abacus
An imprint of
Little, Brown Book Group
Carmelite House
50 Victoria Embankment
London EC4Y 0DZ

An Hachette UK Company
www.hachette.co.uk

www.littlebrown.co.uk

For Hannah

. . . .

And all sway forward on the dangerous flood
Of history that never sleeps or dies,
And, held one moment, burns the hand.

W.H. AUDEN
'To A Writer on his Birthday'

Contents

Contents

List of 1923 Maps

Author's Note

Most words associated with imperialism are loaded, of course. A number of writers in 1923 were well aware of this. With one exception, I've not expunged offensive words or phrases from direct quotations from contemporary sources, and for clarity I use the 1923 names for places.

Converting historical amounts of money to 'modern' values is far from simple. Different ways of calculating – cost of 'staples', average wages, inflation, the size of the economy – produce different answers. Perhaps it is easiest if we bear in mind that the average male factory-worker's wage in Britain in 1923 was about £200 per year. There were 12 pence ('d') in a shilling ('s') and 20 shillings in a pound.

This book includes extensive quotation from contemporary sources, which, together with pertinent secondary sources, are acknowledged with a number in the relevant position in the text. In order to keep the book to a manageable size, the corresponding details, including suggestions for further reading and a complete bibliography, can be found on and downloaded from my website www.matthewparker.co.uk.

Introduction

Only sympathy and knowledge are needed to complete
that stupendous edifice of Empire ... whose noble
example may well be the prelude to the Federation of
the World.

LIM BOON KENG,
Chinese community leader, Singapore[1]

On Saturday 29 September 1923, the Palestine Mandate became
law and the British Empire reached what would prove to be its
maximum territorial extent.[2]

Now the British Empire covered nearly 14 million square miles, 150
times the size of Great Britain and a quarter of the world's land area.
Four hundred and sixty million people, a fifth of the world's population,
woke that morning as subjects of Britain's King-Emperor George V.

One Fine Day is a new way of looking at the British Empire. It is
not encyclopedic; instead, travelling from east to west with the rising
sun – with occasional returns to London for the Imperial Conference –
it aims to immerse the reader in that moment, focusing on particular
people and stories from that day, gleaned from contemporary newspapers, letters, diaries, official documents, magazines, films and novels.

This takes in the new, more independent, attitudes of the Dominions to the empire, resistance and demands for change centred on Rotan Tito in the Pacific, Jawaharlal Nehru and Mohandas Gandhi in India, Tan Cheng Lock in Malaya, Sayadaw U Ottama in Burma, Harry Thuku and A. M. Jeevanjee in Kenya, Herbert Macaulay, Kobina Sekyi and Joseph Casely Hayford in West Africa, and the huge influence of Marcus Garvey across Africa and the Caribbean.

At the same time, we encounter colonial doctors, educators, policemen and officials, many now at best uncertain about the imperial mission.

On the centenary of its territorial zenith, the shared history of the British Empire is being vigorously debated, not just in Britain, but from Australia to Barbados. At the same time, autocratic imperialism – most notably in Russia and China – is on the rise. In many ways, the issues of a hundred years ago – only three or four generations past – are with us still: discussions around cultural and ethnic identity in a globalised world; how to manage multi-ethnic political entities; the persistent influence of racism; the divisive co-opting of religion for political purposes; the dangers of ignorance, cultural arrogance and self-interest. In other ways, most obviously in terms of technology, it is an alien world.

Perhaps most strange, however, is that only a hundred years ago one small country off the coast of Europe was the ruler of the largest empire in world history. Twenty-five years before, the Victorians had produced a stamp with a map of the world and the legend 'We hold a vaster empire than has ever been'. But under the terms of the Treaty of Versailles, Britain had now absorbed a further 1.8 million square miles and an additional 13 million subjects. As well as Palestine, Jordan, Iraq, Cameroon, Togo and Tanganyika all came under rule from London. Other areas in Africa and the Pacific were granted, within the empire, to the British white-run Dominions and the 'cadet' imperialists of South Africa, Australia and New Zealand.[3]

In keeping with the vision of former Colonial Secretary Winston Churchill, Palestine was now the keystone of a geopolitical and strategic arch that stretched from Cape Town to Cairo, across the Middle East and down to India, Burma, and all the way via Malaya to Australia and New Zealand. With a puppet ruler and British garrison installed in Persia, and Egypt under an entirely bogus 'flag of independence', you could now walk from Cape Town to Rangoon without ever leaving British-controlled territory.[4]

Prime Minister Stanley Baldwin's Foreign Secretary, former Viceroy of India Lord Curzon, declared that 'The British flag has never flown over a more powerful empire.' Technological advances in aircraft and bombs meant that vast territory could now be controlled on the cheap. There was talk of the British Empire, now the sole global superpower, becoming a 'federation of mankind', a structure for benign world government. The New Zealand Prime Minister William Massey, arriving in London that Saturday, 29 September, for the forthcoming Imperial Conference, told the press that 'The British Empire is today more necessary than ever to the welfare and peace of the world.' South African Prime Minister Jan Smuts called the British Empire 'the widest system of organized human freedom which has ever existed in human history'.[5]

But the Great War, while dramatically expanding the size of the empire, had changed everything.

This period became known to contemporaries as 'The Aftermath', and the shadow of the war fell over every part and aspect of the empire: military, political, financial, racial, psychological. The war had seen the empire at its most useful ever for the mother country – the huge contribution of money and nearly 2.5 million men from India, the Dominions and the African colonies had arguably made the difference between victory and defeat for Britain. As Major-General Sir Frederick B. Maurice, founder of the British Legion, declared in a lecture in the summer of 1923, the war had 'displayed the unity, the majesty, and the power of the British Empire to a degree which surpassed the expectations of the most ardent of the pre-war imperialists'. The editor of the *Observer*, in an article published on 30 September, described the 'Empire's world-wide rally in the war' as 'an immortal epic unsurpassed in history'.[6]

But in 1922, during the Chanak Crisis, when Prime Minister David Lloyd George had, without consulting, pledged the Dominions to fight against Turkey if war broke out again, they were outraged, and determined that only their own parliaments could decide war. So now the idea of a common foreign policy and unquestioned military alliance was under threat. The Imperial Conference of Dominion leaders, starting the following Monday, promised to be highly charged.

The war had also wrecked the international trading and financial system on which Britain's prosperity had been built. In September 1923, Rudyard Kipling, who famously had urged the United States to take up the 'White Man's Burden', gave a bad-tempered interview to the *New York World*: America, he said, 'came in the war 2 years, 4 months and 7 days too late, botched the Versailles Treaty for us, and withdrew without assisting any further. She has our gold, but we have our souls.' Indeed, there had been a tectonic shift in the distribution of gold reserves. In short, much of the world's gold was now sitting in Fort Knox or in the basement of the New York Fed. For its part, Britain was saddled with a vast war debt, including £900 million owed to the United States. New York was in the process of replacing London as the world's leading capital market.[7]

Mainland Europe was the best market for British exports, and had almost always been far more important than the empire. But this market had pretty much ceased to exist: post-war Europe was in ruins, with devalued currencies, hyperinflation and political chaos. Rival militias, including Hitler's Nazis, were fighting in the streets. Optimists hoped that the overseas markets of the empire could come to the rescue, but this would require them to grow substantially in population and wealth.

In the meantime, Britain was suffering high taxation and unemployment and ever harder cuts to government expenditure, including on defence. Among British political and military leaders, there was concern that particularly in these severely straitened post-war financial circumstances, the empire was now just far too big, 'a huge bladder waiting to be pricked', as German wartime propaganda had alleged.[8]

To make matters worse, in order to avoid antagonising the Americans, in the forlorn hope of debt reduction and with an irrational belief in the 'special relationship', Britain had just ended its treaty with Japan. It had also agreed to limits on its key strategic asset, the Royal Navy. The empire had never made strategic sense, with its closest allies on the other side of the world, but this now left the Far Eastern possessions, including Malaya, Burma and even Australia, intensely vulnerable to an expansionist and insulted Japan.

In other ways, the First World War, ostensibly fought against German autocracy and in the name of freedom, had cracked the foundations of the empire. Before the war, imperialism had been the familiar form of government for much of the globe. Now, 'empire' for many was a dirty word, conjuring up a 'vision of conquest, of domination, of the oppression of the weak'. The future seemed to belong to alternative forms of government – the nation state, democracy, communism, fascism. In Britain itself, 1918 had seen the ushering in of (almost) mass democracy for the first time, with a universal male franchise and votes for most women over thirty. Was real democracy at home compatible with autocratic imperialism abroad?[9]

For many defenders of British imperialism, the villain of the piece was US President Woodrow Wilson and his talk of 'self-determination' at Versailles. Although Wilson, a dyed-in-the wool segregationist and imperialist, had aimed his rhetoric at the imperial graveyard of central and eastern Europe rather than at Western overseas possessions, it 'struck at the roots of the British Empire' and encouraged anti-colonial forces around the world.[10]

Furthermore, a new, nuanced form of empire emerged from the Versailles Conference: the mandate system for ex-Axis imperial territories. Although in many ways a fig-leaf for an imperial land-grab, the League of Nations mandates were established in principle as a form of 'trusteeship', 'government in the interest of the governed' – territories were to be administered for the benefit of their populations with the express goal of moving them towards self-government in the near future. Such an idea could not be contained, and was soon being applied to the British Empire as a whole. This led to the reluctant granting of political reforms in India, Burma, Ceylon, Nigeria and elsewhere. On Saturday 29 September, the streets of Lagos were thronged with Nigerians celebrating the landslide victory of black Africa's first ever political party. Soon the imperial authorities realised that giving in to demands for reform merely stoked the demand for further constitutional changes. And in the light of these mandate and trusteeship ideas, was the empire's only purpose now to dismantle itself? Had it become nothing more than a 'self-liquidating concern'?[11]

So at its greatest ever extent, the empire was suffering a crisis of confidence, beset by debts and doubts. What *was* the empire, and what was it for?

Apart from the public-school-university elite who made up most of the senior colonial manpower, most British people's direct engagement with the empire came through supporting the efforts of missionaries, or through migration. There were few families who did not have at least one member who had migrated from the UK. But neither activity was dependent on direct imperial control of overseas territories.

In theory, the empire generated economic gain through producing raw materials, providing an outlet for capital, and importing finished goods from Britain. But, again, did this really require a hugely expensive imperial infrastructure? Britain's most important raw material import was cotton, most of which came from the United States; some of the most profitable investment was in South America, particularly Argentina; only a sixteenth of the imports of Malaya, the richest colony, were from Britain. Despite appeals to 'buy British', there was not a single colony that imported more cars from Britain than from the US, which turned out cheaper and better models.

The mass of red ink on a map of the world from September 1923 might give the impression that the empire was in some way homogeneous. Nothing could be further from the truth. The empire covered incredibly diverse parts of the world from frozen wastes to bustling cities to the thickest tropical jungle. It also took many forms: dominion, Crown colony, protectorate, mandate, sphere of influence. Some, like Malaya, were rich; others desperately poor. Jamaica had become almost derelict after the collapse of the sugar price the year before (Britain imported 90 per cent of its sugar from outside the empire anyway). In places like the

West Indies, imperial rule spanned all of recorded history; in others it had been established for only a few years, if that. In parts of Africa and the Pacific the British ruled over pre-industrial societies, while in India and Ceylon, for example, Britain was just the most recent of a string of imperial rulers of civilisations far older than Europe's. Many colonies' internal dynamics were a honeycomb of different and often conflicting religious, social, military, civilian and business interests. Above all, unlike many empires before, there was precious little coherence, unanimity or consistency of purpose from the metropolitan centre. All that could unite it, it was decided, was shared loyalty to the monarchy. This, it was hoped, could provide a visible embodiment for an otherwise diffuse and fragmented entity. The central vehicle of monarchical influence was the royal tour. Hence throughout the early 1920s the young, photogenic Prince of Wales – the future Edward VIII – would be sent on an almost endless global odyssey of 'palm and pine'.

Imperial cheerleaders in Britain promoted and justified the empire as a form of international altruism. The manifesto of the British Empire Union, while extolling the 'unifying influence of the Crown', was to teach the young to see the achievements of the empire in 'maintaining peace and bringing order, health, knowledge, improved conditions of life to formerly ignorant and primitive people'. These claims – around Pax Britannica, the rule of law, medicine, education and development – are all scrutinised here. None are as simple as they look. We see the First World War causing more deaths in East Africa than generations of 'tribal warfare'; the failure of courts in Kenya to provide justice for black victims of white violence; how in the Pacific, doctors, thinly stretched and presiding over a dramatic population collapse, were mainly dealing with diseases imported by whites; how in places, such as Malaya, education was being deliberately retarded in order to satisfy commercial needs and to prevent political opposition; how development – particularly in places under indirect rule in India, Malaya or Northern Nigeria – was seen by the coloniser as a mixed blessing at best. The British Empire Union might have added to the list of virtues the protection of minorities. But this, too, is complicated. In

many cases, such as Ceylon, Burma, Trinidad and Malaya, minorities
were only there because of the needs of the empire, and policies to protect them often made divisions worse.[12]

The empire was also seen in many quarters in Britain as an expression of racial pride and a result of racial superiority. 'We hold these
countries,' one empire-builder wrote in 1922, 'because it is the genius
of our race to colonise, to grade, to govern.' The issue of race – and
racism – dominated the empire. Nineteenth-century ideas of a social
Darwinian hierarchy of races, and race as a biological rather than cultural concept, had been widely discredited. In 1921, Indian politician
V. S. Srinivasa Sastri had secured from the Imperial Conference a
statement on the equality of races within the empire. But old attitudes
still dominated. A few years later, Sastri wrote to a supporter about a
meeting he had had with a senior civil servant in the Colonial Office.
'He depicted the struggle going on at present between two rival ideals
of the British Empire,' Sastri wrote. 'The one tending towards the
equalities of races and communities, the other insisting on the maintenance of white supremacy. The latter idea, till recently undisputed,
even now is in practice dominant, and prevails in most matters of
importance.' In reality, ideas of white supremacy remained a guiding
structural principle of the empire.[13]

This racist ideology was a coping stone of empire, explaining and
justifying white rule, while at the same time undermining the colonised's agency and self-respect. As Jamaica's first Prime Minister
Norman Manley would write, 'The Empire and British rule rest on a
carefully nurtured sense of inferiority in the governed.' In his country,
he saw this as creating 'turgid lethargy' and 'a culture of dependence'.
Jawaharlal Nehru wrote how 'surprisingly most of us accepted it as
natural and inevitable' that Indians were second rate. 'Greater than
any victory of arms or diplomacy was this psychological triumph of the
British in India,' he suggested. The French West Indian political phi-
losopher Frantz Fanon would write that because colonialism involved a
'systematic negation of the other person' it forced 'the people it dominated to ask the question constantly: "In reality, who am I?"'[14]

On a wider level, across the world, including among the indigenous populations of the white settler colonies, empire, globalisation and the 'challenge of modernity', had disrupted or destroyed traditional social structures and arrangements, with severely deleterious effects, from a crime wave in Burma to alcoholism among Aboriginal Australians to a refusal even to raise families in the Pacific Islands.

But things were changing. The edifice of white supremacy was starting to crumble. The defeat of the Italians in Africa in 1896, and then the victory of Japan over Russia in 1905, had seen white power overcome by the hands of the so-called lesser races. African-American leader W. E. B. Du Bois spoke of a worldwide eruption of 'colored pride'. The Japanese victory, he wrote, had 'broken the magic of the word "white"'. For Nehru in India, it 'diminished the feeling of inferiority' from which many of his compatriots suffered.[15]

Just as significant for colonised peoples was the cataclysm of the First World War, which made a mockery of the narrative of progress built around Western technological modernity. How could Europe continue with its claim of a 'civilising mission' when it could not contain its own barbaric violence? It was a huge blow to the all-important white prestige as well as to the confidence of the rulers.

At the same time, influential politicians and writers – Edward Blyden, Marcus Garvey, Joseph Casely Hayford, Gandhi and Tagore in India, and many others – were spreading a message of indigenous pride, ingenuity, intelligence and beauty that actively opposed the racist ideologies put forward by the colonial regimes. Booker Prize-winning novelist Chinua Achebe would write that 'Nigerians were taken out of our history and dumped in someone else's history'. Now anti-colonialists were urging the teaching of African history in schools, encouraging the appreciation of African art and music and the wearing of traditional dress, setting up African churches, newspapers and literary societies. The same process was underway in India, Ceylon, Burma, the Caribbean and elsewhere. Strong pan-Asian and pan-African movements were emerging.[16]

It was a fascinating balancing act for the colonised and the subject of great debate and even division. At its heart was the question: how do we compete through taking on the successful techniques of the West, without losing our own culture and identity? Education was a key site of debate: as Sierra Leonean teacher Adelaide Casely Hayford would ask, 'How can we educate and enlighten the African child without taking him too far away from his native environment?'[17]

Across the empire, colonial officials were witnessing a new confidence in the colonised. In Kenya, where previously 'the native employee was respectful and obedient ... now he has become openly insolent, disobedient and even menacing'. In Malaya, there were complaints that Chinese people were no longer serving Europeans first in shops, or stepping aside when Europeans were walking in the streets.[18]

Of course, anti-colonial interests were as varied as the empire itself and by no means homogeneous even in a single place. They did share a common opponent in the 'Empire' but this meant radically different things in different places. Nevertheless, networks existed underneath the official channels. The example of Ireland inspired Indians who in turn encouraged Burmese and Africans. And this moment in time does shine a light on some striking similarities – how from Canada to Africa to the Pacific there was a new post-war indigenous generation turning against those of their fathers or grandfathers who had signed away their land rights, aped the British or collaborated for their own benefit in some other way; and the growing importance of religion in shaping and inspiring local nationalisms as well as dividing indigenous communities in India, Sri Lanka and elsewhere.

In September 1923, it should be stressed, there was comparative tranquillity and widespread optimism about the future of the empire and world peace and prosperity after the 'War to end all wars'. There was a strong expectation that the United States would join the League of Nations.

Recent troubles and unrest in India, Iraq, Egypt, Ireland and elsewhere had abated or been crushed. At the end of the previous month, the victory in Ireland of William Cosgrave's pro-Treaty party over

Eamon de Valera's republicans had confirmed the Irish Free State as a Dominion of the empire, an arrangement believed to be a permanent and acceptable solution to an age-old problem.

The new 'trustee' relationship between coloniser and colonised, which included a widely professed concern for the well-being of 'native' people, together with new ideas about racial equality, promised a glorious and more humane future in a consensual empire, now increasingly being referred to as the British 'Commonwealth'. Here, equals would participate freely in what Lim Boon Keng called 'the greatest human enterprise in the world's history'. Of course, no one knew then that this moment was the empire's territorial zenith, that it was on the brink of a precipitous decline and that the 'sympathy and knowledge' 'needed to complete that stupendous edifice of Empire' would remain out of reach.[19]

PART ONE

THE SUN RISES

1

Consuming Ocean Island

There can be no civilization without population,
no population without food,
and no food without phosphate.

New Zealander ALBERT ELLIS[1]

B ritish Resident Commissioner Herbert 'Reggie' McClure woke
on the morning of 29 September 1923 to a dilemma that Franz
Kafka, currently writing *The Castle*, would have appreciated. McClure
was in charge of Ocean Island or, in local parlance, Banaba. He was in
an impossible and bizarre situation.

It was here, on that day, that the sun first rose over the British
Empire. Ocean Island was a place described as 'Eastwards as far as ship
can sail ... up against the gateways of the dawn.' Just a short distance
from the international dateline, this tiny island of 2.5 square miles,
6 miles in circumference, with a population of only 1,000, was now
in a surreal dilemma. It had been discovered that the island's entire
soil, thanks to almost unique geological factors, was pretty much pure
phosphate, an immensely valuable, even crucial resource for the wider
empire. So the soil was being dug out – the actual physical body of

the island was being removed in the hundreds of thousands of tons, shipped away for ever. As the very ground beneath their feet was disappearing, the island's inhabitants were making a stand, just as the company running the operation was now demanding more acreage for its excavations, and that the Resident Commissioner should help secure the agreement of the locals.[2]

The situation in Ocean Island is a microcosm of many of the challenges and dilemmas facing the empire in late September 1923: new resistance from the colonised across the empire; impossibly conflicting interests between government, the governed and business; issues of race, culture, labour, education, health, 'trusteeship'. But most of all – a crucial issue from Canada to Kenya and from Burma to southern Africa – land. And here it was *in extremis*. The land of Ocean Island, tiny as it was, wasn't just being 'nationalised', expropriated or purloined, it was being physically abducted.

McClure knew what had gone on over the past two decades, how the British officials in charge of Ocean Island, while in theory administering an impartial system, in practice had had to choose between their integrity and their careers.

Until the beginning of the twentieth century hardly anyone outside the region had known or cared about Ocean Island. McClure himself, who had had a long career stretching from the Boxer Rebellion in China to Australia and then nearly twenty years in Kenya, later admitted that when he was appointed Resident Commissioner (RC) on Ocean Island in 1921, he had no idea where it was.[3]

While the group of Pacific islands to the east had in 1892 been declared the British Protectorate of the Gilbert and Ellice Islands, Ocean Island, on its own, isolated 500km to the west, had been ignored. Then, at the turn of the century, a New Zealander, Albert Ellis, working for the Pacific Islands Company, a business trading in coconut products and guano, took a second look at a block of supposed fossilised wood being used in his Sydney office as a doorstop. The lump was from Nauru, which lies 250 miles to the west of Ocean Island. Tests showed it to be almost pure rock phosphate, an immensely valuable commodity used to make fertilisers. Nauru had been declared German, when in 1886, for reasons of faraway realpolitik, a line had been drawn delineating German from British spheres of influence in the Pacific. So in early 1900, Ellis headed for nearby Ocean Island, on the off-chance that it might have the same money-spinning geological origin.

All his hopes were met and more. 'There is phosphate *everywhere*,' he wrote in his diary. What's more, it was phosphate of the highest quality in the world.[4]

There were plenty of rival companies who would leap on the money-making opportunity the island offered. Ellis had to do a deal with the Banabans as fast as he could.

The Banabans were one of the world's great survivors. They had to be. Their home, like most of the rest of the Gilbert and Ellice Islands, was small – land was at a premium – and infertile. The phosphate soil was of no use as a fertiliser until it had been industrially processed.

Most of all, the island was starved of water. In the centre of Ocean Island were limestone caves in which sparse rainfall gathered. But in times of drought this would become insufficient for drinking purposes, let alone for watering crops or the coconut palms on which the small population largely depended. Desperate measures undertaken included heading out into the wider ocean in canoes with receptacles to chase rain clouds.

By general agreement, families were kept small – birth control methods included abortion and infanticide – and food sources such as giant taro and pandanus, elsewhere considered too unappetising or laborious to process, were mainstays. So, since first arriving as migrants from Micronesia 1,500 years before, the Banabans had survived against the odds in this inhospitable spot.

Across the region, sustained contact with the outside world long pre-dated the arrival of the imperial flag. For several decades from the 1820s, the waters of the central Pacific hosted whaling ships. By the 1840s there were more than 600, mostly American, following the

THE PACIFIC

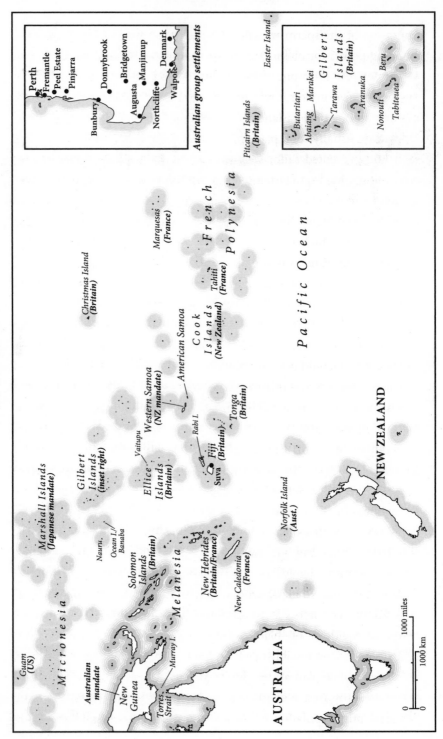

Guam
(US)

Marshall Islands
(Japanese mandate)

M i c r o n e s i a

Australian
mandate

New
Guinea

Solomon
Islands (Britain)

Gilbert
Islands
(inset right)

Nauru.
Ocean I./
Banaba

Christmas Island
(Britain)

M e l a n e s i a

New Hebrides
(Britain/France)

New Caledonia
(France)

Ellice
Islands
(Britain)

Vaitupu

Western Samoa
(NZ mandate)

American Samoa

C o o k
I s l a n d s
(New Zealand)

Marquesas
(France)

F r e n c h
P o l y n e s i a

Tahiti
(France)

Rabi I.

Tonga
(Britain)

Fiji
(Britain)
Suva

Norfolk Island
(Aust.)

Pitcairn Islands
(Britain)

Easter Island

P a c i f i c   O c e a n

Murray I.
Torres
Strait

AUSTRALIA

NEW ZEALAND

1000 miles
1000 km

0
0

Inset (top): Australian group settlements

Perth
Fremantle
Peel Estate
Pinjarra
Bunbury
Donnybrook
Augusta
Bridgetown
Manjimup
Northcliffe
Denmark
Walpole

Australian group settlements

Inset (bottom): Gilbert Islands

Butaritari
Abaiang
Marakei
Tarawa
Aranuka
Nonouti
Tabiteuea
Beru

G i l b e r t
I s l a n d s
(Britain)

migration of the sperm whales. The Pacific islands became important stopping points for picking up provisions, crewmen and the company of women. At least one ship would call per week at Ocean Island during the season and it was not unusual to have two or three vessels moored off one of the islands at the same time.

Trading usually took place on board ship where it was quicker and safer and prevented sailors deserting. Islanders sold coconuts for the crew to eat and also to fatten the pigs kept on board; also fish, fruit and vegetables, hats, mats, fish hooks, and curios such as spears fashioned from shell and wood. Sex was for sale at the same price as a woven hat, a mat or half a chicken.

Iron of any kind was sought by islanders, also ready-made metal tools. But soon one product dominated the exchange. At some point, probably in the early 1820s, tobacco was introduced to the Gilberts, previously innocent of its appeal. By the 1850s the entire region was hooked: men, women and children smoked, chewed and ate the drug whenever they could get hold of it.

For the whalers and other traders, it was good business. A compact, cheap and easily transportable product now commanded a huge profit margin. Handicrafts that had taken many months to produce could be acquired for a small plug of inferior chewing tobacco. Even well-chewed pieces from the 'spit-box' were highly prized by the islanders. Robert Louis Stevenson, who lived in Abemama in the Gilberts for several months in 1888, reported that when trade goods were displayed to the wives of the island chief, including ribbons, tinned food, perfumes and dresses, 'they had but one idea – tobacco, the island currency, tantamount to minted gold'.[5]

Alongside the whalers, who would occasionally take on men as crew, labour recruiters started appearing among the islands. There were notorious incidents of 'blackbirding': inhabitants of the easternmost Ellice Islands were forcibly taken on board and shipped to guano mines in Peru or coffee plantations in Central America. Others were tricked with false promises. Nonetheless, up to a quarter of the Gilbert and Ellice Islands' population of 30,000 at some point worked away from home, the most popular destinations being the plantations of Fiji and Tahiti, and from the 1860s Samoa, where the Hamburg firm J. C. Godeffroy und Sohn were investing huge sums in cotton and coconut plantations. Most islanders worked for a season, then returned home to share their experiences of Europeans, Americans and the wider world.

After peaking in the 1850s, the Pacific whaling industry declined, and some captains moved to trading in coconut oil, an essential ingredient of soap and candles. The emphasis was soon on copra – dried coconut flesh from which oil could be extracted. This became big business, driven by entrepreneurs from Sydney and Liverpool, as well as German companies. Among them was Albert Ellis's Pacific Islands Company (PIC).

Thus by the end of the nineteenth century almost every islander was selling his or her surplus production into an international market, and had been introduced to the ways of wider commerce and wage labour. Men like Albert Ellis saw this process as both inevitable and, particularly combined with Christianity, to the definite benefit of the islanders.

Ocean Island, however, was the poor man of the region. Apart from abundant firewood from the fast-growing calophyllum trees that formed a thick forest on the island's central upland, they had little surplus to trade. And in the 1870s and again in the 1890s the island was struck by two of the worst droughts in its modern history.

A whaling ship that stopped at Ocean Island in 1873 found the Banabans starving and out of pity took twenty-four to another, less hard-hit island. Two years later a labour recruiter found the situation on the island so bad that 'practically all the children died'. To reduce the number of mouths to feed, female children were being killed. From a population of over 1,000 in 1870, by the time of Ellis's visit, thanks to emigration, imported diseases and starvation, there were fewer than 500.[6]

Having gone ashore with two colleagues from his company and discovered the island's rich deposits, Ellis began negotiations with a man called Temati, whom Ellis called the island's king, as well as with another 'chief', both illiterate. In the meantime, his doctor colleague busied himself treating islanders suffering with yaws – tropical skin ulcers. Ellis promised, through an interpreter, that his company would build water tanks and a distillation plant so that the island would never again lack for water. He pledged that they would bring medicines to deal with the serious syphilis problem (a legacy of the whalers). What he demanded, and got, was exclusive mining and trading rights on the island for 999 years in return for an annual payment of £50 in trade goods from the company store that would be established.

In fact, Ocean Island did not have a king – each of the four villages had its own chief – and even if it had, he would have had no right to agree to the contract as land was held by individuals not the chief. But the deal, fateful for the Banabans, was done. Two days later, on 5 May 1900, Ellis raised a flag – actually a blue ensign – declaring 'its never failing message of good cheer for the natives', and announcing that the island 'belonged to her Majesty'.[7]

Although there were objections, the monopoly was licensed thanks to a well-connected chairman and directors of the PIC in London, and in September 1901 a British man-of-war turned up at Ocean Island officially to raise the flag and Banaba became part of the Gilbert and Ellice Islands Protectorate.

Despite the immensely generous terms that Ellis had secured, the company at first struggled to raise capital for the project. Then William Lever – later Lord Leverhulme – who had interests in the Pacific copra business, stepped in and took a large stake. It turned out to be one of his best-ever investments. In 1902, the PIC became the Pacific Phosphate Company (PPC) and started doing individual rental deals with land-owners on Ocean Island (thereby admitting that the original contract was nonsense). Then the phosphate began to flow. Ellis had, of course, known the key markets for the island's phosphate – Australia and New Zealand. Both had created an economic model for themselves, even a *raison d'être*, as the agricultural powerhouses of the empire, supplying the vast British market with food. Wheat was Australia's biggest export and New Zealand already had millions of sheep. But there was a snag: the two countries weren't actually very fertile. Both had large areas of soil with deficiencies in nitrogen, phosphorus and sulphur. A later New Zealand Minister for Agriculture confessed that there were very few areas in his country where crops or pastures could be grown without phosphate.

The Ocean Island deposits, formed from sedimentation over millions of years as the island rose above and then fell below the sea level, had a particularly high quantity of calcium phosphate that, when subjected to sulphuric acid, unlocked a valuable source of phosphoric acid, the key ingredient of all phosphorus-bearing fertilisers. This 'superphosphate' radically improved the capacity of plant roots to absorb minerals and water from the soil, increasing crop yields and fostering the growth of grass fields for grazing. Land previously considered useless could be made home to prosperous farms.

For Australia, it was seen as a strategic as well as an economic necessity. Billy Hughes, Prime Minister from 1915 to 1923, would write: 'Without a sure and reasonably cheap supply of phosphate our agriculture must languish and instead of peopling our vast unoccupied interior population will continue to hug the seaboard where they will be comparatively easy prey to any predatory power.' Sir James Mitchell, who as a dynamic Premier of Western Australia wanted to increase the population there for the same reason, would declare: 'Gold brought these men to Western Australia, and superphosphate will keep them here.'[8]

Some 25,000 tons of phosphate were shipped from Ocean Island to Australia in 1903, and it was less than half the price of the bone meal used previously. Cheaper fertiliser not only meant bigger profits, it also lowered the price that the British consumer paid for their food. This chimed with the aspirations of pretty much every modern British government. In addition, it helped British industry, who could then keep productivity high by paying lower wages to its workers. Thus the Ocean Island mining concern became a key cog in an international system of unquestioned benefit to the wider empire – or, as Ellis might have put it, to civilisation itself. It also had very significant vested interests keen on keeping the supply going, as British officials would soon discover.

From a start with a few men with pickaxes and baskets, the mining operation rapidly increased its mechanisation and scale of production. As well as local Banabans, men were recruited from the nearby Gilbert Islands, and skilled or semi-skilled workers from Japan. Within a few years there were 350 Japanese and 700 Gilbertese managed by about eighty white employees, almost all from Australia or New Zealand. Wages for everyone were significantly higher than anywhere else in the region.

The company in this respect could afford to be generous. The PPC was soon making a fortune, paying dividends of up to 50 per cent. By 1908 it was shipping 200,000 tons of phosphate a year, mainly to Australia and New Zealand but also to Japan and further afield. The value of the phosphate sent to Australia alone was more than £300,000 per annum. The previous year the company had done a deal with the Germans on Nauru Island to mine there as well. Nauru was bigger than Ocean Island but had phosphate deposits of less depth and quality. Reflecting Ocean Island's importance, the seat of government – and the Resident Commissioner – of the Gilbert and Ellice Islands Protectorate was moved there in 1908. As part of its deal with the British government, the company was paying a royalty of 6d a ton to this local administration, which, together with customs duties and shipping charges, made up about half of its revenue. As was the model across the empire, private enterprise was paying a significant portion of the cost of government.[9]

The diary from 1906 of a young woman, Lilian Arundel, visiting her father, the company's manager, gives a snapshot of the island just before this transitional moment. She noticed the 'striking contrast' between the comfortable dwellings of the European residents and those of the native Banabans and imported workers. Europeans had electric light until 10 p.m., sewerage, telephones, and deliveries of ice, wood and coal. Most food was from tins, but once a fortnight a steamer from Sydney would bring fresh meat, fruit and vegetables. Although the

company had built a plant that produced 400 gallons of water a day, it
was still at a premium, so most washing was done in salt water with just
a fresh water rinse. In the two European settlements now established,
there were 'hospitals, a dispensary, recreation and mess rooms'. All this
created work for the locals, and with the water supply secure, Banabans
who had left the island began to return and the population started to
recover.[10]

Lilian Arundel enjoyed the warm but breeze-refreshed climate and
had great affection for the Banabans, being particularly impressed by
their extraordinary fishing skills. Exploring the island, she came across
'dense green foliage', 'many beautiful flowering trees' and 'luxuriant,
trumpet-shaped hibiscus flowers, scarlet, pink, cream and white'.
Overall, she found the island a place 'with freedom, romance and
beauty unequalled in any other part of the world'.

There was one note of caution: since the start of mining, 'it is
remarkable what a lot has been done since then, and what a vast undertaking it is now'.

With further investment in machinery and port facilities, the undertaking just grew and grew. In 1909 an acting Resident Commissioner,
Arthur Mahaffy, took over for six months. He had visited the island
in 1896 and was now amazed by the scale of the operation and the
changes to the landscape. On arrival he 'found four or five 6000-ton
steamers waiting to carry away the very ground on which I stood'.
And this was the rub. In the mined-out areas, nothing remained
except spikes of coral rock. In theory, the land was to be returned to
the Banabans once the company was finished with it, but it was now
utterly worthless, a sterile soil-less wasteland. Furthermore, although
the company had promised not to encroach on food-growing areas or
to destroy food-producing trees, the spirit of this had not been adhered
to. Mining had carried on right up to the trunks of valuable trees,
fatally exposing their roots, and land not rented whose perimeter had
been mined to a depth of 10 feet or more had become unproductive as
well as sometimes difficult to access.[11]

Mahaffy complained about the living conditions of the workers but was most struck by this effect of the mining: he realised that it was rapidly making the island uninhabitable. He suggested a vigorous programme of land reclamation and tree planting on the mined-out land, but found the company unresponsive. The locals, Ellis argued, were too lazy to look after new trees. Furthermore, although the company conceded that the mined land was 'of little use to the natives unless trees are again planted on it', they argued that 'concern or financial provision for the long-term welfare of the Banabans was premature on the grounds that by the time the island was worked out, perhaps a century hence, the native inhabitants of Ocean Island' – already few – 'may not improbably have wholly disappeared'.[12]

But the islanders were not quite ready to disappear so conveniently.

Their 'main idea', reported Mahaffy's successor as Resident Commissioner, 'seemed to be to preserve the island for their descendants; they said that they had been foolish in the past in disposing of their land, but now realised the mistake they had made, as they had no idea when the company started operations that it would result in the devastation of the island'. Even Ellis, who by now was the company's manager on Ocean Island, admitted that 'they had no adequate idea what they were letting themselves in for'.[13]

The Banabans now steadfastly refused to lease any more land to the company. 'They asked what they should do when the big steamers carried away all their land,' reported the *Sydney Morning Herald* in 1912, 'yet it is inconceivable that less than 500 Ocean Island-born natives can be allowed to prevent the mining and export of a product of such immense value to all the rest of mankind.'

The new Resident Commissioner, John Quayle-Dickson, had come from South Africa, where he had fought in the Boer War and had thereafter been an adviser on native affairs. Described by a subordinate as a 'haughty old man from the Veldt', his career so far had been characterised by administrative and financial incompetence. But he knew enough about money to question the vast scale of the dividends the company was paying against benefit to the islanders. In fact, looking at tons per acre extracted and profit per ton, the company was making something like

£14,000 on land that had cost them less than £20. By 1913, the mining operation had cleared a profit of £1.75 million and paid the Banabans less than £10,000. Furthermore, it was clear to Dickson, as it had been to Mahaffy, that the mining operation was making the Banabans' island home, at some point in the near future, uninhabitable.[14]

Dickson felt that the money being offered for further land was totally inadequate. He suggested that the company should pay £100 an acre, proper compensation for loss of trees, and a royalty per ton into a fund for the Banabans towards the cost of relocation should they be forced to find somewhere else to live. Effectively, he took their side, backing their refusal to give up further land, and 'made the strongest representations to the colonial office in favour of the oppressed land-owners'. He also sent Ellis photographs of the destruction that his company was causing.[15]

This irritated the company and embarrassed the Colonial Office (CO), and very soon Dickson was removed, demoted and sent to the remote Falkland Islands, possibly the empire's most dismal posting. Dickson even had to pay his own fare. He retired soon afterwards; 'his heart', he wrote, 'was broken'.

How much his removal owed to administrative incompetence rather than his support for the Banabans is not clear. Certainly, among those enjoying the vast dividends of the PPC were some of the most powerful and well-connected men in the empire. Whatever the truth, his sacking would be used by the company as leverage over succeeding Resident Commissioners.

The Colonial Office now negotiated in London directly with the company, and in fact many of Dickson's suggestions were adopted. Under new proposals, in addition to the 6d per ton to government, another 6d a ton would be paid into a trust fund for the Banabans; land was to be replanted after mining and there was to be compensation for the loss of food-bearing trees. The rental price per acre was to rise from £40 to £60, depending on the land's phosphate worth. Under these terms, the company wanted to lease a further 145 acres, in addition to the 105 already held.

A number of questions had recently been asked in Parliament about the government authorising the original 1900 deal and it had been pointed out that many of the directors of the company had recently 'held positions of trust' in the Pacific or the Colonial Office (the company chairman Lord Stanmore was a former High Commissioner for the Western Pacific; another director was a former permanent Under-Secretary of State for the Colonies). It was alleged that the royalty of 6d a ton was based on the company's statement that the phosphate was worth 10s a ton, when in fact the actual price was over £2. All this came amid accusations in the House of Commons of 'unjust taxation, ill-treatment of natives, and general mal-administration'. Calls for an independent investigation were rebuffed for now, with the explanation that 'the position of the Government is difficult in this matter, seeing that the arrangement was made with the natives before the British Government had anything to do with the island'. (Many years later, this excuse would be reprised.) Nonetheless, this public scrutiny prodded both the company and the CO to offer better terms.[16]

The man sent out to replace Dickson and to persuade the islanders to accept this new deal was a rising star of the Colonial Office. As he put it, 'because of my success in the past with native races I had been chosen to bring the Ocean Islanders to reason'.[17]

Unlike most Colonial Office officials, Edward Eliot had not followed the usual path of private school then university. His father was a curate in Wiltshire and his family's funds were limited. Priority was given to his brilliant brother Charles, eight years older, who won all the prizes at Eton, and having read Greats at Oxford became a high-flying diplomat, speaking twenty languages. In 1901 Charles was appointed Commissioner for Kenya, then the British East Africa Protectorate. He was responsible more than any other one person for the situation in Kenya during the second half of 1923 that so dominated coverage of the empire in the British press. By September 1923 Sir Charles Eliot was British ambassador to Japan.

His younger brother Edward had to forgo university and instead left England aged eighteen with £50 in his pocket. For two years he worked as a rancher and in a railway gang in Argentina, then he became an overseer on a sugar plantation in British Guiana. Through a friend of his brother he got a junior job in the government there, which led to an appointment in the Gold Coast at the time of the brutal war against the Asante. Having risen quickly through the ranks, he was promoted again to Deputy Governor of Trinidad. In 1913 he was transferred to Ocean Island, where, he later wrote, 'I met my Waterloo.'

It was clear that the company was in a hurry to acquire more land, so Eliot immediately got to work. 'With no knowledge of its iniquitous past history,' he later wrote, 'I eventually managed to persuade the younger generation on Ocean Island that the terms I had to offer would turn them into a rich community.' It helped that he demanded, and got, an undertaking from the company immediately to pay a backdated contribution to the new Banaban fund for July 1912 to July 1913, totalling £4,743. This could be spent on improving the island, or anything else subject to Eliot 'being satisfied that it was not used for any wasteful purpose'. He also secured a promise that the company would not subsequently demand more land and that the Banabans would not be forced to leave the island without their consent.

Although Eliot pointed out that the phosphate was of no value to the islanders if the white man did not buy it from them, many of the older men refused to part with any more land at any price. But enough of the younger Banabans signed the deal that the company now had sufficient land to continue their operations 'for a number of years to come'.

The other important factor was Dickson. He had established the position of Resident Commissioner in the eyes of the Banabans as a defender of their interests. This belief was transferred to Eliot. They trusted him. When he asked them to sign, most of them did.

Eliot almost instantly regretted this success. He had had vague doubts about whether the situation was 'not fair and straightforward'. With the deal already done, Eliot started to probe. He ordered an independent survey of the mining areas and discovered that encroachments on to unleased land and wanton destruction of trees was commonplace. He looked into the original 1900 agreement and interviewed its signatories, concluding that the sum of £50 a year was 'ludicrous', 'worth more like £15 in overpriced trade goods'. It was 'an iniquitous agreement made by the PPC with a totally illiterate community of natives', 'done with the knowledge of permanent officials of the Colonial Office'. His conclusion was that the CO official who had approved it was hoping 'that the Company would show appreciation ... in a tangible manner'.[18]

He also discovered that the Banabans, whom he patronisingly described as a 'delightful', 'docile, friendly and childlike' people, were far from unaware what was being done to them: now 'no Banaban would work at any price for the hated Company which was despoiling their island', he reported.

Hitting back at the company, he forced them to change their policy of selling goods in their store at a discount to white employees. When he discovered that the company had been making 'thousands of pounds a year' out of selling water to the locals, he demanded that they 'provide one gallon of fresh water per diem whenever necessary at the price of three farthings per gallon'.

Not all his efforts were successful. He later wrote: 'I pressed them to improve the housing conditions of the Gilbert and Ellice labourers. The local Manager of the Company told me in my own house, and before my wife, that if I tried to force them to spend what they considered unnecessary money, the Company would call on the Colonial Office to remove me, as they had removed my predecessor.'[19]

With the Great War over, in late 1919 Eliot left on leave back to England. In June the following year the Pacific Phosphate Company was nationalised, bought out by the governments of Britain, Australia and New Zealand, who formed a new organisation, the British Phosphate Commission (BPC), which would run profit-free operations on both Nauru (taken from the Germans at the beginning of the war) and Ocean Island, and supply the phosphate to imperial farmers at cost price, about half the market value. Despite complaints in the House of Commons from the Tory benches that this was a 'socialistic policy', the purchase was made for £3.5 million. The BPC would continue to

contribute to the Banaban fund, and pay for British administration in
the islands, and it took on many of the old company's bosses, including
its MD, Alwin Dickinson, who became UK Commissioner, and Albert
Ellis, who was appointed New Zealand Commissioner. Although
articles specified that governments should not interfere in the running
of the new commission, the industry now had an even more direct
line to the Colonial Office, and was more than ever 'for the greater
Imperial good'.[20]

Edward Eliot was urged to return to Ocean Island to explain to the
Banabans the changes because they had shown such trust in him. He
refused, as 'my natives there would ask me certain questions which
I was not in a position to explain'. He had no faith in the new commission honouring the terms of the agreement he had facilitated and
realised that he had pushed the Banabans much closer to having to
abandon their island. His only hope was that 'the commercial atmosphere of Ocean Island would have so affected the Banabans' that they
would lose their ties to their ancestral land. As his successor Reggie
McClure would discover in 1923, this was far from the case.

Eliot's refusal to return in 1920, he later wrote, 'sealed my fate as far
as my future in the service was concerned'. 'The authorities were anxious to keep me in harness to muzzle me', and for the following seven
years he languished in roles of ever-decreasing importance. September
1923 saw him in charge of the tiny Caribbean island of Dominica; it
wasn't quite the Falkland Islands but it was still a backwater of a backwater. He loved the beauty of Dominica but, he later wrote, the zest
had gone out of him and he had lost his faith in the Colonial Office.
From his time in 'the Ocean Island farce' he had 'received a scar which
will not heal this side of the Styx'. The 'sorry tale', as Eliot put it, had
managed to cost him both his integrity and his career.[21]

Reggie McClure and his wife Dorothy arrived at the beginning of
1922, and the new Resident Commissioner had immediately made a
good impression. He was far more genial and relaxed than the 'satur-
nine' Eliot or 'haughty' Dickson – he was thought to be 'humorous

and kind' – and he soon proved himself accomplished at sorting out disputes among the workers or between the commission and its employees.[22]

In 1919, complaining about the high prices in the commission's store, the Japanese workers had gone on strike demanding a 20 per cent increase in wages. So they were replaced with Chinese labourers shipped out of Hong Kong. Gilbert and Ellice Islanders performed the tricky job of manning the boats that took the phosphate to steamers waiting beyond the reef.

The mined-out areas of the island were by now a desiccated industrial moonscape of dust and limestone pinnacles, 'a wilderness of blazing rocks where never a blade of green could grow for cover from the sun's blistering glare', as a British official described it. Heat from the exposed white coral blasted into the air, dispersing clouds that might otherwise have provided much-needed rain. Work in these areas was both unpleasant and hazardous. The official correspondence reported that on 3 August 1923 a Chinese worker, Cheung Po, was killed when a piece of rock fell on his head. McClure gave him his name; to McClure's superiors he was known only as Coolie No. 360. Apparently 'Chinese overseer No. 322' had warned him that his position was not a safe one, but he had been ignored. The white overseer, Mr Clow, 'arrived on the scene a few minutes afterwards and hurried the coolie to hospital', McClure reported, 'but I understand he died on the way'. A compensation payment to his family of £19 4s was sent to the Secretary for Chinese Affairs in Hong Kong.[23]

Workers were issued with no sort of protective equipment, and the dust from the excavations and the crushing plant caused frequent respiratory diseases. This was made worse by the lack of rainfall. This had been particularly bad during the war, and much of the island's vegetation had died, including the desultory attempts at replanting mined-out areas. Happily, McClure later wrote, 'there was no actual want of water for drinking by reason of the existence of the condensing plant which the forethought of the Pacific Phosphate Company had caused to be constructed'.[24]

Almost no Banabans worked for the BPC, but instead hung on living on the viable land that remained to them. During 1922 and 1923, large concrete-lined reservoirs were constructed for each of the four Banaban villages, as had been done earlier for the two European settlements. The population continued to rise, families allowed to grow in size. Each reservoir cost about £450 in labour and materials, money which came from their Banaban fund. From 1920 onwards, this had an income of about £5,000 per year, and was worth just short of £20,000 by the end of 1923. McClure wrote that the Banabans were 'probably the richest natives in the world'. Expenditure was suggested by the Banaban council of elders, the Kaubure, subject to approval by McClure. In each of the three years before the end of 1923, the new Banaban hospital received about £500, as did the Banaban school. In 1923, £340 was paid to 'Old Banabans' at a rate of about £5 each, on the basis that they would not be around to enjoy the benefits of the fund in later years.[25]

Then, on 29 September 1923, a letter arrived at the Colonial Office from the British Phosphate Commissioner Alwin Dickinson, addressed to the Colonial Secretary, the Duke of Devonshire. Plans were afoot to build a cantilever at Ocean Island that could deliver the crushed phosphate at a rate of 400 tons an hour directly into the holds of steamers waiting in the deep water beyond the reef. To make this worthwhile, new drying and crushing facilities would be needed. To feed them, the commission needed more land, specifically 'about 150 acres in the Northern Area', the richest of the yet-unexploited deposits. Would His Grace approve this and 'inform the Resident Commissioner accordingly by telegraph and ask him to render his assistance in the negotiations with the native land owners?' At the bottom of the letter a Colonial Office official had wearily written: 'This will raise the whole question of the future of the Banabans and the position of Ocean Island.'[26]

This was followed by another letter from the BPC, dated 29 September, anticipating debates at the Imperial Conference due to start the following Monday. They knew the tricky subjects of imperial preference and a self-sustaining empire would be discussed. The commission stressed the immense value of the deposits of Ocean Island and Nauru and pointed out that they 'no doubt constitute over 80% of the quantity of phosphate available within the Empire'. To fail to support the BPC and instead be forced to buy elsewhere was only draining imperial coffers to the benefit of rival powers.[27]

McClure did not have a direct line to Devonshire. He reported through the High Commissioner of the Western Pacific based in Fiji, 1,200 miles away. As well as being Governor of Fiji, the High Commissioner had responsibility for the Solomon Islands, the Gilbert and Ellice Islands, the New Hebrides, Tonga and Pitcairn. On 29 September 1923, the man in this post was Sir Cecil Hunter-Rodwell. After Eton and Cambridge, he had fought in the South African War and then stayed on in the South Africa High Commission before being sent to Fiji in 1918. He is best known now for a later posting in Southern Rhodesia from 1928. When asked by a Jesuit missionary for funds to build a hospital for the black community there, he replied, 'Why do you worry about a hospital? After all, there are too many natives in the country already.' The comment was overheard by young Robert Mugabe, who never forgot nor forgave it.

The CO sent the BPC request for more land to Rodwell, who passed it on to McClure. The Resident Commissioner replied that the 'application involves interference with one village [Buakonikai] and commencement of alienation of entire best food producing area both within 5 years. It is almost inevitable that eventual removal of Banabans elsewhere must follow. Anticipate vigorous initial protest by Banabans.' During negotiations, he softened the blow by excluding parts of the village and 50 acres of the best food-growing land, but it made no difference. 'I have failed to secure consent of Banabans to any further extension *whatever* of existing mining areas,' he reported.[28]

McClure could see the islanders' point of view. If the extension of the mining areas went ahead, they 'would have found themselves insufficiently provided with indigenous foods and the problem of their ultimate disposal would have become acute'. He reminded his

superiors that the Banabans had been promised that they would never
have to leave '*without their full consent*' (emphasis in the original). He
also reported a new centre of resistance. While in 1913 it had been
the older men who had argued against giving up land, now it was
the young men, and new leadership. Rotan Tito, from a landowning
family that had been one of the first to convert to Christianity, had
been educated by missionaries in the Gilberts and was literate, articulate and determined. He made it absolutely clear to McClure that the
Banabans desired 'to remain in undisputed possession of the remainder
of their land for ever'. This meant, as McClure spelled out, that once
the current mining areas were exhausted, the activities of the British
Phosphate Commission 'shall automatically cease'.[29]

Upon 'questions of Imperial requirements in the matter of valuable
fertilizer', McClure wrote, he was 'not qualified to speak'. But he knew
that he and his fellow British officials on Ocean Island were in an
impossible situation.

2

'The Great Inter-Britannic Council'

> Without its overseas possessions the United Kingdom is
> merely a small group of islands off the coast of Europe;
> with them, it has become one of the poles of the
> human race.
>
> ALBERT DEMANGEON,
> *L'Empire britannique*, Paris 1923[1]

Early in the morning on Saturday 29 September 1923, the plump, balding figure of William Mackenzie King, Prime Minister of Canada, disembarked from the steamer *Montcalm* in Liverpool. He was met by the Canadian High Commissioner and a gaggle of journalists. It was a 'great privilege', King said, to have 'the chance to confer with the British Prime Minister and the Prime Ministers of the Dominions'. The purpose of the forthcoming Imperial Conference, he said, was to 'safeguard the permanence of the empire'. Canadian loyalty, he went on, 'can be taken for granted', and he had 'great pride in the British Empire – that it has stood for peace, justice, and good will among men'.[2]

New Zealand Prime Minister William Massey and South African Prime Minister Jan Smuts were already in London and that afternoon would meet British PM Stanley Baldwin in Downing Street. Massey had arrived the day before, the journey having taken him only thirty days rather than the usual six weeks. According to the press reports he was looking 'particularly well' as he announced that 'If anything happened to break up the Empire, world chaos would ensue.' Stanley Bruce, Australian PM, interviewed a couple of days earlier as he passed through the Suez Canal, said his desire was 'to ensure a strong and virile British Empire which should be the precursor of a world-alliance'.[3]

Prime Minister Smuts, who had moved from Boer general in the war against Britain to ardent imperialist, was delighted by the British gains from Germany that had at last created the 'all-red' route from the Cape to Cairo, what Smuts called 'a great white Africa along the eastern backbone'. The empire, he declared, had 'emerged from the awful blizzard of the War quite the greatest power in the world'.[4]

He was right. The collapse of the rival empires of Russia, Germany, Austria-Hungary and the Ottomans, and the retreat into isolation of the United States, had left the British Empire the sole global superpower. The population of her vast territories at 460 million far exceeded that of Russia (about 135 million), the United States (about 112 million) and France (93 million). And then there was the informal empire of trade and investment beyond the imperial frontiers. London, the world's most populous city, was the centre of global business and information, a shipping and cable hub communicating news, opinion, values and ideas across the world.

Contemporary neutral observers seemed to concur. Sorbonne professor and self-styled 'colonial geographer' Albert Demangeon, in a book just published in Paris, wrote that 'the idea of the might and solidity' of the British Empire 'impresses itself upon the mind'. For him, it was trade above all – 'the gold and diamonds of South Africa; the wool, wheat, butter, and meat of Australia; the wheat, fish, and timber of Canada; the sugar of the West Indies; the rubber and tin of Malaya; the wheat, cotton, jute, rice, and tea of India' – that had established British global supremacy. Indeed, within the empire was produced a quarter of the world's wheat and around half its rice, wool, chrome and tin as well as 60 per cent of its rubber and 70 per cent of its gold.[5]

But for Demangeon, the 'most original type of British settlement' were the cosmopolitan entrepôts such as Aden, Singapore and Hong Kong, 'suction pumps, gathering to themselves the commerce of vast regions'. In fact, four out of five of the world's busiest ports were in the British Empire, with Hong Kong, clearing nearly 40 million tons a year, at the top of the list above London, New York, Liverpool and Singapore. What's more, very nearly half of the vessels using Hong Kong harbour were under the British flag, part of an unmatched merchant fleet of more than 2,000 ships over 3,000 tons. It was this 'commercial genius', Demangeon concluded, that had made the British Empire 'the largest, the richest, and the most populous colonial empire that the world has ever seen'.[6]

German academic Johannes Lepsius, writing in the August 1923 edition of *Current History*, a well-respected monthly magazine published by the *New York Times*, predicted that the African colonies of Portugal, Belgium and Italy would soon fall into the hands of the British Empire. 'There remain the French possessions as *piece de resistance*,' he wrote. 'Their fate will be decided by the next European war.' For Lepsius, the primacy of the British Empire – what he called the 'Sea Continent' – was down to naval power. 'Britannia rules the waves,' he wrote. 'England lives in a different element from all land powers. She intervenes in the affairs of continents from another dimension.'[7]

In September 1923 Britain had a powerful army and air force, but its greatest strength was indeed at sea, with almost twice the number of battleships and battlecruisers as its nearest competitor, the United States, as well as far more destroyers and submarines. In the shipyards of Birkenhead, two new state-of-the-art battleships, the *Rodney* and the *Nelson*, were under construction. Each was to have nine triple-turreted 16-inch guns, capable of firing shells of 2,500lb. The world's first purpose-designed aircraft carrier, HMS *Hermes*, had completed its sea trials the month before.[8]

This vast fleet guarded the five key strategic points of the empire – Dover, Gibraltar, Suez, the Cape of Good Hope and Singapore – supported by additional oil storage facilities and other naval infrastructure at Hong Kong, Kingston, Malta, Aden, Port Said, Freetown, Rangoon and Colombo.

To demonstrate the power and strategic reach of the Royal Navy, a 'Special Service Squadron' consisting of the world's biggest warship, the *Hood*, along with another battlecruiser and six light cruisers was at Devonport, making final preparations before setting off on a world tour that would take in West, South and East Africa, India, Ceylon, Malaya, Australia, Fiji, Canada and Jamaica. At every stop there would be march-pasts, sports matches and tours of the ships given to local dignitaries as well as those, such as Indian students, whom it was considered wise to impress with the magnitude of British firepower. In all, 2 million people around the world would be shown around the warships.

The army, too, had a global presence. As well as a large contingent in India, there were garrisons of various sizes in Malta, Gibraltar, Egypt, Sudan, Palestine, Iraq, Burma, Singapore, Hong Kong, Shanghai and Jamaica. Although smaller than in 1918, the Royal Air Force in 1923 had forty-three squadrons, of which eight were on imperial duty in Iraq, six in India and four in Egypt and Palestine.

In general, defence spending had been cut back very hard over the previous three years (although the Royal Navy escaped the worst of it). But this was justified in two ways. First, Cabinet in August 1919 had laid down the ten-year rule – no major war was likely for a decade. The only European power from whom there was anything to fear, it was decided, was France. (In the *Observer* newspaper of 30 September 1923, France is described in a worrying tone as 'a far more dominant military power in Europe than Germany ever was before the war'.) Second, new technology developed during the war offered far greater efficiency for less outlay. Barbed and electrified wire was pressed into service on the

Northwest Frontier; new wireless technology vastly increased the effectiveness of military units; across the empire improved motor vehicles were deployed, including armoured cars that provided greater defence, mobility and firepower. Most of all, huge developments in military aircraft provided reconnaissance and photography services as well as machine-gunning and bombing from the air. First used in Sudan in 1916, then in Somaliland and Afghanistan three years later, attack from the air on enemies or their homes and flocks quickly became part of the frontier routine for what we would now call counter-insurgency operations, and at far less cost than the traditional artillery-and-mule-train punitive column, and it still delivered, in the parlance of the day, a great 'salutary moral effect'. In 1920 widespread resistance to British rule in Iraq had been suppressed by Vickers Vernon biplanes, whose pilots included Arthur Harris, then a young squadron leader. Perhaps the most effective military weapon of post-1919 imperial policy was the De Havilland DH9A, capable of air-to-ground machine-gun fire, as well as carrying bomb racks for 20lb bombs, and all for only £300 a piece.[9]

Such successes were a great boon to the infant RAF as the three services fought for resources. To stimulate public enthusiasm for the new force, an annual RAF tournament was established at Hendon aerodrome in north London, where visitors could watch as aircraft dropped incendiary bombs on a model of an African village.

There had been half a dozen Imperial Conferences of varying sorts between 1887 and 1921. Very much the white top table of the empire, leaders from Canada, South Africa and Australasia discussed improving shipping and cable communications and inconclusively mulled over imperial constitutional and tariff issues. In the meantime, amid much speechifying, they were taken to cricket matches, shown around the latest battleship and lavishly wined and dined.

The 1907 conference had started calling those white-dominated parts of the empire 'Dominions' rather than colonies – a significant step – but it was at the 1917 Imperial War Conference that the agenda shifted most notably. One of Lloyd George's first acts having become Prime Minister in early December 1916, after calamitous loss of life on the Western Front, had been to summon the Dominion Prime Ministers to London. The plea was for more men. He got what he wanted, but at the cost of promising the Dominions further freedoms from the empire. In effect, their massive wartime contribution was, for these countries, a proxy 'war of independence'.

Two Indians had been invited to the 1917 conference, which previously had been exclusively white. Lloyd George successfully persuaded them that India should contribute even more men and money. In 1921, in respect for its wartime efforts, India was awarded an official delegation, albeit one led by the British Secretary of State for India. The two Indians were a fairly 'enlightened' royal, the Maharaja of Cutch, and a thoroughly moderate Anglophile (at this time), V. S. Srinivasa Sastri. Sastri had attacked repressive legislation in India but had left the Indian National Congress in protest at the policy of non-cooperation and had founded the rival pro-British Liberal Party. As it turns out, he would be back in London in late 1923 with very different attitudes, formed not from British policy in India but in East Africa.[10]

For the 1923 conference, the Indian delegation had two men, selected by the Viceroy for their unswerving loyalty. Representing British India was Sir Tej Bahadur Sapru, a member of the Viceroy's Executive Council and prominent member of the Indian Liberal Party. For the 'native princes' there was Jey Singh, Maharaja of Alwa. Prime Minister Baldwin would introduce him as 'widely known as an enlightened ruler, deeply interested in the educational and material progress of his state', but in fact he was in the process of bankrupting his kingdom with his passion for grand palaces and motor cars. He would spend his free time during the conference and its attendant events shopping in Park Lane for Rolls-Royces to add to his fleet.[11]

The most notable new arrival for the 1923 conference was William 'W. T.' Cosgrave, representing the Irish Free State, the empire's newest Dominion. After the bitter Anglo-Irish War, a ceasefire had been declared in July 1921 and a treaty negotiated that while giving the new

Irish Free State far greater independence than envisaged by previous campaigns for Home Rule, still kept the new state firmly in the empire with Dominion status. The Sinn Féin republican constitution of 1919 was repudiated, and the Royal Navy kept access to strategically important naval facilities (which had been vital against the U-boat threat during the First World War). King George V remained head of state with a Governor-General as his representative.

The treaty was ratified by the Irish Dáil on 16 January 1922, but only by a very narrow majority. Although the June 1922 General Election showed majority opinion emphatically pro-treaty, Eamon de Valera, the republican leader, resigned, the IRA split, and civil war broke out. With superior forces, resources and popular legitimacy, the Free Staters overwhelmed the republicans, who laid down their arms at the end of April 1923. The end of violence was a huge relief across the empire, particularly in Australia and New Zealand, which had substantial Irish populations.

The leader of the pro-treaty party was now William Cosgrave. Having played an active part in the Easter Rising of 1916, he had been sentenced to death, commuted to penal servitude for life. From his prison in Wales he won two elections as a Sinn Féin candidate, and was released in 1919. Although a close friend of de Valera, he adopted the pro-treaty position, and following the deaths of Arthur Griffith and Michael Collins in 1922 had found himself leading the party and head of the new state, carefully titled the President of the Executive Council.

In the elections of August 1923, the pro-treaty party had again come out on top. 'The victory of the Cosgrave Government in the Irish Free State is a victory for the Empire,' wrote the nephew of the Irish nationalist politician John Redmond the following month. 'It marks the turn of public opinion in Ireland from separation back to Imperialism ... Ireland stands where she has always stood – part of the empire, whether she likes it or not – but, as a matter of fact, she does like it.'[12]

On 10 September, the Irish Free State had been formally admitted to the League of Nations. *The Times* reported a 'generous outburst of applause for first public appearance of Irish delegates ... a tribute to the good sense of Mr Cosgrave' who 'is so English-looking that it is hard to believe that he is the head of an Ireland which by his quiet courage has been brought back from histrionics and confronted with facts. He made an excellent impression.'[13]

Cosgrave would be warmly welcomed by the Imperial Conference as well. 'We realise our responsibilities and are prepared to shoulder the common burdens,' he would announce to the assembled delegates. 'With these words,' the *Irish Times* admiringly reported, 'President Cosgrave ended a chapter and turned a new page in the history of Ireland.' The same issue quoted South African leader Jan Smuts, who like Cosgrave had fought the empire, been defeated and then had been welcomed back into the fold courtesy of a liberal treaty. The presence of Cosgrave at the conference, Smuts declared, was 'an outstanding proof of the power of imperial good-will'. The dreadful 'Irish Question', it seemed, was at last settled.[14]

On the agenda of the conference was foreign policy and imperial defence, improvements in trade and communication, and emigration. Several of the Dominion leaders had already made it clear that they were hoping for increased preference for their products in the British market, by far the largest for imported food in the world. Massey boasted that his exports, in no small part thanks to superphosphate, had more than doubled from £23 million ten years ago to £47 million now. New Zealand, he said, 'is rapidly becoming the dairy farm of the Empire', but he was angry that a recent contract for supplying beef to the army and navy 'went to a country outside the Empire'. What was the point of being in the empire if free trade dominated? he asked. Similar sentiments were expressed in newspapers from Australia to Kenya to Jamaica. The Dominion leaders also wanted capital for development – Mackenzie King mischievously pointed out that US investment in Canada would soon exceed British – and immigrants of 'good British stock'.[15]

On the migration issue, there was broad consensus that the population of the empire was inefficiently distributed. Britain, at 43 million, had 8 million too many people. Schemes were already underway. Amid fears about demobilisation, the Overseas Settlement Committee had been established in 1919. In 1922, the government passed the Empire Settlement Act, whereby the imperial government agreed to spend £3 million a year to help emigrants with costs of passage and settlement, sharing expenses with Dominion governments. Part of the motivation was to prevent manpower being lost to the empire through migration outside its borders. In 1916, the Royal Colonial Institute had sponsored a tour of Australia for novelist H. Rider Haggard to investigate settlement there of British ex-servicemen. Rider Haggard would declare that 'Every drop of Anglo-Saxon blood is so precious that every drop of it should be preserved within the Empire.'[16]

So here was a virtuous circle: Britain would supply men and money to develop the empire's far-flung resources, thereby alleviating domestic unemployment and at the same time creating bigger markets for its exports and ensuring a supply of reliable and efficiently produced food and other primary products. Britain's surplus and potentially politically restless urban proletariat and demobilised troops would be regenerated into sturdy colonial farmers who would, if needed, come to Britain's aid again as effective soldiers. Here was migration as a generator of race power.[17]

There was even a suggestion of a 'self-sustaining and self-contained Empire, without dependence on any other country for anything'. 'The resources of the Empire are as great as those of the United States,' the President of the Board of Trade would tell the conference. The Empire Development Union, formed in 1922, had collected statistics showing that the empire could be self-sufficient. 'All red trade routes', *The Times* commented, would 'rivet closer the bonds of Empire'.[18]

This immense potential wealth, all within the borders of the empire, was to be showcased at the vast Empire Exhibition, scheduled to open in six months' time. All the Dominion leaders were lined up to visit the site at Wembley, then on the outskirts of London, the following Saturday.

Work on the 216-acre site had been underway for eighteen months under the aegis of a general committee led by Edward, Prince of Wales (his contribution would be marked by a statue of him made out of Canadian butter). At the 1921 Imperial Conference, the Prince had told delegates that the project would include a 'great national sports ground'. Football was considered the best way to draw the attention of the working class to the undertaking and Wembley Stadium had been completed in April 1923 in time to host the FA Cup Final between Bolton Wanderers and West Ham. By the end of September, according to the *Daily Mail*, 'the greater part of the machinery hall, which extends over an area six times as large as Trafalgar Square, is already covered, and so is the almost equally extensive Palace of Industry'. The Australian and Canadian Pavilions were far advanced, and 'white minarets are also showing above the roof of the Indian Pavilion'. The Dominion leaders could not help but be impressed by what promised to be 'the greatest exhibition the world has ever seen'.[19]

Once completed, the exhibition would contain pavilions representing almost every territory of the empire, as well as medical displays demonstrating the advances made under imperial rule. The purpose, as would be outlined in the official programme, was to 'foster inter-imperial trade ... To make the different races of the British Empire better known to each other, and to demonstrate to the people of Britain the almost illimitable possibilities of the dominions, colonies, and dependencies overseas.' For Colonial Secretary the Duke of Devonshire, the hope was that it would 'open the eyes of the world to the tremendous material resources contained within the ambit of the British Empire'. The September issue of *United Empire* magazine saw the exhibition as one of the few and 'most hopeful' signs of 'the world's return to sanity and progress', as well as a chance for schoolchildren to learn about 'an Imperialism that stands for service no less than for profit'.[20]

Newspapers and magazines from 29 September and the days around it, published in Britain and across the empire, were dominated by reports on the hopes for the Imperial Conference, what the *Daily Mail* called 'the great inter-Britannic Council'. There was universal agreement that the Dominion leaders, because of the support of their

countries during the war, had earned the right to be listened to carefully and consulted on imperial foreign policy. Indeed, India and the
Dominions had already been assured an 'adequate voice in foreign
policy' and a 'constitutional overhaul of the imperial system ... based
upon a full recognition of the Dominions as autonomous nations of
an Imperial Commonwealth'. The Dominions were now 'sister nations
with Great Britain'. At the same time, everyone agreed on the importance of imperial unity.[21]

What this 'unity' actually meant in practical terms was much less clear.
As the *Spectator* magazine of 29 September commented, 'the manner in
which the Treaty of Versailles was signed left the question of Dominion
status confused'. The British representatives had signed for the empire,
not mentioning Britain, but the Dominions had signed on behalf of
their countries, not mentioning the empire. This had then led to the
Dominions being admitted to the League of Nations as independent
units. How was it possible, asked the September 1923 issue of *Round
Table* magazine, to 'reconcile imperial unity with national freedom'?
Or as the *Irish Times* put it, to square the circle of 'the full independence of [the empire's] several parts with the oneness of the whole'?[22]
    A lot had changed since 1914, when George V, without any con-
sultation, declared war on Germany on behalf of the entire empire.
Across the Dominions, the war, while to an extent uniting the wider
empire, had sharpened internal divisions and stoked anti-imperial
sentiment, most notably over the issue of conscription. In October
1914 in South Africa, where Dutch-speaking Afrikaners formed a clear
majority among the whites over the 'English', two of Prime Minister
Louis Botha's senior commanders and about 11,000 men refused to
invade German South West Africa and took up arms against the government. Botha's personal authority brought the revolt to an end in
January 1915. Some 77,000 whites and 44,000 South African blacks
eventually served in Europe, but almost all the whites were from the
'English' sector.
    In Canada, thanks to a huge wave of migration shortly before the

war, there was a sizeable contingent born in Britain. These men made up the vast majority of those who rushed to enlist in 1914: 70 per cent of the first detachment of the Canadian Expeditionary Force was British-born, and they still made up half the manpower in 1918. It didn't go unnoticed that the least keen to volunteer were the French Canadians. In fact, although they made up 35 per cent of the population, French Canadians would supply only 5 per cent of the troops fighting abroad. When conscription was introduced in 1918 (with many easily exploited exemptions) there were anti-recruitment riots in Quebec which left four dead.[23]

New Zealand was the first Dominion to introduce conscription for overseas service, in June 1916, voted by Parliament with a large majority. Ironically, this was where the measure was least needed. About half of the eligible male population of 240,000 volunteered, of whom 92,000 passed the medical boards. Only 32,000 men were conscripted.[24]

But young men were under immense pressure to volunteer. 'Shirkers' became a target of abuse. Sports clubs banned single men of military age. White Feather Leagues spread across the country. Men who had been rejected for military service on medical grounds found themselves having to wear badges in public.

In New Zealand, resistance to conscription came from Catholics, Irish, Quakers, socialists and some groups of Māoris. In 1918, 111 Māoris were imprisoned for refusing conscription and treated harshly, though they were released after the war. Overall, enlistment among the Māori was at about half the rate of the Pākehā (non-Māori New Zealanders).

Opposition to conscription united the left and led to the formation of the New Zealand Labour Party in 1916. Peter Fraser and others of its leaders were imprisoned for sedition. Nonetheless, the new party won a quarter of the vote in 1919 and would increase its share again in the 1922 election.

As the brutal war dragged on it required, as New Zealand historian W. P. Morrell wrote, 'a continuous exercise of the imagination to realize that New Zealand was at war on the other side of the world'. By 1917, after terrible losses at Passchendaele, even empire-loyalist Sir Joseph Ward, whose Liberal Party was in ruling coalition with the Reform Party, felt that 'the Dominion could send no more men to feed the guns'.[25]

But it was in Australia that the conscription issue had most divided a country. Fifty thousand men had enlisted in the Australian Imperial Force by the end of 1914. Protestant clergymen were vigorous recruiters. One Anglican minister declared, 'we are British first and Australians second'. As elsewhere, the first volunteers were the British-born, the ultra-patriotic and the unemployed. Marching bands, patriotic speeches and plenty of free drinks were deployed across the country to help the recruitment effort. As in New Zealand, there was pressure from the public as well. Edward Eliot on Ocean Island noticed an influx of Australians at the beginning of the war. He called them the 'shirker class ... ready to work for any salary ... simply to escape the war'. Back in Australia, he wrote, 'pointed remarks were made by the girls about young men in mufti'.[26]

From the earliest days there was resistance to the war effort from pacifists, Irish and organised labour. The Melbourne Trades Hall Council called on all unionists to ignore recruiting cards. Organisations opposed to recruitment and the war in general included the Women's Peace Army, formed in Melbourne in July 1915, led by Vida Goldstein, a noted suffragist and pacifist. Soon afterwards a branch was formed in Brisbane. During one meeting there, the authorities notified the organisers that they would be arrested if they sang the anti-war song 'I Didn't Raise My Son to Be a Soldier', an offence under the new War Precautions Act, which banned statements likely to prejudice recruiting. (It was also used to order strikers back to work, and towards the end of the war to ban the waving of red flags.) A key organiser and speaker of the Peace Army was Adela Pankhurst, a daughter of Emmeline, who had arrived in Australia the year before, due to estrangement from her family and to escape police harassment. In October 1920 she would be one of the founders of the Australian Communist Party.[27]

The heavy losses during the failed Gallipoli campaign of the nine months after April 1915 sharpened divisions. For Billy Hughes, Prime Minister from October 1915, Australia could now 'put on the toga of manhood' thanks to the 'sweet purifying breath of self-sacrifice'. Meanwhile the Labor movement was demanding punishment for the 'ghastly ghoulish gamble of Gallipoli'.[28]

Far worse was to come in France in 1916, in particular at the battle of Pozières, part of the Somme campaign. In all, the Australians suffered 28,000 casualties in July and August 1916 alone. Consequently, the force's leaders called on Hughes to introduce conscription for overseas service.

Hughes was personally in favour, but two thirds of his Labor Party, particularly the unionists and those of Irish descent, stung by the brutal reprisals after the Easter Rising of April 1916, disagreed. The party split, with Hughes expelled and taking with him most of the able parliamentarians. The rest of the party then moved steadily leftwards and against 'King and Empire'. In 1918, at its federal conference, it would call for full Australian self-government, and an end to the honours system, state governors and the legal process of appealing to London.

In October 1916 there was a country-wide referendum on conscription. To Hughes' surprise, it was rejected by a small majority of just under 65,000 votes. There followed a period of even more intense political polarisation and bitterness. Leading anti-conscription campaigners were arrested and imprisoned or tarred and feathered in the street. Hughes started calling those opposed to the war 'foul parasites'. Nonetheless, a second referendum voted down conscription again, and by a larger margin than before.

So uniquely among the war's belligerents, the Australian 'Diggers' abroad would all be volunteers. In total 416,000 came forward, of which 330,000 fought overseas, with 60,000 losing their lives and 160,000 wounded.

The end of the war did not see the end of the stark divisions in Australian society, which were further exacerbated by industrial unrest. In Brisbane in March 1919, partly in protest at the continuation of the War Precautions Act, 2,000 Bolshevik 'red-raggers' marched waving banned red flags and singing revolutionary songs. The next day 7,000 supporters of 'King and Empire' staged a counter-demonstration amid violent clashes. In 1921, a crowd of between 2,000 and 3,000 marched in Sydney singing 'The Red Flag'. A Union Jack was burned then trampled underfoot. A week later there was a huge counter-march organised by the Returned Soldiers' and Sailors' Imperial League that drew over 100,000.

In both Dominions there was a new emphasis in school curricula on the heroes of empire – Nelson, Wellington et al. In New Zealand, Massey, Ulster-born and an ardent Anglophile, demanded that a new syllabus should inculcate imperial patriotism, 'especially through the study of great men from whom the race had sprung'. He wanted specific reference made to the 'heroes' of the Great War including Douglas Haig and David Beatty, and to the personal, military, political and racial qualities which were believed to have contributed to British victory.

At the same time, New Zealand and Australian children were now lined up on Monday mornings to salute the flag and then, with their right hands on their breasts, to vow to obey parents and teachers, and to be loyal to king and empire. In New Zealand, after the arrest in June 1921 of Hedwig Witzel, a student at Wellington Teachers College, for distributing subversive literature – 'The Communist', a pamphlet of Australian origin – there was a compulsory oath of loyalty for teachers as well.

From some quarters, objections to these measures were ongoing. The Sydney *Sun* of 23 September 1923 reported complaints in the Brisbane legislative assembly – a Labor bastion – about 'children bowing down to the flag, about which they know nothing'. The weekly *Australian Worker*, whose circulation had peaked during the conscription crisis, where it was firmly in the 'No' camp, but which was still going strong, in its 26 September 1923 edition denounced flag-saluting as a 'farce' and 'compulsory hypocrisy'.

Despite this, even on the right there was a change of attitude towards

the empire, particularly in Australia. The efforts and sacrifices of the
Diggers, as Hughes pronounced, had allowed Australia to 'enter into
a family of nations on a footing of equality' and created what Keith
Hancock (who in 1923 became the first ever Australian to be elected
to All Souls) would call 'heightened self-consciousness'. 'The old feeling of subservience to England', journalist Keith Murdoch wrote, had
gone, to be replaced by what he called 'Australianism'. While the hard
left continued to rail against the 'chains of empire', Conservatives,
while not disputing that Australia's future lay within the empire, were
determined to make Australia's own particular interests heard. Hughes'
successor from February 1923, Stanley Bruce, who presided over the
first all-Australia-born Cabinet, would continue this new 'Australia
first' policy.[29]

'The average Australian regards this and all other Imperial
Conferences with more suspicion than enthusiasm,' warned the writer
of an article published on 29 September 1923 in the *Nation and
Athenaeum*, 'An Australian view of the Imperial Conference'. 'It is not
that Australians are anti-British or disloyal to the Empire', it went on,
but they did not want an 'Imperial foreign policy' when a super-Cabinet
in London could overrule the sovereignty of the Australian Parliament
or elector. They didn't want to be ordered to go to war again.[30]

Exactly a year before the Imperial Conference, this new independence, as well as the Dominions' sensitivity at being taken for granted,
had been illustrated in spectacular style by the Chanak Crisis. In
September 1922, Turkish troops led by Kemal Pasha, having driven
back a Greek invasion, were closing in on the neutral zone in the
Dardanelles occupied by the British Army at Chanak. Neither France
nor Italy were prepared to help Britain prevent the Kemalist forces
from going on to take command of the Straits, so at a Cabinet meeting
late on Friday afternoon, 15 September, on the urging of Secretary of
State for the Colonies Winston Churchill, it was decided to ask the
Dominions for armed assistance. Telegrams were dispatched, and a
press release prepared as a threat to Kemal.

But Churchill had failed to factor in that it was by now the weekend.

The result was that the Dominion leaders heard about the appeal for help from newspapers before the telegrams had been decoded. Canadian Prime Minister Mackenzie King was told about it by a reporter from the *Toronto Star* while giving a speech in the city.

In relatively loyal New Zealand, the Cabinet decided in just a few minutes to send military aid, and the next morning 12,000 volunteered for service. Elsewhere, though, it was a different story. South Africa did not even reply to the request. Mackenzie King insisted that it was a matter for the Canadian Parliament. In Australia, Hughes complained that 'If Britain only consults the Dominions when they are committed, then all talk about the Dominions having a real share in deciding foreign and imperial policy is empty air.' Meanwhile the *Australian Worker* newspaper railed against the possibility of 'more graves to dig beneath alien skies' and urged that 'the most strenuous opposition be offered to Australia's participation in any war outside the Commonwealth'.[31]

In the event, the assistance was not required as an armistice was declared between the Greeks and Turks, and the new Treaty of Lausanne, ratified in August 1923, overturned the draconian measures of the earlier Treaty of Sèvres. This time, however, Dominion representatives were not asked to contribute their signatures, and the whole episode cast a sour pall over the Imperial Conference.

There was also another recent treaty with repercussions for the conference, and the potential shape, or even survival, of the Commonwealth in the future. It was over a seemingly trivial matter – the allocation of fishing rights between Canada and the United States. A deal was done, resulting in the Halibut Fisheries Treaty. Commercial treaties made by members of the empire with other powers were previously always also signed by a British representative but, according to an article published during the conference by *Nation and Athenaeum* titled 'The Emancipation of the Dominions', Canada and the US told the British government that 'as respects Canada the signature of Mr Lapointe (minister of marine) alone should be sufficient, as it affects solely Canada and the United States'. In a piece published on 29

September 1923, Sir John Foster Fraser, star columnist for *Empire News* and self-confessed imperialist who believed 'the safety of the world largely depends upon the continuance of the Empire', found this new development a great cause for concern. What if a Dominion signed a bilateral treaty that not only excluded the rest of the empire but actually went against the interests of another Dominion or Britain itself? 'Looking facts straight in the face,' he wrote, 'I see in this new move of separate treaties by the Dominions a process which will lead to the disintegration of the Empire.'[32]

The *Daily Mail* of 29 September reported a speech just given by Neville Chamberlain, Chancellor of the Exchequer. 'The Dominions were young nations, but in a generation or two they would be among the powerful peoples of the world,' he declared. 'If we only remained united ... we should be a world Power to whose influences no man could put a limit.' This, then, was the rather fragile hope of the British as they welcomed the Dominion leaders to London.

3

The Metropole

Melodrama is the latest cult in London.

Daily Mirror, 29 September 1923

'**A**lready the leading hotels are well filled with Overseas delegates and their numerous experts and secretaries,' reported the London *Evening Standard* on 29 September. 'The Savoy, Hotel Cecil, Hyde Park Hotel and the Carlton are at the moment true "outposts of Empire".'

The delegates might – or might not – have wanted to avoid nearby Hyde Park. According to a newspaper report published the following day, 'the conditions obtaining' there 'were a disgrace to the nation'. 'In broad daylight,' complained the Bishop of London in his capacity as president of the London Society for the Promotion of the Public Morality, 'persons are to be seen openly mis-conducting themselves and committing acts of the grossest indecency.' The society had conducted ten nights' observation in Hyde Park, employing 'men of great experience', and discovered '746 cases of impropriety, indecency and immorality'.[1]

Also to be avoided, according to a newspaper report of the 29th, was

'London's Black Colony'. Since the war 'some hundreds of coloured men' had 'established themselves in the net-work of streets west of Tottenham Court Road'. Their 'haunts', readers were told, 'are nothing less than hotbeds of evil . . . many of the blacks are involved in the drug trade, and nearly all are armed. Razors are their favourite weapons, and all-night orgies are their recreation.' Scotland Yard was doing its best to 'bring these pests to justice' but 'one difficulty is that as most of the negroes are British subjects they cannot be dealt with by deportation orders'.[2]

The delegates, particularly those with an international outlook, would be on safer ground making their way to Polytechnic Hall, Regent Street, where Captain Noel's film *Climbing Mount Everest* was being shown that night. Noel had been a member of George Mallory's failed expedition the previous year, and the film was part of a fund-raising effort for the next attempt in 1924. 'Though defeated this time, still our climbers will not accept defeat,' the narration of the film ends in sonorous tones.[3]

Alternatively, the delegates could visit the New Oxford Theatre, where Howard Carter was giving a lecture on the discovery the previous November of the tomb of Tutankhamun. That's if they were unafraid of the now famous 'curse'.

Theatre highlights included Fred and Adele Astaire (his older sister) at the Queen's Theatre in *Stop Flirting*, which included numbers by George Gershwin. It was Fred's first appearance in the West End and his big break, although in 1923 Adele was the real star. Prince George, Edward's wayward younger brother, saw the show scores of times and wrote her long, infatuated letters. Overall, though, the theatre on offer was somewhat dominated by 'villains and heroes, sinister adventuresses and virtuous heroines'. 'Melodrama is the latest cult in London,' declared the *Daily Mirror* of 29 September. 'Is it because we find in melodrama the mirror of the rather hectic and explosive times through which we are passing?' the paper asked.

Although far from ignoring news from Europe or of the Imperial Conference, the mass-market newspapers gave plenty of space to

high-society weddings and crime of all sorts. Most of the papers of
the 29th carried the story of the end of a trial of two con-men who,
claiming they were representing some ladies who were setting up a
subscription for a wedding gift for Princess Mary, purloined £12,000-
worth of pearls from an Indian visitor, Mr Allibhoy M. Jeevanjee. All
the papers called Jeevanjee 'an Indian pearl merchant'. In fact he was
the richest man in Kenya, mainly thanks to property in Nairobi, and a
key player in the restless Indian community there.[4]

Perhaps the story that month that had aroused most prurient interest was that of the trial of Marguerite Alibert, a thirty-two-year-old
French woman, ex-prostitute and gold digger extraordinaire. After a
string of rich lovers, including during the war the Prince of Wales (who
had foolishly sent her passionate letters, which she'd carefully kept),
she had married twenty-two-year-old Prince Ali Fahmy, a wealthy
Egyptian playboy. In July 1923, after furious arguments in a room at
the Savoy hotel, she had shot him three times. The trial for murder in
September should have been an open-and-shut case, but she was sensa-
tionally acquitted. Her lawyer's tactic had been to appeal to every racial
prejudice he could. Fahmy was cruel, promiscuous, bisexual. He had
forced her to have 'unnatural' intercourse and beaten her mercilessly.
Beneath his respectable exterior, the Egyptian was an animal, a beast
who preyed on white Western women to degrade them and destroy
their values of decency.

So it was a good time for Edward, Prince of Wales, to be out of
the country. Newspapers from 29 September from across the empire
reported on his visit to his ranch in Alberta, Canada, purchased on his
first trip there four years earlier. Now he was travelling privately rather
than officially, but, the *Mail* reported, he had just hosted 500 people
for a picnic lunch followed by an 'exhibition "stampede"'. According to
another paper, 'this young man's enjoyment of his own land in Canada
is agreeably democratic and helps to cement the empire together ...
everywhere he appeared he strengthened his popularity and won new
hearts by his democratic bearing and agreeable personality'. Ernest
Hemingway, then in Toronto, wrote to Ezra Pound on 6 September,

'The Prince gets here on Tuesday. Prince Charming, the Ambassador of Empire, the fair haired bugger.'[5]

The Times had, for that time, a small circulation of just over 100,000. But the paper was very much aimed at those most interested in the empire – the military, those in colonial service, and overseas investors and traders. More than any other paper, it detailed naval, air force and army promotions and movements, including a large section on the Indian Army. Readers of its edition of 29 September learned that the Atlantic fleet of seventy vessels was conducting training manoeuvres off the Moray Firth. There was a report on the battleship *Malaya* and the First Baltic Squadron. The flagship of the Mediterranean fleet the *Iron Duke* had just arrived at Gibraltar from Malta. The start of the 'Cold Weather training season of the Army in India' was announced. The Royal Ulster Rifles were being posted to join the British army of occupation in Cologne, taking with them two packs of beagles.

From Edinburgh came news of the establishment on the castle esplanade of an equestrian statue in bronze of Earl Haig. The statue was a gift from Sir Dhunjibhoy Bomanji of Bombay, 'a Parsi gentleman'. Lady Haig and her two children were present at the ceremony. Lady Bomanji, 'in handing over the statue said that India yielded to no one in admiration for Earl Haig'.

In Dundee there was the unveiling of a stained-glass window in memory of Mary Slessor, 'the Scottish factory girl who, inspired by the example of Livingstone, went out to the West Coast of Africa'. 'Mary Slessor did much to civilize the natives of the West Coast, being largely instrumental in bringing about the abolition of the slaughter of twin babies and other inhuman practices.'

There were copious details of shipping insurance rates, arrivals and departures as well as information on Cook's tours to Egypt and elsewhere. Reading that edition of *The Times* today there's a real feel of Britain's global reach, even among the trivia, personals and advertisements. Officers recently returned from Baghdad have presented herons and a vulture to London Zoo, all of them obtained on hunting expeditions. A lady asks, can anyone recommend an ayah (nanny) for the journey to Bombay? An RAF flying officer, on flying duties in Quetta, India, wants exchange with a flying officer in Iraq. A government official returned from West Africa seeks an opening home or abroad. Aged forty, single. 'Good knowledge colloquial Arabic. Knows Egypt, South Africa, Australia, Canada.' The School of Oriental and African Studies is advertising lessons in 'Arabic, Turkish, Persian, Hindustani, Chinese, Japanese, Swahili and other important languages, as well as the history and religions of the East and of Africa ... special facilities are offered for merchants, missionaries, and others.' 'For Sale', reads one somewhat alarming advertisement, 'beautifully marked Wild Cat (Cerval), also one baboon, recently arrived from East Africa. Both are very tame.'

It is striking that apart from adverts for domestic staff and notices of marriage, births, entertainment and sport, there is absolutely no mention of anyone female, with the exception of a brief report that the (unnamed) 'wife of a farmer in Newry' has given birth to her twentieth child. There is not even a mention, covered by most other papers, of the election of the first woman to be chairman of the Council of the Trade Union Congress, Margaret Bondfield. The *Evening Standard* expresses the hope that Bondfield will make progress in sorting out the boiler-makers' dispute, which has been running for six months, to the great detriment of the shipbuilding industry. This dispute is covered in *The Times*, with the observation that only eighty-five out of 250 berths on the Clyde were occupied by new vessels on most of which work was suspended. This is part of a gloomy article headlined 'Trade Outlook', which gathers together news from the various industries of the country. Sheffield reports on the cutlery industry, Bradford on wool and textiles, Glasgow on shipbuilding, South Wales on coal, Stoke on pottery, Leicester on 'hosiery'. Everywhere the 'immediate outlook' is 'obscure' and 'much machinery remains idle'.

A strong impression is given that the empire is now a better bet. 'YOU CAN LEAD A HEALTHIER AND HAPPIER LIFE at Zebediela, the premier Orange-growing estate in South Africa' proclaims one advertisement. 'Native labour' was plentiful for 'field and house work'. Smuts himself would tell the Imperial Conference that he did not want unskilled labour as they had this in great numbers. Instead, the immigrant to South Africa should be 'a man of the overseer type, or a man with a certain amount of capital, however small'. The Canadians, too, would prefer immigrants with capital. In a report prepared by the head of the Department of Immigration just prior to the Imperial Conference, there was a plea for 'quality rather than quantity first'.[6]

During the last decades of the nineteenth century, two thirds of migrants leaving the British Isles had gone to the United States, but this had fallen away in the twentieth century. By the early 1920s, in part due to new government support and subsidies, 70 per cent ended up somewhere in the empire – about a third to Canada, a quarter to Australia and the rest elsewhere. The years 1920 to 1924 saw an inter-war high, with a net outflow of some 144,000 a year (with Scots, Welsh and Irish highly disproportionately represented). During the first nine months of 1923, departures to other parts of the empire totalled 68,789 men and 38,065 women.[7]

This gender disparity did give cause for concern, and efforts were underway to correct it. The majority of migrants leaving the UK had always been young males, and numerous societies had sprung up during the nineteenth century to promote the migration of women both to alleviate the perceived problems created at home by 'surplus' women and for the 'civilizing' influence they were thought to bring to colonial society. With 740,000 war dead, this 'problem of surplus' had become more acute, leaving the country in late 1923 with an excess of 1.9 million women over men. For some this threatened 'morality', for others a rise in militant feminism. So, in 1919, the existing voluntary female emigration societies were collapsed into the Society for Overseas Settlement of British Women (SOSBW), a new 'central and advisory body' for voluntary organisations involved with female migration. From 1920, this quasi-governmental organisation of 'responsible women' with 'first-hand experience of ... empire migration' was recognised as the women's branch of the Overseas Settlement Committee. The chair of its executive committee was Gladys Pott, previously a vigorous campaigner against female franchise. September 1923 found her returning from a fact-finding mission around Australia. Shortly after her return she gave a talk to the Royal Colonial Institute. 'Of course it is easier for the man to fend for himself, to live roughly, to fight nature, and to be self-dependent,' she told her audience at the Hotel Victoria. 'Yet for true Empire building, the man must only precede the woman, not live without her ... the destinies of race and empire lay in women's hands.'[8]

According to a Cabinet report prepared for Colonial Secretary Devonshire just prior to the Imperial Conference, 'Australia has shown the greatest zeal and energy of any of the Dominions' when it came to encouraging migration, in terms of contributing to schemes for assisted passage and establishing land settlement programmes. 'Unfortunately,' the report continued, 'the progress being made under these schemes is disappointing.' Clearly, all was not well.[9]

For Gladys Pott, the advantages of emigration to Australia and the Dominions in general, as she outlined for her audience, were the climate, the space, 'the less rigid conventions of Dominion life' without the restrictions of 'constant subservience to a tradition ... [and] above all the greater importance of the individual, where each unit counts in a way that he or she cannot hope to count in this crowded country of our own'. One 'scheme' had particularly caught her eye, whereby women and families needn't just follow, but could be in at the outset. This was Group Settlement, 'one of the most interesting experiments that has taken place'.[10]

4

'Australia Unlimited'

I love a sunburnt country,
A land of sweeping plains,
Of ragged mountain ranges,
Of droughts and flooding rains.

Australian poet
DOROTHEA MACKELLAR[1]

S eptember 1923 saw the publication of perhaps D. H. Lawrence's
most autobiographical novel, *Kangaroo*, which tells the story of an
English married couple arriving in Australia, their everyday life staying
for a few months near Sydney and their impressions of the country, its
people and its relationship to the empire. It is a strange, worried and
conflicted work that would garner mixed responses from Australian
readers and reviewers.[2]

Lawrence himself and his wife Frieda had arrived at Fremantle at
the beginning of May the previous year. During the war, mainly on
account of Frieda's German nationality, they had experienced public
hostility and police harassment, so they had been on self-imposed exile
from Britain since 1919, first in Europe, then Ceylon. The aim had

been to end up in the United States, but they decided, after leaving Italy, to head east. Ceylon was not a success. Lawrence struggled to cope with the heat and the feeling he always had that the 'dark swarming people' were 'jeering at him'. He concluded that the 'natives' were 'in the living sense lower than we are. But they are going to swarm over us and suffocate us.'[3]

On the boat to Ceylon they had met and got on well with a number of Australians, which inspired their next move. 'I believe Australia is a good country, full of life and energy,' he wrote to a friend.[4]

In English literature, Australia had long been a convenient and exotic site for the disposal of characters, sometimes to return (for example, Magwitch in *Great Expectations* and Arabella in *Jude the Obscure*). For Lawrence, in his novels and plays up till now, it had also provided the potential for regeneration and redemption, a place of modern outlook and robust health, in contrast to a war-damaged Britain of constraints, conventions and grim industrialisation.

In fact, Lawrence, in his frequent letters and then in his novel, displays deep ambivalence about what he discovered in Australia. Lawrence found the Fremantle 'air beautiful and pure and sky fresh, high', but the town itself 'a queer godforsaken place: not so much new as non-existent'. A friend from the boat set them up in a guest house 16 miles out of Perth, but they only stayed for three weeks. Lawrence found the surrounding bush alarming and frightening, 'a strange, vast empty country ... with a pre-primeval ghost in it'.[5]

At the end of May they sailed to Sydney. Although he admired the beautiful harbour, the city, with its ugly sprawl of tatty bungalows and rubbish casually flung everywhere, was 'raw and crude ... without any core or pitch of meaning'. The 'London of the Southern hemisphere', he wrote, appeared to have been 'made in five minutes, a substitute for the real thing. Just a substitute – as margarine is a substitute for butter.'[6]

It was also expensive, and the Lawrences were short of money, so they quickly relocated to a rented house at Thirroul on the coast about 40 miles south of Sydney. Perched on a cliff overlooking the Pacific, here they would swim naked in the sea and enjoy the 'boomingly crashingly noisy ocean'. Frieda, in particular, loved it. 'I feel I have packed all old dull Europe in the old kit bag and thrown [it] in the sea,' she wrote to a friend.[7]

Here, on 3 June, Lawrence started *Kangaroo*. He needed the money, despite earlier successes. By now he had published, among other novels, essays, plays and poems, *Sons and Lovers*, *The Rainbow* and *Women in Love*. Only five weeks later, *Kangaroo*'s 150,000 words were pretty much completed – something of a tour de force of rapid composition. Throughout the novel, and in his own letters, Lawrence examines Australia and Australians.

'There seems to be no inside life of any sort,' he wrote to a friend on 22 June, a complaint that echoed that of many Australian clergymen at the time, who railed against American influence in the form of cinema, jazz music and 'cheap and nasty' magazines. Instead of the Church, they complained, Australians preferred the picture house, the racecourse, dancehalls and the beach. The sun 'had defeated religion in Australia', one conservative wrote. (Similarly, the New Zealand *Truth* newspaper of 29 September 1923 complained that 'In our New Zealand cities the cabarets and the extravagant living they promote are often a menace to weak and pleasure-driven youth.')[8]

For Lawrence, it stemmed in part from a derivative British culture being transplanted on to a weirdly alien, 'aloof' landscape, 'as if the people were not really here: only accidentally here'. 'The land has a fourth dimension,' he wrote to Frieda's mother. 'The white people swim like shadows over the surface of it.' Sydney at night-time 'seemed to be sprinkled on the surface of a darkness into which it never penetrated'.[9]

The plot of *Kangaroo* revolves around the stark political polarisation in Australia after the war. Extremists on both political wings try to recruit the protagonist to their cause. He is introduced to Kangaroo, the nickname of a charismatic lawyer and ex-army officer who is the leader of the 'Diggers', a quasi-fascist group based around ex-servicemen. His plan is to 'have another sort of government for the Commonwealth – with a sort of Dictator'. The character is based in part on Sir Charles Rosenthal, an Australian ex-general, militarist and staunch anti-communist who in 1921 founded the King and Empire Alliance. He is also taken to meet the union men on the left plotting socialist revolution. There are violent clashes between the two groups.[10]

In the novel and his letters, Lawrence also explores the relationship of Australians to British incomers and to the empire as a whole. Some are almost painfully deferential, seeing the English as possessing superior sophistication and worldly knowledge. Others are more guarded, sometimes superior, sometimes insecure, never really trusting the English. 'You're a stranger here,' one Australian tells Lawrence's protagonist. 'You're from the Old Country. You're different from us.'[11]

The same character declares that he'd rather have the British Empire 'ten thousand times over' than a 'red republic', even though he doesn't like 'sharing a bed' with 'a crowd of n******s and dagos'. Although he resents Australia being bossed around by anyone, including the 'Mother Country', without imperial protection 'the Japs [would] come down this way. They'd squash us like a soft pear.'[12]

At times Lawrence succeeds in feeling 'Australian . . . a new creature'. But mostly he feels 'very foreign with the people, although they are all English in origin'. So his 'pilgrimage' continued. On 4 September, Lawrence and Frieda left for San Francisco, en route to New Mexico.[13]

When it was published in September 1923, there was much not to like in *Kangaroo* for Australian readers and reviewers. For one thing, some found it tedious and dull (it does, indeed, betray the speediness of its composition). Others, despite it being written by an Englishman on a fairly brief visit, talked of it as 'a great Australian novel'. Reviewers on the whole recognised the character of their countrymen and women that Lawrence had drawn, as well as the contemporary political division and the interesting and pertinent questions Lawrence asks about Australian and imperial identities and loyalties.[14]

When, after several delays, Australian Prime Minister Stanley Bruce finally reached the UK for the Imperial Conference, he was interviewed on the train from Dover to London. 'The purpose of the British Empire', he said, was to develop cooperation among its members.

For him this meant securing investment, markets and migrants for Australia. In fact, he wanted 100,000 Britons a year to start new lives in his country.[15]

Before the war, although colonial governments – at state level in Australia – had encouraged and subsidised 'desirable' migrants from Britain, the imperial government had refused to intervene in what it considered an area of free enterprise. The change after 1919, when the imperial government embarked on a vigorous programme of state-aided migration, had seen objections raised from those who didn't want to see the home country depopulated of its young men, now in short supply. But the huge growth in unemployment from 1920 onwards had convinced most that Britain did indeed have a large surplus and redundant population with all the threats to political stability that this entailed.

From the outset, however, there were two potentially conflicting aims – to build up the strength of the manpower of the Dominions, and at the same time get rid of those who were unwanted or who had failed for whatever reason at home. The Dominions wanted the most useful; the mother country wanted to offload the most useless.

Here, though, was a solution. Whether demobbed soldiers or urban industrial unemployed, the migrants would have a definite destination – the land. Those enfeebled by urban squalor – wartime medical checks had shown a stunning third of British men physically unfit for service – would be regenerated by the fresh air and bracing hard work of rural life. The heroic ex-soldiers would be rewarded with the chance to become independent, landowning yeoman farmers, the bedrock of a moderate, sensible, stable liberal democracy, far removed from the trade unionists, immoral artists and hopeless criminals and layabouts of the cities. Rider Haggard was certainly decided: 'Prosperity will follow the feet that tread the fields, rather than those which trip along pavements,' he declared. Gladys Pott, chair of the women's branch of the Overseas Settlement Committee, concurred: 'We are all agreed that successful settlement overseas implies encouragement of settlement upon the land rather than in crowded centres.'[16]

For Australians, this also made sense. There had been a drift to the cities; new arrivals could replace missing workers in the important agricultural sector, and therefore not threaten Australian jobs. Even more importantly, a growth in the country's inland population of sturdy Anglo-Saxon farmers might make the difference in what was widely considered an existential threat to the country. Some six weeks or so into his stay, D. H. Lawrence had written to a friend in England. Australians, he reported, 'are terribly afraid of the Japanese. Practically all Australians, and especially in Sydney, feel that once there was any fall in England, so that the Powers could not interfere, Japan would at once walk in and occupy the place.'[17]

Fear of Japan, and more generally of what was called the 'yellow peril' – the millions of Asians to the north of Australia – pre-dates even the formation of the Commonwealth in 1901. Until the 1860s immigration was fairly unrestricted, with Chinese on the gold fields, Afghan and Sikh cameleers, Malay and Japanese pearlers, and Pacific Islanders labouring on sugar plantations in the tropics. But efforts had been made by individual states, with measures such as a head tax on Chinese entering the colony or restrictions on how many Chinese could be legally carried by each arriving vessel. Federation offered the chance to construct an Australia-wide immigration policy. Indeed, this was one of its key attractions.

With Japan already identified as a 'future war menace', it was considered undesirable to have a large immigrant population that might act as a fifth column. More generally, at a time when ideas were prevalent about a hierarchy of races – what we would now call white supremacism – it was seen by white Australians as essential that non-whites be excluded lest Australia be 'swamped'. What was needed, the *Sydney Morning Herald* demanded, was 'a stone wall against the danger of race pollution'.[18]

For legislators of the new Commonwealth, it wasn't a question of whether Asians should be excluded, but how. The Labor leader John C. Watson suggested a simple formula blocking the immigration of 'any person who is an aboriginal native of Asia, Africa, or of the islands thereof'. But this was awkward, as Indians were fellow subjects of the empire, and at the time Japan was being courted by Britain as a partner against Russian expansion in the Far East. The compromise – or, more exactly, ruse – that was decided on was the 'Natal Formula' – a literary test in any European language. The Japanese consul in Sydney was unimpressed, saying it was still 'racial, pure and simple'. Similar policies were adopted around this time in Canada and New Zealand as well.[19]

But the 1901 'White Australia' policy, which would become a cornerstone of Australian politics for generations, did little to allay strategic fears. In 1905 Japan had pulled off the stunning victory over Russia and begun a process of expansion. The First World War had demonstrated Japan's new naval power. Japanese vessels had guarded Australian and New Zealand troop ships heading for Europe and patrolled the Pacific, as well as serving in the Mediterranean. And at the end of the war, all the German islands north of the equator were in Japanese hands, bringing their power much closer to Australia.

In 1920, the Australian Department of Defence issued a report that noted that 'the great natural resources of Australia, coupled with the sparseness of her settlement, render her desirable in the eyes of any nation with a limited territory and a large population'. The enormous coastline, and the concentration of people and industries on the seaboard, made Australia 'peculiarly vulnerable to attack'. It went on to estimate that Japan, with a population of 76 million, could easily put an army of 600,000 in the field and had the shipping to be able in one convoy to transport an army of 100,000 and 'could land troops at almost any place desired on the Australian coast'.[20]

These concerns were shared by journalists, opinion-formers and politicians. At the 1921 Imperial Conference, Hughes had pointed out that Australia had a coastline three times the length of that of the United States, but with only 5 million to defend it against America's 100 million. His successor Bruce would call Australia 'the most potentially rich, uninhabited country on the face of the globe'. The

Agent-General for Western Australia, C. P. Colebatch, in a lecture at the Royal Colonial Institute in London, expressed concerns that 'Close to our northern shores are teeming millions of coloured folk ... In many cases the War has caused a strange awakening amongst these people – they are beginning to realise the congestion of their own countries and to cast envious eyes upon the fertile and empty territory within their easy reach ... If we would keep Australia for this Empire and for this race, we must people it while it is yet ours.'[21]

So for this reason too, Australia not only needed population, but it needed it on the land, away from the existing, vulnerably situated coastal cities (part of the thinking behind the inland siting of the new capital, Canberra). It should be in 'ungarrisoned' areas, identified as in the north (closest to the danger), sparsely populated Western Australia and the vast empty interior.[22]

For some, this was not just defensive but in fact inspirational. People looked at the United States, with a similar mainland area to Australia (about 8 million square kilometres/3 million square miles) but with more than twenty times the population, farms and factories from coast to coast and an undisputed invulnerable global power. Why should Australia not be the same? Bruce himself reckoned Australia could and should have a population of 100 million. Others suggested 200 million or more. Rider Haggard considered Australia had 'all that is necessary for the development of a great and powerful nation' and immense agricultural potential.[23]

Joseph Banks, scientific expert on James Cook's first voyage to Australia, had described the continent as the most barren he had ever encountered, despite arriving at Botany Bay at its most verdant time. Pre-war experts had written off as hopeless the arid 'Dead Heart' at the centre of Australia. But didn't the wonders of superphosphate, huge irrigation schemes like the new Murray River project, and the successful development of new strains of drought-resistant wheat and other crops change all that?

Shortly after the war, E. J. Brady – then known, if at all, as a jobbing poet – had a runaway bestseller, *Australia Unlimited*. 'Cradled and reared in the bush,' he wrote, 'I flattered myself that I knew the Australian Continent better than most people.' For him, Australia was like 'a song written – but unsung'.

To outsiders ('alien souls'), the bush was strange, off-putting, 'predominantly melancholy'. But 'to the sane, healthy native-born it is a mother of everlasting youth and beauty, and the freest, richest, happiest land on earth'. He had travelled all over the country and everywhere found 'Wonder, Beauty, Unequalled Resource. Under the arid-seeming plains I saw the possibilities of marvellous tilth . . . The whole continent has proved to be a vast storehouse of mainly undeveloped Wealth.' The arid, undeveloped north-west was, he decided, just like Utah. Some readers, he conceded, might find his 'outlook over-optimistic', but he hoped that his book's 'shortcomings may in part be atoned for by its patriotic intentions'. Australia could become, he wrote, 'the richest and most powerful . . . nation of the world . . . The breed that stormed and held the heights of Anzac will grow stronger and more self-reliant as their generations follow.'[24]

To express doubts about this glorious, strategically secure future was now to be unpatriotic. When a geographer, in a text book published in the same year as *Australia Unlimited*, pronounced that even with hugely expensive irrigation, artesian wells and unlimited fertiliser 'Little can ever be done to reclaim this vast arid region', he found his book banned by Western Australia University Library and there were calls for his dismissal from his post at the University of Sydney. The consensus, certainly in Bruce's government, was for expansion and exploitation, specifically of primary agricultural production – what Brady called the 'oldest, most permanent and important feature of our material development' – at almost whatever the cost.[25]

To attract the hundreds of thousands of migrants this vision demanded – white, of course, and preferably Protestant British – the full paraphernalia of promotion was deployed. Through subsidies, fares were equalised between the UK and Canada and Australia (the Canadians, it was thought, had before the war won the race to receive more settlers thanks simply to being closer and therefore cheaper to

get to). Sir Joseph Cook, High Commissioner in London, told who-
ever would listen that Australia was the 'land of the better chance',
a place of 'sunshine and laughter'. Under him in London worked the
Migration and Settlement Office, whose personnel toured the United
Kingdom all the way to the Hebrides but in particular the 'country
districts' to recruit rural workers. Backing this up was a huge effort
involving pamphlets, posters, newspaper and magazine advertisements,
films, lantern slide shows, exhibitions and lecture tours. In images and
texts, the message was of a bucolic idyll of an attractive homestead set
in rich rolling farmland. By 1924, forty-one promotional films with
titles such as *Australia Calls* had been shown throughout Britain via
some 1,650 outlets, often organised by Labour Exchanges and Poor
Law Guardians, who weren't shy of twisting arms to get unemployed
workers off their dole list. Independent agents, operating on commission, worked the fertile grounds of poor urban districts. 'Farmboys'
were recruited from orphanages and broken homes.[26]

Under the terms of the Empire Settlement Act, the large majority
of those who took up the offer received grants or loans to help with
the costs of the passage. Under-twelves travelled free. These 'Assisted'
migrants had to undertake to stay for at least two years. Ex-servicemen
also received help with passage and settlement costs. In the twelve
months leading up to September 1923, there were 36,827 net arrivals
in Australia of whom 27,774 were assisted. It was up on the previous
year's figure of just over 24,000, but far from the 100,000 desired and
expected.[27]

Part of the problem, it seemed, was stories appearing in British newspapers of 'droughts, strikes, dingoes and tales of woe from returned
misfits', as Australians in the New Settlers' League saw it. The NSL had
been founded in March 1921 as a voluntary organisation committed
to providing aftercare to immigrants by ensuring they were welcomed,
given accommodation when they got off the boat, then employed and
integrated into their new communities. Soon they had hundreds of
branches country-wide and thousands of volunteers and were publishing
handbooks – circulated in the UK – with advice for the new arrival.[28]

In keeping with the official policy, the NSL did everything to keep the new settlers on the land rather than letting them drift to the cities, even if the migrants had to 'rough it at the beginning' and not be too fussy about their initial job. 'If for any reason whatsoever your first position is terminated, on no account return to Perth before consulting the Local Representative of the League,' ordered the Western Australian edition of the handbook. 'With few exceptions', they were assured, they would find Australians 'very friendly and ready to assist', and were given hints on how to interact with Australians. 'Don't criticise your new surroundings or try to make out that things are better done in Britain,' the handbook cautioned.[29]

In fact, the NSL had a second job to do as well as looking after new arrivals – to 'preach always the gospel of immigration' to an often doubtful Australian public, to impress upon them 'the vital importance of immigration to the national safety of the Commonwealth; to the maintenance of a White Australia; to the effective occupation and use of the land; and to the per capita reduction of the National Debt'. 'If a person of our own flesh and blood is willing to give up home, relations and friends and come 12,000 miles to this country to become an Australian it is up to us to give him a helping hand,' implored the general secretary of the Queensland branch of the NSL. For many, the 'helping hand' was proffered with great generosity, particularly by the volunteers of the NSL. In other places, the welcome was less warm.[30]

5

'A Moron from Whitechapel'

South West thou are the land of pests
For fleas and flies one never rests.
E'en round me now mosquitoes revel,
In fact they are the very devil.
Sand flies and hornets just as bad,
They nearly drive a fellow mad.
There's the scorpion and the centipede
And stinging ants of every breed.

'The Group Settler's Lament'[1]

At the end of September 1923, one sensational murder case dominated newspapers across Australia. In the Arncliffe district of Sydney, a young man – seventeen or eighteen – called Leonard Puddifoot had, in broad daylight, killed a boy of five while in the process of attempting sexual assault. Part of his defence, it was reported, was that because of the boy's long fair curls, Puddifoot had thought he was a girl. Despite it being 'A Deed that has sent Sydney Shuddering', on 22 September he was sentenced to just three years' hard labour for manslaughter.[2]

There were public protests and outrage in the press at the leniency of the sentence – 'a satire of justice' – and numerous calls for the 'surgeon's knife'. While such stories – and reactions – were of course standard fare in popular newspapers across the empire, this one in Australia took a particular twist. Puddifoot, it was immediately stressed, was an 'Immigrant Boy'. It quickly emerged that he was from Watford near London and had arrived the previous August as an assisted migrant. As the papers endlessly repeated the grisly details of the case, Puddifoot was soon 'the gawky abnormality from Britain', 'a loutish degenerate, recently imported from England' and eventually 'a hulking, morbid importation from the Dear Old Motherland, whose junk, in human form, has been flooding Australia with unmentionable crimes'. When a similar case hit the headlines the following year, suspicion of recent British immigrants was immediately raised.[3]

The *Australian Worker* of 26 September agreed that Puddifoot had received too light a sentence and suggested that more vetting should be made of intending emigrants, though 'no doubt the cheap-labor lovers will object to such a proposal'. The Labor Party (ALP) was often accused of opposing immigration – an unpatriotic stance because of its importance to national security – but denied this, replying that the time was simply not right. Unemployment had risen sharply in 1921, up from 6.5 per cent to 11 per cent in a year. The ALP Conference of October 1921 carried a motion: 'Labor opposes all further assisted immigration'. Otherwise, wasn't the problem of unemployment simply being shifted from Britain to Australia? The rate fell slightly by the end of 1923, but earlier that year the Australian Workers Union had contacted British Labour Party leader Ramsay MacDonald asking him to make it widely known that Australia was 'overrun with unemployed' and that British immigrants were being fooled by recruitment agents' promises of high wages; instead immigration was a ruse to help employers lower pay rates. The same issue of the *Australian Worker* reported that 'England is sending about 500 boys a month to Australia', aged fourteen to eighteen years. For some, youth migration offered a group most likely to 'in a short time become real Australian citizens in the fullest sense'. For others, the attraction lay in the fact that they could be paid much less than older married men.[4]

The *Nation and Athenaeum* article of 29 September, 'An Australian view of the Imperial Conference', summarised the viewpoint of the 'average Australian' as 'frankly hostile or, at best, indifferent' to questions of migration and settlement. The industrial worker was afraid of an overstocked labour market, while 'the countryman is himself land-hungry and is not eager to share with outsiders what little good land is available for settlement'.

On 29 September 1923 there were a number of vessels at sea carrying British migrants to start new lives in Australia. The *Esperance Bay* had sailed on 29 August, the *Orsova* on 15 September, the *Omar* on 21 September. The largest group of migrants were from the quadrilateral bounded by Inverness, Glasgow, Hull and Liverpool, with London next. Some migrants had a small amount of capital – perhaps £20 or £30. Assisted migrants were usually unemployed and impoverished, although in theory they had passed medical tests and were in good health. Ex-servicemen usually had money from pensions but were often suffering from the after-effects of wounds, poisonous gas or 'shell-shock'.[5]

For many on board, this was the first time they had left their home districts, let alone the country. Few had experience of life on board a ship. For the voyage of five or six weeks all assisted migrants travelled third class, where most cabins had six or eight berths. Mothers and children were separated from men. Toilets were few. So it was crowded and unhygienic, which often caused enmity between passengers. There was little scope for exercise. It was unsettling but also liberating, just as the migrants themselves alternated between high hopes and deep anxiety about their new lives to come. Those who could afford it often spent the time gambling and drinking (one migrant arrived penniless and almost naked, as he'd literally bet his shirt and lost). Others engaged in ship-board romances. Some of the boys, previously malnourished, took to the regular supplied meals with such gusto that they suddenly outgrew their clothes.

The first port of call was Fremantle, Western Australia. One migrant remembered the dock-workers shouting at the Britons lining the rail: 'Go away – there's no work for you!' Here, the New Settlers' League had commandeered a large warehouse to accommodate the migrants on their first nights off the boat. It contained nearly a hundred beds ranged close together. It soon acquired a bad reputation for discomfort and dirt and insect infestations, being nicknamed the 'Buggy House'. The commission, headed by William Windham from the Ministry of Labour and including Gladys Pott, chair of the Society for Overseas Settlement of British Women, sent to investigate migrant conditions would report that for the migrant these early days, 'after the excitement and novelty have worn off and illusions with which he may have set out have been dispelled, is likely to be the most difficult and testing time in his career'. The commission estimated that a fifth of all migrants after this period still, 'for one reason or another, find difficulty in settling down'.[6]

Promotional literature had plenty of examples of migrant success stories. The *New Settlers' League Handbook to Western Australia* quoted a recent arrival declaring that 'The people seem very sociable and are not so "classy" as they are in the Old Country.' The report of the SOSBW tells of the story of a young woman who had emigrated in 1922 and the same year married an Australian, Jack: 'The glorious sense of space and freedom in the bush districts of Western Australia can only be truly realised by those who have lived and worked in large cities and disliked them, all clatter and smoke . . . The life here is so free and easy. There is no mistress and maid (in the English meaning). Jack is as good as his master.'[7]

'So many contradictory statements have latterly appeared as to the state of the labour market in Australia that authentic information is welcome,' reported the *News of the World* on 30 September 1923. They had received a letter from a recent migrant at Burra, South Australia: 'There is plenty of work here . . . there are quite a number of English lads round about the Burra, and from what they tell me, none of them has yet regretted coming out.'

But the *News of the World*, like most press, preferred bad news stories, of which there was no shortage. A boy of sixteen, the son of a

Midlands boot maker, just arrived, 'Went straight up country to farm jobs.' He was back in Melbourne a week later. He had been allotted a bed in a shed on the farm. Lifting a dirty old blanket, he was horrified to find a nest of tarantulas.[8]

Many Australians looked to exploit the incomers, demanding more work and paying lower wages than locals would have accepted, and most at risk of exploitation were 'farmboys' like this. Many became intensely homesick, and employers complained of excessive bed-wetting. By the end of 1924 there had been five suicides among the farmboys, the last being James Smith, a boy of fifteen from Glasgow, who shot himself in the head. 'Lonely Migrant Commits Suicide' was the headline in the *Mercury* of 3 December 1924. This caused shock at home and questions were asked in the House of Commons.

A worrying number of migrants gave up and headed back home. An investigator in 1924, noting Australian 'dislike and antipathy' towards the incomers, found one shipload with seventy-one 'disconsolate' families returning to Britain. Perhaps there would have been more had they been able to afford it, or were not disallowed visas on the grounds that they had not served the two years demanded by the terms of assisted passage.[9]

The *Western Mail* carried an article by a reporter who had interviewed several among a group of 900 people returning to England. One, a 'fresh-faced mother nursing a sturdy little baby', complained, 'we are treated as foreigners, as "pommies" – people on a lower social scale. I love Australia ... but instead of being received as the mothers of Australia's future sons, we were ostracized.'[10]

The census of 1921 had recorded only 8 per cent of Australians born in Britain, against 85 per cent born in Australia, the highest ever proportion. The war had not only stopped immigration, contributing to this figure, but had also, by increasing Australian 'self-consciousness' and distinct national identity, in many cases made arrivals from Britain no longer 'new chums' but 'foreign immigrants'. Furthermore, the sacrifices made for Britain during the war in some quarters contributed to 'resentment' among Australians of 'those imperial ties which had entailed war's devastation'. More generally, 'Pommies' were now treated with suspicion or even hostility, as Lawrence described in *Kangaroo*.[11]

One garment worker from Manchester, having experienced hostility, explained, 'if you were a Pom and wanted to remain English in your outlook, they didn't care for you'. Instead you should 'become "Australianised" as quickly as possible, which I did and fitted in. My mates were Australian lads.' Within months he was watching Australian rules football on Saturday afternoons with his new local friends.[12]

For many others, though, there was confusion and disappointment. 'Why in God's name do we from the Motherland find such a wall of prejudice against us?' wrote an ex-service Scot in Melbourne to the Overseas Settlement Department in London. 'We from the Old Motherland are considered "dirty pommies" and by no less than those who were recently "pommies" themselves.'[13]

Most challenging though, and for different reasons, was the ambitious scheme in Western Australia known as Group Settlement. In his *Unlimited Australia*, E. J. Brady called his chapter on Western Australia 'Miserablest Country' after the explorer William Dampier's description of it, and then set out to prove the opposite: in fact, thanks to its abundant rainfall, the south-west of the state, he wrote, when cleared of timber, 'becomes a splendid natural pasture' with potential to 'give employment and wealth to millions'.[14]

The Premier of Western Australia, Sir James Mitchell, had earlier been Minister for Agriculture and overseen a vast expansion of the state's wheat belt. But he was unhappy that dairy products were still being imported from Victoria and Tasmania. In 1921, unemployed workers were given land in the south-west near Manjimup. They were to clear it in groups and establish dairy farms. The favourable response to the scheme encouraged Mitchell to adapt it for British immigrants. In fact, he became so gripped by the idea that he came to be called 'Moo-cow Mitchell'. Anyone pointing out the many potential difficulties was dismissed as a 'croaker'.[15]

In the spring of 1922 he made his only trip to Britain, preaching the gospel of Group Settlement. The scheme, which would be officially approved by London in February 1923, involved Western Australia taking 75,000 British immigrants over five years. Out of these, 6,000 married men with families – the larger the better – would, after gaining experience for a year working on existing farms, be selected in groups of twenty for settlement in the state's forested south-western region. To manage them, there would be an experienced local foreman.

Each Group Settlement would consist of twenty 'blocks' of 25 acres each. The land would be cleared by mutual effort and then a block allocated to a settler by a ballot system. Then dairy farming would start, which had the advantage of being a year-round activity, unlike wheat or fruit farming, and of being supposedly the easiest type of farming to learn.

Except for surveying costs, the land would be free, though preparation expenses – securing a water supply, fencing, building houses, tools, stock – would be accounted as debt to be paid off in thirty years, with interest for the first five years partially paid by the state and the UK government. Wages would not be paid, but settlers would receive a subsistence allowance of 10s a day.[16]

The scheme would have the crucial advantage of creating an instant community, along the lines of an English village, making 'possible a social life, the absence of which is one of the great obstacles in the way of outback settlement', as the *West Australian* newspaper approvingly noted on 29 September 1923. The scheme was also available to local applicants, who by late 1923 would make up just under half of the number of 'Groupies'. Left-wingers were positive, calling it 'as near Socialism as you can get in a capitalist society'.[17]

Mitchell received a warm welcome on his promotional tour of the UK, particularly from the Northcliffe papers, the *Mail* and *Evening News*. Northcliffe had toured Australia in 1921 and promised to become 'Australia's finest immigration agent'. His efforts were so appreciated that one of the new settlements would be named after him.

Ten thousand copies of the *New Settlers' League Handbook to Western Australia* were printed and the majority shipped to London for distribution around the country. With advertisements for super-phosphate and a cover showing a pastoral scene of lush farmland, the handbook had an introduction by Mitchell himself. Western Australia, he wrote, had only 350,000 people in 640 million acres. 'Do you realise what this means to you in your over-crowded British Isles? It means that if you desire elbow-room, a clear blue sky, with glorious fresh air and sunshine; if you want to become your own master; if you want to have your own farm, here is where your fortune lies. I say to you – Come to Western Australia and grab the opportunities that await you!' It was no place for an 'idler or drifter', he warned; instead the work required was what 'A Man's Man' should want to do. A new settler was 'expected to have some backbone of his own'. There was also an appeal to racial pride, to help hold Australia 'inviolate for the white races'.[18]

The first casualty of the scheme was the plan for immigrants to spend a year gaining experience on existing farms. Few farmers could afford the upkeep of an inexperienced incomer and his family; others failed to keep their side of the bargain to provide a whole year's train-ing, instead using the immigrants as cheap seasonal labour, laying them off when they were not immediately required. At the same time, some immigrants were impatient to fulfil their dream of becoming independent landowners.[19]

The result was a huge demand for land that saw many novice settlers going from the 'Buggy House' at Fremantle straight out to blocks that had been over-hastily surveyed and on which little preparation work had been done. A Devon man, R. Fowler, described how he and his wife were taken straight to 'Tin sheds ... we called them shacks.' 'My wife thought she had come to the Last of her days, her heart was in her mouth straight away, have we to Live in this? I said, of course *yes* just for a while.'

When the time came for the balloting, he got what he called a 'Swamp Block'. This was 6 miles from their camp of tin shacks, which meant getting up before 4 a.m. in order to be there '20 past 7 sharp, if you were a Minute Late you had to make it up, My word they were days. Wet, no name for it. Some weeks we were working in water up to our knees slashing down Scrubb, Mulocking Roots out best way we Could, Cold Soaked into the Skin, go back at Night to our Old Shacks, all water logged, cold, shivering.'

As well as directing the work, the foremen had a great challenge in managing the group dynamics, and certainly some were better than others. 'We were treated like a Dam Lot of Dogs,' complained Fowler. 'Foremans would chew your heads off, that's not the way to do that . . . and tell you you B. *Pommys* as they Call us people out here.'[20]

Helen Woolmer was the wife of a British veteran who had found it impossible to find work in post-war London. 'After a terrific struggle, selling every single thing we possessed to buy food, even my engagement and wedding ring, my Husband decided to make a break, & a bid for a new and better life for us and our children, & to migrate to Australia. We had glowing accounts of the bright and prosperous future which awaited us in Australia . . . bitter was our disillusionment.'

Helen, her husband John and two small children spent three days at the 'dreadful migrants' home at Fremantle' and were then sent to Northcliffe, three and a half hours' journey south of Perth. Like Fowler, they were greeted by tin shacks, but there weren't enough, so the families had to share (although the foreman got one to himself). There were no toilets and the water supply consisted of a small creek. Access was by a rough bush track; there was 'no doctor or hospital, no beds or blankets, no milk, no fruit. In these shacks women & children laid on the bare earth covered with sacks, while the men slept out in the bush.' Their baby daughter and young son contracted dysentery, then they became covered in sores, 'through improper and insufficient food'. Then her husband fell gravely ill with pneumonia and pleurisy. At 'starvation point' the family threw themselves on the mercy of the Red Cross in Perth.[21]

Some were even less lucky. At the end of 1923 a young English couple arrived at Group 98 near Northcliffe. She was pregnant with their first child. At the time the group consisted of a double row of two-family huts facing each other over a cleared space. All around behind the huts were tall trees that they were assigned to bring down.

It was strikingly unsanitary. There were two toilets – one for men and one for women, each consisting of an open pit with a sapling balanced on forked sticks serving as the seat. Some of the settlers, however, were content to empty their chamber pots – a chopped-down kerosene tin – outside their huts. Almost inevitably, there was an outbreak of gastroenteritis, which killed their first baby. Dressing in their best clothes, and carrying nothing but the dead child, they walked off the group never to be seen again.[22]

Northcliffe was situated in virgin forest of immensely tall and thick karri trees, some of the toughest wood in the world, difficult enough even for experienced timber workers. Almost all of the 'groupies' here were British immigrants, none of whom had handled a saw before, nor even lit a wood-burning stove. The timber, once brought down, could not be sold as there was insufficient transport to take it away. To get rid of the stumps, a hole had to be drilled, then filled with gelignite with a cordite fuse. The challenge was to light this then run away fast enough to escape the debris from the blast. A visitor to Northcliffe remembered that 'the claustrophobic effect of the heavy karri country' together with the isolation 'blanketed the area and the people with an air of pessimism'. A settler admitted to hospital in a delirious state, a doctor later recollected, had a constant preoccupation: 'Trees, trees, trees – you never see anything else but trees.'[23]

The monotony and isolation brought severe homesickness, particularly for those who had previously been city dwellers. An Australian remembered hearing from the British women in his group how they missed 'the simple things such as the ringing of church bells, the cries of the fishmongers, the coal men and the rabbit merchants, the bells of the muffin and crumpet man ... the milk vendors pushing their little carts along the cobbled roads'. The men 'told me of the warm local pubs, the factory siren, the music halls, and the roaring crowds of football patrons'.[24]

But a little further north, where lumbermen had been at work for some years, it was a different story. Jack Murdock was born in Walthamstow in 1907, and the same year his family had migrated to Western Australia, settling near Fremantle. In his memoir, he described his parents as traditional cockneys of 'very humble circumstances' who had migrated as they were 'young, healthy and venturesome, and heartily detested the class distinction rampant in England at the time'. Both were 'terrifically honest and battlers'.[25]

In September 1922, the family had joined the new Group Settlement 31, south of Manjimup. The Group had twenty huts, one for each family, as well as an equipment store and stable. Four miles away was Jardanup (later Jardee), a town built around a large saw mill. This provided shops and entertainment. To feed the mill, the nearby hardwood karris had been professionally cleared, meaning that the settlers only had to cope with the more manageable jarrah and marri trees, and they were also provided with timber for building.

Murdock's account is full of praise for the first settlers' initiative, energy and improvisation. Women made cushions, curtains and rugs out of old flour sacks. Empty butter boxes, kerosene cases and gelignite cases 'were invaluable, and were put to a great variety of purposes'. Kerosene tins provided the basis for buckets, food bins, washing-up dishes, shower baths, firegrates and dust pans. They were even made into wardrobes, bookcases and cupboards.

It was never boring on Group 31, Murdock wrote. Instead 'There was a virile, almost humorous feeling in the camp as though things were a bit rough, any obstacles that arose, they were tickled pink to overcome.'

A model farm was established with seven cows and six pigs, and, following generous application of superphosphate, the first pasture was planted. Soon they 'had plenty of beautiful sweet smelling hay and ensilage', and cows were put out to pasture.

But here things started to go wrong. However lush the pasture growth, 'the animals became skinnier and scruffier. We dared not leave harness, hats or clothing lying about. The cows would chew the lot up.' One of Murdock's friends left his motorbike and sidecar near a field, and the cows got out during the night. 'Next morning he found the seat and lining stripped bare. Every piece of the upholstery had been chewed up.'

'I don't think the top echelon of our governing body gave a thought to any experiment to find out what mineral deficiencies there were in the soil,' Murdock later wrote. There was only so much superphosphate could do. Various 'licks' were tried without success and the lack of minerals also caused temporary sterility in the cattle, as well as resulting in cows calving at the wrong time of the year. The 'wonderfully fertile soil' advertised in Britain by the *Settlers' Handbook* had proved anything but.

Looking at the surviving settler diaries, it's difficult not to be awestruck by how hard they worked, clearing the land, travelling miles by foot or horse and cart to collect tools or food, fixing things, digging, fencing, ploughing, planting and tending vegetables. One typical diary entry ends: 'miserable day'. Others relished the struggle. Len Cooke, a young Englishman, wrote to his parents back in Britain that he was 'working 14 hours a day', living on endless cold mutton and bread and jam, but having a 'jolly experience . . . it has been very interesting & have learnt a great deal'.[26]

In late 1922, Morris Munday, a twenty-nine-year-old Western Australian, applied to become a Group Settler. He favoured the Manjimup area, but was told by an official who 'worked somewhat like a war-time recruiting officer' that it was the Peel estate or nothing. During the war, Munday had volunteered and embarked for Europe in October 1915. Thanks to a shortage of shipping he didn't return until late November 1919. Not long after that he married a Lilian Parker. 'After sampling two or three different vocations,' he wrote, 'I thought the call of the Group Settlement Scheme appealed as a likely step to becoming a farmer . . . So taking the plunge we set off in the beginning of 1923 to join group No. 47 Peel estate.' The couple had with them a six-month-old daughter, Gwen, Lilian's father and a part-fox terrier dog, Bob.[27]

The No. 47 Group was situated on what was somewhat discouragingly named 'The Corner Swamp'. On a small piece of dry ground, the group moved into army-surplus bell tents. Father Parker, as Lilian's dad was known, was accommodated in a 'hand-made bush shed'; the other three plus dog shared a tent. 'Cooking arrangements were most primitive, an outside rock-built fire place.' The water supply was so dark that it stained clothes, and food 'would emerge from the pot with an unappetizing blackish colour'.

The south-west, of course, had been favoured for development because of its high rainfall compared to most of the rest of the continent. In theory, effective drainage ditches had been built prior to the occupation of the blocks by settlers, but much of Morris's block was under several inches of water. Most of the soil was pretty much pure sand; in other areas were bulrush marshes lying on a dark peaty loam. Here were none of Northcliffe's ferociously hard karri trees: instead there were soft banksias, 15 feet tall, 6 to 8 inches in diameter. Using a horse with a chain attached, and with a settler chopping at the shallow roots, they could be pulled out fairly easily. The bulrushes were more of a challenge. One method was the use of 'the old-fashioned scythe', a 'slow and laborious work'. Another was to plough, but 'each small piece' of the thick, compact roots, 'even after being broken up with the plough ... would quickly send up fresh growth'.

In the meantime, Gwen spent her days in a large packing case placed partly in Father Parker's shed and partly in the open air. 'This at least allowed her to move around in safety from inquisitive reptiles such as dugite snakes (which were fairly plentiful) and goannas.' Goannas are large carnivorous lizards with sharp claws and teeth and a fearsome appearance. Dugite snakes, known only in Western Australia and the western parts of South Australia, can grow to over 6 feet, but most are a little smaller. They are highly venomous.

In September 1923, having spent six months in their army bell tent, the family moved into a newly built four-roomed jarrah-wood house. Morris Munday got ill, but Father Parker stepped in and took up the slack on his son-in-law's strictly allocated work. The same month saw the completion of wells that meant the brackish black water was replaced by 'beautiful clear drinking water'.

But preparing the land for dairy was not going well. There had been great hope placed in a species of subterranean clover that was not only excellent fodder with exemplary nitrogen-fixing properties, but also grew well in poor, arid soils. It was one of those new crops that gave so much hope to the believers in 'Unlimited Australia'. But the soil of the Peel estate proved to be beyond even its abilities. As Munday wrote, 'despite many attempts to grow clover and other feed the result was complete failure ... Unfortunately for the group settlers, pasture does not flourish in sand.' Now 'the settlers began to realise that dairying on the Peel estate was not going to be a success. One by one the families left until officially Group No. 47 came to an end.'

As early as the end of 1923 people were already talking about the 'failure' of the Peel estate. Along with the poor soil, flooding over wide areas meant that pasture was destroyed and the large amounts spent on seed and manure were wasted.[28]

Morris Munday would stay on the Group longer than most, and after three years and three months he produced his first cream. In the meantime, Lilian had had two more children, another girl then a boy. But by then they had had enough. Like many others, Morris gave up and returned to the city.

This 'drift to the cities' was, of course, exactly what the authorities had hoped to avoid. There they would compete with Australian workers for jobs; it also undid all the purposes of rural settlement – national security against the threat of Japan, primary production for export, the creation of the agrarian idyll of family-based, politically stable small homesteads.

No one suggested that the solution to this problem might be to improve conditions on the Group Settlements. Instead what was needed was a more rigorous weeding out in Britain of those who did not have what Sir James Mitchell had called the 'backbone' to succeed in the challenge. A New Settlers' League Conference held in Perth in August 1923 resolved that 'the methods in England of examination of immigrants are farcical, indicating a systematic attempt to expel unemployed from England irrespective of consequences'. In effect, failures were blamed on the weaknesses of the settlers, rather than on the scheme itself. The New Settlers' League pronounced it 'astonishing how a person who fails to make good by laziness or some other equally bad complaint immediately blames the country'.[29]

This strength of feeling reflects what was now becoming an inescapable fact: the Group Settlement scheme was failing. Settlers had run up debts to the local storekeepers on the security of their blocks, but now the storekeepers were threatening foreclosure. At the same time the prices for dairy had fallen steadily. By the time of the publication of the Windham commission's report in May 1924, 31 per cent of the immigrant Group settlers and 49 per cent of the Australian-born had walked off their blocks. Soon, much of the laboriously cleared land had returned to nature.[30]

'We are pouring people onto the land, in the hope that some will stay,' wrote G. L. Wood, a senior lecturer in economics at the University of Melbourne, in what he called a 'plain statement of the issues involved in migration within the Empire as they are seen from the Australian angle'. In an article published a little later, he surveyed the failures of the previous few years, the 'salutary correctives to the assumptions that boundless empty spaces await the plough of the settler'. It wasn't just Western Australia that had proved to be less than the proponents of 'Unlimited Australia' had hoped. Schemes across the country had disappointed. One in New South Wales, part of a grand 'Million farms' project, had land that only supported one sheep per 20 acres.[31]

Then Wood got to the crux: Britain wanted to get rid of its urban proletariat, but Australia wanted agricultural workers, 'the class of labour that Britain could least afford to lose'. What was now needed, he wrote, was 'a frank admission of the costly failure of the attempt to make efficient farmers of industrial workers'.

Wood's article includes a graph showing distribution of population by nationality between rural and urban districts. In terms of the ambitions for rural development, the British immigrants do not come out well; of many nationalities only the Greeks have a higher proportion in the cities. In second place as the desired rural dwellers, behind Germans, are Italians.

Whatever the Australian hostility to 'Pommies', there was far more prejudice against southern European immigrants. They were somehow considered not quite as white as, say, British or Scandinavians. There was a similar view of a 'hierarchy of whiteness' in the United States at this time, where legislation was going through to limit immigration from southern Europe in favour of 'Nordic' races. In Australia, an investigation into immigration made a sharp distinction between the 'knife-wielding, inferior Sicilian' and the 'blonde, intelligent, hard-working, assimilatable Alpine'. Fairly unsuccessful attempts were made to recruit migrants from Scandinavia.

But as the doors to the United States closed, so more southern Europeans headed for Australia. State governments had to stress to their publics that they had not encouraged or assisted 'these classes of immigrants' who were arriving on their own initiative. Many Italians joined already established communities in the northern canefields of Queensland, 'becoming a menace to the Britisher ... monopolizing the sugar industry and gradually outnumbering the British Farmer'.[32]

Wood takes issue with this view, describing Mediterranean immigrants as 'of a virile and adventurous type'. They were for the most part hard-working, law-abiding agriculturalists. They also often came with capital, unlike the majority of British migrants who arrived with neither money nor farming experience and ended up leading the dreaded 'drift to the cities'. 'It must be admitted', concluded a Sydney magazine article on 'Italian Immigration', 'that a healthy-bodied hard-working Italian who is prepared to live laborious days in the bush is preferable to a moron from Whitechapel or Soho who prefers to walk the city streets.'[33]

6

'The Dream of the Heart'

It was essentially a silk hat and morning coat occasion,
all the overseas Premiers looking very trim and
smart . . . India excited much attention. The gorgeously
bedecked secretary to the equally resplendent
Maharajah of Alwar . . . lent a touch of colour to
the scene.

Evening Standard,
on the first day of the Imperial Conference[1]

A successful war against America was quite out of
the question.

CABINET SECRETARY MAURICE HANKEY[2]

At the beginning of September 1923, a massive earthquake devastated Tokyo and nearby Yokohama. Combined with the effects of the resultant fire, as many as 150,000 were killed and the homes of half a million destroyed. The news was greeted with horror in Britain, but also with a certain amount of schadenfreude. 'Terrible as is the destruction of life and property in Japan,' wrote one reporter, 'it will prove an important factor in the world's peace as it will give pause to the military caste in that country.'[3]

For the fifty years from 1860, after the Second Opium War, Britain had been the undisputed master of the East, with more investment in China than everyone else put together as well as control of more than two thirds of the foreign trade, worth £53 million.

But following the Meiji Restoration in 1868, Japan had rapidly reformed and industrialised. In all things, the aim was to cherry-pick the 'best of the West'; this meant, among other things, the examples of American industry, the German Army and the British Royal Navy. It seemed the only way to avoid the humiliating fate of most of the rest of Asia and elsewhere.

By the beginning of the First World War, a modern railway network connected all the major cities, and foreign trade from new, state-of-the-art ports had grown an astonishing thirty-fold. Japan was now a major importer of raw materials and exporter of finished goods, along the British model. For Japan, achieving status as a modern power meant having colonies as all the others did. And this was not just for symbolic reasons: it was motivated by the same needs as others. Japan's population had grown from 35 million in 1873 to 55 million in 1918 (over the same period Britain's had risen from 31 million to 45 million). This drove the need for new territories for migration, raw materials, and markets for capital and finished goods.

A successful war with China had seen the takeover of Taiwan/Formosa and China's former vassal, coal- and ore-rich Korea. At the beginning of the First World War, Japan seized the German-leased territory of Shandong and presented a list of 'Twenty-one Demands' to China's leader. It was a blatant statement of imperial intent. Most were resisted, but China had to concede to Japanese dominance in Shandong, Manchuria and Inner Mongolia.

Ever since the Meiji Restoration, Japanese leaders had tried to secure acknowledgement from the West that they were peers in the international community, but had been consistently rebuffed. At the Versailles Conference, the Japanese delegation were treated with contempt, sat at the far end of the long table facing the representatives of Ecuador and Guatemala. At the top of the Japanese agenda had been a motion to enshrine racial equality. In defence of his 'White Australia' policy, Billy Hughes had fervently argued against it, but it passed nonetheless. Then President Wilson, with immigration issues of his own, decreed that the vote was annulled as there were some strong objectors.

Along with much else, Japan had also adopted a Western-style constitution with parliament, prime minister and ministers. But the restored emperor, considered divine, was the executive ruler of the state and ministers were responsible to him; a parliament could criticise and obstruct but not rule. The emperor also directly commanded the armed forces, who soon became the most powerful group in society. As early as 1871 the military establishment was ignoring civilian orders. After successes in wars against China and Russia its status and independence only increased.

But even liberal Japanese intellectuals saw racist European and American imperialism as a greater threat than any drift towards authoritarianism at home. Nagai Ryuturo, a Christian journalist who championed universal suffrage and women's rights, and favoured socialism, also sought to raise the alarm against what he called 'the white peril'. 'If one race assumes the right to appropriate all the wealth, why should not all the other races feel ill-used and protest?' he asked.[4]

The war gave Japan the opportunity rapidly to increase its influence and trade in China at the expense of the British. Before the war, Britain had supplied 62 per cent of China's cloth imports and Japan 13 per cent. Between 1914 and 1918 Japan's share of foreign trade in Shanghai (a British colony in all but name) doubled, and by 1923 the figures for Chinese cloth imports were 35 per cent British and 52 per cent Japanese.

In the meantime, Tokyo had become a mecca and centre of a transnational intellectual network for nationalists from India, Burma, Ceylon, French Indo-China, Dutch Indonesia and elsewhere. Here was a potential nursery of coordinated, multi-colony resistance to British rule. Japan's example offered new hope for colonised, non-white people across the world.

So, by 1923, Japan seemed to pose the greatest threat – commercially, politically and militarily – to the British Empire in the Far East.

This threat had been made worse by two recent, interlinked developments. Back in 1902, Britain had signed a treaty with Japan that had allowed the Royal Navy to redeploy five battleships from the Pacific to face the German threat in home waters. The treaty with Japan was renewed and expanded in scope twice, in 1905 and 1911. But when it came up for renewal in 1921, the United States intervened.

US–Japan relations were strained, to say the least. Following the Chinese Exclusion Act of 1882, the gap in the supply of cheap labour had seen large-scale Japanese immigration to the United States, particularly California. Between 1901 and 1908 some 127,000 Japanese entered the US. But there was a backlash, with the formation of the Asiatic Exclusion League in 1907, calling for America to be a 'white man's country'. President Roosevelt pressurised Japan's leaders into promising to issue no more passports for Japanese workers wanting to migrate to the US, Japanese children in California were forced into segregated schools, and discriminatory legislation on land ownership and leasing was passed. As with the 'White Australia' programme, Japanese officials protested against 'racial' policy.[5]

There was also rivalry over China, which empowered nationalistic elements in Japan. 'We are unable to remain calm when America is showing herself a hypocrite, a wolf in sheep's clothing,' fumed the *Yorodzu* newspaper. 'After trampling Hayti and San Domingo under her foot, she now attempts interference with Saghallen, incites a revolt in Korea, and hostility towards Japan by China. At such a rate the American attitude towards Japan will soon be worse than towards the blacks. No wonder Japanese blood has reached boiling point.'[6]

It was in this context that a clear message was sent to London that Washington would view the renewal of the Anglo-Japanese treaty 'in any form' as an unfriendly act. The threat to British interests in the region from France, Russia and Germany – the original motivation for the 1902 treaty – had evaporated, so against whom, the Americans asked, would the alliance be directed? US naval planners' worst-case scenario was the Japanese and British fleets combining against them in the Pacific. But at the same time, Sir Charles Eliot, British ambassador to Japan, warned that if the treaty were not renewed it would result in Japan taking on 'an attitude of resentment and a policy of revenge'. There was no good option. Lloyd George called it the 'biggest decision' Britain had had to make 'since 1914'.[7]

The security of the empire depended on Britain's naval supremacy over any potential enemy. There was an acknowledgement that it would be ruinous for Britain to enter an expensive arms race against the United States, and furthermore that 'A successful war against America was quite out of the question.' There was also an assumption of American goodwill towards Britain, based on common language, origins, political systems and the 'Anglo-Saxon race'. In fact, two thirds of Americans were not of English stock, and not far beneath the surface there was fierce rivalry over oil, communications, shipping and commerce, where the Americans were capturing previously British markets while keeping their own firmly closed. Nonetheless, among the British establishment there were hopeful ideas of a 'special relationship' and even a great Anglo-American union. Lloyd George in 1921 assured his Cabinet, 'the people who govern America are our people. They are our kith and kin.' The 'non-white' Japanese, in contrast, Lloyd George suggested, 'might have no conscience'. For Foreign Secretary Curzon, the Japanese were 'not at all an altruistic power' but instead 'restless and aggressive'.[8]

The decision split the empire and demonstrated that a truly global power almost inevitably had distant territories with conflicting strategic imperatives, making a shared foreign policy impossible. Australia and New Zealand, long anxious about the vulnerability of their small populations and wide-open spaces, urged renewal of the treaty. 'If Japan is excluded from the family of great Western nations – and, mark, to turn our backs on the Treaty is certainly to exclude Japan – she will be isolated,' the Australian PM warned, 'her national pride wounded in its most tender spot.' But Canada took the opposite view. It was essential for Canadian security that Britain and the United States remained friendly powers, which an alliance with Japan clearly threatened. If the treaty renewal went ahead, they declared, they would not be bound by it. Effectively, this would mean the 'premier' Dominion jumping ship from the empire.

This threat proved to be decisive for decision-makers in London. In the event, the ending of the treaty with Japan, considered by Australia and New Zealand the best guarantee of their security, would be folded into a wider international agreement on naval arms reduction, the Washington Treaty, finally ratified a month before the 1923 Imperial Conference. Under its terms, battleship tonnage of both the US and UK was not to exceed 525,000 tons. Japan was limited to 300,000 tons. The proportions were 5:5:3, with Italy and France set at 1.75.

The Japanese delegation fought hard against the implied inferiority of the 5:5:3 ratio, and only accepted it with a new provision – that none of the powers would be allowed to construct new naval bases north of Singapore or west of Hawaii. Nonetheless, they remained, as the Australians had feared, resentful about the ending of the treaty and the ratio, described by one Japanese critic as 'Rolls Royce, Rolls Royce, Ford'. One journalist called for Japanese expansion, 'to break the worldwide monopoly ... the special sphere of influence and the worldwide tyranny of the white races'.[9]

In fact, Japan had done well out of the treaty, the United States poorly, Britain perhaps the worst. The empire had global strategic responsibilities and therefore potential threats. It needed considerably more ships than anyone else. In contrast Japan, for all the umbrage taken, looked like the rising imperial power, well above France and Italy in the new pecking order. For its part, the United States, unlike Japan, had two ocean commitments. It could have easily out-built its rivals, but instead the imposed ratios delivered to Japan marginal naval supremacy in the Western Pacific. The ban on naval bases left Hong Kong defenceless, also Guam and the Philippines. As a senior US naval strategist complained in the summer of 1923, 'The United States has yielded the possibility of naval equality in this region.'[10]

The treaty, then, had alienated Japan and pushed it into a more aggressive and expansionist policy without in any way constraining its power in the Pacific. The restraint imposed by the treaty with Britain was gone. Hopes were expressed at the time of a pay-off – perhaps some debt forgiveness or that the 'good but scarcely intimate relations of the British Empire with the United States will be widened into close and extensive co-operation'. But the British Empire got nothing from the Americans in return for choosing their friendship over Japan's. The isolationist US was in no mood to make treaties or commitments; as Hughes had acknowledged at the 1921 conference, 'If Australia was asked whether she would prefer America or Japan as an ally, her choice would be America. But that choice is not offered to her.'[11]

Shortly before the 1923 Imperial Conference Curzon would admit that 'the strategic position of Japan has been greatly strengthened as a result of the Naval Treaty'. At the conference itself, the Australians and New Zealanders pushed for funding for the new Singapore naval base, an idea that had been agreed on in 1921, but for which money from the Treasury had not been forthcoming. The scheme, for a heavily armed and lavishly equipped 'Gibraltar of the East', was resurrected, but doubts remained. For one thing, there was concern that the spine of British power – the dreadnought and battlecruiser – had become obsolete in the face of developments in submarines and air power. There was also a suggestion that the Royal Navy, under the new restrictions, would not have enough ships to furnish the base. First Lord of the Admiralty Leo Amery assured delegates that the Royal Navy would have the bulk of its force in the Mediterranean ready to rush to Singapore, and that the threat of air power against the fleet was much exaggerated.[12]

The threat of Japan in the East was one part of a wider discussion at the conference of the empire's vulnerability. In some ways, the post-war settlement had improved the empire's strategic position – the vital Suez lifeline was now protected from the east by the Palestine Mandate, and the overland route to India, once threatened by Napoleon, was secured by the British Mandate in Iraq and a strong position in Persia. But these extra responsibilities had stretched resources nearly to breaking point. To enforce the Iraq Mandate against widespread opposition had cost, as well as thousands of lives, nearly £30 million a year from 1920 to 1922, far more than the UK's health budget (leading to the abandonment of ambitious irrigation schemes in the Euphrates valley designed to make the region a breadbasket, the 'Oriental Canada').

Together with commitments in Ireland, Egypt and the 60,000-strong garrison in India, this had left the army, as the Chief of the Imperial General Staff Sir Henry Wilson put it in 1920, 'spread all over the world ... far too scattered. In no single theatre are we strong enough.' Soon afterwards the Liberal leader in the House of Lords, Marquess Crewe, a former Secretary of State for the Colonies, told Curzon during a debate on Mesopotamia that 'the people of this country are not prepared to play fairy godmother to all undeveloped parts of the world. The country simply could not afford to pursue such a policy.' Wilson reckoned that Britain now needed an army twice the size of that of 1914. Nonetheless, the military budget went on shrinking, from £300 million in 1920 to £114 million in 1923. One of Wilson's last public appearances before his assassination by the IRA in June 1922 was to give a lecture entitled 'The Passing of the British Empire'.[13]

There was, of course, an alternative 'world policeman' in the form of the new League of Nations. With its commitment to peaceful arbitration in place of armed conflict, the League enjoyed wide popularity in the years immediately after the war. In October 1918, a British 'supporters' club' had been formed, the League of Nations Union. Its first chair was Gilbert Murray, brother of Hubert, Governor of Papua. By 1920 the union had 60,000 members across the empire, including branches in every Australian city, and a new chair, Lord John Cecil, who had been the first government supporter of the idea of a League.

Cecil saw the union's role as educating people away from old opinions about foreign nations. 'In a democratic age, everything depends on public opinion,' he wrote. 'This means that the public must have an opinion on international affairs, and that its opinion must be right.'

Lecturers were sent across the country – one of whom was a young Vera Brittain – extolling the virtues of the League. Brittain called it 'the one element of hope and progress contained in the peace treaties'. The Union's parliamentary secretary was up-and-coming young Conservative MP Oswald Mosley.[14]

The League was also sold as the best insurance policy the empire could ever buy. 'We have a small army and a vast Empire,' one of its supporters pointed out; 'it is immensely important to us to preserve our status quo by the peaceful methods of arbitration and international co-operation rather than by the maintenance of armies and navies which a return to the Balance of Power would force upon us.'[15]

The League of Nations Union was supported by the middle class and lower middle class, women and free churches. It was opposed by Conservatives and the military. Churchill would later declare of the Union: 'What impresses me most about them is their long suffering and inexhaustible gullibility.'[16]

However, not all on the left were won over by the League of Nations. Ramsay MacDonald, outlining the foreign policy of the Labour Party in a 1921 pamphlet, pronounced that the League should be the 'focus of our contacts with Europe' instead of 'sectional alliances or guarantees', but acknowledged that the organisation needed 'the confidence of all the important nations', by which he meant the United States, who were still refusing to join and whose participation was crucial.[17]

Philip Snowden, who would in 1924 become Labour's first Chancellor of the Exchequer, saw the League as tainted by association with the Treaty of Versailles, which he described as 'not a peace treaty, but a declaration of another war'. With Germany excluded, the League looked like an Allied alliance to hold Germany in an inferior position. H. G. Wells, taking the same line, called the League 'a sham world parliament'.[18]

The League had notched up some successes, for instance mediating between Yugoslavia and Bulgaria over a border dispute and thus avoiding war. But in September 1923 it caved in to demands from Italy's leader Benito Mussolini over an argument with Greece that had involved Italian warships bombarding a defenceless town in Corfu. Mosley would later write that this failure 'wrecked' the League.[19]

Nonetheless, it was too big an electoral risk for British politicians to ignore the League, so fulsome support was expressed in public, and the government remained formally committed to the League framework to solve international crises through negotiation. In private, though, they expressed deep cynicism about its capacity and continued to conduct a foreign policy based on deals between the major powers.

There was another factor that fuelled this attitude. Hard-headed politicians realised that the League would only really be effective if backed by actual force. In post-war Europe, this meant the French Army and the British Royal Navy. Thus over-commitment to the League risked increasing Britain's already perilously stretched strategic obligations. Prime Minister Andrew Bonar Law, taking over after the fall of Lloyd George at the end of 1922, echoed the words of Marquess Crewe: 'We cannot act alone as the policeman of the world.'[20]

Unsurprisingly, this over-stretch prompted the domestic press and politicians to request more material contribution to empire defence from the Dominions. In the build-up to the Imperial Conference, newspapers from *The Times* to the *News of the World* had complained that Britain had 'thus far shouldered practically the whole burden involved in coping with the naval, military, and aerial needs of the Empire'. If the Dominions wanted to 'take a greater share' in foreign policy, it was only 'natural and fitting that they should bear their part in defence', argued *The Times*.[21]

At the conference, the First Lord of the Admiralty Leo Amery spelled out the huge disparity in contributions to imperial naval expenditure: Britain annually spent per head of the population 26s 8d, Australia 8s 2d, New Zealand 4s 7d, and Canada a meagre 1s 4d.

Massey and Bruce were certainly embarrassed by these figures, and made vague promises to increase their contributions. But Bruce, while acknowledging that 'Australia knows that any future for her except within the Empire would be utterly precarious', told a dinner of businessmen in London: 'You brought us into existence. You have some responsibility for us and cannot shirk.' At the conference itself, he argued that 'the major responsibility for the Empire is Britain's ... it is proper that Britain has a greater share'.[22]

A central ambition of the conference was the creation of 'a united understanding and common action in foreign affairs'. Massey was in favour. Bruce wanted to secure the whole-hearted commitment of the empire to Australia's defence, but did not want to alienate those Australians who had what *The Times* called a 'deep-rooted fear of "entanglement"' in Europe'. He had already announced Australia should be given a proper opportunity to express an opinion upon imperial policy before the course taken by Britain be determined. In London, he told Foreign Secretary Curzon privately, 'We do not want a repetition of the 1922 episode, when we were nearly involved in a war with Turkey at Britain's back, without really knowing what was going on.' In effect, he wanted all the advantages of imperial partnership, but at the same time increasingly looked to assert a measure of independence.[23]

Thus it all came back to the central dilemma, as outlined in September 1923's *Round Table* magazine: how to 'reconcile imperial unity with national freedom'?

There were also practical considerations. In the New Zealand Parliament questions had been asked about how this newly acquired 'voice upon foreign policy' would actually work – 'the machinery for it is defective', one MP argued. Massey suggested that an Empire Council could be created, or that Dominion leaders should meet more regularly. Others proposed that High Commissioners should be invested with the power to agree or not to urgent foreign policy actions. Certainly, the current set-up would not do. As Curzon's principal adviser, Eyre Crow, had already privately argued, 'it is ... not possible to delay all action until the Dominions have been consulted and have agreed upon a common decision'. But the conference failed to agree any new machinery that would solve this problem.[24]

During the conference, Foreign Secretary Lord Curzon gave the delegates an extensive overview of British foreign policy across the world with a clear ambition to bring the Dominions and India 'on board'. Earlier that year he had talked up the need for a 'common policy in international matters', so that the Foreign Minister could speak 'not only for Great Britain alone, but for the whole of the British Empire ... Think of the addition to his power and strength that will result if, in speaking, he knows – and the world knows – that there lies behind him the sentiments and the might of the British Empire as a whole.' If New Zealand and Australia – fearful of Japan – were on the whole compliant, the rest were distinctly not. Ireland wanted nothing to do with British foreign policy; although Smuts was sympathetic, he was soon to be yesterday's man as South Africa had already become increasingly secessionist and republican; the Indian government now insisted that the Indian Army was not available for imperial adventures 'outside the frontiers of India'.[25]

The key opponent of any moves towards a centralisation of imperial decision-making and policy, however, was Canada's Mackenzie King. As well as being dependent on Anglophobic French Canadian votes, King himself distrusted British politicians and press. He had arrived at the conference already annoyed by the publication in Canada of an Admiralty memorandum urging increased Canadian naval expenditure, as being an attempt to influence public opinion over the head of his government. Shortly before his departure for London he had received a letter from the Prime Minister of Saskatchewan warning him: 'Australasian and British imperialistic propagandists ... are straining to stampede us into a participation in big naval expenditures (& so commit us to Imperial Wars, irrevocably).'[26]

In reply to Curzon's plea for a united foreign policy driven by London, King replied that, for him, foreign policy fell into two areas: local and of particular interest to a Dominion or to Great Britain; or related to the empire as a whole. Thus Europe was the business of Great Britain, and the South Pacific of Australia, New Zealand and Britain. Anything that might suggest the existence of a single imperial entity in defence or foreign policy should be struck out of the conference's

conclusions. 'It is not true that the Empire is indivisible,' King pronounced. 'It is divisible, and very distinctly divisible. It is divisible
geographically, racially, politically, and in a thousand ways ...'[27]

Leo Amery, for one, was furious at this direct attack on the military
and political unity of the empire. When he accompanied King to the
naval inspection at Spithead, he could not help saying to the Canadian,
as they watched the fleet pass by, 'That is why you are Prime Minister
of Canada, and not at best one of the Senators of the American State
of Ontario.'[28]

Though privately he might have held a more nuanced position – he
said after Chanak that 'if a great and clear call of duty comes, Canada
will respond' – King was not to be moved during the conference.
Outlining the defence of the empire in terms of land forces, the
Secretary of War Lord Derby appealed for a 'complete agreement' as to
what steps should be taken in the event of an attack on any one part
of the empire, and also for an idea to be given on what assistance each
part could and would provide. King replied carefully that, of course,
there should be cooperation on training and equipment, but, he went
on, 'I think I ought to make it clear that as to what extent Canada
would participate in a war at any time must be considered a matter
which her own Parliament will wish to decide.'[29]

Derby was shocked. 'I appeal to two assumptions which I hope
are not ill-founded,' he exclaimed. 'First of all, that, if any part of the
Empire, wherever it is, is attacked, the whole Empire will rally to the
support of the part so attacked. Secondly that it will rally to the fullest
extent of its power.' Not so, replied King. Canada would not have, for
example, participated in the threatened war with Turkey over Chanak.
It was all down to the merits of the individual case, and would be
decided by Canada's Parliament.

Having killed off the idea of a common imperial policy, and of the
empire as a solid military alliance, King now took aim at the authority of the conference itself. Curzon had referred to it as a 'Cabinet'.
'We at this table cannot be too careful not to assume powers which
we have not got,' countered King. 'We have no right, as I see it, to

regard ourselves a Cabinet shaping policy for the British Empire. We are here as the representatives of Governments, deriving what power we have from that circumstance and that fact alone.' So, the Imperial Conference, the only existing body for imperial cooperation over high policy, was in fact little more than a talking shop.[30]

With no effective executive, no common foreign policy and no military alliance, what was the empire? Was it held together by nothing more than a 'sentimental tie'? King himself, fond of empty rhetoric, gave a speech at a dinner on 2 October, replying to a call for imperial unity. 'It had not been agreements, or charters, or treaties, or Constitutions, that had made for the unity of the Empire,' he said. 'It had been the vision of the mind and the dream of the heart.'[31]

Empire News columnist Foster Fraser ended his piece on 29 September on a thoughtful note. 'It is within the range of possibility that Great Britain may find herself at war and one or other of the Dominions may decide we are not in the right or at any rate think it advisable to remain neutral . . . the strings which tied the Dominions to Great Britain were slackened and then loosened altogether.' 'The only link of an official character which binds us together,' he concluded, 'is that the King is sovereign of all parts of the empire.'

7

The 'Prince of Hearts' – 'Pivot of Empire'

In a little tight naval uniform which clung close to
his figure he did not look above 15, a quite pathetic
little person.

Foreign Secretary LORD CURZON on the
Prince of Wales, leaving for his tour of Australia[1]

The King and his heir had a difficult relationship. King George
was poorly educated, unimaginative and a dour character,
obsessed with etiquette, punctuality and correct dress. Christmas at
Sandringham, the Prince of Wales wrote, consisted of 'an atmosphere
of restriction, killjoy pompousness ... and the most complete and utter
boredom'.[2]

The Prince later complained of distant and inattentive parents, and
an isolated childhood. He was privately taught at home, even though
his tutor urged that he and his younger brother Albert be sent to a
prep school to meet other children. The King always refused. In his
teens, Edward attended several naval colleges, where he was frequently

bullied. On one occasion his fellow cadet 'persecutors' performed a mock re-enactment of the beheading of Charles I. The Prince later remembered that he 'kept bursting into tears'. [3]

At Oxford, the shackles came off to an extent, even though he had an equerry and valet in attendance. He later admitted he was drunk most of the time and was 'initiated into the more sophisticated pleasures of carousing'. This continued in London, where he became a fixture at parties and nightclubs.[4]

The Prince volunteered in August 1914 and served as a staff officer in the Grenadier Guards. No one wanted to see the heir to the throne killed or, worse, taken prisoner, and he was kept well back from the front line. In a letter to his then mistress Marion Coke, at the time of Passchendaele, he wrote, 'I do so resent being kept back, tho' really I loathe going forwards and am terrified far more than anyone else could be.' But although not experiencing combat, he saw enough of the war to learn something of its horrors and comradeship.[5]

In early February 1918, he met Freda Dudley Ward, a recently married woman with two young daughters. She became one of the two great loves of his life. His father disapproved strongly of this liaison, as well as of his son's liking for fashionable clothes, cocktails and nightlife. They tried to get him married off, but the Prince declared that he was 'determined under no circumstances to contract a loveless marriage'.[6]

Most importantly, father and son differed on the role of the monarchy. In November 1918, the Prince wrote to his father: 'there seems to be a regular epidemic of revolutions & abdications ... which certainly makes it a hard & critical time for the remaining monarchies'. Indeed, among the many fallen European royals were two first cousins of the King – the Tsar and the Kaiser. Although 'ours' was 'by far the most solid', to keep it so, the Prince argued, would require getting in 'closest possible touch with the people'. The King's opposite viewpoint was expressed by one of his senior courtiers in a letter to the Prince: 'the Monarchy must always retain an element of mystery. A Prince should not show himself too much. The Monarchy must remain on a pedestal.'

The Prince, who hated formality and ceremony, and saw the monarchy in need of urgent modernisation, couldn't have disagreed more.[7]

With his open and unstuffy attitude, together with his slightly frail 'little boy lost' good looks and unmarried status, the Prince became one of the most photographed 'celebrities' in the world, perfect fodder, along with Hollywood stars, for the increasingly popular illustrated magazines. Soon his image was appearing as well on thousands of postcards and chocolate and biscuit boxes. His brother Albert even suggested that part of the King's rancour was based on jealousy of his son's enormous popularity.[8]

Prime Minister David Lloyd George, ever a canny operator, was of course aware of this popularity and the success so far of the Prince's domestic appearances, even in potentially hostile parts of the country such as industrial towns or mining villages. He suggested that the Prince should tour the empire to thank, on behalf of the King, the various countries for their contributions to the war, and that this would do more for imperial unity 'than half a dozen imperial conferences'. The King agreed, seeing it as good experience for his son, and it would also, of course, keep him away for a while from London nightclubs and Mrs Dudley Ward. In fact, the Prince would write to her pretty much every day of his travels.[9]

Canada, as the premier Dominion, would be first, followed soon afterwards by a trip to New Zealand and Australia, then another one to India, with stops at smaller territories on the way. Before he left, the Prince was given training in speech-making by Winston Churchill. He also received a strict note from the King's secretary, urging him to 'do & say the right thing. The Throne is the pivot upon which the Empire will more than ever hinge. Its strength and stability will depend entirely upon its occupant.'

In August 1919, the fast battlecruiser the *Renown* left Portsmouth. On board with the Prince was a retinue of about twenty. Edward Grigg, former intelligence officer and editor of *Round Table* magazine, and according to the Prince 'a great imperialist', was on board as political adviser and speechwriter. The Prince's speeches, the Colonial

Secretary Lord Milner suggested, should stress his 'appreciation of the political institutions of the Empire and of the very vital place which the Crown takes as the modus of the whole web'.[10]

On the whole, the tours of the 'white' Dominions were a resounding success. In Canada there had been considerable anxiety about the Prince's reception in Quebec, whose largely Francophone community had traditionally shown little enthusiasm for king and empire, and, recently, the war effort. But huge enthusiastic crowds awaited him, and his speech, made in French and English, went down well. 'His clear boyish voice has a quality of sympathy and sincerity which makes the speaker one with his audience,' reported *The Times*' Canada correspondent. The Prince was greatly relieved, though privately to Freda he described the French Canadians as 'a rotten priest-ridden community who are the completest passengers & who won't do their bit in anything & of course not during the war!' The enthusiastic welcome in Quebec was repeated across the country. In Toronto there was a crowd of 50,000 who 'yelled and screamed and cheered'. The Prince wrote to his father: 'People seemed to go quite mad.'[11]

In New Zealand there was a railway strike timed to coincide with his visit, supposedly fomented by Sinn Féiners, but the overall welcome was warm. Louis 'Dickie' Mountbatten, the Prince's nineteen-year-old cousin, who had pulled out all the stops to get on the trip, reported that the country was 'quite the model Dominion that one has always heard it to be'. The Prince had been more nervous about Australia. Weren't the cities 'full of bolshies and Sinn Féiners?' he asked. Indeed, many on the left had been appalled by the news of his visit. He was coming, the *Socialist* newspaper exclaimed, 'for the express purpose of creating a psychology in Australia which was favourable for militarism and capitalism'. Several unions resolved to boycott the trip, but these spectacularly failed to materialise. In supposedly left-wing Melbourne, half a million people lined the route of his 8-mile progress through the city to Government House, where the Prince was introduced to the assembled bigwigs as the 'great ambassador of empire'. He was soon dubbed 'Prince Charming' and 'The Prince of Hearts'. The mothers, especially, warm towards him,' reported an unnamed female Melbourne journalist. 'His slight, boyish form appeals to their maternal instincts.'[12]

The Prince's frailty was part of his appeal but, in fact, it was all too real. The person fated to play this seemingly crucial role of 'pivot of empire', the embodiment of the only factor that united the disparate parts of the empire, was chosen, of course, by birth rather than merit. And in many ways the Prince fell short. As he himself admitted in a letter to Freda: 'I'm not half big enough a man to take on what I consider is about the biggest job in the world.'[13]

The role required a robust physique and stamina that the Prince simply did not possess. 'If only the British public really knew what a weak, powerless misery their press-made national hero was,' he wrote to Dudley Ward, 'they would have a nasty shock.' Even at the end of the relatively sedate New Zealand tour, speechwriter Grigg found him reading 'with an air of profound dejection' an article in the *Wanganui* newspaper which called him 'the coping stone of Imperial federation'. 'I never saw a coping stone in worse condition,' Grigg wrote in his diary. The frantic official schedule of endless travel, speechifying, photocalls, dances, banquets and other events took their toll. 'Midnight often found me with wearied brain and dragging feet, the orchestra blaring out the by now hackneyed tunes,' the Prince later wrote. Particularly emotionally exhausting were the frequent inspections of injured veterans of the war, 'and everywhere the sad visits to hospital wards, every step bringing me face to face with some inconsolable tragedy calling for a heartening word from me'. Soon after his arrival in Australia, it was necessary, on his doctor's orders, to cancel an entire week of events so that the Prince could rest.[14]

In Western Australia he was sent to inspect the site of the new Group Settlements. On a rickety track in heavy rain, his train derailed. Thankfully, having recently had to stop to avoid a cow on the line, it was running at low speed. Even so, the Prince's carriage and the one ahead crashed over on to their sides and slid down the embankment with 'a terrifying clatter'. Fortunately, again, the embankment was not too steep, otherwise, according to Mountbatten, the accident would almost certainly have been fatal. The Prince found himself flat on his back with most of the contents of the compartment on top of him. He was able to extricate himself through a window, having grabbed the 'precious cocktail shaker' and some cigarettes. The Prince made light of it, declaring, 'Well, anyway, at last we have done something which was not on the official programme.' But he was badly shaken, writing to his mother, 'I live so much on my nerves nowadays ... I just loathe a train now and have "the wind up me" the whole time!'[15]

In theory, the long journey eastwards was supposed to be restful, but now the Prince found it hard to sleep on a train. So he arrived at Adelaide 'absolutely worn out', worried that he could go on no longer 'without the top of my *head cracking like an egg*'. Accompanying journalists from the *Morning Post* and *The Times* reported that he had lost his voice, looked pale and ill, and that his speeches had become rambling and incoherent: 'Renewed sign of nerve strain ... very disturbing.'[16]

It didn't help that he stayed up late, smoked and drank far too much and ate little, obsessed as he was with his weight. He was also unable to accept that he was on show all the time – 'a performing animal', as he put it. Throughout these Dominion tours he often caused offence at balls by dancing with the prettiest young women – often one in particular for most of the night – instead of all the daughters of those of highest rank. When on a later trip his ship stopped at Japan on the way home, the British ambassador, Sir Charles Eliot, found the young Prince profoundly bored and tired but still full of indiscretions, loudly pronouncing that the British Governors of Singapore and Hong Kong – his last two stops in HMS *Renown* – were 'fossilized clerks who ought to be kept in a cupboard in Whitehall'. There was also an awkward incident at a dance. The Prince, it was now well known, was apt to try to procure 'informal companionship' at every stop on his tours. Eliot reported to Curzon back in London that the Japanese, 'with their usual excess of precaution, subjected every female thing that could come near him to a medical examination ... There was nearly a terrible scandal because two missionary ladies who wished to present him with a Japanese Bible were hurried off by the police on the grounds that they had not been inspected and disinfected.'[17]

In New Zealand and Australia, the Prince often failed to hide his boredom with what he called 'the usual hot air addresses'. He snapped at people or cancelled visits at the last minute that had taken weeks of preparation. He was also complaining and moody in a childish way. Alan Lascelles, who would join his entourage at the end of the year as assistant private secretary, later wrote: 'his mental and spiritual growth stopped dead in his adolescence, thereby affecting his whole consequent behaviour'.[18]

'Each day I long more & more to chuck this job & be out of it & free for you,' he wrote to Freda, whom he often addressed as 'Mummie'. 'The day for Kings & Princes is past, monarchies are out of date,' he wrote. Perhaps his least favourite part of the role was dealing with what he called 'natives'. In Panama, passing through the canal, Mountbatten reported, 'HRH shook hands with coloured men, a thing an American would never have done, which roused them to still greater enthusiasm.' But from Barbados the Prince wrote to Freda, 'I didn't take much to the coloured population, who are revolting.' He hated the frequent displays in Fiji, Samoa and elsewhere of traditional dancing, music or art, calling them 'native stunts'. In his expertly ghost-written autobiography, published in 1951, he described the Māoris as 'what was most novel to me in New Zealand'. In several places 'they gathered to meet me in their native garb, chanting folk songs, and performing warlike dances called *hakas*'. But in his letters of the time to Freda, he described the Māori ceremonies as 'long and tedious ... inane Maoris danced & made weird noises'. When the women kissed his hand, he was 'revolted'. Close to the border between Western and South Australia, a group of about a hundred Aboriginal Australians had been assembled to meet the Prince. 'They are the most revolting form of living creatures I've ever seen!' he reported to Freda. 'They are the lowest known form of human beings & are the nearest thing to monkeys I've ever seen.' Sadly, what the Aborigines made of the Prince was not reported.[19]

Despite all this, the tours of the Dominions seemed to have served their purpose. In Australia, even the *Australian Worker* newspaper was won over to his charm, calling him a 'pleasing figure head'. *The Times* reported: 'he has done here Imperial service of the highest usefulness'. A local journalist observed that 'the Prince has silenced criticism of the Monarchy for current lifetimes'.[20]

One typical Canadian wrote to Grigg after his tour there, saying the Prince 'symbolizes the unity of the whole empire'. But it would perhaps have been more accurate for him to have written 'the white-dominated part of the empire'. Some of the praise for the Prince inadvertently acknowledged this. 'The Prince is among us,' exclaimed the *West Australian*, 'an ambassador Royal from the centre of the Empire, and propagandist in the cause of imperial unity, making the kinship of race felt keenly.' There is an interesting report from *The Times*, when the Prince was in Melbourne. The 50,000-capacity cricket ground had been packed for a 'physical training' display by no fewer than 10,000 local children. For the correspondent, this was the most impressive sight so far. They had the 'ordered discipline of veterans', he wrote, and what's more, 'The great majority were fair-haired, witnessing that they were probably of the purest Anglo-Saxon stock in the world to-day.'[21]

On his return from Canada after his first tour, the Prince had told his parents that the most appreciated part of his speeches was when he announced, 'I regard myself as belonging to Great Britain and Canada in exactly the same way.' The King warned him that that would mean he would have to be an Australian in Australia and a New Zealander in New Zealand. The Prince replied, and why not? 'Of course, in India there would be no question of it as I happen to have been born a white man and not a native.'[22]

Indeed, when the Prince got to India, it would be a very different story.

8

'Dying Races'

Where there have been fewest changes, important
or unimportant, salutary or hurtful, there the
race survives.

In the South Seas, ROBERT LOUIS STEVENSON[1]

The most important event of the year in Australia, reported the
London *Observer* on Sunday 30 September 1923, was not the
fall of Billy Hughes and his replacement by Stanley Bruce in February,
nor schemes to promote immigration from Great Britain. It was the
holding of the Pan-Pacific Science Congress in late August and early
September in Sydney and then Melbourne.

The Congress included delegates from the United States and Japan
as well as the Dominions and European colonial powers. Hopes were
expressed that 'the strong bond of brotherly feeling between the men of
science from different nations' would promote peace in the region and,
as a Japanese delegate pointedly told the introductory session, 'dispel
misunderstandings ... it was altogether ridiculous to suggest that
Japan entertained hostile ambitions towards Australia'.[2]

The distinguished scientists discussed local seismology (rather presciently for Japan), livestock diseases and invasive species. But of most interest to the public were the sessions on diseases and anthropology, the latter under the chairmanship of one of the most distinguished and influential anthropologists of his day, Alfred Haddon of Cambridge University.

By 29 September, the delegates had scattered: some back home, others to view the Great Barrier Reef and report on its economic potential, or, like Alfred Haddon, to investigate the lives of Aboriginal Australians in Western Australia. But the startling conclusions from the Congress continued to be debated in the press and at public meetings. In fact, the data presented during the meeting challenged much of the accepted justification for the British and other empires in the Pacific.

The *Observer* headline said it all: 'Dying Races'. The indigenous peoples of the region under European rule were, it was declared, facing rapid extinction.

For some, this development, however regrettable, was in the natural order of things. The 'collision of races', brought about by improved communication, missionary activity and the expansion of commerce and empire, had created a Darwinian drama in which only some would survive. 'Every change in civilisation dooms sections of mankind to extinction,' wrote the Sydney *Evening News* reporting the conclusions of the Congress. 'They may be excellent folk in their way, but if they are not the toughest, biologically, they are not the "fittest".'[3]

However, little of this fatalism was evident in the presentations made by the medical experts to the Congress. One after another they expressed despair, shame and bewilderment at the appalling statistics of population collapse among the indigenous peoples of the region. Wasn't the spread of Western 'scientific' medicine supposed to be one of imperialism's proudest boasts, one of its most indisputable claims to legitimacy? (Hubert Lyautey, in 1923 the Resident-General in Morocco, had famously gone so far as to declare, 'La seule excuse de la colonization c'est le médecin.') So why, then, was the Pacific, as the *Observer* of Sunday 30 September described it, 'a reservoir of diseases' including 'cholera, plague, malaria, leprosy, beri-beri and influenza'?[4]

The medical and anthropological delegates frequently quoted from a book published in London in February 1923, *Essays on the Depopulation of Melanesia*. This book, in which missionaries, government officials and researchers reported on the chain of islands from New Guinea to the borders of Fiji, including the Solomons and New Hebrides, defined the content and tone of this part of the Congress. The writers' contributions, combined with the delegates' own research across the wider Pacific, did indeed paint a grim picture of demographic collapse.[5]

The leading medical speakers were both young Australians: Dr John Cumpston, aged only thirty-three, was the Chief Medical Officer of the Commonwealth; Dr Raphael 'Ray' Cilento, from a poor Italian immigrant background, was at thirty years old the newly appointed head of the Australian Institute of Tropical Medicine following a string of scholarships and stints working in New Guinea and Malaya.[6]

Cilento started his presentation to the Congress and assembled journalists with what he called the two prominent features of the populations of the Pacific regions – 'one, their considerable numbers, as emphasized by the early explorers, their high state of development, and their great natural abilities'. The second feature was their 'constant and rapid diminution since the white man had taken possession'. He then launched into a series of startling statistics that were duly reported by the journalists present. The inhabitants of French-controlled Tahiti, estimated in 1774 to number 150,000, had been reduced to only 10,000 twenty-five years later. The Māoris had decreased from 120,000 in 1840 (when the British took over) to just 40,000. Moving on to the new Australian New Guinea Mandate territory, Cilento gave the example of one district seeing an annual excess of deaths over births of nearly 300 in a population of less than 10,000, and 'this in by no means a bad year'. Cilento concluded that the 'ultimate fate of the Polynesian and Melanesian races would be extinction unless measures were taken'.[7]

Cumpston took the same approach, opening his first presentation with grim statistics from New Caledonia, a French Melanesian protectorate. Cumpston declared that an 1853 indigenous population of 70,000 had shrunk to not much more than 20,000 by the present day in September

1923. The New Hebrides just to the north, run since 1906 as an awkward and dysfunctional condominium between France and Britain (dividing on lines of Catholic–Protestant/Francophone–Anglophone as per rival missionary penetration), had seen comparable losses. Drawing on the contributors to the *Essays on the Depopulation of Melanesia*, in particular missionary Reverend William Durrad and Swiss anthropologist Felix Speiser, Cumpston declared, 'As to the fact of depopulation there can be little doubt.' In many places, previously thriving communities were reduced to 'a miserable handful of people, herded together in one village, with hardly any children, and they will soon be altogether extinct'.[8]

Although there were specific factors affecting some places more than others, the doctors at the Congress and the authors of the *Essays on the Depopulation of Melanesia* also largely agreed on the key reasons for this population catastrophe. What's more, there was a wide acceptance that most of them were, as Everard Thurn, the former Governor of Fiji from 1904 to 1911, wrote in his stinging preface to the *Essays* (quoted by Cumpston), 'a direct, however unintended, consequence of the settlement among them of Europeans'.

Thurn, by late 1923 seventy-one years old and the president of the Royal Anthropological Society, saw European penetration as 'unavoidable'. But those who had arrived with a view to 'developing and exploiting the land' had sometimes been 'callous and even brutal'. Furthermore, he wrote, efforts on the part of 'missionaries and Government representatives to save the islanders from the worst effects brought on them by the in-rush of Europeans', though 'well-intended', had been 'sometimes mistaken, ill-calculated and inadequate'.[9]

The biggest factor, almost everyone agreed, was imported diseases. 'The history of the island groups of the Pacific is a long series of epidemic tragedies,' Cumpston told the Congress. For tens of thousands of years, Australia and Oceania had been fairly isolated from Eurasia and Africa, and suffered from a smaller number of infectious diseases. It was not really until the late seventeenth and early eighteenth century that the region saw sustained European contact. This brought, among other diseases, dysentery, measles, tuberculosis and pneumonia with, Cilento told the Congress, 'the most tragic and appalling results'. As well as lacking immunity, the indigenous communities of course had no expertise with which to treat these new diseases, their efforts to do so often making them worse. The local people quickly understood the link between disease and the white man's arrival by sea: in the Cook Islands, if you were ill, you would say 'I am shippy'.[10]

As well as bringing diseases, the whalers and early traders also sold the indigenous peoples alcohol, opium and, as we've seen in the Gilberts, tobacco. Alcohol, according to Felix Speiser on the New Hebrides, 'kills directly through poisoning and indirectly through sickness and quarrelling ... its baneful influence has been almost as great as tuberculosis'.[11]

Most destructive, though, were metal weapons including firearms, 'by means of which', one anthropologist wrote in the *Essays*, 'the comparatively harmless warfare of the natives is given a far more deadly turn'. This pattern was repeated across the region. In the Solomons, a Royal Navy surveyor reported at the end of the nineteenth century, 'rifles and especially tomahawks, during the last forty or fifty years, have largely increased the fatal effects of head-hunting; so that where one man's head was taken in olden times, three or more are taken today'. Some villages were 'almost annihilated'. Speiser on the New Hebrides wrote that 'in old days the wars were not very serious ... and as a rule fighting ceased when each side had lost five men', but the rifle had introduced 'a terrible war of extermination'.[12]

Perhaps the most extreme example was New Zealand. Because of the cold and treacherous waters around the two main islands, it was not populated until the thirteenth century, a thousand years after even remote Easter Island. The Polynesian adventurers who settled there became known as the Māori to the Europeans who started arriving in numbers early in the nineteenth century. Uniquely for indigenous people, the Māori were represented at the Congress in the person of Peter Buck, or Te Rangi Hīroa. Described by the *Sydney Telegraph* as 'one of the outstanding personalities at the congress', he had served as a Māori member of Parliament, and had fought with distinction at Gallipoli. In a speech reported by the *Waikato Times* on 29 September, he declared, 'We had our own ideas of chivalry and warfare, and I am convinced that they were much superior to yours. The native fighting was hand to hand, where you saw your enemy face to face, and the wounded were safe after they had fallen in battle.'

The introduction of firearms, however, changed inter-tribal warfare from something seasonal, ritualistic and involving few deaths into something altogether different. Several Māori chiefs made visits to London, where they were much feted and given valuable gifts, which on returning home via Sydney they invariably sold to buy muskets. For the first time, warfare ranged across the whole country, and what became known as the Musket Wars, fought during the first four decades of the nineteenth century, depopulated whole districts. European land speculators moved in, and by 1860 the Māori were outnumbered by the Europeans, or Pākehā. A further 2,000 were killed in an unequal war in the 1860s against British troops, supported by artillery, cavalry and local militia.

Across the region there were occasional violent clashes between incoming Europeans and locals, with the latter invariably coming off worst against superior firepower. Hardest hit was the New Hebrides to the south of the Ellice Islands, which was blessed, or cursed, with sandalwood forests, a fragrant and beautiful timber that commanded an astronomically high price back in Europe. Unlike the whalers, the sandalwood traders found they needed to go onshore. According to Felix Speiser, the traders were 'the same riff-raff as the whalers'. 'If the whites ventured ashore, they wrought havoc like wild beasts.' On one occasion in 1842 thirty natives, old men, women and children, were shut in a cave and burned alive. The local people had responded, and 'provided the whites with a welcome pretext to wage an almost systematic war of extermination against the natives'. Speiser wrote of an 'attested case' from 1861 when a man from Tanna Island in the south of the group was shut up on board with sailors suffering from measles so that he would spread the germ. A third of the population of Tanna Island was reported subsequently to have died of the disease.[13]

What Speiser called 'the agencies of extermination' also included the 'blackbirders', forcible labour recruiters who hit Melanesia particularly hard from the 1860s through to the 1890s. In some cases islanders were marched at gunpoint on to ships supplying labour to Australia, Fiji, Chile and elsewhere. It was effective slavery, and only about half made it back home. These outrages were vigorously brought to the attention of the wider world by missionaries, who had started to penetrate the region from the 1830s. But they too, it turned out, were an agency of extermination.[14]

Florence Coombe was until 1919 a teacher at the missionary school on Norfolk Island, halfway between New Caledonia and New Zealand. This was run by the Melanesian Mission, which had driven missionary activity in New Zealand since the 1840s and had expanded its activities in the Pacific islands in the following decade. Coombe wrote about travelling around the region in the mission's supply ship, the *Southern Cross*, a 100-ton schooner. In the New Hebrides, she said, 'Everywhere are traces of a formerly large and strong population. What is left? Villages with only 30 to 50 inhabitants apiece, and amongst them not half a dozen babies. Magic and poisoned arrows have been doing destruction for generations, and sheer ignorance and laziness account for the scarcity of children.'[15]

But she was wrong. It wasn't such practices which had been carried on for centuries without any of the radical fall in the population now being experienced. In fact, it was her ship. As the Mission's Rev. Durrad, oft-quoted by the doctors at the Congress, wrote, 'It has to be confessed that the "Southern Cross" is one of the chief agents in the distribution of pneumonia germs.' Everywhere the *Southern Cross* sailed, death followed. Durrad experienced this himself having been deposited in the Solomons by the vessel, when 'severe illness' and numerous fatalities followed the ship's visit. This was plain, too, to the local people, who soon stopped sending out canoes to welcome the visiting missionaries because of the 'unusual sickness being connected with this new teaching'. So for Durrad, 'What should have been one of the happiest of experiences was converted into one of the most tragic. The message of the Gospel was stultified by the terrible sufferings of the people.'[16]

Some, though not all, of the missionaries also insisted on decency, that people be fully clothed, even small children. For Durrad, this was the greatest of 'all the evil customs introduced by civilisation'. The problem, he explained, was that the clothes were never dried, washed nor changed and therefore became 'utterly insanitary'. Felix Speiser declared, 'one of the most pathetic contrasts in the islands is the lithe and glossy skin of the healthy native and the dirty over-dressed Melanesian masquerading as a white man'. It was also suggested that the copying of European-style buildings, with thick walls and poor ventilation, contributed to the poor health of the islanders, as did eating imported tinned food rather than the traditional fresh staples.[17]

Missionaries across the region continued to campaign against the 'blackbirding' labour trade, in part because those who returned were disruptive, having 'picked up the white man's vices without any of his good qualities'. This campaign, along with imperial rivalry, had led to a wave of annexations twenty or so years earlier. As Everard Thurn explained, the mission of the new High Commissioner of the Western Pacific was to 'protect the islanders against aggression by British subjects'. (A similar justification had been used, much earlier, for sending a British Resident to New Zealand.)[18]

Indeed, following the assumption of direct responsibility across the region by the imperial powers, the labour trade was now regulated, and in most places destructive inter-tribal warfare was ended. Nevertheless, the indigenous populations continued to fall. Cumpston told the Congress the tragic story of Fiji. In 1875, King Thakombau of Fiji went to Sydney with his two sons to consult with the Governor on the terms of British annexation (this had been pushed by Australia, who feared German ambitions). They returned on a Royal Navy vessel to be met by a full assembly of chiefs from all the Fijian islands. But they brought from Sydney the measles germ. The king's son fell ill, as did every one of the assembled chiefs. 'The final outcome,' said Cumpston, 'was the death of about 26 per cent of the entire population of the Fiji group.'[19]

In preparation for the Congress, Cumpston had sent out a questionnaire to the health departments of every Pacific island group and
the countries bordering the ocean. From the answers he received, it
was clear that several of the imported diseases, including gonorrhoea,
dysentery, pneumonia and new strains of leprosy, had now become
endemic. The most destructive of these, however, was tuberculosis: Dr
Kitson in the Gilberts described it as a 'great scourge'; it was now also
'the principal cause of death among the natives' in Fiji.[20]

Other endemic diseases, though not usually fatal, lowered the resistance of the sufferer, as well as sapping energy and vitality. In places
hookworm was 'universal', as was 'yaws' (a form of tropical ulcer),
particularly among children. On some islands filariasis, a parasitic
roundworm disease spread by mosquitoes, affected about a quarter of
the population. In Samoa, the figure was nearly 60 per cent. Faulty
hygiene and sanitation were to blame in large part, Cilento told the
Congress, but the situation had been worsened by changes wrought by
the Europeans. The growth of the copra trade had seen villages relocated from the interior to the less healthy coasts. Or larger settlements
had sprung up centred on the new churches and schools, facilitating a
more rapid transmission of many diseases, as the fortuitous quarantine
effects of population dispersal were removed. Worse, though, were
the labour camps that served mines and plantations. Workers were
often accommodated in crowded and insanitary conditions, creating
micro-environments favourable to the spread of disease, worsened by
alcoholism and industrial pollution. The diseases were then carried
back to their own families and villages. Imported labour also spread
infections: Cumpston gives the examples of a steamer from Tonkin
bringing Chinese workers, introducing meningitis to Thursday Island;
and leprosy, he said, was brought by a Chinese worker to Nauru
in 1911.[21]

Labour migration was just one part of the growing inter-
connectedness of the Pacific, and indeed the wider world, some of
it driven by imperial authorities, such as military recruitment, and
some by private individuals, such as traders. Growing commerce and

more efficient infrastructure linked places previously isolated from one
another. For example, plague was carried from Hong Kong in 1864
to Bombay two years later, Cape Town in 1900 and Nairobi in 1902,
then on to West Africa. The most spectacular and deadly example is of
course the Spanish influenza pandemic that killed at least 50 million
people after the end of the First World War, demonstrating along the
way the fallibility of Western medicine. Perhaps nowhere was the tragedy deeper than in Western Samoa.[22]

Samoa had had a tendency to political fragmentation, rival groups
based on families and geography. As elsewhere, warfare had been made
far more deadly by the introduction of firearms in the mid-nineteenth
century, and also by the arrival of American, German and British
warships, taking sides in the civil warfare. Only a timely hurricane
in 1888 had prevented German and American navies embarking on
open conflict.

The situation was calmed by the Tripartite Convention of 1899,
under which the archipelago was divided between Germany and the
United States, with Britain in compensation winning substantial
concessions from Germany elsewhere in the Pacific and as far away as
West Africa.

The US was in an expansionist mood, having just seized Guam and
the Philippines from Spain, and was busy planning a trans-Isthmian
canal. It was the age of A. T. Mahan and his highly influential books
on the importance of sea power. American Samoa, the two smaller
islands to the east, became in effect an enormous naval base. Secretary
of State John Hay, who would shortly deliver the Panama Canal Zone
to his country, called Samoa 'the Gibraltar of the Pacific'.[23]

The colony was run as a military project by the navy, which sent
out a series of short-lived, incompetent and sometimes corrupt administrators. Most disastrous was Commander Terhune. 'The natives are
very charming people, but very childish,' he reported. 'They are of the
Stone Age and are not capable of managing their affairs with wisdom.'
The Samoans strongly resented being under effective martial law
rather than civilian government, and when Terhune banned marriage

between Americans and Samoans there was open rebellion, known as 'Mau'. Terhune had in part been trying to protect Samoan women from callous and often bigamous American sailors, but the measure was perceived as simply racist. When several of his senior officers sided with the Mau, in November 1920 the unstable Terhune committed suicide. His replacement tried to improve the situation by establishing a new school board, improving healthcare and building roads, but the Mau movement continued, leading to further protests and arrests in 1922, by which time Mau influence was being felt on the larger islands of Western Samoa.[24]

Here the Germans, led by Wilhelm Solf, a liberal and highly competent administrator, had, from the outset in 1900, very carefully left intact Samoan political and social structures. At the same time, thanks to a generous subsidy from Berlin, they had established a schools system, constructed infrastructure and a hospital, and trained Samoan nurses. Solf also developed plantation agriculture, centred on copra but including coffee and rubber.

At the beginning of the First World War, on instructions from Britain as 'a great and urgent imperial service', New Zealand troops had occupied Western Samoa. For the duration of the war the new military governor, Colonel Robert Logan, carried on 'as far as lay in his power' on German lines, clearly recognising that the 'Germans understood the natives and their wants better than he did'.[25]

Then, on 7 November 1918, a ship arrived, the SS *Talune*, which had sailed from Auckland via Fiji and Tonga. On board was the deadly Spanish flu virus. New Zealand had been hard hit – in all, 8,600 would die (with the Māori affected at a rate six times worse than the Europeans, thanks to poor diet and housing). But the *Talune* was not quarantined, with disastrous results. As well as infecting Fiji and Tonga, nearly 90 per cent of the Western Samoan population went down with the virus, with nearly a quarter dying – the worst rate in the world. Those who survived were often left severely weakened. In nearby American Samoa, where quarantine was rigorously imposed, there was not a single death.

At the end of 1920, despite objections from the New Zealand Labour Party, Western Samoa was declared a League of Nations mandate, and in January 1921 the first civilian Governor arrived. Robert Ward Tate was a romantic in the Stevenson tradition, believing Samoa 'veritably a Garden of Eden, or rather could be, if there were no white men'. But he was met by a population reeling from the epidemic and furious that they had not been consulted about the mandate. Tate was delivered a petition addressed to George V demanding that they be ruled by Britain or the US rather than lowly New Zealand, and there were threats of a boycott of British goods.[26]

Tate managed to have the petition withdrawn, and undertook various improvements to medical facilities, water supplies and roads, but dissatisfaction remained. In part this was because the flu epidemic had destroyed trust in the administration, so that even simple projects, such as the eradication of the rhinoceros beetle (which attacked the coconut plantations), were treated with suspicion and non-cooperation. Furthermore, the New Zealand administration was seen as expensive and wasteful, and was criticised for failing to consult the Samoans on spending priorities. A second petition, which did make it to London, requested that 'We and our children who have been educated are quite sufficient to perform the various duties of our Administration.' Tate added a comment that the idea the Samoans could govern themselves 'need not be considered seriously'. According to a visitor, Somerset Maugham, Tate 'regarded the natives as wilful children'.[27]

In May 1923 Tate was replaced by G. S. Richardson, a good army organiser but with no experience of 'non-self-governing peoples'. He declined to investigate the anthropological literature left behind by the Germans. Richardson, like Tate, considered Samoans 'destitute of reasoning power', 'backward children'. But he had genuine concern for the well-being of native peoples made explicit in the doctrine of the 'sacred trust', undertook an extensive tour and tried his best to learn Samoan. With his arrival, the tempo of paternalistic 'uplift' increased. Alcohol was banned, and in an effort to improve the Samoans' health, education and productivity, a host of new rules were drawn up, some incredibly trivial, which if ignored, incurred heavy penalties. One Samoan high chief was exiled to another part of the islands for failing to comply with a 'village beautification' directive to remove a hibiscus bush growing on his own land. In all, this aggressive paternalism, although it delivered, among other achievements, the lowest infant mortality rate in the Pacific, made Samoans feel rule-bound and infantilised.[28]

The report of the New Zealand Chief Medical Officer to the Science Congress contained an interesting final comment. 'Water supply systems,' he explained, were being installed 'on sanitary lines in the principal villages, and the natives were required to find one-third of the cost. It had been found that they appreciated and valued a system, thus partly paid for by themselves, more than one provided wholly by the Government.'[29]

Elsewhere, Cumpston told the Congress, there had also been some progress and successes on the medical front. In the Dutch East Indies, an outbreak of smallpox had been controlled thanks to 'systematic and careful vaccination'. The Dutch medical authorities had also successfully treated 300,000 people suffering from yaws, using arsenical compounds. This was just being started under British imperial auspices in Papua and, Dr Kitson reported, the Gilbert Islands. The success of the treatment increased the popularity of European medicine and at the same time imposed new demands on the scanty resources.[30]

But by far the greatest effort in the region, rather to the embarrassment of the imperial medical authorities, was being made by an American private philanthropic organisation, the Rockefeller Foundation.

9

'The Man with a
Million Patients'

Although he had already given vast sums to educational programmes and medical research, John D. Rockefeller had first
become involved in large-scale public health programmes back in 1909,
with a $1 million donation to fund an aggressive campaign in the
American South. The target was hookworm, 'the germ of laziness' –
seen as a key factor in the famously low productivity of the poor whites
of the South (which therefore provided meagre returns for Northern
capital and was an obstacle to integration into the national economy).[1]

Hookworm eggs deposited in human faeces on the ground hatch
into tiny larvae that burrow through the skin on contact and migrate to
the lungs, from where, having caused reflex coughing and swallowing,
they reach the small intestine to which they fasten themselves and start
sucking blood. In many cases, particularly among the malnourished,
they can cause severe anaemia, leading to a general debility and fatigue.

The programme was three-fold – survey, cure and prevention, the
last an education campaign to drive understanding of the role of faecal
contamination of soil in the hookworm lifecycle. More than 700,000
people were treated and, though not eradicated, the problem was much

reduced. The rate of deaths from chronic anaemia fell drastically. Among children, the worst sufferers as they often went barefoot, a significant improvement in school attendance and literacy rates was also noted.[2]

In 1913, it had been decided to roll the programme out across the world. Driving this was Frederick T. Gates, the Rockefeller lieutenant who handled their philanthropic activities. Gates wrote to his fellow Baptist John D. Rockefeller explaining that the 'channels of intercourse opened up by the missionaries' had been worth to 'our own land' in increased trade a thousand times what the missions had cost. Large-scale public health programmes, he suggested, could achieve the same result of aiding American commercial penetration. Hookworm was present in a global band of tropical territories – for instance the West Indies and the Pacific – of increasing interest to the United States. It was also one of the few diseases afflicting the tropics that had an identifiable cause and a known treatment effective enough to be considered a 'cure'. The hope was that it would make such dramatic improvements that people would abandon superstition and outdated medical concepts and embrace scientific medicine as superior. From here it was a small jump, Gates suggested to Rockefeller, to them accepting the transplantation of Western civilisation in general – what he called 'our improved methods of production and agriculture, manufacture and commerce, our better social and political institutions, our better literature, philosophy, science, art, refinement, morality and religion'.[3]

So, in 1913 the Rockefeller Foundation established the International Health Board with a massive fund of $50 million. Widespread surveys of hookworm infection were soon underway including, from 1916, in Fiji. Here, in part to make up for the collapse of the indigenous population, a large number of Indian workers had been imported to labour on the plantations, and now Indians made up 30 per cent of the population. The Indian diaspora was seen as an agent of spreading hookworm (and other diseases); furthermore, hookworm-induced anaemia and consequent poor productivity among the Indian sugar workers was now seen as an economic liability for the colony.[4]

The Rockefeller doctors had found that in Fiji's wet districts hookworm infection rates were as high as 89 per cent in Fijians and 93 per cent in Indians. Forty thousand, a quarter of the population, were subsequently dosed with the vermifuge oil of chenopodium.[5]

In May 1920, Dr Sylvester Lambert had arrived in Papua New Guinea. A very large man, weighing over 100kg, he was immediately named 'Bogabada' (Big Belly) by the locals. Born in New York State, and a graduate of Johns Hopkins University, he had worked as a medical nurse and doctor for American companies in Mexico and Costa Rica. His first posting for the Rockefeller Foundation had been in northern Australia in 1918. Here the state authorities had lobbied hard to be included in the Foundation's hookworm programme, in part to convince people that the tropical north was suitable for white settlement, and thus presented no challenge to the 'White Australia' policy. Lambert found the white population with low rates of infection – under 10 per cent (the exception being mine-workers in unhygienic labour camps and the many children who went to school barefoot) – but the Aboriginal Australians, or more exactly those he could reach on the nearby reserves, showed rates more like 90 per cent. He used tobacco as a bribe to persuade them to take the foul-tasting purgatives.

Together with four assistants, he then spent two years in New Guinea, starting in Papua then moving north to the Australian New Guinea Mandate. While he led teams into the bush and the mountains, his wife Eloise, whom he described as 'of pithy stock', stayed in the two main towns with their young daughter. Across the two territories there had been complaints about the poor productivity of anaemic plantation workers. An Australian plantation owner told him, 'It's God's blessing that you Yankees are jogging up the Government a bit. Half a million natives, maybe, and not half of 'em fit to lift a bloody hand.'[6]

In all he covered 5,000 miles, sometimes on horseback or by canoe but mainly on foot, along the way catching malaria and battling snakes, spiders and crocodiles. Finding infection rates of around 60 to 70 per cent, he treated the locals with the oil of chenopodium vermifuge followed by a purge of Epsom salt (magnesium sulphate). 'With great gusto they swallowed down the nasty oil in a spoonful of sugar, and smacked their lips,' he wrote. 'They laughed over the bitter purge that followed.' Usually trade tobacco served to purchase provisions and oil the process, except in the high mountains, where salt was king and tobacco unwanted. Here, Lambert secured potatoes, yams, bananas, sugar cane, various fruits and two chickens for the price of two tablespoons of salt.[7]

Using his 'prize number', a large bottle of adult hookworms pickled in alcohol, everywhere he explained the lifecycle of the parasite, persuading people to dig latrines deep enough so that hookworm larvae could not climb out, and ensure they were covered to keep flies at bay. This was not always necessary. In a village high in the mountains of New Britain never before visited by a white person, he found perfectly dug latrines. When he asked who had taught them this, the villagers simply replied, 'It is the custom.' Elsewhere, though, 'there was no attempt at sanitation . . . They lived like animals, and like animals they died.' Often he would need two interpreters for his lectures, and so undertook to learn pidgin English, with some success.[*8]

Along the way he trained local indigenous assistants who continued the campaign, but he usually 'rejected the mission-trained boys, who were too often slackers, liars, and hypocrites'. After New Guinea he worked his way through the Solomon Islands, and by early 1922 he was back in Fiji, where he saw that the earlier campaign had largely failed to reduce hookworm infection rates.[9]

The problem was, he wrote, that the oil of chenopodium 'was not coming up to our expectations'. This was in part because of the complicated way it needed to be deployed. Then he read an article in the November 1921 edition of the *Journal of the American Medical Association* suggesting the use of tetrachloride, a close relation of chloroform. He experimented on four Indian hookworm sufferers. One

---

* His description of John D. Rockefeller: 'Master belonga me him make im altogether kerosene, him make im altogether benzene. Now he old feller. He got im plenty too much money.'

expelled 244 hookworms after just a single dose. By the end of the
years, the hookworm project around the world had switched to the
more effective treatment.[10]

For the next decade, Lambert would criss-cross the South Pacific.
In Tonga he 'groaned over dirt and flies and the ignorance of simple
hygiene' but was very impressed with the queen, a huge woman over
6 feet tall and weighing 300lb; in Western Samoa he found Governor
Richardson devoted and honest in his desire to be 'father to his flock'
but 'rather self-satisfied ... I longed to tell him that he was doing too
much for the Samoan, feeding him with modernism faster than he
could digest it'; the New Hebrides Condominium – or 'Pandemonium'
as it was nicknamed – was the most chaotic, dangerous and lawless
island group, with warfare and forced labour recruitment continuing,
and missionaries still being killed. Reporting the destructive rivalry
between the different missionary groups, Lambert found himself
sometimes wondering 'if civilization had done these people any good at
all'. But under his direction some half a million were treated across the
Pacific. Lambert became known as the 'Man with a Million Patients'.
By the mid-1930s, hookworm would hardly be mentioned in medical
reports.[11]

The huge efforts of Lambert and the Rockefeller Foundation were
acknowledged by the Pan-Pacific Science Congress, but there were criticisms and doubts as well. The American medical representative from
the Philippines, Professor Frank G. Haughwout, argued that spending
vast sums on low-hanging fruit such as hookworm in order to make a
flash impression, while intestinal diseases were a much greater problem
and the 'average industrial or plantation physician' often lacked training or even a microscope, was a mistaken priority. Others also agreed
that the money could have been better spent on fighting more deadly
diseases, but of course to take on, say, diarrhoea would have involved
the hugely expensive and unglamorous construction of water and
sewerage systems. The Foundation had always approached its work on
disease as a self-contained technical problem with a technical solution.

But, as the wider Congress acknowledged, this ignored the social, cultural and economic contexts – data on hookworm from Fiji showed that the fundamental problems were poverty and malnutrition.[12]

The Foundation had always been careful to get itself invited into a foreign imperial territory, and to involve the authorities by asking for financial contributions and an undertaking to continue their work. In September 1923 Lambert was busy organising a survey in Tonga, and securing from the authorities there a token contribution of £100 towards their expenses. But inevitably on the part of the European powers there was jealousy of the extraordinary resources available to the Foundation's doctors, and suspicion that American cultural and economic influence was being extended by the programmes to the detriment of their own. (Lambert was careful to praise the cooperation he received from most British officials in the Pacific, adding, 'If a Britisher had come to an American colony and assumed the critical role to which my job compelled me, he would have been tarred and feathered and ridden out of bounds.') Furthermore, the Foundation was a new and unfamiliar creature – a private effort, which could be done on a whim, rather than one that was public and at least vaguely accountable.[13]

By now the Foundation had realised what the missionaries had always known – that medicine was an almost irresistible force in the penetration of non-industrialised countries. In 1921, after work in more than sixty countries, a Foundation leader told Rockefeller, 'We have seen an attitude of cold curiosity as to what our real motives might be give place to an implicit trust which opens all doors.' A Nicaraguan lawyer called the Foundation's public health programme in his country 'one of the many "advance guards" of American conquest'. A report on its activities in the Philippines noted that doctors could go where soldiers could not, and that 'for the purposes of placating primitive and suspicious peoples medicine has some advantages over machine guns'. Submission to public health programmes allowed for the widespread surveillance and control of subject populations, even their bodies. It also implied submission to the superior medical theories and practices of Western medicine and, by implication, an acceptance of alien authority. Even the doctor-patient relationship fitted this model, with the doctor as the authority and the patient submissive.[14]

The novelty of the programme also prompted afresh the most fundamental questions about Western medicine's role in colonised territories. Was it purely altruistic, to better or even save the lives of anyone regardless of their utility to the coloniser? Or was it, more cynically, 'soft power' to convince indigenous peoples of the benevolence and superior technical abilities of the West, while at the same time sustaining the health of the cheap local worker on whom the whole economic case for empire depended? Even Lambert had his doubts. Writing a health survey report on Western Samoa in late 1923, he described 'the average white man' in the South Seas as 'sitting in the shade and talking about the "lazy native" and criticising the government for not compelling (always the same word) the native to this theory or that which will benefit him (the white man) and never a thought for the native himself'.[15]

Of course, imperial medicine had begun as an attempt to protect European soldiers stationed overseas from the diseases that killed far more of them than combat ever did. The first European hospitals were usually situated in or adjacent to forts. Only occasionally did European doctors minister to local rulers, and many Europeans sought the assistance of local physicians, both because of the scarcity of European doctors and the belief that locals would know better how to deal with local diseases. With European medical theories dominated by 'folk remedies', there was no 'medicine gap'.

But in the mid- to late nineteenth century the status of Western medicine and its confidence had grown, driven by advances like the work in bacteriology of Louis Pasteur and Robert Koch (both committed imperialists) from the 1860s to 1880s. New understanding of the transmission of diseases also led to an acceptance that however much Europeans and their families were segregated from the local populations, they could only be protected if local people were also treated. Thus 'native' hospitals had started appearing.[16]

In 1899 schools of tropical medicine had been founded in London and Liverpool and courses run in many other universities across Britain, Europe and the United States. Specialists in certain tropical diseases soon emerged. Their primary aim was to end the status of tropical countries as 'a white man's grave'. William Gorgas, the American doctor who by ridding Panama of yellow fever made the achievement of the canal possible, wrote in 1909 that his work should be looked on 'as the earliest demonstration that the white man could flourish in the tropics and as the starting point of the effective settlement of these regions by the Caucasian'.[17]

Gorgas had done little to tackle the diseases that affected the West Indian workers on the canal, who were seen as expendable and who consequently died at a far higher rate than the whites. But in many other places this was not an option: European-owned mines, factories, ranches or plantations in the Pacific were worthless without a good supply of reasonably healthy local labourers. Thus an imperative of imperial medicine became capacity to work (with consequent bias against women and children). The acknowledged founder of tropical medicine, Sir Patrick Manson – who had died in 1922 – famously described the effects of beri-beri as 'it kills off the planter's coolies like flies and makes his plantations unprofitable'. The charter of the Rockefeller Foundation was 'the well-being of mankind throughout the world' but in their 1923 annual report they describe the effects of hookworm as 'reducing economic efficiency, causing unhappiness, and increasing mortality' – a revealing order of priorities. Hookworm infection rates were very often described in terms of lost labour productivity.[18]

To stress the economic benefits of medicine was also, of course, a pitch for more money from those who controlled the purse strings, a tactic that would be pursued by the doctors at the Congress. Pleading for more resources, Cilento declared that 'economic, as well as humanitarian, considerations' should be taken into account. Felix Speiser wrote that the population collapse in the New Hebrides should 'be regretted both from a humanitarian and a commercial standpoint'.[19]

But they also appealed to what they hoped was a new mood about trusteeship and responsibility. Much was made at the Congress of Australia's 'urgent duty' and 'obligation to mankind' as a 'public trustee' of the New Guinea Mandate. The population crisis was, it was concluded, 'the most serious obstacle to the duty accepted by the Mandatory Powers of promoting the material and moral well-being and social progress of the inhabitants'. Former Governor of Fiji Everard Thurn, in his introduction to the *Essays on the Depopulation of Melanesia*, described how the issue of 'inter-relations of white men and "natives"' had recently become 'of very great and ever increasing imperial importance'. Britain, he wrote, had 'almost unintentionally assumed more or less control over a very great part of the tropical lands'. Previously only a few colonial administrators understood the obligation but, he suggested, 'as a nation, we are now fully realising that, in assuming control of these lands, we have saddled ourselves with the duty of providing as well as may be for the welfare and comfort of the earlier occupants'.[20]

Suggestions to counter the huge losses to disease included better regulation of labour conditions and checking of workers before they returned home to spread infections. Ray Cilento, who before the end of the year would give up his prestigious job in Australia to return to work in New Guinea, made an impassioned plea for a huge increase in training for district officers and missionaries, and a massive expansion of medical personnel and facilities including properly equipped surgeries and mobile field units. Cumpston, too, called for a huge increase in medical resources, to provide free vaccination, clean water, medicines and dressings. The message from both young Australian doctors came across loud and clear: the existing facilities to deal with the health crisis in the Pacific were shamefully inadequate.

Furthermore, it was the territories under British imperial control that were suffering most from understaffing and underfunding. Sylvester Lambert complained that in Papua, medical services were 'ridiculously inadequate', with only five trained doctors, a couple of nurses and two European dispensers responsible for 300,000 people spread across 90,000 square miles. In general, he described European doctors in the

Pacific (most of whom were British) as 'either lazy and incompetent time-servers or good men baffled by overwork and the whims of local government ... from sheer boredom and despair many of them became quacks and drunkards'. A young nurse, Edith Grinchloin, sent to Fiji under the auspices of the Overseas Nursing Association, sent back a horrified report on the main hospital in Suva: 'you can imagine what a shock the place was to us, when I tell you instead of finding a hospital the buildings are simply a collection of dusty barns ... no more suitable for a hospital than a dog's kennel ... the whole lighting system is a huge farce ... treatment is done often in semi-darkness, no hot water'. Lambert had been there in 1922. He described the hospital as 'a creaky old shack tinkered up somehow'.[21]

Older and more experienced heads knew that this was not going to change any time soon. A former island Governor, Sir William MacGregor, writing in the *Essays*, worked on the assumption that no administration 'for financial reasons' would be able to 'provide a staff of qualified medical practitioners sufficient to meet all the requirements'. For Everard Thurn, this was part of a wider parsimony on the part of imperial authorities in the Pacific, with 'the number of Government representatives resident in the islands throughout the year quite inadequate to enforce British law and justice throughout this chain of widely scattered islands'. (The islands were dubbed the 'Cinderellas of the Empire'.)[22]

What was so frustrating, even shameful, for Cumpston and Cilento was that most of the diseases that 'cause so much suffering and premature death among the native races' – yaws, malaria, hookworm, dysentery, filariasis, gonorrhoea, syphilis – 'present no difficulties which money and trained men cannot remove' with methods of treatment and prevention well established. Cumpston's final words to the Congress showed his furious frustration: 'If half the cost of a modern battleship were expended over a period of five years on providing proper hygienic conditions for the native races within the shores of the Pacific, all these diseases could be completely eradicated.' Newspapers reported that this comment was met with the loudest applause of the Congress.[23]

10

'Subtle and Even More Deadly Influences'

Then we came along with the *pax Britannica* . . .

HUBERT MURRAY, September 1923[1]

The star of the show, however, the Congress's biggest fish, was Hubert Murray, Governor of Papua, one of the empire's best-known and, at the time, most respected imperial officials. A large, 6ft 3in ex-champion amateur boxer, rower and rugby player, he was still an imposing figure in September 1923, aged sixty-two. His presentation to the anthropological and hygiene section was the Congress's most widely reported speech in the newspapers.

Murray's background and allegiances are curious. His father was a rich Irishman who emigrated to Australia and became a successful politician and extensive landowner. His first wife died and he subsequently married Agnes Edwards, the English governess of his three children. She produced two further boys, Hubert then Gilbert.

Born in Sydney, Hubert was sent to the city's grammar school, then, at seventeen, to England. Despite being expelled from Brighton

College for punching a master, he finished his education in Germany, then attended Oxford where he read Greats. Having then trained as a lawyer, he returned to Sydney and practised for a while as a barrister, but he struggled as Australian clients and solicitors disliked his lordly manner.[2]

In January 1900 Murray sailed to South Africa as a volunteer for the Boer War. He saw little action, apart from having to burn Boer farms ('a task he hated'), but did come away with an impression of the British officers as utterly affected and incompetent. He didn't think much of his fellow Australians back home either. There, booksellers thought he was joking when he asked for high-brow volumes. In the meantime, his English-born mother was referring to Australians disparagingly as 'colonials' and urging both her sons to shun the nation's 'trivialities' and 'stagnation'. 'You must never think of this country for your career – break your heart and waste your talents,' she told them.[3]

His brother Gilbert chose to live his whole life in England, and became extremely prominent in academia, the League of Nations and humanitarian circles. Hubert chose Papua.

In 1904 he took up a judicial position in the colony, which was in the process of being transferred from British to Australian control. Murray was unimpressed with the British colonial officials there, who handed over full charge to the Australian government in 1906. Having been made acting Administrator in 1907, Murray was Lieutenant Governor from 1909 all the way to 1940. Like Sylvester Lambert, he would spend his working life in the Pacific.

Murray had written a book about Papua, published shortly before the war and well received, and in 1923 was writing another. He was thinking hard about the role of his government and the impacts of colonialism and modernity on the people of Papua.[4]

For what he said to the Congress, he drew on his own books and pamphlets as well as the *Essays* and other recent ethnographical works on the region. 'History in Papua is barely a generation old,' he began. It was 'but a short time to study the effects of European settlement on a primitive population'. However, there seemed to be clear factors that might have caused an increase in population, just as there were obvious factors in the opposite direction. The establishment of peace and the abolition of tribal warfare, improved sanitation in the villages, transport infrastructure that meant supplies could be moved to areas suffering famine, and medical treatment – 'all these tend towards the preservation of life and the increase of population'. Having 'a contrary effect', Murray continued, 'the most obviously evil of civilization's gifts are, I suppose, diseases, drink and drugs, especially opium', and also the wearing of European clothing, 'a fertile source of sickness and death'. 'Improved communication', he conceded, 'is not always an unmixed blessing, for it facilitates the spread of epidemics which might otherwise have been localized.' But there were, he suggested, 'other more subtle and even more deadly influences' having 'a contrary effect'.[5]

Practical measures he had adopted to counter the obvious 'evils' included a rigid prohibition of the sale of alcohol and opium to the indigenous population, and an edict forbidding the covering of the upper half of the body. Dealing with imported disease was more difficult. A careful system of quarantine had kept out smallpox and the plague, though not influenza. For those suffering from venereal diseases, there was 'arrest and compulsory treatment'.[6]

In keeping with Treasury orthodoxy, the colony was meant to be self-supporting, receiving only 'a pittance towards the cost of administration' from the Australian government. So to bring in revenue Murray had encouraged Europeans to develop plantations, mainly in copra or rice. It was a model prevalent across the empire where revenue from customs duties on exports of plantation products and imports of European manufactured goods made up more than half the government income. Administrators needed European businesses to pay their costs, and businesses needed the governments to protect their interests. And with indigenous plantation labourers being paid in cash, they could now be taxed simply. Murray had introduced a head tax in 1919, but with the unusual proviso that the money raised was kept separate from general revenue to be expended only on areas considered by him to be of direct benefit to the Papuans.[7]

The tax, while raising money for medical facilities and schools, also gave Murray leverage. His flagship policy for reversing population decline was to give tax exemption to any man with four surviving children. Their mother, meanwhile, would receive an annual payment of 5s, with an additional shilling for every living child in excess of four. Although he admitted the census data was scanty, Murray told the Congress that he believed these measures were working, and that Papua's population was at last growing again.

But the 'other more subtle and even more deadly influences' were a much more complicated matter. On population decline, Cilento had alluded to the 'indisposition of the natives to have families'; Cumpston had mentioned 'social factors and psychological factors'. Murray spelled these out.[8]

Before the white man came, Murray said, the Papuan lived in a state of more or less constant war with neighbouring villages and tribes; he had to be prepared to fight for his life at a moment's notice; he had no metals, and he had to cultivate the land, to build houses and canoes, and to make weapons with no better implements than sticks and stones and shells. 'His life, therefore ... was rather a strenuous one. Then we came along with the *pax Britannica*, telling him he must not fight or collect heads any more, and providing him with steel tools which enable him to do his work in as many days as it used to take weeks. And the result is that the necessity for strenuous action was gone, and the tenor of his life is changed for the worse.' The chief activities of his life, Murray went on, 'the delight, for instance, of head-hunting and the joys of the raid – are lost to him forever'.[9]

The reverend missionaries Durrad and Hopkins, in the *Essays*, agreed. In the Solomons, where headhunting was 'the very keystone of the social structure', now 'the men simply loaf about and smoke in idleness'; with life made easier by 'money, wages, tools etc.' 'there is a temptation to slackness which the stress of existence corrected in the old days. The white man is the black man's burden,' Hopkins concluded: 'unless he uses great restraint, his presence saps the black man's independence'. Across the islands, there was a 'decrease in vitality'.[10]

Everywhere, Murray continued, after 'the sudden advent of modern civilization in a primitive community', 'old native traditions and customs tended to become disintegrated and to disappear'. In some cases, Murray said, this was a 'good thing'. 'Cannibalism and head-hunting must go, regardless of any social disorganization that may follow.' Other traditions were disappearing because of obsolescence, he suggested, giving the example of the 'institution of the *Kula*, in the Trobriand Islands, on which Dr Malinowski has recently written'.

Published the year before, Bronisław Malinowski's *Argonauts of the Western Pacific* is now credited with founding a new discipline of social anthropology. Having spent the war years among the Mailu people on islands off the coast of New Guinea, he wrote about, among other things, their extraordinary trading system, the *Kula*, now dying out, whereby long and dangerous trading missions were undertaken in small canoes. He analysed its huge cultural importance and, more widely, how social and cultural institutions served basic human needs. 'Every human culture gives its members a definite vision of the world, a definite zest for life,' he wrote, but when that culture is destroyed, so is the zest for life.[11]

Murray's point was that however important the *Kula* was for 'teaching social disciplines and skill in seamanship', it had been superseded by modern methods, in this case the steamer, just as 'the mail coach was superseded by the railway'.[12]

In more obvious ways, the old order had been undermined. If a chief's authority depended on his knowledge of witchcraft and magic, Swiss anthropologist Felix Speiser wrote, then 'this power falls with his conversion ... all the cords which had united the people into a community and tribe under a recognised head were snapped'. Contact with the white man revealed the 'weakness of its civilisation' and undermined 'the native's confidence in his ancestral religion and the magic of his tribe, and makes his traditional institutions appear rather absurd to the younger men'. Instead there is a 'pitiable attempt to ape the white man'.[13]

Many of the customs might seem to us 'ridiculous', Murray told the Congress, but whether ridiculous or not, they had been the social cement that made the difference between a community and a horde of men, providing 'refuge and protection' in times of stress and trial. The suppression or modification of 'native' habits and institutions destroys 'the complex web of custom and institution which constitutes native society, causing the native to lose interest in life, and so to bring about the gradual extinction of the native himself, for if he has nothing to live for he will die'. This 'deadly' effect, Murray said, was long realised by those engaged in the task of native administration, but had been 'recently made widely known by the writings of Dr Rivers'.[14]

W. H. Rivers was the guiding force behind this new emphasis on culture and psychology as a significant factor in the population collapse in the Pacific, as well as in other imperial issues and challenges around the world. He was the editor of the *Essays* and contributed the final piece on 'The Psychological Factor'. It was his last published work, as he died in June 1922 at the age of only fifty-eight.

He is best known now as a shell-shock doctor during the war, his patients including Siegfried Sassoon and Robert Graves. As a young man he had travelled the world as a ship's surgeon, before working in London hospitals in neurology and psychology. But his career took a different turn when in 1898 he was asked to join an anthropological expedition to the Torres Islands, south of New Guinea.

Leading the expedition was Alfred Haddon, who in September 1923 would be the chair of the anthropological section of the Congress. Along with Rivers, among the small team he recruited were C. S. Myers (who would also later work on shell-shock patients) and Charles Seligman, who by 1923 would be one of anthropology's best-known names. Up until this point, anthropology had largely been produced from an armchair – an amalgamation of travellers' and missionaries' reports. Now, as Haddon put it, the ambition was to create 'a laboratory in the field'. In other ways, too, the expedition would prove to be revolutionary.

The purpose, as defined by Haddon, was to investigate the psychology 'of a lower race'. The word 'race' was often used in a confused way; for instance, people spoke of the 'English race' (indeed, there was a wildly pro-empire magazine of that name published in London in September 1923), and in late-Victorian science there were competing theories about how many races the world contained and what constituted their 'essential' characteristics. At this point, European scientists all still agreed that human beings were naturally unequal, even to the extent of a Negro brain weighing less than a European one, and that there was a hierarchy of races. In the Pacific, it was widely believed that lighter-skinned Polynesians were superior to darker Melanesians (Melanesia meaning 'black islands'), who in turn were superior to Aboriginal Australians. In general, it was believed that the 'higher races' – i.e. Europeans – had superior concentration, reasoning and self-control, while the 'lower', 'less evolved' races were closer to animals in that they had superior eyesight and hearing, were more instinctive and lacked individuality. This theory, of course, explained, and perhaps even justified, the vast differences in wealth and technology between human societies.[15]

The expedition brought newly developed tools to measure sense perception and reaction to stimuli. These included colour wheels and wools for testing vision, ohrmesser for hearing, Galton's whistle for distinguishing frequencies, and fourteen scents in test tubes. There was also a tachistoscope to measure reaction time. These tools offered the chance to make deductions about otherwise unobservable neural processes and a properly scientific and objective way to understand the differences in the brains of, say, a European and a 'primitive savage' – and perhaps, through studying a 'less evolved' human, to gain insight into how evolution worked.

Most of the work was carried out on Murray Island, one 'little touched by the artificial hand of European civilisation', but where most people spoke pidgin English, thanks to work on nearby oyster beds. Rivers arrived ill from sunburn and seasickness and the kindliness with which he was treated by the local people stayed with him for the rest of his life.

Some of the machinery worked better than others; some had been damaged in transit. Nevertheless, the findings were revolutionary. One by one, primitivistic stereotypes were collapsed. Rivers, working on colour perception, exploded the notion that the 'savage' was endowed with powers of vision exceeding civilised people. Furthermore, he wrote, 'in intellectual concentration, as in many other psychological processes, I have been able to detect no essential difference between Melanesians and those with whom I have been accustomed to mix in the life of our own society'. Hearing, touch and reaction times were also shown to be pretty much identical with Europeans. Differences were down not to some sort of racial essentialism, but to the environment or individual variability. Rather than lacking individuality, the community of Murray Islanders contained characters as diverse as any English town. Furthermore, Myers reported, the Scottish schoolteacher on Murray Island had found the children there superior in mathematical ability to those of an average British school.[16]

'An intimate and friendly acquaintance with savages breaks down many prejudices,' Haddon would write. He was impressed by the definite system of morals extolled by the elders: truthfulness, diligence, generosity, kindness to relatives, discretion in dealing with women, and a quiet temper. Instead of what the theorists of the primitive mentality would describe as a slavish obedience to traditional rules, he saw the indigenous culture as flexible and dynamic rather than oppressive, conservative and static.[17]

The ground-breaking expedition marked the beginning of an important shift that would slowly transform 'race' from a biological into a cultural concept. Ultimately it would be discarded as a tool of science altogether.[18]

The 1898 'Headhunters', as Haddon dubbed his team in his account of the expedition, would go on to inspire and train a new generation of anthropologists. Malinowski, who would come to the same conclusion that 'the native mind works according to the same rules as ours', called Rivers 'the patron saint of field work' and dedicated his magnum opus to Charles Seligman.[19]

*

From cutting his teeth with the 'Headhunters' through almost all his subsequent anthropological work, Rivers specialised in families. Originally aimed at researching heredity in physical and neurological attributes, his painstaking construction of genealogies of his subjects soon led him on to the key question of children.

Infant mortality was a terrible scourge. The Rev. Durrad in the *Essays* reported baptising 145 children over eight years. All had survived the earliest years, but only sixty-six of the 145 were still alive. One teacher he knew had six children of whom only two were still living. Durrad blamed this in large part on poor parenting – 'the total ignorance of scientific nursing', defective hygiene, feeding the babies too early on the standard diet of chewed taro or yam. For the Rev. Hopkins, on the other hand, at fault was parents giving their babies 'tinned instead of natural milk and rice instead of the chewed native food'. 'There is a great opportunity for women's work here,' he concluded. Most agreed, though, that high infant mortality was endemic and preceded the arrival of Europeans. (In fact, an earlier report into Fiji found imported infections the primary cause for infant mortality.)[20]

Rivers' focus was different, however. For him, the key factor was not the death rate but the birth rate. Across his Melanesian research, the family trees he constructed all told the same story of a drastic fall in family size over the three or four generations from the earliest European contact.

His most thorough work was at Eddystone Island (now Simbo) and Vella Lavella, both in the western Solomons. Here he documented over three generations a huge increase in childless marriages, from 20 per cent to 50 per cent on the former, and from 12 per cent to 70 per cent on the latter. From an average of well over two children per marriage two generations ago, it had fallen the next generation to less than one and a half, and in the present generation to less than one child per marriage.[21]

In his piece 'The Psychological Factor', Rivers summarised the conclusions of the other essayists as to how disease, European clothes, food, firearms, alcohol, unhealthy houses and labour recruitment had contributed to the depopulation of Melanesia. But, he argued, 'first and foremost' was 'loss of interest in life'. European magistrates and missionaries had arrived to rule and direct the lives of the people and discovered customs and institutions they considered to be heathen or 'contrary to the principles of morality', and had promptly banned them, whether they be the highly complicated organisations around ancestor worship, or dancing that 'gave opportunity for licence'. Thereby, Rivers wrote, 'the people were deprived of nearly all that gave interest to their lives'. This, he argued, was 'quite as important, if not more important than the material side of life in the production of native decadence'.[22]

The result was the creation of a people with no interest in life, 'prey to any morbid agency'. Everyone had noted, he wrote, how 'a native who is ill loses heart at once. He has no desire to live.' But his research had shown that they also increasingly declined to bring children into this new barren, meaningless world.

The specific case of Eddystone in the Solomons stood out. Here most of the material factors were absent: there was little imported disease, no missionaries, little labour recruitment or imported firearms and alcohol, but, he wrote, 'no one could be long in Eddystone without recognising how great is the people's lack of interest in life and to what an extent the zest has gone out of their lives'.

To blame, he concluded, was one simple edict by the British government – the banning of headhunting. Rivers described this practice as forming 'the centre of a social and religious institution which took an all-pervading part in the lives of people'. The heads themselves were needed to propitiate ancestral ghosts on occasions such as building a new house for a chief or constructing a canoe, as well as at funerals. The actual headhunting only lasted a few weeks, with only a couple of hours' fighting, but this was just the culmination of a process that lasted years. There were frequent rites and feasts around the process of canoe building, as well as the expedition itself. In all it was 'a social and religious institution which took an all-pervading part in the lives of the people'.

Rivers also studied, though less thoroughly, similarly falling birth rates in the New Hebrides. Although he conceded that the absence of men at marrying age away on plantation labour, as well as venereal diseases that could cause infertility, were factors, they were 'trivial or of slight importance as compared with voluntary restriction'. Melanesians were familiar with means of effecting abortion and contraception, practices that had shown a 'marked increase'. 'The people say,' Rivers wrote, '"Why should we bring children into the world only to work for the white man?"' Measures which, before the coming of the European, were used chiefly to prevent illegitimacy, 'have become the instrument of racial suicide'.[23]

Rivers ended his essay with a plea: 'that something must be done, and done quickly, to give him that renewed interest in life to which the health of peoples is mainly due'.

No indigenous Melanesian voice was heard either in the *Essays* or at the Congress. Instead the various doctors, missionaries, anthropologists and government officials did their best to provide solutions.

Hubert Murray suggested that some new activity be found to take the place of headhunting and bloodshed. Rivers addressed this directly: could pigs not be exchanged for human sacrifices and skulls? This would of course negate the need for canoe construction, but perhaps that important cultural tradition could be directed towards canoe racing or some other sport?

Felix Speiser offered the satisfactions of good, honest labour on the plantations as something to fill the void. Indeed, he argued it should be compulsory. Murray disagreed, suggesting instead that 'native production' should be encouraged, indeed even compelled 'for their own benefit'. Rivers and others agreed that the Melanesian should be 'given a real interest in the economic development of his country' to 'work more for himself and less for the white man'. European purchase of land should be restricted, even if the sale was the wish of the 'native' owner.

And here was the rub. Almost all the measures suggested for the improvement of the Melanesians' conditions involved some form of compulsion, of 'father knows best', of treating them, indeed, as a 'child race' – all factors identified as causing psychological damage.

Murray's regime, with its rules around clothes, food and the most intimate aspects of life, was later described as 'no more than a well regulated and benevolent type of police rule'. The parallel with Richardson's regime of aggressive paternalism in Western Samoa is obvious. These restrictions were widely resented. One example is the ban on alcohol. From New Zealand (where Māoris were not allowed to buy it) to the New Hebrides, to flout this rule and to drink became a way to recover self-respect, a flag of rebellion.[24]

This dilemma posed deep questions for the imperial authorities, missionaries and doctors in the Pacific, and, indeed, in the wider empire. Was it possible to fulfil the mandate of occupation – 'to promote the material and moral well-being and social progress of the inhabitants' – without in some way making them feel infantilised and humiliated even to the point where they didn't want to bring children into the world? Was there a colonial model that could achieve this, or was colonialism itself to blame?

The recent researches of previous 'Headhunter' Charles Seligman threw interesting light on this. Since the Torres Strait expedition, Seligman had done further work in New Guinea, Ceylon and the Sudan. In the latter, his research included collecting accounts of the dreams of local people, as well as their interpretations of them. This started an interest that would last for many years and at first involved research across Europe. Then, in early 1923, he set up some twenty researchers – who became known as 'Seligs' – to continue the work further afield. Most were anthropologists but there were also some moonlighting colonial officials. They were sent across the empire to Nigeria, Sudan, the Gold Coast, Nyasaland, Uganda, Malaya, the Naga Hills of north-eastern India and the Solomon Islands.[25]

What they discovered was that the dreams of 'primitive' people, held by some to have little 'inner life', were remarkably similar to those of an average European. Seligman, who would lecture on the research in 1924 and later talk about it on BBC radio, concluded that 'the unconscious of all these races is qualitatively much the same'. Most astonishing was the similarities of different peoples' 'dream dictionaries' – how they were interpreted. To dream of losing a tooth meant the imminent death of a close friend or family member whether you were in Africa, India, Britain, Germany or Hungary. Dreams of flying were a favourable omen from Indonesia to Austria. If raw meat appeared, this was a prophecy of impending death or bad luck for Irishmen, Solomon Islanders and West Africans alike. Hungarian anthropologist Geza Roheim described the dream collection as evidence of 'the fundamental unity of the human psyche'.[26]

But there was one noticeable difference between the dreams of the coloniser and colonised that was consistent across a huge range of subjects from chief to lowly peasant and across all the various different colonial systems of the empire.

In September 1923 researcher James Mills wrote to Seligman from the Naga Hills, describing the dream of a twenty-five-year-old man in which one of the 'white Sahibs' gave him a cylinder of salt, 'interpreted to mean someone will laugh at me'. In November, Mills wrote again describing a dream he had collected that featured himself as the owner of a frightening elephant. T. T. S. Hayley, researching in Uganda, reported a dream in which a young man, Okuja, dreamt he was once again a child at the mission station. 'L. G. Amery (the missionary) put him on his shoulders and took him far away. He then threw Okuja into a deep hole and so he died.'[27]

Seligman was soon remarking on 'the very large part played by white officials in these dreams'. And almost always it was in the context of humiliation, reproach or violence. In another dream collected by Hayley, a Ugandan dreamt of being given ten strokes with the cane by the District Commissioner. Even a chief – Philip Oruro, an educated man and a Christian – dreamt that 'Bwana D.C. beat the behind of Won pacho Asanasio Pule [a village chief] hard . . . ' Hayley noted 'how heavily the affairs of administration and fear of the district commissioner hang upon the mind of a native chief'.[28]

The dream collecting continued for some years, but very soon researchers were coming to an important conclusion. Whatever the particular imperial situation, or the status of the dreamer within it, colonised minds were anxious, even damaged.

In pioneering the idea that administrative and missionary meddling with indigenous customs could inflict life-threatening psychic wounds, Rivers in 'The Psychological Factor' came close to this same conclusion. Revealingly, he reported that there was one group who had sustained their child-rearing levels and general 'zest for life' – the unconquered. 'There are still certain parts in Melanesia which as yet the footprint of the white man has not reached, and others where, after successful encounters with punitive expeditions, the people still believe themselves to be a match for the invader,' he wrote. 'Here the old zest and interest in life persist and the people are still vigorous and abundant.'[29]

So could the deleterious effects of empire in the Pacific, between twenty and fifty-odd years old, or indeed sustained European contact for a century or so, be reversed? Speiser wrote of the ideal of some missionaries to try to 'isolate their people from the influence of the world and keep them from contamination in Utopian conditions of perfection'. This 'museum policy' would involve banning 'all products of civilization', such as clothes, tools and imported food, so that the 'natives were thereby compelled to make for themselves mats and clothing, weapons and furniture' as well as do more 'wholesome' garden-work, rather than be idle. But he deemed it 'impossible to separate the people from the world'. 'The only truly just act', he wrote, 'is for us to withdraw from the group, and let the natives manage their own affairs. As this would involve the destruction of the people [through a resurgence of warfare], the only alternative is for us to stay.'[30]

Hubert Murray, in his soon-to-be-published book on Papua, declared it 'out of the question that we should withdraw from the territory'. Someone else, 'who might be worse, would immediately take our place. The material fact is that we are here, and shall remain here; and that we and the Papuans must consequently make the best of one another.'[31]

In his earlier book, Murray asserted that the interests of Papuans and the Europeans he had encouraged to develop the territory coincided. Although it would be hypocritical, he wrote, to 'pretend that Europeans generally came to Papua with the object of benefiting the Papuans. But I think that, in fact, European settlement has had that effect.' Ten years later, he took a more nuanced view in his weighing up of the pros and cons of empire. Has the presence of the white man done more harm or good to native races in general? he asked. 'The probability is that the Papuan in his native state was far less happy and care-free than we imagine,' he suggested. 'He was tightly bound by the rules of hard-and-fast conventions which governed practically the whole of his life, he was the constant prey of superstitious terrors, he not infrequently suffered from want of food, and he was exposed to ever-present danger of attack. On the other hand, he had no Government to work for, no tax to pay, no jail to fear, and no imported diseases to suffer and to die from.'[32]

Sylvester Lambert, who agreed with Rivers that 'decay of custom and a lack of will to live' were 'important killers', found himself in late 1923 when in Tonga wondering whether 'civilization had done these people any good at all'. Was it better, he asked, under 'the ancient communism, with nobody rich, nobody poor, in a self-contained island group that fought away intruders'? Elsewhere, though, he asserted that it was the Europeans' 'job to lift them from the stone age to the bomb age'. Murray was similarly conflicted. The task of his government, he wrote, was to 'preserve the Papuans', but also, contradictorily, to change them 'from a non-industrial to an industrial people'.[33]

The compromise position, Murray outlined, was to restrain the rapacity of the plantation owners and to steer development in the interests of the indigenous inhabitants and primarily through their own efforts. This approach would win him much applause: Alfred Haddon, who would write his obituary, described him as 'one of those outstanding administrators of whom the British Commonwealth may well be proud ... he devoted himself entirely to the well-being and peaceful progress of the natives'.[34]

But what were the 'interests of the natives'? As early as 1904 Murray had become interested in anthropology when he met Charles Seligman when on his Papua expedition. For some years he had been lobbying the Australian government for the appointment of an anthropologist to help his administration. He wanted 'someone with the capacity to acquire the art of "thinking black" or "brown" which it is said "requires more sympathy and insight than is given to most men"'. Such a man, he hoped, would be able to give guidance on 'how best to reconcile the native public opinion (so far as it exists) with ... the policy of the Government in particular'. It took some years of haggling over the cost, but eventually, in 1920, an appointment was made – anthropologist Dr Walter Strong, who had been part of Seligman's expedition but had stayed on as a general medical officer.[35]

This was a ground-breaking move for the region, and Murray was much praised for it by speakers at the Science Congress. This was reflected in the anthropological section's final resolution that the 'preservation, progress and welfare of the native population of Oceania ... can best be carried out by a policy based on the investigation of native conditions, customs, laws, religion and the like'. This was not just of 'academic interest', 'but points the way to a sympathetic method of dealing with and governing such people'. (It would also, happily, help develop an 'intelligent native labour policy', 'induce a contented frame of mind in the workers', and thus be 'of definite economic importance'.)[36]

In practical terms, the resolution called for a chair of anthropology to be established in Sydney (which would eventually happen three years later), and a general expansion of anthropological training and personnel across the region, which was divided up in terms of responsibility for this between the European imperial powers, Australia, New Zealand, the United States and Japan (the last two sharing responsibility for Micronesia, which included the Gilbert and Ellice Islands).

There was, everyone agreed, an 'immense difference between their culture and ours'. Even experienced men on the spot, like Rev. Durrad, confessed to their frequent bafflement. The hope, then, was that this new science of anthropology, based, according to Murray, on the 'principle of the ultimate unity of the human race', could bridge the gap of understanding. Anthropology's rising star, Bronisław Malinowski, made the same appeal at the end of his 1922-published book. 'The Science of Man', as he called it, 'should lead us to tolerance and generosity, based on the understanding of other men's point of view.' The alternative would be a continuation of the fundamental failure of understanding that had led to so much strife and grief.[37]

11

Grimble in Paradise

Arthur Grimble loathed Kipling. In early 1914, when as a twenty-five-year-old he was applying for the position of cadet in the Pacific imperial administration, 'The cult of the great god Jingo was as yet far from dead.' Most English households of the time took it for granted, he wrote, that 'the Almighty was Anglo-Saxon' and 'Dominion over palm and pine . . . and anything far-flung . . . was the heaven-conferred privilege of the Bulldog Breed. Kipling had said so.'[1]

For Grimble, though, it was 'presumptuous to speak of our right to own an empire'. Instead, he set himself apart from what he called his uncles' generation, with their walrus moustaches, talk of leadership and firmness, and for whom Stalky, terrifyingly, 'represented their idea of dauntless youth'. 'I was a tallish, pinkish, long-nosed young man,' he wrote, 'fantastically thin-legged and dolefully mild of manner.' If his potential employer, the Colonial Office, wanted leadership in the same sense as Kipling and the uncles, he was 'scuppered'.[2]

His interviewer in the gloomy Downing Street warren of the Colonial Office, 'owlish' with heavily tufted eyebrows and dressed in tails, quickly picked all this up. Reaching for an atlas, he whipped over the pages until at last he found the Gilbert and Ellice Islands. 'Here we have them: five hundred miles of islands lost in the wide Pacific.

Remote ... I forbear, in tenderness to your feelings, from saying anything so Kiplingesque as far-flung. Do we agree to say remote and not
far-flung?' He traced the tiny atolls with his finger. 'Remote ... and
romantic ... romantic! The lagoon islands, the Line Islands, Stevenson's
Islands! ... Do we stake our lives on Stevenson, *not* Kipling? Do we
insist upon the dominion of romance, *not* the romance of dominion?'[3]

The young Grimble squirmed a bit on the mention of romance.
But, he later wrote, having applied to the Colonial Office for a job in
part so that he could marry his sweetheart Olivia Jarvis, he chose the
Pacific islands 'blindly, for the only reason that they were romantically
remote'. He had read Stevenson's 1896 essay collection *In the South Seas*
enough times to be able to quote it from memory. He hoped that he
would be working for heads of departments who 'harboured a hidden
passion for the writing of R.L.S.'[4]

But there was one other crucial influence behind his choice: anthropologist William Rivers.

Grimble had been born in Hong Kong, son of a well-off Admiralty
contractor. After boarding school in England from the age of ten, he
read law, literature and languages at Magdalene College, Cambridge.
He had a natural flair for languages and also dabbled in literary societies. But most importantly, he met and was inspired by Rivers, who
encouraged his interest in anthropology, supplying him with reading
lists, advice and tutorials. Rivers was then working on his *History of
Melanesian Society*.[5]

Grimble was offered a cadetship in the Gilbert and Ellice Islands
(he was the sole applicant for the position) and only a couple of weeks
later he and his new wife Olivia were on their way to Ocean Island via
Sydney. Grimble would end up serving nineteen years in the Gilberts –
longer than any other colonial officer in history bar one. Throughout
this time he was on the frontline of all the anthropological dilemmas
discussed at the Congress as well as, it turned out, the Kafka-esque
land issue on Ocean Island.

He would become a household name in Britain in the 1950s on
the back of the success of two books he wrote about the Gilbert and

Ellice Islands as well as radio programmes on the BBC. In the books, he comes across as charmingly self-deprecating, but also truly engaged in the lives of the Gilbertese. He was once described as one of the 'nicest colonial administrators in history'. Only after his death and an epic court case brought in the late 1970s by the Banabans against the British government and the British Phosphate Commission would his reputation take a sharp downwards lunge.[6]

The voyage to Sydney lasted two months, then they transferred to a steamship for the seven-day journey to Ocean Island. The filthy vessel 'reeked of dead shark, putrid oyster and rancid copra from stem to stern', and at night cockroaches gnawed away at the dead skin of their feet. When they woke, 'the ball and heel had been stripped pink'. Compensation was had from lying on deck at night as the steamer churned through the South Pacific, overhung 'by a firmament of flaming stars ... just as the travel books had promised'.[7]

As a cadet officer, Grimble was paid £300 a year and was on probation for three years; to become part of the permanent administrative staff he had to pass examinations in law and native language. The then Resident Commissioner, Edward Eliot, had Grimble tutored in Gilbertese (in which he quickly excelled), moved him round the various departments to gain experience, and advised him to learn local manners and etiquette. 'We are here to learn their customs, not to teach them ours,' Eliot told Grimble.[8]

After a year and a half, the young cadet was told he was leaving Ocean Island to take up the duties of district officer at Tarawa, with responsibility for the nearby atolls of Marakei, Abaiang and Maiana. The Grimble party now included not just Olivia but also their first daughter, Joan Ruth, aged eleven months, plus Faasalo, a nursemaid originally from the Ellice Islands.

The 250-mile eastwards voyage to Tarawa was unusually bad, taking eighty hours in very rough seas. Within an hour, all four of the Grimble party were being violently sick. The Australian captain of the steamer offered his passengers the usual cure for seasickness: pork fat from a brine barrel. This brought on a stream of vivid swearing from

Olivia. As Grimble put it, 'her voice rang clear as a bugle on two words that girls born in Queen Victoria's reign simply did not know'. The captain looked at Grimble for a moment. 'Cripes . . . she's a fair bosker, ain't she son? . . . She'll do alright in the islands.'[9]

But it would be a struggle. Apart from a Father of the Sacred Heart mission, and a medical officer who was hardly ever there, they were the only Europeans on Tarawa. Mail from home could take eight months to arrive. There were no refrigerators, no fresh milk, butter or meat. Unlike Ocean Island, whose phosphate riches meant regular steamers, bringing goods, mail and produce to a cash-paid workforce and around fifty white families, Tarawa was, Grimble wrote, 'desperately poor'. Its sole exports – copra and shark fin, worth only about £25,000 a year – were meagre enough to merit just two steamers a year to collect. These would bring fresh fruit and potatoes, but most of it had rotted on the journey from Sydney. There were tins, but with a couple of exceptions all they contained, be it onion, pea, cabbage, bean or potato, tasted identically of 'iron filings boiled in dishwater'.[10]

The sandy coral soil, loved by coconuts and pandanus trees, was impossible to grow vegetables in. The Grimbles dug trenches and filled them with compost to raise tomatoes or beans, but if it rained, the compost disappeared underground. If there was a dry spell, it was unrealistic to water the vegetable plants as the household was limited to two buckets of water a day for all purposes. Often, imported chickens refused to lay and quickly died off from the parasitic gapeworm. Goats rarely provided milk or kids.

So the family shared the islanders' staples, coconut and 'swamp taro', whose 'unhallowed starchiness' even Olivia's determined efforts in the kitchen could not alleviate. There was the occasional local pawpaw or pumpkin, and sometimes rice from the one trade store, run by an ancient half-Gilbertese, half-Austrian called Old Anton; 'bush eggs' could be purchased from locals at the rate of three for a stick of tobacco; and there was fish from the lagoon. The jelly-like flesh of green coconuts proved to be good food for their infant. Toddy, the sweet sap of the coconut blossom, provided vitamins.

There were other compensations. Because Tarawa had previously been the seat of the Resident Commissioner, there was a large, handsome two-storey wooden house with a deep veranda shaded by louvred shutters. Situated on the semi-circular atoll's southern tip, from this new home the Grimbles could gaze along the palm-fringed white sand beach or look out across the turquoise lagoon. It was hot, but as Grimble wrote, quoting Stevenson, the Gilberts had a 'superb ocean climate, days of blinding sun and bracing wind, nights of a heavenly brightness'.[11]

As a district officer, with a pay rise to £400 p.a., Grimble had responsibility for some 5,000 on Tarawa and around the same number on the three nearby atolls, all living in lagoon-side villages of thatch and rough timber. His job, as he described it, was 'correspondent, sub-accountant, customs authority and postmaster-general', as well as spending time on 'island tours, village tours, countless interviews, work with the Native Courts' and plenty of 'surprise-packets'. He was 'a pretty tired man by nightfall'.[12]

His territory, he knew, was 'less than a drop in the ocean of Empire economy . . . forgotten by the Colonial Office'. But, for now, he clearly loved his new job. What made the biggest impact, though, was not the balmy heat, nor the beach-fringed lagoon, but the friendliness of the local people. They were, he wrote, 'gentle and merry', 'naturally' kind and courteous, a 'race of princes in laughter and friendship, poetry and love', with an 'amazing affection for our race'. Grimble put this down in part to Gilbertese origin myths of pale-skinned ancestors, who now lived in the Land of Matang. Thus Grimble was frequently called 'the Man of Matang'. (Pale skin was much valued among Gilbertese women, who would bleach their skins with coconut oil.)[13]

Olivia was now pregnant again, with the baby due in January 1917. According to Grimble, it would be the first white baby born on the island, and this caused much excitement. Olivia, he wrote, was 'greeted like a beloved goddess wherever we went'.[14]

In the course of his work, Grimble was noticing that there were numerous land disputes on Tarawa. Before the establishment of the protectorate in 1892 there had been frequent fighting between different clans and groups. This had been ended, but many issues were left unresolved. Grimble suggested to his superiors that he establish a Land Commission, but for now, nothing was done. Grimble also used his time to do as much anthropological research as he could. The interest he showed delighted the older Gilbertese to the extent that he was invited to join the Tarawa sept of the royal and priestly clan of Karongoa, becoming, effectively, 'kin'. This involved being tattooed with serpents on both arms from the palm to just above the elbow. The pain, he wrote, was like the sting of five hornets, but he was not allowed to show any reaction. Instead two young girls, each holding an arm, squealed and moaned on his behalf.[15]

The baby, Rosemary Anne, was born in January 1917 and the following month the family was moved south to Abemama, where Grimble was to replace a retiring district officer. Here, their accommodation was a three-roomed thatched house. 'It was a lonely life for any white woman prone to sitting down and twiddling thumbs,' Grimble wrote, 'but Olivia was not a twiddler.' Soon she had – unofficially of course – commandeered the little-used women's prison to establish a mother and baby clinic. Local women came at first out of curiosity, then for the positive results she was achieving armed with little more than a childcare book by Dr Truby King and a medical guide issued for sailors beyond the call of doctors. The result, said Grimble, was 'the dissemination of a very reasonable knowledge of pre-natal hygiene and infant welfare among the women of Abemama'.[16]

Grimble himself, though, was struck by the first of what would be many attacks of amoebic dysentery. He suffered without proper medical care for several months at the end of 1917 before being evacuated to Ocean Island weighing only a little over 7 stone. Then, with his family, he took sick leave in Australia, before returning to Abemama in May 1918, leaving Olivia and the children behind for the birth of their third daughter, Monica Hope.

There was something of a manpower crisis by this point. Prior to the war there were usually five district officers working under the Resident

Commissioner at Ocean Island. But several had enlisted (Grimble volunteered several times but was always turned down), and in October Grimble, now reunited with his expanded family, was needed to take charge of all the central and southern islands of the Gilberts group. Thus he was posted to Beru, unofficially the capital of the south.

The Grimble party arrived at the island in heavy seas. The party now consisted of the three girls, three nursemaids, a cook, a 'houseboy' and his wife, together with an orderly and a clerk. They also had all their luggage, boxes of office material, twelve guinea fowl, forty-eight chickens, six goats and a terrier called Smith. There was no ship's entrance to the lagoon, so all had to be conveyed by a rickety old steam launch towing lighters for 5 miles in a growing storm. With the goats perched on the peaks of the luggage, 'as if back in their native highlands', and the children howling and soaked to the skin, after two hours they made it to the beach thanks to the skill of the Gilbertese boatmen.[17]

But when they reached the district officer's house, they found it semi-derelict. All amenities such as beds, stoves and pans, and even its veranda, had been shipped out with the departing previous occupant. Olivia, Grimble reported, was unfazed, commenting that it was 'just another of those Gilbert and Sullivan twists that added zest to life in the islands'. (The only time she was driven to tears was when they discovered shortly afterwards that they had caught crab lice off borrowed beds.) A new house, proudly using only 'native' materials, was quickly erected, then rebuilt again when on Christmas Eve night a gale lifted off the whole roof: 'The lamp went out. We knelt in gross darkness, with our wailing progeny about us, while the gale lashed down upon our roofless heads.'[18]

The stint at Beru constituted the earliest memories of Rosemary, Grimble's second daughter. She remembered the roof being blown off, but admitted she had little understanding of how difficult life was for her parents. Instead she recalled 'the lagoon edge where we played, cool shadows beneath the coconut palms, and water that was warm and green and crystal clear ... In the evenings wood smoke and at night mosquitoes.'[19]

The southern Gilberts were very different from Grimble's earlier postings in the north, and in a way that was not to his liking. He described Beru as 'highly indoctrinated'. While the northern islands retained much of their pre-Christian character, in the south the Gilbertese were firmly converted and the five islands were effectively run by the evangelical Protestant London Missionary Society (LMS).[20]

The society had operated in Samoa from the 1820s and the following decades had seen Samoan converts spread out across the region, arriving in the southern Gilberts in the 1870s. Catholic missionaries followed the next decade and on some islands sectarian disputes were pursued enthusiastically as a new expression of traditional rivalries.

Soon the pastors were powerful, thanks to their monopoly of education and interference in local politics. They ended inter-island warfare and protected their flocks from malicious labour recruitment as well as mediating in disputes with traders. But they also introduced a penal code that aimed to put an end to 'heathen practices'. A particular target was 'native dancing', thought to 'promote sorcery, jealousy, adultery and drunkenness'. Fines levied for even the most minor infractions provided much of the income of the missions.[21]

By Grimble's time, the LMS had achieved a position of dominance across the five islands. Its local leader since 1900 was William Edward Goward, a 'stocky, pink faced, white haired figure'. Thanks to 'government lassitude', Grimble wrote, Goward had been 'politically speaking, their dictator for the previous twenty years'. He was 'flaming with energy, stubborn as a mule, puritanical as a Pym, arrogant as a cardinal'. His word was law: all 'Native Courts' and village councils were under his control through Protestant deacons. For most of the last twenty years the thinly stretched imperial authorities had been happy to let him get on with it.[22]

Grimble did acknowledge the missionaries' achievements of widespread literacy and also peace and order, all accomplished with next to no assistance from the government. But the rules and restrictions they introduced he condemned as 'a moral and anthropological crime of the first magnitude'. For one thing, they had 'not improved the morals of the Gilbert Islanders', he would tell an Australian journalist the following year. 'Their old laws of morality and family discipline have been a good deal knocked about, to the detriment of the race.' Taking the example of 'offences against sexual morality', he pointed out that the old way was for the man to be tied to a log and floated out to sea, and the woman throttled to death. With these punishments banned in favour of imprisonment, adultery had increased, and 'morality had run to seed'. (Elsewhere Grimble pointed out that the ban on polygamy had caused numerous suicides by second wives.)[23]

In the same way, he argued in a letter to Western Pacific High Commissioner Rodwell, what he called the 'fanatic dogma of clothes' – the neck-to-ankle 'Mother Hubbards' the pastors insisted women wear – 'has taught a certain number of natives to harbour thoughts about the female body. It has planted a seed of corruption where once there was only innocence.' The result was, he reported, a steep rise in the 'vices of sexual curiosity, fornication amongst juveniles, and (worse than all else) self-abuse'.[24]

The rules against 'pagan' practices had, he wrote, 'rooted out much that was beautiful and useful in native custom'. Grimble had loved the traditional dancing he had seen in the northern islands, in particular the *Ruoia*, 'a magnificent harmony of bodies, eyes and arms – even of hands and fingertips – swinging, undulating and poising in perfect attunement, through a thousand graceful attitudes to the organ-note of fifty voices chanting in absolute rhythm'. As well as beautiful, the dances were also useful, vital even, 'the sole historic document of the islands, the sole common bond of sympathy between them'. Dancing chants were a 'literary vehicle', telling the stories of ancestors, 'and once a native forgets his ancestors he may be said to have lost his "hold"'. Dancing was useful, too, for keeping people away from idleness and 'mischief'. Where dancing had been suppressed there was more thieving and 'vice' than on the islands where it was still extant.[25]

Grimble later remembered, when in Tarawa, coming across an old man, alone in a canoe shed, holding a skull in the crook of his elbow, blowing tobacco smoke into the skull's jaws. He told Grimble that the spirit of his grandfather, who had shown him much kindness, was at that moment inside the skull, and the tobacco was a gift of love. Grimble also told the story of a man who had had a shrine with five generations of skulls. Each evening he would anoint them with oil. 'I spoke to them, and they answered me, and I was happy with them.' But the Christian pastor had ordered him to throw them away. He refused, saying, 'They are my roots and my trunk.' The next day a crowd had come from the church and stamped them into small pieces.[26]

Belief in spirits had survived. Grimble's daughter Rosemary remembered that even in 'indoctrinated' Beru, 'magic and magical presences, benign or evil, were a part of life. Every aspect of daily existence, every object, wish, thought, condition, action and purpose, good or bad, was governed by its own set of charms and spells.' But, Arthur Grimble believed, veneration of benign ancestors had gone, leaving only fear of vindictive spirits. It was all part of what he called 'the chaos of conflict between the old and new religions'.[27]

Grimble did intercede with the LMS to defend traditional pastimes and succeeded in getting some Catholics on to the 'native courts', but by mid-March 1919 he was again suffering from amoebic dysentery and colitis, 'sulkily on my back again ... at the end of April, I was living on two glasses of milk and water a day, very weak, and savagely sorry for myself'. He recovered enough to help with the birth of their fourth daughter in June, two months early, but was struck down again in October. A passing steamer took him to Ocean Island, its captain promising to be back in six weeks for the rest of the family. But the ship did not return until four and a half months later, by which time Olivia had also succumbed to dysentery, they had run out of rice, flour and potatoes, and their daughter Rosemary had become seriously ill with blood poisoning. When she finally met up with her husband at Ocean Island in May 1920, Olivia was painfully thin.[28]

Much to his surprise, and pleasure, Grimble had been appointed acting Resident Commissioner in the absence from Ocean Island of Eliot on leave, until in August he and his family also went on leave. As he had served six years, their passage to Sydney was paid for, as well as a contribution of £60 towards their onward fares to England. By now, Grimble had saved £280 out of his pay; £120 of it went on winter clothes for the children and accommodation in Sydney while they waited three weeks for a ship. The quicker route via Suez was too expensive, so they went round the Cape on an old and dirty vessel. At several stops they were delayed by strikes, everyone got ill 'in the endless hugger-mugger of that horrible craft', and it would be November by the time they reached London, with only £80 left.[29]

There followed visits to family and friends; Grimble went to Cambridge to see his mentor William Rivers, 'that colossus among anthropologists'. With his help, Grimble had his first article 'From Birth to Death in the Gilbert Islands' published early the next year in the *Journal of the Royal Anthropological Institute*. The piece remains 'essential reading for students of Gilbertese social organization'.[30]

Meanwhile, the family debated what to do next, having decided that 'the climate of the Gilberts was cruel to growing children'. If the family stayed in England, Grimble would need nine months' leave to visit them for just three months, and this was only permitted after another six years' service. They had an idea to locate Olivia and the girls in Sydney, only two weeks from Ocean Island. This, however, would require borrowing £800 to pay for the move. Grimble went to the Colonial Office to check that he wasn't going to be posted elsewhere having taken on this large debt. The first official he saw was markedly unhelpful. 'We know nothing officially of wives and families in the Colonial Office,' he told Grimble. 'We deal with officers in the field as officers, not husbands or fathers. And we never give guarantees not to move them from post to post.' A second official was more sympathetic and even apologetic. Something was now being done for wives and families of officials in Africa, he explained, but the Pacific part of the empire was too poor 'to pay for improvements'. Nor could he guarantee that he might soon be moved nearer to home, but Grimble was generously praised for his work so far and promised another stint as acting Resident Commissioner.[31]

He and his wife, through a family friend, had been offered a job running a small hotel. They were sorely tempted. But, as Grimble wrote, 'our six years in the Gilbert Islands had put me in love, not with the people alone but, beyond them, with the colonial service as a way of life'. His resignation letter went unsent. Borrowing a further £150 for the passage ('emigrant class again'), he sailed for Sydney on his own early in 1921. He would not see his children again for seven years.[32]

12

'Empire Bunk'

For Grimble, much of the three months on Ocean Island as acting RC was taken up with supervising repairs on the residency for the arrival of Reggie McClure and his wife Dorothy. Interestingly, Grimble commented that among the Banabans he missed 'the gay and spontaneous mass-friendliness I had learned to expect from villagers over in the lagoon islands'. He put this down in part to the segregated living space of the fifty or so Europeans, many with families; 'the white man and the brown . . . tended to meet each other seldom except in the relationship of employer to employed'.[1]

In August 1922, Grimble at last got the go-ahead to start on his Land Commission, unravelling the complicated disputes across the island group. It would be an intensely lonely time for him, but also in some ways the most rewarding. Returning to the Gilberts having recently been in England, he was struck anew by how they were 'lost in an immensity of ocean' and 'on the route to nowhere'. He often wondered, he wrote, what on earth he was doing there 'whenever I thought of my family in England'. During this period he had a number of pieces published in *United Empire* magazine. One was a poem which extols the beauty of a Pacific atoll sunset, but ends, 'But I would back to England once again / (Where lush things grow – where even Summer ends) / To firelit books; to all the dear, clean things / Whose memory makes us always English men.'[2]

The same magazine published a piece he wrote on 'Women as Empire Builders'. The treatment of his family by the Colonial Office obviously rankled. In it, he praised the 'practical, unassuming, gallant women' who were the wives and mothers of the children of officers in the 'British Imperial Colonial Service' for whom 'home' was at their husband's side wherever that may be. This devotion, he wrote, might cost them dear under a system which 'makes provision ranging from little to absolutely nothing for their comfort' even though it was on their sacrifices that 'the foundations of Empire are built'. For one thing, the 'natives' much preferred being ruled by married men, particularly if, like Olivia, their wives threw themselves into childcare work. For another thing, the 'homely peace that hums around them' was of inestimable help to their husbands. 'Everyone who knows the tropics is aware that they are full of dark corners where a white man simply cannot live alone,' Grimble explained. Solitary white men 'soon begin to feel a sense of appalled isolation ... Many good men have gone under in this condition (I have known several) into rank madness.'[3]

Harry Maude, a Cambridge-trained anthropologist who worked under Grimble for three years in the late 1920s, recalled being told by Grimble that it was 'only his complete absorption in the Gilbertese life surrounding him and the kindness of his many Gilbertese friends, particularly among the old men, that kept him going'. The Land Commission involved the investigation of history and genealogy and the principles on which the society rested. Land could change hands for all sorts of interesting reasons. In effect, it was applied anthropology on the Rivers model. Grimble channelled this into further articles for anthropological journals. He became a Corresponding Fellow of the Royal Anthropological Institute, guided by Rivers, then after his death by Alfred Haddon. Grimble shared the Congress's emphasis on the importance of understanding. 'Most young administrative officers appointed in London', he wrote, 'go out to their posts with no useful foreknowledge whatever of the primitive societies with which they will deal.' Most 'native grievances' were caused by 'ignorance of native customs'.[4]

Grimble started his Land Commission work at Butaritari, the northernmost Gilbert of any size. But his happiest time was at Marakei, the next atoll to the south, described by Harry Maude as 'a circular garland of coconut palms and coral sand set around a sapphire lagoon'. Here he found a knowledgeable and cooperative group of elders led by Taakeuta, 'teller of histories', who was impressed by Grimble's competence in classical Gilbertese, his interest in their ancient customs and his careful checking with them of everything he noted down. This was where he did his very best anthropological fieldwork.[5]

His stay on the island, however, ended very badly. Grimble's Land Commission had found against a man who had purloined his orphaned niece's valuable inheritance of 20 acres of good copra-growing land. The uncle was, as Grimble described it, a 'sorcerer', and soon afterwards Grimble was told that he had been cursed with a spell to fall ill within a week and die within three. Grimble hoped that he wouldn't be struck once more by dysentery and therefore give the sorcerer credence. 'No white man had ever yet been known to succumb to Gilbertese magic,' he wrote. 'The whole confidence of the brown men in the white race rested ultimately on that one fact.' And who would have faith in his Land Commission judgements if he was shown to be susceptible to spells? Two days later he woke before dawn feeling 'as if an ice-cold hand with red-hot fingernails was tearing out a hollow space between my kidneys and my solar plexus'. [6]

The 'spell' had involved spiking Grimble's night-time coconut toddy with a large infusion of cantharides beetle (sometimes known as Spanish fly). In small doses it is considered an aphrodisiac, but in large amounts it is a potent toxin causing organ damage including extensive blisters on the bladder, leading to days and nights of excruciating pain. Desperate not to be seen to have succumbed, Grimble had the weekend to recover before his next appearance on the Land Commission, but by Sunday night he could not even sit up. Then there was a lucky break: a fierce storm blew over about half the dwellings on the island, and everyone was concerned with this, giving Grimble a week to recover. With no doctor for a hundred miles, he dosed himself with tinned milk, olive oil and bicarbonate of soda. Although he was by now 'six feet of skeleton clothed in nothing but skin', he managed, just about, to appear reasonably unaffected the next time he faced the crowds at the Land Commission. Still, he reckoned it took him three years to recover fully.[7]

In April 1923 he was called back to his routine district duties. As part of a general retrenchment, Rodwell was reducing the Gilbert and Ellice Islands district officers from five to two, as well as selling their ship. This was despite Rodwell's region running a healthy budget surplus, requiring no subsidy from London. As Grimble explained, 'the good taxpayers of Britain would simply hate the idea of paying for a single thing I am doing in or for the Gilbert Islands!' McClure had lobbied hard for Grimble to be kept on, even though Grimble had several times requested a transfer to less of a career dead-end, neglected, distant and poor part of the empire.[8]

So, in September 1923 Grimble was back at Tarawa, when Olivia arrived from England. She had inherited a small legacy earlier in the year and had decided to spend it all on visiting her husband. Unfortunately, their reunion after more than two years was overshadowed by the recent tragic death from pneumonia of the infant son of the latest cadet trainee. Both the cadet and his wife blamed the senior medical officer, Dr Kitson (who had responded on behalf of the Gilberts to Cumpston's questionnaire for the Pan-Asian Congress). Kitson, they alleged, through 'wanton neglect' was the 'killer of their son'. Grimble suggested that lack of medical facilities on the island might have contributed, but Kitson was clearly not to blame – he was himself sick beyond hope of cure and semi-comatose in his bed. He would die a week later of Bright's Disease. Nevertheless, the 'hate and despair' the young parents nursed 'defied all consolation, and seemed to flow from them through the station like some dark river'.[9]

At least Grimble got Dr Kitson to Ocean Island to a proper hospital before he died. This was thanks to the arrival of the Fiji government's motor launch, which was being lent to the Gilbert and Ellice Islands to take Grimble on a tour of the colony in the place of McClure, who was suffering from ill health. It was also to convey round the islands the American doctor Sylvester Lambert and his team of Fijian microscopists looking for incidence of hookworm. Grimble had heard of the Rockefeller Foundation's 'princely sums of money' being 'poured into aid for the medical services', and also of Lambert's reputation as a 'selfless worker' and a plain speaker.[10]

Lambert, who by September 1923 had seen as much of the British Pacific Empire as anyone, found the colony somewhat dismal. In the 'highly missionized Ellices' there was much 'religious confusion'; in the Gilberts he was depressed by the 'usual squabble' between the London Missionary Society and the Catholics and 'native teachers' who 'fanned up religious mania'. Most depressing, though, were the few white inhabitants. 'White colonists of the Gilbert group needed a doctor more than the natives did,' he wrote. 'Monotony of life there must eventually depress the health of every European.'[11]

At each stop of the tour, Grimble would take Lambert and his team into the big meeting house (*maneaba*) and introduce them to the assembled people. In one, at Vaitupu in the Ellice group, Grimble had the task of thanking the people for their gift of 20 good copra acres towards the cost of maintaining a new school. As 'a matter of course', Grimble conveyed the thanks not of the Colonial Secretary (which the locals, he said, would not understand) but of King George. Afterwards Grimble exclaimed to Lambert: 'Wasn't that a wonderful gift of land for the school, doctor? It's going to save hundreds of pounds a year on the ration account.'

'Wonderful,' Lambert replied. 'And oh boy, your speech about it! You sure can pull that Empire bunk over these people to perfection.'[12]

Nonetheless, Lambert respected Grimble, describing him as 'an ethnologist who had made useful discoveries'. Reading Grimble's contemporary letters and his anthropological essays, written on the spot in the 1920s, alongside his 1950s books produced for the general reader, of course throws up some contrasts. The books paint a romanticised picture of the islands and their inhabitants: some of the more brutal traditions, outlined in his anthropology, such as the coming-of-age ceremonies for young men involving extensive burning, are glossed over in the later books; the position of women – who as wives could be lent to brothers or friends or handed over to older men in return for grants of land – is barely mentioned.[13]

But his anthropological work is also 'romantic' in that it celebrates an idealised past of hierarchy and respect for elders. A tradition he particularly admired was that of a young boy going to live with a grandfather or great uncle. 'The object ... was to provide for his aged relation a companionship and support which [the boy's father], as a busy breadwinner, had no leisure to afford. It was a very sensible arrangement, calculated to promote high reverence in the young for the old and responsible for a great family solidarity.'[14]

Like many administrators of the early 1920s, Grimble's attitude to the changes being wrought to the old systems was confused and contradictory. 'Pax-Britannica', he wrote, 'really did mean the dawn of newer, richer life for the Gilbertese' as it stopped the incessant warfare. He told of meeting a very old woman, with dozens of descendants, who without the intervention of the British to stop the war in Tarawa would have been killed. While they were talking, a great-granddaughter arrived after a visit to a neighbouring village. 'See that!' the old woman exclaimed. 'This woman arrives from walking in the north, yet no man has molested her.' Before 'the coming of the Flag', she explained to Grimble, 'If we wandered north, we were killed or raped. If we wandered south, we were killed or raped. If we returned alive from walking abroad, our husbands themselves killed us, for they said we had gone forth seeking to be raped.'[15]

But, Grimble lamented, change, though inevitable, had been imposed too quickly, endeavouring 'in a single span to bridge the abyss between savagery and modernism'. This had wrecked the 'native character' leading to the disappearance of what he called 'the native gentleman with his primitive yet perfectly clear cut standards of conduct and ... the birth of the native snob; a being ashamed of his ancestry, ashamed of his history, ashamed of his legends, ashamed of practically everything ... the fine courtesy and respect paid in pagan days by young to old are dead with disuse ... this is the seed of all insubordination'.[16]

What was needed was a firm guiding hand. Harry Maude would later write, 'Grimble became a benevolent patriarch', sure that he knew what was best for the Gilbertese. Both the Banabans and Gilbertese, Grimble wrote officially in 1920, 'demand the paternal form of admin-istration if anything is to be made of them'. Elsewhere Grimble called Gilbertese 'children, and at bottom very well-disposed children'.[17]

When he became Resident Commissioner at the end of 1925, Grimble would rule the islands in the 'aggressive paternalism' model of Richardson and Murray. Rules were drawn up covering everything from the upbringing of children to the care of dogs, pigs and fowls. In his opinion, such was the 'ruin of the ancestral system' thanks to changes wrought by modernity that the Gilbertese could no longer look after themselves in any way. Grimble would also reverse the policy of teaching English in the Ellice Islands schools, as it might inspire the 'natives' with ambitions which they could never fulfil, and thus become the potential cause of political unrest, producing 'a class of youth both economically useless and socially dangerous'.[18]

So at once Grimble could write that the Gilbertese had 'a natural dignity and taste which set them apart from others' (so much so that they must have descent from 'ancient Egyptian, Babylonian or Chinese cultures') but at the same time work on the assumptions that the islands would remain isolated and impoverished and that, apart from a small elite trained as clerks or interpreters, education in English would 'produce no appreciable effect whatever upon the collective dirtiness, inertia, improvidence, and domestic unenlightenment of the people'.[19]

According to Grimble himself he was much loved by the Gilbertese. Several families were happy for their children to take his daughters' names and thus become a version of god-children to him. And cer-tainly it had been noticed by his superiors that he was the foremost expert on 'native custom' and had won the trust of many. This is partly why, despite many requests to be moved elsewhere, he was too useful to spare. Indeed, he was already being lined up as the person 'most competent' to deal with the thorny question of the future of the phosphate-rich Banabans.[20]

For now, however, Resident Commissioner Reggie McClure remained in the hot seat. A few weeks after the request of 29 September 1923 for further mining land had been made, McClure wrote a long missive to the Colonial Office via Rodwell in Fiji. In this he worked through various possible solutions to the dilemma of the clash between the clearly stated wishes of the Banabans to remain in their ancestral home and the demands of the wider empire for their valuable phosphate.

First, he pointed out that much of the phosphate in the mining areas the commission already had was yet to be worked out. Rather than making a lunge for the untouched parts of the central region where the phosphate was at its richest, the miners could continue for at least ten years, or maybe longer, on the current areas, which would be 'a convenient method of shelving the problem of the ultimate disposal of the Banabans'.

Hope had been expressed, he wrote, by his predecessor Edward Eliot that during this period the 'commercial atmosphere' of Ocean Island would have dispensed with the Banabans' 'sentimental tenacity to their lands' and thereafter the BPC could ship them happily off elsewhere and move in on the last areas. But he did not believe this change of attitude to have occurred in the ten years since the Eliot agreement of 1913 and did not foresee it happening any time in the future.

The problem was the women. Although the young men, in particular Rotan Tito, were now the spokesmen for the majority, 'behind them and most formidable of all is the feminine influence on which everything depends and which is entirely re-actionary. Education will undoubtedly affect the future point of view of the Banaban boys but unless the girls are to be educated up to their level I confess that in my opinion the feminine influence in the matter of land will be just as re-actionary 20 years hence and just as supreme as it is now.' (Later, it would be the women who would tie themselves to trees as the diggers moved in on their last remaining lands.)

Another option was for the CO to grant the current request for a further 150 acres, with a firm promise to request no more, and with an underhand hope that when the Banabans realised that this still made their land uninhabitable they would 'by a process of what can only be described as indirect pressure' welcome removal to a new home. McClure could not stomach this. 'I would strongly deprecate the adoption of such a policy,' he wrote.

The third option was for the CO strictly to keep the commission to its existing areas, thereby allowing the Banabans to 'inhabit their island forever'. But McClure's many years working in the empire saw him rule this out. *'Assuming always that Imperial interests are to prevail,'* he wrote (his emphasis), there was no escaping the uncomfortable fact that the Banabans were going to have to leave at some point. The challenge, then, was how to make it as painless and 'humane' as possible for the islanders. Maybe another island could be selected soon and it could be done over a long period, he suggested.

He stuck to his opinion that the Banabans would never willingly consent to such a move, but then produced a torturous justification that chimed with Grimble's views on the detrimental effect the modern world had had on the Banabans. The colonial overlords had 'responsibility for the health and morale of a native race'. The current situation was doing them no good, he argued. Because they had money, they were buying and consuming 'exotic in preference to indigenous foods', the preparation of which was becoming 'an unknown art'; there was 'no necessity for effort in the matter of existence'; 'luxuries are too easily obtainable'; 'life is altogether too easy an affair; native crafts languish'. Furthermore, 'constant contact in a confined space with a comparatively large European and Asiatic community is not necessarily beneficial to a native race'. Thus, the removal of the Banabans so that the destruction of their island could be completed, against their oft-expressed wishes, could be seen somehow as rescuing them from the ill effects of the imperial intrusion.[21]

The Colonial Office reaction was to suggest that Rodwell meet with a representative of the commission to discuss the problem. After some delays, Albert Ellis himself appeared on the scene and met Rodwell at Fiji headquarters at Suva.

Whether the two men were always of like mind or whether Ellis did an extreme job of persuasion is impossible to say. But the agreement they came to, as reported back to London, was quite extraordinary. Rodwell asked to proceed 'without consulting H.M.G. in any way on the following basis'. The commission was to be given mining rights for ninety-nine years over the entire island, excepting 'native reserves'. These were to be cleared of Banabans within twenty years and another island in the Gilbert or Fiji groups purchased for them out of their Banaban fund. The Resident Commissioner was to be moved away from the island to make it clear that His Majesty's Government was 'practically handing the whole island over to the Commission' and that the Banabans should move to 'another habitation where their welfare would be a primary instead of a secondary concern of administration'.

Ocean Island was now to be a purely commercial concern. 'Too much weight' had been given to the 'sentimental attachment of the Banabans to Ocean Island', which, Rodwell suggested, was 'of relatively recent growth'. If it wasn't for the BPC 'they would either have drifted away or become extinct through disease and starvation. That their presence should be allowed to become a bar to the exploitation of an important product, the discovery of which may be said to have saved them from extinction, seems scarcely reasonable.'

A firm hand was called for, Rodwell concluded. 'No useful object is to be gained by negotiation with the Banabans and the only course is to present them with a firmly but considerately worded ultimatum' – or, as he later clarified, 'the High Commissioner will order the Native owners to evacuate the area'.[22]

On receipt of these suggestions, Colonial Secretary Lord Devonshire snapped and delivered to Rodwell a firm slapping-down. Marked 'Confidential Urgent', his telegram in reply tersely reminded the High Commissioner that the original concession granted to the Pacific

Phosphate Company under which the BPC was working 'imposed obligation to respect rights of inhabitants of Ocean Island. These rights extend to full ownership of land and minerals thereunder.' Any transactions with 'natives' must accept that the land rights were at their disposal. His Majesty's Government would not be party to anything that was not clearly to the benefit of the 'native proprietors'. 'Native interests cannot be sacrificed in order to secure any advantage financial or other.' It was the most explicit statement of Banaban rights in the history of the phosphate industry: it appeared, then, that lofty, disinterested London had ridden to the rescue of its powerless distant trustees embattled by local and commercial forces.[23]

But it wasn't over. The powerful phosphate interest would not give up. And with McClure in poor health and nearing retirement anyway, the next and most unfortunate stage of the negotiations would fall to Arthur Grimble.

13

Forster and Nehru

Saturday 29 September 1923 found E. M. Forster visiting Thomas Hardy at his home, Max Gate, a mile or so outside Dorchester. Forster had been introduced by Siegfried Sassoon four years earlier and made a number of somewhat reluctant trips. Many of Forster's fellow contemporary writers, including Virginia Woolf and D. H. Lawrence, admired Hardy greatly, particularly for his poetry, but Forster found the old great man of letters over-anxious to make a good impression and a boring conversationalist, particularly when he talked about books. He was also, for Forster, almost comically morbid.

On a recent visit, Hardy had taken Forster to a dark spot in the garden to see the graves of his deceased pets, each with a small tombstone, now mostly ivy-covered. All, it seemed, had perished violently: 'This is Snowball – she was run over by a train ... This is Pella, the same thing happened to her ... This is Kitkin, she was cut clean in two.' Forster asked whether there was a railway near. 'Not at all near, not at all near,' Hardy mumbled in reply. 'I don't know how it is. But of course we have only buried those pets whose bodies were recovered. Many were never seen again.' Forster later wrote to his mother that he had found it hard to keep a straight face – it was all so much like Hardy's novels and poetry.[1]

On the late September trip the weather, as in London, was very much 'Indian summer' territory, unseasonably warm and bright, though the thousand pine trees Hardy had planted around his property for privacy made the house and garden of Max Gate dark and gloomy. But Hardy was cheerful for once. 'The brother of one of his servants was being buried the first day, John Morley [previously Secretary of State for India] the second, so he was in good form,' Forster noted.

Talk turned to the Prince of Wales. 'Mrs H.' – Florence, his second wife – was 'rather scornful', Forster wrote in his diary. 'The middle classes as a whole seem turning against the P. – say he drinks and is in an "unhealthy state". His omission to marry makes them uneasy.'[2]

Forster had recently published an article about the Prince's visit to India. Unlike most of the coverage in the British press, he had taken the Indians' point of view. In fact, in the liberal press he was considered something of an expert on Indian matters, thanks to his two visits there – one in 1912–13 and one in 1921–2 – and the fact that he stood outside the Anglo-Indian establishment. Numerous other pieces on India were published. That his trips had straddled the war gave him a special insight into the huge changes that had occurred.

He later wrote that to visit India had been 'the great opportunity of his life'. It had also, of course, provided the inspiration for his masterpiece, now considered 'one of the great novels of the twentieth century', *A Passage to India*. Two weeks after the visit to Hardy, Forster noted in his diary that he had 'written a little to my damned novel'. He had sent the first twelve chapters to his publisher back in May, and been offered £500 in advance of royalties – 'good terms', he noted in a letter to an Indian friend. It had proved hard going – sometimes he wanted to 'spit and scream like a maniac' (he would never write another novel) – but now it was nearing completion. Its publication the following year would cause a sensation.[3]

Newspaper coverage of Indian affairs on 29 September 1923 was dominated by the latest arrest of Jawaharlal Nehru, amid what *The Times* called 'Sikh Agitation in the Punjab'. Since soon after the end of the

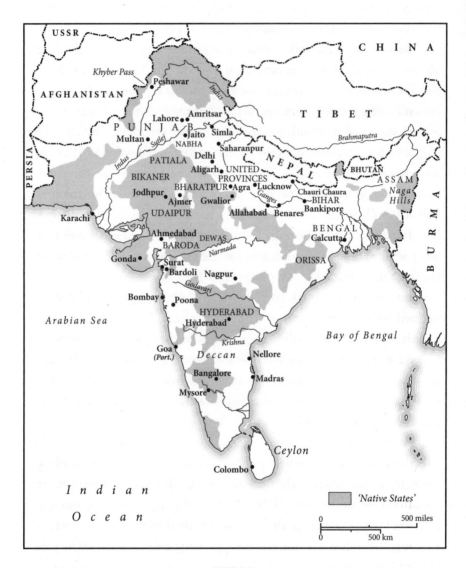

USSR

CHINA

Khyber Pass

Peshawar

AFGHANISTAN

TIBET

Indus

PERSIA

Lahore Amritsar

PUNJAB

Multan Jaito Simla

Sutlej NABHA Saharanpur

Brahmaputra

Delhi

NEPAL

PATIALA

BHUTAN

Aligarh UNITED

BIKANER PROVINCES Lucknow

ASSAM

BHARATPUR Agra

Naga

Jodhpur Ganges Chauri Chaura

Hills

Ajmer Gwalior BIHAR

BURMA

UDAIPUR Allahabad Benares Bankipore

Karachi

BENGAL

Ahmedabad DEWAS Calcutta

BARODA

Narmada

Gonda Surat

ORISSA

Bardoli Nagpur

Godavari

Bombay Poona

Arabian Sea

HYDERABAD

Hyderabad

Bay of Bengal

Goa Krishna

(Port.) Deccan Nellore

Bangalore

Madras

Mysore

Ceylon

Colombo

Indian

'Native States'

Ocean

0 500 miles

0 500 km

INDIA

war, a reformist Sikh 'Akali' movement had been campaigning and demonstrating in an effort to secure the transfer of Sikh gurdwaras (places of worship) from government-appointed managers and the traditional clergy (many of whom were corrupt and considered less than devout) to elected Sikh bodies. On several occasions violence had broken out and the movement had been declared illegal. 'Meanwhile,' *The Times* continued, 'extremist newspapers are supporting the Akalis by conducting a violent campaign of incitement and making outrageous attacks against British officials associated with Nabha State affairs.'

Nabha State was a small principality in the Punjab whose Maharaja had expressed support for the Akali campaign and for the non-cooperation movement and had thus been deposed by the colonial authorities. This had led to further protests, and a declaration of support from the Indian National Congress. Jawaharlal Nehru and two other senior Congress leaders had travelled to Nabha State to observe the latest demonstration at a place called Jaito.

Soon after their arrival, Nehru and his Congress companions were stopped by the police and an order served on them, signed by the British administrator, calling on them not to enter Nabha territory, or to leave it immediately. Nehru insisted he was not part of the demonstration, merely an observer, and 'we could not vanish suddenly into thin air'. Anyway, the next train from Jaito was many hours away. Thereupon all three were arrested and taken to the local jail.

That evening, wearing home-spun cloth and Gandhi caps, hand-cuffed together with a chain from the cuffs held by a policeman leading them, they were taken to the railway station. 'This march of ours down the streets of Jaito town', Nehru later wrote, 'reminded me forcibly of a dog being led on a chain.' Still handcuffed together, they spent a long night in a slow-moving train before being delivered to Nabha jail, where all three were kept 'in a most unwholesome and insanitary cell'. Sleeping was on the floor, Nehru wrote, 'and I would wake with a start, full of horror, to find that a rat had just passed over my face'. All three prisoners were in the process of catching typhus.[4]

According to Sir Michael O'Dwyer, former Governor of the Punjab, writing in *Current History* at the end of 1923, the local authorities had shown 'neither tact nor firmness in handling the [Akali] situation'. Instead, 'they have shifted rapidly from conciliation to repression and back again from repression to conciliation in a manner which has caused despair to their friends and aroused contempt and defiance from their enemies'. Indeed, many others had already identified this official vacillation as a contributing factor to the tumult of the previous four years, a period Nehru described as 'the most troubled years that India had known since the Revolt of 1857'. It was also a period that had seen, in Nehru himself, an utter transformation.[5]

'An only son of prosperous parents is apt to be spoilt, especially so in India,' Nehru began his autobiography, written in the mid-1930s, during another spell in prison. His father, Motilal, of Kashmiri descent, was a lawyer, specialising in Hindu inheritance cases. He hadn't travelled to Britain to train, unlike his contemporary Gandhi, but had become very successful and, as his daughter later wrote, had 'earned fabulous sums, lived lavishly and sometimes extravagantly'.[6]

The death of his elder brother had left Motilal with a large extended family to house and educate. He moved his residence from the crowded Indian part of Allahabad to the 'civil lines' – the European quarter with its wide streets and bungalows set in large gardens. When Jawaharlal was ten, the family upgraded to a huge, double-storied mansion amid vast grounds. Once extensively renovated, it boasted electricity, a riding ring and stables, a swimming pool and tennis court, and garages for Motilal's carriages and growing collection of motor cars. Manned by an army of servants, and full of Persian rugs, Dresden china and Venetian glass, it was by some distance the city's most lavish mansion.

This became a centre of the city's social life, welcoming guests most evenings. There were no racial or religious barriers. For Motilal and Jawaharlal's elder cousins, religion 'seemed to be a woman's affair'. They were, Jawaharlal remembered, 'cheerfully agnostic'. Indeed, the mansion was divided into two, one side Western, where Motilal entertained, and one Indian, where the more orthodox women members of the household could retain their eating and living habits and perform the family rituals. Motilal freely broke conventions over what Brahmins could eat and who with, enjoying meat, wine, whisky and cigars. When he travelled to Europe he refused to undertake the usual ceremony of purification on his return. Even as a student in Allahabad he had been 'attracted to Western dress and other Western ways' at a time when it was uncommon for Indians to take to them except in big cities like Calcutta and Bombay. And as his wealth grew, his son wrote, 'our ways became more and more Westernized'.[7]

Motilal did, however, attend some of the early sessions of the Indian National Congress. Founded in 1885, the Congress was a loose union of disparate regional and local associations and was dominated by Western-educated high-caste Hindus. Although most delegates were from areas where Western education was most available – Bengal, Bombay, Madras – there were men from all parts of the sub-continent. Helped by the huge growth of infrastructure in the second half of the nineteenth century – 25,000 miles of railway, 35,000 miles of telegraph lines, the post system, cheap printing and the spread of the English language – Congress was the first articulation of the idea of India as a public realm or even as a state along European lines.[8]

According to his son, Motilal gave Congress his 'theoretical allegiance', but at this point he took little interest in its work. For one thing, he was too busy with his career, but he also had a 'trace of contempt' for 'politicians who talked and talked without doing anything'. Indeed, the early Congress was essentially a debating society, with little institutional organisation or permanent financial support. It was studiously loyal to the Raj, and steered clear of controversial issues.

For his part, Motilal was a 'nationalist in a vague sense of the word, but he admired Englishmen and their ways ... He looked to the west and felt attracted by Western progress,' his son later wrote. 'He had a feeling that his own countrymen had fallen low and almost deserved what they had got.'[9]

From his cousins, however, Jawaharlal learned a different attitude. Often their talk would be of the 'overbearing character and insulting manners of the English people', of how Englishmen were always acquitted by juries of their countrymen, and of the humiliating rules banning Indians from certain railway carriages and even benches in public parks. One of the cousins was the 'strong man of the family' and loved to pick a quarrel with an Englishman, 'or more frequently with Eurasians [meaning people of mixed race] who, perhaps to show off their oneness with the ruling race, were often even more offensive than the English official or merchant'.[10]

Jawaharlal wrote that he learned to resent the presence and rudeness of the 'alien rulers'* but that he had 'no feeling against any individual Englishmen'. He had seen his father entertaining English friends, and from the start he had had English governesses and tutors. Although from his mother and aunt he would hear stories from the Hindu epics, the *Ramayana* and the *Mahabharata*, and from the Muslim controller of the household Munshi Mubarak Ali stories from the *Arabian Nights*, most of his reading was British. *The Jungle Book* and *Kim* were firm favourites, then, later, H. G. Wells, Conan Doyle, Thackeray, Scott and Dickens. He considered Jerome K. Jerome's *Three Men in a Boat* 'the last word in humour'. 'In my heart I rather admired the English,' he later wrote.[11]

The house was full, but the cousins were much older, and Jawaharlal had no siblings near his own age (a sister was born when he was ten). Educated at home, he had no school-friends either. So it was a lonely childhood, he wrote. 'I was left a great deal to my own fancies and solitary games.'[12]

In a way, it was preparation for the next step. In 1905, aged fifteen, Jawaharlal started at Harrow School, northwest of London. Two years later he went to Trinity College, Cambridge to read Natural Sciences. Apart from one trip home in 1908, he was away from India and his family for seven years.

At Harrow he was one of only four or five Indian boys, all of whom were sons of royalty. He was intensely homesick, and felt different from

---

* The Indian census of 1921 would report just under 157,000 Europeans in India of whom 45,000 were women. The men included about 60,000 troops and just under 22,000 in government service.

Ocean Island Banaban dancers in happier times.

Phosphate mining on Ocean Island left a blistering, sterile wasteland.

Dominion leaders would not have appreciated the patronising tone of this cartoon from the front page of the *News of the World*, 30 September 1923. An impoverished and colony-deprived Fritz looks on.

The Imperial Conference of 1923 displayed the empire's disunity and lack of purpose.

There was a massive publicity campaign to drive migration of white Anglo-Saxons to Australia, but there the Left saw the new arrivals as lowering wages and taking locals' jobs.

The Prince of Wales' train derailed in southwestern Australia near the site of a Group Settlement. Although unhurt, the accident contributed to the Prince's nervous exhaustion.

Anthropologist Charles Seligman in Papua New Guinea. In late 1923 he was running an empire-wide programme of recording and analysing the dreams of local people

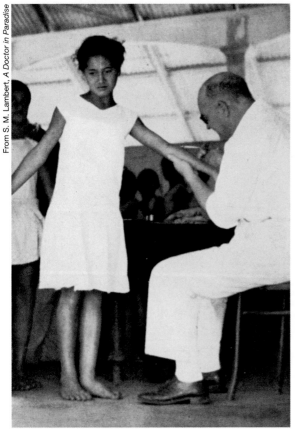

Dr Sylvester Lambert administering vaccines in the New Hebrides. His battle against hookworm in the Pacific region on behalf of the Rockefeller Foundation led him to be known as 'the man with a million patients'.

The Prince of Wales meeting leaders of the Chinese community in Singapore. He was struck by their dominant position across Malaya.

Loke Yew, one of the pioneering Chinese entrepreneurs who made a fortune from tin mining in Malaya. Most of his children were sent to Scotland for their education.

E. M. Forster and Syed Ross Masood, to whom he dedicated his masterpiece, *A Passage to India*.

Forster in 'native dress' at the court of the Maharaja of Dewas, where, he wrote, 'to check the idleness, incompetence, and extravagance is quite beyond me'.

Jawaharlal Nehru with his father Motilal before their rejection of European clothing. Having been educated at Harrow and Cambridge, on his return to India he described himself as 'perhaps more an Englishman than Indian'.

Nehru in rough-spun *khadi* addressing a meeting. He admitted that he was at first 'terrified of public speaking' partly due to his lack of fluency in Hindustani.

The 'crawling order' in Amritsar in action. For many Indians, the strictures of martial law were even worse than the massacre itself.

Hugh Clifford as a young man in Malaya. His conflicted attitude to the British Empire there would shape his long colonial career.

Clifford, in full gubernatorial regalia meets chiefs in Kaduna, Nigeria.
By this time, he was in poor mental health.

the other students, not because of race but because he felt much older and more worldly than his British contemporaries. But he worked hard and threw himself into activities like sport. His headmaster declared him 'a thoroughly good fellow'. E. M. Forster, who had attended Tonbridge School in Kent a decade earlier and had hated it, later wrote that public-school boys went into the world with 'well-developed bodies, fairly developed minds, and undeveloped hearts ... for it is not that the Englishman can't feel – it is that he is afraid to feel. He has been taught at his public school that feeling is bad form.' Nehru took a different view: 'The teaching of the West has made me value restraint a great deal.' Indians, he wrote, 'are continually indulging in emotionalism and lessening our activity thereby'.[13]

As well as Japan's victory over Russia, Nehru was also 'stirred' by news of events in India following the disastrous partition of Bengal in late 1905. While Muslims were largely supportive of the measure, the 'babus', as the British called the educated Hindu Bengalis, led the opposition to the partition, and the protest took a much more direct and populist tone than the usual meetings and petitions. Agitators spread out from Calcutta into the districts, urging the boycotting of British goods and *swadeshi* – the use of India-produced articles instead. Hindu learned men – pundits – were recruited to give the campaign religious backing. Protests spread to Hindu communities in Bombay and the Punjab.

It was the first great nationalist campaign, and the widespread adoption of the boycott suggested that politics now at last included 'the masses' rather than just a tiny educated elite and wealthy businessmen and landowners. 'For the first time since the Revolt of 1857 India was showing fight and not submitting tamely to foreign rule,' wrote Nehru, following events from England. Motilal was not so sure. For him, the 'background' of the boycott and *swadeshi* movements 'was a religious nationalism that was alien to his nature'.[14]

At Cambridge, the Indian students had a debating society, which hosted visiting Indian politicians and mulled over the latest developments at home. Much discussed was the split in Congress following the agitation against the Bengal partition, which had occasionally descended into communal violence. On one side were the radical 'extremists', led by Bal Gangadhar Tilak, well known for his imprisonment in 1897 in connection with covering up for the killers of two British officers. Tilak deplored the British education system that ignored or belittled Indian – or, more exactly, high-class Hindu – culture and history, and advocated an extension of the boycott to include non-cooperation in the functions of the Raj – in administration, defence, the payment of taxes. The aim was to achieve 'Swaraj' or self-rule for India. He became known to the British as 'the father of Indian unrest'. On the other side, the moderates, led by Gopal Krishna Gokhale, wanted reform through constitutional means within the framework of British rule. Gokhale had high hopes that the new Liberal government in London would deliver meaningful constitutional change for India. At the Congress session of 1907 at Surat, amid chaotic and even violent scenes, the Tilak party was roundly defeated. Soon afterwards Tilak was convicted of sedition and shipped off to prison in Burma.

The Morley-Minto reforms of 1909 (named after the Liberal Secretary of State for India and the then Viceroy) modestly extended the franchise and substantially increased the numbers of elected and nominated Indians on the provincial and central legislative councils of the Raj. The aim, according to a Government of India dispatch, was to co-opt 'the aristocratic elements in [Indian] society and the moderate men' and isolate the 'extremists'. The reform was structured through complex electoral arrangements so that various interest groups – religious, professional or economic – would be represented. It was far less than Gokhale had hoped for, and Congress as a whole deeply regretted that it gave separate electorates to Muslims.[15]

Motilal Nehru, who had been at the Congress session at Surat, shared these concerns, particularly about the religious divisiveness of the communal franchises, which, like the censuses for many years, demanded that Indians identify as one particular religion. This, many others also felt, encouraged different groups to see themselves in competition with each other, and to politicise and publicise what were previously private religious rituals. Nonetheless, he stood, and was elected to the new United Provinces legislature. Now very much a man of the establishment, he was one of the very few commoners invited to attend the Durbar of King George V. For the occasion he had his son send out a full court dress from London. According to Jawaharlal, his father was a 'moderate of moderates' at this time. He put this down to his grounding in law and constitutionalism, and his revulsion against anything that resembled religious revivalism: he 'utterly disliked many old social customs, caste and the like'.[16]

While at Cambridge, Jawaharlal had an allowance of £400 a year, about half a professor's salary, but still ran up debts that had to be met by his father from gambling and enjoying 'a soft life and pleasant experiences'. After university he moved to London to study for the Bar, and meanwhile travelled widely around the UK and Europe. He kept in touch with home, writing separate letters to his mother and father, the former in Hindi, the latter in English.

In London he became interested in the political issues of the day – women's suffrage, Ireland, socialism – but falling in with old Harrovian friends increased his expensive and luxurious habits. He later wrote that he was 'trying to ape to some extent the prosperous but somewhat empty-headed Englishman who is called "a man about town" . . . a soft and pointless existence'. In 1912, having been called to the Bar, he returned to India. 'I am afraid, as I landed at Bombay,' he wrote, 'I was a bit of a prig with little to commend me.'[17]

His sister Nan remembered that for days before his return the entire household was in a fever of excitement making preparations to welcome him back. 'Jawaharlal was, when he returned to India, somewhat of a "fop",' she recalled. 'Like a great many others who belonged to the educated classes, "Bhai" (brother) as I call him grew up in complete ignorance of the misery and poverty that was the lot of the majority of the people of India. He had lived a comfortable, luxurious life.'[18]

On his return, he worked initially as his father's junior. He found India 'politically very dull'. Tilak was in prison, leaving the extremists leaderless; the moderates had been 'rallied' to the Morley-Minto scheme; Congress attracted little attention. At the end of the year he attended the annual Congress meeting at Bankipore and was unimpressed: 'It was very much an English-knowing upper class affair where morning coats and well-pressed trousers were greatly in evidence.' It seemed more a social than a political occasion.[19]

Although pleased to be home with his family, he felt a 'mongrel' after seven years in England, 'a queer mixture of the East and West, out of place everywhere, at home nowhere'. He later said that at this time he was 'perhaps more an Englishman than an Indian. I looked upon the world almost from an Englishman's stand-point.' (Even years later, in November 1921, at the height of the non-cooperation campaign, he admitted to Gandhi that he still admired the British in many ways, 'and in many things I feel even now that an Englishman can understand me better than the average Indian'.) India did not seem to fit his previous ideas. He joined the High Court, but found the work, and the company, insipid. The British he came across were 'dull and narrow-minded. Even a bright young Englishman on coming out of India will soon relapse into a kind of intellectual and cultural torpor,' he later wrote. He blamed the 'ever-rotating and never-ending files', the 'high-bound bureaucratic and despotic system of government' and the same-old activities at the club. The Indian official working with him 'is not likely to fare better, for he tries to model himself on the English type'. An 'official and Service atmosphere' dominated middle-class life.[20]

When the war came, it was almost a relief from the boredom.

A couple of months after the 1912 return of young Nehru to his homeland, thirty-three-year-old E. M. Forster arrived at Bombay. It was a tradition for King's College men to join the Indian Civil Service (ICS) or the Bombay Burmah Trading Corporation, so he had a number of contacts, one of whom was Malcolm Darling, a particular friend and regular correspondent. Darling had been appointed by the ICS as tutor and guardian to a young prince who was now the Maharaja of Dewas, a small princely state in central India. Part of the tutelage had involved extensive travel around India and Burma, and the two had become very close. Forster later wrote that when Darling had first taken up the role, 'he had the feeling of racial superiority which was usual among Englishmen at the time. In a few months he lost it, and it never returned.' In fact, 'the young Englishman and the still younger Indian were full of hope and felt themselves to be symbols of their respective countries, and the pledges of a happier political union'.[21]

The experience of the voyage out suggested that Darling was in the minority. The ship was full of Indian Army officers and their wives. Forster found the women on board 'pretty rotten, and vile on the native question'. They all agreed one must not speak politely to 'natives', as 'they would despise you if you did'. 'Never forget that you're superior to every native in India, except the Rajas, and they're on an equality,' he was told. When Forster let one of the wives know that he was going to stay with a non-royal 'native', she gasped and quickly changed the subject.[22]

This 'native', and the inspiration for the trip and for Forster's interest in India, was Syed Ross Masood, to whom *A Passage to India* is dedicated. After leaving Cambridge, Forster did some magazine writing, travelling and tutoring, inherited some money, and in 1905 published his first novel, *Where Angels Fear to Tread*. He lived in Weybridge with his mother, his father having died when he was an infant. In 1906, Forster was taken on as a Latin tutor for seventeen-year-old Masood, who was applying to Oxford.

The contact came through his mother, who was friends with the wife of Theodore Morison, a distinguished Anglo-Indian official who in typical style had retired to the Surrey suburbs. Morison had been principal of the Muslim Anglo-Oriental College at Aligarh, United Provinces, founded in 1875 by Masood's grandfather, Sir Syed Ahmed Khan. The college's objective was to educate students by restoring pride in their Muslim culture but at the same time emphasising the compatibility of Islam with modern Western knowledge. Khan had been pro-British and anti-Congress, declaring it as having no benefit to the elite Muslims concentrated in the United Provinces. He was representative of a community that felt under threat – from Hindu revivalism, education policies and the expansion of local government on the elective principle. His college would be the engine behind the formation in 1906 of the All-India Muslim League, with its demand, granted by the Morley-Minto reforms, of a separate communal Muslim electorate.

Khan's grandson Masood had been educated at Aligarh, and following the early death of his intemperate father in 1902 had to all intents and purposes become Theodore Morison's ward. Masood at seventeen was already an imposing figure, well over 6 feet tall with a deep and sonorous voice and a princely manner. He was extravagant and generous, and seemed to live in a constant state of heightened emotion. He and Forster quickly became close friends, and over the next few years would see a lot of each other, including travelling in Europe together. By now, Forster was firmly in love, though when he made an awkward advance, it was politely rebuffed.[23]

Forster later wrote that Masood had woken him up out of his academic and suburban life and shown him new horizons and a different civilisation. They often spoke of India. Like his grandfather, Masood was full of nostalgia for the glories of the Mughal Empire, its art and poetry. 'Ah that I had lived 250 years ago,' he would exclaim, 'when the oriental despotisms were in their prime.' He painted a picture of an aristocratic India where friends were more important than duties, 'Hence the confusion in Oriental States,' Masood explained to Forster. 'To them personal relations come first.' It was exactly Forster's philosophy. Masood also talked of the slights and ill treatment that Indians could expect from the British in India, and sometimes 'flew into a passion against Anglo-Indian prejudice'.[24]

Before meeting Masood, India for Forster was 'a vague jumble of rajahs, sahibs, babus and elephants'. Now Forster threw himself into reading about Indian art, literature, music, religion and history. After Oxford, Masood moved to London to study for the Bar, and Forster was a frequent visitor to his house, which always seemed full of Indian friends, or more exactly an Indian entourage, for Masood regarded the world, Forster wrote, 'as a roomful of secondary persons with himself feeling intensely in the centre'. Forster was almost always the only European in the group, and seemed to the Indians unusual for an Englishman – sympathetic, interested, patient. One later said, 'We thought him like an angel.' Meanwhile, he and Masood started planning to visit India together.[25]

In late 1910, Forster published *Howards End*. Although he had had success with *A Room with a View*, this was the moment of Forster's 'arrival', and it secured his entry into the Bloomsbury set. The novel sets up oppositions – between inner and outer life, emotion and reason, culture and business – that the central and most sympathetic character, Margaret Schlegel, attempts to reconcile. Forster would later write that his initial aim in *A Passage to India* was to build 'a little bridge of sympathy between East and West'. In *Howards End*, Margaret wants to build 'a rainbow bridge' between herself as a cultured intellectual and her husband Mr Wilcox, a businessman. 'Only connect! That was the whole of her sermon. Only connect the prose and the passion, and both will be exalted.'[26]

The Wilcoxes are 'imperials'. They have made their money out of rubber from West Africa, where one of their sons is sent to work. The Schlegels have a typically metropolitan intelligentsia's disdain for such people. They would at times 'dismiss the whole British Empire with a puzzled, if reverent, sigh'. It bores them, and they ridicule the idea of empire as a divine mission. Wilcox has 'carved money out of Africa, and bought forests from the natives for a few bottles of gin'. He is a 'destroyer'; imperialism 'is the vice of a vulgar mind'. Margaret's efforts to 'Only connect' ultimately end in failure.[27]

Masood had firm ideas about what should be the subject of Forster's next novel. 'You know my great wish is to get you to write a book on India,' he wrote. 'You are about the only Englishman in whom I have come across true sentiment . . . even from the oriental point of view.' By the beginning of 1912, Masood was back in India, practising law. He urged Forster to come and visit. Thanks to the success of *Howards End*, he could now afford to do so. [28]

*

At Bombay, Forster was met by Baldeo, a servant who would accompany him throughout his visit. This had been organised by Rupert Smith, another ICS friend Forster had met on holiday in Greece, who was now an assistant magistrate in Nehru's home city of Allahabad. Much of Forster's six-month tour of India was predictable and touristic. In fact, his itinerary was not that different from that undertaken by the Prince of Wales in 1921–2. He took in the Taj Mahal, Peshawar on the Northwest Frontier, where the 'fine fierce youths' seemed a bit 'of the stage', the cave temples of Ellora, 'more amazing than anything in a land where much amazes', Simla with its view of the Himalayas (if it hadn't been cloudy), Gwalior, the fortress city on a rock, traditionally reached by elephant, the spectacular Jain temples at Mount Abu.[29]

But he had a key advantage over Adela Quested, his naive character from *A Passage to India* who arrives wanting to see and experience 'the real India'. He had Masood, and other Indian friends he made in London through him.

His first stop was Aligarh, where Masood was staying. It was a journey of 900 miles from Bombay, and thanks to a missed connection at Agra it took two days. Collected by Masood from the railway station, Forster collapsed into bed only to be roused moments later as a crowd of friends arrived at the house to drink tea and chew betel. This continued all week, with friends arriving day and night. Forster loved it, and felt plunged into Indian life.

He soon realised that he had unwittingly arrived at a centre of political activity and energy. Previously, Forster later wrote, Aligarh College 'could be described as pro-British … Then a change took place, and under the influence of college graduates Mohammed and Shaukat Ali' Aligarh rejected the stance of Masood's grandfather and 'took to Nationalism and Pan-Islamism (two diverse yet not incompatible aims)'. There were student strikes and anti-British secret societies. Japan was much admired among Masood's circle, as a power that had stood up to the Europeans, but more important in Muslim India was the Ottoman Empire, the only surviving Islamic power, the seat of its 'universal' caliphate, and the guardian of the Islamic holy places of Mecca,

Medina and Jerusalem. But the empire had been crumbling for a long time, was hopelessly indebted to European capitalists, had recently been defeated by Italy in North Africa and was now under attack from the Balkan League. If it were to disappear, Indian Muslims, some feared, 'would become like unto Jews – a mere religious sect whose kingdom was gone'. A Muslim might believe the Crusades were still in progress, Forster later wrote. 'He can observe what he has lost in North Africa and Central Asia during the last twenty years.' Now there was a growing belief that Britain was no longer a safe custodian of Islamic interests, bringing support for Turkey and opposition to Britain into step.[30]

At the forefront of this movement in India were the Ali brothers, Mohammed and Shaukat. Both were Aligarh graduates; Shaukat, a cricket obsessive, had captained the college team. Mohammed had moved on to read modern history at Lincoln College, Oxford. Their mother, Abadi Begun, had been the driving force behind their education and brought them up to resent British rule. The brothers had recently established a magazine, *The Comrade*, which promoted Indian Muslim kinship with Turkey based on their shared Islamic faith and the greatness of their common Islamic culture in the past. On one occasion, Forster came across Mohammed Ali in the *Comrade* offices on the verge of tears. 'I am absolutely miserable,' he cried. 'The Bulgarian army is within twenty-five miles of Constantinople!' Masood, though not religious, was of the same mind, at one point declaring that all the money raised for the college – he was now a trustee – should at once be sent to Turkey to support their war efforts.[31]

After Aligarh, Forster and Masood travelled to Delhi to stay with Dr Mukhtar Ahmad Ansari, who was also prominent in Muslim politics. (Intelligence reports suggested he had been meeting with 'suspicious Turks'.) Ansari had studied medicine in Britain – Nehru had met him in London in 1905 and described him as 'a smart and clever young man with a record of brilliant academic achievement' – and was now almost the only Muslim practising Western medicine in India. A few weeks after Forster's visit, Ansari would depart for Turkey, leading a

Red Crescent medical team, funded through *The Comrade*, to help
with the wounded and refugees from the latest Balkan war.[32]

Ansari's house in Delhi was tiny and once more full of visitors who
would even crowd into the bedroom shared by Forster and Masood,
sitting on the beds, the floor, each other's laps. Poor relations crouched
in the background ready to run errands or collect food, tea or betel.
Ansari's wife, who kept purdah, would send gifts of cigarettes or scent.
Forster wrote to a friend on 2 November: 'I am in the middle of a very
queer life, whether typically Oriental I have no way of knowing, but it
isn't English.'[33]

Most important for the future was Forster's meeting with a very different sort of Indian, the Hindu Maharaja of Dewas, who as a young
man had been tutored by Malcolm Darling (who described him as 'the
oddest mixture of prince and imp'). Forster's stay in Dewas, 500 miles
south-west of Delhi, included a lavish wedding, for which he had to
wear Indian dress, and a banquet with dishes that 'tasted of nothing till
they were well in your mouth, when your whole tongue suddenly burst
into flame'. He and the Maharaja became close friends.[34]

Later in the trip he rejoined Masood in Bankipore, where he had his
legal practice. Forster didn't like the city, but again there was always a
host of Masood's friends around. At a dinner on one occasion he found
himself in the unusual position, for him, of talking politics, explaining
that the British Empire's foreign policy was 'based not on hatred of
Islam but a fear of Germany'. The Indians present were impressed, one
of them declaring that the British Empire might last for ever so long as
it produced gentlemen like him.[35]

The time spent with British people was less happy. After Delhi,
Forster travelled to stay with Malcolm Darling at Lahore, where he
was now a magistrate. He was delighted to meet so many Indians at
their dining table, and Darling's wife Josie 'could display the unstinted
warmth that India appreciates', but it soon became clear that in the
Anglo-Indian centre of Lahore they were very much the exception.[36]

His friend Rupert Smith had invited him to Allahabad to see the
annual bathing in the sacred spot where the Ganges and the Jumna

(Yamuna) meet and, according to tradition, a third stream springs up from underground, a story Forster loved and saw as 'an allegory of human relationships'. In the care of a friend of Masood's and his two nephews, Forster visited on the way the Buddhist sites of Buddh Gaya and the caves of the Barabar Hills, later to become the Marabar Caves in *A Passage to India*. Part of the journey to the caves was on elephant, then they climbed on foot 'in much heat and emptiness'. 'The caves are cut out of the solid granite [with] a small square doorway,' Forster reported in a letter to his mother. Inside were 'oval halls' where candle-light showed 'the grain of the granite and its reds and greys. The nephews tried to wake the echoes, but whatever was said and in whatever voice the cave only returned a dignified roar.'[37]

In Allahabad, Rupert Smith himself was off-putting. When an Indian friend of Forster's came to lunch, Smith refused to speak to him. After four years in India Smith had come to 'dislike every class of Indian except the peasant'. In Benares, Forster had an introduction to an English schoolmaster who told him all his plans were 'simply not done', and that much of what he said was 'seditious'. Like Smith, he kept telling Forster that the 'toiling *ryot* [peasant] is the real India'.[38]

The Anglo-Indians Forster met on this pre-war trip would form the basis of their hugely unflattering portrayal in *A Passage to India*. He had found the attitude he had encountered on the boat out to be widely prevalent. 'Mixed up with the pleasure and fun', he wrote soon afterwards, 'was much pain. The sense of racial tension, of incompatibility.' From his close friendship with Masood, he perhaps understood more than many Englishmen the intense affront that British racial attitudes caused Indians, and he came away from India with a realisation that here friendship between an Indian and an Englishman was eccentric, to say the least. This, of course, would be a central concern of *A Passage to India*, through the relationship of Aziz and Fielding.[39]

Forster, writing soon after his return to England in 1913, put this down to several factors. One was the preponderance among the Anglo-Indians of 'public-school men' with 'undeveloped hearts', 'who go forth into a world of whose richness and subtlety they have no conception'. Another was the 'new type of official' in India, who was 'worked harder, was less independent, and less in touch with the Indian socially. He could get back more easily to England for his leave, owing to improved steamer service.[40]

One Anglo-Indian Forster visited was less conventional. May Wylde, who had been a childhood friend of Forster's, had, against much opposition, established a girls' school in Hyderabad. She was very unlike the usual memsahibs. She would drive everywhere at a furious pace, and sit down to haggle in shops. Wylde was rather dismissive of Forster's pride in having sampled the 'real India' and she thought him 'prejudiced against the British official: too inclined to blame him for the lack of close intercourse between British and Indians, when the fault lay with the *purdah*-system'. Later, she told Forster's biographer Philip Furbank: 'Morgan had got a few introductions to Indian homes in north India. Later on I heard one or two comments on his visits. They had wondered what the English visitor wanted to know. They did not find him as easy to talk to as the Englishmen who live in India.'[41]

Forster, of course, imposes much of his world-view on his experiences of India. In Jodhpur, he wrote, he had found a unique situation of Anglo-Indian harmony. Here, the English community 'had none of the indifference to their surroundings that is considered good form elsewhere' and men and women shared the same club as the Indians, 'and under its gracious roof the "racial question" had been solved'. He put this down to the sheer beauty of the city and its surroundings, and because 'each race had made concessions. Ours seemed more sensitive than usual, the Indian more solid. A common ground for friendship had been contrived.' It is the oppositional landscape of *Howards End*, with the Indians as emotion and poetry, and the British as reason and prose. Perhaps Forster's view was coloured by the effusiveness and heightened emotions of the Indian he knew best – Masood – and his own repressed nature.[42]

In fact, Forster was honest about his lack of understanding of India after this first visit. 'India is full of wonders,' he wrote to a friend, 'but she can't give them to me.' He would call his collection of essays about this trip 'Adrift in India'. 'Plunging into this unknown world' had given him 'pleasure', but also 'bewilderment'. Time and again the landscape and the people had refused to fit into familiar categories, to make sense. At one point, Forster was alone with a cart driver searching for some famous ruins. To make conversation, he asked the driver 'what kind of trees those were, and he answered "Trees"; what was the name of that bird, and he said "Bird"'. It was very hot and they could not find the ruins. 'The track we were following wavered and blurred, and offered alternatives; it had no earnestness of purpose like the tracks of England. And the crops were hap-hazard too – lunging this way and that on the enormous earth, with patches of brown between them. There was no place for anything, and nothing was in its place. There was no time either. All the small change of the north rang false, and nothing remained certain but the dome of the sky and the disk of the sun.'[43]

This was, of course, written for an English reader; and India is defined little more than as not-Britain. However, for all these caveats, it was with some justification that Forster would claim that he 'had seen so much of the side of life that is hidden from most English people'. His letters following the trip are full of his love of India and his urgent desire to return. And he had started writing *A Passage to India*.[44]

14

'Loyal India'

At the beginning of the First World War, when Viceroy Hardinge announced, without consulting a single Indian, that India was also at war with the Central Powers, the response was an effusion of expressions of loyalty to the empire. 'On the question of loyalty to the British Government all people are united,' declared the *Tribune* newspaper on 26 August 1914. In London, *The Times* ran articles headlined 'Loyal India'.[1]

Jawaharlal Nehru remembered it slightly differently. 'There was little sympathy with the British in spite of loud professions of loyalty,' he wrote. 'Moderate and Extremist alike learnt with satisfaction of German victories. There was no love for Germany, of course, only the desire to see our own rulers humbled. It was the weak and helpless man's idea of vicarious revenge.'[2]

There was similar schadenfreude from elsewhere. Days before the outbreak of hostilities, the Lahore-based *Zamindar* newspaper predicted 'a universal war in which all the great Empires of Europe will be involved'. Having 'portioned' Asia and Africa, now, 'with no hunting grounds left', they were turning on each other. 'The result of it all will be that the giant which has so far been ruining Asia will now be engaged in ruining himself.'[3]

The entry of Turkey into the war in late October, followed by the declaration of Jihad by the Sultan the following month, saw the shutting down of the Ali brothers' newspaper *The Comrade*, and their internment as 'Pro-Turkish agitators' soon afterwards. It remained a 'sore point', as the president of the Muslim League declared the following year, 'that the Government of our Khalif should be at war with the government of our King-Emperor'. In fact, after the war, the fate of Turkey, far from being a mere 'sore point', would be a key political issue.[4]

Nehru reported 'from the second year onwards news of conspiracies and shootings'. A German attempt to ship arms from the United States came to nothing, and in February 1915 a planned rebellion in the Punjab, having been thoroughly infiltrated by agents working for the British, was swiftly closed down, with fourteen conspirators arrested and a handful of weapons and home-made bombs recovered. It was all rather anti-climactic but the immediate response was a wave of further arrests and the introduction of the Defence of India Act, based on Britain's draconian and unpopular Defence of the Realm Act. This gave the authorities added powers for censorship and detention without trial. Nearly 1,000 print titles were banned in India. Alongside this measure ran a programme of propaganda that saw the distribution of 4 million leaflets and 331,000 posters, what Nehru called 'ceaseless and unabashed propaganda on behalf of the Allies ... we tried to discount it greatly'.[5]

In his letters from Cambridge there had been frequent references to his marriage. He insisted that he did not have to marry a Kashmiri, and that he did not want to marry 'a total stranger'. However, by 1912, a suitable girl, Kamala Kaul, had been found from a reasonably wealthy Kashmiri family living in Delhi. Kamala was moved to Allahabad to live with relatives, and was entrusted to the Nehru family's English governess to learn a bit about their Westernised ways, and to get to know her future groom. When she was seventeen, in 1916, they married, and moved into a separate apartment in the family home.

In the same year, Jawaharlal Nehru joined both the new Home Rule Leagues. Tilak, released from prison in 1914, had established one

in the west of India, and Mrs Annie Besant, the Theosophist leader
and advocate of 'Indian freedom', the other. The Home Rule Leagues
called for self-government within the empire and broke new ground
in promoting themselves, using newspapers, pamphlets, posters and
illustrated postcards, as well as substantial speaking tours. According
to Nehru they did attract newcomers from the middle classes, 'but
they did not touch the masses'. Nehru himself was 'terrified of public
speaking', partly because he doubted his capacity to speak at any length
in Hindustani. Around this time he did, though, make his first public
speech in English. He also organised a meeting in Allahabad calling for
the release of the Ali brothers.[6]

Compared to later movements the Home Rule Leagues were moderate and poorly supported. Nonetheless, they rattled the British
authorities enough for them to ban their leaders from several provinces
and issue a prohibition on students attending their meetings. And in
early 1917 Mrs Besant was interned under the Defence of India Act.
This, wrote Nehru, 'stirred even the older generation, including many
of the Moderate leaders'. His father now joined the league, though
another leading moderate and then an Indian member of the Imperial
Legislative Council, V. S. Srinivasa Sastri, Nehru wrote, 'failed us
completely' by declining to protest against the internment. Unlike the
other key moderate, Sir Tej Bahadur Sapru, Sastri refused to sanction
boycotts or passive resistance as he believed it would compromise his
strictly constitutional approach and, particularly during wartime,
would alienate friends of India in Britain, 'whose sympathy is our chief
hope in the present political situation'.[7]

Meanwhile, the former 'extremist' Tilak had rejoined the Congress
along with his supporters who had quit at the split in Surat in 1907,
making it more united and energetic than it had been for many years,
although this did alienate some moderates.

Even more importantly, the end of 1916 saw Congress forge the
'Lucknow Pact' with the Muslim League, which included agreement on
separate electorates and a joint demand for the status of India to be that
of 'an equal partner in the Empire with the self-governing Dominions'.[8]

For the British authorities, whose oft-stated purpose for their rule in India was to prevent age-old Muslim–Hindu tensions from breaking out into open bloodshed, this was a dangerous and undermining move. Now, the new shout was '*Hindu–Musulman ki jai*' ('Hail Hindu–Muslim unity'). For Nehru, it was an exciting development. 'The atmosphere became electric,' he wrote, 'and most of us young men felt exhilarated and expected big things in the near future.'[9]

It was at the Lucknow Congress meeting that Nehru first met Mohandas Gandhi. Having studied law in London, Gandhi had moved to South Africa in 1893 and had led Indian struggles against white settler racial policies. By developing a new tactic – *satyagraha* – of direct but non-violent confrontation with the authorities, as opposed to the conventional constitutional political methods of petitions, meetings and press campaigns, he had secured from the then South African Minister of Native Affairs Jan Smuts pretty much all he had demanded. When Gandhi sailed from Durban in July 1914, Smuts remarked, 'The Saint has left our shores; I sincerely hope for ever.'[10]

Gandhi had yet to make his mark in India. Nehru, then twenty-seven, twenty years younger than Gandhi, was less than impressed. 'All of us admired him for his heroic fight in South Africa,' he wrote, 'but he seemed very distant and different and unpolitical to many of us young men.' Much of what Gandhi said seemed to Nehru to be medieval and 'revivalist'.[11]

Gandhi was a vocal supporter of the war effort, and in 1918, although a pacifist, would even work tirelessly as a recruiting agent for the army. 'We are, above all, British citizens of the Great British Empire,' he declared. 'I have faith in the virtues of the English nation ... I know the English have done great harm to India, but I believe it to be beneficial to live with that nation. Comparing vices and virtues, I find that the virtues are great.'[12]

Like others in India, and across the Dominions, he viewed the war as an opportunity to have the mother country in India's debt. *Zamindar* declared that as 'compensation for the services of Indians during the war', 'we are convinced that self-government will be granted to this country'. Nehru reported this as well: 'there was everywhere', he wrote, 'an expectation of great constitutional changes'.[13]

In the same *Zamindar* article there was hope that the experience of fighting in Europe would teach Indian sepoys that 'there is no difference – except in colour – between Indians and Europeans'. For all the Indian supporters of the war effort, it was seen as an opportunity for national honour and for recovering racial pride, so injured by discrimination at home and across the empire. Gandhi's vision of British and Indians treating each other as equals required, in his opinion, an uplift of Indians' views of themselves as well as a change in the British attitude of superiority. Volunteering, he declared in a recruitment speech in June 1918, 'will give us honour and manhood ... the courage and strength which they will acquire will transform all the villages'.[14]

In addition, Gandhi saw military training as fostering the qualities he considered essential for nation-building, and for *satyagraha* – discipline, bravery, resilience, fellowship. He also noted in a recruitment leaflet of July 1918, 'we shall learn the use of weapons ... we will be unfit for Swaraj [self-rule] ... if we do not regain the power of self-defence'. Also, from his experience in the South African War, where he'd worked in an ambulance unit supporting British combat troops fighting the Boers and been decorated for his efforts, Gandhi had acquired a view of the battlefield as a space of brotherhood free of racial discrimination, recalling how the 'lovable' Tommy had shared his rations and water with his Indian stretcher-bearers. Shared experience of combat offered the possibility of a future 'free of racial distinctions'.[15]

As well as creating the impression of a debt owed by Britain to India, the war in other important ways created the conditions and accelerated changes on which later momentous developments depended. While most Indians suffered from sharp rises in taxation and food prices, 'Industrialisation had spread and the capitalist class had grown in wealth and power,' Jawaharlal Nehru wrote. Manufacture expanded in cotton, sugar, engineering and chemicals. Cloth mills in Bombay and Ahmedabad, mainly Indian-owned, thrived, in some cases trebling their profits thanks to the disappearance of foreign competition. The jute mills were kept busy supplying material for sacks and sandbags (previously most raw jute had been shipped to Dundee for manufacturing). The recently established Tata Steel Company, wholly Indian owned and financed, increased its output from 31,000 tons in 1912–13 to 181,000 in 1918–19, and was going through a process of massive expansion.[16]

The war also saw the promotion of Indians to positions of collectors, magistrates and police inspectors to fill the gaps left by Englishmen who had returned to fight. In 1915, the Congress president declared that 'the idea of re-adjustment is in the air'. In the Imperial Legislative Council, Madan Mohan Malaviya stated in early 1917, 'I venture to say that the war has put the clock ... fifty years forward, and I hope ... that India will achieve in the next few years what she might not have done in fifty years.'[17]

With provincial Governors warning that wartime hardship risked provoking rebellion at a time when India was severely denuded of British troops, there was a call from Delhi at the end of 1916 for urgent political concessions. The then Secretary of State cautioned against radical change during wartime, but his replacement from July 1917, the 'radical Liberal' Edwin Montagu, grasped the nettle. On 20 August 1917 he announced in the House of Commons that government policy was now for 'increasing association of Indians in every branch of the administration and the gradual development of self-governing institutions with a view to the progressive realization of responsible government in India as an integral part of the British Empire'.

This was no manifesto for self-government, and it was clear that the pace of the change would be firmly in British control, but nonetheless it was an important shift in policy. Nothing even vaguely in the direction of self-government had ever before been envisaged for a non-white colony.

Montagu later claimed that by his announcement he had 'kept India quiet for six months at a critical period of the war'. The new Viceroy Lord Chelmsford described it to the pugnacious Governor of Punjab Sir Michael O'Dwyer as 'a political truce ... for the purpose of allaying the political situation existing in the country'.[18]

In September, Montagu ordered the release of Mrs Besant, and in November began a five-month tour of the sub-continent, meeting among others Gandhi, Mrs Besant and Muslim leader Muhammad Ali Jinnah and receiving advice and requests from a huge variety of interest groups. All the Indians demanded control over everything except naval and military matters, including 'the power of the purse, so that it is practically responsible government at one fell swoop'. He also noted that 'revolutionary or not', none of the Indians he spoke to showed any sign of wanting to be removed from 'connection with the British throne'. He was concerned, however, that 'owing to the thinness with which we have spread education', the people he met had 'run generations away from the rest of India'. To empower them, then, would be just to create 'another and indigenous autocracy'. The vast majority of political activists were high-caste Hindus. What might happen to the religious minorities and the masses?[19]

The end of the war saw no improvement in the economic situation and harvests remained disastrously poor, with the failure of the monsoon in 1918. Famine, malaria and influenza killed millions in the three years from 1918. There were something like 11 to 13 million excess deaths during this period. Prices stayed high and trade was disrupted. The Punjab was hit hard, and ill feeling remained from what Nehru called 'press gang methods' of army recruitment. Villages and districts had been given quotas, with water for irrigation being cut off if targets were not met. Over half of all recruits had come from the Punjab (home to the so-called 'martial races') and men were now returning, as nationalists had hoped, newly politicised. Nehru described them as 'no longer the subservient robots they used to be. They had grown mentally and there was much discontent among them.' There was also a new pride among the men. 'Who calls me now a coward base, / And brands my race a coward race?' goes a limerick popular among the returned soldiers. 'I'll brook no more such scoffing word: / My King himself has washed the shame / That fouled so long my stainless name.'[20]

Meanwhile, the Montagu Declaration had been given a guarded welcome. While committees in London worked out the details of a new constitution, among the Indian middle classes, Nehru reported, people talked with assurance of self-determination and self-government. There was great hope that India's epic wartime contribution to the empire would be rewarded as promised.[21]

But then came Rowlatt and Amritsar.

In late 1917, a commission under the Scottish judge S. A. T. Rowlatt had been set up to look into the wartime conspiracies and recommend measures to deal with the problem in the post-war period. Although only a tiny minority of political activists had been involved, the British remained haunted by the threat of revolutionary violence. Furthermore, with the Defence of India Act due to expire six months after the end of the war, all those held under its provisions would have to be released. There was also a concern that returning soldiers would be easy targets for agitators and that forthcoming constitutional changes might make the passing of 'coercive' legislation difficult. The committee report, delivered in August 1918, recommended that in cases of emergency, detention without trial and trials without jury should continue to be allowed.

For Nehru, these were 'drastic provisions for arrest and trial without any of the checks and formalities which the law is supposed to provide. A wave of anger greeted them all over India, and even the Moderates joined in this.' Indeed, in early February 1919, arch-moderate Srinivasa Sastri made a powerful speech in the Legislative Council, denouncing the proposed 'Rowlatt' Bills as entirely contradictory to the liberal spirit of the Montagu Declaration. 'Very slight incidents', he argued, had put the government in a panic, 'to which all alien Governments are unfortunately far too liable'. In fact, anyone undertaking any political activity, such as addressing a meeting, even a moderate such as himself, would become suspect. The result would be 'such a lowering of the political tone in this country, that all your talk of responsible govern-ment will be mere mockery'. In summary, he deemed the proposed new legislation a 'callous disregard of liberty'.[22]

Gandhi weighed in against the proposed Rowlatt Bills, calling them 'so restrictive of human liberty, that no self-respecting person or no self-respecting nation could allow such legislation to appear on its regular statute book'. On 2 March, the *Bombay Chronicle* published his manifesto for action, which included the wording of a vow for those undertaking the *satyagraha* to pronounce: 'in the event of the Bills – subversive of the principles of liberty and justice – becoming law we shall refuse civilly to obey these laws and such other laws ... and we further affirm that in this struggle we will faithfully follow truth and refrain from violence to life, person or property'. *Satyagraha* is 'essentially a religious movement', Gandhi explained. 'It is a process of purification and penance. It seeks to secure reform or redress of grievances by self-suffering.' This included embracing arrest and imprisonment.[23]

Gandhi then began a speaking tour, taking in Madras and the United Provinces. In Amritsar and Lahore also, huge crowds turned out to hear speakers denouncing the proposed 'repressive' legislation now being drawn up based on the Rowlatt Committee's report.

Montagu himself privately wrote to Viceroy Chelmsford that he 'loathed' what was essentially the retention of the Defence of India Act in peacetime, but reluctantly sanctioned the legislation under pressure from the Viceroy and his officials, in particular hardliners like Michael O'Dwyer in the Punjab who had been less than welcoming to the Montagu Declaration.[24]

So, on 18 March 1919, the 'Rowlatt' Act, more properly the Anarchical and Revolutionary Crimes Act, was forced through the Imperial Legislative Council by 35 votes to 20. All Indian members present (some had absented themselves) voted against and a number resigned from the Council in protest. Although the Indian members had succeeded in watering down some of the measures, the impotence of constitutional politics was there for all to see. Mass mobilisation was now the only alternative.

The Act's supporters had made a serious mistake. The legislation, which was repealed three years later, was never even used (in part because the government already had widespread powers of arrest and censorship), and it united Indians of all religions and regions against what was now called 'the Black Act'. In a report on the years of unrest after the war, Deputy Director of the Government Intelligence Bureau P. C. Bamford concluded that 'it is to be regretted' that the government took so long to explain the details of the Act to the people at large, because in the meantime 'rumour distorted its provisions'. It came to be believed, he explained, that the police now had the power to invade the sanctity of the home, that weddings and funerals would be taxed and that four men sitting together could be arrested. Newspapers, Bamford complained, did little to quell the rumours, and the result was that people who usually took no interest in political questions were persuaded 'that a dangerous weapon was being prepared against their liberty and peace of mind'. In fact, opposition to the Act did gather together a wide range of grievances and anxieties: high prices and rents, drought, epidemics, the issue of the Khilafat and Turkey, the widespread dislike of the police.[25]

On 24 March, Gandhi called for a national 'hartal' to take place on the second Sunday after vice-regal assent to the Bill, 6 April. This was to be 'a day of humiliation and prayer' and a twenty-four-hour fast, which also included the closure of all shops, businesses and markets – essentially a general strike.

Nehru read Gandhi's proposals and felt 'tremendous relief. Here at last was a way out of the tangle, a method of action which was straight and open and possibly effective. I was afire with enthusiasm, wanted to join the Satyagraha Sabha immediately.' His father, though, was 'dead against this new idea'. According to Nehru's sister, their father tried to stop Jawaharlal 'rushing headlong into the political arena'. He was horrified by the idea of his son going to prison and even spent a night himself sleeping on the floor to see how it felt. For now, the father and son were in conflict.[26]

In several places, the hartal went ahead a week early on 30 March. In Amritsar, a crowd of 40,000 heard speakers denouncing the Act. While everything went off peacefully there, in Delhi the arrest of two *satyagraha* volunteers who were trying to persuade sweetmeat sellers to close their stalls led to violent confrontations between protesters, police and British soldiers that ended with the troops opening fire and killing at least eight people.

In a letter of 3 April to the *Bombay Chronicle* about what he called the 'Delhi tragedy', Gandhi explained that protesting arrest missed the point: 'the essence of the [*satyagraha*] pledge is to invite imprisonment'. He went on to express the hope that all speeches on the coming Sunday 'will be free from passion, anger or resentment'. The movement, he stressed, depended on 'self-restraint'.[27]

But to Gandhi's dismay there was violence in the Punjab and Gujarat. Confessing to a 'Himalayan miscalculation' in suggesting civil disobedience to a people not yet ready for it, he called off the campaign. And it wasn't just his abhorrence of violence. He knew it played into the government's hands. After all, what better justification for the continuation of British rule, and indeed 'emergency' legislation, than 'mob violence'?[28]

15

Amritsar

In Amritsar, the hartal of 6 April passed off peacefully, but British officials were rattled by its reach, its efficient organisation and its demonstrations of unity between Muslims, Hindus and Sikhs. The city's Deputy Commissioner Miles Irving sent a report to Punjab Governor O'Dwyer asking for reinforcements. O'Dwyer decided that the two *satyagraha* leaders Drs Kitchlew and Satyapal should be removed from the scene. On the morning of 10 April they were both summoned to Irving's house in the European quarter outside the old walled city, arrested and secretly deported. When the remaining *satyagraha* leaders heard the news they organised a crowd to go to Irving's house to deliver a petition calling for the two men to be released.

The European quarter, or 'civil lines', were separated from the city by the railway, across which stretched a couple of narrow bridges. On the orders of Irving, the bridges were blocked by a small number of British and Indian soldiers on horseback. But they were driven back by the weight of the crowd, and one British trooper, struggling with his panicking horse, fired his rifle into the advancing people. As the soldiers retreated, the crowd came across a pile of bricks which they started throwing. Soon afterwards, reinforcements arrived, more shots were fired and ten people were killed, with more wounded. Two British men, one a railway guard, the other an electrician, found themselves isolated on the wrong side of the railway and, despite begging for their lives, were beaten to death with clubs and stones.

The crowd now fell back to the city, where visible symbols of colonial authority – the post office, telephone exchange, churches, the town hall – were attacked, looted and burned. At the National Bank, doors and gates were hurriedly barred, but the crowd broke in and the two Europeans there were stabbed and bludgeoned to death. Another bank was attacked and its sole European employee killed, thrown from the balcony into the bazaar below then set on fire. Men in the crowd shouted that those killed on the bridge had been avenged. A missionary, Miss Frances Sherwood, was rushing round the city trying to shut down the missionary schools she ran when she was set upon by a crowd, beaten and – mistakenly – left for dead. Another woman had a narrow escape.

That evening, as Europeans sheltered in the fort outside the city in a state of panic and confusion, reinforcements, including aircraft, quickly appeared. The following day saw the arrival of General Reginald Dyer. Irving told him that they were facing 'the greatest calamity since the Mutiny'. In the city, reported an Indian factory manager, it was now 'quiet, but every person looked depressed and terrified'.[1]

Although martial law had not yet been proclaimed, Dyer took charge. Water and electricity supplies to the city were cut off, aircraft flew low over the rooftops, and there were house-to-house searches looking for ringleaders of what was seen by the British as an organised and determined movement to kill all Europeans in and around the city and carry the rebellion throughout the Punjab.

On the morning of the 13th, Dyer led a force of 400 troops, supported by two armoured cars, through the city, broadcasting a proclamation in Urdu and Punjabi that there would be an eight o'clock curfew and that all meetings and gatherings were prohibited. But later that day, Dyer received information that a gathering – estimated at 1,000 – was taking place nonetheless at Jallianwala Bagh, an expanse of public land of about 6.5 acres.

Dyer saw this as a direct challenge to his authority and assembled a force to respond. Troops were stationed at all the city gates, then Dyer led ninety men, supported by two armoured cars, towards the Jallianwala Bagh. Apart from Dyer, his two bodyguards and two other officers, none were British. There were twenty-five Gurkhas and twenty-five Baluchi sepoys as well as a further forty Gurkhas armed only with kukris.

By now, there was a large crowd in the Jallianwala Bagh. In one corner, speeches were being delivered from a raised platform. Few could hear what was being said, and most were not there for the speeches anyway. A cattle and horse fair and the Sikh Vaisakhi festival had brought a lot of people into the city from rural areas. The Bagh was a place to relax, chat to friends and for their children to play. Dyer's earlier march through the city had left out large central and eastern areas: many had not heard the proclamation making such a gathering illegal; others believed it had been sanctioned.

So when Dyer marched his men into the Bagh (the entrance was too narrow for the armoured cars), he was confronted with a much larger crowd than he had expected. The immediate estimate was 5,000, in fact it was more like 15,000. Within thirty seconds he had formed up his troops and ordered them to open fire. No warning was given.

Dyer's bodyguard, Sergeant W. J. Anderson, later described how 'when fire was first opened the whole crowd seemed to sink to the ground, a whole flutter of white garments'.[2]

For ten minutes they continued shooting, expending 1,650 rounds from their Lee-Enfield rifles. 'The fire control and discipline of the native troops was first class,' Anderson reported. The crowd immediately fled, but the Bagh was surrounded by walls and the backs of houses, and there were only two narrow exits, which quickly became choked with dead and dying bodies. Some tried climbing the walls, but many were shot down. When eventually the firing stopped, a 'low moaning' could be heard from the wounded and dying. In all, some 500 to 600 were killed and 1,500 to 1,800 wounded. Among the dead were two women and fifteen boys under the age of fifteen. His work completed, Dyer marched his troops out of the Bagh; no provision was made for the wounded.

The reasons for this infamous massacre, which more than anything shaped the state of India at the end of 1923, would be much debated over the following years and, indeed, ever since. The government-led inquiry would place the blame on General Dyer alone. He had made 'an error of judgement'. Churchill would famously describe it as 'without precedent or parallel in the modern history of the British Empire ... an event that stands in singular and sinister isolation'. Others disagreed. Gandhi refused to blame Dyer on his own; instead, he blamed the 'system that produces General Dyers'. Indeed, the sometimes over-lapping and even contradictory reasons why the General ordered the shooting shine a light on the edifices of British rule in India.[3]

The first factor was a failure to understand. Dyer did not react to the crowd in front of him – peaceful, unarmed, mostly apolitical and there by accident. Instead he saw a murderous mob, carefully and deliber-ately organised to attack Europeans, particularly women, and to set in motion a new general rebellion against British rule, a new Mutiny, the spectre that haunted the Anglo-Indian community.

His action, for all its extreme effect in terms of the number killed, was firmly in the tradition of exemplary violence established in India after the 1857 rebellion, when hundreds were publicly and gruesomely executed as an example to potential new rebels. This policy contin-ued through the rest of the nineteenth century, most notably in 1872 after the 'Kuka rebellion'. In the classic manual for colonial military officers published in 1896, *Small Wars: Their Principles and Practice*, author C. E. Callwell argues that 'The lower races are impressionable. They are greatly influenced by a resolute bearing and by a determined course of action.' Dyer himself had been involved in the protracted and bloody fighting after the conquest of Burma in 1885, and agreed with Callwell's thesis that a short, sharp blow, 'which may shock the humanitarian', was in the long term more effective than cautious meas-ures. Later defending himself, Dyer explained that he 'meant to strike hard as a lesson' to deliver 'a sufficient moral effect' on the whole of the Punjab.[4]

Indeed, Dyer's defenders would later point to the 'Moplah' or 'Malabar' rebellion in southern India in 1921 as a proof of the effectiveness of his approach. In August 1921, in an area of largely Hindu landowners, backed by the British, and Muslim peasants, a small-scale protest about evictions and a confrontation with armed police was treated by the authorities with hesitancy and caution, determined as they were to keep the army under control and avoid another Amritsar. The result, pointed out hardliners like Michael O'Dwyer, was that while the rebellion in the Punjab had been crushed in a few weeks, leniency in Malabar allowed the insurrection to spread and continue for months with far greater loss of life than had occurred at Dyer's hands. In the end, 2,339 rebels were killed, along with some forty Indian Army troops. Communal violence saw some 10,000 Hindus murdered, with forcible conversions, women raped and temples desecrated.[5]

The overwhelming motivation for Dyer, however, was fear. Ever since the Mutiny, European communities in India were acutely aware of their vulnerability. In their view only 'prestige' protected them from the Indian masses. (Dyer later said that he could have dispersed the crowd without firing, but they would have laughed at him and he would have lost 'face'.) In Amritsar after the events of 10 April, the British were terrified, and quickly evacuated their women and children to safer hill stations. It was the attack on Miss Sherwood, with its possibility of sexual violence, that had rattled them the most. And Dyer too, suddenly finding himself confronting a vast crowd with only fifty armed men, panicked. 'The crowd was so dense that if a determined rush had been made at any time, arms or no arms, my small force must instantly have been overpowered,' he told the later inquiry. When a group of Indians tried to make for the exit behind his troops, it was interpreted as an attack and they were gunned down. 'I was very careful of not giving the mob a chance of organizing,' Dyer said later. 'I sometimes ceased fire and redirected my fire where the crowd was collecting more thickly.'[6]

Forster's friend Malcolm Darling had been near Amritsar at the time. Shortly afterwards he wrote Forster a long letter. 'We're in a bit of a mess out here,' he reported. 'Racial hatred in towns leaping in a twink to pillage and murder, murder too of the most horrible kind.' Two of the British bank workers killed he had known slightly. 'You can guess the effect of the Amritsar murders. They were awful, Morgan,' he wrote. 'But it was the way they tried to batter the women to death. One, a friend of Josie's, who had ridden into the City to save *Indian* girls (Christian) was set upon and knocked down ½ dozen times before she was left for dead.' 'Heaven knows what produced so sudden a flare,' he went on. 'Some say it's Bolshevist gold, others that it was all spontaneous. One thing is clear – the big towns hate us.'[7]

Darling described the British response on the 13th as 'panic and cruelty – the two go together ... they shot down hundreds, mostly zemindars [villagers], there by religious hazard (Bhaisakh Day). I have seen the place – a death trap. 5 or 6,000 there, the kernel of them thoroughly seditious, but the majority lookers on, mooching about as zemindars do. Enter infuriated general ... and then – 1500 rounds. God it makes me sick to think of it. Yet I was told by my chief 10 days later "people at the Club (Lahore) say you ought to be court martialled for criticising".' The British closing ranks, he concluded, 'had got the wind up'. Forster himself, writing later in the year, described the massacre as an 'example of public infamy'.[8]

Two days later the secretary of the YMCA, S. K. Datta, visited the scene with a friend. The bodies had now been taken away, but the 'testimony of blood remained', the friend wrote. 'Datta stood weeping and saying, "This ends the British connection with India."'[9]

For some, however, including Gandhi, what followed in the subsequent weeks was even worse than the shooting itself. Even though the system of civil administration and courts was still working, martial law was declared on 15 April. It would not be lifted until 9 June.

To the satisfaction and relief of those Europeans who had sheltered in the fort in fear for their lives after the riots and murders of 10 April, the people of the city were now subject to retributive terror and physical and psychological humiliation. Gandhi would call it 'slow torture, degradation and emasculation ... calculated, malicious and soul-killing'. Still reeling from the horrors of the massacre, the inhabitants of Amritsar now saw armed police on every corner and long lines of cavalry patrolling the streets. Indians were ordered to salaam any European they encountered. Those who failed to do so, or were too slow about it, were locked up or taken to the army camp outside the city and forced to practise salaaming for hours. The street where Miss Sherwood had been attacked was closed off by British soldiers, while its residents were brutally interrogated to find the identities of her assailants. Any Indians passing along the alleyway had to do so crawling on their bellies.[10]

Under the provisions of martial law, the authorities had sweeping powers of arrest, detention and summary, exemplary punishment. Over 500 were arrested without warrant and many were kept imprisoned without even being told the charge against them. The British were searching for their imagined grand conspiracy, and those in custody were subject to extortion, abuse and torture. At the end of the alleyway with the 'crawling order', a whipping post was set up. Here seven men, the youngest only thirteen, who were suspects for the attack on Miss Sherwood were tied up and viciously flayed, even though they had not been tried, let alone convicted.[11]

Martial law also allowed the authorities to put the province into 'lockdown'. There was strict censorship of the press, no one was allowed to leave, and Indian journalists and politicians wanting to investigate the rumours of the massacre were turned away at the border or quickly deported.

'The Punjab was isolated, cut off from the rest of India,' wrote Nehru. 'A thick veil seemed to cover it and hide it from outside eyes ... Odd individuals, who managed to escape from that inferno, were so terror struck that they could give no clear account.' But when what Nehru called 'the long horror and indignity of martial law' was lifted at last, Indian politicians and journalists could investigate for themselves, including Gandhi and Motilal and Jawaharlal Nehru.[12]

Jawaharlal spent a week in Amritsar at the beginning of September interviewing some 150 witnesses and visiting the key locations. He saw the bridge where the British had first opened fire on 10 April, the burned-out ruins of the National Bank, town hall and post office, the 'crawling lane' and, of course, the Jallianwala Bagh itself.[13]

In general, he found the people of the city reticent, at least at first, 'in a funk and afraid of publicity', 'in mortal terror of the police'. But a doctor told him of tending to a 'stout boy' of about eighteen who had been shot near the bridge, leaving 'his intestines and abdominal viscera turned out and lying in the dusty road'. The boy was given water which had revived him enough to blurt out: '"there is no hope for my survival, take care of the brother who is lying by my side". He stopped, then gasped brokenly: *"Hindu–Musulman ki jai"* and expired.'[14]

In the 'crawling lane' he was told that a 'respectable' woman had been raped in a neighbouring house, and much more about the 'General misbehaviours of tommies'. On being made to crawl on their bellies 'after the manner of snakes and worms', he noted: 'Assert as fact that people [were] forced by butt end of rifles.'

In the Jallianwala Bagh, where he made several visits, Nehru saw numerous bullet holes in the walls, including many as high as 30 feet off the ground. He heard about the 'remarkable case' of a small boy who had remained on an open roof thinking the shooting was fireworks, and escaped unhurt with the walls around him riddled with bullets. Nehru deplored the 'total lack of medical arrangements' for the wounded, and discovered that among the dead there were several young boys whose fathers had died fighting for the British in the war.[15]

Writing some years later, Nehru put the 'tragedy' of those lives lost down to misunderstanding and panic. 'A sudden fear overwhelmed the authorities and the English people generally.' This made them see danger everywhere and a 'second mutiny with all its frightful massacres'. It was a 'blind, instinctive attempt at self-preservation at any cost [which] led them to that frightfulness, of which Jallianwala and the Crawling Lane of Amritsar have become symbols and bywords'. In his autobiography, Nehru added a coda to his Amritsar story. Later in the year, on a sleeper train from Lahore to Delhi, he found himself in a compartment almost full except for a top berth into which he slid. He soon discovered that he was among braying Indian Army officers, including Dyer himself, who boasted to fellow passengers that he could have reduced the city 'to a heap of ashes, but he took pity on it and refrained'. 'I was greatly shocked', Nehru wrote, 'to hear his conversation and to observe his callous manner.'[16]

While the news of the massacre had spread quickly round Punjab, it took far longer to reach the rest of India, and even longer to have its impact in Britain. Originally, *The Times* had reported on 19 April '200 casualties' amid news of other unrest in the region. The Punjab government, led by Michael O'Dwyer, who had approved Dyer's action straight afterwards, were in no hurry to give out details, and even Secretary of State Edwin Montagu was given a partial account of what had happened. Nonetheless, in May he ordered an inquiry into what he called Dyer's 'savage and inappropriate folly'. This would eventually start in October, led by a Scottish judge, Lord William Hunter, with a committee of three Indian and three British lawyers and civil servants. This led some Indian nationalists, including Gandhi, to hope that justice would be done and restitution made.[17]

But together with the hated Rowlatt Act, the Amritsar events threatened to scupper the great 'liberal' moment designed to shore up British rule by consent – the introduction of the much-awaited Montagu-Chelmsford constitutional reforms.

16

'The Moment of Moments'

In his letter to E. M. Forster of 11 July 1919, the liberal and pro-Indian magistrate Malcolm Darling expressed deep concerns about the forthcoming constitutional change. 'What's going to happen?' he asked. 'Democracy? For India, with her 300 million illiterates – God's truth we must be possessed.' But with 'Home Rule so much in the air' he reckoned that nothing but democracy would satisfy, 'the only way out of the mess Montagu and his gang have got us into'.[1]

At this time, moderate politician V. S. Srinivasa Sastri was in the middle of a long visit to Britain, meeting politicians, newspaper editors and opinion formers. It was his first time in England and he was amazed how 'India and her troubles vexed only a few persons'. Most Englishmen admitted their complete ignorance of India 'with almost the pride with which he might confess an amiable weakness'. Sastri, while conceding progress should come in stages rather than in a single bound, pleaded for an element of responsibility in the central government of India and for fiscal autonomy for the country. India wanted to be an equal partner in the empire, he said, and not a dependency. Meanwhile, prominent Indian lawyer Satyendra Prasanna Sinha took up the position of Under-Secretary of State under Montagu and was raised to the peerage (the first ever Indian in both cases) to steer the reform legislation through the Lords.[2]

The Montagu Reforms, passed by the House of Commons in December 1919 as the Government of India Act, would, in fact, be a strange and uneasy mixture of democracy and continuing autocracy. The central and provincial legislatures were enlarged and freed of their official appointed majorities. These would be voted for by an expanded franchise of 5.5 million property holders, as well as all returned soldiers. (The enfranchisement of women was left to individual provinces to decide; apart from in Madras, the number of women allowed to vote was less than 1 per cent of the female population.) In Delhi, a bicameral legislature was established to debate the actions of the government who retained control of foreign affairs, the military, criminal law, currency and income tax. In the provinces, there was greater change. In a system known as dyarchy, a wide range of government areas were devolved and transferred to elected Indians – health, local government, education, public works, agriculture. The Act also committed the government to the gradual Indianisation of both the Indian Civil Service and the officer corps of the Indian Army.

For many Indian nationalists, this was a severe disappointment. The new central legislature had no powers to reject or pass legislation without the consent of the Viceroy, who also retained emergency powers to push through new bills. In the provinces, the local Governor and his bureaucrats kept control over 'sensitive' areas including justice, the police, prisons, finance and censorship. Although it was conceded that many of the newly enfranchised were illiterate, it was still seen as an insult that only 10 per cent of the adult male population now had the vote. And the pace of change was too slow: the Indianisation of the ICS was envisaged to be complete only by the 1980s, and the whole process was dependent on the 'good behaviour' of the new Indian politicians and ultimately controlled by the Viceroy and London. It all fell a long way short of the demand – a decade old – for equal status with the white Dominions.

French 'colonial geographer' Albert Demangeon praised the reforms as containing 'the germ of a revolution: it marks the end of a tradition of autocracy inherited by Britain from the Great Mogul and the beginning of a system by which Indian affairs will be conducted in conformity with the wishes of the country's own representatives'. But Indian nationalists were divided. A number of moderates, of whom Sastri and Tej Bahadur Sapru were the most important, formed their own new party, the National Liberal Federation, and boycotted Congress sessions called to discuss the reforms, not wishing to be associated at all with any hostile reaction to the work of British statesmen with whom they looked to cooperate. Sastri deemed rejection of the reforms and 'the constitutional position gained' as 'suicidal'.[3]

Furthermore, although they shared the extremists' ultimate goal of self-government for India, the moderates saw a continuation of British rule 'for some years' as further positive exposure to liberal elements in British history and tradition, which they deemed essential for facilitating a thorough change in Indian social conditions and values. Social reform – Sastri, for example, was a fervent campaigner against child marriage – could even be jeopardised by over-hasty political change, should it leave social conditions undisturbed while ushering in a new type of political authoritarianism.[4]

Others, particularly those who had been active in the Home Rule Leagues, deemed that the reforms merely demonstrated that the 'bureaucrats were not prepared to give up materially any fraction of the power which they have enjoyed', as a Bombay newspaper complained.[5]

With the moderates still staying away, this would be discussed at the National Congress session at Amritsar at the end of 1919, described by Nehru as 'the first Gandhi Congress'. Tilak was still a large presence but, Nehru reported, 'the majority of the delegates, and even more so the great crowds outside, looked to Gandhi for leadership. The slogan *Mahatma Gandhi ki jai* [Hail to Gandhi] began to dominate the Indian political horizon.' Gandhi used his popularity astutely to push through resolutions that previously had little support. One was to state regret and condemnation of the violence committed by Indian crowds during the Punjab disturbances. When this was initially defeated, he threatened to withdraw from Congress, for this was for him crucial to 'success in the future'. 'I say if there was no violence on our part . . .

these troubles would not have arisen. But the Government went mad at the time; we went mad also at the time. I say, do not return madness with madness, but return madness with sanity and the whole situation will be yours.' The resolution was passed.[6]

On the reforms, Gandhi commented that they could be 'considerably improved' but needed 'a sympathetic handling rather than summary rejection'. They might even, he said, produce a 'new spirit of respect, trust and goodwill'.[7]

But six months later, Gandhi had entirely reversed his position.

The Hunter Committee investigating the Amritsar massacre had started carrying out interviews in November 1919, but didn't speak to any Indians who weren't government employees or allies. Although it did confirm that there had been no 'prearranged conspiracy', condemned the 'crawling order' and extensive public floggings, and censured General Dyer, it was otherwise seen as a whitewash by Indian nationalists who wanted wider redress, including criminal prosecutions, for the punishments and humiliations of the martial law period led by Punjab Governor Michael O'Dwyer. The three Indians split with the committee and published their own minority report that starkly warned that Dyer, 'by adopting an inhumane and un-British method of dealing with subjects of his Majesty', had done 'great disservice to the interest of British rule in India', adding: 'This aspect it was not possible for the people of the mentality of General Dyer to realise'.[8]

It was news from the inquiry, reported in Indian newspapers, that at last brought the gravity of the Amritsar massacre to the attention of the British public. 'Breaking' the story on 13 December, the *Guardian* reported that there had been 400 to 500 casualties. Nine days later, Labour MP Josiah Wedgwood, great-great-grandson of the 'original Josiah' and one of the most high-profile parliamentarians in Britain, rose in the House of Commons to condemn the massacre as having 'destroyed our reputation throughout the world'. Wedgwood, who had fought in the South African War and in France, Gallipoli and East Africa in the Great War, saw the British Empire, particularly 'our own special invention' the self-governing Dominions, as a potential force for world peace. After all, no one could imagine these states going to war against each other. He believed that Dominion status should immediately be granted to Ceylon, India, Burma, Palestine and Ireland. (Labour Party policy, as outlined in their 1918 manifesto, was that the 'great Commonwealth of all races, all colours, all religions and all degrees of civilization that we call the British empire' should move in the direction of 'Local Autonomy and "Home Rule" All Round'.) But the massacre now threatened all of that. 'National honour' had been wrecked. How can we now criticise the Turks for the massacres in Armenia, the Americans for the current epidemic of racist lynching, the Belgians for the Congo atrocities, or the Germans for Belgium? Wedgwood asked. 'This damns us for all time.'[9]

And in India, he predicted, 'you will have a shrine erected there and every year there will be a procession of Indians visiting the tombs of the martyrs ... by this incident you have divided for all time races, races that might otherwise have loved one another'. The Montagu Reforms, he said, might have laid a foundation for real cooperation, 'but that has now been destroyed'.[10]

Wedgwood claimed in his speech that the vast majority of the British public shared his horror and outrage at the massacre. Nonetheless, General Dyer and hardline Governor Michael O'Dwyer had vociferous supporters in the right-wing press and the Conservative Party.

O'Dwyer was replaced as Punjab Governor and Dyer was forced to resign from the Indian Army after the Hunter Report was finally published in March 1920, but the General arrived back in England in May in a defiant mood. 'I shot to save the British Raj,' he told the *Daily Mail*, 'to preserve India for the Empire, and to protect Englishmen and Englishwomen who looked to me for protection.'[11]

The same month, Montagu approved Dyer's forced resignation from the Indian Army and handed over his case to the Army Council. Meanwhile, the right-wing press campaigned to clear his name.

With the country split, Dyer's case came before the House of Commons on 8 July. Both General Dyer and former Punjab Governor O'Dwyer were in the gallery as Conservative MPs followed the line that his action had been timely and justified, and that the Hunter Committee's verdict that there had been no organised conspiracy had to be wrong. A former Indian Army officer, Lieutenant General Sir Aylmer Hunterweston, pointed out that back in 1857 it had been the 'natural reluctance to take the immediate and drastic action necessary to check the Mutiny in its inception' that had led to the 'terrible sufferings and the heroic deaths of British women and children'.[12]

Sir William Joynson-Hicks, life-long campaigner against nightclubs, indecent literature and votes for women, also backed Dyer and warned that his censure would bring 'far worse political troubles in India in the near future'. 'After they have read your speech!' interrupted Wedgwood. Joynson-Hicks had just returned from a tour of India and came bearing letters from Anglo-Indian women, including one from Miss Sherwood herself in which she wrote: 'I am convinced that there was a real rebellion in the Punjab, and that General Dyer saved India and us from a repetition of the miseries and cruelties of 1857.' Joynson-Hicks also reported that his views were shared by 80 per cent of Indian civil servants and 90 per cent of Europeans in India. With the session becoming ever more acrimonious, with antisemitic abuse being hurled at Montagu, Hicks told the Secretary of State that he had 'entirely lost the confidence' of the Indian Civil Service and the British Army in India.[13]

It was about more than Dyer's decision. It was also a sacred principle of the empire, as Unionist MP Edward Carson explained. 'You must back your men ... to give confidence to those faithful and patriotic citizens who have ... won for you and kept your great Empire beyond the seas.' The feeling, the Chancellor of the Exchequer Austen Chamberlain later recalled, was of 'A Jew, rounding on an Englishman and throwing him to the wolves.'[14]

For Montagu, it was about what he called 'modern ideas of what an Empire means'. 'Are you', he asked, 'going to keep your hold upon India by terrorism, racial humiliation and subordination, and frightfulness, or are you going to rest it upon the goodwill, and the growing goodwill, of the people of your Indian Empire?' He condemned Dyer's defence that his motive was to teach a 'moral lesson to the Punjab' as 'the doctrine of terrorism'. He also attacked the 'crawling order', the compulsory salaaming of officers and the widespread public flog- gings as racial discrimination and 'frightfulness'. Instead, he pleaded, Indians must be seen as partners in the commonwealth, rather than subordinates.[15]

He was supported by Labour Party speakers. Wedgwood called for Indians to be given the same rights as Englishmen or Australians. 'If you persist in treating Indians ... as though they were an inferior people ... you are ruining the British Empire.' 'I want to see England embracing all these people,' he went on, 'not only Indians, but as they come along in the scale of civilisation, the black men of Africa, as well as the Jews of Palestine and the Egyptians of Egypt. I want to see them all as proud of being British citizens as the men in the Roman days were proud of being Roman citizens.'[16]

The motion to uphold the censure of Dyer was passed by 230 to 129 votes, but the General was allowed to resign without any disciplinary action. This, however, was not enough of a compromise for the House of Lords, who debated the issue under the motion 'This House deplores the conduct of the case of General Dyer as unjust to that officer, and as establishing a precedent dangerous to the preservation of order in face of rebellion'. Like Edward Carson, the supporters of the motion concentrated not so much on Dyer as on the principle that 'One of the mainstays of our Empire has been the feeling that every officer, whose duty it was to take action in times of difficulty, might rely ... upon his superiors standing by him.' The alternative would have 'a most demor- alizing effect'. Although opposed by some senior figures in the Lords, including Curzon, the motion passed 129 to 86.[17]

Together with the vocal press and public support for Dyer in Britain, the debates in both houses of Parliament 'destroyed the last vestige of faith in the government', as the Indian National Congress later reported. There was certainly a conciliatory policy now being pursued in India: there was an amnesty for all political prisoners not involved in actual violence; on the suggestion of O'Dwyer's successor as Governor of the Punjab, pensions were paid to those wounded and the relatives of those killed at Amritsar; and a new Viceroy, Lord Reading, known for his liberal sympathies, was appointed (one of his first acts was to undertake a visit to Jallianwala Bagh on the anniversary of the massacre). But it was too little, too late. Support for Dyer among the British community in India, the right-wing press and Conservative 'die-hard' MPs in London had caused irreversible changes.[18]

For Gandhi, the key issue was the demonstration that Indians, and Indian lives, were considered of lesser value than those of Europeans. His vision of Indians as equal subjects in the British Empire looked to be in ruins. Dyer's action was not, as the Army Council had decided, 'an error of judgment', Gandhi said, but 'criminal incapacity and heartlessness', 'an insufferable wrong'. 'To my amazement and dismay,' he proclaimed, 'I have discovered that the present representatives of the Empire have become dishonest and unscrupulous ... I can no longer retain affection for a Government so evilly manned as it is now-a-days.' The answer was for Indians to withdraw their cooperation from the government.[19]

On top of the Rowlatt 'Black Act', and what was now being referred to as the 'Punjab Atrocities', another grievance had grown significantly in size. The defeat of the Ottoman Empire had caused fresh worries about the caliphate's temporal guardianship of the Islamic holy places. During the Versailles Peace Conference, Montagu had fought against the dismemberment of Turkey, and had shipped in Indian Muslims, including the Aga Khan, to argue this case. From India, several delegations, which included Forster's acquaintances from before the war Mohammed Ali and Dr Ansari, had travelled to London to argue for the continuation of the caliphate (they also pressed for the reining in of Jewish immigration to Palestine). Rebuffed, they started organising a Khilafat Committee and proclaiming the British Empire an enemy of Islam.[20]

From exile in Tokyo, then Afghanistan, Maulana Barkatullah, a veteran pan-Islamist, urged Indian Muslims, by embracing Bolshevism, to look to Russia to tear up any harsh treaty on Turkey, rather than trusting to the 'savage wolves of Europe'. In the comparative safety from censorship or arrest in London, the Islamic Information Bureau and the Central Islamic Society urged a pro-Turkey unity and kept in touch with activists in India.[21]

There, the Ali brothers, called 'firebrands' by intelligence officer P. C. Bamford (who fiercely regretted their release from prison in the amnesty), told a string of public meetings that there was a choice between remaining British subjects and being Muslims, subjects of the empire or of God. Tearfully, they exclaimed that the honour of their faith should be defended even at the cost of their lives, or their mothers' lives. Another influential Muslim community leader who, like the Ali brothers, was followed everywhere by the police and his every utterance noted down, urged his listeners in February 1920 to die for their religion, 'and even though they had no firearms, they could well make use of bricks'.[22]

Montagu often pointed out to the Prime Minister that there were 80 million restive Muslims in India, three times the number in Arabic Asia, but he was shut out of the negotiations that produced the Treaty of Sèvres. When details of the treaty's brutal partition of the Ottoman Empire became public in May 1920, they caused, Bamford reported, an 'outburst of Muhammadan feeling' which 'found expression in the Press and on the platform'. Forster, trying to explain in a London-published liberal magazine to a baffled British public what this strange fuss was about, wrote that Indian Muslim sentiment about Turkey was 'decent, human, and even if it cannot be furthered it should not be wantonly insulted – which is what we have done'.[23]

For Gandhi, it was 'the moment of moments'. Already he had joined deputations of Khilafat leaders delivering addresses to the Viceroy, and, as Nehru wrote, the Khilafat Committee 'came more and more under his influence and began to flirt with his ideas of non-violent non-co-operation'. Nehru remembered a meeting in early 1920 when Gandhi, eyes 'blazing' 'with a fierce energy and determination', pledged Hindu support for the Turkey issue, but with strict provisos. 'This is going to be a great struggle against a powerful adversary,' he told the assembled

Muslims. 'If you want to take it up you must be prepared to lose everything, and you must subject yourself to the strictest non-violence and discipline.'[24]

Thus, when in June he returned the medal won helping establish an Indian Ambulance Corps while serving in South Africa, he wrote to the Viceroy that although he remained a 'devoted well-wisher of the British Empire', as a staunch Hindu who wished to live on terms of closest friendship with his Muslim countrymen he had to stand by them in their hour of need. Therefore, he wrote, he was withdrawing his support for the Montagu Reforms, and launching a new campaign of non-cooperation. Thanks to the Hunter Report, he added, both Muslims and Hindus had lost faith in British justice.[25]

What non-cooperation meant for Gandhi was a gradual process of removing the Indian support on which British rule depended. First, Indians should resign titles, honours and seats in local political bodies, then withdraw from posts in the civil services of government, the police excluded. Next was to take children out of schools or colleges aided or controlled by the government, and establish instead national schools and colleges. In the same way, British courts should be boycotted and replaced by private arbitration courts. Soldiers should refuse to volunteer for overseas service in Mesopotamia, where the Iraq rebellion was beginning. No one should vote or stand in the forthcoming elections, and foreign goods, particularly cloth and alcohol, should be boycotted, and there should be a drive towards home-spinning and weaving to make up the supply of cloth that Indian-owned mills could not provide. The last stages, which he hoped would not be necessary, would be for Indians to resign from the army and the police and refuse to pay taxes. All steps should be accompanied by a strict regime of non-violence.

This emphasis was echoed by the manifesto of the Central Khilafat Committee. Pressure 'must be peaceful and moral'. (Gandhi considered Britain to be, uniquely among European nations, 'amenable to the pressure of moral force'.) 'We must evoke a sympathy by suffering,' the manifesto continues. 'We wish to cultivate a world opinion in favour of our cause by inviting suffering on ourselves.' Muslim–Hindu unity was essential, the Khilafat Committee stressed. Muslims had 'realised by bitter experience that too often have the bureaucracy played the one against the other'.[26]

Not everyone celebrated this new alliance. Among others, Sastri considered the Khilafat movement a religious issue outside the remit of Congress. Furthermore, he declared that he had 'no obligation to suffer for a religion not one's own', and that Gandhi's support had given the Muslim community a strength and 'potentialities for mischief' it would otherwise have lacked.[27]

In the same way, the Khilafat movement itself was not supported by all Muslims and alienated important sections of the community. A dissenting voice at a conference in Lucknow in early 1921, the Bengal Muhammadan Association, declared it would preach the advantages and benefits of loyal cooperation 'to save the Muslim community from the foolish and nauseating movement of Mr. Gandhi'.[28]

Nonetheless, the Khilafat movement had united many in the Muslim community who previously had nothing in common. And the 'Hindu-Muhammadan combination', relentlessly driven by Gandhi, was, as intelligence officer Bamford put it, 'dominated by a most mischievous anti-British spirit'. Muslims, who made up the bulk of the army, had been considered a loyal bulwark against Hindu nationalism. But the new common cause with Hindus now presented the most serious challenge to British rule since the Mutiny.[29]

Jawaharlal Nehru had greeted the Montagu Reforms with scepticism. Writing in late 1919, he accepted that efforts to improve 'the material condition of the people' had, at every turn, been checkmated by 'the inherent difficulty of progress in a country under alien domination'. But the reforms offered little more than 'toy responsible government', and he pronounced himself 'doubtful if anyone besides Mr Montagu is enamoured of them'.[30]

Dismissing as a solution for India 'Orthodox Socialism' as 'seldom enamoured of progress', Nehru concluded that 'we are a communal people and when the time comes perhaps some form of communism will be found to suit the genius of the people better than majority rule'. Here Nehru shows the growing influence of Gandhi, who saw the village and pre-industrial Indian traditions as the building blocks of a new nation (in the same article Nehru described Gandhi as a 'saint'). According to his sister, Nehru's 'outlook on life, both politically and socially' had been much changed by the time he was spending with Gandhi. Nehru's own account of his political journey, however, focuses on what he described as a life-changing incident in June 1920, when he was thirty-one years old.[31]

Prior to this, Nehru confessed, he had been 'totally ignorant of labour conditions in factories or fields'. His politics had been of his class, the bourgeoisie. India's peasantry was seen as irrational and passive – 'resigned to their miserable fate and sat upon and exploited by all who came in contact with them – the Government, landlords, money-lenders, petty officials, police, lawyers, priests'. But that June he encountered a group of peasants who had travelled into Allahabad to seek help with resisting exactions from and ejection by their landlords. They persuaded Nehru to spend three days in their villages, far from the railway or even proper roads. The visit was a 'revelation'; 'we found the whole countryside afire with enthusiasm and full of strange excitement', Nehru wrote.

In fact, in the area between Lucknow and Benares, peasant movements – 'Kisans' – had been organising, with 100,000 joining in the early part of 1920, and tens of thousands attending demonstrations. Seeking support from urban Congress politicians like Nehru seemed to be a step forward, as one organiser explained: 'if we could link our Kisan movement with some established organization, or gain the support of well-to-do groups and lawyers, then this movement would become the future of India'.[32]

For his part, Nehru could see the advantage for the nationalists in bringing these new organisations into the fold, as, Gandhi apart, nationalists had failed to mobilise 'the masses'. Over the next months, Nehru made frequent tours of the countryside, enjoying exhausting his constantly accompanying police, CID men and junior British officials, and gaining hugely in confidence as a public speaker in Hindustani.

Most importantly, he wrote, 'a new picture of India seemed to rise before me, naked, starving, crushed, and utterly miserable'. He learned for the first time the gross imbalance of power in rural India, with the big landlords 'propped up' by the British government. Nehru was profoundly moved by what he called 'the degradation and overwhelming poverty of India', and ashamed not only of his 'easy-going and comfortable life' but also his and his fellow city politicians' former ignorance, how 'cut off we were from our own people'. From now on he would be totally absorbed in politics 'to the exclusion of everything else'.[33]

Back in Allahabad, Jawaharlal shed his immaculate suits to don rough hand-spun and woven cloth, *khadi*, and rejected the lavish meals served at the Nehru mansion in favour of simpler fare. He had completed his transformation from 'priggish' 'man about town' to conviction politician, Gandhi's chosen and favourite disciple and an all-India figure to be reckoned with.

All of this threw his father, Motilal, into a state of confusion. Back in 1917 he had been part of a delegation of United Provinces (UP) politicians who met Montagu on his tour of India. Then Montagu had been told that a time-frame to self-government over twenty years was acceptable. But the Amritsar massacre and its aftermath had 'made his blood boil', and after the publication of the Hunter Report 'whitewash' he wrote to his son that they should 'raise a veritable hell for these rascals'. Nonetheless, he remained unsure about non-cooperation, unlike his son, and worried how it would work in practice, particularly in the case of elections due in November.[34]

The Calcutta Congress Conference in September 1920, called to debate Gandhi's suggested policy of non-cooperation, would prove to be Motilal's personal turning point. The policy was opposed by many of Motilal's former political bedfellows, but the Congress, and Motilal – overwhelmed, according to Bamford, by the 'towering personality of Mahatmaji' – narrowly backed boycotting the elections and launching non-cooperation. According to Jawaharlal, Calcutta was the beginning of the Gandhi era in Congress. The whole look changed; 'European clothes vanished and soon only khadi was to be seen ... the lower middle classes became the new type of Congressman.' The language used was Hindustani, and there was 'a new life and enthusiasm and earnestness'.[35]

After the Congress, Motilal resigned his position in the UP government and gave up his legal practice. As Jawaharlal wrote, joining Gandhi in his campaign meant 'a total break with his past life ... not an easy matter when one is on the eve of one's sixtieth birthday'. Motilal's Savile Row suits went on a bonfire: now it would be only *khadi*. The wine cellar was disposed of, and the Nehru mansion's vast retinue of servants culled. The horses and carriages were sold, and his youngest daughter removed from her British school. It was a break, too, from old friends and political colleagues.[36]

The November elections, the first under the new reforms, were clearly affected by the non-cooperation campaign. The polls went off peacefully, and in only six cases out of 637 was election impossible because there was no candidate. But most of those who normally would have stood withdrew, and only about a quarter of those eligible to vote did so, with the turnout varying hugely: in parts of Madras it was over 50 per cent, in other places as low as 5 per cent. A British journalist in a township outside Allahabad reported: 'there was nothing to show that this was the red-letter day in the history of modern India which was to initiate her people into the great art of self-government ... From eight in the morning till past twelve not a single voter had presented himself in the course of the whole day.'[37]

In December at Nagpur a full Congress session, attended by more than 14,000 delegates, confirmed the decision from Calcutta, with many earlier waverers now coming on board. The session also saw the adoption of a new constitution, masterminded by Gandhi, that created for the first time a permanent paid executive, the Working Committee, reorganised the party nationwide, and initiated vigorous fund-raising activities. One dissenting voice was that of Labour

MP Josiah Wedgwood, on a six-month tour of India, who warned that non-cooperation would alienate sympathisers in Britain. But, as Nehru wrote, 'non-co-operation was now a mass movement, and it was led by a man of commanding personality who inspired devotion in India's millions'. 'If there is sufficient response to my scheme,' Gandhi declared, 'you can gain Swaraj in the course of a year.'[38]

Socialist leader Jayaprakash Narayan, then a young man, would forever speak of the 'tradition of 1921', calling it 'the most glorious page in the living history of our national revolution'. For Jawaharlal Nehru, it was a moment when a 'demoralized, backward, and broken-up people suddenly straightened their backs and lifted their heads'. There was a 'tremendous feeling of release, a throwing off of a great burden, a new sense of freedom'. Accompanied everywhere by 'innumerable spies and secret-service men', he toured the United Provinces, declaring that India 'had resolved to shake off the slavery' of 150 years of British rule. Looking back, he later wrote of that moment: 'I had a flame-like quality, a fire that burned within me ... and drove me relentlessly forward.'[39]

Meanwhile Gandhi, often accompanied by one or both of the Ali brothers, criss-crossed the country, addressing huge crowds of what Bamford sneeringly described as the 'completely ignorant and uneducated', urging non-cooperation to achieve Swaraj. The British connection should be kept up, Gandhi said, 'but only if the British should give up behaving as our superiors'. Mohammad Ali declared that 'If Muslims wish to maintain Islam they should join hands with the Hindus and free their country first.' Addressing a Muslim crowd, Gandhi warned that Englishmen were 'casting evil eyes on your religion'; a largely Hindu gathering elsewhere was urged that 'if you wish to protect the cow you should either mend or end this Government'. All were told that it was an 'unholy act' to cooperate with the government-run courts and schools and that government titles were 'dirty things'.[40]

Already Montagu had warned Viceroy Chelmsford that Gandhi could not be arrested, however seditious his speeches or writings. 'If you move against him,' he wrote, 'he will hunger strike and die in prison, and then I don't know where we shall be.' In February 1921, Montagu read the report of Labour MP Ben Spoor, who had been touring India with Josiah Wedgwood. The good news was that 'Hardly anyone in India wants separation from Great Britain.' But Gandhi was 'worshipped', Spoor wrote. 'His influence cannot be over-estimated ... Nobody in India, European or Indian, thinks it would be wise to touch Gandhi ... meanwhile non-cooperation appears to be getting more dangerous.'[41]

The campaign created a massive nationwide network of activists for the first time. Ten million rupees were collected between April and June. Hundreds of lawyers, like the Nehrus, withdrew their services from the government's courts; thousands of students boycotted their schools or colleges. In Bengal alone, 24,000 students walked away from their degrees. A boycott of foreign cloth saw imports halve, and the temperance campaign caused, in places, severe shortages in government tax income. Some lesser taxes went unpaid; the strict forest laws were widely flouted.[42]

Those Indians who continued to sell foreign cloth or liquor were picketed, and on occasions even attacked by arsonists. Social pressure was put on those who did not give up their government jobs. Bamford cited a case of a doctor who refused to treat the child of a continued 'co-operator'. A teacher staying at his post was stoned; some schools that did not 'nationalize' were burned down.

The campaign gathered up a lot of unrelated grievances. There was a wave of strikes in the public services such as post, telegraph and railway, as well as in the textile and jute factories of Bombay and Calcutta, and the tea plantations of Assam. Most had nothing to do with the political demand for Swaraj, and while swelling the 'movement', remained out of the direct control of Congress.

Gandhi, and Nehru too, took every opportunity to preach the doctrine of non-violence. Nehru declared that 'Englishmen' wanted to see riots so that they could 'wipe you out', 'shoot you in thousands'. 'Peaceful methods' provided 'no handle, no grip, no opportunity for forcible suppression'. The programme of non-violent political protest also gave the campaign moral superiority. It would, Nehru hoped, be India's gift to the world. In stark contrast was the behaviour of the British, for whom, Gandhi wrote, 'violence is the keystone of the Government edifice'. And, of course, 'mob' violence would quickly alienate those from the ranks of the Indian moderates and vested interests who, so far, had come on board.[43]

There was violence, sometimes on a small scale, sometimes much more. The worst, the flaring up of an ancient grievance into the 'Moplah' or 'Malabar' rebellion (already described), was blamed by the British on Khilafat agitators. In all, British intelligence counted fifty-four major instances of riot or violence during the year. And Europeans were targeted, frequently insulted, and sometimes victims of personal violence. After every outbreak, Congress leaders condemned the violence. As Bamford astutely noted, 'Gandhi was faced by the difficulty, after having brought the pot to the boil, of keeping it boiling without allowing it to boil over.'[44]

For its part, the Indian government, led from April by the Liberal Viceroy Lord Reading, displayed restraint, often in the face of contradictory advice from London, some provincial Governors and the army. Nehru was threatened with arrest for sedition, but no move was made against him. The hope was that the non-cooperation campaign, if unprovoked, would run out of steam or collapse from its internal contradictions.

Jawaharlal Nehru had one concern about Gandhi's leadership. As a student at Cambridge he had been angered by a visiting Indian Hindu politician speaker who made repeated references to the 'spiritual mission of India', calling it 'God's chosen country . . . The Mohammadans here were, naturally, not very pleased with him.' In his autobiography Nehru several times expressed his distaste for 'the exploitations of the people by the so-called men of religion', and declared that the 'outward ways of religion' did not appeal to him.[45]

Now he found himself troubled by the spectacular growth of the 'religious element' in nationalist politics. 'I did not like it at all,' he wrote. Muslim religious leaders took a prominent part in the Khilafat movement and gave it, Nehru wrote, 'a definite religious tinge ... Many a Westernised Muslim, who was not of a particularly religious turn of mind, began to grow a beard and otherwise conform to the tenets of Orthodoxy.' This reversed a previous trend towards 'new ideas and a progressive Westernisation'. Hindu swamis were also at the forefront, and along with Moulvies and Moulanas were condemned by Nehru for giving a religious twist to everything that 'prevented all clear thinking'. On history, economics and sociology they were 'all wrong'.

But it was Gandhi more than anyone who was influencing this direction by 'continually laying stress on the religious and spiritual side of the movement', Nehru wrote, and some of Gandhi's phrases, such as his frequent reference to Rama Raj as a golden age about to return, jarred with Nehru. According to Bamford's intelligence report, during Gandhi's meetings 'unscrupulous agitators were circulating to the credulous masses stories of divine attributes and miraculous powers. These were readily believed and thus the Mahatma's influence was strengthened by a spurious divinity.' But Nehru conceded that Gandhi's approach worked, giving him 'an amazing knack of reaching the heart of the people'.[46]

The first 'Gandhi' Congress session at the end of 1920 had seen the departure from the movement of Muhammad Ali Jinnah, previously a strong advocate of Hindu–Muslim unity. 'I will have nothing to do with this pseudo-religious approach to politics,' he had declared. It was nothing more than 'working up mob hysteria'. Gandhi's leading colleagues in the Congress Working Committee – Motilal Nehru, Deshbandhu (C. R.) Das and Lala Lajpat Rai – were also not 'men of religion' and considered political problems purely on the 'political plane'. But they, like Jawaharlal, had given up their jobs and donned the *khadi*, and thus had also plugged into and benefited from the traditional Indian respect for the ascetic 'Holy Man', as Nehru admitted.[47]

Nehru also differed from Gandhi on the Mahatma's rejection of all things modern and Western – including modern machinery and medicine – in favour of a return to an idealised Indian past based on the village. 'Most of us were not prepared to reject the achievements of modern civilization,' Nehru wrote, 'although we may have felt that some variation to suit Indian conditions was possible.'[48]

For now, Nehru did not worry himself too much with these concerns, being too 'absorbed and wrapt in the movement'. Pressure was now coming from provincial Congress committees to advance to the later stages of the non-cooperation programme – non-payment of taxes and forcing resignations from the police and army. In fact, non-payment was already underway in some places, and in September the Ali brothers were arrested for 'tampering with the loyalty of troops', having earlier declared it unlawful for any Muslim to serve in the army. At the time, Gandhi had called this 'premature. It is the last, not the first step.' But following the arrests, Gandhi, writing in *Young India* in October, changed his tune, deeming it 'sinful for any Mussalman or Hindu to serve the existing Government whether as a soldier or in any capacity whatsoever'. And still the government lacked the nerve to arrest him.[49]

A British report in September noted that 'disturbances in places so widely apart ... indicate a growing contempt for law and order'. The Governor of United Provinces, surveying widespread strikes, anti-rent campaigns and demonstrations, described the situation as 'the beginning of something like revolution'.[50]

Meanwhile, news had come through that the long-delayed tour by the Prince of Wales was now scheduled for the end of the year. Congress immediately announced that if the trip went ahead, 'in spite of the growing unrest and discontent', there would be a total boycott of the tour.[51]

E. M. Forster was now back in India, staying with Masood in Hyderabad. A week before the Prince's visit started he wrote home: 'It is disliked and dreaded by nearly everyone. The chief exceptions are the motor-firms and caterers who will make fortunes, and the non-cooperators and extremists, who will have an opportunity for protest which they would otherwise have lacked.' For Nehru, 'matters had at last come to a head'.[52]

17

'An Organisation of Real Power'

E. M. Forster had returned from his first trip to India feeling liberated. He continued his reading about India and wrote extensively, in articles and book reviews, about Indian art, architecture, literature and religion, often confessing to his relative ignorance. He particularly championed the work of poet and polymath Rabindranath Tagore, the first non-European to win the Nobel Prize in Literature. But on his 'Indian novel', he was stuck. He managed to get down a couple more chapters, but then put it aside. To unblock himself, he wrote *Maurice*, the story of a homosexual relationship which he knew could not be published in his lifetime.

But on *A Passage to India*, Forster remained blocked, and the advent of the war brought a deep depression and an abandonment of the hope for creativity. Through connections, Forster got a job at the National Gallery, where the more valuable artworks were being put into storage to be safe from bombs. Forster joked to his friends that if he was killed in an air-raid, he would die, 'appropriately, among second-rate masterpieces'.[1]

In 1915, Masood married, which made Forster rueful, writing in his diary: 'I wish very much that he had felt, if only once, what I felt for him.' He was also receiving slights about his lack of 'war work', so volunteered to join the efforts of the Red Cross in Alexandria. This was the supply base for the Dardanelles campaign, and Forster's job was as a 'searcher' – asking in the hospitals for information on missing men.[2]

In Alexandria he worked hard and impressed not only with his efficiency but also in the unaffected sympathy he showed to the injured servicemen, playing cards, chess or taking dictation of letters. For his part, Forster was struck by the soldiers' lack of vindictiveness towards their Turkish enemies.

In his spare time, Forster gave lectures and piano recitals, taught English and did some local journalism. He enjoyed the climate and swimming, but struggled to find affection for the country or its inhabitants. Since 1882 Egypt had effectively been run by the British Consul-General, although officially it was still part of the Ottoman Empire. The British in Egypt rarely fraternised with either Egyptians or the cosmopolitan commercial, legal and cultural classes and officials. The Egyptian elite looked to France for inspiration (and spoke French). The British rarely ventured away from their clubs, tennis parties and horse-racing events. When the Turks joined the war on the German side, Egypt was declared a British protectorate, though no Egyptian was consulted on anything important. In fact, the Egyptians and British regarded each other with loathing and contempt. As the war dragged on, recruitment of Egyptian fellahin for labour battalions became more and more compulsory, and requisitions of grain and domestic animals widespread. The price of cotton, a key resource for the British economy, was fixed to the detriment of the grower. And with a quarter of a million, sometimes ill-disciplined, empire troops stationed to guard the Suez Canal imperial artery, there were frequent clashes.[3]

Forster found the landscape of Egypt 'flat, unromantic, unmysterious'. It was the 'pseudo-East', he wrote to Masood, 'vastly inferior to India, for which I am always longing in the most persistent way'. Egyptians were 'exasperating in the extreme'. Nearly a year after his arrival, he wrote to Malcolm Darling expressing worries that, having turned up inclined to be 'quite free from racial prejudice', he now feared that he had become as bad as the Anglo-Indians, finding himself feeling 'intense dislike' of anything 'Arab'. 'What does this mean?' he asked. 'Am I old, or is it the war, or are these people intrinsically worse? ... It's damnable and disgraceful and it's in me.'[4]

Forster pulled strings to avoid conscription and would remain in Egypt until January 1919. In October 1917 he had his first 'full physical encounter' (as his biographer P. N. Furbank puts it) with a soldier on the Alexandria beach. Soon after that he befriended a young tram conductor, Mohammed el-Adl, who had learned English at an American Mission School, and was impressed by what he saw as Forster's very un-English politeness. They started a relationship, and Forster lent him money when he established his own business, and paid for medical treatment when he fell ill with TB.[5]

Back in England, Forster found himself no longer the famous name he was before the war, and his royalties and income from investments much reduced. He churned out journalism and book reviews – including more pieces on India – and was briefly literary editor of the Labour Party newspaper, the *Herald*. In the meantime, there was bad news from Egypt.

At the end of the war, most Egyptians had expected the protectorate to end and, with the Ottoman Empire defunct, for them to be a fully independent state on the European model. A delegation (*wafd*) of distinguished Egyptians met the British High Commissioner and laid out this desire, indicating that they were to travel to Versailles to secure the support of US President Wilson. The British were 'liberty loving', they said, and the President was an advocate of self-determination. The High Commissioner responded cautiously, aware that wartime privations had caused distress and anger across Egypt's 13 million population, but the Foreign Secretary Curzon was having none of it. In March 1919, two months after Forster's departure, the delegation's leader, Said Zaghul, was arrested and exiled to Malta.

This showed how little the British understood Egyptian feelings and how poor was their intelligence and understanding. The arrest was followed by waves of demonstrations – many taking on a religious Islamic tone – riots, strikes and sabotage. The sizeable imperial military force still in Egypt from the war responded rapidly as martial law was declared. Crowds were machine-gunned, including from the air, and in eight weeks 1,500 Egyptians were killed. Empire troops were notably 'trigger happy', and not averse to torture and extortion.[6]

Forster's friend Mohammed el-Adl was a victim of this ugly mood. Forster had already heard that he had fallen ill with consumption. In May, Mohammed was harassed after refusing to buy a gun from two Australian soldiers, who then returned with a warrant for his arrest for trying to buy a gun. He was sentenced to six months, and was now, he wrote to Forster, violently anti-British.[7]

Forster, who knew that imprisonment could well be fatal for el-Adl's weak state of health, wrote a furious letter to the *Guardian*, declaring that the uprising had been the result of the British treatment of the Egyptians during the war, in particular labour recruitment. He also contributed to a Fabian Society pamphlet on Egypt put together by Leonard Woolf, who had recently returned from seven years' colonial service in Ceylon, an experience that had led him to denounce 'the bloodshed, atrocities, and economic exploitation which have made the word imperialism stink in the nostrils of most people'. Forster called for Egypt to become a League of Nations mandate, and hit out at the British 'profound distrust of Orientals'.[8]

Once the outbreak had been suppressed, Said Zaghul was allowed to return to Egypt, and to travel to Versailles. But he failed even to gain an audience with Wilson, who had been told by the British that Zaghul's new Wafd Party was riddled with Bolsheviks and Islamic fundamentalists. Egypt, for now, remained a British protectorate.

While Forster had been in Egypt, he had received an invitation to visit the Maharaja of the Princely State of Dewas, whom he had met through Darling on his first Indian trip. Then unable to leave the Red Cross, Forster was delighted when in February 1921 a second invitation came, this time to stand in for six months for an employed Englishman on sick leave. Forster wasn't sure what his duties would be – 'Prime Minister or something', he told friends – but seized the chance to return to India.

Before he left, he was given riding lessons by Leonard Woolf, a skill deemed essential for his new job. Virginia Woolf noted in her diary on 1 March, 'Morgan goes to India and I think forever. He will become a mystic, sit by the roadside and forget Europe.'[9]

After a long voyage and then an overland journey, encountering numerous muddles along the way, Forster arrived at Dewas feeling 'rather dazed and dreamy' but delighted that he was the only European for many miles around. 'Life here will be queer beyond description,' he wrote.[10]

The princely states now made up a third of India's area, and a little more than a fifth of its population. All were advised by British political agents of one sort or another. In total there were 693, if you included Nepal and the Shan states of Burma. Some were tiny, not much more than a town and its surrounds; others much bigger, the largest being Hyderabad, with a similar size to France and population to Egypt. Dewas, near Indore, was small, only 446 square miles, home to some 80,000. There was neither railway station nor industry, the principal products being wheat, millet and cotton. It was also, Forster had noted on his earlier visit, far from scenic, unlike many other places he had seen in India.

Having spent most of his previous visit in the company of Muslims, Forster had been keen to learn more about Hinduism, and he was confronted at once by the Holi festival of the Shudras, the lowest of the caste groups. This consisted in the main of practical jokes and horseplay, including exploding cigars, sofas that gave you an electric shock, and being showered with red dust. It was all fascinating and confusing, made more so by Forster's very scant understanding of Urdu and Marathi, the language of the court. On 6 April he wrote to his mother, 'Everything that happens is said to be one thing and proves to be another ... I live in a haze.'[11]

As it turned out, he was to be not 'Prime Minister' but the Maharaja's private secretary. This would include a motley portfolio of responsibilities – the palace garden and tennis courts, the guest-houses and the electricity generator – as well as mail and accounts. But above all he was to be a companion to the Maharaja, seven years his junior, with whom he had on his pre-war trip struck up such a close friendship. Forster described H. H. Sir Tokoji Rao III, as he was officially known, as 'high-spirited', 'proud' and 'one of the sweetest characters on earth'.[12]

Forster quickly noticed changes from his earlier encounter. For one thing, no one was wearing European clothes. On his previous visit the Maharaja often had done. Forster interpreted this at the time as a backward step.

He soon realised that the Maharaja's finances were in a parlous state. Bills and salaries were going unpaid, and the state was seriously in debt. The books were chaos, with 'faery budgets, such as might occur in the parliaments of Gilbert and Sullivan'.[13]

A large part of the problem was the new palace and gardens. Already under construction on Forster's first visit in 1912, they were still being built in a desultory way, and parts erected ten years ago were now falling down. In the grandly planned gardens, costly fruit trees were dying for lack of water because the expensive irrigation scheme didn't work. 'We live amongst rubble and mortar,' Forster wrote to his mother. The cost had 'drained the life of the State', and Forster worried that the Maharaja might have to raise taxes: 'if he overtaxes the cultivator in these days, it means trouble'.[14]

Among the Maharaja's subjects, as elsewhere in India at this time, there was widespread want and destitution. Agriculture was impoverished and the cost of living had risen by 100 per cent over the last few years. Most of the 'cultivators' were in debt to money-lenders, sometimes as a consequence of expensive weddings.[15]

Nonetheless, the Prince lived extravagantly (about a quarter of the state's revenue was for the 'Chief's Establishment', five times the amount spent on education). A visiting neighbour prince was treated to a meal with thirty-five courses. For another one, the Maharaja brought in singers all the way from Bombay (they missed their train and arrived too late). No expense was spared when it came to religious festivals. When the Maharaja went to Nagpur for a conference, he was accompanied by elephants, horses and a huge retinue of servants. 'To check the idleness, incompetence, and extravagance is quite beyond me,' Forster wrote to Malcolm Darling.[16]

Although uneasy about the profligacy of the court amid such severe poverty, Forster got on very well with the Maharaja and lived comfortably in the half-built palace, full of warped pianos and broken telephones, and in which sparrows flew about at will. Forster had three rooms, which had been equipped with European-style furniture, and he had arranged for his servant from his previous trip, Baldeo, to join him in Dewas. The electricity sometimes failed, but the palace was free of smells and bugs and open to the breeze. The heat didn't bother him, although, he wrote to his mother, 'the fate of ink is desperate'. When water ran low, he would insist that Baldeo bring some for his bath from the ornamental fountain, so it sometimes arrived complete with fish.[17]

When he wasn't trying to prevent wandering cows from eating what little vegetation was growing in the gardens, he rowed on the lake, wrote extensive letters to friends and family, and tried to do what he could with the chaotic accounts. He spent several hours each day with the Maharaja discussing politics or religion, and read to him essays by Arnold and Macaulay.

Not long after his arrival he tried to arrange an assignation with a young Hindu workman of about eighteen but, believing the Maharaja had learned about it, offered to resign. However, the Maharaja was sympathetic, suspecting that Forster's tastes had been formed by his contact with Muslims in Egypt, and instead set him up with the palace barber.

Several months in, Masood came to visit. He was now Director of Public Instruction in Hyderabad, having been persuaded that law was too politically dangerous. He was embarrassed by and critical of the chaos of the Maharaja's domain. 'Our incompetence distressed him more than it could me,' Forster wrote, 'because he saw it as an extreme example of his country's inefficiency.'[18]

Certainly, with marked exceptions, the princely states were well behind the rest of India in all-round development. The British had maintained the princes after the East India Company was effectively nationalised in 1858, and thus secured their support. But the laissez-faire policy of indirect rule meant that the states were neither modernised nor integrated into the rest of India. Allowed to continue to run on 'traditional' lines, they often now stood as examples of the failure of 'traditional India', so revered by Gandhi.

'I don't believe in native states any more,' Forster told the Woolfs during a visit soon after his return from India. He had just written an article titled 'The Mind of the Indian State'. Forster had now taken on a new public role as an interpreter of India for the British reader. The princes, he wrote, 'can exalt and depress their own subjects at will [and] regard the State revenue as their private property'. Ironically, he pointed out, subjects of the princes actually had less independence and freedom than those of direct-ruled British India. 'Agitators don't exist there,' he told Virginia Woolf of the Indian states. 'If they come, they disappear.'[19]

Jawaharlal Nehru, writing about his arrest in September 1923 in Nabha State, was equally damning. The Indian states are 'well known for their backwardness and their semi-feudal constitutions', he said. 'They are personal autocracies, devoid even of competence or benevolence. Many a strange thing occurs there which never receives publicity.' Forster quoted 'certain Anglo-Indians' as speaking of the states with 'morbid envy': 'They stand no nonsense over there ... they clap agitators all right into prison without a trial, and if your servant's impudent you can strafe him without getting hauled into the Courts.'[20]

The British welcomed the support of the princes as 'counter-weights against the new Nationalism'. Forster pointed out that 'only Democratic Indians' thought of themselves as Indian. 'In the princely states the majority still say, I am Afghan, or Persian, or Rajput; my ancestors entered the country under so-and-so.' Instructions had been sent out to the political agents and advisers, who previously had 'laid down the law on all conceivable subjects', now to treat the princes of India 'as if they were princes and not naughty boys'. (That said, the political agent for Dewas, encountered by Forster, was 'bad-mannered', 'whiskified and fishy-faced, and obviously a bully'.)[21]

For their part, it was not in the interests or tradition of the princes that India should become a nation, and they applauded any attempt to suppress nationalist aspirations. The threat to their positions came not from the British but from Indian critics outside their realms. 'There is no anti-English feeling,' Forster wrote of the princes he met. 'It is Gandhi whom they dread and hate.' In mid-1921, the princes, worried by criticism of them in the British India newspapers, urged the Viceroy to strengthen the Press Act. Against the wishes of the legislature, Reading pushed the measure through.[22]

However, the British could not entirely ignore the backwardness, inequality and wastefulness of many of the princely states. As part of the Montagu-Chelmsford reforms of 1919, they had created a Chamber of Princes, consisting of the rulers of the larger states, and lesser princes who became members through election. It was, Forster wrote, 'one of the many stillborn children of Lord Chelmsford'. It was ignored by the rulers of the largest states: someone like the Nizam of Hyderabad was not going to hobnob with chieftains who might be far less powerful than his own vassals. Even being in the same room was extremely tricky, 'lest they compromise their prestige'. The British hoped that the Chamber would bring 'ideas and enlightenment to many a prince', but it was 'nothing more than a forum for anti-nationalist resolutions'. 'They forget the common enemy as soon as they see each other,' Forster continued, 'while the New Spirit knocks with increasing irritability on their door.'[23]

After 1919, it had, however, become fashionable for the princes to talk of liberalisation and constitutions. Even in Dewas the Maharaja was putting together a new constitution, with a council of advisers and representative bodies from different interest groups in the state. But close scrutiny revealed it to be little more than window-dressing: all power remained firmly in the hands of the Maharaja. 'Politically,' Forster wrote, 'we are still living in the fourteenth century.'[24]

In Dewas, the Maharaja had managed so far to exclude 'agitators'.
However, 'disciples of Gandhi' were to be found shouting 'subversive
slogans at us over the border'. The problem, Forster wrote, was that
Dewas, and other states he visited, were 'so slackly administered'. The
Maharaja, with his incompetence and extravagance, was ruining his
people. Writing to Malcolm Darling, Forster asked: 'If fate in the form
of any political party should ask Dewas a Question, what answer could
Dewas give?'[25]

The Maharaja, for all his faults as a ruler, was 'one of the sweetest
and saintliest men I have ever known', Forster later wrote. Before he
left, Forster was invested with the second-highest honour of the state,
the Tukojirao III Gold Medal. He was given a temporary version and
promised that in time the real medal would be struck. Forster wasn't
holding his breath.

He then visited English friends in India and had two more months
in Hyderabad with Masood. 'I have passed abruptly from Hinduism
to Islam and the change is a relief,' he wrote home. He admitted that
he was baffled by Hindu rituals. In contrast, Muslim India, although
'not as subtle or suggestive as the Hindus', had 'definite outlines and
horizons . . . I can follow what they are saying.'[26]

There was much talk of the impending visit of the Prince of Wales.
All agreed that the timing was bad – a ceremony celebrating the tie
between India and Britain just at the moment when it was under revi-
sion. Forster thought the visit 'ill-omened', even 'impertinent'. 'You
can't solve real, complicated and ancient troubles by sending out a
good-tempered boy; besides, this naïve slap-the-back method, though
the very thing for our colonies, scarcely goes down in the East.' In fact,
the visit would intensify existing problems, while also presenting the
government with the 'challenge of persuading hundreds of millions of
people not to be rude'. Forster knew about the threatened boycott from
Congress. 'If there is a general response,' he warned, 'this expensive
royal expedition will look rather foolish.'[27]

So why was it going ahead? Apart from those who might gain

materially 'scarcely anyone in India wanted the Prince of Wales to come'. Someone suggested to Forster that it was the Prince himself keen to make the trip. On this Forster was doubtful. He reckoned it was about prestige. The visit had already been delayed once – the Prince was supposed to have opened the new legislatures back in February, but he was too exhausted from his Australia trip, so his place had been taken by the Duke of Connaught. To delay twice would be 'unseemly ... it would look as if they doubted India's enthusiasm; it would look what it was, in fact. Prestige can only be maintained by pretending it has not been questioned.'[28]

Forster was right to be sceptical of the suggestion that the Prince wanted to come to India. Nothing could be further from the truth. For one thing, since his return from Australia in October 1920 he had been enjoying the company of Mrs Freda Dudley Ward, fox-hunting and steeple-chasing, and the London season of 1921, 'one of the gayest in my memory'. 'How I'm loathing and hating the thought of India,' he wrote to his mother. To his mistress he lamented that no new disaster had occurred in India that might have stopped his going. Wasn't his brother Bertie better suited to the India trip, he asked, 'where it's all apparently so pompous as he's rather pompous himself!'[29]

But when the Prince suggested to his father he ask Lloyd George whether the trip was really necessary, the King replied, 'I don't care whether the Prime Minister wants you to go or not. I wish you to go and you are going.' The King later said that if the Prince had failed to undertake the tour, it 'would have meant an end of our government there'.[30]

The army – its British contingent understrength – and most of the provincial Governors, embroiled in dealing with non-cooperation, were against the trip. But the King's view was shared by Viceroy Reading and Secretary of State Montagu: that it would be disastrous for prestige 'if we let it be believed that the conditions of India were such that the Heir Apparent to the Indian throne could not visit'. In addition, Reading hoped that it would be good for the relationship with the

Indian princes, whose support was so vital against Gandhi, and would reassure Indian nationalist moderates and boost the flagging morale of the British serving in India. Montagu believed that a successful tour would bolster his position, under fire from Conservatives for his reforms and his condemnation of General Dyer.[31]

In September, the Prince received a letter from Achyutandanda Purohit, a member of the All-India Congress Committee of Orissa, usually a 'hotbed of loyalty'. 'Once', he wrote, 'people used to smile with incredulity if anybody talked against British Justice or British rule. But now, believe me, Noble prince, not one sincere man through-out the length and breadth of the Indian Empire will be found, who is not – despaired of British justice, who does not, attribute his rank poverty to British rule, and who does not desire a radical change of the system of Government in this land.' If the Prince wanted to do anything of real benefit to India, he should cancel the tour and redirect the money it was going to cost towards 'feeding the dying hungry and clothing the shivering naked'.[32]

Gandhi, writing in *Young India* the following month, said the trip and the Prince himself were being 'exploited for advertising the "benign" British rule' and that it was a 'crime' to spend extravagantly from the Indian exchequer on 'a mere show' when millions were starving. The moderate Srinivasa Sastri, however, in the *Times of India* in November, predicted that India 'will show herself in her usual character ... of profound loyalty and attachment to the Throne'. People understood, he went on, 'the crucial and delicate part played by the Crown in the British Constitution' and 'realize fully that it forms the link by which the Empire is held together'.[33]

The Prince and his entourage left Plymouth on 26 October 1921, once more aboard the *Renown*. Against the opposition of most of the staff members, 'Dickie' Mountbatten was once more in the party. They stopped at Gibraltar and Malta, and then Aden, where they were greeted with a banner reading 'Tell Daddy We Are All Happy Under British Rule'. On 17 November, with some trepidation, they reached Bombay.[34]

The tour was planned in two halves. The first took the Prince northward from Bombay through the 'native states' of Rajputana to Nepal and then across to Calcutta. From there they were to sail to Burma, then return to Madras, then head north to Delhi and Peshawar, and then across the Sind desert to Karachi. In all, it was to take four months and cover 41,000 miles by land and sea.[35]

The initial reception at Bombay was better than most had dared hope. There was a respectable crowd, despite the notices posted across the city urging, in Gandhi's name, a boycott or hartal. Gandhi himself was in the city, presiding over a huge bonfire of Western clothes. He had urged that the hartal should be peaceful, but about an hour after the welcoming crowds had dispersed, violence broke out. From Government House, the Prince reported, 'one could hear the sounds of distant rioting and occasional shots'. According to Mountbatten, the non-cooperationists were 'enraged at the failure of their propaganda', and took it out on Parsi and Christian Indian communities. In addition, Europeans and those wearing European clothes were attacked. Shops were looted, and liquor stores burned to the ground. Trams were overturned, and soon there were armoured cars on the streets. In all, some 400 were injured and twenty killed, including one European.[36]

Gandhi was appalled, writing that the 'Swaraj I have witnessed during the last two days has stunk in my nostrils'. He called on Indians to go home and pray for forgiveness, while himself undertaking a penitential fast. The accompanying British press, in a pattern to be repeated through most of the tour, emphasised the positive reception and downplayed the actions of what they called the 'hooligan element'. The Labour Party *Daily Herald* argued that the fact that the Prince's visit 'should be made the occasion of violent hostile demonstration is deplorable and disastrous'. The left-leaning *New Statesman* said that Gandhi's 'prestige' had received a 'double blow': 'Half the population of the city disobeyed him by gathering to welcome the Prince with remarkable enthusiasm; while the other half, or at least another fraction, disobeyed him equally, and much more seriously, by resorting to violence.'[37]

The Prince spent a week in Bombay and its environs, which now had armed soldiers on every street corner, visiting polo matches and attending balls (where he surprised everyone by his willingness to shake hands). Then the Prince and his entourage of a hundred or so British and Indians (including ten princes or their sons) boarded their train to head north into princely Rajputana. The royal train was, Mountbatten noted, 'easily the most magnificent one that we have ever had', beating those in Australia and Canada hands down. Its eleven gigantic coaches, painted a creamy white, with the Prince's arms in the centre of each one, had only four cabins, and included a magnificent dining room. In fact there were three more trains: one for the more junior members of the entourage, one for the press, and one to lug around landaus and carriage horses, and twenty-five polo ponies. All this was duplicated for when the party encountered a narrow-gauge railway, at which point all had to be transferred, including the 400 pieces of baggage that had been landed from the *Renown*, as well as food and the office equipment provided for the press. Because the departure was ten minutes late according to the meticulous schedule that had been devised, the trains set off at 55mph. When his carriage began to rock, the Prince, no doubt remembering his derailing in Australia, ordered that it should not exceed 35mph.[38]

Princely India would be very welcoming to the party, with large crowds everywhere and no sign of the 'Gandhists', but also full of elaborate protocol – the endless exchanges of *pan* and *itl*, the giving then returning of presents – at times very strange, and often disturbingly extravagant. At Baroda they were treated to a show of fighting cocks, acrobats and 'rustic scenes'. 'Altogether my head was in a whirl at the wonder of it all,' Mountbatten noted in his diary. At Udaipur the route was lined by irregular troops wearing breastplates and other pieces of armour and carrying shields and long curved swords, as if, Mountbatten wrote, they had 'stepped back into the Middle Ages'. Then they were shown a fight staged between a leopard and a boar. At Bikaner there were fire-walkers and people, including young children, walking unharmed on sharp blades.[39]

At Baroda they were shown the state jewels, which had their value attached on a ticket, 'as in a shop'. They were also shown a life-size solid gold gun mounted on a solid silver carriage. In Udaipur they saw the feeding of the royal pigs. 'I regret to say that even when there is famine in the town the pigs are not neglected,' wrote Mountbatten. 'There are times when I do sympathize with the Bolsheviks.' In fact, everywhere there was a display of the ruler's wealth and the expense that had been gone to in order to entertain the Prince, regardless of the poverty of the ordinary people, suffering, as Forster had seen in Dewas, from poor harvests, indebtedness, high prices and depressed trade. In Bharatpur, a night pageant, which involved having a hill specially built on which to place a pavilion for the royal audience, cost nearly £60,000. Mountbatten reported that a procession of 'infantry, cavalry, camel corps, elephant batteries, motors, etc. went by like toys at Hamley's Christmas fair'. The Maharaja, he learned, owned at least ten Rolls-Royces and two 'of the most magnificent modern Daimlers, which cost him £9000 and £12000'. The Prince later wrote of the 'appalling' 'contrast between the excessive wealth of ruling Princes and the abysmal poverty of the masses'.[40]

At every stop, hunting was laid on for the Prince. On one occasion he found himself chasing buck across rough ground in a brand-new Rolls-Royce. Most lavish was the shoot laid on in Nepal, which was rumoured to have cost £300,000. But the Prince, apart from pig-sticking, had little taste for hunting, preferring polo or steeple-chasing. In Patiala, a rare black panther had been taken from the zoo, doped and set out under bushes for him to 'bag'. When they heard that the Prince was not shooting they returned it to the zoo and revived it.[41]

Mountbatten soon noticed that their night-time journeys by rail were guarded all the way by 'line watchers'. Six hours before the royal train was due to pass, locals were ordered to tie up all cattle and camp out along the line every 100 yards on alternate sides. Keeping warm with only dried dung fires, the watchers, many with their families, each had to do a six-hour stint. Mountbatten worked out that it took over 3,000 'unfortunate shivering natives' to guard a single night's journey, 'their only reward being that if they carry out their duties properly they will not be evicted by their sardar'.[42]

The Prince's tour was, of course, a security nightmare for the authorities. After all, as with Viceroy Hardinge, seriously injured in a 1912 assassination attempt, it only took one person to throw a home-made bomb. Orders came from Delhi that all crowds should be kept at least 15 yards away from the royal procession, the route of which was lined with police and soldiers facing away from the Prince, batons and other weapons in hand. In some places only schoolchildren or those with tickets were allowed anywhere near. In Lahore, the route from the railway station to Government House, only 2.5 miles long, was guarded by 3,000 troops as well as extra police, with three aeroplanes circling above. Standing by to proceed to any incident were five motor lorries, filled with armed infantry equipped with Lewis guns, as well as three tanks and three armoured cars. There were a number of scares. The Prince's staff learned of at least two cases in which people had been offered more than 1,000 rupees to throw a bomb at the Prince. In Peshawar, the Chief Commissioner took alarm at a threat to assassinate the Prince and redirected the procession through the back streets. The Prince was furious, convinced that everyone would consider him a coward.[43]

More than that, the heavy security, in some places augmented by local British residents brandishing rifles and machine-guns, was resented by the Prince as keeping well-wishers away and preventing him from meeting – and charming – ordinary Indians. At his first public address in Bombay he had announced that he wanted to 'appreciate at first hand all that India is . . . I want you to know me and I want to know you'. But how could he win the hearts of ordinary Indians, he asked in a letter to the King, when he was always cut off from them by rows of soldiers or police?[44]

'I greatly regret that [the situation in India] should have changed so much for the worse since we were there only 10 years ago,' the King replied. 'The War & the situation in Turkey & Montagu's reforms have no doubt produced the unrest which now exists . . . ' Furthermore, the informal style that had succeeded so well in the white Dominions was not the right approach for India, the King explained. Instead 'elaborate displays and pageantry' – what the Prince always called 'official rot and pompousness' – was best for 'impressing the Oriental mind'.[45]

In Australia and New Zealand, as we've seen, there were a few attempts at boycotts of the Prince's progress, but all had pretty much been swept away by the excitement generated by the famous visitor. But India was different. Here, in a number of places, the boycotts would be great successes for the 'Gandhists', and spectacular humiliations for the Prince.

On 28 November, the royal party reached Ajmer, a small island of direct British rule surrounded by huge areas of princely states. 'Here,' noted Mountbatten, 'the reception was not so good as other places. It really does begin to look as though the only doubtful part of the tour is going to be British India.' The British authorities had, of course, been alarmed by the riots in Bombay, but also by the highly successful hartal carried out in the old capital, Calcutta, on the same day, a sort of dress-rehearsal for the Prince's arrival there. According to Forster, 'awed Englishmen' gave eyewitness reports that 'the volunteer organization was perfect ... and displayed a calm enthusiasm that was very impressive, and an efficiency that could only come from careful preparation. The discovery that Indians can run a great city without European assistance filled the Calcutta merchants with dismay.' Bamford's intelligence report had a different version – that the volunteers had succeeded only through an 'intolerable state of coercion and intimidation ... action against the organisation responsible could no longer be delayed'. The Governor of Bengal agreed. The non-cooperation movement 'had built an organization of real power ... this it will be necessary to break if decent administration is to be restored'.[46]

It was time for a crackdown.

18

'An Orgy of Arrests'

At the end of November, Congress volunteers were declared illegal, at first in Bengal, then across India. Next came what Jawaharlal Nehru called 'an orgy of arrests and convictions'. There were raids on Congress and Khilafat offices throughout Bengal, UP, Assam, Bihar, Orissa and Punjab. Those the officials called the 'ringleaders' were picked up first: Lajpat Rai in Punjab, Deshbandhu Das in Bengal and both Jawaharlal Nehru and his father in UP.

The Congress Committee of United Provinces, of which Jawaharlal had just been made general secretary, ignored the ruling on volunteers and even published their names in the daily newspapers. 'The first list', Nehru proudly wrote, 'was headed by my father's name.' Reporting to Delhi, the Chief Secretary of the Provincial Government later explained, 'They had thrown down an open and flagrant challenge in defiance of Government and there was no option but to arrest them.'[1]

Late in the afternoon of 6 December, while Nehru was working in the Allahabad Congress office, an 'excited clerk' approached him to say that police had surrounded the building and had come in with a search warrant. Nehru admitted that he was excited too, 'for it was my first experience of the kind', but he did his best to appear cool and collected, instructing the office workers to continue as normal while the police carried out their search. Meanwhile, he heard of arrests being carried out across the city, and decided to see what was happening at his home.[2]

Reaching the Nehru mansion at around 6.30 he found the family gathered in 'father's room'. Motilal was having his now customary evening bread and milk, while giving out directions. Both he and his son were to be arrested, Motilal said. 'On the whole, everyone was taking matters very cheerfully,' Jawaharlal wrote in his diary. 'Only mother had a lost expression. Kamala behaving admirably.' His daughter Indira, who had just turned four, 'made quite a nuisance of herself objecting to her food and generally getting on people's nerves'.[3]

News of the forthcoming arrests had spread and a crowd had gathered outside the compound. It was briefly addressed by both men, who were then driven to the district jail. There they were separated and Jawaharlal sent to Lucknow.

To the 'Citizens of Allahabad' he declared, in an address published in a newspaper on 8 December, 'I go to jail with greatest pleasure.' He went on to implore compliance in the 'complete Hartal' on 12 December, the day of the Prince's visit, and stressed as vital 'an atmosphere of non-violence'. There was a chance, he said, to make 'the name of our city immortal in our annals'. The same paper carried his message to the UP Congress Committee: 'There can be no compromise or parleying with evil. This struggle must and can only end in complete victory for the people.' He urged that the work of the committee should not suffer.[4]

However, shortly afterwards all fifty-five members were arrested en bloc while holding a committee meeting. The arrests were on a huge scale: not only the leadership, but ordinary volunteers were also incarcerated, some 30,000 in December and January. Many, Nehru wrote, 'were carried away by the wave of enthusiasm and insisted on being arrested'.

Soon the jails were full. In Bengal, the authorities were forced to convert a disused dockyard into a prison. Elsewhere, there were plans for the construction of prison camps. 'The whole of India is a vast prison,' declared Deshbandhu Das from Bengal. 'I feel the handcuffs on my wrists and the weight of iron chains on my body.'[5]

The resources of government were being taxed to their utmost. And the arrests had the effect of 'warming waverers into outspoken opposition', as intelligence officer Bamford reported. It became about 'the issue to the rights of public association and public meeting', and when the 'sons and relatives of Moderates began to fill the prisons, the Moderates very quickly made themselves heard'. The mass arrests had decapitated the movement, and Nehru admitted that with 'the absence in prison of all the trusted workers, a feeling of confusion and helplessness spread'. But this was only 'superficial', Nehru wrote. 'There was still thunder in the air and the atmosphere was tense and pregnant with revolutionary possibilities.'[6]

Meanwhile, the Prince had left the safety and reassuring comfort of the princely states and was now in the heartland of Indian nationalism and agrarian protest. At Lucknow, where the crowds were 'moderate' at best, word came from the police that there was an attack planned on the Prince's car. Mountbatten took his place, 'fingering his six-shooter', but when they came to the 'ugly part of the town, the entire procession leapt forward at 50 miles an hour and so we got through safely to the palace'. A visit to the university was greeted by an embarrassingly small turn-out of students. 'I prefer native states to British India,' Mountbatten noted.[7]

At the next stop, Allahabad, as one of the Prince's party put it, 'we went from cold to frost'. The arrest of the Nehrus and other Congress leaders had clearly backfired. The Prince, riding in a state carriage wearing full-dress uniform, was met, he later wrote, 'by shuttered windows and ominous silence along the troop-lined, deserted streets. It was a spooky experience.' He was driven to the university to be met by a near-empty hall.[8]

Even the super-loyal *Times of India* had regrettably to report that 'Allahabad has failed in its welcome to the Prince. There is no use blinking the fact that the non-co-operators have scored their first success.' In a city the size of Allahabad, a crowd of 70,000 would be expected, but there were a few thousand at most, and they were largely British. The British press, also, had to report what they called 'the first check to a triumphant tour'. The reason, it was reported by the *Telegraph*, was 'intimidation and terrorization of the most shameless kind'.[9]

At Benares, another university visit was a further and almost worse humiliation. 'It would have been humorous if it had not been so sad,' the Prince wrote to the Viceroy afterwards. The university authorities had tried to cover up the almost-total student boycott by bringing in Europeans, high school boys and boy scouts. 'I suppose they hoped I would never get to hear,' wrote the Prince to Reading. 'What a BF [bloody fool] they made of me,' he concluded.[10]

'I'm very depressed about my work in British India,' the Prince wrote to his father three days later from Nepal. 'I don't feel that I'm doing a scrap of good; in fact I can say that I know I am not.' Calcutta, the end of the first leg, was little better. Ten thousand arrests had been made in the ten days prior to the Prince's visit, and security measures included a 'civil guard' of gun-toting Europeans supported by armoured cars. Amid closed shops and vehicle-free streets, almost all the 5,000-strong crowd were Europeans or 'Asiatics'; people expressed surprise at how many lived in the city. 'A temporary stop had been put to all the activities of a great city,' Nehru later wrote. 'It was hard on the Prince of Wales; he was not to blame, and there was no feeling against him whatever. But the government of India had tried to exploit his personality to prop up their decaying prestige.'[11]

The British and much of the Indian English-language press continued to stress the positive: even if the official drive-pasts were ignored, Indians still came out to watch the Prince play polo; it was only the intimidatory tactics of a few extremists that was keeping the crowds away. *The Times*, for example, in an article published at the end of the year, avowed that 'The visit of the Prince of Wales has served to demonstrate that changing India, for all its conflict and seeking and suffering, is still at heart loyal to the Crown.'[12]

In his article 'A Prince's Progress', published in London in January 1922, Forster, in his new public role as an interpreter of India, attempted to correct the record. The non-cooperation movement, he wrote, was not made up of a tiny minority but enjoyed support across all India and from Indians of many different backgrounds; moderates had been brought on board by the widespread arrests; the tour had been a failure and a 'waste of money'; it had only created opponents; Indians were unimpressed by the Prince's 'royal aspect'; they were just not interested in him. As for the hartals, empty streets and arrests – 'It is sad that the pleasure of a young man should be spoilt, but it is sadder that hundreds of other young men should be in prison on account of his visit to their country.'[13]

In fact, the Prince himself was of the same mind. In private letters to Secretary of State Montagu and Viceroy Reading, he said that he 'deplored' the exaggeration and 'camouflage' that was the dominant feature of press coverage of the various receptions and events. 'People at home are being given the wrong impression,' he went on. 'They think my tour is a success, and I must reluctantly tell you that it is no such thing.' In almost all of the cities of British India, the Prince wrote, he had been met by 'hartals and more or less emptied streets'. He was 'angry and insulted' by the student boycotts. The 'vast expenditure' on the tour had been 'absolutely wasted'. In fact, he concluded, the tour was 'worse for the Empire ... than no tour at all'. Each of the hartals, the Prince wrote to his mother, even if they only partially succeeded, were a 'feather in Gandhi's cap and the lowering of British prestige another peg'.[14]

After the Burma leg of the tour, the Prince's party returned to Madras to be met with more trouble. The route to Government House had been 'uncommonly well lined with natives', but soon afterwards a riot broke out. A cinema decked with British flags was attacked and burned, trams and cars stoned, and pictures of the Prince and Union Jack flags trampled into the ground. Only after the deployment of bayonet-wielding British soldiers and armoured cars firing machine-guns was order restored. Unlike in Bombay, the rioters had penetrated the European quarter. In fact, Mountbatten, in Government House, could hear the commotion, 'almost within view of my bedroom window'. At least five rioters were killed.[15]

Uncharacteristically, the *Daily Express* reported the riot in dramatic terms: 'Bayonet Work in Madras, Leinsters Scatter the Gandhist Riots, Grim Scene of the Royal Route'. Once he saw the article, Montagu was forced to have a word with his friend, *Express* proprietor Lord Beaverbrook.[16]

Madras's Governor later reported that the 'visit had done little lasting good'. It might have deepened the loyalty of those already loyal, but had 'no effect whatever on those who are at present in open hostility to the British government ... the whole visit was regrettably inopportune'.[17]

Two days later, Mountbatten paid a visit to Madras's Theosophical Society headquarters, run by a friend of his sister, Baroness de Kuster, 'a nice little person full of enthusiasm ... she spoke so enthusiastically of David [as the Prince was known to his family] that I wonder if she had ever met him'. Dickie asked her if she had. She replied, '"No, not here, but I have often met him on the astral plane." I was too astounded to laugh.' She then told Dickie that it had lately been revealed to Mrs Besant that 'David's last incarnation had been in the body of Akbar, the great Moghul Emperor of India ... David was not over-pleased at the idea of having been a "black man"'.[18]

Much of the second leg was through princely states, where 'Gandhi's menacing influence disappeared', the Prince later wrote. 'Here there was a way of life, almost feudal and sometimes barbaric ... impervious to the growing uproar in British India.' Elsewhere, the party kept a keen eye on the crowds, weighing their ethnic make-up and looking out for 'Gandhi caps'. And the authorities redoubled their efforts to stage-manage the Prince's appearances. It had already been noticed in Lucknow that the government had laid on lorries bearing notices: 'Come and See the Prince and Have a Free Ride'. In Agra, the journalist from the *Statesman* noted that the official route contained 'a large number of country folk who had been brought to Agra by the landowners to help swell the throng of loyal natives. There were also delegations of students of all ages, and girls and boys of various educational institutions, in the charge of European teachers.' Taxi drivers had been given money to keep working, but had all returned it and stayed at home. A demonstration against the Prince was dispersed by a police baton charge. In Lahore, 'country folk' had been offered free transportation into the city, and enticed by a huge fair, with lantern shows, merry-go-rounds, bands and dancing.[19]

'I can't understand why Gandhi, the man who is causing all the trouble, has not been arrested & deported,' the King complained in a letter to his son. 'Are the Government frightened of him or what?' Forster reported the bafflement of the native princes – why couldn't the Prince 'just ask for Gandhi's head upon a charger?' If not, was this what modern monarchy meant? 'Gandhi was still out,' wrote Nehru, 'issuing from day to day messages and directions which inspired the people . . . The Government had not touched him so far, for they feared the consequences, the reactions on the Indian Army and the police.' Viceroy Reading was also aware of the large international press pack travelling with the Prince. The arrest of Gandhi would be global news.[20]

Then, as Nehru wrote, 'the whole scene shifted'. On 5 February 1922 at Chauri Chaura, a village near the border of India and Nepal, a demonstration had turned violent, with stones thrown at the local Indian police, who had responded with gunfire, initially into the air then, when stones and rocks continued to batter them, into the crowd. Eleven people were killed and many more injured. The outnumbered police then retreated to their station, which was set on fire. Just over twenty were burned alive or hacked to death trying to escape. Gandhi, hearing the news and that the crowd had been chanting his name, was mortified. A week later, while on a penitential fast, he called off the non-cooperation campaign.[21]

Although the 'Bardoli Resolution' that officially ended passive resistance was passed by the Congress Working Committee, Nehru and many other Congress and Khilafat leaders were angry and disappointed at what Nehru called 'the stoppage of our struggle at a time when we seemed to be consolidating our position and advancing on all fronts'. All because 'an excited crowd of peasants . . . had attacked a police outpost, set fire to it, and killed a few policemen who were there'. But for Gandhi, the 'brutal murder' was the last straw after the violence in Bombay, Madras and elsewhere. 'Our people', he wrote to Nehru in prison, 'were getting out of hand and were not non-violent in demeanour.' Nehru, for his part, blamed the general violence on 'numerous agent provocateurs, stool pigeons and the like who crept into our movement' who 'indulged in violence themselves or induced others to do so'. But he also admitted that with 'almost all our good men in prison', 'organisation and discipline was disappearing'.[22]

Just as news of the Bardoli Resolution was reaching London, Tory 'die-hard' MP and former Dyer supporter Sir William Joynson-Hicks moved a vote of censure in the House of Commons on Montagu, accusing him of 'criminal betrayal of every white man and white woman in India'. Montagu, Joynson-Hicks said, held the opinion that 'a Government, though bad, if free is better than a Government, though good, if autocratic'. Hicks' own view and that of his friends, he went on, was that 'in a country like India it is far more important to give them good government, though it be autocratic, than to give them free government'. After all, there had been no trouble in the autocratic Native States: 'It is the form of Government that India has had for 2,000 years. It is the form of Government that India understands.'[23]

He then accused Montagu of encouraging the extremist party and 'his friend' Gandhi, in effect siding with the 1.5 million educated people in trying to stir up the 300 million illiterates to discontent. 'The position of affairs during the Prince of Wales's visit is now becoming known,' he said, before reading a letter from a Calcutta insurance broker working for a British company, who alleged that 'the "Raj" ceases to exist here and Swaraj mob or Khilafat rule takes its place'. It was time, Hicks concluded, for the imposition of proper law and order.[24]

He was seconded by fellow hardline Conservative Rupert Gwynne, who had also defended Dyer. Gwynne pointed out that since the beginning of the reform process there had 'been more bloodshed, more disturbance, and more destruction of property than in the preceding 60 years under the old cumbrous system'. Why hadn't Gandhi been arrested? he asked. The view that Montagu's 'continued occupancy of his position is a grave peril to the country and the Empire, is held by a great many Members of this House', he concluded.[25]

Montagu's reply was somewhat faltering: Gandhi was about to be arrested until he called off non-cooperation. Law and order in India was the responsibility of the Viceroy and provincial Governors, who had to be trusted to know what they were doing. No further reforms would be granted until India had proved itself worthy, which was a long way off.

The Prime Minister Lloyd George stressed his government's commitment to its 'trusteeship' in India. 'If Britain withdrew her strong hand,' he said, 'there would be chaos, confusion, and desolation indescribable. Anyone who reads the history of India just before we went there can see that.' There was no question of 'fully-fledged' democracy in India any time soon. After all, he said, democracy was only a recent experiment in the West. His support for his Secretary of State, however, was less than fulsome.[26]

Just over three weeks later, Montagu was gone. The pretext for his forced resignation on 9 March was a technical issue about the publication of a private memorandum. In reality, it was about Lloyd George appeasing the Conservative right at a time when his coalition was looking fragile. Montagu's view was that his head had been presented on a charger to the die-hards. They had never liked his reforms, his Jewishness or his seeming inability or unwillingness to forcibly suppress the non-cooperation movement. The humiliation of the Prince at the hands of the nationalists had been the final straw.

Srinivasa Sastri, the moderate Indian politician who had sincerely wanted to make the Montagu Reforms work, was disconsolate at the resignation. 'In the long history of our British connection, no one has loved India more, no one has sacrificed more for her,' he wrote. 'No one . . . has had a more thorough or sympathetic knowledge and appreciation of her problems or her ambitions.'[27]

According to Montagu's wife, when he resigned his office 'he seemed, in saying good-bye to his work for India, to lose the greater part of his interest in life; he was never the same man again'. An official in the India Office encountered him in the House of Commons, 'wandering about in a homeless and friendless kind of way ... A tragic figure.' He would die from causes unknown just over a year and a half later, at the age of forty-five.[28]

The day after Montagu's resignation, Gandhi was arrested at last. With civil resistance stopped, and non-cooperation wilting away, Nehru wrote, 'after many months of strain and anxiety the Government breathed again, and for the first time had the opportunity of taking the initiative'. Gandhi was tried for sedition for articles he had written for *Young India* over the past two years and sentenced to six years in prison.

The day before the trial, the Prince had embarked from Karachi. 'The feeling of relief is predominant,' reported the journalist from the *Statesman*. 'The authorities ran the gravest risks in bringing His Royal Highness to India, and it is a matter of universal congratulation that nothing in the nature of a direct personal outrage has marred the success of the tour.' Nonetheless, it had demonstrated the acute unpopularity of the British in India. 'The reception accorded to his royal highness has been such as to make every true friend of this country hang his head in shame,' the journalist concluded.[29]

Safely ensconced on ship en route to Colombo, Ceylon, the Prince wrote of his 'great relief'. 'It has all been very tricky indeed,' he informed the King, 'and the uncertainty of a good welcome at each place was rather a strain.' However, he was delighted by the 'splendid news' of the fall of Montagu, 'that despicable man' who had 'given in and pandered to the natives', and the arrest of Gandhi – 'two events [that] are easily the best things that have happened to India for many years'. Gandhi's long prison term was further cause for celebration: 'We shan't hear any more of Gandhi for 6 years by which time he may be forgotten!'[30]

Montagu's replacement, who despite the change of government would still be Secretary of State for India in September 1923, was Conservative peer Viscount Peel. He inherited a very different situation in India from that of the 'glorious page' of 1921.

Lord Lytton, Governor of Bengal, wrote to London in August 1922 that since March the atmosphere had begun to change. 'Everything has been calm and quiet,' he reported. The monsoon had been good, crops were promising, agitation had died down, and 'the non-cooperation movement has completely collapsed since the arrest of Gandhi'.[31]

Gandhi's cancellation of the non-cooperation campaign in February had had the effect of reopening the partially closed breach between moderates and 'extremists' in Congress, as well as schisms in the ranks of the non-cooperators themselves. With the removal from the political arena of Gandhi in March, the various elements in the Congress which his personality had held together began to disintegrate. Most seriously, with the end of the close cooperation between Gandhi and the Ali brothers, who were also for now still in jail, relations between Hindus and Muslims became strained.

In his intelligence report, Bamford described the disappointment among Muslims at the Bardoli Resolution, and how 'almost immediately signs of Hindu-Muslim friction appeared'. Muslims felt they had been exploited 'merely to further the Hindu aim of Swaraj', Bamford reported. There was a joke circulating in the Punjab: Swaraj meant Swab ('ashes') for the Muhammadans and Raj for the Hindus.[32]

From his prison cell, Jawaharlal Nehru looked on in dismay. The end of non-cooperation had 'brought about a certain demoralisation'. Now 'the fine ideals of the movement . . . were being swamped by petty squabbles and intrigues for power'.[33]

Both Nehru and his father had been sentenced to six months, Motilal for being an illegal volunteer, Jawaharlal for promoting the hartal. As political prisoners they were kept separate from ordinary criminals. In fact, the Nehrus and two of their cousins had their own shed, about 20 by 16 feet. They were allowed to receive books, clothes and food, as well as regular visitors from outside. After three months, the sentence on Jawaharlal was overturned and he was released. But six weeks later he was back in prison, this time on a sentence just short of two years for having picketed a merchant in Allahabad who had been selling imported cloth. At his trial he had declared, 'I shall go to jail again most willingly and joyfully.'[34]

His father was no longer there and this time the rules were stricter and the conditions much more cramped – less moving around was allowed and he was in a barrack of fifty men. He found the lack of privacy hard to endure, but made every effort to keep himself mentally and physically fit, exercising as much as possible and reading voraciously – British and Indian history, as well as English poetry and essays; also Dickens, Turgenev and Tolstoy, and, somewhat surprisingly, the *Harrow Association Record*.

Meanwhile, both Congress and the Khilafat Committee were carrying out inquiries into the workings and success or otherwise of the non-cooperation campaign. Their findings were far from unanimous, but it was generally agreed by both investigations that the campaign had failed, and that India had not been ready to take this path. Least successful was the call for the return of titles: of the 5,186 Indian title holders, only twenty-four had resigned their honours. Very few government servants had left their posts, even when under heavy social pressure. Some 200 lawyers had withdrawn their services, but the legal system continued to function, and the alternative arbitration courts generally had a short life, in part because they had insufficient authority to enforce their orders. Most barristers soon returned to work in the mainstream courts, 'after the pinch of want was felt'. The temperance campaign, although badly affecting government income from duties in some places, had led to a sharp rise in the manufacture of illicit liquor.[35]

More successful was the boycotting of imported cloth and the surge in home-spinning. But this was in part due to post-war overstocking and the steep decline in Indian purchasing power at the time. Imports soon resumed. Although many students had withdrawn from government-backed institutions, and there was widespread establishment of 'National' schools, these had suffered from poor discipline, and in terms of curricula made no real break from that prescribed by the Education Department.[36]

With the publication of the reports at the end of 1922 (the Congress one being written by Motilal Nehru), nationalist leaders began to look round for a different approach. Deshbandhu Das started to argue that Congress should participate in the next elections, due in November 1923, and won the support of Motilal Nehru. The aim was to secure control of the legislatures, and then wreck them from within. When this policy was defeated in a Congress vote, at the beginning of 1923 they formed the Swaraj Party.[37]

The issue of participation in the elections now split the nationalist movement in two. 'No changers' argued that it would confuse the masses, and could lead to collaboration. 'Changers' pointed out that the alternative approach had failed, and there was no other way forward. This sharp disunity saw donations to Congress funds slump dramatically and membership fall away.[38]

By 1923, the Khilafat movement was in similar disarray. There was the same deep division over council entry, and the organisation had also suffered from serious allegations of the misappropriation of funds.

Kemal Pasha's victory over the Greeks in August 1922 had been celebrated across Muslim India. Kemal, it was declared, was 'a hero at the head of a band of heroes' who had saved the Khilafat from ignominy and shame. But in November, Kemal deposed the Sultan and removed all non-spiritual power from the position. (In 1924, it would be abolished altogether.) This, Bamford wrote, 'completely took the wind out of the sails of the agitators'. 'Ordinary people', he reported, 'see Kemal Pasha as a viper whom they have cherished in their bosoms and who rewarded them by removing their spiritual head.' Freedom of the holy places from foreign influence and control remained an issue, but this was now 'confined to the irreconcilable extremists'.[39]

At the same time, there was growing suspicion of Congress among Muslims, and general disengagement. In 1921, nearly 11 per cent of Congress delegates were Muslim; by 1923 it was under 4 per cent. This was mirrored on the ground. In March and April 1923 there were serious communal riots in Amritsar, Multan and other places in the Punjab. More followed in May; through June and July there were riots in Muradabad and Meerut, Allahabad and Ajmer. All created tit-for-tat communal hatred, and a cycle of violence, recrimination and retaliation. Alongside this there sprang up new religious groups aimed at converting Muslims to Hinduism and vice versa.[40]

Jawaharlal Nehru was released from prison at the end of January 1923. As ever, he was sickened by the inroads religion was making into politics. On both sides, he explained, 'political reactionaries' had emerged as 'the principal communal leaders'. 'We seem to have drifted back to a state of affairs which prevailed in Europe during the dark ages when to think rationally was considered an evil,' he told a UP conference near the end of 1923. 'I think it is time for persons who wish to regard ... the exercise of rational thought as essential for human progress, to protest with all their might against all kinds of bigotry and superstition.'[41]

For much of 1923 Nehru was involved with municipal work in Allahabad. He also had a role in the central Congress organisation, where he tried unsuccessfully to heal the rift over council entry, while urging more training and discipline for party workers. But he also spent much more time with his family and went about his work, he admitted, 'with something of [an] air of detachment'. In August, his father was unwell. Jawaharlal wrote to a friend, 'I am weary and sick at heart.' In September, as we've seen, he was arrested at Jaito. Although soon released, he came away with a nasty case of typhus from the prison, which would lay him low for some months.[42]

September 1923 also saw a special session of Congress at Delhi to resolve the issue of council entry before the elections in November. Thanks in part to the acquiescence of Mohammad Ali, who had just been released from prison, Das secured support for his Swaraj Party contesting the elections. Ali did, however, express his concern 'about the Councils capturing the Swarajists instead of the reverse'. Furthermore, Das, hoping to attract moderate votes, now argued that instead of simply wrecking, government resolutions deemed 'for public good' should not be opposed.[43]

Reporting the Congress, *The Times* noted 'a spate of treasonable chatter' and 'extravagant speeches' that called on a 'manifestation of national will as in the French revolution'. If you didn't know the 'character of the Indian intelligentsia', it went on, 'you would be amazed at the apparent weakness of the Government of India, who permit the open formulation of revolutionary schemes under their very noses in their new capital'. But those in the know 'understand and appreciate the patience exercised by its Government' because '99 per cent of all this torrent of treason that is poured forth at the National Congress is only froth and bubble'. Congress was divided, and 'farther than ever from practical politics'. Civil disobedience 'is quite dead'.[44]

The real danger, *The Times* suggested, was not the attempt to capture and wreck the councils, but in 'the recrudescence of the old communal antagonism between Hindu and Moslem ... There have been many deplorable instances of friction between the communities.' At the Congress itself there were serious quarrels between Hindu and Muslim volunteers, which on one night ended in a fracas. *Current History* magazine reported communal rioting in September at Saharanpur and Gonda, at Agra, Calcutta, Ahmedabad, Amritsar and Nellore, the last between Sunni and Shiite Muslims.[45]

With 'the fundamental cleavage between Hindu and Moslem as wide as ever', *The Times* concluded, only the 'guiding hand of British administration' was preventing 'disastrous developments'. As long as the division continued, it must 'not only justify, but necessitate, the continuance of strong British control in India'. Nehru's version of this was slightly different: 'Divide and rule has always been the way of empires.'[46]

But even the *Daily Herald*, while explaining that a Labour government would aid and foster self-government, warned that 'it was not the business of the British democracy to aid the disintegration of India, which would assuredly happen without efficient government and defence, or to leave Indian agriculturalists to the tender mercies of money-lenders and capitalists ... Socialists should avoid the danger of acclaiming every wave of India unrest as a welcome factor in world revolution.'[47]

Bamford ended his intelligence report with positive news for the British authorities. Good crops and improved economic conditions had damped down agitation, now 'confined (except in Burma) to the comparatively small irreconcilable elements from which every country, to a greater or lesser extent, suffers'. Back in 1921, he wrote, Gandhi 'had raised all India to a pitch of enthusiasm and united effort which it had never attained previously and which – with its widely divergent communal interests – it will possibly never reach again'. Jawaharlal Nehru came to the same conclusion. 'Our movement was at a low ebb,' he wrote of the situation in late 1923. 'The magic moment had passed.'[48]

19

Chinese Malaya

We, men of Kwangtung and Fukien, remote from
our homesteads, join in spirit in longing for our dear
fatherland. Still resting here, united and happy, in
the State of Selangor. We feel joy in the land of our
adoption, the mother of our trade.

Chinese community leaders' address to a departing
British colonial officer, Kuala Lumpur[1]

Battered by their experience in India, the Prince of Wales's party
were anxious as they neared Malaya. There were rumours
of rebellion: that the powerful Chinese Triad gangs were going to
kidnap the Prince; that the large Indian population were planning a
fresh hartal.[2]

The *Renown* anchored off Port Swettenham just after lunch, and at
tea-time the High Commissioner of the Federated Malay States (FMS)
and Governor of the Straits Settlements Sir Laurence Guillemard – 'a
nice old man', according to Dickie Mountbatten – came on board to
pay his official call. Soon after that the Prince and his entourage were
barged to the shore, where they were met by the 'usual notables' and

the four Sultans of the Federated States – Perak, Selangor, Negri (now Negeri) Sembilan and Pahang. All were closely accompanied by their British Residents. Dickie was impressed with the Malay royalty's jewels and, in particular, their 'solid gold lace trousers'. Thereafter they drove in a cavalcade the 30 miles to Kuala Lumpur, the capital of the FMS. The Prince was accompanied by the Sultan of Perak, 'who was educated at Oxford and is quite a nice little fellow', Mountbatten noted in his diary.[3]

According to an accompanying Australian journalist, there had been no need to worry about the loyalty of this particular part of the empire. In spite of the 'blistering heat', which, he reported, was far greater than in India, along all of the 'perfect English road' every wayside habitation was hung out with flags, and the occupants gathered in the verandas or on the roadside in their best clothes. For the first part of the journey Indians predominated, but the Chinese increased in numbers steadily as the party neared the capital, until the Prince found himself driving slowly through streets flanked by modern, well-built houses tenanted wholly by Chinese. It might have been 'a bit of China itself'. All were dressed in their best silks and bowed politely as the cars passed.[4]

That evening a ball was held at the centre of the British community, the mock-Tudor Selangor Club. Pretty much the entire 'European' contingent was in attendance, with the ballroom cooled by huge blocks of ice, into which fresh flowers had been frozen. The Prince stopped the dancing when a Chinese torch-lit procession paraded outside its windows, with crawling dragons, a car full of Chinese beauty queens, and companies of children carrying lighted lanterns.[5]

The following morning, most of the party motored to a rubber plantation – the key, now, to the colony's extraordinary wealth and importance. Here there were 'miles and miles of systematically planted rubber trees'. For Dickie, 'the view became distinctly monotonous after a few miles', the boredom only alleviated through watching the Indian 'coolies' laboriously tapping the trees.[6]

The *Renown* now moved on to Singapore, where the Prince and his party found that the seats of the cars waiting for them were so hot that

SIAM

PERLIS

KEDAH

PENANG
George Town

*Indian
Ocean*

Taiping
Kuala Kangsar
Ipoh
PERAK

KELANTAN

*South
China Sea*

Kota Bharu

TERENGGANU

Kuala Terengganu

Kuala Lipis

M A L A Y A

PAHANG

Kuantan

SELANGOR

Port Swettenham   Kuala Lumpur

NEGRI
SEMBILAN

Port Dickson

Straits of Malacca

MALACCA

Malacca

JOHOR

Sumatra
(Dutch East Indies)

Johor

Singapore

0 _____ 100 miles
0 _____ 100 km

MALAYA

they were impossible to sit on; instead, Mountbatten wrote, they had 'to crouch above them trying to look unconcerned'. Here, the Prince met the hugely wealthy office bearers of the Chinese Chamber of Commerce, and was greeted with another Chinese torch-lit procession.

The Rajas aside, the only Malays presented to the Prince were 'tribal dancers', '400 wild warriors from Borneo', wearing jackets covered with fish skin and 'strange necklaces of bones, shells and stones', who chanted a welcome while brandishing their spears.

To coincide with the Prince's visit there was a 'Malaya-Borneo exhibition'. This emphasised 'native' traditional production by Malays and Dyaks over the activities of the large immigrant populations from India and China. The stress was on romantic primitivism. In pride of place was a replica 'native' village of straw huts built on stilts. Dickie, ever on the lookout for touristy knick-knacks, purchased a 'genuine old Malay *kris* from Perak and a small war gong from Brunei'.[7]

It was a very brief visit, as Mountbatten conceded. But in that short time what he had seen – the Indian 'coolies' grindingly tapping rubber, the impressive Chinese Chamber of Commerce, the bejewelled Malay Rajas, with the rest of the Malay population portrayed as backward peasants – provided a revealing snapshot of the huge complexity and strangeness of this, the empire's richest colony. It was impossible to ignore that in the areas they visited, in particular the towns and cities, the huge bulk of the population, of every class, was, bizarrely, not Malay but Chinese. As the tour's official account noted, the most striking impression was how 'the Chinese predominate'.[8]

The colonisation of Malaya is foremost a Chinese story. A thousand years before the first European penetration of the Malaya region, the Chinese were there, in the shape of Buddhist pilgrims. These were followed by Chinese traders, diplomats and pirates. The first firm report of Chinese settlement in Malaya comes in 1349, from a trader who found Chinese living on the island of Tumasik, later known as Singapore.[9]

For now, however, the key regional strategic position was Malacca, with a fine port and astride one of the narrowest points of the Straits of Malacca. Founded in around 1400, Malacca soon became a thriving entrepôt for the trading of goods from China, India, Arabia and the Indonesian archipelago, including spices, porcelain, tea, sandalwood, musk, pearls and fabrics. Malacca trade was dominated by the Chinese, and some settled there.

Malay-Chinese relations were not always happy, however. The Sultan exacted heavy tolls on the merchants, who also suffered from occasional ill treatment ashore. So when a Portuguese fleet arrived in 1511 to attack the town, the five Chinese junks in the harbour sided with the invaders and helped ferry the European troops ashore.

The Portuguese in Malaya found a multi-ethnic community, built up by the ebb and flow of local empires and extensive trading networks. By the late sixteenth century Malacca had a sizeable Chinese population, with their own district and a 'Kapitan Cina' to manage the community and represent its interests. But Portuguese attempts to run the entrepôt as an exclusive monopoly led to most Chinese and Arabic traders going elsewhere. By the time the Dutch conquered the city in 1641 there were only around 300 Chinese still living there.

For the Chinese, it wasn't much better under Dutch control. The monopolistic policy of the Portuguese was continued; all trade was to be in the hands of the VOC Company, with only meagre commissions on offer. By the time of a census in 1678 there were still only 500 to 700 Chinese in or around the town, although they were comparatively prosperous: making up only 10 to 15 per cent of the population, they owned at least a quarter of the town's buildings and enslaved people.[10]

'The country must have a larger population,' the Dutch Governor of the town declared, 'especially of industrious Chinese.' He wanted farmers as well as traders. The local Malays, he regretted, were 'too inert, idle and lazy'. Chinese merchants were certainly weakened by the trade restrictions, but they still had better contacts, and unrestricted access to Chinese ports, unlike their European competitors. By 1750, the Chinese population of Malacca had increased to over 2,000. A new arrival a few years later was Tan Hay Kwan, the great-great-grandfather of Tan Cheng Lock, who would be the leader of the

Chinese community in Malaya in September 1923. Tan Hay Kwan
was from a wealthy family in Fukien Province. Migrating to Malacca,
he quickly established a flourishing junk trade in the Straits of Malacca
and the wider Indonesian archipelago.[11]

Tan would live to see the Dutch supplanted in Malacca and across
the Malay Peninsula. Their policy of restricting trade killed the goose
that laid the golden eggs, and by the end of the eighteenth century the
Dutch East India Company was bankrupt, in no small part because of
their inability to prevent the smuggling of goods out of the region by
merchants of the rival English East India Company.

The establishment – under the aegis of this company – of Penang by
Captain Francis Light in 1786 and of Singapore by Stamford Raffles
in 1819 had a huge impact on Chinese trade and settlement in Malaya.
After only a year there were sixty Chinese families in Penang, and the
shops in the bazaar were almost all run by them. By 1794 there were
3,000 Chinese, described by Light as 'the most valuable of our inhabitants', useful as planters, traders and artisans. Only ten years later,
the Chinese population had increased a further four-fold, making up
nearly half the town's inhabitants.[12]

Crucially, the Chinese were, according to Light, the 'only people
of the east from whom a revenue may be raised without expense
and extraordinary efforts'. They were 'indefatigable in the pursuit of
money, and like the Europeans, they spend it in purchasing those articles which gratify their appetites'. They were also 'excessively fond of
gaming'. 'Farms' were established for opium and gambling. Under this
system, the right to collect agreed levels of taxes for the consumption
of certain commodities was given to the highest bidders, who made
their profits by collecting more revenue than was required to cover the
costs of buying and running. For the English, it avoided the difficulty
of collecting direct taxation from an alien and largely transient population, and most importantly was fabulously lucrative: these farms
soon provided over half the colony's revenue. This allowed the English
to reduce import duties to next to nothing, which further stimulated
trade and immigration.[13]

The case of Singapore was even more dramatic. Established from the outset on the principle of free trade, it was an instant success as an entrepôt and grew rapidly. According to an early leader of the colony, the Chinese formed not only the largest but the 'most industrious and useful portion of the Asiatic part of the population'. Peerless as traders and artisans, the Chinese soon dominated agriculture as well. By 1860 there were 50,000 Chinese in Singapore, against 13,000 Indians, 11,000 Malays and 2,500 Europeans and North Americans.[14]

Looking back at early Singapore during the 1919 celebrations of its centenary, a spokesman for the Chinese Chamber of Commerce expressed his community's 'admiration of the sterling qualities of foresight and fortitude of that great Empire-builder, Sir Stamford Raffles'. Unlike the Portuguese and the Dutch, Raffles had 'no narrow-minded spirit'. Instead he made the port 'a free one ... throwing open its portals to every nationality, granting equal rights and equal opportunities to all'. A British historian of the early development of Malaya, in a book published in 1925, concluded that the Chinese had demonstrated a 'strong partiality for British rule ... They keenly appreciated the security, justice and freedom from molestation which they enjoyed in British territory.'[15]

In 1824, Malacca was handed over to the British as part of a deal that divided up local spheres of interest. Two years later, the port settlements of Penang, Singapore and Malacca were combined to form the Straits Settlements. In 1841, Hong Kong was annexed, creating a Penang–Singapore–Hong Kong axis. In 1867, after the effective nationalisation of the English East India Company, the Straits Settlements became a British Crown Colony, and all their cosmopolitan inhabitants British subjects.

In Malacca, Tan Choon Bock, the grandson of the Tan family pioneer, would expand the family business and, when the traditional junk became obsolete, move his operation into steamships. He refused to tender for the gambling and opium farms, as he believed it to be tainted money. Nonetheless, he was wealthy enough to buy a Dutch-era mansion in Heeren Street, literally the 'Street of Gentlemen' but referred to locally as the 'Street of Millionaires'. (It has now been renamed after his grandson Tan Cheng Lock.) As with the other Straits Settlements ports there was free trade, and fresh Chinese migrants, suffering at home from unemployment, landlord exploitation and overpopulation, continued to pour in.[16]

As early as 1815 Chinese tin miners had arrived in Lakut in Selangor. The Malayan Peninsula had one of the richest remaining seams of this rare and important metal, and the industry quickly expanded over the following decades. The Malay rulers, with sparse populations mainly involved in subsistence agriculture and fishing, were encouraging – to exploit these resources they needed capital and labour, and the Chinese had plenty of both. By the 1860s there were Chinese mining settlements all across the south-western states, with the new town of Kuala Lumpur among the largest. Losses to malaria were colossal – at one newly cleared mining site, all but eighteen of a party of eighty-seven were killed within a month. But new arrivals made up the numbers. The Malay rulers left the leading Chinese entrepreneurs, appointed Kapitan Cina, to their own devices, including running farms for gambling, opium, pawnbroking and liquor, as well as maintaining law and order and building infrastructure.[17]

Some of the huge migration of Chinese into Malaya came from kinship – a family member would establish a foothold and then recruit relatives for business operations. But the majority was through the credit ticket system, known as the 'coolie trade', whereby workers would be recruited by labour brokers, agencies (both Chinese and European) or just the captain of a junk, who would pay their passage. Arriving at Penang or Singapore, the worker would be effectively sold to an employer, and be required to work for them at whatever wage they cared to fix, until the debt was paid off. The 'coolie trade' was characterised by inhumane treatment during recruitment as well as transportation and in the final labour destination. The 'coolies' were known as *Chue Tsai*, or 'piglets'. The system was described as the 'pig business'.

*

The British authorities of the Straits Settlements, now reporting to the Colonial Office, had inherited from the English East India Company a policy of strict non-interference in mainland Malaya. The combination of factors – commercial, strategic, humanitarian, the 'man on the spot' – that led to this policy being reversed after 1870 and the peninsula being effectively brought into the empire reads almost as a tick-list for how, sometimes for contradictory reasons, so much of the world had come to be coloured red by late 1923. Some are particular to the region, for sure, but most can be applied in different proportions across the history of the vast empire of September 1923.

The Chinese-driven tin boom meant certain areas of land suddenly for the first time became hugely valuable, turbo-charging local rivalries as well as succession disputes among the Malay royalty, aristocracy and local chiefs. In the late 1860s and early 1870s there was bloodshed in Perak over a succession dispute and a civil war in Selangor as rival alliances of Chinese and Malays fought for control of the tin mines. On several occasions the conflict spread to Penang and Singapore in the form of clashes between rival Chinese gangs. Meanwhile, the French were tightening their grip on Indo-China, and there were concerns that they, or another rival power, could use the chaotic situation as a reason to step in to 'restore order'.[18]

As tin production collapsed, Chinese and European commercial interests in the Straits Settlements urged the colonial government to intervene. A group of British entrepreneurs had acquired tin concessions from the Viceroy of Selangor, and asked for peace to be restored and 'stable government' established for them to be able to develop them.

After much vacillation, the Colonial Secretary instructed the Governor to report on conditions in the Malay States to discover if the British could play a part in restoring peace. Going far beyond these cautious instructions, the Governor arbitrated a settlement, and in 1874 installed British Residents in the south-western states of Perak, Selangor and part of what would become Negri Sembilan. These were now 'protectorates'. The Sultans and senior chiefs were instructed to act on advice from their Resident in all questions other than those 'touching Malay Religion and custom'. This included handing over control of revenue, which would now fund a civil list for the Sultans and senior chiefs. A brief flurry of armed resistance was defeated by British troops. After a decade of banditry and bloodshed, peace and law and order was imposed.

The spread of 'Pax Britannica' now took on a momentum of its own; once the British had decided to 'pacify' and take under their protection the south-western states they could not stop there, leaving 'unquiet frontiers'. Over the course of the next thirty years the process of installing British Residents was extended north, south and east, until the entire peninsula was under British control. Among the first actions of the Residents was to end the 'tyrannical' practices of debt-slavery and compulsory labour in the states, issues that had irked humanitarians in the Straits Settlements and back in Britain. They would also gradually implement much-needed sanitation and anti-malaria measures in the towns. With peace and the rule of law established, in theory, the resources of the peninsula were now ripe for easy exploitation.

Travel writer Isabella Bird was in Malaya in 1879. 'Whatever enterprise I hear of in the interior is always in the hands of Chinamen,' she wrote; 'the more I see of them the more I am impressed by them. These States would be jungles with a few rice clearings among them were it not for their energy and industry.' Well into the twentieth century, almost all the richest men in the Malay States were Chinese. Yap Swan Seng had arrived in Malaya from China in 1864 and worked as a tin miner in Negri Sembilan before moving to Kuala Lumpur in 1870, where he soon owned a string of mines and employed over 7,000 'coolies'. His residence occupied the greater part of a street in the town. He became the town's Kapitan Cina in 1889. He was conspicuously loyal to the empire, donating $10,000 during the South African War to the Transvaal War Fund, and also gave considerable funds to supporting healthcare for the poor of Kuala Lumpur.[19]

The newly rich Chinese tin barons competed to travel around in the smartest carriages and to fund the most expensive religious processions and temples, but most also used their wealth to acquire more Westernised lifestyles, buying European or American furniture, clothes and cars, and hiring European architects to design their new houses. For the very richest, only marble imported from Italy would do. Most spectacular, and still standing in downtown Kuala Lumpur, was the 'villa residence' of Loke Yew. As a humble farmhand, he had emigrated to Malaya aged thirteen to seek his fortune. Having worked ferociously hard in a shop in Singapore, he had invested his savings in a mine in Perak and struck a rich seam. Arriving in Kuala Lumpur in the late 1880s, he invested in numerous ventures, including Tan Choon Bock's Malacca-based Straits Steamship Company, and took over the farms for gambling, liquor, pawnbroking and opium. In 1889 he went into partnership on a number of tin mines with the most prominent and wealthy member of Malaya's Indian Tamil community. K. Thamboosamy Pillai had been born in Singapore in 1850 and came to Selangor in 1875 working as a clerk for the first British Resident. He rose to become state treasurer and then left government service to work in tin mining with Loke Yew, as well as investing in real estate, money-lending and construction.[20]

Loke Yew went against Chinese custom of the time in that he was a serial monogamist. He had four wives one after the other and eleven children, several of whom were sent to Aberdeen in Scotland to be educated. He was also unusual in that he considered his daughters' education to be as important as his sons'.[21]

Education in Kuala Lumpur was an unsatisfactory and inadequate hodge-podge. The original Chinese school, catering to many different dialects, was mired in disputes about which Chinese language should be used. There was a tiny school for the sons of Malay royalty and aristocrats. The first English-language school in Kuala Lumpur had been set up by an English vicar, but in 1892 it only had thirty-eight pupils (twenty-five Chinese, three Tamil, two Malay, six Eurasian, two Sinhalese).

In late 1892, Loke Yew, K. Thamboosamy Pillai and Kapitan Cina Yap Swan Seng convened a public meeting calling for the establishment of an English secondary school. They each promised to contribute

$1,000. Supported by the Sultan of Selangor and the colonial government, the new Victoria Institution was opened in 1894 with just under 200 pupils – 104 Chinese, sixty Indian, twenty-four Eurasian and ten Malay. Thereafter it expanded rapidly. Neither Yap Swan Seng nor Loke Yew spoke English, but they were determined that the next generation would have what was now becoming an essential attribute for government service or the mercantile sector.

This was the peak moment for the Chinese tin millionaires. From 1874 to 1898, Malaya accounted for 55 per cent of global production, and this was dominated by the Chinese. The industry's success drove wider development and mass immigration that transformed the peninsula. Restrictions imposed on Chinese migration to the United States and Canada in the 1880s further increased the appeal of Malaya, where, of course, there was no white working class to complain about being undercut on wages. By 1911, the mining states of Selangor, Perak and Negri Sembilan had more Chinese than Malays. Over the next ten years, up to the census of 1921, 1.5 million Chinese arrived to work in Malaya. Of these just over half a million stayed.[22]

From the earliest days of the British takeover of the Malay States, the Chinese communities found that the British had decidedly ambivalent attitudes to their predominance and economic success. Frank Swettenham, one of the first Residents (none of whom spoke any Chinese language), echoed the admiration of Isabella Bird for the industry of the Chinese. They were, he said, the 'bone and sinew' of the Malay States. Indeed, well into the twentieth century, revenue for the colonial government was almost entirely dependent on the production and consumption of the Chinese, through export duty on tin and taxes on opium and gambling. But this dependence was resented. The Chinese, Swettenham continued, were 'the bees who suck the honey from every profitable undertaking'. It was an affront to the British sentiment of white superiority. 'They must know their master,' Swettenham declared.[23]

Swettenham was a key early figure in the process of Kuala Lumpur changing from being a town entirely controlled and populated by the Chinese into the centre of British colonial power – and British society – in the Malay States. From 1882 he was active, in collaboration with the Kapitan Cina, in installing massive storm drains and anti-malarial works as part of a replanning of the town, with wider streets, brick buildings and a central square or *padang*. Within a few years this square was surrounded by the edifices of imperial power: a church, the government printing press, law courts, the police station and the Secretariat, which from 1896 housed the growing bureaucracy running the newly federated Malay States. On the opposite side of the *padang* stood the Selangor Club, which would be visited by the Prince in 1922. The government buildings and the court were in a 'Saracenic' style, with Arabic-shaped doorways and minarets, in a concession to Malaya's Muslim culture. The club, though, was mock-Tudor. Opening its doors in 1884, it had no racial exclusion; K. Thamboosamy Pillai was a founding member and on the committee for some years. There were also Eurasians and Chinese.[24]

However, the British community, swollen in the 1890s by an influx of coffee planters from Ceylon (where the crop had been wiped out by a fungus), only considered about half a dozen non-Europeans to be their social equals. These included the local Malay Sultan, also Loke Yew, Yap Swan Seng and K. Thamboosamy Pillai. All four had contributed funds to the development of the town, including the new botanical gardens and even the Anglican church. All hosted senior British administrators for lunch at their mansions, one occasion being described as 'highly convivial' and perfect for 'cooking, wines and service'. Pillai's curry tiffins became legendary. Loke Yew and Yap Swan Seng would converse with their British guests in Malay or through interpreters. Records from this time of big European weddings and dances indicate that these four were usually invited. For now, they were still valued for their warm hospitality as well as their wealth and influence in their communities.[25]

But as the town, now connected to the coast by a railway, grew in administrative importance and population – 30,000 by 1900 – dividing lines grew starker. The first British Resident had built his house, for defence reasons, on high ground on the opposite side of the Klang River to the Chinese-Malay settlement. The area around it was later reserved for civil servants, and as they were all white, it became a European enclave. A government-sponsored guide to the Malay States commended Kuala Lumpur as 'it does not require the European and Asiatic to live side by side'. (Illustrating the growing sensitivity about their relations with Asians, this comment, which appeared in the 1920 edition, was expunged for the edition of 1923.)[26]

Early on, a separate European ward was set up in the general hospital, and in 1897 the first hotel catering exclusively for Europeans was opened by the widow of a government officer. Already, a rival to the theoretically colour-blind Selangor Club had been established. The Lake Club, as it was known, excluded all non-Europeans. (It was also very expensive to join, thus shutting out all but the white elite.) A similar process was happening elsewhere. The Perak Club in Taiping had been established in 1881 with government support conditional on it being open to all Europeans and some Eurasians and Asians in government service. In 1891, elite members withdrew to form their own highly expensive white-only New Club, and a visitor noted with regret 'the formal separation of class and caste'.[27]

By 1923 there were only two remaining Chinese members of the Selangor Club, neither active. Asians, particularly if they were not English speakers, had found that they preferred to form their own clubs. In Kuala Lumpur there was a Chinese Athletic Club, and for the very rich the Choon Cheok Kee Loo Club, known by the British as the 'Chinese Millionaires Club'. Luxuriously furnished, it had the highest subscription rate of any club in the town. Tamils had the Tamil Physical Culture Association; Malays had the Sultan Suleiman Club. Under the patronage of Yap Swan Seng, the Chinese community set up its own hospital. It was now a sharply divided population.

20

'A True Malayan Spirit'

Victor Purcell, twice severely wounded in the Great War and a prisoner for its last year, from 1921 spent the entire rest of his career working as a government officer with the Chinese communities of Malaya. He wrote in his history, *The Chinese of Malaya*, that there were important 'obstacles to Chinese understanding of Europeans and vice versa ... the Europeans and Chinese were out of contact with one another in every sphere except that of common material interest'. He noted, with deep regret, that all British opinions expressed 'are concerned with the value or otherwise of the Chinese as merchants, cultivators, or workmen, in fact as persons who might be useful or otherwise to the Europeans who had taken over control of these Malaysian parts'. Nothing was ever expressed, he wrote, of a Chinese person's 'social qualities, his moral refinements, his aesthetic judgments'. 'It is almost hopeless to expect to make friends with a Chinaman,' Swettenham had declared. Indeed, the relationship between the British and the Chinese would increasingly be about rivalry, prejudice and a failure to understand – what a leader of the Chinese community would call 'a lack of sympathy and knowledge'.[1]

From the outset, of course, the British were in competition with the Chinese for the rich trade and resources of Malaya. For all the

brilliance of Chinese entrepreneurship, and their early privileged control of cheap and effective labour, the British had two key advantages:
better access to capital and to modern machinery, and the fact that,
ultimately, they now held the levers of power.

It suited the colonial authorities initially to allow the Chinese to
continue to run the financial and bodily risks of pioneering tin extraction, policing their communities and managing the complicated task
of collecting tax revenue. But as the British bureaucracy grew, and
the country was sanitised and opened up by railways and roads, the
Chinese found themselves increasingly pushed into subordinate roles,
politically and commercially.

Agency houses representing London companies had been set up
in Singapore and Penang in the late 1820s and 1830s. They soon
expanded into the entrepôt trade as well as finance, shipping, mining
and plantation agriculture. Many of the Chinese 'merchant kings'
found themselves relegated to middle men between the Europeans and
local producers. (The Malacca-based Tan family steamship business
was taken over by a European company; by 1923 shipping in Singapore
was dominated by British companies.)[2]

Not all European attempts to challenge Chinese dominance succeeded. In the 1880s there was a determined effort to take over some
of the amazingly lucrative tin business. But the Europeans lacked the
Chinese prospecting experience as well as easy access to the essential
Chinese labour, at that time controlled by *Kongsis* (what the Europeans
called 'secret societies'). They also had excessive overhead costs for their
European managers. Most sustained huge losses.

Nonetheless, inroads were made over the next decades. As surface
deposits were exhausted, tin extraction at a deeper level came to require
large, expensive equipment, and the Europeans' readier access to capital began to tell. Eu Tong Sen, the largest mine-owner in Perak with
a labour force of 12,000, was part of a group of Chinese businessmen
who in 1907 tried to float their Eastern Smelting Co. in the London
market to raise capital for mechanisation and to expand their foundry.
That the effort failed was attributed to the composition of the board

of directors, including Eu, who were 'exclusively Asiatic'; the company was eventually sold to British interests in 1911. By then the Chinese still controlled over three quarters of the tin business, but by the mid-1920s this was down to under a half.[3]

By this time, rubber had narrowly supplanted tin as the key export from Malaya. In the late 1870s seedlings had been brought from Brazil, via Kew, and planted in the botanical gardens of Singapore and Kuala Kangsar, Perak, then offered to British ex-coffee planters in Selangor. However, they showed no interest and so pioneering the new crop would fall to Tan Chay Yan, a kinsman of the Malacca Tan family. In 1895, he planted Malaya's first commercial rubber estate on 40 acres near Malacca. Three years later, he formed a syndicate of Straits Chinese and planted several thousand acres nearby.[4]

Driven by the expansion of the United States automobile industry, the price of rubber doubled in five years after 1900, and British investors piled in. From 6,000 acres in 1900, land planted in rubber rose to over a million in 1913. By 1923 Malaya was responsible for half the world's rubber production, 75 per cent of which went to the United States.[5]

Chinese entrepreneurs from Malacca, Singapore and Kuala Lumpur, including Loke Yew, were behind much of the expansion, but three fifths of the larger estates were under European management and control by 1923. It was capital intensive: it required five to seven years after planting for the trees to become productive, and here again European merchant houses in Singapore and Penang had greater access to the money of the London market. This meant that most investment came from Britain. In addition, the colonial government, in handing out generous loans and the best land near railways or major roads, privileged European, particularly British, companies. It also set up a Tamil Immigration Fund to stimulate and organise recruitment of estate workers. In fact, for a while the British had favoured Indian 'coolies', 'creatures far more amenable to discipline and management' than the 'sturdy and independent' Chinese, as one British planter pronounced. (It had been Kuala Lumpur's K. Thamboosamy Pillai, of curry tiffin fame, who back in the 1880s had been contracted to bring over the first tranche of Indian workers to build the railways.) By 1923, nearly 80 per cent of the labour on rubber plantations was from southern India. The clear message was that the Chinese no longer had a monopoly on the importation of cheap labour.

Rubber was now about wider imperial policy, about the point of the empire. It generated wealth for British companies and their shareholders (some enjoying staggering dividends of up to 300 per cent); it also provided a strategically essential product in times of war, and in times of peace a crucial source of overseas credit in the shape of US dollars. When the price fell a little in 1921–2, the scheme to reduce output and thus – successfully – to raise the price was engineered to benefit European companies over Chinese producers.[6]

A parallel process had been underway to assert British colonial political control and, for various reasons, to enforce stricter racial boundaries. The 'farms' for opium, gambling and so on were gradually abolished and revenue-raising transferred to British bureaucrats. The 'secret societies' were broken up and legislation introduced to reform the 'coolie trade' which, while satisfying humanitarian demands from all quarters, further loosened the Chinese grip on labour supply. The Kapitan Cina position was abolished. State councils, consisting of Malay aristocrats, Chinese leaders and British officials, were created, along with sanitary and municipal boards and later legislative councils for the Federated Malay States and Straits Settlements, again with appointed members from the various communities. But all were from the outset controlled by the British and there was a process of the Chinese finding themselves dislodged from key positions and consulted less and less.

Originally, Europeans had prided themselves that compared to the southern United States and other parts of the British Empire, in particular South Africa, there was relatively little overt racial segregation in Malaya. Trains, government rest houses, churches and most hotels were not segregated. In the Singapore Raffles Hotel, established and run by the Armenian Sarkie brothers, non-Europeans ate in the same dining room as Europeans, but were not allowed on the dance floor. This limited segregation did not occur in hotels in the FMS.

But in 1904, after significant expansion of the railway network, separate, less comfortable first class carriages were introduced 'For Chinese', even though they paid the same fare. There was a barrage of complaints; an English vicar warned that the policy was bringing in a new system of 'race prejudices and distinctions'. Elite Chinese, many of whom had European employees and were accustomed to being seen as equals by the British, took great offence.[7]

The Selangor Chamber of Commerce, which included prominent Malays, Tamils and Eurasians, and was chaired by Loke Yew, petitioned to have 'this obnoxious distinction' removed. They were told that the separation had become necessary because European women had been offended by the lack of manners of some Chinese and had complained to the general manager. Loke Yew responded by having printed, at his own expense, thousands of leaflets laying out rules of etiquette to be observed by Chinese travelling first class: offer seats to ladies; avoid 'coarse conversation'; don't take off shoes and squat on the seat; don't smoke or chew betel nut when women are close, or 'clear one's throat promiscuously'.

The 'For Chinese' signs were removed, but instead the more comfortable first class carriages were now 'For Europeans only'. This raised the extremely delicate question of what constituted being 'European'. The *Malay Mail* (whose British editor at that time moonlighted as Loke Yew's real estate agent) sarcastically advised anyone intending to travel to have his genealogy and birth certificate ready in case his European pedigree was questioned by a railway porter. It also raised the awkward question of skin colour being privileged over being a British subject. For instance, Germans would be allowed, but someone of mixed parentage, however Western-educated and proud to be a British subject, risked humiliating exclusion.[8]

Although by various means – mainly access to certain platform areas – all but the most elite Asians and Eurasians were excluded from first class, the overt distinction was removed. Nonetheless, significant damage had been done.

More serious and long-lasting was the introduction in the same year of a new policy of excluding non-whites from the civil service and commissioned grades in the police. This issue would still dominate Anglo-Chinese relations in late 1923. To qualify to serve had always been conditional on being a 'natural born British subject', and on passing an examination held in London that was structured to favour those from public-school and Oxbridge backgrounds. Some non-European British subjects did have this background, and in the 1880s and 1890s successful applicants included a Sinhalese, a Eurasian from Ceylon and a black West Indian. All had been educated at Cambridge.

In 1904, however, Frank Swettenham, by then the senior British official in the FMS, warned that the efficiency of the civil service was being compromised by the number of non-Europeans. The argument, backed by the then Governor, went that it was an 'indignity' for a European to have a non-European as his superior, and furthermore that the Malay aristocracy would find it 'very unacceptable' to be 'advised' by an Asian or African. Indians, the Governor reported, caused 'hopeless disorganization'. The Colonial Office agreed that future candidates should be 'of European descent'. When, in 1911, a Eurasian argued that he should qualify, the rule was changed to 'of pure European descent on both sides'.[9]

This measure particularly angered Western-educated non-Europeans born in the Straits Settlements Crown Colony – and therefore 'natural born British subjects'. The message was clear to them that they were no longer to have an equal stake, and equal rights, in the country of their birth, however useful and loyal they had been to the empire and British interests. The leader of this group was Lim Boon Keng. Born in Singapore in 1869, he had been the first Asian to win one of the newly instigated 'Queen's Scholarships', thanks to which he read medicine at Edinburgh University, graduating with a first-class degree in 1892, before a year's scholarship as a research fellow at Cambridge.[10]

Returning to Singapore, he got involved in private practice and partnership, with a European, in a dispensary business, but also, as was expected of a Queen's Scholar, started a career in public service, including on municipal health boards, advisory committees and, aged twenty-six, a position as the nominated Chinese member on the Straits Settlements Legislative Council. But a combination of factors – the humdrum powerlessness of the Council under an official majority, segregation on the railways, the ban from 1904 on Chinese participation in the civil service (what he would call 'the operation of the colour bar policy') – led him to resign in disgust from all his government positions.[11]

Although a third-generation Singaporean, Lim had ever since his return from Britain been very China-focused. He was part of a cultural nationalist movement among Malayan Chinese that, seeing its identity threatened by proximity to Malays, Indians and Europeans, looked to reinvigorate traditional Chinese values among the diaspora. Literary societies were formed to study classic texts; the Confucian Revival Movement was founded in Kuala Lumpur. Lim was involved with publishing the first Chinese-language newspapers and magazines in the Straits Settlements. He believed that the promotion of Chinese culture and language and the practice of Confucianism would improve the lives of Straits Chinese, who were suffering, he said, from 'marked traits of restlessness . . . encouraged by the individualism which permeates modern European thought and institutions'.[12]

But he was also an ardent reformer, as early as 1899 cutting off his queue, or pigtail, symbol of loyalty to the Manchu dynasty. In a lecture to the Malacca Literary Society he took pride in the fact that the 'Chinese race' were characterised by 'arduous and continuous application to work', in contrast to the 'Malay people in their simple blissfulness'. But the Chinese were being held back, and made to look weak and backward in the eyes of Europeans, he said, by the 'vices' of opium, prostitution and gambling, as well as antiquated funeral rites, wasteful wedding ceremonies and general treatment of women, including foot-binding. The 'freedom and education of our women folk' was crucial, he went on. (In 1899 he had been a co-founder of the

Singapore girls' school, the first of its kind among Chinese communities in south-east Asia.)[13]

In early 1912, the colonial government abolished the Queen's
Scholarship scheme, under whose auspices some twenty or more
Chinese boys had followed Lim to university in Britain. Lim pub-
licly complained that 'the original spirit of Raffles had been lost'. In
May 1912, he addressed a meeting of twenty-two prominent non-
Europeans. 'We will never be allowed to be more than subordinate
servants, clerks, and so on, under men who think their white skins are
the sole sign of born rulers and administrators,' he said.[14]

But the outbreak of the First World War saw Lim rally to the flag.
He rejoined the Legislative Council and carried out a series of lecture
tours, encouraging support from the Chinese community for the war
effort. These lectures were published in 1917 as a book, *The Great
War from a Confucian Point of View*. 'As a people, we are indissolubly
attached to the British Empire. Her interests are ours – her enemies are
ours too,' Lim declared. This was not just through geographical accident of birth, but also through shared values of 'political aspiration'.
'The Empire today is the monument of the greatest human enterprise
in the world's history,' he said. No longer 'ruled by despotism', 'it
stands as the most magnificent democracy in the world'. The secret of
its success, he suggested, 'lies in the just and liberal treatment of subjects belonging to alien races'.[15]

However, alongside all this were sharp criticisms of 'the discrimination based entirely on the question of the colour of the skin, irrespective
of the social status, education or culture of the individuals concerned'.
At one point he stated: 'Asiatics in the Straits Settlements demand
equal opportunities and equal treatment.' Thus the peroration at the
end of one speech had a key caveat. The empire 'may well be the prelude
to the Federation of the World' (a Confucian aim), but 'sympathy and
knowledge are needed'.[16]

The hope, as elsewhere, was that by demonstrating 'loyalty and
devotion' to the empire, they might prove 'worthy to claim and to
enjoy the liberties and privileges of free men'. The Chinese community,

together with the Rajas and the colonial government, did contribute hugely towards the war effort, raising enough money for fifty-three warplanes, 250 'coolie' workers and even a battleship, HMS *Malaya*. Lim was given an OBE for his efforts.[17]

But the years after the war would prove to him a disappointment. There was no move to change the second-class status of non-Europeans or to break down the 'colour bar'. But what seems to have brought things to a head for Lim was the issue of a university. He had called for one in Singapore more than twenty years previously. In 1919, a multi-racial committee was established pushing for at least a college to be set up, to act as the nucleus for a university. The government charged them to raise $2 million before the government would contribute $1 million. Within a year they had raised $2.4 million and hopes were high that at last, belatedly, the project would go ahead. After all, there were already universities in Hanoi, Bangkok and Rangoon.

But the British authorities, in the person of Director of Education Richard Winstedt, stalled on every pretext available. It was increasingly clear that the Malayan government, looking at India where universities were producing discontented young nationalists, wanted nothing of the sort in Singapore.

Lim and his fellow campaigner, wealthy Singapore businessman Tan Kah Kee, each of whom had donated $10,000 to the university fund, gave up, and in 1921 established Amoy University in Fukien Province, China. Here, both decided, would be a better opportunity for providing a higher education for the Chinese of south-east Asia. Lim departed to be its first president. At his final Council meeting, Lim was praised by a British official for his leadership of the Straits Chinese community, 'the backbone of the permanent inhabitants of the colony [who] in time to come, must take a greater share in the government of this colony'. Lim wasn't going to wait and see. Instead, he stayed away from Malaya for twenty years, running the university and deploying his considerable medical, administrative and political skills in service of Sun Yat Sen and the Chinese government.[18]

Leadership of the Chinese community now fell to Tan Cheng Lock.

Later known as 'one of the founding fathers of Malaysia', Cheng Lock would share many of Lim's views and complaints, but with a crucial difference.

Tan Cheng Lock's grandfather, himself the grandson of the Tan merchant pioneer from the 1770s, had died in 1880 and left an awkward legacy, to say the least. He had further enriched the family from proceeds of shipping, real estate and agriculture (though he continued to shun the opium and gambling businesses). He treated his household, and his children, with brutal strictness, and to his horror, his sons, as young teenagers, reacted by adopting playboy lifestyles of gambling and intoxication. Cheng Lock's uncle became an opium addict, and his father an alcoholic. On their father's death, both wayward sons found themselves disinherited. The huge fortune was placed in a reserved trust estate, and the sons only got a small allowance plus, for Cheng Lock's father, permission to live in the Heeren Street family mansion.

So Tan Cheng Lock, born three years after his esteemed grandfather's death, grew up in a household in straitened circumstances and with a father disgraced by the terms of the will and consumed by bitterness. Every evening at seven, after a few glasses of whisky, he would pour a torrent of abuse at his own father's portrait in the family's ancestor shrine. And far from changing his ways, he continued to drink and, according to Cheng Lock's daughter, Alice Scott-Ross, never did a day's work in his life. If money got too tight, he would sell off some of the family furniture or other heirloom pieces.

There were four boys and three girls, Cheng Lock being the third son. But one elder brother died aged three falling out of a rocking chair, and the eldest, the great hope of the family, a brilliant student who hoped to become a doctor, was killed by typhoid fever, aged seventeen. Cheng Lock, at fourteen, now found himself with huge responsibilities as the eldest son.

Their mother, from a well-to-do Straits-born Chinese family, who passed her time every day playing cards (*cherki*) for small stakes with her friends, never had a close relationship with Cheng Lock. She was a great one for favourites – first the eldest son, then, on his death, the youngest one, who was 'infallible in her eyes'. For Cheng Lock, she 'did not manifest even an iota of affection'. Nor was it a close marriage between Cheng Lock's mother and father. When he was in his early sixties, she decided to resign from 'marital duties' and procured a mistress for her husband, a girl of eighteen. But his passion was for whisky not women, and after two years she was sent back to her parents.

'My father grew up into manhood without much affection being bestowed upon him,' Cheng Lock's daughter Alice wrote, in a biography based on his unpublished memoir, as well as her own recollections. He emerged from this childhood and family a non-smoking teetotaller, determined to restore his illustrious family's tarnished reputation, 'very serious minded and pessimistic' and with his 'innermost emotions well concealed and under control ... the only manifestation of his feelings would be his irritability if things turned adverse', his daughter Alice wrote.[19]

But he loved his home town of Malacca. It had long ago given up its strategic and trading pole position to first Penang, then Singapore. For one thing, the fine port of the Portuguese and Dutch eras was now silted up and effectively defunct. Nor could it now match the wild energy of Singapore, where not only Malays, Chinese and Europeans but also Armenians, Syrians, Jews, Americans and Arabs were arriving, striving, working and trading. But Malacca was 500 years older than Singapore, and its almost equally diverse people had been mingling and inter-marrying for generations. Out of the commercial slipstream, Cheng Lock's Malacca backwater was relaxed, calm and tolerant. For rich Straits Chinese it was an agreeable place to retire. Alice, growing up there in the 1920s, remembered the almost complete lack of 'interracial ill-will'. On Temple Street, a Malay mosque, an Indian temple and a Chinese temple stood side by side. All carried on their worship with no 'hatred, malice or disrespect' for the other religions. The Malays even allowed the Chinese to sell pork outside their mosque.

Tan Cheng Lock would often express his pride in the fact that his family had been in Malacca for five generations – two centuries. He called the town his *negeri bertuah* (Malay for 'blessed homeland', or 'lucky state'). While its silted-up port and decaying Dutch-era mansions might cast minds back to a more vibrant past, its centuries of diverse people genially muddling through, for Cheng Lock, informed his political vision of the future for his country.

After the English school in Malacca, where he won a scholarship, Cheng Lock was sent to Raffles Institution in Singapore. This school had undergone many changes since its foundation in 1823 and it was now an English-language secondary school. It was run by a Derbyshire-born teacher, R. W. Hullet, who was credited by Cheng Lock as taking a great interest in his progress and instilling in him a life-long love of literature. Lim Boon Keng had studied here a decade earlier; when Lim's father died and the money for fees dried up, Hullet had stepped in to ensure that Lim could finish his education. Tan Cheng Lock described Hullet as 'a truly great man'.[20]

Cheng Lock worked hard, hoping to study law in Britain, but did not quite make the academic grade for the then still-running Queen's Scholarships. Instead he took up Hullet's offer of a job as English literature teacher at the school. He was very good at his subject, but had little else to commend him as a teacher. Aloof, impatient and quick-tempered, on one occasion he slapped a child until he bled. On another, he injured his hand throwing a glass at some rowdy schoolboys.[21]

Although he had formed 'close ties of friendship' with European colleagues at the school, for a non-European, pay and promotion prospects were poor. After six years, Cheng Lock had had enough. In 1908 he took up an invitation, engineered by his mother, to work as an assistant manager on his cousin's rubber plantation close to Malacca.[22]

It was a tough job, with very long hours in extreme heat supervising the rubber tappers. Like most, he caught malaria, from which he would suffer repeated relapses. But he was good at his job, even if he was 'very strict and seldom smiled, and was feared by estate staff and labourers alike'. He would spend his evenings voraciously reading (he would later have a library of nearly 3,000 books, many endlessly re-read and heavily annotated).

He was soon working in a more senior position for another firm. In 1910, in partnership with a rich Malacca Chinese, he floated his first company. Over the next two years he was involved as a partner or director in another couple of rubber companies with a diverse group of other investors.

His rise in wealth and prestige can be seen through the family alliances. Part of his duty as eldest son was to organise the marriages of his sisters before planning his own. The rule, his daughter wrote, was that 'both parties must be equally financially well-established'. The first was to a salaried clerk in a British firm. By the time of the turn of the third sister, it was into a 'wealthy family in Singapore'.

He had by now attracted the interest of colonial officials, in part, apparently, because of his excellent command of English, and in 1912 he was appointed as a Malacca Justice of Peace and then also a Municipal Commissioner. In this capacity he was spotted by Yeo Tin Hye, the hugely wealthy leader of the town's Hokkien community. Yeo had a sole teenage daughter, Yeok Neo, one of only three of his children out of thirteen to reach adulthood, to whom he was devoted. Impressed by Cheng Lock's polished eloquence and commanding presence, he decided to arrange a marriage. It was made clear that the daughter, against Chinese tradition, would have a hefty inheritance.

According to Alice, her father had earlier fallen in love with a maternal cousin who was 'attractive, gentle and fused with immense femininity'. But she had been promised as an infant to another cousin. Apparently, it took him many years to get over her. But, as his daughter explained, 'one's choice in life was limited to a certain degree'.

Tan Cheng Lock, following Lim, would later campaign against the Chinese tradition of madly extravagant weddings, which, as in India and elsewhere, delivered so many people into the hands of the moneylenders. But his wedding in 1913 went on for two weeks, with lavish parties and processions, and with the bride in an elaborately hand-embroidered Mandarin costume, 'adorned with magnificent jewels'. On the fifth day, he actually met his bride for the first time. According to his daughter Alice's biography, on lifting her veil he found her 'a plain-looking woman'.[23]

The following year, Tan, having rapidly expanded his business portfolio, found himself with severe liquidity problems. His wife's inheritance came to the rescue, and the substantial remainder under his prudent management, along with ever-increasing directorships in rubber companies, would provide enough wealth for him to be able to concentrate on public service.[24]

On the outbreak of war, as well as, like Lim, undertaking fund-raising, he resuscitated the Chinese company of the Malacca Volunteer Corps and served as a private for five years. He also took on more positions on public boards.

After the war he frequently hosted dinners for Europeans – fellow directors of companies, or government officers. With his wide command of literature, philosophy and political theory, both Chinese and European, he was an interesting and impressive host. Alice recalled women in long dresses and men in tails, with her and her brother and two sisters on show and on best behaviour, dressed 'like China dolls'. After dinner, the guests would often play roulette for small stakes, with the winnings going to the children to spend on sweets or at the Japanese-run toy shop.

More fun and relaxing were the frequent visits of James Fairweather, a young Scot working for the Agriculture Department. He had organised for dog-lover Cheng Lock the importation of two Alsatians from England. A 'lonely bachelor', he became a close family friend and for three years, until he was posted away, visited daily and often stayed for supper. 'Our home was open to him,' Alice remembered; 'he was even-tempered, accommodating and patient'. As a result of his 'good-nature' he was the frequent victim of pranks by the children. 'We would claw all over him', pulling his tie again and again and unlacing his shoes. On one occasion the children tricked him into falling into a hole they had dug and then camouflaged on the beach. 'Just imagine', Alice wrote, 'the uproar which exploded from us, peals of laughter and hilarity.'[25]

In 1920, Cheng Lock played host for a lunch at the Heeren Street mansion for the latest Governor, Sir Laurence Guillemard, on a tour of his new domain. Normally such occasions were strictly about pleasantries, but Tan in his speech, given to an assembly of British officials and thirty-two of the Chinese local elite, caused an uproar by adopting the policy of congratulating the new Governor for 'wise and important reforms so badly needed' that he had yet to implement. Tan spoke up for 'that portion of the population of this country who are British-born, British subjects, and loyal subjects, whether they are Malays, Eurasians, Indians or Chinese'. They were 'part and parcel of the Empire', he said. But 'British subjects should be British subjects in fact as well as in name ... unfortunately they are debarred from entering the Civil Service of the country.'[26]

At the beginning of 1923, the Straits Settlements Legislative Council was enlarged to thirteen officials and thirteen unofficials, with a Malay representative for the first time, two Indians, and the Chinese contingent raised from one to three, with the newcomers from Penang and Malacca. Tan Cheng Lock, aged forty, was appointed the new member for Malacca.

The British view, as expressed in a history published in 1925, was that the Chinese had 'no desire to assume the wearisome task of governing themselves'. They had no interest in politics, so long as their business was not interfered with. In the case of Tan Cheng Lock, this could not have been more wrong.[27]

The Legislative Council remained little more than a forum for rubber-stamping – the Governor held the casting vote – but Tan threw himself into its workings as no Asian member had done before. He continued Lim's campaign to overturn segregation in the civil service, and blamed the fact that 'real participation in the Government and administration of their country, is banged, barred and bolted to them' for having driven away 'highly capable and ambitious men of the type of Dr. Lim Boon Keng'. That he had 'left to give his services to China' had been 'such a loss to this country'. Furthermore, he asked, wasn't the colour bar the 'very antithesis of Queen Victoria's Proclamation of 1858 which decreed that "our subjects of whatever race or creed be freely and impartially admitted to offices in Our Service"?' To the argument that the Chinese in Malaya were transient, with no political investment in the country, he replied with the case of his own family's 200-year history in Malacca, which actually pre-dated the British, and the fact that an increasing number of Chinese were Malaya-born and 'regard this country as their permanent home'.[28]

He also took issue with the tokenism that often saw solitary Asians appointed to boards, committees and councils, but still excluded from any real participation in the running of the government. They were little more than 'dummy figureheads', he argued in a speech in late 1923. Instead, the government was under 'autocratic control', leaving the people of the colony 'utterly devoid of an effective constitutional means of repelling the invasion of our rights'.[29]

Tan argued that there should be Asian representation on the Executive Council, where the decisions were actually made, and that unofficials such as himself on the Legislative Council should not only be in the majority, but also be elected, and thus have a proper mandate from those they sought to represent. He pointed to political reforms underway in India, Burma and Ceylon, 'placed on the high road towards responsible government', while Malaya remained stuck with the system of nomination and official majority.[30]

All this was much in line with what Lim had been arguing before he departed, but Tan Cheng Lock also had a wider vision that went beyond his role as a representative of the Chinese community. In the Council, he often made the case for government support for impoverished Portuguese Eurasians, Malay fishermen or economically 'out-distanced' Malays in Singapore. In contrast to Lim, he wanted Malayan Chinese to identify first and foremost as Malay, with a multi-ethnic nationalism, 'a true Malayan spirit and consciousness ... to the complete elimination of racial or communal feeling'. Indeed, 'racial categories', he declared, should be consigned to 'the limbo of oblivion.'[31]

This 'Malayan consciousness among all the races' would be built on common full citizenship, a shared language – English, which should

be taught in all schools – common affection for Malaya and shared
loyalty to the British Empire, he declared in October 1923. And he
wanted British executives and merchants living in Malaya to be part of
this vision of the future, to see it as their home rather than just a place
to make money then depart from. The ultimate aim, he said, should
be a united self-governing Malaya – the Straits Settlements and the
Federated and Unfederated States – with a capital at Kuala Lumpur
and 'with as much autonomy in purely local affairs as possible'.[32]

His innovative suggested first steps towards this vision indicated that
he had understood the mistakes made during Indian political reform
processes. He called for the addition to the Legislative Council of
three unofficials to give them a majority, one each from the three main
communities – Chinese, Indian and Malay. While remaining in the
imperial framework of 'native representation', the proposal eschewed
the divisive Indian model of communal electorates. (In Ceylon, too, a
communal voting system had stirred up antagonism between Sinhala
and Tamils.) Instead, there should be 'mixed electorates' of Europeans,
Eurasians, Chinese, Indians and Malays to elect each member, who,
despite being a member of one of the three main races, would then
represent the trans-ethnic interests of all of colonial society.

Tan Cheng Lock somewhat presciently warned that to remain with
the current 'defective and archaic constitution', rather than forging
a Malaya united across all races, risked fatally weakening the country against external threat. But his eloquent speeches and blizzards
of memoranda got nowhere. For one thing, he did not command a
mass following, nor was he part of an organised political movement.
And the British officials, used to humdrum business in the Legislative
Council, simply ignored him. After one ground-breaking speech, the
next speaker addressed expenditure on the mental asylum, while the
one after that covered an unsatisfactory court building in Penang. One
British official, Education Director R. Winstedt, was heard complaining that Tan's speechifying was making them late for lunch.

The time would come, of course, for Tan Cheng Lock and his vision
of a multi-ethnic self-governing Malaya, but now, utterly frustrated, he

concluded that the entire system of colonial rule was 'evil, sinister and degrading'.[33]

Victor Purcell, who worked for many years with the Chinese community in Malaya, later wrote that 'It is one of Malaya's great misfortunes that the Malayan governments cold-shouldered Mr Tan ... and before the Second World War gave no encouragement at all to the Malayan-born Chinese to regard themselves as citizens of Malaya.'[34]

21

'Schizoid Rule'

It is said that a white man, who has lived twelve
consecutive months in complete isolation, among the
people of an alien Asiatic race, is never wholly sane
again for the remainder of his days.

HUGH CLIFFORD, *In Court and Kampong*[1]

Sharing Tan Cheng Lock's desire for English to be taught in all
Malayan schools was Mohammed Yunus bin Abdullah, the sole
Malay member of the new Legislative Council and the acknowledged
leader of the Straits Settlements Malays. A former government worker
and newspaper editor, he was demanding that English be taught in Malay
schools. At the time there were thirty English-teaching schools in the
FMS, but they were all in towns, where less than 6 per cent of the Malay
population lived. Of the 10,000 enrolled pupils, there were fewer than
700 Malays. In rural districts there were only vernacular schools (poorly
attended and funded – the education budget only took up 1.5 per cent of
the government revenue). Should these schools not be teaching the Malay
children English? Yunus bin Abdullah asked. How else were his people
going to avoid missing out on the cosmopolitan prosperity of the colony?[2]

But for a long time, the British had been wary of Malays learning English, an attribute increasingly essential to making a life outside the village. The widespread view, as expressed by an unofficial member of the Council, was that Malays should be taught 'the dignity of manual labour, so that they do not all become clerks and I am sure you will not have the trouble which has arisen in India through over-education'. The Malays, Mohammed Yunus was told by Education Director Richard Winstedt, were peasants engaged in agricultural pursuits, and if their education was improved and they learned English this 'would be likely to have the effect of inducing them to abandon those pursuits'. This would lead to 'economic dislocation and social unrest'.[3]

To which Mohammed Yunus responded in a most critical speech: 'The Malay boy is told you have been trained to remain at the bottom, and there you must remain.'

So here education, a much-vaunted advantage of colonialism, was a tool of social maintenance rather than mobility. What the colonial authorities were looking to maintain was the strange, self-fulfilling policy of racial distinctions they had imposed on multi-ethnic Malaya, a social and economic order based on race. Chinese were to be miners and shop-keepers, Indians rubber-tappers and Malays farmers and fishermen. The role of the British, they believed, was to hold the balance between the separate and functionally disparate communities, and keep each in its place.[4]

Ironically, the Malays, 'trained to remain at the bottom', were considered the most important sector of the population by the colonial authorities. British Malaya was about the Malays, not the Chinese or Indians who, out of sight, carried out industrial production and trade. Eighty per cent of British cadets were set to learning Malay with only 10 per cent to Chinese and 5 per cent to a southern Indian language – Tamil or Telegu. This was when the population consisted of 1.6 million Malays, 1.2 million Chinese and 500,000 Indians. There was a feeling of a duty of care, *noblesse oblige*, to the Malays that was not felt towards the others. In part, this was because the Malays were generally well liked by the British; they were also considered 'indigenous' (in fact only 60 per cent were residents for more than forty years, the rest immigrants from Indonesia). But most importantly it was down to the 'indirect rule', 'trusteeship' arrangement with the rulers of the Malay States.[5]

Nowhere in the empire illustrated more vividly the contradictions within the current 'Big Idea' of trusteeship. To keep the Malays on the land was to preserve the pre-colonial social structure, the faults of which were used to justify British intervention in the first place. British policy towards Malaya, not just in education but across the board, has been described as 'schizoid'. Perhaps no one better personifies this than the contradictory and complicated figure of Hugh Clifford.[6]

In September 1923, Clifford was the Governor of Nigeria, making him one of the most important and influential men in the empire. He had previously been Colonial Secretary (effectively the Governor's number two) in Trinidad, then Ceylon, and then Governor of the Gold Coast. After Nigeria, he would have two more senior governorships. There was no more experienced colonial officer in this period, nor one with, on paper, a more distinguished career. But he started out in Malaya, where he served for twenty years, and it would be this time, which he much later described as the 'happiest and most interesting of my life', that would decisively shape his attitudes to almost all facets of empire, as well as providing all the material for his successful novels and short stories. He would dramatically return there at the end of his career.

Born in London in 1866 into the junior branch of an old aristocratic family, Clifford attended a private Catholic school and, although he had ambitions to become a journalist, at this point looked destined to follow his father into the army. But then his cousin, Sir Frederick Weld, who was Governor of the Straits Settlements, offered him a job as a cadet in the Malayan Civil Service. So, in 1883, aged only seventeen, he found himself in Perak.

Even as a very young man, Clifford was an imposing figure. A colleague from his Malaya days described him as 'a big, heavily boned man. His eyes were large and luminous, set rather deep, in a massive, rather bullet shaped head. There was power in his attitude, his gestures and voice.' Pretty much throughout his career he would do everything at full pelt – sport, work, driving fast. He smoked furiously, too. He was also vain, and was appalled when he lost his hair very young. Convinced that constantly wearing a hat against the sun prevented his hair from growing back, he would go out bareheaded at every opportunity. (Reportedly, he was the inspiration for Noel Coward's 'Mad Dogs and Englishmen'.) This continued throughout his long years in the tropics. When he was in his thirties, his doctor in Ceylon was Lucian de Zilwa. He was fond of Clifford. Most senior colonial officers would insist on a British doctor, but 'Clifford was indifferent to such considerations ... he had no racial prejudice whatsoever.' But de Zilwa described Clifford as 'obstinate about one thing: he would go bareheaded in the blazing sun, although he was quite bald'. The doctor had to treat blisters on his scalp. His wife and the doctor tried to make him wear a topee, but without success. De Zilwa later mused: 'I feel that the tragedy of his eventual mental breakdown might have been averted if he had a little fear of the Sungod.'[7]

Arriving in newly 'protected' Perak in 1883, Clifford was employed as the secretary for Hugh Low, one of the pioneering Residents, and set to learning Malay. After eighteen months he was fluent enough to pass the exams and hugely impress his teachers with his natural linguistic ability. He took on a junior job in northern Perak, by which time he had learned the requisites of 'Residential' rule: tact and patience (the first Resident of Perak had been assassinated in 1875 having tried to change too much too quickly), lots of money (the Sultans and chiefs had to be compensated for the loss of their debt-slaves and given generous incomes), and, where necessary, prompt military action.

Soon afterwards, trouble broke out in the independent eastern state of Pahang. There were disputes over mines; a British subject – a Chinese man from Hong Kong – had been murdered, and European concession-mongers were bullying the Sultan and causing disruption. Clifford, aged only twenty-one, was summoned to Singapore to be briefed by the Governor on 'a special mission of some delicacy and

difficulty'. He was to persuade Pahang's ruler to accept British protection and a Resident. Apparently no more senior officer could be spared
for the long task.[8]

He arrived in Pahang in March 1887, and would spend nearly two
years there, 'to a degree unequalled by any of my brother officers . . . in
almost complete isolation from men of my own race', thrown entirely
upon Malays for companionship.[9]

For Clifford, this time was a 'privilege'. Living and eating as a 'native',
he loved the 'excellent Malay curries', the river close at hand to swim
in, 'hosts of amused and amusing Malays with whom to gossip, chaff
and chatter; chess and a kind of Mah-jongh to play with little Chinese
paper cards'. 'Each hour brings fresh insight', he wrote, 'into the mys-
terious workings of the minds and hearts of that very human section of
our race, which ignorant Europeans calmly class as "n*****s".' It was,
he later wrote, 'the most impressionable period of my life'.[10]

Clifford would write an autobiographical story about a white man
marooned among Malays. He was aristocratic, 'a masterful son of the
dominant race'. But 'circumstances and inclination had combined
to well-nigh denationalise him, to make him turn from his own
kind, herd with natives, and conceive for them such an affection and
sympathy that he was accustomed to contrast his countrymen unfa-
vourably with his Malayan friends'. For any European, this was 'not a
wholesome attitude . . . but was curiously common among such white
men as chance has thrown for long periods of time into close contact
with Oriental races, and whom Nature has endowed with imagina-
tions sufficiently keen to be able to live into the life of the strange folk
around them'. Leonard Woolf, who would work for Clifford in Ceylon,
reported the widely held assumption that in Malaya, Clifford had 'gone
native'. (There are a couple of mentions of a young Malay woman,
Miriam, who might have lived with Clifford at this point. 'Going
native' was often a euphemism for taking a local lover.)[11]

However, Clifford did not neglect his mission. Securing agreement
from the Sultan of Pahang that he should enter into a treaty with
Britain to secure his protection from outside threat was fairly easy and

delivered by April. But the Sultan resisted the idea of direct interference, until at last in September he agreed to have a British 'political agent' with consular powers, a role Clifford immediately undertook. Then, just over a year later, the Sultan agreed to have a 'British Resident' along the lines of the west coast states – to be consulted on all matters save 'Malay religion and customs'.

So, 'at a preposterously young age I was the principal instrument in adding 15,000 square miles of territory to the British dependencies in the East', Clifford later wrote. Governor Weld was delighted, writing to a friend that 'Young Clifford' had been the instrument of opening up 'utterly disorganized' Pahang to 'commerce, peace, and civilisation', thanks to his 'tact, prudence and firmness' along with 'great physical powers of endurance in arduous and even to some extent dangerous journeys, often living on native food for weeks together'. Clifford was even congratulated by the Secretary of State.[12]

By now, though, he was severely ill. It might have been malaria, or possibly syphilis, something that could have contributed to what would be called his 'cyclical insanity'. Either way, he was invalided back to England at the end of 1888, returning to Malaya in 1890.

He was then appointed Superintendent of a large region of 3,000 square miles in the interior of Pahang, an area reckoned the wildest of the state, without a single mile of road. The population consisted of riverside Malay villagers, a handful of Chinese miners, 'a band or two of sulky Australian prospectors, sorely discontented with the result which they were obtaining; and an odd thousand or so of squalid aborigines, living in dirt and wretchedness up in the mountains'.[13]

Based in a one-room hut precariously balanced on stilts on the bank of a river, he spent most of the first year travelling by raft, looking to 'establish a personal influence among them, which, in a new land, is the first, surest foundation of British rule'. There were moments when he was overwhelmed with the excitement of being the first white person who had ever set foot in a place.[14]

Two years into his posting, a group of chiefs organised a rising with the object of restoring the old system of government. Clifford suspected that they had the tacit support of the Sultan. Clifford was part of a small force that expelled them from the state, action that included using artillery fire on a stockade full of women and children and then a 'few days spent in burning miles of villages; in impounding flocks of cattle; in writing the anger of the Government plainly on the place, so that even an illiterate people may read it closely'. Two years later, he was the leader of a 'bushwhacking' expedition into the as yet independent states to the north to root out the rebels. With four European officers, a hundred Sikhs and a handful of Malay trackers, he spent two months harrying the rebels until the final handful were captured, ill, emaciated and covered in sores.[15]

Clifford's fellow Malayan Civil Service officer Frank Swettenham wrote how 'a really good fight is the acme of man's enjoyment ... the thrill of battle, the quickening pride of race ... the shock of arms and the ecstasy of victory'. Clifford's view could not have been more different. The fighting might have been 'inevitable' and brought 'the wished-for peace more speedily', but it was 'a heart-breaking little war', a 'depressing business', 'squalid and petty'. 'A man to go bush-whacking', he concluded, 'should have no insight, no sympathy, no imagination' – precisely the qualities Clifford considered requisite for colonial administration. (The political officer character in his story 'Bushwhacking' had a brief crisis while crossing an icy river, 'a momen-tary lack of faith in the mission of the white races'.)[16]

After a short leave in England, during which he married, he returned to Pahang as Resident. For a few months in 1900 he was Governor of North Borneo, which was run by a London-based chartered company. It was a brutally extractive operation and Clifford soon resigned in dis-gust. 'You do not look upon much of our enterprise in a manner that is sufficiently mercantile,' the company's director responded. This brief experience would shape Clifford's later dealings with 'big business' in the colonies he ran.[17]

After another return to Pahang, Clifford was invalided home in October 1901. He had supposedly been poisoned with ground glass in his food. Whatever the actual cause, he was extremely ill, and not fully recovered until 1903. Eager to return to Malaya, he was instead posted to Trinidad. This came as a great blow. 'It was severing a link that binds me to the life which I love,' he wrote the following year. It was twenty years since he had first arrived in Malaya; his time there, 'from boyhood to middle age', had 'wedded me to Malay'. The move to the Caribbean was like a divorce.

The new posting also struck at one of his strongest principles – that good administration depended on a close link and deep understanding from long experience between ruler and ruled. 'Deprived of the light of intimate, first-hand knowledge that in the East had become so sure a guide,' he wrote in Trinidad in 1904, 'I stand today bewildered in the half-darkness of a new experience.'[18]

Developments in Trinidad had required new blood in the top echelons of the Colonial Service there, and Clifford was still one of the Colonial Office's upcoming bright young men. But the CO was almost certainly motivated to move him by the slightly 'gone-native' nature of some of his now widely published writing about Malaya, and its undoubted ambivalence about the 'imperial mission' there.

Clifford's writing career had started with his abortive effort to produce a dictionary of the Malay language. He'd got as far as 'G' before a completed rival edition was published. In early 1896, on his return to Pahang, he had written a number of pieces for the *Straits Times* newspaper. When these were collected into a book, they caught the attention of magazines in London, and thereafter his stories were frequently published in *Cornhill*, *Living Age* and the prestigious *Blackwood's*. These were then issued in book form with critical and commercial success.

The money was important. As well as a wife to support, Clifford had a son, Hugh, in 1897, then two daughters, Mary and Monica, soon after. Kipling in India, Rider Haggard in Africa and others elsewhere had been prospering through writing about the distant and 'exotic' parts of the empire. In 1895, Joseph Conrad had published his successful first novel *Almayer's Folly*, set in Malaya and Borneo, at that time new fictional territory. Clifford reviewed Conrad's book for a Singapore newspaper, criticising his depiction of Malays and his

general ignorance of the country. 'Well I never did set up as an authority on Malaysia,' Conrad responded. Indeed, Conrad wrote about Asia
from his experience – the deck of a ship – and his fiction would rarely
venture outside the heads of European characters.

Clifford had a different ambition, to foster true understanding. 'My
stories deal with natives of all classes – I have tried to describe these
things as they appear when viewed from the inside,' he wrote in the
preface to his first short story collection. 'I have striven throughout to
appreciate the native point of view, and to judge the people and their
actions by their own standards, rather than by those of a White Man
living in their midst.' In a later collection, his expressed hope was that
the reader would see Malays as real people, however 'foreign to the
everyday experiences of Europeans'. All his efforts would be justified,
he wrote, if 'I have succeeded in conveying a true picture of my friends,
in awaking a greater sympathy for them, and so have brought them
ever so little nearer'.[19]

Reviewing Clifford's *Studies in Brown Humanity* (1898), Conrad
paid a glowing tribute to his understanding of the people about whom
he wrote, while gently criticising his literary style. Clifford then wrote
to Conrad, embarrassed by his earlier criticism of *Almayer's Folly*, and
a correspondence and friendship was established. (Clifford would be
instrumental in having both *Nostromo* – Conrad's 1904 masterpiece –
and *Chance* – his commercial breakthrough in 1913 – commissioned in
the US, the latter being dedicated to him 'for his steadfast friendship'.)
Clifford, knowing that he was not in Conrad's league, wanted literary
help, and Conrad remained impressed by Clifford's ability convinc-
ingly to portray non-Europeans, something he admitted he could
not match.[20]

Clifford's stories and novels sometimes feature white protagonists
and explore the relationships between the coloniser and the rest.
Sometimes a white narrator is told a story by an elderly Malay. But
most of the characters and protagonists are Malay and there is an
anthropological and romantic urge, like Arthur Grimble's, to capture
and describe a pre-European way of life that was rapidly disappearing.

Indeed, he claimed that most of the stories were based on fact, and they do contain anthropological elements – myths and proverbs, wedding etiquette and other traditional customs, dream interpretations.

In the forewords and prefaces he wrote for his books he was always careful to express his enormous affection for Malays. A typical villager of the interior was 'good-natured and easygoing, courteous of manner, soft of speech, and caressing by instinct'. Throughout his career, Clifford would try to engineer a return to Malaya.[21]

But over and above personal contact, Clifford, and many other British colonial officials, felt a genuine affection for the values and virtues inherent in Malay rural life as he saw them. Aged thirteen, Clifford had had something of an epiphany while visiting the senior branch of the family's estate at Ugbrooke Park in Devon. He was driven in a dog-cart by his father to visit the tenants. Here, it seemed, was a near perfect social organisation and one unchanged for generations. The men in the 'Big House' had a responsibility, so that if, for example, a tenant woman was widowed and found herself in difficult circumstances, she was 'tided over'.[22]

So, like many colonial officers, Clifford was nostalgic for an aristocratic system where everyone knew their place. He was very Conservative – when the Liberals won their landslide in 1906, he described their MPs as an 'appalling collection of extremists, cranks, faddists, false sentimentalists and haters of their country'. He viewed colonial societies through the prism of the aristocratic system in full retreat at home. For Malaya, this meant describing the rule of the Sultans as akin to feudalism, with barons and yeomen. Malay rulers had the 'characteristic qualities of the English gentleman', he wrote, loving pageantry and the 'country pursuits' of hunting, fishing and other sports.[23]

But all this is riddled with contradictions. In fact, much of what Clifford wrote and spoke about Malaya – and, later, other places – pulled him apart in different directions.

Almost nothing holds together. For example, he wrote from close personal experience about the great differences between the Malays of

the various regions and states and how the large immigrant populations from Sumatra and Java had added yet more diversity – in culture,
dialect, dress and much more – but then opined grandly about 'The
Malay' as a homogeneous thing. He affirmed that 'racial characteristics'
were the result of 'environment and circumstances' rather than innate,
but then declared that the Siamese, 'as anyone who is acquainted with
the two races will at once acknowledge', were 'the intellectual superiors of the Malays'. For all his professed love for Malays, he sometimes
described them as 'slovenly', 'listless', 'indolent', 'the cattle of mankind'.
In other instances they were hard-working and brave, 'ever wont to
take their chance of danger'. It makes no sense.[24]

Most unstable was his attitude to the 'Big Idea' of the British as
imperial 'trustees' and the supposed indirect rule over the Malay
States. His first boss, Perak Resident Hugh Low, told him that the
'fiction ... that the Residents are merely advisers must be kept up'. In
the preface to a later volume of stories, Clifford admitted that 'passing
under the protection of Great Britain, was barely distinguishable from
annexation'. 'The Chiefs know', he wrote elsewhere, 'that, cloak it as
we will, we are there to wrest the power they have misused from their
unwilling grasp.'[25]

As he well understood, the giving of pensions to the Sultans and
chiefs, some way above their traditional levels of income, had to a large
extent ended their 'feudal' relationship with the people. They didn't
need the peasantry to provide them with income, and the peasantry –
under Pax Britannica – didn't need them any more to protect them
from outside attack, internal violence or crime. The whole system,
which in theory he was 'protecting', had been hollowed out.

Clifford constantly and increasingly returned to the question of
whether this was a good thing, and whether his own substantial role in
its implementation was justified, twisting and turning to keep his conscience clear. Clifford was at the same time adamant that the imperial
intervention had been beneficial to the Malay people, and also highly
ambivalent and defensive about it. 'The boot of the white man', he
wrote in an early collection, 'stamps out much of what is best in the

customs and characteristics of the native races ... reducing all things to that dead level of conventionality, which we call civilisation.' In the following volume, he wrote, 'we English have an immense amount to answer for', and expressed his anxiety 'for the good and the bad we have done – both with the most excellent intentions'.[26]

In a lecture given in London in 1902, Clifford told his audience at the Royal Colonial Institute that 'A plebiscite taken today would return an overwhelming majority in favour of our rule as against the ancient regime ... the vast bulk of the Malays have attained to a measure of contentment and happiness unprecedented in their history.' The main justification for the British intervention, to which Clifford returned again and again, was the 'vile misrule' of the Malay Rajas and chiefs, who were somehow 'noble' and 'savage' at the same time.

But ambivalence, or more exactly defensiveness, is persistent. In a much later collection published in America as well as in Britain, having reminisced about his role in 'adding 15,000 square miles' to the empire, he wrote that his 'share in the business stands in need of some explanation or defence, if readers who are not themselves Britishers are to be persuaded that I am not merely a thief upon a rather large scale'. Declaring that the rule of the Rajas and chiefs was 'one of the most absolute and cynical autocracies that the mind of man has conceived; and the people living under it were mercilessly exploited and possessed no rights either of person or of property', he expressed the hope that the stories he told of pre-British days would help justify the imperial takeover.[27]

The stories in this 1916 collection – all, Clifford claimed, based on fact – do contain romantic tropes: the unspoilt nature and the people's intimate relationship with it; the 'untroubled peace and quiet almost unimaginable to a modern European'; the 'wild days before the coming of the white men'; the beautiful young, and nearly naked, women. But in other places they are decidedly unromantic. The Aboriginal 'Sakai' are covered with 'leprous-looking skin disease', and their lives are depicted as a struggle against sickness and malnutrition. They are treated appallingly by the Malays who rob and enslave them. In one story titled 'Droit de Seigneur', a chief demands the attractive new wife of a peasant, who is killed when he resists. In another, we learn of the 'diabolical ingenuity' of the earlier widespread use of torture.[28]

In one story, 'A Malayan Prison', Clifford himself makes an appearance at the end. The 'horrible gaol-cages of Independent Malaya' are described in gruesome detail through the experience of an innocent man whose suffering makes him beg for death. Clifford claimed to have met this man, but was at that time 'powerless to affect his deliverance'. 'Readers of this true tale will perhaps realize how it comes to pass that some of us men – who have seen things, not merely heard of them – are apt to become rather strong "imperialists" and to find it at times difficult to endure with patience those ardent defenders of the Rights of Man, who bleat their comfortable aphorisms in the British House of Commons and cry shame upon our "hungry acquisitiveness".' The Liberal call might be that 'self-government is better than good government', but 'thousands of my friends in Malaya would passionately dissent'.[29]

Nonetheless, doubts remained. During the war, H. Egerton, the first Beit Professor of Colonial History at Oxford, had written a pamphlet as a riposte to German propaganda. In this, he held up Malaya as an example of the very best imperial practice. 'By conserving old feudal institutions as far as possible,' he wrote, 'and by dealing gently with local prejudices and by acting through the medium of the native rulers, British residents at the courts of these rulers have been able to bring about a material and moral improvement to which it would be difficult to find a parallel elsewhere; while they have been able to avoid that break with the past which so often has produced disastrous results in the history of native races.' Clifford was not so sure. The 'natural', he wrote, was being replaced by the 'artificial'. 'The Malay in his natural unregenerate state' was a 'more attractive individual than he is apt to become under the influence of European civilisation'. Although British rule 'relieves them of many things which hurt and oppressed them ere it came, it injures them morally almost as much as it benefits them materially'. The Malays on the west coast, the first brought under protection, were now, he said, 'sadly, dull, limp, and civilised' compared to those whose customs were still 'unsullied by European vulgarity'. Under protection, he wrote, 'the Malay' was apt to become 'morally weak and seedy, and to lose something of his robust self-respect'.[30]

This goes to the heart of the 'trusteeship' question, as debated by Arthur Grimble, Hubert Murray and the 'Dying Races' Congress in Australia: to preserve and protect from the outside world – the 'museum policy' – or to reform, banishing age-old unacceptable practices, and risk doing unpredictable damage?

In the Malay States it was an awkward, contradictory mixture of both. The peasants were encouraged to stay on the land in order to sustain the traditional structure of Malay society, nostalgically seen as nobly medieval, while at the same time, as Clifford wrote, such were 'the horrors of native rule' that 'the only salvation for the Malays lies in the increase of British influence, and in the consequent spread of modern ideas, progress, and civilisation'. The British presented themselves as paternalistic tutors of the Malay 'natural gentleman', yet tutelage, if successful, could only lead to the destruction of the perceived medieval society through development.[31]

Education sits at the heart of this contradiction. Rural Malays were encouraged to attend vernacular schools – and by 1923 efforts were at last being made to improve the quality of the teachers – but they were not taught English; only, as Education Director Winstedt put it in reply to Mohammed Yunus bin Abdullah, to become 'More intelligent farmers and fishermen'.

Clifford himself was ambivalent about even this level of education. There were, he noted, 'many lamentable instances of Malays who have been educated out of this self-respecting reserve'. Visiting a village in Pahang when Resident, he identified three types of Malay men: 'the old men whose wisdom is their own and of its kind deep and wide; the middle-aged tillers of the soil, whose lives are set in so straitened a rut that they cannot peep over the edges, and whose wisdom is of the field and the forest'; and the 'swaggering youngster, grown learned in the mysteries of reading and writing, fresh from our schools'. But their 'knowledge is borrowed, extraordinary imperfect of its kind, and fortified by the self-confidence of ignorance'. The first two types, he reported, were 'gradually dying out', being replaced by the last. This, Clifford wrote, 'sometimes tempts one to ask the heretical question whether European systems of education are really as practically educative as the unsystematic transmission of accumulated knowledge and tradition which they superseded'. He would take this conflicted attitude with him across the empire.[32]

'The great wheel of progress', he wrote in a later story, caused people of the 'weaker races' to take 'wrong turnings at every step, and go woefully astray. Let us hope that succeeding generations will become used to the new conditions, and will fight their way back to a truer path.' But he didn't suggest what this 'truer path' might consist of. The Malays, of course, had their own ideas.[33]

22

'Fatherless Young Chickens' and 'Pale Strangers'

Pulau Pinang hath a new town
And Captain Light is its king.
Think not of the days that are gone
Or you will bow low your head and your tears will flow.

Quatrain of the 'Men of Kedah'[1]

Towards the end of 1923, a young Malay translator, Zainal Abidin bin Ahmad, wrote an article for the *Malay Mail* entitled 'The Poverty of the Malays'. 'That they are poor in money matters goes without saying,' he wrote. But they were also 'poor in education, poor in intellectual equipment and moral qualities, they cannot be otherwise but left behind in the march of nations'.[2]

An attitude of paternalistic trusteeship such as that held by the British towards the Malays must depend on the relative powerlessness of the subject population. By the end of the nineteenth century, the Malays were seen, even by some of themselves, as passive, lazy, incompetent and unable to rule. But this staple colonial attitude is conspicuously absent from earlier writings. In the 1830s there was fierce fighting between the British and the Malays outside Malacca, and the Sultan of Kedah made a determined effort to drive Captain Light's British out of Penang. There was little talk then about the feebleness of 'The Malay'.[3]

For various reasons this had changed by the end of the century. The sharp growth in population and prosperity of the Straits Settlements cities, together with their transfer to the Crown in 1867, had altered the relative power of the British and the Malays. More widely, the nineteenth century saw a growing gap in technology and wealth between the Europeans – particularly the British – and the rest. This was combined with, and contributed to, a shift in thinking on race. Earlier multiple explanations of human diversity were replaced by a Social Darwinist theory of innate differences and inevitable struggles. This gave the dominance of the world by European peoples a moral purpose – it was inevitable, natural, and beneficial to the progress of all mankind. It was this confidence that underwrote the last great burst of imperial expansion at the end of the nineteenth century, in Malaya and, of course, elsewhere.

The Malay States, having been destabilised by the huge growth in tin mining, were in the years after 1874 literally and figuratively disarmed and the submission of their leaders either purchased or compelled by force of arms. At the same time, mass immigration of cheap and effective labour from China and India excluded Malays from the country's growing prosperity.

In October 1894, a Straits Chinese newspaper published a series of articles under the title 'Why are the Malays Withering Away?'. In theory written in a spirit of friendly criticism, they alleged that the reasons for Malay educational and economic backwardness included the decadence of their traditional leaders, interested only in women, opium and gambling, their lack of energy and ambition, their slavish adherence to outmoded traditions and their hostility to anyone who showed exceptional talents. The articles provoked anger and counter-blasts against the Straits Chinese, but there was no denying that in the Straits Settlements, the majority of the Malays formed an economically depressed and educationally inferior class, in particular in Penang and Singapore with their highly competitive Chinese majorities. Any clear-sighted Malays could plainly see that their society had been left behind in the modern world, and was failing to compete with the other races in the country.[4]

In Singapore, the richest and most influential Malays were in the main of some sort of Arab descent. Up until the end of the nineteenth century they were successful traders in tobacco, as well as brassware from Birmingham and haberdashery from Leicester. In addition, Singapore was a key shipping point for the Haj. Dutch colonial authorities in Indonesia restricted this passage to Mecca as they believed that returning Hajis were subversive socially and politically, but the British were less stringent, so Indonesians travelled first to Singapore. This pilgrimage industry was in the hands of Singapore Arabs and contributed significantly to their wealth.

These elite Muslims saw the economic and educational backwardness of most fellow Malays as a discredit to the wider Muslim world and the Muslim religion itself. In 1906 a group, almost all with educational links to Mecca or Cairo, launched a ground-breaking periodical *Al-Imam* (The Leader). The new journal announced its mission in its first issue: it was to 'arouse those who sleep' from the 'slough of apathy and indolence'. The ills of the Malay community were pronounced: backwardness, dominance by foreigners, complacency, laziness, disunity. Plenty more such self-laceration followed in subsequent issues. There were calls for more skills in craftsmanship and agriculture, an expansion and reform of education, and for unity, but 'the one thing that will strengthen and realise all our desires is knowledge of the commands of our religion. For religion is the proven cure for all the ills of our community.'[5]

Malays were Sunni Muslims but influenced by local traditions which included mysticism and magic. In the villages, rituals were still performed to ensure a good catch of fish or plentiful harvest, as well as to banish evil spirits. Such 'superstitious' practices, editorials in *Al-Imam* argued, should be purged. This 'purification' of Islam was not just for its own sake: traditional Islam as practised in the states was leaving Muslims open to criticism of obscurantism by the West and holding back social and economic change.

The group around *Al-Imam*, and its successor *Neracha*, soon came to be known as Kaum Muda ('Young Faction') in opposition to the official religious hierarchy, personified by the village *uluma* and backed by the Sultans and chiefs, known as Kaum Tua ('Old Faction'). To be Kaum Muda was to espouse modernism in any form and go against tradition; to be Kaum Tua was to be in favour of all that was familiar, unchanging and secure.

The Kaum Muda established reformist madrasah and published pamphlets promoting its agenda. These stimulated debates at a village level about whether, for example, it was acceptable to wear trousers and a tie, to take interest from post office savings banks and rural cooperatives, or to pray at the local *keramat* (spirit shrine).[6]

The Malay ruling elite in the states, stripped of all power save 'Malay religion and custom', had flexed their muscles in this last remaining area, establishing authoritarian rule over the religious hierarchy. So an attack on the traditional structure was an attack on them, and some reformist teachers were arrested or exiled, and publications censored. But this was not possible in the directly run Straits Settlements – 'one of the major benefits of British rule', as one reformer commented.

Part of the Kaum Muda manifesto, in common with the founding principles of Aligarh College in India, was the idea that Islam was not hostile to knowledge and progress as exemplified by the West. Education should include a pure Islam purged of embarrassing local traditions and esoteric accretions, but also modern secular knowledge. New schools should teach English as well as Arabic, and modern educational subjects. There should also be greater freedom for women to receive education and participate in public life. All of this, they argued, would allow Malays to compete with those who currently ruled and dominated them.

It has been suggested that the comparable Islamic reformist movement in Indonesia was a sort of pre-nationalism. To an extent this is true for Malaya, but the Kaum Muda never put forward a political programme, nor organised in such a way as to attract mass support for political nationalism. But its publications did include reports from the wider pan-Islamic world (as well as following the inspiring rise of Japan) and, at a time when few Malays recognised allegiance outside their state or Sultan, suggested a wider unity based on religion and common experience of colonial rule. Furthermore, their insistence on the equality of all men before God, and on a more individualistic approach to religion, was subversive of the existing political as well as religious order. In time, the movement would take a more secular and radical direction.

Also in its infancy was a new secular Malay nationalism based around the Sultan Idris Teacher Training College. Founded in 1922, it brought together some 400 of the best graduates from Malay vernacular schools in a residential setting in Perak. The following year it established its own magazine. In time, influenced by Indonesian nationalism, it would become a nursery for a radical Malay intelligentsia critical of Malay feudalism as well as British imperialism, but for now, its students concentrated on little more than the development of a modern Malay literature and literary and debating groups as a stimulant to progress. The training college did bring together Malays from across the peninsula, and its British headmaster stressed loyalty to Malaya over the individual states, but at the end of 1923 its students remained wedded to the idea of Malay inferiority. As one of its students, Zainal Abidin bin Ahmad, quoted above, wrote in the same article for the *Malay Mail* about his fellow Malays: 'Their literature is poor and unelevating; their domestic surroundings from childhood are poor and seldom edifying; their outlook on life is poor and full of gloom ... In short, the Malays cut poor figures in every department of life.'[7]

Meanwhile, the Malay secular press consisted of just one daily paper, the *Lembaga Melayu*, published by the British proprietor of the English-language *Malaya Tribune*, and edited by Yunus bin Abdullah.

For all his frustrated anger in the Legislative Council at the issue of English teaching in Malay schools, his paper was only ever very mildly critical of government policy and took the view that Malays should take the responsibility of helping themselves.

So in Malaya there was less opposition to colonial rule than perhaps any comparable place in the empire. The British had pretty much succeeded in leaving the ordinary Malay peasant's life unchanged, apart from the improvements of freedom from partial justice, forced work and exactions from the chiefs and Sultans. Although some had started, despite official disapproval, growing rubber, most were, as the Malay expression has it, 'the frog beneath the coconut shell' – knowing no other world and content with his immediate surroundings. A British official could pronounce in the Federal Council, without too much fear of contradiction, that Malaya had 'no politics' and was 'one of the very few territories in the world to-day where there is no real poverty, no unrest, no oppressive taxation, and no racial ill-feeling'. In contrast to India, wrote Victor Purcell, 'We did not feel ourselves in the presence of a hostile nationalism.'[8]

A couple of years later, a Malayan writer declared that 'Malays are quite satisfied with present arrangements, as they know full well that if they get rid of the British, they will be worse off under some other power who would be sure to overrun the country ... it is dangerous for fatherless young chickens like ourselves ... to move about alone where there are hawks and eagles hovering about ready to pounce upon them.'[9]

Despite this, the British community in Malaya had a reputation for leading lives that were surprisingly anxious and unstable. Riding the coat-tails of Conrad, Clifford and a handful of others, Malaya had become fashionable reading, resulting in a flurry of publications including travellers' accounts, guide books, novels and stories. None, though, were more popular than the short stories of W. Somerset Maugham, the undisputed king of British letters, admired across the spectrum. George Orwell would call him 'the modern writer who has influenced me most'. Around September 1923 his Malaya short stories, garnered from a recent trip he had made there, were being published about every other month in Hearst-owned magazines that sold in the millions. Before paperbacks, these magazines constituted fiction's mass reach. Maugham's success made the British community in Malaya perhaps the most famous, or infamous, in the empire. His millions of readers would be given a very particular take on life in the British community in Malaya which would shape popular perceptions in Britain and the United States, not just of that particular colony but of the wider empire. The British in Malaya were embarrassed and furious.

In the two decades after 1901, the 'European' community (of whom over 80 per cent were British) nearly tripled to some 15,000, fairly equally distributed between the Straits Settlements and the Malay States. The new men worked in planting, mining, finance and commerce. It was part of a huge expansion of population thanks to mass immigration – alongside a booming export economy.

By late 1923 Malaya's trade exceeded the aggregate volume of all the other British colonies and protectorates combined. The value of the exports per head of population made Malaya the richest country on earth. In a book published in 1923, an American traveller, Hermann Norden, described Malaya as the 'land of King Rubber and Prince Tin'. In Kuala Lumpur, whose population had grown from 30,000 in 1901 to 80,000 twenty years later (with 2,500 Europeans), he admired the 'substantial houses and villas standing in gardens along the borders of lakes and rivers'. The beautiful European quarter of the city, he remarked, suggested an aristocratic European or American resort rather than the tropics.[10]

In just two years, the number of motor cars in Kuala Lumpur had trebled to over 4,500. A cold storage company had established a branch supplying butter, beef, mutton and vegetables from Australia, there were two large hotels and a department store – John Little's – with electric lifts and fans, and a café which quickly became a social centre for European women.[11]

Most Europeans enjoyed a higher standard of living than they would at home. While in Britain post-war middle-class families would have considered themselves fortunate to have one servant, for a European home in Malaya it was deemed essential to have seven: a cook, a gardener, a chauffeur/mechanic, a 'boy' who performed general household duties, a water carrier (who would also clean the toilets or commodes), an ayah or several to look after young children, and a washerman.[12]

All this prosperity, as the American traveller Norden noted, was, of course, floating on a sea of cheap labour. He visited a tin mine near Ipoh where he saw 'vast machinery of the most modern type in use; steam and electric power hoists, hydraulicking and dredging'. But close beside, he noticed, there were still numerous 'Chinese coolies with pick and shovel'. Underpaid Chinese workers, many in ruinous debt, continued to do the hard and dangerous work on the ground.[13]

The rubber plantations were worse. Here the labour force, almost all Indians, while undergoing the physically draining procedures of planting and tapping, were accommodated in overcrowded estate 'lines' in conditions that promoted viral infections, hookworm and diarrhoeal diseases. Beatings were commonplace and suicide another major killer. In 1920, a separate health branch within the FMS Medical Department was established to oversee living conditions on the estates and drive the construction of stone-built accommodation, deep pit latrines and the means to supply running water. A minimum wage, albeit low, was established, but at the end of the decade death rates were still sufficiently high to prompt a Colonial Office investigation.[14]

The international price of rubber, like all commodities, slumped in mid-1921 but was recovering well by September 1923. In the meantime, fortunes had been made, with planters retiring with nest-eggs of up to £100,000. The richest were those who had established plantations early, floated them as a company and seen their shares increase in value up to eight-fold as European investors flooded in.

Most of the Malayan Civil Service (MCS) were English, but a little more than a third of the 'European' planters and miners were Scots. Newspapers of 29 September 1923 reported a concert given by the Associated Scottish Pipers of Malaya, who 'rendered a selection of

Highland Marches'. (Papers of that day also mentioned a recent debate about the Singapore naval base, fighting between Triad gangs in the city, the severe injuries to three young British men and two women who, after leaving a dance at the Raffles Hotel, drove their car off a cliff, and the suicide of a mining engineer in a Penang hotel.)[15]

The great new wealth of the 'unofficial' members of the European community, however, had put the British civil servants in an awkward position. Previously in the rubber districts the district officer would have been the undisputed leader or *Tuan*, from his position and the fact that he would have been the highest-paid European. As such he was expected to entertain local visitors and give more support than anyone else to local charities. But this was no longer the case and the newly rich planters could now entertain on an unbeatable scale. Some Chinese, too, were living lavishly on a level out of reach of the government servants and at the same time pushing up prices.

More widely, the colonial officers were expected to put on a show, to live in a manner befitting their status as governors and their perceived innate superiority. How else were they to retain the respect of the Asian population? It was all about prestige, believed to be the magic formula that sustained and justified British rule. But it was expensive – everyone needed servants, a car, imported food, smart tails or white monkey jackets for dinners at Government House – and after the war, after numerous complaints of penury, a salary commission was appointed to investigate.

The Governor himself pointed out to the commission that the 'official who would be quite prepared to travel third class in England must perforce travel first class here'. The investigators agreed that an official had to live in 'a more luxurious style', 'whether he wishes to do so or not'. Otherwise he would 'diminish the credit of the Service in the eyes both of unofficial Europeans and of the native communities'. The government officers were given a hefty rise in salary, making them the best-paid officials in the empire. Fortunately, government revenue was more than up to the task.

However, there still remained a small number of 'poor whites', the largest group of which were train drivers, brought in with the expansion of the railways. Largely working class, they were excluded from the clubs and social activities enjoyed by the privately educated planters and officials. They were paid about the same as they would be in Britain, but because of the higher cost of living were compelled to work up to twelve-hour shifts to match the income of even the most junior MCS cadet. 'We are on the same level as the Asiatic,' one embittered train driver told the salary commission. Their wives could not afford to shop at John Little's or the Cold Storage, so instead would be seen haggling in the Chinese shops. It was all a bit unseemly. 'Unless a European can earn a wage on which he is able to live decently as a European should, he merely brings discredit and contempt upon the British community,' pronounced the commission. The solution implemented by the General Manager of the Railways was to replace what the commission called this 'class of poor whites' with non-Europeans, mainly Eurasians from India.[16]

There was a similar challenge when the brief rubber slump of 1921 threw a number of young British men out of work. Hermann Norden was in Singapore at the time, and reported 'Handsome young Englishmen, still dressed in the whites of the tropics, though whites no longer immaculate, who come into the clubs and hotels to borrow small sums from any who will lend. A white man without resource in a yellow man's country is always a tragic sight.' *Planter* magazine agreed that 'the spectacle of unemployed Europeans' threatened to 'destroy European credit and prestige in a native country'. The government quickly stepped in with a fund, including grants and help with passage away to England or Australia.[17]

Apart from failing to live 'decently as a European should', there were other ways in which the all-important carapace of prestige could be damaged. As elsewhere, the war had hurt white prestige; efforts were made to censor cinema that showed whites as crooks, or white women as lewd. The white community were by all reports heavy drinkers. Victor Purcell admitted that the per capita consumption of whisky 'was no doubt higher in Malaya than it was in Britain, but one has to consider the extenuating facts of a higher per capita income and a more trying climate'. He confessed he drank a 'very great deal' but never became a 'soak'. Public drunkenness, though, was damaging. When two planters received fines for unruly behaviour and assaulting a Chinese barman in a railway restaurant car, they were berated by *Planter* magazine for behaviour which 'degrades the European in the sight of the Oriental'. But what was perhaps most damaging, and most complicated, was sexual behaviour.[18]

Male homosexuality was in theory taboo, despite the fact that a career in the colonies 'attracted an unusually high proportion of men who had good reason for wishing to avoid marriage at home'. Beyond Suez was seen as offering expanded opportunity, in terms of a more liberal attitude and the widespread all-male brothels and young impoverished boys plying their trade on beachfronts and in bars. Maugham, according to one biographer, 'always maintained that the most memorable sexual experience of his life had been with a local boy on a moonlit night in a sampan in Malaya'.[19]

Nonetheless, homosexuality was strongly condemned at this time, and those found out publicly would be ostracised by much of the rest of the European community. There are mixed reports on its prevalence in Malaya. One informant to a social historian estimated that in the 1920s two thirds of European men had homosexual relations with Asians. Another said that it was extremely rare. In the 1930s the diary of a professional Chinese catamite fell into the hands of the police, resulting in an official inquiry, the disgrace of several prominent persons and the suicides of two implicated in the matter.[20]

At the end of the nineteenth century, concubinage by European men with local women was no longer in fashion in India (where in the eighteenth century, a third of British wills left everything to Indian wives), but it was still widely practised in Burma, Malaya and most of the African colonies.

Before the First World War, it was the norm in Malaya for young bachelors in isolated local districts, whether officials or planters, to have 'native' mistresses. Pioneering Resident Hugh Low had a Malayan wife. His protégé Hugh Clifford was sympathetic to the plight of a young man 'long removed from all intercourse with women of his own race'. In his semi-autobiographical novel *Since the Beginning* (1898), he wrote of a young official who is seduced by a Malay woman provocatively bathing near his houseboat. He is overwhelmed by 'burning admiration of her beauty'; her touch gives him 'wild emotions'.[21]

To blame, many thought, was the unmarried status of almost all colonial officers in their twenties. In fact, at home, it was the custom for middle-class men to wait until 'well established' before taking on a bride, usually in their late twenties at the earliest. In Malaya, even the inflated salaries did not cover the expense of a wife until many years' service had been completed. This was still being debated in late 1923. In a letter to the *Planter* magazine of August 1923, a doctor in the Malay States pushing for higher salaries to enable earlier marriage asked its readers to sympathise with 'the young assistant standing all day over Asiatic labour, many of them working with breasts and bodies exposed to the sun, surrounded by women to whom a few dollars are a fortune for which they would sell the best of themselves, and exposed to all the insidious temptations of the heated tropical zone'.

Not everyone agreed. Sir Harry Johnston, a pioneer explorer in East Africa, was appalled to see even the best and most hard-working colonial officials in Uganda taking on patently exploitative and unequal sexual relationships, which he saw as undesirable and demoralising on all sides. In Burma in the 1890s the Governor expostulated that the same rules at home, in terms of decorum and respect, should apply in the colonies, whatever the challenges faced by isolated unmarried men far from home.

For a long time, though, there was from senior officials a sympathetic approach to 'youthful transgressions'. The Colonial Office's opinion was that a man's private life did not concern the government unless it caused a public scandal or it involved a married woman.

But by 1923 concubinage was much less common for several reasons. In 1908, a shocking incident had come to light that would prompt official action on the issue. An acting District Commissioner in central Kenya, Hubert Silberrad, had found on taking up his post in 1905 that he had inherited from his predecessor, C. W. I. Haywood, two local girls called Nyambura and Wameisa. Haywood had paid forty goats for each of them (mistresses were usually arranged as a business transaction with the male members of a girl's family). Wameisa, who was no more than twelve, was reluctant to be handed on, but had little choice but to consent. Nyambura was given a monthly wage to stay with Silberrad. Then a third girl became involved, Nyakayena, the twelve- or thirteen-year-old wife of a Masai policeman, Mugalla. He contracted out Nyakayena to Silberrad, but then seems to have changed his mind, leading to a fracas at Silberrad's kitchen door, which ended up with the Kenyan being locked in the guardroom for the night on the grounds of insubordination.

This was all too much for a neighbouring, non-official English couple, who removed the young girls from Silberrad's house and complained to the Governor. After a legal inquiry into the situation, which focused on the imprisonment of the policeman as the most discreditable part of the affair, Silberrad was demoted by a year and sent on five months' leave in England (where he married). Haywood was 'severely admonished' but allowed to continue his duties.

This was insufficient punishment in the eyes of Silberrad's neighbours, who wrote a letter to *The Times*. This led to a debate in the House of Commons, which united Conservatives with 'pro-native' Liberal humanitarians in condemnation. Josiah Wedgwood was one of the MPs demanding action.

The result was the Crewe Circular of January 1909, a confidential dispatch that declared that 'native concubinage' constituted a 'grave injury to good administration'. By indulging in the practice a man could not avoid 'lowering himself in the eyes of the natives, and diminishing his authority'. The Marquess of Crewe was the Secretary of State for the Colonies in Asquith's Liberal government. He warned of 'summary punishment' for actions which 'have resulted in scandal and grave discredit to the service'.[22]

In Malaya, a few married their mistresses rather than give them up. Others entirely ignored the order, or just became more private about it. Alec Waugh, who travelled in Malaya in the 1920s, wrote that 'there is fairly often a Malay girl who disappears discreetly when visitors arrive'.[23]

But there was undoubtedly a steep decline in concubinage by 1923. Earlier, in isolated districts 'up-country', the majority of single European men would have had a local mistress, perhaps as many as 80 per cent. But by the mid-1920s, according to one estimate, it was less than a quarter.

This was not down entirely to the Crewe Circular. The period also saw a hardening of racial boundaries, a process that saw Eurasians no longer counted as Europeans in the censuses, weeded out of the civil service, and generally shunned (Eurasians reacted by forming their own united, endogamous and separate community). Now Europeans who 'went native' – that is, lived openly with local women (and thus risked creating more of the worryingly racially ambiguous Eurasians) – were socially ostracised.

There was also a change in attitude to the use of prostitutes in the towns and cities. Previously, while in Britain campaigners at the end of the nineteenth century were successfully forcing the criminalisation of prostitution at home (and thereby ending the earlier compulsory medical checks), in Malaya there was a widespread view that European men could enjoy considerably more sexual freedom, the main justifications being the climate (which 'aroused passions') and the scarcity of European women. It was a rite of passage for an incoming young man to visit the brothels of Malay Street in Singapore, or Petaling Street in Kuala Lumpur. Preferred were the Japanese, or the thirty or so European prostitutes, all from southern, central and eastern Europe (any British prostitute discovered would be immediately deported because of the damage she did to British prestige).

The idea of an Asian being able to use a white prostitute had caused anguish to some, and at the beginning of the war the European brothels were closed down. In 1919, at the request of the Japanese

Consul-General in Singapore, the Japanese brothels followed suit. Of course, this did not end the practice, but merely pushed it underground, as evidenced by the severe problems with VD in the following years once the medical checks had ended. But, as with Asian mistresses, it was now something to be done discreetly.

The most important factor in the changing behaviour, however, was the significant increase in the European female population of the Straits Settlements and the Malay States. For a long time, living conditions were not considered suitable for European women. But by September 1923 the threat of malaria had been reduced and even smaller towns had amenities like Cold Storage shops and clubs. Railways, cars and roads had reduced the isolation of 'up-country'. By the time of the 1921 census, a third of the European population were women, and just over half of men in their early thirties were married – a large increase over just ten years before.[24]

Allowing men to be able to afford to marry earlier had been a big part of the successful campaign for higher salaries. The Reverend W. E. Horley, chairman of the Methodist-Episcopal Committee on Public Morals, had been part of this, arguing that wives from home would help deal with the social problems in the white male community of prostitution, concubinage, suicide and alcoholism.

Although there was a 'fishing fleet', most marriages were contracted back at home on leave. Incoming wives were expected, alongside the traditional restorative and nurturing functions, to produce pure-bred children, provide adornment at dinners, teas and garden parties, and police their men to stop them transgressing. Men who fell into 'bad ways' were strongly advised to find a European wife to sort themselves out.

Wives were expected to reproduce – as much as possible – the supposedly wholesome middle-class domestic and social life of home, to recreate the familiar and exclude the foreign. Amid a mass of Asians, they were to reinforce white prestige, understand that they were the elite purely by virtue of their race, and throw themselves into the activities of the small European community. A guide for new wives going out to the colonies warned that 'the part you play in the life of the community is as much the subject of scrutiny by your elders as the quality of your husband's work in the office or in the district'.[25]

According to a letter sent to *Planter* magazine in 1923, the difference in 'moral conditions' prevailing in a district with white women compared to one without was almost too obvious to state. Lillian Newton, who was living in Singapore in September 1923, later told an interviewer that when white women were present, men dressed smarter, looked after themselves better and modified their language and behaviour. By stabilising the community, she said, the women helped prevent white men from going 'troppo' (having a breakdown – a point, of course, made by Arthur Grimble in his 'Women as Empire Builders' article), sinking into alcoholism, or 'going native', all of which 'let the side down' and were a threat to white prestige.[26]

Not everyone agreed that the influx of wives was an uncontested force for good. Some husbands were ambivalent, one describing the memsahibs as 'necessary nuisances'. The Governor in Singapore, Sir Laurence Guillemard, was concerned about junior officers marrying and therefore not being able to spend long periods in the rural interior getting to know the people there. Wives were a distraction, a block between the British official and the 'native'. Clifford, who brought a wife out to Malaya in 1896, had shared this concern. In 1923 Guillemard decreed that only unmarried cadets should be recruited, and those who married on their first four-year tour would not be entitled to the extra allowance given to married officials.[27]

The arrival of the wives usually saw the rejection of the 'keeps', as Asian mistresses were known. Some were given lump sums or regular pensions, sometimes very substantial. Others were simply dumped and told to make themselves scarce. Similarly, any resulting children might be provided for or not. Returning to Malaya with a bride from Britain was easier for government officials, who would probably be posted somewhere else anyway, or could request to be. It was more awkward when you were a miner or a planter tied to a particular location. There were, according to an anonymous letter from a woman to the *Malay*

Mail, 'countless disillusioned brides' confronted with their new husband's previous lovers or even children. This was part of a series of letters on the subject. 'A Woman' condemned the double standards of sexual morality, but pointed out that it was the same at home. Another female correspondent, 'All White', was resigned to the fact that 'few men are pure on their marriage ... I'm not a prude', but was appalled that men might 'prefer black to white ... this is truly what hurts us women'.[28]

Regardless of their personal attributes or past achievements, wives in Malaya were the personal dependants of their husbands, and were ranked solely in terms of the status held by their husbands, be they in government or business. They were expected not to work – it was considered bad for their health and it would reflect badly on their husband.

There were a very small number of single European women, some deliberately looking for husbands, and a handful of nurses and teachers. A tiny number went to Malaya as children's governesses, but it was restricted by the difficulty they suffered from being as a white person part of the all-Asian domestic staff.

Single women were generally under pressure to get married, and with the ratio of men to women still two to one they had plenty of bachelors to choose from (young wives, of course, also attracted admirers). Hardly any white women married Asians, which would have led to ostracisation, unless it happened to be a Malay royal (as did occur on one occasion).

Although at the end of 1923 a small number were still 'roughing it' up-country, most wives, like their husbands, would be enjoying a higher standard of living than at home. But, as the contemporary *Handbook to British Malaya* warned: 'The chief disadvantage for ladies is often the lack of interesting occupation during the day.' In the larger towns, where there were European stores, they could go shopping during the morning, or visit friends, 'but in the smaller stations or on estates or mines, life is apt to be monotonous ... time hangs heavily on her hands'. Thanks to the persistent but entirely erroneous belief that women suffered more than men from the tropical heat, wives were advised that 'the climate is unsuited to housework, and too much sewing or reading may have its effect on the eyesight . . . The afternoon is usually devoted to a siesta, which most ladies find necessary in a hot and somewhat enervating climate.'[29]

Adding to the tedium was the homogeneous, conformist and exclusive nature of white society by this time. In a newspaper article titled 'First Impressions', a newly arrived wife wrote in March 1922: 'I think my first feeling was that I had never before been a member of a community of which such a large proportion came from one class, was the product of one form of education and whose outlook on life therefore was so uniform.' One of the duties of wives was instructing new arrivals with practical advice on, for instance, water filters, cockroaches or dealing with servants. But it also involved the transmission of the unwritten norms of behaviour. The rules for wives were summed up by one woman as 'Everybody does this, nobody does that.' This process contributed to a maintenance of the status quo and an inhibition of independent thought or action.[30]

A small number of women, often flying in the face of their husbands' disapproval, were involved with charitable or voluntary welfare work, such as the Young Women's Christian Association and the Girl Guides, but friendships with Asian women were rare to the point of non-existence. For one thing, few European women learned Malay or Chinese, and, apart from the wives of some rich Chinese like Tan Cheng Lock, hardly any Asian women spoke English.

Some women wrote of long-lasting relationships with servants. One, Cynthia Koek, told of how she took on a young boy in the early 1920s, trained him up and taught him English, and how this helped him get a good job as head chef in a Singapore club. When, during the Second World War, the Koeks were interned by the Japanese in Changi Prison, he brought them dried food and other essentials. Others, though, did not engage with them as people. One woman later wrote of her staff that they 'didn't seem to exist, they were sort of background, there for my benefit. What I missed and how I regret it now!'[31]

Even within the 'European' community there was self-imposed

isolation. Non-English wives felt the English looked down on them, while in turn Scots, Americans and Australians were considered by the English too 'casual' and 'egalitarian'. Again and again, guides for colonial wives warn of the greatest downside to life and threat to happiness and health: loneliness.

As part of their role to create 'normal family life', wives were expected to have children, and most did. But even this did little to fill the empty hours, as infants would be cared for by *amahs* (nursemaids). One mother remembered that her role with her babies was little more than intervening to stop the *amahs* giving them small doses of opium to placate them when teething. Another, Ida Bryson, wrote to a friend, 'You can have very little idea of the enormous grip which the average *amah* gets on a child even with the mother about most of the time.'[32]

It got worse when the children reached five or six. Here came what was dubbed the 'Tragedy of the East' and 'one of the chief disadvantages of the European's existence in the Tropics'. The *Handbook to British Malaya* spells it out: 'it is inadvisable to keep [European children] in the country after the age of six'. Part of this was social: they would be spoiled by the number of servants; there were 'very limited . . . opportunities for association with other children' (i.e. white children); and educational facilities 'suitable for European children do not exist'. This meant, of course, they didn't want them to go to local schools where they would have to associate with Asian children, maybe even be surpassed by them in schoolwork – therefore damaging prestige. But the most persuasive was the medical evidence.[33]

The *Handbook* suggests that after the age of six, European children in a tropical climate 'tend to become anaemic'. In an article for the *Lancet* titled 'Problems of Acclimatisation' published in August 1923, a Dr Andrew Balfour of the Wellcome Bureau summarised the latest research. In the tropics, puberty came at least a year earlier and growth, though rapid, was 'unaccompanied by increase in weight and strength. Hence the "weedy" European child so common in the hot moist tropics.' Furthermore, the climate put the children's 'nervous systems' in 'a state of unstable equilibrium', the result being that 'illness, fretfulness and peevishness are common and a condition approaching hysteria may even be encountered. One is inclined', Balfour concluded, 'to regard such manifestations as of serious import for the welfare of the race.'[34]

However heartbreaking for parents and, of course, the children themselves, most families in Malaya acted on the advice to send their six- or seven-year-old children away. The 1921 census shows 600-odd European under-fives becoming about 150 five-to-nines, fewer than a hundred ten-to-fourteens and even fewer later teenagers. The lack of 'opportunities for association with other [white] children' thus became a self-fulfilling prophecy.[35]

The 'Tragedy of the East', apart from anything else, presented European women with divided loyalties between their roles of wife and mother. Indeed, many would stay over for a few more months at least after leave in England, and the 1921 census shows that about a third of married women were back in England with the children rather than with their husbands in Malaya.

The *Lancet* article wasn't just about children, but also looked at the latest research into (white) adult reaction to life in the tropics. Hot climates, it suggested, might 'upset the menstrual cycle in white women' and lessen their fertility. The 'chief stress of the Tropical climate', however, fell on the 'nervous system ... and this is the system which presents the greatest barrier to white colonization'.[36]

'At first tropical heat stimulates', the doctor explained. But this was followed by 'depression, and if this depression be exaggerated we get the neurasthenic condition – so often associated with loss of memory'. Other symptoms included 'increased knee-jerks, sleeplessness ... and starting at a sudden noise'. This condition had many names, including 'Malayan Head', 'Punjab Head', etc. After three or four years in the tropics, it had been noticed, white men no longer displayed as much energy in their work and many became nervous or irritable and found it difficult to concentrate or remember even important appointments. The rate of suicide was also very high. Dr Balfour pointed to recent medical data from Dutch Indonesia, which suggested that in a year, out of 189 cases of disease on account of which leave was granted, 111 were 'examples of psychoses or psycho-neuroses'.[37]

Dr Balfour concluded that 'the hot and humid tropics are not suited to white colonization and never will be'. The handbook on 'Life in Malaya' is less downbeat but comes to the same conclusion: 'The climate, while not so black as it is often painted, is not such as would induce many to make it a permanent place of retirement.'

Thus, there was no question of white planters or businessmen and their families making Malaya their permanent home, as Tan Cheng Lock was urging. They were always, as Dr Lim had pointed out, 'birds of passage'. But at the same time, a return to Britain, stripped of the plethora of cheap servants and the automatic racially superior status, held few attractions.[38]

Somerset Maugham had already travelled to the Pacific and China in successful searches for material, and his two trips to Malaya were motivated by the same impulse. And, as before, he was accompanied by his secretary/partner Gerald Haxton, a semi-alcoholic American who provided Maugham with the most important relationship of his life.

When not overly drunk, or committed to some high-stakes gambling, the good-looking Haxton was, unlike the shy and prim Maugham, garrulous and charming. With Haxton's help, Maugham secured numerous letters of introduction and heard lots of stimulating stories.

Often Maugham would turn up with a letter of introduction at some remote spot, rather embarrassed to be imposing himself on his host. But he was always welcomed by people lonely or bored with their usual circle and keen to hear news from home from a fresh face. After a few whiskies, Maugham later wrote, 'they unburdened themselves ... People tell you things they would not tell an acquaintance of 20 years.' These 'things' became the basis for Maugham's bestselling Malaya stories. His 'passage [in Malaya] was clearly marked by a trail of angry people', Victor Purcell later wrote. 'It was charged against him that he abused hospitality by ferreting out the family skeletons of his hosts and putting them into his books.'[39]

While collecting material, Maugham wrote in his notebook as he went along, including a number of character sketches of those he met. The people are generally 'melancholy' and 'morbid'. There is 'A Planter' – 'There is something pathetic about him. He lives alone in a very untidy bungalow. On the walls are innumerable pictures of women in all states of undress.' A Resident in North Borneo tells him of his alcoholism. Another, though he has been in Malaya for thirty years, 'speaks little Malay and takes no interest in the country or in anything else but doing his work ... and getting away as soon as he is entitled to a pension'.[40]

The desire to go home, but a dread of its resultant fall in status, is a recurring theme. Maugham wrote of the British expatriates: 'They are bored with themselves, bored with one another. They look forward to their freedom from bondage and yet the future fills them with dismay.' In his novel *The Painted Veil*, written after his trip to Hong Kong, a character (whose face is a 'mask' as she sends her third son off to boarding school in England) is the daughter of a colonial Governor: 'Of course it was very grand while it lasted – every one stood up when you entered a room and men took off their hats to you as you passed in your car – but what could be more insignificant than a colonial governor when he had retired? Dorothy Townsend's father lived on a pension in a small house at Earl's Court.'[41]

In general Maugham, sharing the widespread snobbishness towards colonials, found the British of Malaya to be middle-brow-at-best suburbanites, over-promoted to the status of master race in the East. (Noel Coward would call Malaya 'A first rate place for second rate people'.) They were a 'less adventurous generation' than the pioneers, Maugham decided, and 'You would have to go far to find among the planters a man of culture, reading or distinction.' Most of them 'drank too much ... read nothing worth reading ... If you were interested in the things of the spirit you were a prig.' Instead, 'They were eaten up with envy of one another and devoured by petty jealousies. And the women, poor things, were obsessed by petty rivalries. They made a circle that was more provincial than in the smallest town in England. They were prudish and spiteful.' Most of the memsahibs if they were back home, Maugham commented, 'instead of having a house with plenty of servants and a motor car, would … be serving behind a counter'.[42]

Maugham was by no means critical of the imperial project in Malaya. He praised the 'planters and administrators' who, 'with all their shortcomings, have after all brought to the peoples among whom they dwell tranquillity, justice and welfare'. But in his stories he delighted in prising open the cracks in the prestige façade and exploring the strains and stresses involved in maintaining 'white supremacy'.[43]

Most of the Malaya stories, like the earlier ones set in the Pacific, involve a male narrator being told of an incidence of transgression against colonial discipline when its protagonists have become undone by trespassing over the rigid boundaries they have set for themselves. Boundaries are a recurring motif: the 'trim lawns, so strangely English, and the savage growth of the jungle beyond'. Alcoholism, adultery and inter-racial sexual relations are central to most of the Malaya stories. In 'The Force of Circumstance', first published in February 1924, a seemingly ideal marriage breaks down when the new English wife discovers her husband's previous Malay lover and children. 'I think of those thin, black arms of hers round you,' says the wife, 'and it fills me with a physical nausea.' In 'The Letter' (April 1924), a man is murdered by his married white lover when she discovers he is living with a Chinese woman. In one story, 'The Yellow Streak' (August 1925), an Englishman of seemingly impeccable pedigree – the right school and regiment – lives in almost mortal fear of it being discovered that he has a half-Malay mother, explaining his dark complexion as down to a 'Spanish grandmother'. 'Before the Party' (December 1922) tells the story of a British official in Malaya who, because of his drunkenness, is ordered to go home to bring back a wife to straighten him out. But the official, who like Clifford refused to wear 'sun-helmets … very bad for the hair', relapses and is eventually murdered by his wife.[44]

In general, Maugham depicts the British in Malaya as prematurely aged by the climate, but at the same time psychologically stunted. The narrator of one story describes 'middle-aged gentlemen' as 'speaking and acting like schoolboys. You might almost think that no idea has entered their heads since they first passed through the Suez Canal.'[45]

The first tranche of Malaya stories was collected together and published in book form as *The Casuarina Tree* to great commercial and critical success. Cyril Connolly described it as one of the key books of the 'modern movement' because 'he tells us – and it has not been said before – exactly what the British in the Far East were like, the judges and planters and civil servants and their womenfolk at home'. Unsurprisingly, those depicted begged to differ. The stories, Maugham later wrote, 'earned me considerable criticism and hatred. On my return visits to many of those places a lot of doors were rudely slammed in my face, I was publicly insulted, and some even threatened to do me bodily harm.' Even years later, by which time several of the stories had become successful plays or films, a Singapore newspaper noted the 'intense and widespread prejudice against Somerset Maugham in this part of the world'. At fault was his 'cynical emphasis on the same unpleasant things' – 'murder, cowardice, drink, seduction, adultery ... No wonder that white men and women who are living normal lives in Malaysia wish that Mr. Maugham would look for local color elsewhere.'[46]

At times, Maugham would apologise for misrepresenting the 'ordinary people' in Malaya, 'ordinarily satisfied with their station in life'. At other times he would claim, with some justification, that all the stories were based, at least, on things he was told on his travels. Old Malaya hand Bruce Lockhart, while denying that the scurrilous stories were 'in any way a true reflection of British life in Malaya as a whole', conceded his admiration for the 'accuracy or the brilliance with which Mr Maugham has described certain exceptional aspects of European life in the East'.[47]

It was noticed by critics at home that the 'oriental' stories contained virtually no Asian characters. Maugham would later defend himself, writing that 'all the depictions that had been made of either Chinese, Indians or Malays were merely superficial impressions combined with a lot of conventional prejudices'. The tiny few depicted, though, are interesting. In 'P&O' (February 1923), where a planter is punished on a voyage home for deserting his long-time Asian mistress, two 'little Japanese gentlemen' are described playing deck quoits. In their tennis shirts and white trousers 'they looked very European' and even called the score out to each other in English. This sight fills the central character 'with a vague disquiet. Because they seemed so easily to wear a disguise there was about them something sinister.' In 'The Letter', a lawyer's Chinese assistant also dresses immaculately as a European, with 'white ducks' and shiny patent leather shoes, as well as speaking 'beautiful English'. He ends up blackmailing one European and compromising the professional integrity of another.[48]

Was being 'European' and 'separate' – the dress, the language – these characters seemed to ask, nothing more than a performance?

Despite these few examples, the Maugham Malaya stories pretty much occur in a 'European' bubble. Anthony Burgess defended him for this, writing that 'Maugham cannot be blamed for making his stories centre on ... Europeans, since they were the only people he could really get to know.'[49]

In his notebook, Maugham shared this ignorance of local people across the 'European' community. Watching a crowd in a provincial town, he saw that 'through that press of people passes the white man who rules them. He is never part of the life about him.' The British colonial official, planter, trader was there, but not quite there: 'a pale stranger who moves through all this reality like a being from another planet ... he is the eternal exile. He has no interest in the place.' Alec Waugh, the tireless traveller, came to the same conclusion, writing of the English in Malaya in the 1920s: 'They make no attempt to assimilate into the character of the country they occupy ... An Englishman living in Penang is as little affected by the presence round him of the Malays, the Tamils, and the Chinese as is his elder brother in South Kensington by the slums that are west of Hammersmith.' 'The British Europeans had no interest in the welfare of the country,' remembered Tan Cheng Lock's daughter, 'except where it affected their businesses or own immediate well-being.' It is not the climate, Maugham's writing suggests, that causes the frequent cases of 'neurasthenia', alcoholism and suicide, but the isolation, rootlessness, alienation and boredom of a group taking no interest in the community around them.[50]

Clifford had seen this coming, and what he saw as its dire threat to 'good government'. As early as 1897 he worried that in the first-protected states of Selangor and Perak it was possible for a European to spend weeks 'without coming into contact with any Asiatics save those who wait at table, clean his shirts and drive his cab'. His concern was that the Malays would be governed by men who 'cannot expect to have more than a surface knowledge of the people whose destinies are in their hands'. Clifford himself, as Resident of Pahang after 1896, now with a wife in tow, found himself already spending more time on paperwork and socialising with the growing European community than on meeting and communicating with local Malays.[51]

Dr Lim, in his wartime book, also commented that 'the gulf separating the groups has become wider every year'. He blamed this on discriminatory behaviour, previously alien to Malaya, learned by the white bureaucracy, he suggested, while working in Africa, India or China.[52]

This all made some nostalgic for the old days of the 'man on the spot', the valiant adventurer and scholar-ruler who lived among the 'natives', learned their language, traditions and medicine and counted them as friends. The first federation agreement in 1895 had brought an administrative and judicial centralisation that diminished the independence of the Residents. Clifford complained that he was now subject to the tyranny of the telegraph and 'how at the end of that infernal wire there sat men whose business was to impede me with instructions concerning matters which they imperfectly comprehended'.[53]

Centred on Kuala Lumpur, an elaborate and extensive bureaucracy had grown up, in finance, public works, lands, mines and police. Its executive ranks were all Europeans. Because of the exclusivity of the Malayan Civil Service, positions that could have been filled by Malays went to British cadets. (There would be a Malayan Administrative

Service formed for locals, but its recruits had little power, and would never be put in charge of Chinese or Indians.) This meant that as early as the turn of the century, the FMS with a population less than a fifth the size of Ceylon had twice as many European administrative officers, not counting those in professional and specialist departments. By 1925, shortly before the return of Clifford, the MCS had 258 members, against 86 for the Gold Coast, 118 for Kenya and only 297 for the whole of Nigeria.[54]

The newcomers were of a different type. A new recruitment policy privileged academic achievement over family connections (which had served Clifford, among others, well). This meant that the majority of recruits were graduates and nearly half of the total from Oxbridge. None of the 'pioneers' like Swettenham and Clifford had even been to university.

It was part of an effort by the Colonial Service to smarten itself up, to become more conformist and aloof than the sometimes ramshackle and certainly more heterogeneous characters who had been the pioneers in Africa and Asia.

Effects of the change in the size and make-up of the bureaucracy meant that district officers now had to refer even the most trivial matters to their official superiors, and spent more and more time on the mounting paperwork rather than roaming their districts. There were complaints, also, that too many civil servants concentrated on office politics to further their careers, rather than getting to know the people in their charge.

This state of affairs was seen as having serious security implications. In February 1922 a Malaya Political Intelligence Bureau was established, modelled on its Indian equivalent. Its director, writing in early 1923, bemoaned the lack of information coming in from district officers – able to 'communicate to the Bureau, so little of the common talk of the people'. The Chinese community, who had their own entirely independent street names in the cities they dominated, was even more opaque. New night schools established for the poorest of the Chinese community were seen by the British as breeding grounds of anarchism and communism. As with concerns about plots being hatched in the Indian bazaars, fears filled the void left by ignorance. 'It is difficult to prevent the feeling that more is going on under the surface than we are actually aware of,' read one intelligence report.[55]

When Clifford eventually returned to his beloved Malaya, he would find the administration bloated, anxious, inward-looking and with no roots in the lives of the people.

23

An Empire of Sport

There will be a perfect planet
Only when the Game shall enter
Every country, teaching millions
How to ask for Leg or Centre . . .
When the cricket bags are opened
Doves of Peace fly forth instanter!

NORMAN GALE[1]

It is immediately striking when reading newspapers from around the empire on 29 September 1923 just how much space is given over to sport. Wherever you were in the empire, you could read the football results from England and Scotland, even the lowest national divisions, as well as reams of information about local sporting activities. Indeed, one paper, the weekly *Ceylon Observer* of 30 September, carried no local news at all apart from sport. There's plenty, though, on cricket, including a report of the 'Brilliant Bloomfield Victory Over Tamils'. The highlight was an impressive six hit by the Tamil top scorer P. Saravanasnuttu, 'a big whack that cleared the trees and landed on the roof of the Home for Incurables'.

French 'colonial geographer' Albert Demangeon was baffled by the British obsession with sport, which he dismissed as 'unremunerated physical activity'. 'Throughout the Empire on Saturdays,' he wrote, 'the open air life reigns supreme.' Indeed, it did.[2]

Arthur Grimble reported that on Ocean Island every Saturday at 2.30 p.m. a cricket match was contested by the Company and the Government. The Company players were almost all Australian – and always won – while the Government team, apart from a couple of Englishmen, consisted of 'native' police and Fijian soldiers. The wicket was made of coconut matting. According to Grimble, the island's elders approved of 'kirikiti' as it replicated some of the excitement and comradeship previously found in warfare. Ocean Island also had a golf course, where the balls were painted red so as not to be lost in the bleached coral wastelands of the excavations. (In Entebbe, Uganda, the jeopardy for golfers was provided by grass ticks, which necessitated players wrapping kerosene-soaked rags around their legs. On tiny Tristan da Cunha, the golf course only had one hole.)[3]

On Saturday 29 September 1923 there was a horse race meeting at Randwick in Sydney, which the Prince of Wales had visited on his trip to Australia, and lost money by betting, as he always did, on the low-odds favourite. According to newspapers, 80,000 spectators were there to see the gelding Ballymena that was owned, trained and ridden by New Zealanders come in at 25-1 and take the premium race prize money of a staggering £9,000.[4]

In Ceylon, where, Michael Ondaatje wrote, there was a 'mania for gambling', race tracks were to be found all over the island. 'If you sat in the grandstand all bets were five rupees,' he remembered hearing about the 1920s. 'Then there was a two-rupee enclosure and finally, in the middle of the track, the "Gandhi enclosure" where the poorest stood. From the grandstand you could watch them leaving like ants a good hour before the last race having lost all their money.'[5]

In Hong Kong, the saying went that the colony was really run by the Jockey Club. All the Treaty Ports had race tracks. The grandstand of the Race Club in Shanghai, a British colony in all but name, was one

of the largest in the world and had unmatched facilities. At the end of
the nineteenth century access to it had been restricted to the membership, which excluded Chinese. In response, Chinese racehorse owners
opened their own tracks – both fully integrated. Losing spectators,
Shanghai Race Club was forced to change its policy.[6]

Tennis, described by Leonard Woolf from his experience in Ceylon
as a 'sacrament', is being played everywhere. (In Africa, courts were
often made from beaten-down earth from ant nests.) At a mission station in Kenya there is a knock-out football tournament, named after
the head missionary John Arthur, whose efforts to 'make the devil let
go of these people' involve teaching them football and cricket. Happily,
he reported, 'Amongst schoolboys the passion for the tribal dance [has
been] largely sublimated by the love of football.' In Nigeria, a young
British nurse, Mary Lucas, is learning golf. In Accra, in the Gold
Coast, the European suburb, with its 'well watered golf-course and
tennis courts', gives the impression of 'the selecter parts of Surbiton
or Cheltenham', while in the city itself there are now eighteen football teams.[7]

In Trinidad, an exhibition match is being played in front of 'a crowd
of gigantic proportions' to mark the return of West Indian players from
their recent tour of England. Five of their number were Trinidadians,
including Learie Constantine (who, much later, would become the
first black member of the House of Lords). The constabulary band
'enlivened the match with attractive items'. When the Acting Governor
arrived, they struck up the National Anthem, after which he presented
each of the five Trinidadians with a gold watch, a silver cigarette case
and a gold scarf pin. The West Indies team captain had expressed
his gratitude for the warm reception they received in England and
declared, 'the true credit really lies with English cricketers who came to
our part of the Empire and taught us the game'.[8]

It was a universal belief of the British that regular exercise was
mandatory for maintaining health and morale, as well as personal and
public control. Energetic team sports were beneficial to keep fit, build
team spirit, and offset any tendency to 'nerves' or mental breakdown

due to alienation, isolation and loneliness. They were also thought to sublimate sexual urges in young men. 'This need for bodily exercise forms part of a kind of national system of hygiene,' explained Demangeon. A visitor to Nigeria noted that 'the whole of English life in West Africa revolves very properly round the problem of Keeping Fit ... The great god Fitness has five forms or fetishes under which He can be worshipped with little balls: the princely fetish is Polo, and then in descending order of merit Golf, Tennis, Cricket and Football. The last is slightly plebeian.'[9]

As well as of benefit to the coloniser, sport was seen as integral a part of the civilising mission as law, religion or education. Games, particularly cricket (run by the ICC, the Imperial Cricket Conference), were elevated to the status of a moral discipline, vital for fostering 'British qualities' of discipline, fair play, endurance and team spirit. By introducing sport, it was hoped that Asians, in particular, might improve their physical abilities and their character, and acquire qualities such as sportsmanship.

Sport drove dress reform for girls and women. Mi Mi Khaing, a teenager in Burma in 1923, remembered that her relatives disapproved of basketball, preferring tennis where you could wear a *longyi*. She played nonetheless, although she wasn't allowed, unlike some other girls, to dispense with her traditionally formal and cumbersome *sadone* hair arrangement.[10]

In Malaya before the war, traditional dress meant that for girls, only gentle stretching exercises were possible. But by the 1920s a revolution had occurred. Chinese and Malay vernacular girls' schools were able to play basketball, volleyball and badminton thanks to a relaxing of restrictions that now allowed them to wear shorts and short-sleeved shirts. Girls' cycling and swimming competitions also flourished. (In Britain, however, women's football, hugely popular during the Great War, had just been banned by the FA.)[11]

In Malaya, football clubs were the preserve of working-class Malays. There were forty clubs in Singapore alone, organised into a league. This attracted the disapproval of the Kaum Muda reformist press, who ran a campaign against football. While its defenders claimed it kept youngsters off the streets and taught them teamwork, the *Neracha* newspaper retorted that poor Chinese immigrants were becoming 'our masters, our rich merchants, our rulers' and that the spare time of young football-enthusiast Malays would be better spent in studying, and teamwork learned by communal prayer.[12]

The widespread adoption of Western sport by the colonised across the empire on one level underlined Western superiority, and flattered the colonisers. But it also challenged colonial structures by teaching the doctrine of equality and fair play. Inter-ethnic sport also undermined the idea of white superiority. In Malaya, once Asians and Eurasians were allowed into the athletics championship in 1922, none of the overall winners for the next six years was a Westerner.[13]

In many instances, sport broke down the barriers between Europeans and the rest, and also between different ethnic groups. 'Where we have such a cosmopolitan population,' wrote a Malayan journalist, 'the various racial elements are brought into friendly contact by no medium more effectually than that of sport.' A traveller in Burma in 1923 went to a sports club to find 'Tennis in full swing ... the players being two Englishmen in the regulation white flannels, a Burman in pink silk lungyi and orange gaung-baung, another young Burman in European kit, and a Madrasi doctor. On a seat watching the play sat a Burmese woman, a Eurasian girl, and the D.C.'s wife.' Even at the height of the 'anti-Indian agitation' in Kenya, 'Nairobi Club continued playing cricket with Asiatic elevens, apparently oblivious of heated opinions in the backwoods that they were doing anything subversive of "white domination".'[14]

A leading promoter of Parsee cricket in India, who was made an honorary member of the MCC, told an interviewer that Indian cricket was 'the child of progress of the friendly embrace of the East and the West ... let the providential alliance of India and Britain be cemented', he declared, 'by one grand Imperial game'.[15]

It was not always such a happy picture. In many places sports clubs remained racially segregated. Where teams had been multi-ethnic, the 1920s saw some become tied to a particular community – for example football teams in Malaya and cricket teams in Ceylon, which were increasingly Tamil versus Sinhala. There was an ugly incident in Burma at the end of 1923. The Governor had ordered that all clubs remove colour bars, but the Rangoon Rugby Club still fielded an all-white team. However, they only had one opposition, the garrison, who were short of players and therefore recruited U Tin Tut. He was a civil servant who had been an officer in the war, was a member of the English Bar, and had played rugby for Dulwich College and Cambridge University. He was easily the best player on the pitch. But after the game he was refused the use of the showers and told that only Europeans could enter the clubhouse. This incident caused a great stir among Burmese officials and journalists, and huge damage to race relations.[16]

Nonetheless, sport did, by 'means of shared enthusiasms', often foster that elusive goal of imperial unity, or even purpose. 'English cricketers are playing against Parsees and Mohammedans at Karachi while a team of Maoris are testing the best of our Rugby footballers at home,' wrote the English author of *Character and Sportsmanship* in the mid-1920s. 'By such threads are the best bonds of union woven.' Indeed, the spread of British sports was an enduring achievement of imperial power.[17]

John Sydenham Furnivall, who worked as a colonial officer in Burma from 1903 to 1931, married a Burmese woman and served the government after independence, went further. Noting how the Burmese passionately loved football and became very adept at it, he pronounced its introduction by the British as pretty much the only item on the credit side of imperial rule in Burma.[18]

PART TWO

THE SUN SETS

24

The Lost Kingdom

'I was hated by large numbers of people – the only time in my life I have been important enough for this to happen to me,' wrote George Orwell (then Eric Blair) of his time in Burma. 'As a police officer I was an obvious target and was baited whenever it seemed safe to do so. When a nimble Burman tripped me up on the football field and the referee (another Burman) looked the other way, the crowd yelled with hideous laughter. This happened more than once.'[1]

Orwell, an enthusiastic and reportedly skilful footballer, author of several stories about Burma, much journalism and memoir and the coruscating novel *Burmese Days*, had empire in the blood. He was born in India, where his father Richard Blair worked in the Opium Department of the civil service. Orwell's great-grandfather had been a wealthy slave- and plantation-owner in Jamaica. His paternal grandfather had been a Church of England vicar in Calcutta and Tasmania and had married in Cape Town. On the other side of the family, Orwell's mother had grown up in Moulmein, Burma, where her family had been timber merchants for two generations.

Aged one, Orwell travelled to live in England with his mother. He would hardly see his father until he was eight, when Richard – eighteen years older than his wife – retired and returned to live with the family in Henley. By that stage Orwell was at a boarding school on the south coast.

As a child, Orwell was a member of the Navy League, the patriotic cheerleaders for naval history, national pride and the arms race with Germany. He later wrote, 'the earliest political slogan I can remember is "We want eight [dreadnoughts], and we won't wait."' The League, 100,000-strong, ran essay-writing competitions, published maps full of the red of the empire, held displays and exhibitions, and provided schools with textbooks about the importance of the navy for international supremacy. Orwell was also a voracious reader of *Gem* and *Magnet* magazines, home of Greyfriars and Billy Bunter, stories of public-school boys with shameless snob-appeal, much inspired by Kipling's *Stalky & Co.*; for Anglo-Indian families like his, Orwell later wrote, Kipling was like a 'household god' ('I worshipped Kipling at thirteen,' he remembered). Alongside the goings-on of Billy Bunter and friends were colonial adventure stories – or, as Orwell later put it in his essay 'Boys' Weeklies', 'at the outpost of Empire the monocled Englishmen are holding the n*****s at bay'. (The Indian boy at Greyfriars, known as 'Inky', was 'the comic *babu* of the Punch tradition'.) Like the massively popular children's novels by Edgar Wallace, W. E. Johns, 'Sapper' and G. E. Henty, *Gem* and *Magnet* aimed to instil patriotism, reverence for royalty and authority and a view of all foreigners as vicious or stupid. 'The outlook inculcated by these papers,' Orwell later ruefully reflected, 'is that of a rather exceptionally stupid member of the Navy League in 1910.'[2]

Orwell's first appearance in print was in the *Henley and South Oxfordshire Standard* on 2 October 1914 – a short patriotic poem entitled 'Awake! Young Men of England'. It ended, 'If . . . you do not enlist by the thousand, / You truly are cowards indeed.' He was only eleven, and at a prep school, St Cyprian's, near Eastbourne. This establishment was remembered by fellow pupil Cecil Beaton as a place of constant hunger and cold. For Cyril Connolly, a friend and contemporary of Orwell there, the school's message was 'character, character, character'. 'Muscle bound with character,' Connolly later wrote, 'the alumni would pass on to the best schools, reporting their best friends for homosexuality and seeing them expelled, winning athletic distinctions ... and then find their vocation in India, Burma, Nigeria and the Sudan, administering with Roman justice those natives for whom the final profligate outflow of character was all the time predestined.'[3]

'When I was fourteen or fifteen I was an odious little snob, but no worse than other boys of my own age and class,' Orwell remembered. At Eton, on a scholarship, he appears to have been part of the awkward squad, rejecting 'the Empire, Kipling and Character'. 'I loathed Kipling at seventeen', he wrote, but 'enjoyed him again at twenty'. By then, though, he was an imperial servant.[4]

According to most biographers, there had been hope, particularly from his mother, that he would win a scholarship to Oxford, but his poor academic performance at Eton had made this impossible and the family could not afford it otherwise. By now, to enter the Indian Civil Service required a university degree. So instead he crammed for six months in his parents' new home of Southwold – a favoured retirement spot for less well-off ex-colonials – for the exams to become an officer in the Indian Police. September 1923 finds him an Assistant Superintendent in Burma – as he would later write, 'part of the actual machinery of despotism'.[5]

The Indian Police had a poor reputation in the liberal press, but Orwell did not have the technical bent to go into forestry, infrastructure or medicine, and at least the police wasn't the perhaps even more discreditable Opium Department where his father had worked. Bill Tydd, who would closely follow Orwell into the Burma Police, described the organisation as offering a wide variety of duties and good career prospects, thus after the war attracting 'the attention of many young men casting around for an interesting and congenial career'.[6]

Orwell had existing family links to Burma – his maternal grandmother still lived in Moulmein. Roger Beadon, who was one of the two other police cadets arriving at the same time as Orwell, was the same – his father was still working in the Burmese colonial government or in business there. Another policeman, a couple of years ahead of Orwell, A. Meer-Nemo, said in his unpublished autobiography 'A Burmese Bobby' that he had chosen the Indian province of Burma because it was 'much less starchy than India, and the Burmese were a friendly, jolly people'. There was the impression that Burma was less overcrowded, caste-ridden and religiously divided than India proper. (In fact, officials there would receive a special 'Burma allowance' to compensate them for the even greater difficulties Burma presented.) Biographer Bernard Crick put Orwell's career choice down to 'simply following in his father's footsteps . . . which was then, after all, a most ordinary thing to happen, in any class or condition whether the boy welcomed it or not'.[7]

Jacintha Buddicom agreed, but only up to a point. She had met Orwell in 1914 when she was playing in her garden with her brother Prosper. They saw a tall boy in an adjoining field standing on his head. 'This was a feat we had never observed before,' Buddicom wrote. They asked, 'Why are you standing on your head?' Orwell replied, 'You are noticed more if you are standing on your head than if you are right way up.' He was eleven, Prosper ten and Jacintha thirteen. Along with their younger siblings, they all became close friends, often holidaying together. Prosper and Eric would play tennis and go fishing and shooting. 'We, me and Eric *talked*,' Prosper wrote. They were both 'inveterate readers', sharing books, writing poetry, talking of going to Oxford, and exchanging letters almost every week while away at school.[8]

Buddicom admitted that Eric, aged about fifteen, developed a crush on her. He wrote poetry comparing them to Romeo and Juliet and declared 'My heart belongs to your befriending mind.' According to her memoir, this was not reciprocated. For one thing, he was younger than her – 'The two years between a girl of 17 and a boy of 15, as a beginning, are just the wrong two years.' She wrote that 'among all the boys we knew, Eric was one of the most interesting, the best informed, the kindest, the *nicest*' (her emphasis). But he was not 'quite so good-looking as the handsomest'.[9]

Her version in her memoir of why Orwell went to Burma is that his mother Ida – 'vivacious, spirited, rather pretty . . . rather left wing' – supported by Jacintha's mother, fought an unsuccessful battle with Ida's much older 'dour, discouraging husband' over their son's future. His mother wanted Eric to go to university. According to Jacintha, Eric – 'a born scholar, a boy who lived for books' – wanted this as well and 'would have worked so hard to gain an almost-certain scholarship'. But 'Old Mr Blair had been "Indian Civil", and Indian Civil was the only career he would tolerate for his son. It was the last thing Eric wanted, but the tramlines were laid down . . . And Eric was exiled to the Burma Police.'[10]

After Jacintha's death, a huge hoard of letters was discovered that gave this account a new twist. Her memoir, it appeared, had not told the whole story. In the summer of 1921, the two families rented a house together in rural Hertfordshire. Eric and Jacintha became 'inseparable', and while admiring a sunset, shared their first kiss. This soon proceeded to 'heavy petting', described by Jacintha as 'some intimacy but not full intercourse'. She later told an Orwell biographer that Eric had asked her to marry him, which she had turned down. Then, on 4 September when they were out walking, he tried to take it further. At only 5 feet to his 6 feet 4in, Jacintha had shouted, screamed and kicked before running home with torn knickers and skirt and a bruised hip. 'He had ruined what had been such a close and fulfilling relationship since childhood,' she later wrote in a private letter, 'by trying to take us the whole way before I was anywhere near ready for that.' Jacintha refused to see Eric again for the rest of the holidays, and when some version of the incident reached the two mothers, it produced a lasting breach between the two families.[11]

Orwell would write her three letters from Burma; she replied to the first in brief but not the others. She did not keep any of them. Many years later, Orwell wrote to her: 'You were not so tender-hearted to me when you abandoned me to Burma with all hope denied.' The incident must have informed Orwell's misery and self-disgust when in Burma.[12]

Having passed the entrance examinations (though nearly failing on the horse-riding test), Orwell, still only nineteen years old, sailed from

Birkenhead on 27 October 1922. The journey, his first time abroad, took about five weeks. He got a taste for what he was in for from the attitudes of the planters and colonial officers on board returning from leave. Then, on the way to Rangoon, the boat stopped at Colombo. On the dock he saw a white police sergeant viciously kick a 'coolie' who was clumsily carrying a suitcase. His fellow passengers watched the scene with 'no emotion whatever except a mild approval', Orwell later wrote. 'They were white, the coolie was black. In other words he was sub-human, a different kind of animal.'[13]

He was shocked. But, as he would soon discover, Burma would be far worse.

The aggressive imperial expansion of Burma after its reunification by the Konbaung dynasty in the mid-eighteenth century had seen it annex the Shan and Kachin areas to its east and then expand southwards to Mons and Tenasserim and west to Arakan, Manipur and Assam. This last gain in 1816 brought the militaristic Burmese Empire up to the borders of British India, prompting war in 1824.

The fighting lasted two years, and cost 15,000 Indian and British lives, many from disease, particularly among the expeditionary force that captured Rangoon at the beginning of the monsoon season and found itself trapped. However, when it was eventually relieved, this force, helped by an armoured steamer and the new Congreve rockets, advanced swiftly northwards towards the capital Mandalay, prompting Burmese surrender.

As well as being forced to pay a huge indemnity of 10 million rupees (£1 million), Burma gave up all their recently conquered territories in the west – Assam, Arakan, Manipur and the Tenasserim Peninsula. In Assam and Manipur pro-British Rajas were installed. But the British withdrawal from Rangoon left those in the south – primarily Karens – who had sided with the British exposed to Burmese vengeance, which took the form of indiscriminate killings and the burning of villages.

If both sides had been to blame for the outbreak of hostilities in the 1820s, the next war thirty years later was entirely down to the British.

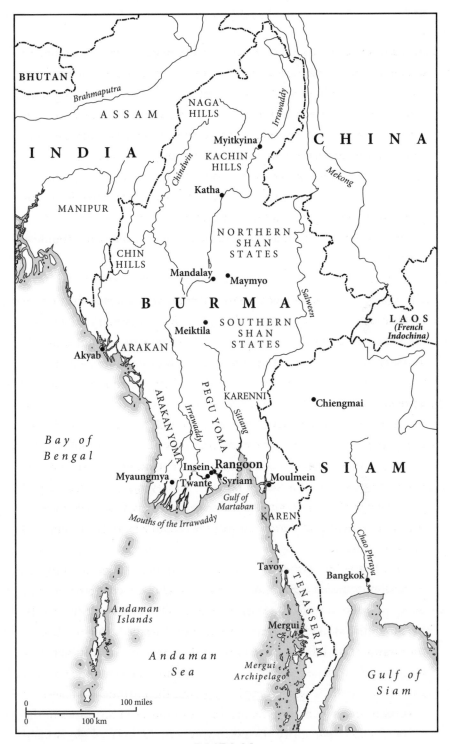

BHUTAN

Brahmaputra

ASSAM

NAGA
HILLS

INDIA

CHINA

Myitkyina

KACHIN
HILLS

Chindwin

Irrawaddy

Mekong

MANIPUR

Katha

NORTHERN
SHAN
STATES

CHIN
HILLS

Mandalay • Maymyo

Salween

BURMA

Meiktila

SOUTHERN
SHAN
STATES

LAOS
*(French
Indochina)*

Akyab

ARAKAN

KARENNI

•Chiengmai

*Bay of
Bengal*

ARAKAN YOMA

Irrawaddy

PEGU YOMA

Sittang

SIAM

Myaungmya

Insein

Rangoon

Twante

Syriam

Moulmein

*Gulf of
Martaban*

KAREN

Chao Phraya

Mouths of the Irrawaddy

Tavoy

Bangkok

*Andaman
Islands*

TENASSERIM

Mergui

*Andaman
Sea*

*Mergui
Archipelago*

*Gulf of
Siam*

0   100 miles

0   100 km

BURMA

It was triggered by the fining of a couple of British ship captains in Rangoon for customs violations. The Governor-General of India demanded that the Burmese rescind the fine and sack the local governor. They quickly accepted, but by that time the 'volatile' 'man on the spot' had blockaded the coastline anyway, and then seized Rangoon. This time the opposing forces were less evenly matched, particularly in terms of weaponry, and after a palace coup deposed the Burmese king they sued for peace, handing over the whole of Lower Burma. (The British took advantage of the chaos in the Burmese court to advance a further 50 miles northwards, thus securing some valuable teak forests.)[14]

The new king, Mindon Min, who had been summoned from a monastery to replace his brother, did his utmost to avoid further confrontations with the British (he refused his advisers' urging that he take advantage of the Indian Rebellion to recapture parts of the south). He also attempted to reform and modernise. Students were sent abroad as far as Europe, telegraph lines were laid and new factories established to produce modern weapons. He centralised the administration of what was left of the country, simplified the taxation system and diminished the power of the hereditary gentry. But he died in 1878, and left his succession uncertain – he had 110 children, including forty-eight boys. In the event his most senior surviving wife arranged the marriage of her daughter Supayalat, who was known as violent and unpredictable, to one of the sons, Thibaw, by another wife. Thibaw, only twenty years old, was weak and, it was hoped by the court and his new mother-in-law, pliant to their wishes.

Thibaw rounded up and imprisoned most of Mindon's other children. In February 1879, along with other potential trouble-makers, they were massacred, probably on the order of Supayalat. To avoid spilling royal blood, they were strangled or wrapped in blankets and bludgeoned to death. According to some accounts, they were then thrown in a ditch and trampled by elephants. Shortly afterwards, Thibaw was crowned king.[15]

The British were appalled, and the press in Rangoon, Calcutta and

London reported the gruesome details. (In fact, this practice was far from unknown in Burma – Mindon Min's brother had killed about a hundred of his family on his accession.) Intervention was called for, and troops were sent to the border near Prome. But Britain was entangled in military action in Afghanistan and Zululand, so invading Burma was seen as a step too far. Still, most important for the future was the conclusion the British came to that the Burmese would welcome escape from seemingly murderous royal government.

When the final war came in 1885, it was down – like so many of Britain's imperial conquests – to business, and to the desire to stop France. Thibaw had set up monopolies in sugar and salt, damaging the now valuable trade between Upper and Lower Burma. He had also been entertaining envoys from the French, who had been establishing control over Indo-China. There were rumours that the French were going to set up a bank, build railways and furnish the king with arms.

The pretext for the British invasion was a large fine imposed on the Glasgow-based Bombay Burmah Trading Corporation for illegally exporting timber from Upper Burma without paying the correct royalties to the King. The British demanded it went to arbitration and that Mandalay should receive a British Resident, along the lines of the 'protectorate' status of the Indian and Malay princedoms. Thibaw refused. On the orders of Lord Randolph Churchill, the Secretary of State for India, the British marched on Mandalay almost unopposed, and arrested and deported the king. Burma then became a province of British India.[16]

When this was presented as a fait accompli to the British Parliament, Scottish Liberal William Hunter argued, 'Burmese people, like all other people, would rather bear the vices of their native rulers than the virtues of foreign officials.' Liberal Welsh MP Henry Richards denounced the annexation as 'an act of high-handed violence for which there is no adequate justification'. He also presciently warned that 'By suddenly overthrowing the existing government, it looks as though we have consigned the country to ... a prolonged anarchy.'[17]

Both would be proved right. It had taken 10,000 soldiers to conquer

Upper Burma, but soon there were 40,000 deployed, attempting with great difficulty to impose control. It turned out that Thibaw's 'mad, bloody and exasperating reign' had not turned the Burmese against their king. Instead there was fierce guerrilla resistance, along with widespread lawlessness. Long-time bandits suddenly found themselves hailed as patriots. The British responded with brutal repression; as one officer put it, 'We simply wiped out the village and shot everyone we saw ... Burned all their crops and houses.' Some semblance of order was not restored in parts of the country till as late as 1890.[18]

The invaders had had a pliant half-brother of Thibaw on stand-by in Calcutta whom they could have installed as a puppet, but as well as being expensive, it was believed that the monarchy was discredited beyond repair. But by removing the king, the British destroyed at a stroke the linchpin of the entire religious, political and social structure of the country.

The Buddhist religion was central to life in Burma. There was a monastery in every village, where the boys learned their letters. The monks, revered by the villagers, kept an eye on the manners and morals of the village and enjoined the people to obey the law and to pay their taxes. Religious life was centred on Mandalay, where there were as many as 10,000 monks, or *pongyis*. From there the king had spread his patronage to hundreds of monasteries across the country. With a non-Buddhist power now in charge in the city and the king gone, the entire system of education and religious instruction collapsed almost overnight.[19]

Like the Malay farmer, the Burmese cultivator under the new British rule was freed of many previous restrictions. Under the old system he had been liable to compulsory labour, was restricted in selling his produce and subject to rules that reduced his freedom of movement, dress and marriage. People were now freer to make money, but also to disregard previous social obligations. The villages lost their communal spirit; dances, festivals and races died out, in part due to measures to suppress gambling. Communities became individuals.[20]

For a decade or so after the conquest, British officials were hardly ever seen, but by the turn of the century British rule had become more intrusive, causing Burmese to feel more keenly the humiliation of the conquest of their once-great empire, and they were 'hurt very often by a constant assumption of superiority' by the British. Even well-meaning efforts by veterinary, school or sanitary inspectors, or the introduction of vaccination and other welfare measures, were treated with suspicion and irritation. A rapid succession of British officials enforced the measures with a system of law – the Indian Penal Code – alien to the legal traditions of the Burmese. For the British part, there was a failure to understand: 'the workings of the Burman mind are a sealed book to the European', a visitor wrote. 'The average Englishman is slow to realise that an outlook different from his own is even possible.'[21]

Efforts to restore Burmese pride and identity began in 1906 with the Young Men's Buddhist Association (YMBA). Its founder and first president was U May Oung – a moderate, Cambridge-educated, London-trained barrister. The initial members were mostly students, who met to discuss religious matters and ways of reviving Burmese literature and culture. It first gained real traction when in 1916, under the more radical leadership of U Thein Maung, also a barrister, it launched a campaign of protest against the European habit of wearing shoes in the pagoda precincts. By 1918 the issue of footwear in the temples had become a symbol of anti-British sentiment. The British certainly saw it as political: 'no self-respecting Englishman will consent to obey it,' reported a British official, 'since in obeying he is doing exactly what the *pongyis* want him to do – namely lowering himself in the eyes of the majority of the native population.'[22]

The Burmese had little direct involvement in the First World War. Some 4,500 military police, mainly Indians, volunteered for service in Europe and an 8,000-strong Burmese labour corps served in Iraq. But it still had a detrimental effect. Shipping shortages paralysed the rice industry, leading to unemployment, peasant dispossession and conflict between cultivators, landowners and money-lenders. At the same time, as elsewhere, the tax burden increased dramatically. Nascent Burmese nationalism also felt the impact of the Easter Rising in Ireland, the

Bolshevik revolution, and President Wilson's call for self-determination.

What generated most umbrage and activity, however, was the exclusion of Burma from Montagu's India reforms. 'Burma is not India,' the Joint Select Committee on the Government of India Bill had decreed. 'Its people belong to another race in another stage of political development ... the desire for elective institutions has not developed in Burma.'[23]

An outraged YMBA, now the primary political organisation, held mass meetings to protest, and sent a delegation to London demanding Burma's inclusion in the reforms – and, at the same time, its separation from India. (There was also a separate Karen delegation, urging continued British rule and protection.) The YMBA delegation, led by U Thein Maung, made contact with sympathetic journalists and Labour MPs, and eventually got an audience with the government. Colonel Wedgwood (who would shortly visit Burma and outrage the European community by removing his shoes to visit a temple) pressed the YMBA case with Montagu, who candidly admitted that he knew little about Burma.

The Governor in Burma, Sir Reginald Craddock, responded to the pressure by extending his scheme of establishing district councils that would take over some of the work of the British Deputy Commissioners. But he insisted that Burma was in terms of political development a generation behind India, with far fewer competent Western-educated locals. When this was rejected as utterly inadequate, he blamed 'Mr. Montagu with his magical midwifery across the Bay of Bengal', which had disturbed the Burmese from 'their placid contentment'.[24]

Another delegation from the YMBA arrived in London in May 1920. This time, as much through government disinterest in the Burma 'backwater' and distraction with other seemingly more pressing concerns, the delegation secured agreement that Burma would be granted constitutional reform and dyarchy along the lines of India. There would be a largely elected Legislative Council, with a wide franchise of adult taxpayers and responsibility for local government, health, education, public works, agriculture and forests delegated to Burmese ministers.

This, wrote Burmese historian Thant Myint-U, 'was more than anyone would have expected or even dreamed of just a few years before'. But, he went on, it 'already fell far short of rising nationalist aspiration'. For in the meantime, 'virtually overnight politics went from placid to passionate'.[25]

The catalyst was the establishment of a new university in Rangoon, essentially an upgrade of an existing college that had previously been affiliated to Calcutta University. To raise standards, entry and graduation requirements were made far harsher. There had been little consultation with the Burmese, who were pretty much excluded from its managing bodies. On 1 August 1920, the YMBA convened a meeting in Rangoon of some 400, including a number of *pongyis*. The moderate U May Oung was condemned for having supported the measure.

The upshot was a boycott launched on 4 December. It was the first open challenge of nationalism to British rule (and is now a National Day in Myanmar). The boycott soon spread to government and missionary schools and saw the establishment of national schools free of British control. Although the boycott petered out after a year or so, it spread far and wide ideas of Burmese self-reliance and nationalism, previously the reserve of a tiny Westernised urban elite.

The following year, the YMBA was superseded by the General Council of Burmese Associations (GCBA). Under a younger and more radical leadership, it was less Westernised, more in touch with ordinary Burmese, and more willing to cooperate with the *pongyis*. Buddhist monks, leaderless since the fall of the king and ill-disciplined, had seen their status drop as education was taken over by the government and missionary schools. Teaching in the national schools had brought them back into the picture. Some moderate YMBA leaders had been unwilling to mix politics with religion. In India, Congress support was mainly among the middle class and business and professional people, but in Burma this class was much smaller, and was dominated by Indians and Chinese, so educated nationalists had little choice but to ally themselves with the *pongyis*. In addition, in the towns monks lived in monasteries of several hundred members, so were easy to organise for demonstrations or meetings. Every village had at least one monk, giving the nationalists a ready-made political network.[26]

And in the same year, from across the sea, came a new leader. Born in Arakan in 1879, Buddhist monk Sayadaw U Ottama had been inspired by Japan's victory over Russia to move to Tokyo in 1907. He had already studied in Calcutta, travelled round India and visited France and Egypt. In Tokyo, he taught Pali and Sanskrit and mixed with the congregation of nationalists from across the region.

After further travels, which included careful consideration of the tactics of the Indian National Congress, he returned to Burma in 1921, and immediately assumed leadership of the 'political *pongyis*'. A gifted speaker, he was, like Gandhi, adept at tailoring his message to his audience. He told villagers, '*Pongyis* pray for Nirvana but slaves can never obtain it, therefore they must pray for release from slavery in this life.' He argued that Buddhism was threatened by alien government, and by his country's large non-Buddhist Indian immigrant population. (Similarly, in Ceylon, militant Buddhist nationalism, stimulated by antipathy towards the British 'barbarians', came to be directed too against the sizeable non-Buddhist population, in particular the large Tamil minority.) While the GCBA at this time started advocating Home Rule, including an elected majority in the Legislative Council in control of the purse, to be achieved through non-cooperation and boycotts along the Indian Congress model, U Ottama went further, pushing for non-payment of taxes and complete independence, repeating his refrain, 'Craddock Get Out!' For this he was imprisoned in late 1921 for ten months – supposedly the first person in Burma to be arrested for making a speech. As soon as he was released the following year, he continued in the same vein (he would be arrested again in 1924). Priests, reported a British visitor in 1922, are 'today preaching the doctrines of Communism in their temples ... and spreading sedition in the rising generation'. Visitors 'can hardly fail to remark the attitude of the young Burman of the town towards Europeans. It is "Burma for the Burmese" today, just as recently it was "Ireland for the Irish".'[27]

An admirer of Gandhi, U Ottama advocated non-violence. But among the 100,000 *pongyis* in Burma, resort to force was not rejected in principle, and monks were often involved. At the beginning of 1922 there was a pitched battle between several hundred monks and police in Rangoon.

Shortly afterwards, the Prince of Wales arrived, midway through his tour of India. He'd experienced his hartal and boycott humiliations in Allahabad and Benares, but it was prior to the violent scenes in Madras. The GCBA and the 'political *pongyis*' had called for a boycott of the visit, but before his arrival the nationalist leadership and their most active followers had been interned far from Rangoon and Mandalay, and newspapers had been forbidden 'under Section 144 of the Procedure Code even to mention the word "boycott"'. However, reported the chief secretary, 'a few days before the Prince's arrival ... notices [were posted] warning the people to take no part in the celebrations as the Government would seize the slightest pretext to have the crowds shot down, as had happened in Bombay. These had a distinctly bad effect.'[28]

The Prince and his party, nonetheless, received a warm welcome from the largely Indian population of Rangoon, and at stops during the railway journey to Mandalay were greeted by village headmen and their entourages, Mountbatten reported, 'kneeling in a prostrate position on a little carpet – sometimes for half an hour or more in the heat'. But in Mandalay, where men working on the preparations had been threatened, and the special new royal barge had been destroyed by ill-wishers at least once before it was completed, the procession route was only 'moderately well filled' and in places 'devoid of people' except for the heavy police presence. Where there were crowds, they remained standing and silent. Mountbatten put this down to their 'ancient behaviour in the presence of royalty', and the sparse numbers to the fact that the majority in Mandalay were Burmese, 'more easily intimidated than the rest of the inhabitants'. 'Burma may have its troubles but it is many times more loyal than India, anyway at the moment,' Mountbatten concluded, adding, 'It is a most confusing country.' He did notice, however, that more than anyone else, the *pongyis* 'held aloof'.[29]

Soon after the departure of the royal party, a Burmese theatrical group that had disobeyed the boycott order by performing a *pwè* for the Prince – described by Mountbatten as 'one of the usual attendant stunts' – was attacked by a group of *pongyis* armed with knives, stones and sticks. Several actors were seriously wounded.[30]

Outbreaks of violence, political or otherwise, were by no means restricted to the *pongyis*. If on the Pacific islands the destruction of old social structures and traditions expressed itself in an unwillingness to have children, in Burma it was manifested in an unmanageable crime wave.

In the wake of the suppression of the insurgency following the conquest of Upper Burma, there had been a decade of comparative calm. But from 1904 to 1913, minor offences had risen by 40 per cent, while the murder rate climbed to 32 per million in 1910 then to 42.9 by 1920 (in Britain at this time, it was at about 4). Three or four times more people were sentenced to rigorous imprisonment than in any other province of India. The British kept building more prisons, but they quickly filled up. To make room, magistrates were encouraged to sentence men and boys to whipping rather than incarceration.[31]

In 1921, it was noted that during the preceding decade the population had risen by 9 per cent but increase in serious crime 'ranged from 31% in the case of murder to 109% in the case of robbery and dacoity'. Dacoity was defined in the Indian Penal Code as 'an assembly of five or more persons intent on committing robbery with violence'. What this meant on the ground was roving bands attacking villages, burning, raping and looting. Villages that agreed to give the bandits sustenance and shelter instead were subsequently subjected by the authorities to collective fines. Others fortified themselves with earthworks and walls of cacti. The police report for 1922 told of 'The existence of gangs of dacoits reported from all parts of the province; and the use of firearms in dacoity continued to increase.'[32]

There were hopes that the elections in November 1922, under a new system seen by the British as a generous concession, might help invest truculent elements in the future of their country. But with demands consistently running ahead of concessions, the *pongyis* and the majority of nationalists declared a boycott, with only a few moderates, inspired by the Swaraj Party in India (and sharing Motilal Nehru's suspicion of religious nationalism) agreeing to stand. The elections saw minimal voter turnouts, in many places as low as 7 per cent. How much of this was down to boycotts enforced by the *pongyis*, who beat with small canes anyone breaking the injunction, or down to mistrust of the British, disinterest or lack of understanding on the part of the Burmese has been much debated. Burmese historian Tin Tin Lay argues the latter: 'The British brought us democracy. It was the first time we had tasted it. We had never even heard of it before the British came, and we were not ready for it. I am ashamed of the Burmese people . . . we are so very, very ignorant. We are always looking for someone to blame, so we blame the British.'[33]

As the crime rate continued to climb, the elections had clearly failed to lance the boil, and might even have contributed to further unrest. Against the advice of U May Oung, who had argued that it was divisive, the scheme reserved communal seats for Karens and Indians. The 'Tribal areas' of the Kachin and Chan Hills in the east were excluded altogether, remaining under the direct 'protection' of the Governor. For the British this was part of their duty to protect minorities; to Burmese nationalists, it was divide and rule. The effect was of sharpening religious and ethnic divisions already being stoked by militant Burmese Buddhism. Communal violence would not be long in coming.[34]

Much thought and ink was expended on attempting to understand the origin and true nature of the appalling crime wave. Was it political, or just common-and-garden criminality? Or some combination of the two?

U May Oung lamented the time it had taken to introduce political reform and blamed the surge in crime partly on the dislocating effects of the increasing poverty and landlessness of Burmese peasants, for which the British were being held responsible.

'Burmese Bobby' A. Meer-Nemo, while serving in Mandalay, noted the high prevalence of 'unpremeditated murder'. Fellow policeman

C. Bruce Orr, also serving in the early 1920s, put this down to 'the Burman' being 'liable to fits of uncontrolled violence'. But if this was an inherent trait, it didn't explain how the rise in crime had so outpaced population growth. At fault, some suggested, was the new prevalence of violent Western movies from the United States. Others blamed the increased availability and use of alcohol – previously banned under Burmese rule – for these crimes of passion. As the police record noted, 'The ubiquitous toddy and dhani palm afford unlimited opportunities for illicit distillation in nearly every district.' There were also reports of increasing quantities of 'ganga' making its way to the country from Madras and Siam, as well as cocaine imported from Germany and Japan.[35]

The report of the 'Police Administration of Burma' blamed the judicial system, imported from Britain via India and 'not suited to the country'. It was indeed alien, replacing a local legal tradition of conciliation, arbitration and compromise with impersonal law, individual rights and the sanctity of contract. Most tellingly, 'it must be put down as one of the chief causes of crime, for the simple reason that crime is not punished and that therefore there is no deterrent'. As the Deputy Commissioner of Pegu complained, 'the extraordinarily high standard of evidence required to obtain a conviction, combined with the notorious corruptibility of witnesses and general unwillingness, partly due to political agitation, to co-operate with the police' meant that of those arrested only 36 per cent were convicted. As the hard-pressed governor of the prison system pointed out, 'it is the certainty, rather than severity of punishment that deters'.[36]

The head of the police force had a slightly different take. For him, 'The country is now in a state of transition between the old autocratic rule, in which lawlessness was put down with a strong hand, and democratic rule, in which law and order can only be maintained chiefly by public opinion as in England. The administration of today cannot be as strong as the administration of yesterday unless it receives the support of the public.'[37]

Historian Thant Myint-U takes it back to the fall of the last remnants of the Burmese Empire in 1885, the 'collapse of centuries of tradition ... a break with the ideas and institutions that had under-pinned society since before medieval times'. From that moment, he writes, British Burma was 'adrift, suddenly pushed into the modern world without an anchor to the past, rummaging around for new inspi-rations, sustained by a more sour nationalist sentiment'.[38]

The key cause of the crime wave, British judicial officers decided, was 'contempt for authority, inspired by political agitation'. This included Burmese of course, but ultimately 'authority' meant the alien British rulers. One thing was undeniable, however: rampant lawlessness as well as political rebellion coalesced at the point of their common hostility to the police.[39]

Shortly after the failed election of November 1922, nineteen-year-old cadet policeman George Orwell arrived in Burma.

25

Imperial Orwell

This desert inaccessible
Under the shade of melancholy boughs

As You Like It (Act II scene vii),
frontispiece of *Burmese Days* by GEORGE ORWELL[1]

All first-time arrivals at Rangoon from this period comment on how, still far off the coast, the water turned a 'curious brick red', thanks to the silt poured out into the sea by the mighty Irrawaddy River. Bill Tydd would arrive a few years after Orwell, and was also a probationary District Superintendent of Police. Like Orwell, he reached Burma in November, the best time of year – after the monsoons and before the hottest months. He remembered the river banks, 'low and flat, covered with a thick crop of vividly green plants, my first sight of paddy fields at the height of the growth after the rains'. As they reached the city, he saw on the right bank the black chimneys of the Burmah Oil Company's huge refinery. Then, coming round a final broad sweep of the river, 'I had a fine view of the Shwe Dagon Pagoda ... the gold-covered temple, shimmering brightly in the late afternoon sun, was a marvellous sight'.

Like Orwell, Tydd spent a couple of days in Rangoon meeting senior officials. He remembered the 'variety of people and their dress' in the streets. Rangoon was one of the most cosmopolitan cities in the empire. Its 250,000 inhabitants included 2,000 Europeans and substantial communities of Chinese, Armenians and Iraqi Jews. Well over half, though, were Indians. Except in the outlying districts, Burmese, like Malays in Singapore, were firmly in the minority.[2]

The financial, commercial, industrial and political centre of the country, Rangoon boasted the most modern steam trams, Rowe's department store (considered the 'Harrods of the East') and the smart riverfront Strand Hotel, run by the Armenian Sarkie brothers, owners of Raffles Hotel in Singapore and the Pacific and Orient in Penang. The European elite congregated at the Pegu or the Gymkhana Club. Rich Indians had their own establishment, modelled on the British version, called the Monday Afternoon Club.

The city's roads were a chaotic medley of motor vehicles, garries drawn by skinny ponies, rickshaws, bullock carts and heedless pedestrians. Away from the main boulevards, wrote Paul Edmonds, a visitor in 1922, was a 'rabbit warren' of side streets with 'huddled native shops swarming with people, thick with smells, full of dirty children, pidogs, rubbish and general filth'. Here lived the dock and warehouse workers, and the labour force for the rice mills and oil refinery. Amid squalid conditions, some rooms licensed for nine would hold forty or fifty men. 'Many others slept in the streets,' it was reported, 'so tightly packed that there was barely room for a wheelbarrow to pass.'[3]

Orwell had arrived in Rangoon with another cadet policeman, Alfred Jones. After presentation at the giant Secretariat, the bureaucratic hub of the colony, they made their way to the Police Training School in Mandalay, a 400-mile journey by rail, mostly on a high, flood-proof embankment through intensely green paddy fields as far as the eye could see. They were met at the railway station by Roger Beadon, who would make up the triumvirate of that year's European police trainees. He had come out a fortnight early in order to visit his father, who was working as a mining engineer.

According to Bill Tydd, unlike Rangoon, Mandalay was a Burmese town through and through and for him it had a medieval feel, with various crafts congregating in their own streets – one of wood-carvers, another of silver- and goldsmiths, another of lacquer workers. Tydd was struck by the sight of women running their own businesses, noting, 'they had as much independence and liberty as their western sisters'.[4]

Paul Edmonds described Mandalay as 'a straggling town of squalid streets ... The roads are inches deep in dust and littered with rubbish ... children swarm everywhere.' Orwell agreed. Apart from the picturesque moated fort, it was 'a rather disagreeable town', he later wrote, 'dusty and intolerably hot ... swarming [with] dark-faced human beings'. It had 'five main products', he wrote, 'all beginning with P, namely pagodas, pariahs, pigs, priests and prostitutes'.[5]

Orwell was joining a police force of 13,000, of whom around 1,500 were British officers. (There was also a military garrison of around 10,000 – two battalions of British and ten of Indian infantry.) At the residential training school, an imposing red-brick building, they spent the morning cramming courses in criminal law, police procedure and administrative procedures, then an hour learning Burmese, followed straight away by an hour of Hindustani. Beadon remembered struggling with the languages but that they seemed to come easily to Orwell. Afternoons included parade-ground drilling, with occasional games of football, hockey or tennis. Evenings were spent drinking in the mess, or at the Upper Burma Club, situated in the fort's old harem.[6]

Some new arrivals suffered intense loneliness. Bill Tydd, going through the same process a few years later, told the story of 'a young probationer, unable to bear the homesickness which assailed us all'. He 'stretched out on the rug beside his bed, placed the barrel of his shotgun in his mouth and then pulled the trigger'.[7]

There were seventy Burmese training in the same intake as Orwell, but the three Europeans were automatically senior and apart from them – Beadon said, 'we had one pip and thought ourselves very important'. There was also for Orwell's intake a separation from the other slightly older British men. Having been 'just too young' to serve in the war, 'You felt yourself a little less than a man, because you had missed it,' Orwell wrote. 'Those who had talked about it incessantly.'[8]

So Orwell and Beadon were thrown together, even though they were chalk and cheese. 'I was very fond of going down to the club and playing snooker and dancing,' said Beadon, 'but this didn't seem to appeal to him at all.' Orwell was 'very quiet', not a 'socialite in any way', very far from being 'one of the bright boys of the club'. Instead of drinking, Orwell, 'long and thin and rather lugubrious', would spend his evenings reading. Beadon said he was an extrovert and Orwell was 'entirely opposite'.

Nonetheless, the two men went on motorcycle rides, and on one occasion went on a tiger shoot, with Orwell borrowing the principal's shotgun. Having ridden on their motorbikes 14 or so miles out of the city, they hired a man with a bullock cart who took them, in pitch darkness, off into the bush. 'We didn't see a tiger,' Beadon remembered, 'and I had a sort of feeling that I don't think the gentleman in charge of the bullock cart ever intended that we should. If we had I think possibly Mr. Blair or Orwell would not have existed and I don't suppose I should either.'[9]

On another occasion they went up to the hill station of Maymyo to visit Beadon's father. Orwell later described the 'queer experience' of boarding a train in the 'scorching sunlight' and heat of Mandalay, then stepping out of the carriage at Maymyo at 4,000 feet above sea level 'into a different hemisphere. Suddenly you are breathing cool sweet air that might be that of England, and all around you are green grass, bracken, fir-trees.' With mock-Tudor buildings, it was, a visitor in the 1920s reported, 'conspicuously un-oriental, more like a corner of Surrey than Burma'. Here Beadon and Orwell enjoyed rounds of golf, and Orwell would be posted here for a month in September 1923. He was attached to a British regiment, an experience that prompted a later comment about how the common soldier was the most hated Englishman in Burma – 'They develop an attitude towards "the n*****s" which is far more brutal than that of the officials or business men.'[10]

In January 1924 Orwell passed his exams, and though he still had nine months of his two-year probationary period to run was posted to Myaungmya, a small, primitive and impoverished town in the Irrawaddy delta. Here, he supervised the investigations of serious crimes, observed the interrogations of prisoners, and testified at important inquests and trials. This brought 'him face to face with the darker side of British rule'.[11]

Thereafter he was moved on every six months or so. In Twante, further east in the Delta, he ran his own sub-division. Then, after a year in the Delta, notorious for its dreary landscape and ferocious mosquitoes, Orwell was posted to police stations on the outskirts of Rangoon.[12]

His longest stint was for nine months at Syriam, site of the Burmah Oil Company refinery. Technical expertise was provided by hard-living Americans. Orwell found them to have an 'implied belief that Man is naturally in a state of playing poker & drinking whisky'. Famously they had responded to an edict from the Governor's wife that white officials and residents should marry their Burmese mistresses or cast them out with an unsigned telegram in clear stating 'No c***, no oil.' (Orwell was careful to note, however, that in a 'competition in offensiveness between the two branches of the Anglo-Saxon race – the English are worse'.)[13]

At his next posting, Insein town, just north of Rangoon, home to a sizeable European community and the second biggest prison in Burma, he was visited by Roger Beadon. It seems Orwell was still something of a misfit. 'He had goats, geese, ducks and all sorts of things floating about downstairs,' Beadon remembered, 'whereas I'd keep rather a nice house – it rather shattered me, but apparently he liked that.' Orwell hadn't 'gone native', Beadon was keen to add. 'More "bohemian". Didn't seem to give a damn.'[14]

His penultimate posting was to Moulmein, Burma's third biggest city, where he had nearly 300 men under his command. It was home to his grandmother who, Orwell was rather appalled to learn, spoke no Burmese despite having lived in the country for forty years. After that he was sent north to Katha on the Irrawaddy River in Upper Burma. By far the most beautiful of his postings, this would be the setting for

Burmese Days. Paul Edmonds had visited in 1922 and admired the wild elephants and monkeys on the shore line, the jungle 'very beautiful with the early sun shining through the leaves, and the dewdrops sparkling everywhere'. A. Meer-Nemo, author of 'A Burmese Bobby', had served there three years before. He remembered it as 'pleasant and tranquil'. He enjoyed the 'Rabelaisian' humour of the villagers, though worried about how they were preyed on by con artists claiming supernatural powers. His servants there, he recalled, were 'more friends and members of the family than servants'. Though 'how their minds worked', he added, 'was often beyond my comprehension'.[15]

Orwell would later write that he remembered the landscape of Upper Burma with great fondness. But by now, he had had enough. 'I had already made up my mind that imperialism was an evil thing,' he later wrote, 'and the sooner I chucked up my job and got out of it the better.'[16]

Imperialism in Burma was 'very largely a racket', he wrote afterwards. Not only was it a mechanism for 'exploiting cheap coloured labour' but also, he alleged, 'the Burman has profited very little from the huge wealth that has been extracted from his country'.[17]

British businesses had, indeed, been doing very well from their activities in the country. It was Burma's unrivalled teak resources that had first, long before, interested Britain. Nothing was more ideal for the decks of Royal Navy ships fighting Napoleon. Shortly after the annexation of Lower Burma, all teak trees were declared the exclusive property of the government, and British firms authorised by lease arrangements were soon running the export trade. Supreme among them was the Bombay Burmah Trading Corporation. Originally known as Wallace Brothers, Edinburgh-born traders who had started out in India before getting involved with Burmese tea, it was floated in 1863. Some of its equity was held by Indian merchants, but the Wallace brothers kept a controlling stake. By the 1870s, as well as having other interests in cotton, oil exploration and shipping, it was the leading producer of teak in Burma and Siam. So large were its operations that at one time the company employed a herd of nearly 2,000 elephants to drag the huge logs from steep hillsides down to the Irrawaddy to be carried off to Rangoon and beyond. As we've seen, its dispute with the Burmese king provided the *casus belli* for the conquest of Upper Burma, while its agents had done all they could to stir up concerns about French involvement. (The company is now part of the Wadia group of companies.)[18]

George James Swan of Perthshire established the Irrawaddy Flotilla Corporation in the 1870s, and soon its huge fleet operated a virtual monopoly on large-scale river freight. Needless to say, local boatmen were put out of business.

The oil industry in Burma also had Scottish origins. Burmah Oil Company had its headquarters in Glasgow. In 1908, a pipeline was laid from the northern oil fields to the refinery near Rangoon. In 1923, just under 7 million barrels of oil were extracted, with Burmah Oil Company paying a dividend of 30 per cent. For the princely sum of £5,000, the company had recently employed as a political lobbyist no less than Winston Churchill, out of the Commons after losing the 1922 Dundee by-election to E. D. Morel. Churchill used the Treasury door into Downing Street privately to meet with Prime Minister Baldwin and push the company's interests. (The company is now British Petroleum.)[19]

Other Scottish trading houses exported tungsten, lead, silver, jade and precious stones. In October 1922, a huge ruby was found. Worth £10,000, it was called the Lady Craddock after the Governor's wife. Most of the mining was done by Chinese workers, who were compelled to wear enormous masks entirely covering the head, making it impossible for stones to be swallowed.[20]

The biggest export business, worth four times the value of oil, was rice. After the annexation of Lower Burma, imported convicts and then 'coolies' from India had cleared the jungles of the Irrawaddy delta, planting rice on an industrial scale. The opening of the Suez Canal supercharged the rice export business, with half the export quantity now going to Europe. By 1923, Burma was exporting 3 million tons of rice, half the world's production.[21]

Burmese peasant cultivators, however, enjoyed little of the profits. Collusive practices by British mill-owners kept the price paid to the producer low. Prices for rice exported to India were fixed to India's advantage. The trade was firmly in the hands of the British. William Strang Steel of Glasgow's Steel Brothers was one of several making a fortune from the business. In fact, thanks in the main to indebtedness, the cultivator was worse off than ever.

The clearance of the delta had required capital investment which was not available locally. Instead it was financed by the Chettyars, a class of bankers and money-lenders from Madras. Of course, it only took a sharp fall in price or a failed harvest to put the peasant proprietor into difficulties. A report from 1922 found that in one riverine district 85 per cent of cultivators were in debt with many living hand to mouth and only the luckiest making more than a bare living. The 1921 census shows only a half of Burmese agriculturalists still owning their land, the rest reduced by foreclosure to the status of a landless labourer.[22]

Naturally, the Indian money-lenders were resented. So too were the seasonal Indian 'coolies' who could earn twice the wage in Burma and could therefore undercut local workers. From India too came doctors, engineers and clerks imported by the British as it was easier than training up Burmese. Of the quarter of a million immigrants from India every year, many stayed on, becoming shop-keepers, farmers or merchants. Policeman C. Bruce Orr wrote that 'the Burman' 'disliked all foreigners but chiefly the Indians'. There were also Chinese staying on, many of whom were skilled artisans, and others who became successful businessmen. By 1923 the liquor and pawn-broking sectors were firmly in Chinese hands. Anyone could now see that the richest people were almost entirely non-Burmese. In the meantime, local industries making clothes and household goods were wiped out by cheap imports. As Orwell complained, 'the Burmese are also, little by little, being taken into an era of industrial capitalism without ever being able to become capitalists themselves'.[23]

*

This indebtedness, landlessness and resentment kept the crime wave surging along throughout Orwell's time in Burma. John Stanford, aged thirty-five, was posted to Burma from India in June 1923 as an under-secretary in the government. He soon discovered that 'each district possessed ... an astounding assortment of malefactors – murderers, dacoits, thieves, robbers, house-breakers, forgers, coiners, blackmail-ers ... They seemed to spring up like dragon's teeth.' Instances of violent crime rose steadily, and the murder rate per million – 42.9 in 1920 – was nearly 60 a few years later, almost twice that of Punjab, by some distance the worst Indian province.[24]

The 'Report on the Prison Administration of Burma for the Year 1923' detailed the challenges the system was facing. The thirty central and twenty-three district jails were now inadequate; two more were to be built including a new central jail at Tharrawaddy to house 1,500 prisoners. At Insein, a new 'double drop gallows' had been installed.

The author of the report hit out at critics of the regime of corpo-ral punishment, explaining that 'the Burman' (who made up more than 80 per cent of the prison population) 'is a Mongol, and the Mongolians have always had an element of cruelty in their punish-ments ... the Burman guilty of brutal assaults and the like rather expects a return in kind, and for my part I would not disappoint him'.

There was good news of the success of a pilot scheme to issue tobacco as a reward for good conduct. Due to lack of funds it hadn't been possible to issue prisoners with two sets of clothes and a towel, but they had stayed reasonably healthy. On admission, all prisoners were examined medically, vaccinated and treated for hookworm infection. More than half had put on weight, only 15 per cent had lost weight. 'I maintain that a prisoner generally leaves a fitter man than when he came in,' the report's author wrote. 'No people get closer medical attention than those who are the least meritorious among the community.'

There was a new scheme, he wrote: the Burma Prisoners' Aid Relief fund. 'A small but earnest band of voluntary workers ... Has helped 15 ex-prisoners with jobs or small money grants. The chief problem seems

to be to interest Burmans in the work of the society.' The author wearily
ended, 'This is, I am glad to say, the last report I shall write.'[25]

Increasingly, Orwell found his police work impossible to deal with. A
turning point seems to have come when an American missionary had
been watching one of Orwell's sub-inspectors bully a suspect. A decade
after leaving Burma, Orwell recounted the incident in *The Road to
Wigan Pier*. 'Like most Nonconformist missionaries he was a complete
ass but quite a good fellow ...' The American turned to Orwell and
said, 'I wouldn't care to have your job.' 'It made me horribly ashamed,'
wrote Orwell. 'So that was the kind of job I had! Even an ass of an
American missionary, a tee-total cock-virgin from the Middle West,
had the right to look down on me and pity me.'

The administration of criminal law, he went on to say in the same
book, required 'insensitive people'. 'Even the other Europeans in
Burma', he said, 'slightly looked down on the police because of the
brutal work they had to do.' For him, it became beyond bearing to see
the 'wretched prisoners squatting in the reeking cages of the lock-ups,
the grey cowed faces of the long-term convicts, the scarred buttocks
of the men who had been flogged with bamboos ... I watched a man
hanged once; it seemed to me worse than a thousand murders.' On top
of this, the hangings, beatings and incarcerations were 'in the capacity
of foreign invaders. The Burmese themselves never really recognised
our jurisdiction.' What might have been accepted as a thief justly
punished became 'wanton meaningless cruelty' inflicted by a 'foreign
conqueror'.[26]

The Road to Wigan Pier is a mixture of polemic and autobiography,
as are the three key Orwell writings about his time in Burma – the
short stories 'A Hanging' (1931) and 'Shooting an Elephant' (1936),
and the novel *Burmese Days* (1934). Orwell himself declared them to
be essentially anti-imperialist, writing much later that he was 'against
imperialism because I know something about it from the inside. The
whole history of this is to be found in my writings, including a novel.'
In fact, on close reading, these writings display much more complexity

and nuance, at times even justifying British racist attitudes. In this respect they shine a light not just on Orwell's ambivalence, but also on the sometimes contradictory and complicated attitudes of the wider British left – and what we would now call progressive thought – towards the British Empire and race.[27]

Orwell later wrote of *Burmese Days* that much of it was 'simply reporting what I have seen'. Although not published until 1934, it was begun while Orwell was still in Burma. Set in a small town that is recognisably Katha, it depicts, on the face of it, a situation where everyone is corrupted by the colonial system in which they live. There are no likeable characters. The small British community are unremittingly ghastly. They are snobbish, drunk – downing gin and brandy before breakfast ('booze is the cement of empire', we learn) – and display what Orwell elsewhere called 'vicious colour prejudice'. (Interestingly, a vague exception is MacGregor, the most senior British official: although a crashing bore, he does not drink, dislikes the use of the 'n-word', and tries to calm tempers in the community.) Ellis, a timber merchant with a 'spiteful Cockney voice', is the worst. 'Any hint of friendly feeling towards an Oriental seemed to him a horrible perversity,' the narrator explains. He is 'one of those Englishmen – common unfortunately – who should never be allowed to set foot in the East.' Ellis craves violence, hoping for a rebellion so that he has a chance to kill one of the 'black stinking swine'. 'Look at Amritsar,' he says at one point. 'Dyer knew the stuff to give them.'[28]

The central character, also a timber merchant, is John Flory. He is cowardly, dissolute, self-disgusted and cruel – very much the antithesis of the colonial hero of fiction. He acts at most times as the authorial mouthpiece (at one point he was going to be named George Orwell). Like Orwell, he condemns economic exploitation – 'The official holds the Burman down while the businessman goes through his pockets' – and uniquely displays affection and respect for Burmese and Chinese culture. His best friend is an Indian. But in the end he betrays his friend and his principles, is disgraced, and commits suicide. ('There is rather a large number of suicides among the Europeans in Burma,' the narrator explains, 'and they occasion very little surprise.')[29]

Yet despite the book's outward condemnation of the vicious racism of the British, it has remained widely disliked in Burma/Myanmar. For throughout the book the Burmese and Indian characters are without exception portrayed as corrupt, and in the main feeble. The two principal non-European characters are off-the-peg stereotypes. The villainous Burmese magistrate U Po Kyin, with his 'vast yellow face', is the very archetype of the music hall 'scheming oriental' caricature (*Fu Manchu*, the first of Sax Rohmer's 'Yellow Peril' stories, had been published in 1913, with more following soon after. The first film, *The Mystery of Dr Fu Manchu*, came out in 1923.) His adversary and Flory's friend Dr Veraswami (referred to by Ellis as 'very-slimy') is painfully obsequious and 'understood little of what was said to him'. He is ugly and badly dressed, the narrator tells us, and, uniquely among all the characters, Orwell gives him convoluted English and a 'comical' accent, shown on the page with 'is' becoming 'iss' and 'as' 'ass'. Indeed, he is in many ways 'the comic *babu* of the Punch tradition' that Orwell condemned in his essay 'Boy's Weeklies'.[30]

Checking the proofs for a later paperback edition of *Burmese Days*, Orwell insisted that 'native', a word he hated, was not used in a derogatory way, and that 'Negro' was always given a capital letter; he changed Chinese for Chinaman and Moslem for Mohammedan, hoping, he said, to do 'a little to mitigate the horrors of the colour war'. But 'yellow' is used to describe Burmese skin colour throughout the book, and in the narrator's voice. The narrator also makes frequent animal references: the Eurasians who corner Flory outside the church are 'like a pair of dogs asking for a game'; U Po Kyin's wife's face is 'simian' – and so, endlessly, on.[31]

The nationalist movement in Burma is represented by a newspaper, the *Burmese Patriot*, 'a miserable eight-page rag' cheaply printed, and with a tiny circulation, consisting of news stolen from the *Rangoon Gazette*, and 'partly of weak Nationalist heroics'. When its editor is arrested for libel, he goes on hunger strike, but 'broke down after six hours'.[32]

'No Englishman ever feels himself in real danger from an oriental,' the narrator tells us. In 'Shooting an Elephant' the lone British officer might feel under social pressure, but 'anti-European feeling', if 'bitter', is also 'aimless' and 'petty'. They are in no way a physical threat – 'no one had the guts to raise a riot'. (And of course he is the lone rational person, who knows the elephant does not need to be shot, as opposed to the 'excited' and unreasonable crowd of 'yellow faces above the garish clothes'.)[33]

And as well as feeble, the Burmese are almost all corrupt. As a matter of course clerks steal from government stores; the Burmese police constables are 'knock-kneed, bribe-taking cowards'; Flory's 'keep' steals from him; the hospital is ineffective because the Burmese pharmacist serving the hospital fulfils the doctor's prescriptions with 'bottles filled with water and various vegetable dyes'. A Burmese protester tells the British Deputy Commissioner, 'We know there is no justice for us in your courts', but the problem is identified in large part as the blatant corruptibility of the Burmese actors, either as magistrates or witnesses.[34]

Orwell's fellow probationer Roger Beadon read *Burmese Days* while still serving in Burma. 'I don't think he cared for the Europeans, I can't blame him for some of them,' he said. But portraying all the Burmese as 'corrupt' was 'rather unfair'.[35]

However unworthy of respect the British characters are, as portrayed in the book, white prestige is a real and powerful thing. Flory's girlfriend gains status in her village for having a white 'husband'; for the Eurasians, 'talking to white people' is 'the joy of their life'; when the Indian doctor is framed by his enemy U Po Kyin, he tells Flory, 'all depends upon one's standings with the Europeans . . . I must wait and hope that my prestige will carry me through.' Both he and U Po Kyin are desperate to gain the gold-plated prestige of being elected to join the European club.[36]

When Flory delays returning to the timber-extraction camp in the jungle, 'in his absence everything went to pieces under the incompetent Eurasian overseer'. An important engine breaks down, an elephant gets ill, 'coolies' desert. The white man returns to the camp and immediately identifies the problems and fixes them.[37]

Even more striking (and seemingly out of place in an 'anti-imperialist' and anti-heroic novel) is an episode that occurs at the climax of the story. The British club is under siege by a crowd of 2,000 angry Burmese and someone needs to call out the police. Flory leaps from the balcony, dashes past the picket on the lawn, dives into the river and swims to the police lines. The police, 150-strong and armed only with sticks, have attacked the crowd from the rear but become engulfed. Flory is too, for a while, in the 'animal heat'. The crowd of Burmans 'who could have killed him' don't know what to do with him. Some even 'tried to make way for him, as a white man'.

Flory takes charge, ordering the police to fetch their rifles, then to fire over the heads of the crowd, which instantly disperses, the young men leaping through a gap in the hedge like 'a procession of gazelles' (very much prey rather than predators). Flory encounters an exhausted Dr Veraswami, who had been trying to restrain the crowd. 'It wass hopeless till you came,' he tells Flory.[38]

The whole episode, it goes without saying, is like something from *Gem* or *Magnet* magazine; in Orwell's mocking description, 'at the outpost of Empire the monocled Englishmen are holding the n*****s at bay'. It's a jarring and confusing moment in a complex, strange but revealing novel.[39]

The incident that had led to the protesting crowd concerned Ellis and the blinding of a Burmese boy. Early in the book, the narrator explains that 'Living and working among Orientals would try the temper of a saint.' All of the British, in particular the officials, 'knew what it was to be baited and insulted. Almost every day ... the High School boys, with their young, yellow faces ... sneered at them as they went past, sometimes hooted after them with hyena-like laughter.' Later in the book, Ellis, itching for a fight, reacts to four schoolboys grinning at him with 'deliberate insolence' by lashing out and hitting one in the face with his stick. They all attack him, but he is 'too strong for them'.

They retreat to throw stones, but 'their arms were feeble and they threw ineptly'. The boy is taken to a Burmese doctor 'who, by applying some poisonous concoction of crushed leaves to his left eye, succeeded in blinding him'.[40]

Somewhat surprisingly, this episode with the frankly psychotic Ellis seems to have been inspired by an incident involving Orwell himself. Htin Aung was sixteen when he met Orwell. He would later study at Cambridge, Oxford and Trinity, Dublin and was afterwards Vice-Chancellor of Rangoon University. One of his elder brothers was U Tin Tut, that skilful Burmese rugby player denied use of the clubhouse showers. His father was a district magistrate at Pegu, who in 1923 was the first Burmese to be elected to the club there. According to his son, this wasn't, as *Burmese Days* tells us, the 'Nirvana for which native officials pine', but 'an unpleasant social duty' he would only undertake on sufferance once a month.[41]

Htin Aung would also write histories of Burma, describing 1919 to 1930 as 'the darkest period' of Anglo-Burmese relations (outside actual war), when they were 'bitter enemies, each despising the other', separated by a 'wall of racial prejudice harder than granite' with communications between them riddled with 'mutual suspicion, despair and disgust'.

In November 1924, Htin Aung was a freshman at Rangoon University. Orwell was serving at a police station not far from the city. 'One afternoon, at about 4 p.m., the suburban railway station of Pagoda Road was crowded with schoolboys and undergraduates,' Htin Aung wrote. Orwell came down the stairs to take the train into the city. 'One of the boys, fooling around with his friends, accidentally bumped against the tall and gaunt Englishman, who fell heavily down the stairs. Orwell was furious,' Htin Aung remembered, 'and raised the heavy cane he was carrying, to hit the boy on the head, but checked himself, and stuck him on the back instead.'

He was instantly surrounded by protesting schoolchildren, joined by Htin Aung and other undergraduates. Then the train drew in and Orwell boarded a first-class carriage. 'Some of us had first-class season tickets,' Htin Aung wrote. 'The argument between Blair and the undergraduates continued. Fortunately, the train reached Mission Road station without further incident, and Blair left the train. He must often have pondered on the tragic consequences that could have followed had he not controlled himself. Blair was, of course, merely reflecting the general attitude of his English contemporaries towards Burmese students.'[42]

Indeed, Orwell was honest about how he was angered when 'if a European woman went through the bazaars alone somebody would probably spit betel juice over her dress' and how 'in the end the sneering yellow faces of young men that met me everywhere, the insults hooted after me when I was at a safe distance, got badly on my nerves'. According to a fellow old Etonian who visited Orwell in Burma, he had 'an especial hatred ... for the Buddhist priests, against whom he thought violence especially desirable ... because of their sniggering insolence'. Fellow policeman John Stanford wrote of 'truculent young priests' jeering at him, or staring with 'eyes full of cold menace'.[43]

Orwell himself described a conflicted attitude: he was torn between his hatred of the empire he served and his rage against 'the evil-spirited little beasts who tried to make my job impossible'. 'With one part of my mind I thought of the British Raj as an unbreakable tyranny,' he wrote, 'with another part I thought that the greatest joy in the world would be to drive a bayonet into a Buddhist priest's guts.'[44]

Writing about the empire after his return to 'the cool air' of England, he veered about, often contradicting himself or seemingly changing his mind, even within the same piece of writing. In an article for a French magazine, published in 1929, he condemned the introduction of democracy to India and Burma as a sham, but then went on to write that 'the Burmese are simple peasants, busy working on their land. They have not reached the intellectual level necessary for nationalist activities. Their village is their world, and inasmuch as they are left to till their fields, they don't care too much whether their rulers are black or white.' In the same piece, he suggested that although the British ruled Burma in a despotic fashion, 'it should be borne in mind that it does not mean they are unpopular. The English have constructed roads and canals – in their own interest, sure enough, but the Burmese have profited from them – they have built hospitals, opened schools, and maintained national order and security.' He ended, though, affirming that the relation of the Burmese to the British Empire was that 'of slave to master. Is the master good or bad? That is not the point: enough to state that his authority is despotic and, let us say the word, self-interested.' In *The Road to Wigan Pier*, he declared that British rule in Burma was 'benevolent and necessary', but that 'no modern man, in his heart of hearts, believes that it is right to invade a foreign country and hold the population down by force'. In 'Shooting an Elephant', written in 1936, the British Empire is 'a great deal better than the younger empires that are going to supplant it'.[45]

Ten years after leaving imperial service, he took aim at what he called the 'half-baked, soggy insincerity' of left-wing opinion on empire and its hypocrisy and inertia. 'Every left-wing "intellectual" is, as a matter of course, an anti-imperialist.' It was easy to be witty about the White Man's Burden, Rule Britannia and Kipling's novels. But this, he wrote, was a 'flabby, boneless attitude . . . in the last resort, the only important question is, Do you want the British Empire to hold together or do you want it to disintegrate? And at the bottom of his heart no Englishman . . . does want it to disintegrate.' Everyone who enjoyed the comparatively high standard of living in England was complicit in the empire, Orwell contended, without which England would be reduced to 'a cold and unimportant little island where we should all have to work very hard and live mainly on herrings and potatoes. That is the very last thing that any left-winger wants. Yet the left-winger continues to feel that he has no moral responsibility for imperialism. He is perfectly ready to accept the products of Empire and to save his soul by sneering at the people who hold the Empire together.[46]

Indeed, the leading 'anti-imperial' voices of late 1923 displayed this ambivalent attitude. Leonard Woolf, while declaring that imperialism had 'been accompanied by very serious evils', and was described by Beatrice Webb as an 'anti-imperialist fanatic', wrote that in Ceylon he enjoyed his 'position and the flattery of being the great man and the father of the people ... I became more and more ambivalent, politically schizophrenic'. At one point in his autobiography he mused that 'In the Ceylon jungle village there was still a place or excuse for government paternalism.'[47]

Labour Party manifestos of the early 1920s called for little more than a slightly more rapid path to self-government within the empire. The party's deputy chairman J. R. Clynes, interviewed by *United Empire* magazine in early 1923, suggested that a goal should be more government 'by consent' rather than through the 'application of force', but that the establishment of representative institutions should be governed by 'the standard of education and capacity' of the people concerned.[48]

In September 1923 the Independent Labour Party (ILP) held a seminar to discuss 'Labour and the Empire', with speakers including left-wing London mayors and aldermen. 'To surrender our possessions or protectorates in Africa, the West Indies, the Pacific or elsewhere', one argued, 'was not only to hand back to the native populations their freedom to fight, exploit and enslave themselves, but to induce a scramble for possession of such territories by other powerful nations.'[49]

In general, critics of empire on the left argued that British colonial rule had persistently failed to live up to the ideals of trusteeship – but they didn't challenge the validity of the ideals themselves and the ideas of racial hierarchy and British superiority that went with them.

E. D. Morel, the scourge of the Belgian regime in the Congo, wrote in *The Black Man's Burden* (1920) – a book read by Nehru, who said it 'greatly moved' him – that the 'primitive races' could not escape being 'sucked into the vortex of white economic expansion' and that the 'just equitable, understanding government of the ... politically helpless races of tropical Africa' was 'one of the finest and most unselfish tasks which remain for white men to fulfil in the world'.[50]

Woolf himself, in a 1920 pamphlet, denounced what he saw as the despotic government and economic exploitation of the 'imperialist system' neither 'desired nor understood' by the colonised, but looked to the new mandate system to extend and deepen the application of trusteeship. The effects of European policy in Africa, he wrote, 'have been almost wholly evil'. But there was no question of the European withdrawing 'to leave these non-adult races to manage their own affairs'. The only solution to the problems of imperialism was, it seems, more, better imperialism. Sinhalese critic D. C. R. A. Goonetilleke concluded: 'Leonard Woolf was unconsciously schizoid: the liberal and Fabian shared a skin with the superior white.'[51]

Whatever his later ambivalence, or even defensiveness, Orwell arrived back in England sick, and sick at heart. In Katha he seems to have contracted dengue fever (his health would never really recover). He had decided to take himself in a completely different direction. He had had enough of what he called the 'dilemma that faces every official in an empire like our own ... in theory he is administering an impartial system of justice; in practice he is part of a huge machine that exists to protect British interests, and he has often to choose between sacrificing his integrity and damaging his career'. Back in England, according to a family friend, Orwell was 'far from well, even then. I don't think the tropics suited him, but I think he was also sick with rage. He was convinced that we had no business to be in Burma, no right to dominate other nations. He would have ended the British Raj then and there.'[52]

Orwell carried, he wrote, an immense weight of guilt. He was haunted by 'Innumerable remembered faces – faces of prisoners in the dock, of men waiting in the condemned cells, of subordinates I had bullied and aged peasants I had snubbed, of servants and coolies I had hit with my fist in moments of rage (nearly everyone does these things in the East, at any rate occasionally: Orientals can be very provoking).'

'I had reduced everything', he later remembered of the time of his return to England, 'to the simple theory that the oppressed are always right and the oppressors are always wrong: a mistaken theory, but the natural result of being one of the oppressors yourself. I felt that I had to escape not merely from imperialism but from every form of man's dominion over man. I wanted to submerge myself, to get right down among the oppressed, to be one of them and on their side against the tyrants.' This, then, was the end of Eric Blair, public-school boy and imperial policeman, and the beginning of George Orwell, of *Down and Out in Paris and London.*[53]

26

The Big Shoot

Rangoon had been freshly laid out by colonial architects after the conquest of Lower Burma in the 1850s, but in 1923 there was still a forested area between the old city centre with its massive Shwedagon pagoda and the new city to the south. Here unwary travellers were still being picked off by tigers.[1]

The menace presented by wild animals was real. In Burma in 1923, 111 people were killed – sixty-two by tigers, fourteen by leopards or panthers, sixteen by elephants, nine by crocodiles; the rest perished thanks to bears and buffaloes, with one each accounted for by a wild boar and 'black lizards'. In response, 5,000 wild animals were killed, including 793 tigers, 2,252 panthers and leopards and 1,706 bears. Rewards were offered – 50 rupees for killing a leopard. In all, 85,000 rupees were paid out. There was no reward for the 16,634 registered snake kills, and snakebite accounted for 1,472 deaths.[2]

The figures from India, reported in the British press at the end of September 1923, correspond to the much larger population, but show a similar hazard. Tigers were blamed for 1,603 deaths, leopards 509, wolves 460, bears 105, elephants 55, hyenas 9. Some 20,000 were killed by snakes.[3]

Traditionally, across south Asia, problems with rogue man-eating big cats had been dealt with by local itinerant trapping specialists. But now in many places the responsibility had fallen to the 'white sahib', as seen in 'Shooting an Elephant', and everyone else had been declared a poacher.[4]

Elephants had been a menace to crops and sometimes life in Ceylon for a long time. The British occupation, however, saw the population reduced from 15,000 to 3,000. But in India, where the stock was needed for domestication, they were protected from the 1870s. In Africa, where unlike in Asia the elephants produced valuable ivory, 12,000 a year were killed in the 1880s and 1890s, to provide millions of piano keys and cutlery handles. A conservationist backlash in the 1890s saw the herds spectacularly revive and present once more a severe threat to crops, though it still now took a special, expensive licence from the colonial government to be allowed to kill one.[5]

For the British, who at home had no wild animal threats, with the possible exception of foxes, whose hunting had become as much about pageant and ritual as professional control, shooting and hunting was about sport. Scores were rigorously tabulated. The *Daily Mail* of 29 September 1923 includes the obituary of Lord Ripon, which concentrates on his extraordinary shooting record. There's evidence of overseas trips – eleven tigers, twelve buffaloes and two rhinos – but back at home his 'bag' of birds numbered some 556,000, which included 22,976 pheasants. He had died having collapsed the previous Saturday on Dallowgill Moor near Studley Royal Park, having dispatched fifty-two luckless birds that morning.

His greatest exploit, we read, was downing twenty-eight pheasants in just sixty seconds as a shooting party guest of the King at his Sandringham House estate. Here George V indulged in what his son called 'one of my father's greatest pleasures in life', second only perhaps to his mania for stamp-collecting. At Sandringham, the birds were so lavishly bred that, a visitor reported, 'One sees pheasants everywhere in the park and garden. The place is literally crawling with them.' Shoots were organised on a huge scale with fifty to a hundred beaters. 'A good day's bag was a thousand head, but two thousand was not uncommon,' the Prince of Wales remembered. Some 20,000 birds would be shot there every year through the 1920s.[6]

The King's obvious enthusiasm added to the aristocratic cachet of shooting and hunting. As 'sport' it also shared the idea that a 'Sportsman' was a good, vigorous, manly fellow. The Prince had disliked big game shooting in India – his father on an earlier visit had accounted for twenty-one tigers and eight rhinos – in favour of pig-sticking, and this was latched on to by Robert Baden-Powell, in a book published shortly after the Prince's Indian trip. Pig-sticking, the founder of the Boy Scouts argued, was an excellent training for battle, developing 'an eye for the country, horsemanship, endurance, quick decision and determined attack'. A pig-sticker was a man who 'goes straight, plays fair, rides with courage and judgement'. Baden-Powell hoped that the activity would improve the calibre of the Indian Army and the ICS, which, he considered, was not attracting the same quality of young men.[7]

Baden-Powell also suggested that hunting was a way for the British to encounter ordinary Indians, employed as beaters or grooms. But the hunting activities of the British were sometimes met with hostility. In India, villagers objected to the shooting of peafowl or blue bulls, both revered by Hindus. Sometimes villagers were caught in the crossfire. The worst incident occurred in Egypt before the war. A group of British officers upset the residents of Dinshaway by hunting pigeons for sport. Since the pigeons the officers were shooting were raised by the villagers and served as a local source of livelihood, the villagers sought to protect their property and confronted the soldiers. A scuffle broke out, and an officer's gun was fired – he claimed unintentionally – wounding a female villager who was the wife of a Muslim prayer leader. This provoked further outrage from the villagers, who attacked the British officers. One of the officers managed to escape from the scene and fled back on foot towards the British camp in the intense noontime heat. He later collapsed outside the camp and died, probably of heatstroke. A villager who came upon him there tried to assist him, but when other soldiers from the camp discovered the villager alongside the body of the dead officer they assumed or claimed that he had killed the soldier, and so they shot the villager. The incident, which was followed by numerous arrests of Egyptians and several executions, outraged liberal opinion in Britain and contributed in a large way to the intensely sour relations between British and Egyptians in 1923.[8]

In other ways, the British mania for hunting and shooting had ill effects. In the late 1850s, avid hunter Thomas Austin decided to introduce some European species to Australia, to provide 'a touch of home, in addition to a spot of hunting'. His nephew provided twelve grey rabbits, as well as five hares, seventy-two partridges and some sparrows. Within a decade, the rabbits had become so prevalent that 2 million could be shot or trapped annually without having any noticeable effect on the population. It was the fastest spread ever recorded of any mammal anywhere in the world, and a disaster for agriculture in Australia.

In 1923 pheasants were being introduced to New Zealand, but no one tried to export the quintessential English hunting prey, the fox. Traditional fox-hunting parties with dogs still assembled across the empire, but in Palestine they chased jackals instead. In Argentina and Kenya, it was ostriches. In Shanghai, the Police Assistant Commissioner ran a pack of hounds which hunted at dawn on weekday mornings, following a drag scented by a Siberian bear, courtesy of the city's zoo.[9]

One of the key attractions of empire service, along with the cheap servants, was the possibility of participating in the aristocratic, semi-feudal practice of hunting. For most men, it would have been well out of their reach at home. Not only was labour cheaper – beaters, skinners, bag-carriers, skivvies to ensure your camp table had a clean white linen tablecloth – but targets were often more prevalent. An English newspaper advertisement from 29 September 1923 encouraging emigration to Newfoundland and Labrador, while extolling the 'mineral and forest wealth', led on it being 'The Sportsman's El Dorado'.[10]

Most attractive, though, was the Big Game of East Africa.

Wild animals remained a menace in Africa. As well as destruction by elephants and rhinoceroses, newspapers from September 1923 report the discovery of the remains of a woman eaten by hyenas in Southern Rhodesia, and that 'During the weekend, another lion invaded Nairobi' and was shot only 100 yards from Government House.[11]

But by 1923 the glamour of big game hunting in Africa had gripped the public imagination in Europe and the United States. For many, this was what Africa was about. The year saw the release of a flood of documentary films about the continent: seven premiered in 1923 and another seven the following year, making them the two biggest years for African non-fiction films in cinema history. Titles included *Wildest Africa*, *On the Equator* and *The Wonderland of Big Game*. So prevalent were they that satirists got involved: Stan Laurel's 1923 release *Roughest Africa* poked fun at the blatant staging of zoo animals in fake wild settings (and remains hilarious).[12]

As in the recent spate of cod-documentaries about the Pacific, such as *Headhunters of the South Seas*, the new African films spoke to their audiences' preconceptions about 'natives' and wilfully misinterpreted the purposes of the indigenous ceremonies they filmed, to the fury of Africans not just on the continent but across the diaspora. The films' intention, however, was to create a visual celebration of the white hunter.[13]

This idea had been given a huge impetus by the heavily publicised visit of Teddy Roosevelt, recently retired US President, to East Africa before the war. In theory, it was a scientific expedition, sponsored by the Smithsonian Institution and National Museum, to collect specimens. This allowed the ex-President to enjoy suspended game regulations. In reality, it was an industrial-scale effort to project manliness and white dominance. The expedition shot 512 head of game, including nine rare white rhinoceros. Overweight and a poor shot, Roosevelt left many animals wounded.[14]

Most importantly, East Africa had seen the hunting and exploration frontier (the journeys of Joseph Thomson had inspired Rider Haggard's *King Solomon's Mines*) become the imperial frontier, its game resources contributing to the expansionist urge. Frederick Lugard began his career in Africa as an elephant hunter for the African Lakes Company.

His campaigns in Uganda in the 1890s were partly financed by ivory, of which over £5,000-worth a year was sent to the coast.[15]

Aged twenty-seven, Hugh Cholmondeley, Lord Delamere, crossed into Kenya while on a hunting trip in Somaliland in 1897. The British presence at this point was minimal. But in Kenya he discovered the temperate Highlands, described in a review of one of the 1923 American films as 'No longer Darkest Africa instead a glorious sun-cleansed Africa ... Lands where a man and a woman can live together for two years without a day's sickness between them ... an idyllic oasis ... wherever you look, animals dot the plain, grazing, galloping as in a woodland pasture in Kentucky's Blue Grass region.' Delamere was entranced, and returned in 1903 to buy 100,000 acres. His brother-in-law came too, equipped with £1,500 and a pack of foxhounds. The Mathaiga Club, north of Nairobi, which would later achieve a global reputation for decadence, would have walls decorated with hunting scenes. This was fitting: hunting and 'big game' proved to be part of the genesis of Delamere's project and the advent of the white community in Kenya, and all the mayhem they would bring.[16]

27

Kenya: The Law of Rule

In the forefront stands the steady degeneracy of white stock, soaked from youth, through adolescence, in a culture of hate and disdain, pervading the home, the Colony's public life and the local Press.

WILLIAM MCGREGOR ROSS,
Kenya Director of Public Works, 1905–23[1]

On 29 September 1923, a furious telegram was sent from the Colonial Office to the Governor of Kenya. The message demanded an immediate report on the trial and recently reached verdict on Jaspar Abraham, a well-to-do and well-connected Kenya white settler who had beaten one of his workers, Kitosh, to death. It was coded and sent at 11.25 a.m.[2]

Abraham had employed Kitosh for eighteen months. Previously, Kitosh had run away, but under Kenya's stringent labour laws had been forced to return. Kitosh's reason for his abscondment was the frequent beatings to which he was subjected by his employer. Abraham did not deny this. In mid-June, Abraham sent Kitosh with a mare in foal on an errand to the railway station. Before he returned, Abraham was told by a neighbouring farmer that he had seen Kitosh riding the mare. When he got back, Kitosh found Abraham in a fury (though the mare had suffered no ill effects). According to the trial records, 'Abraham got up, got hold of him, opened a door in the long building and pushed the boy in.' (The 'boy' Kitosh was 'a well-built adult native about 30 years of age and had a small black beard'.) After five other employees had been called on to put him on the ground, Abrahams then got a *kiboko*, a lash made of double-ox hide, and began to beat Kitosh. This continued for fifteen minutes, until Abraham grew tired. He then ordered his employees to continue the whipping, and got furious with them for their obvious reluctance. Eventually Kitosh passed out. Water was flung on him, and then he was taken to a store, being kicked and punched in the head and ribs by Abraham on the way. There he was tied up, with his hands behind his back and his legs fastened to a stick.[3]

After supper, Abraham checked on Kitosh and found that someone had untied him. He tied him up again, but tighter. The kitchen boy took Kitosh some water during the night. He was rolling in pain and said that if he had a knife he would kill himself. Another, later witness heard him weeping. He died at four in the morning.

The post-mortem was carried out by experienced District Surgeon Dr F. L. Henderson, who confirmed that there was no pre-condition that might have contributed to Kitosh's death. 'The injuries were extensive and severe,' he reported. 'There were two cuts with purple bruises around the inner side of the lower lip, abrasions on the right wrist, a distinct swelling on the right groin and numerous horse-shoe shaped marks with dried blood on the outer side of both thighs and buttocks; these marks were half to one inch wide. There were incisions and severe bruisings of the muscles of the buttocks which were congested and full of blood. The same conditions prevailed down the back of the left thigh with considerable haemorrhage. The swelling in the right groin consisted of clotted blood the size of his fist.' The doctor reckoned that Kitosh would have died soon anyway, as his viciously whipped buttocks had become gangrenous.[4]

At the trial in mid-August, Abraham, looking 'well-groomed', denied murder, and manslaughter, but pleaded guilty of inflicting 'grievous hurt'. He was cleared by the white jury of all other charges and he received a prison sentence of just two years.

A memo circulated round the Colonial Office when news of the trial reached London. Annotations were added in various hands. One official wrote: 'This is a revolting case, and, in spite of the Judge's laboured explanations it is clear that nothing approaching justice has been done. If the positions had been reversed and the native had been on trial for a similar offence against the white, who can doubt what would have been his fate? We may expect that the sentence will be severely criticised – and rightly so – both in and out of parliament.' Another commented: 'a verdict of anything less than manslaughter is quite irreconcilable with the facts of the case'.[5]

The case, picked up by humanitarian groups and opposition MPs in Britain, highlighted the violence and coercion underwriting labour relations in the colony, where a whipped African was seen as the equivalent of a spanked child. The Kenya establishment newspaper the *East African Standard* called the murder 'deplorable' but added, 'we do not believe that it is possible for the Native to be properly trained without corporal punishment'.[6]

It also made a mockery of the idea that the British in some way stood for law and justice.

'We have had in the Kenya Colony in the past a deplorable falling away from the honourable British standard which has been maintained, as a whole, throughout the Empire,' a Colonial Office minister was forced to confess to the House of Commons. The white Kenyans, the only settler society over which the government had any real domestic control, were a national and international embarrassment. The Secretary of State for India expressed the opinion that the best option might be to buy them out and get them out of Africa (pretty much what would happen, many unhappy years later).[7]

This was far from an isolated incident. On the memo, one official commented: 'This seems to be a pretty bad example of what has happened too often in the past in Kenya.' He then made reference to recent similar cases, some of which had been raised in Parliament.[8]

These included a Captain Hunter who in 1920 had flogged a man to death, supervised the flogging of a pregnant woman so that she later suffered a miscarriage, and tortured two more men by screwing their fingers in a vice. One of the men ordered to help do the flogging subsequently committed suicide. The white community in Kenya launched a public subscription to meet the cost of Hunter's defence, and he was merely exiled for a short time.[9]

Two years later an R. R. Forrester kicked an employee, Mutito Sanango, so hard that he died of internal injuries. Forrester had to pay a small fine.

John Harris, former missionary in Central Africa and leading light in the Congo Reform Society, and now secretary of the Anti-Slavery and Aborigines Protection Society, wrote to the press and the Colonial Office and petitioned Parliament. 'Too often we are told, in the familiar phrase, this or that case is exceptional, that "the House can rest assured" such a particular case will never occur again,' he complained, 'but, with variations, it does!' In a letter to the *New Statesman*, Harris pointed out that while all-white juries were letting homicides go virtually unpunished, the Kenya settlers were 'demanding the death penalty for natives charged with stealing a goat or a sheep'.[10]

The Trinidadian doctor John Alcindor, since 1921 the president of the London-based African Progress Union, wrote to Colonial Secretary the Duke of Devonshire, pointing out the 'utter inadequacy of the sentence on Abraham for this monstrous crime'. 'Dehumanising treatment of the native on his own soil by his more privileged white fellow-subjects', he warned, 'may result in a lamentable state of affairs for the Empire.'[11]

To blame for all this, wrote an experienced colonial doctor, Norman Leys, who in 1923 was writing for the Woolfs' Hogarth Press a fearsome attack on the white practices in East Africa, was 'the idea that overbears every other in Kenya, the idea of racial dominance, the idea that Africans exist only to labour for our profit'.[12]

*

This culture of entitlement and violence would be integral to British involvement in Kenya. However, the genesis of the colony came from strategic and humanitarian concerns. Exploration and missionary activity from the 1850s, in particular the journeys of David Livingstone, had seized the imagination of the public in Britain, revealed the outline of the East African interior and shone a light on the depredations there of the Portuguese and Arab slave trade in the Indian Ocean. In 1873, a British naval blockade would at last effect the closure of the notorious Zanzibar slave market, by which time, heeding Livingstone's call for 'Christianity, Commerce and Civilisation', mission stations had been established on the East African coast and were soon inland as far as Uganda. At the same time, traders and officially sanctioned missions from a number of European countries were further opening up the interior and, in some cases, making treaties with indigenous people.

The point of view at this time of the Kikuyu, the largest ethnic group native to Kenya, as outlined in a memorandum later presented to London, read: 'We looked upon these men as polite and harmless human beings as compared to the atrocious slave-traders. We extended to them our hospitality and allowed them to pass through our Country.'[13]

South of Mount Kilimanjaro the Germans dominated, while the French were looking to expand their empire eastwards towards the Great Lakes. For the British, Uganda was key: there was a somewhat paranoid concern that a hostile power astride the headwaters of the Nile might be able to dam or divert the river, desiccating Egypt, guardian of the all-important Suez Canal route to India.[14]

Between 1885 and 1900 a series of treaties delineated spheres of influence, which would create British protectorates over Zanzibar, Uganda and what would become Kenya Colony, whose importance was considered little more than as a barrier to German expansion northwards and as a route to the seemingly strategically important Uganda. A private enterprise, the Imperial East African Company, was given a Royal Charter to continue the suppression of slavery and to exploit the new territories. At the end of 1895 it began building a

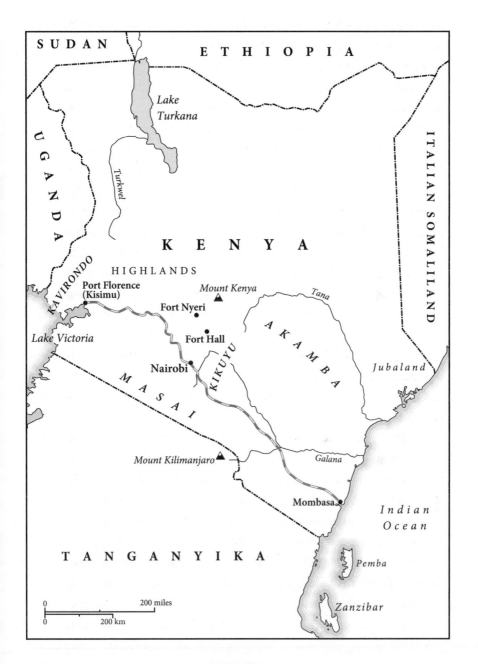

KENYA

railway to run along the line of the long-established though expensive and vulnerable caravan route from Mombasa to Lake Victoria. But the company soon ran out of money, and the British government, under pressure from jingoistic opinion at home, stepped in to run the new territories directly.

The railway, nearly 600 miles long, called in some quarters 'the Lunatic Line', took six years to complete, cost many lives and £5 million, and became the tail that wagged the dog. In the meantime, the British undertook the military conquest of Uganda and the Kenya interior. In Kenya, forts were built along the line of the railway and what were euphemistically called 'punitive expeditions' suppressed opposition around the railway as well as further afield. This opposition could entail attacks on railway workers, missionaries or British officials, or simply a refusal to give up guns, provide porters or, after 1900, pay tax. 'These people must learn submission by bullets – it's the only school,' declared the first Commissioner for the British East Africa Protectorate. 'After that you may begin more modern and humane methods of education.'[15]

There was also action to stop widespread and endemic cattle-raiding and inter-tribal conflicts. Frederick Lugard, writing about his conquest of Uganda and western Kenya, described the scene after a 'tribal raid'. Where before 'you may see peace and plenty, well-tilled fields, and children playing in the sun; on the next you may find the corpses of the men, the bodies of the children half burst in the flames which consumed the village, while the women are captives of the victorious raiders'. Before his advent, he wrote, 'the African knows no peace ... Not against the slave-trade alone are our efforts needed ... The Pax Britannica which shall stop this lawless raiding and this constant inter-tribal war will be the greatest blessing that African has known since the flood.'[16]

Herbert 'Reggie' McClure, who by September 1923 was Resident Commissioner on Ocean Island, arrived in Kenya in 1903, aged twenty. All he knew of Africa, he admitted, was from children's literature like *King Solomon's Mines*. He would remain until 1921.[17]

From Mombasa, he took the train to 'the little tin-roofed town' of Nairobi, then started out on a 100-mile trek to Fort Nyeri. The first 50 miles were across vast plains where 'Game, of all kind, was in plenty', then they 'switch-backed up and down an endless succession of precipitous hills covered, in part, with native cultivation'. As they climbed, they left behind the scorching heat of the plains. Fort Nyeri consisted of a rectangular stockade surrounded by a dry moat in which lay barbed-wire entanglements. Inside were a handful of government buildings and barracks for a company of King's African Rifles (KAR). Over all 'towered Mount Kenya herself, her glaciers sparkling in the sun'. McClure was strongly advised not to venture far from the safety of the fort. Ignoring this, he came under attack one night, though escaped unscathed.

The fort had been constructed following a battle the year before between three companies of KAR and a party of Kikuyu warriors. After the attack on McClure 'it was decided to give these rebellious natives a lesson and a punitive expedition was organised', he wrote. This was the first of three he would undertake over the next few years. A few companies of KAR ventured out, supported by several hundred Masai. The action took what McClure called 'the usual course' – 'some numbers of the rebels were killed, their huts were burned, their gardens laid waste, and their livestock carried off'. The Masai were paid with a cow each. The whole process was 'unedifying' and 'unsportsmanlike' – on the three expeditions, no British officer was hurt in any way – but McClure wrote that they were effective. 'As soon as operations ceased, the enemy and ourselves became the best of friends and, what is more important still, have remained so ever since,' he reported. The theory was of exemplary violence: 'a good sharp knock at the beginnings of things ... half measures were worse than useless'.[18]

A detailed study of 'punitive missions' in one area – around the railway terminus on Lake Victoria – throws up some interesting information. First, it is striking how frequent they were – forty engagements are recorded between August 1894 and December 1899. There is only one definite defeat – in November 1894 a party of seventy Sudanese

troops were ambushed and killed. As McClure reported, British casualties were extremely rare. Only four of the forty clashes resulted in
recorded deaths of local fighters; this totalled just over a thousand. In
the vast majority of cases, a show of force and destruction of homes,
crops and the confiscation of livestock was sufficient (although of
course this could, and did, lead to hunger and even starvation), and
preferable to hunting down guerrillas in the bush. It is also striking
that as the exertion of British power continued, the proportion of
looted cattle handed over to 'native' auxiliaries decreased dramatically,
from 60 to 70 per cent of the haul in 1894–5 to only 10 to 15 per cent
in 1899.[19]

Punitive missions would continue up to the Great War and beyond,
but with much less frequency. Winston Churchill, visiting Kenya in
1907 when Under-Secretary of State for the Colonies, described the
railway's 'trim little stations, with their water-tanks, signals, ticket-
offices, and flower-beds complete and all of a pattern ... one slender
thread of scientific civilization, or order, authority, and arrangement,
drawn across the primeval chaos of the world'. In 1910 McClure was
posted back to Nyeri as District Commissioner, and found it much
changed. The moat was still there but was now cleared of the barbed
wire and surrounded by close-cut lawns and flowerbeds. By the 1920s
Nyeri would have a golf course, two smart hotels and, nearby, the
Aberdare Country Club, a haunt of the 'Happy Valley' set and their
'wild conduct'.[20]

These aristocratic white farmers personified the huge changes that
had occurred to land-holding in the colony. The railway, built for polit-
ical/strategic purposes – to project British power to the headwaters of
the Nile – had left a huge debt. To service this, the railway now had
to carry freight. More generally, the new territories had to become self-
supporting as quickly as possible.

The Uganda Protectorate was a series of kingdoms, of which the
largest and most important was Buganda. It had, to the Europeans,
a recognisable state structure, with a Christianised ruling class and a
productive peasantry. But its only export worth the expense of the long

journey to the coast was ivory, whose supply was dwindling. So British officials and the missionary societies undertook a campaign to establish cotton, distributing seeds and building ginneries. After some initial setbacks, this was a striking success. By the time of the war, cotton was planted on over 400,000 acres and made up 80 per cent of export income. A bumper crop in 1923, the Governor of that time estimated, put £3 million into the pockets of its African producers. Across all of Africa, only Zanzibar (cloves) and the Gold Coast (cocoa) had a higher per capita value of exports. Some of this income was spent on European manufactures, particularly bicycles from Raleigh in Britain, and surplus revenue saw infrastructure improvements and medical campaigns. But European settlement and land purchase was discouraged, in part because the climate was deemed unsuitable.[21]

Kenya was different. Politically decentralised, villages or groups of villages had councils democratically and meritocratically created, but no chiefs, hereditary or otherwise (the British would create chiefs to whom they could delegate tasks of local administration). To the British they seemed disorganised, and the first explorers and missionaries all noted how empty the land seemed. Sir Charles Eliot (brother of Ocean Island's Edward), who arrived as Commissioner in 1900, would write: 'We have in East Africa the rare experience of dealing with a tabula rasa, an almost untouched and sparsely inhabited country, where we can do as we like.'[22]

In fact, there were general and particular reasons for the seeming emptiness of the land. Much of it had inferior soil, light and sandy and lacking water. There were also 'buffer zones' between hostile tribes, particularly skirting Masai areas. In the case of the land immediately north of Nairobi, it had recently been deliberately left fallow by the Kikuyu. In addition, the 1890s had seen a sharp fall in the population due to exceptionally bad outbreaks of rinderpest and smallpox, coinciding with a severe drought.[23]

But Eliot's mind was made up: the local people were too few and too disorganised to produce cash crops for export and thus to provide the vital freight to make the railway pay. The answer was to bring in white farmers. A recruitment campaign followed. First to be appropriated was the land bordering the railway. Then Eliot started handing out grants of hundreds and even thousands of acres to the likes of Lord Delamere for nominal sums or even free of charge. In theory, this was for 'waste and uncultivated' land, but anywhere not defended by 'a documentary title which Her Majesty's Commissioner was prepared to recognize' (no tribe in East Africa had any such documentary title) was up for grabs. Most sought-after was land in the temperate Highlands – 35,000 acres 5,000 feet above sea level, cool and mosquito-free. Delamere saw it as a new Australia or New Zealand. Eliot agreed. Uganda was a 'black man's country', he conceded. But 'the east African highlands are for the most part a white man's country'.[24]

Under Eliot's direction, the Highlands became exclusive to white land-purchasers – effectively a colour bar, aimed, for the most part, against the colony's Indian population. Eliot was told from Whitehall that this would not be 'in accordance with the general policy of His Majesty's Government'. But opposition in London was never strong enough to change practice in Kenya and non-whites remained excluded. In 1908, the Liberal Secretary of State for the Colonies Lord Elgin declared that although, of course, the government did not want to impose 'legal restrictions' based on the race of the King's subjects, it was a 'matter of administrative convenience' that grants of land in the Highlands should be reserved to Europeans. After all, thanks to the temperate climates, this was the only 'limited area suitable for European colonization' (which might have been news to the large European communities living in Mombasa or Nairobi and its environs).[25]

If the punitive raids had established a tradition of violence, the Highlands policy was part of a culture of a slippery-at-best relation to the law in Kenya Colony that would feed into all aspects of its existence.

'When the Whitemen first came we did not understand that we were to be deprived of any of our land, nor that they had really come to stay,' read a petition that would be presented in 1924 by the Kikuyu

Orwell shortly before his departure for
Burma. He later described his teenage self
as 'an odious little snob'.

Militant Buddhist U Ottama,
now considered one of the fathers
of Burmese independence.

George Orwell, back row, third from left, with fellow police officers.
He arrived in Burma at the height of a crime wave.

A punitive expedition in Kenya, with British officers, Sudanese troops and Masai warriors.

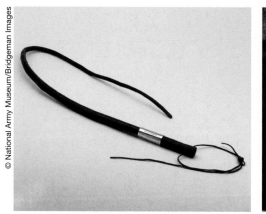

The infrastructure of forced labour in Kenya, the 'kiboko' rhino-hind whip and the compulsory 'kipande' containing particulars of identity and labour record.

Harry Thuku, leader in Kenya of the Young Kikuyu organisation. When asked if he had a message he wanted sent to Britain, he replied, 'Ask the King of England to stop the European settlers using the kiboko on their Africans.'

Zarina Patel

A. M. Jeevanjee, founder of the East African Indian National Congress, stalwart defender of Indian interests in Kenya and the colony's richest man by some distance.

Herbert Macaulay, the 'organising genius' behind West Africa's first political party. Although critical of the colonial government in Nigeria, he remained a fervent admirer of the empire as a whole.

Cambridge-trained barrister Joseph Casely Hayford. He argued that that West Africans were facing 'a national and racial death'.

Members of the Lagos Bar at a race meeting pictured in a magazine published on 29 September 1923. Election winner Eric Moore is the seated fifth figure from the left.

Marcus Garvey, in the uniform of the Provisional President of Africa, is driven through Harlem on his way to his International Convention of Negroes of the World.

Garvey under arrest for mail fraud. He blamed British and French imperialists, worried about his effect on their African colonies, for his conviction.

Adelaide Casely Hayford, who on 29 September 1923 was opening her ground-breaking Technical School for Girls in Freetown, Sierra Leone.

Girls at the Technical School learn the traditional art of basket-making.

Norman Manley, later Prime Minister of Jamaica, in the uniform of an artilleryman.

West Indians stacking shells. Denied combat duties in France and treated as second class throughout, their experience while volunteer soldiers for the empire meant that they returned home angry and radicalised.

Hyderabad's Army Polo team. Sport provided a rare
opportunity for cross-cultural activity.

The hunt assembles in front of Government House, Nairobi.
With no foxes to chase, the prey in Kenya was ostriches.

Association. 'A small piece of land here or there was sold to a few of the first pioneers and to one or two Missions voluntarily by its owners ... we were unaware that our possession of our land would be questioned or challenged. Then from about the year 1902 increasing numbers of Whitemen arrived and portions of our land began to be given out to them for farms until large areas ... had been disposed of in this way.' For land under actual cultivation, they received 'an extremely small rate per acre ... quite inadequate'; anywhere else was simply taken over. 'Had our land been thus robbed by any other native tribes armed with similar weapons as ourselves,' read a later petition, 'Kikuyu would certainly have given their lives for their property, but confronted by people with the latest and most formidable weapons of precision and destruction such an idea was and is unthinkable.'

Local people found themselves shunted on to 'reservations', but even there they had no legal title to the land. Alternatively, they became squatters 'on what', the petition continued, 'had been their own land', growing crops or herding their livestock in return for labouring for the new owner, rather like the manorial/tenant relationship that had been dying out in Britain prior to the war, and which afterwards disappeared entirely.[26]

Eliot's profligacy with land grants stimulated a rush of incomers. From just over 500 Europeans in Kenya in 1901, there were 1,738 in 1908 and more than 5,000 in 1914. An unusually high proportion were aristocrats and 'officer class' like Delamere – their club became known as the 'House of Lords'. In Kenya, they hoped to enjoy prestigious big-game hunting and find a space for values – feudal, aristocratic, anti-democratic – which were being squeezed out at home. A number of farmers also came from South Africa, along with land speculators and adventurers from across the empire.[27]

Concurrent was an influx of government officials and military officers. As we've seen from the Silberrad case that inspired the 1909 Crewe Circular, officials in Kenya had a poor reputation. One district officer reportedly 'combined tax collection with rape'. The officers of the KAR seem part of the same culture. Richard Meinertzhagen arrived in Nairobi in 1902 to join the King's African Rifles to discover that his fellow officers were 'mainly regimental rejects', often drunk, many heavily in debt. He was 'amazed and shocked to find that they all brought their native women into mess; the talk centres round sex and money'. The majority of the rest of the male European population of Nairobi, most connected with the railway, also 'kept a Native girl, usually a Masai, and there is a regular trade in these girls with the local Masai villages. If a man tires of his girl he goes to the village and gets a new one, or in several cases as many as three girls. And my brother officers are no exception.'[28]

Eliot's deputy Frederick Jackson warned the Foreign Office in 1903 that most European settlers were 'a lot of scalliwags' and suggested that Eliot had fallen under the influence of their leader, Lord Delamere. Delamere himself cut a raffish figure with long ginger hair under an enormous hat, shorts and a belt with pistols. A favourite pastime, after a heavy drinking session, was shooting bottles off the bar of the Norfolk Hotel in Nairobi. On one occasion the manager at closing time refused to serve any more drink; Delamere promptly locked him in the meat safe and kept the alcohol flowing.[29]

Another leading light of the colony was Ewart Grogan, an adventurer – and virulent racist – who had ended up in Kenya having, after a challenge in a London nightclub, walked from the Cape to Cairo. In 1907, in front of a cheering white crowd, he violently flogged three Kikuyu men outside the Nairobi courthouse for allegedly having jolted a rickshaw carrying white women. This came to the attention of the Liberal government in London which issued a stern rebuke. Grogan was found guilty of unlawful assembly and sentenced to a month's imprisonment in a private house, where he held court and received gifts from admiring friends.[30]

The doctor Norman Leys, in his book published by the Woolfs in early 1924, called the Kenya settlers 'drunken scoundrels', 'shiftless', 'contemptuous and ignorant'. Leys had been promptly transferred away from the colony in 1910 when he had tried to engage a lawyer to defend the Masai from being moved en masse off their pastoral lands, abrogating a previous treaty. The other great publiciser of the evils of the colony was William McGregor Ross. He had been Kenya's Director of Public Works since 1905, but was forced out in 1923 for persistently opposing measures that blatantly favoured the white settlers over everyone else. A settler-owned newspaper ran a campaign accusing his department of waste and fraud.[31]

Leys and Ross were part of a tiny minority of British officials who swam against the tide. 'Native Commissioner' George Maxwell was another. For opposing pressure from Delamere's faction to 'encourage' natives to leave the reserves and work on their farms, he was branded as 'anti-white', 'nearly Bolshevist', 'saturated with democratic and socialistic ideas', and 'a menace to the prestige of the white man'. The vast majority, from a string of Governors and senior officials to the isolated junior official, largely from similar public-school backgrounds to the big planters, were successfully brought 'on-side'. The white social scene – the races, Governor's balls, shooting parties – was a very small bubble. It didn't 'do' to be 'pro-African'.[32]

In September 1923, McGregor Ross was also working on a book. Like Leys, he had a Scottish Nonconformist background, and as an engineer was technically trained. Both were dismissive of the culture of the public-school amateur among the British settlers and officials in Kenya.[33]

Ross described the white settlers as 'loose, careless, unscrupulous, objectionable swine'. In his book, he told the story of a planter who supervised his workers by sitting on a chair and taking pot shots at them when he felt they were slacking. 'The bullet kicked up the soil near the delinquent one and reminded him that master's eye was upon him. The inevitable mischance soon took place, of course.' A man was shot through the arm, with the bullet entering his chest. The white employer was tried and given a small fine and six months' 'simple imprisonment without hard labour'. The white community rallied to his defence.[34]

Reggie McClure blamed these sort of 'lamentable' incidents on the climate – 'where unintentional slights are liable to be magnified into deliberate insults' – and on the white farmers' furious frustration with the difficulties in securing reliable and sufficient labour. If his capital was gone and he had no income, McClure reported, 'the first thing he loses is his sense of equity as between himself and his native employees. I have seen it happen again and again with good fellows who, had they been in better circumstances, would have been most meticulous in their dealing with white and black.' In his book, he called for the settlers to get 'the true sense of proportion ... and the ability to grasp the other fellow's point of view'. At the same time, he had sympathy for the farmers 'fair and just in their dealing with native labour, completely at a standstill for want of few men from a neighbouring Reserve which teemed with able-bodied natives whose main occupation was dancing'. One farmer, a witness for a Labour Commission in 1913, complained that workers frequently deserted at key times. 'It is hardly surprising', he said, 'if I am in a red-hot state bordering on a desire to murder everyone with a black skin who comes within sight.'[35]

As early as 1907 white landowners were talking of 'a desperate labour situation'. To an extent, they were hoist by their own petard. Norman Leys drew attention to the 'absurd' situation whereby land was alienated because it was 'half empty of people', but without local labour it was worthless. The new aristocratic owners weren't about to get their hands dirty. Pioneer Baron Cranworth called East Africa 'essentially an overseers' country'. For one thing, it would be bad for white prestige, an even bigger obsession of the white community than in Malaya.* So to avoid financial ruin, they were dependent on local people.[36]

For their part, Africans had little incentive to perform wage labour for the whites. Periods of peak demand such as harvest time coincided with their own busiest moments as they were growing on the reserves

---

* Elspeth Huxley, hagiographer of Delamere, famously wrote in *The Flame Trees of Thika*: 'Respect is the only protection available to Europeans who lived singly, or in scattered families, among thousands of Africans accustomed to constant warfare and armed with spears and poisoned arrows. This respect preserved them like an invisible coat of mail, or a form of magic, and seldom failed; but it had to be very carefully guarded. The least rent or puncture might, if not immediately checked and repaired, split the whole garment asunder and expose the wearer in all his human vulnerability. Kept intact, it was a thousand times stronger than all the guns and locks and metal in the world; challenged, it could be brushed aside like a spider's web.'

many of the same crops as the Europeans – maize, wheat, sisal. Pay from the Europeans was low – the settlers, who from the outset were well organised, combined to keep wages down. Workers were ill-housed, ill-fed and ill-treated. Although technically illegal, there was widespread use of punishment whippings. McGregor Ross quoted one farmer admitting to the 1913 Labour Commission, 'I sjambocked the n****r till my arm ached.' Leys wrote that 'the power to flog is supported by public opinion. Natives of course are rarely aware that such practices are illegal and practically never take a European to Court.' Ross also attacked the early settlers – 'colonials of the degenerate type' – not only for 'unjust' and 'severe' punishments, but also for unfair practices such as withholding wages or firing workers or forcing their departure just before the monthly payday. All this 'spoiled the labour market for themselves and their better behaved neighbours' with the result that a 'tradition' was established that working for Europeans was 'liable to be unprofitable – to the labourers'.[37]

The answer for the likes of Ewart Grogan was forced labour: 'we have stolen his land. Now we must steal his limbs.' 'A good sound system of compulsory labour', he argued, 'would do more to raise the n****r in five years than all the millions that have been sunk in missionary efforts for the last fifty ... call it compulsory education ... Under such a title, surely the most delicate British conscience may be at rest.' The Secretary of State for the Colonies could never agree to such a programme being put into actual law, but it was noted in the 1913 Labour Commission report that chiefs, headmen and elders had for a long time been induced by government officials, through bribes or threats, to pressurise those living in the reserves to go out to undertake wage labour for the Europeans.[38]

In the meantime, the British authorities had deployed the key lever of tax. At a banquet given for Winston Churchill in 1907, Delamere made a speech in which he declared that the settlers 'were willing to take up the White Man's Burden as far as the native races were concerned, but they would beg that some discretion be left them to shift the burden slightly according to the exigencies that they had in

British East Africa'. What shifting 'slightly' meant in practice was, as McGregor Ross wrote, 'The White Man's Burden is being borne manfully – but by black men.' As early as 1901 a 2-rupee hut tax was introduced; this would rise sharply over the next few years. If you didn't pay, your hut was burned down on the spot. Then a poll tax was imposed. Taxation on whites remained low, and duties on imports were targeted on articles of 'native consumption'. The result was that the colony's revenue came almost entirely from its non-white population.[39]

This was useful for balancing the books, but perhaps its greater purpose was 'industrial'. After the first few years, collectors (as British district officers were known) would only accept cash as payment. This, of course, forced men (and women and children) into the European wage economy. As the colony's Governor outlined in a speech in 1913, it was essential to keep wages low and taxes high to force 'the native to leave his reserve for the purpose of seeking work'. It was simple coercion.[40]

McClure, in 1923 writing his memoir on Ocean Island 11,000 miles away, set out to concentrate on 'the frivolous side of life' during his long career. But labour coercion in Kenya was one of the few places where he couldn't avoid getting serious. 'Labour for private enterprise is and always had been purely voluntary *in theory* [his emphasis],' he wrote. 'In practice this has not been the case and in that lay the great mistake.' He admitted that he had been 'as great an offender as anybody in this respect'. He wrote how, with the complaints of the farmers ringing in his ears, 'one word from him to a headman and the required number would be found . . . That word was often given, but it had to take the form of a definite order.' 'It was a case of bad beginnings being followed by bad endings,' he concluded.[41]

In fact, after the war unfair taxation and labour coercion would get much worse. And resistance would come from a new quarter.

28

'A Situation of Grave
Peril Might Have Arisen'

Lord our God, it is you who have appointed our leader
Harry Thuku to be over us all. Protect him and let
no danger come near him ... Remember that the
Lord God was able to rescue the children of Israel
from slavery.

Prayer read at East African Association meeting[1]

The situation in Kenya in September 1923 was shaped to a greater
extent by the First World War than anywhere else in Africa.
Imperial Germany's possessions in the Pacific were swiftly and pain-
lessly overrun by Allied troops. With some minor exceptions, it was
the same in South and West Africa. In German East Africa, bordering
Kenya to the south, it was a very different story.

Neither the Governor of Kenya nor of German East Africa wanted to
see a war and there was a clause in a treaty signed in 1885 that allowed
for local neutrality. But on 18 August 1914, the Royal Navy shelled
the radio mast at Dar-es-Salaam, and the city surrendered, with the

Governor disappearing inland. A truce was signed. But the German military commander, Paul von Lettow-Vorbeck, had other ideas. He knew that with the Royal Navy dominant he could never be supplied from home and therefore defeat the British, but he believed that if he tied down Allied troops in the malarial East African bush who might otherwise have been serving on the Western Front, he would be doing his bit for his country.

Immediately after the shelling of Dar-es-Salaam, he launched a small raid into Kenya, which destroyed telegraph lines and railway bridges and penetrated to within 25 miles of Mombasa. It was the only moment in the war that the empire was invaded. The commandos were driven back, but they achieved their purpose. Eight thousand Indian troops, destined for Europe, were diverted. Half were to reinforce the meagre number of KAR in Kenya, half to invade the German colony.

The subsequent landing at the port of Tanga was a fiasco. Forewarned, the Germans had prepared well-organised defences. After two days' fighting against a far smaller force, the British were compelled to re-embark their troops, leaving behind a wealth of guns, ammunition and stores. This set the tone for much of the rest of the war. Von Lettow-Vorbeck ran an expert guerrilla campaign, outwitting a string of incompetent British generals. Large numbers of empire troops were brought in from West Africa, the Rhodesias and South Africa, but the war ended with Lettow-Vorbeck's force undefeated.[2]

Some 11,000 empire troops died, the vast majority from disease and hunger. The worst attrition, though, was among carrier corps. The theatre had no roads for motorised vehicles and no animal transport could survive the tsetse fly. So everything had to be portered. Some 350,000 carriers were recruited for the Allied effort, of whom nearly half were from Kenya.[3]

Llewelyn Powys had arrived just before the war to stay with his brother on his Kenya farm. The purpose was to improve his TB-affected health, but when his brother went off to fight, he was left in charge. He soon heard rumours of an 'appalling mortality' among the carriers, and was not 'in a happy mood' when his local District Commissioner asked him to hand over twelve of his 'boys'. One of those he selected was a Kikuyu called Korombo, a 'friendly plump negro'. Powys wrote that Korombo accepted his decision 'with the characteristic fatalism of the race. Muúngu (God) had caused this protracted fight amongst the white men; Muúngu had arranged that the official should write to me; Muúngu had put it into my head to select him, Korombo, as one of the twelve to be sacrificed.'

Powys heard nothing for a year, except 'the most ghastly stories leaking out concerning the shameful mismanagement of the carrier corps ... thousands upon thousands were dying'. He wondered what had happened to Korombo. Then after two years, the young man reappeared, discharged from his duties. The work of carrying the loads had been 'heart-breaking', he said, and the food abominable – 'he indicated with his cupped hand the exact size of the wretched portion of rice which had been allowed him for each day'.[4]

Many did not return. Estimates are that between 40,000 and 45,000 bearers from Kenya perished from hunger or disease, over 10 per cent of the adult male population. No effort was made to forward unpaid wages to dependants of those who died, nor to provide widow's pensions.[5]

As elsewhere, the war saw a doubling of prices for food. There was widespread commandeering of cattle and sheep for the war effort, with owners being paid well below the fair market value. In 1916, the hut tax was raised to 16s, some eight times its original cost, but wages stayed at pre-war levels. This meant that a man with dependants, say a mother, or a brother's widow, would have to work for three to four months just to pay the tax bill.[6]

In 1918, the country was hit by a severe drought. Llewelyn Powys reported, 'Week after week the country lay prostrate under the blank stare of a soulless sun ... everywhere one came across the carcasses of animals ... The crops never came up.' Some 17,000 tons of foodstuffs were distributed by the government, but 'even so', Powys wrote, 'a great many natives died of starvation. I used to see troops of them moving along the old caravan road, supported by the pathetic illusion that they would at length come to some fat land where there would be enough food for all ... they continued to journey on, day after day, in trailing ant-like lines – tall men, women with milkless breasts, and little dazed, wrinkled children.' The following year, 'Spanish flu' arrived, killing some 155,000.[7]

So, many factors combined to find African Kenyans in the years following the war angry and at a low ebb. Parmenas Githendu Mockerie was at this time in his early twenties. At the end of the 1920s he would be part of a two-man Kikuyu delegation to London, and would be the first Kikuyu to have a book published in English (by Woolf's Hogarth Press). Against the wishes of his parents, he had attended a mission school from the age of thirteen, then night-school in Nairobi, working for a short, unhappy time as a domestic servant for a European family, then in a garage and as a clerk. In 1921 he became a pupil-teacher at the Church of Scotland Mission at Kikuyu. Four years later he would be appointed headteacher at a Church Missionary Society school at Kahuhia.[8]

His attitude after the war was, 'So much for Pax Britannica'. 'It is true that the scourge of inter-tribal warfare and slave-raider's invasion have ceased,' he wrote, 'but the number of men who have been killed in the Great War, in which we were not in the least interested or involved, has probably exceeded the number who were killed in the local warfare for a preceding century.' As for the boast of getting rid of slavery, 'the nation has now been enslaved in their own country'. In the same way, he praised the work done by the Medical Department but pointed out 'the number of our people who succumbed to the ravages of the Influenza, a by-product of the Great War, has probably exceeded the number of all victims of local diseases and pestilence for a whole generation'.[9]

As part of a project to collect Kikuyu tribal laws, folksongs and customs, Mockerie made a tour of the area. Everywhere on the reserves – which he called 'unfenced detention camps' – he found 'the majority of people are poor owing to the expropriation of the best lands which were given to a small group of Europeans'. At Fort Hall, the inadequacy of the land left was 'appalling'. The cows, sheep and goats that used to be kept in the district had died from starvation due to the lack of grazing lands. So, meat supply was 'scanty. Many families spend a year without having tasted any meat and butter', weakening their health. Amid severe overcrowding – 500 people or more per square mile – the land left was collapsing ecologically through over-use. Before the coming of the Europeans, he would later write, 'The land with ravines, the rivers, the forests, the game, all the gifts that nature has bestowed on mankind was ours and above all we had the FREEDOM.'[10]

Part of the impoverishment was down to the absence on Kikuyu land of coffee cultivation. This was pretty much the only profitable crop in Kenya, but 'Africans have been discouraged from growing so as to make it a monopolistic industry for Europeans', a teacher explained to Mockerie. The spurious pretext was to protect European plantations from crop disease.

Mockerie found that many men of working age were away from home for six to twelve months. This left the work of gardening, harvesting, cooking, drawing water, finding fuel and caring for infants on the shoulders of the women and children. 'This results in a high maternal and infant death rate in Kikuyu,' he wrote. A report from September 1923 by the East Africa Women's League detailed a child mortality rate in the first year at 400 out of 1,000 (compared to 83 in Britain). It blamed the native huts, where many were squashed in to alleviate the hut tax, as 'hotbeds of disease and vermin', the severely underfed status of the children, and the lack of 'common surgical cleanliness' during the birthing process. The men bringing in venereal disease contracted while working outside the reserves was also a contributing factor.[11]

Effective leadership in the reserves was in short supply, Mockerie found. He blamed the British, who by creating chiefs had introduced 'a foreign idea' and 'robbed the people of their form of democracy. Chiefs who are nominated by European officials', he wrote, 'cannot win the confidence of the people over whom they are imposed.'[12]

Outside the reserves, he reported a similarly unhappy situation for the Kikuyu. Visiting half-brothers and their families who worked on a European coffee plantation to raise money for hut tax payments by dependants on the reserve, he discovered that they worked from 6.30 a.m. till 5.30 p.m. but still couldn't complete the arduous tasks, picking, weeding or pruning, they were given. There were no wages until thirty days' work had been performed, and sometimes it was piecework, which if uncompleted, went unpaid. In general, Mockerie found squatters 'worried about the future of their children . . . They do not value this method of being employed because some of them have been in employment on the European farms for ten years and still they are poor.' Those who had saved some money resented that they were not allowed to buy land outside the reservations even though Europeans who were not even British subjects could do so without restrictions. A contemporary investigation found that the average European farmer occupied about 500 acres in comparison with the 8 acres held by the average 'native'. This was justified on the grounds that the European made better use of the land, but in fact only 9 per cent of European-held land was under cultivation.[13]

Mockerie inspected schools as well, finding in Nyeri a teacher with a class of sixty and another of eighty. In fact, he was highly critical of the education he received at the 'Christian village school' in Fort Hall. The land, building materials and labour had all been provided by the villagers. The school, only open from 10 a.m. till midday, was put under the supervision of a European missionary, who administered a group of schools from a central headquarters. But he was only able to visit once a month or even a quarter (the first time Mockerie had seen a white man), and 'his visit was not concerned with the education of scholars but with the catechising of the people who were being prepared for baptism and confirmation'. The African headteacher could only teach arithmetic up to one hundred, had a wage of 16s a month (little more than the standard labouring rate) and his subordinates were the oldest students and were unpaid. The only available books in Kikuyu were the Gospels.

The missionaries also stood guilty of commandeering 'large areas of land ... on the pretext that these societies exist for our benefit', Mockerie later wrote, 'but serious differences of opinion arose between the missionary societies and the Kikuyu because of the attempt of the former to interfere with the ancient custom of female circumcision'.[14]

Following the war, there was a new influx of Europeans, including a number arriving on an ill-conceived soldiers' settlement scheme. This saw land in the reserves alienated for their benefit and further increased the demand for labour. 'There appears to be still considerable shortage of labour in certain areas due to reluctance of the tribesmen to come out into the labour field,' read the preamble to the infamous Labour Circular No. 1 of 23 October 1919. With the publication of this circular, McGregor Ross wrote, 'The British government in East Africa had reached the nadir of its recession from established British standards.' 'All Government officials', the circular ordered, 'must exercise every possible lawful influence to induce able-bodied male natives to go into the labour field ... women and children should be encouraged to go out for such labour as they can perform.' In the same way, 'Native Chiefs and Elders must at all times render all possible lawful assistance ... District Commissioners will keep a record of the names of those Chiefs and Headmen who are helpful and of those who are not.' It ended with another threat: 'Should labour difficulties continue it may be necessary to bring in other and special measures to meet the case.'[15]

Shortly afterwards, two Anglican bishops and John Arthur, head of the Church of Scotland Mission, issued a statement in response to the circular. They agreed with its purpose – 'the prevention of idleness' and the meeting 'of the demand for necessary labour' – but pointed out that in the circumstances, a 'native' headman being 'advised' would interpret it as a direct order. It constituted forced labour in all but name. They suggested modifications – women and children should be exempt; it should be carried out directly by British officials rather than through headmen – but concluded that the best way forward was frankly to recognise it as compulsion and legalise it as such.[16]

The following year, the screw was turned tighter still. The circular had ferreted out more workers, but many of them were deserting. So a registration scheme was introduced, whereby every African male over the age of sixteen had to carry a dossier including fingerprints, particulars of identity and labour history from past employers. These were packed into a small tin container known as a *kipande*, that was worn on a chain around the neck. (Locals often called it *mbugi*, or goat's bell, because as one Kikuyu explained, 'I was no longer a shepherd, but one of the flock, going to work on the white man's farm with my *mbugi* around my neck.') Failure to show it to a police officer or official brought six months' imprisonment or a 20s fine. Some 8,000 prosecutions had been made by February 1922. By September 1923 half a million had been registered and in some districts it had been expanded to boys as young as twelve.[17]

The registration programme cost a fortune – some £20,000 a year, against £24,000 spent on all African education – and many Europeans, as well as all Kenyans, disliked it. Ross argued that good employers, who fed, housed, provided schools and good and prompt payment, had no need of the measure, only bad employers, from whom people simply deserted. Now they could be and were tracked down. Of the 3,595 deserters (out of a workforce of about 70,000) in 1921, 77 per cent were traced and punished. The following year the desertion rate fell dramatically.[18]

These oppressive measures did not go entirely unnoticed in London. In particular, the bishops' statement had come to the attention of the Archbishop of Canterbury, who raised the matter in the House of Lords, supported by Lord Islington. In his *Empire and Commerce in Africa*, published by the Labour Research Department, Leonard Woolf took aim at the system whereby chiefs were induced to order men to leave the reserves to work for Europeans. He also drew attention to the inhumane treatment of the workers, particularly when they were shifted about on the railway, 'packed tight into iron-covered goods wagons' in 'inhumane and insanitary conditions'. He gave the example of child labour paid as little as one rupee 'for fourteen days' actual work, without food'. It is 'slavery pure and simple', he wrote.

Both the Labour circular and the *kipande* system were attacked by the Aborigines Protection Society and the Conference of Missionary Societies in London.[19]

In the House of Commons, veteran Scottish Liberal MP James Hogge asked if the *kipande* was a waste of money and every bit as bad as the notorious South African Pass Laws. Winston Churchill replied that it was 'part of the necessary process for developing and organising the country', prompting an intervention by Josiah Wedgwood, who asked, 'Is it not part of the necessary process of enslaving the native worker?'

'Certainly not,' Churchill replied. 'That is a very offensive suggestion.'[20]

Churchill had become Secretary of State for the Colonies in February 1921 and sent out an order that government officials should play no part in recruiting labour for private employers, but this, along with complaints from churchmen and humanitarians in Britain, was widely ignored. With the colonial government, from the top down, in the grip of the Delamere faction, officials who did not toe the line found themselves posted to remote stations and overlooked for promotion.[21]

If pressure for change was to succeed, it seemed, it would have to come from the Africans themselves.

Harry Thuku was born in 1895 into a relatively wealthy land-holding Kikuyu family near Nairobi. His mother was the youngest of his father's four wives. The family had suffered as a result of raiding. One of Thuku's brothers was killed in a Masai attack; before he was born his mother and another brother were kidnapped by Kamba. Both separately escaped and his mother made it home, but the brother was not seen again 'and must have been killed by some of the wild animals'.[22]

In his autobiography, Thuku remembered that in about 1900 'a European had quietly slipped on to our land'. He was nicknamed 'Kibara' 'for he was always beating people'. No one thought he had come permanently, but in 1915 they learned that part of their land had been sold to him by the government. 'Of course it was government policy', Thuku wrote, 'to sell land without telling the occupiers.'

In the meantime, a parcel of about 100 acres had been given in part by Thuku's family to the Gospel Missionary Society, a conservative and evangelical group originating from New England. An American couple, the Knapps, built a church and a school, supported by farming the land. When he was about twelve, Thuku visited the mission where a friend, Wanyoike, was working on the farm. He attended church and was asked if he wanted a job. For a month he worked as a herder, then was invited to attend the school. The education was 'largely religious, and we had to repeat many things by heart from the Bible', but they were taught good English.[23]

Thuku spent four years with the Knapps, becoming a household servant and carer for their young daughter. According to his friend Wanyoike, he was 'under the constant care of Myrtle Knapp who became a second mother to him'. The Knapps hoped that both boys would become qualified for the ministry. This did happen for Wanyoike, but Thuku 'did not wish to be stuck in the Mission for ever' and, aged sixteen, he headed for Nairobi.[24]

His first job was in a small, newly established bank, where his job was sweeping, dusting and carrying messages. This came to an end when he was persuaded by a relative to forge a cheque. 'We were both very foolish,' he later wrote. He was arrested and sentenced to two years in prison. After a couple of months he was moved to Mombasa to work on roads, and then became a servant to the jail's deputy, a Sikh.

Following his release, he got a government job counting huts for the tax, which took him all over the country. Then he started work at the *Leader* newspaper, composing type and learning to print. The paper was very pro-white settler, and reading the articles sent in was an education. 'When I saw something there about the treatment of Africans,' he wrote, 'it entered into my head and lay quiet until later on.' His next job, working in the government treasury's telegraph office, gave him further first-hand insight into the running of the colony.[25]

Thuku wrote how he and his young Nairobi friends deplored the treatment of the wartime carriers, the new burst of land alienation to serve the white soldier settler scheme, the *kipande* registration system, the high taxation and the ongoing forced labour. Thuku was particularly animated by the compulsory labour of young women away from home, and the 'very great' 'number of girls who got pregnant in this way'. Then in early 1921, as the worldwide demand for cash crops collapsed, Delamere's political vehicle, the Convention of Associations, combined to reduce their workers' wages by a third, demanding this reduction be matched for those employed by the government. McGregor Ross, Director of Public Works, refused to do so, arguing that 'nothing had happened to reduce the natives' cost of living, taxation or shop prices'.[26]

Thuku and his friends decided to take action, meeting at a village on the outskirts of Nairobi on 7 June 1921. There they determined to form an association to present grievances to the government, in particular the 'matter of the wages reduction schemed by the Farmers of the Colony'. It was to be called the Young Kikuyu Association, inspired in part by the Young Buganda Association of Uganda, which campaigned against oppression not just by the colonial authorities but also by the despotic chiefs. 'Unless the young people of this country form an Association,' Thuku explained in a letter to the *East African Standard* the following day, 'the Native in Kenya will always remain voiceless.'

In fact, the previous year, a group of senior rural chiefs and headmen had formed the Kikuyu Association (KA) to present their grievances to the colonial authorities. Many of these were shared by Thuku's group – alienation of land, forced labour, the *kipande* – but they were essentially conservative loyalists, dependent for their status on the government and considered 'harmless' by the authorities. Nonetheless, when they presented a petition, a large meeting was arranged for 24 June at a government station near Nairobi. Attending were Kikuyu chiefs and their attendants, missionaries, senior government officials and, arriving uninvited, Thuku and a group of his fellow 'Young Kikuyu'.[27]

The British officials included, it seems, McGregor Ross. Certainly his account reads like that of an eyewitness. Alongside the chiefs in their traditional finery and 'natives in red paint' were the Young Kikuyu 'in imported clothing – the old order and the new, in the native world'. 'The young men acted and spoke with a composure and self-confidence that grated upon the paid chiefs,' Ross reported. Thuku himself 'pointedly' asked if the government would abstain from reducing the pay of the labourers in its employ, and why the Kikuyu could not be given 'as secure a title to their land as all Europeans demanded and got for theirs?'[28]

The meeting broke up with little satisfaction for the Kikuyu, except for a promise that their petition would be forwarded to London once, of course, it had done the round of colonial officials, who would add their own comments. But Thuku had other plans.

For one thing, he decided that any appeal to London would carry more weight if it did not come from the Kikuyu alone. So his organisation's name was changed to the East African Association (EAA). This was announced on 10 July at a meeting in Nairobi attended by some 2,000, during which Thuku was voted into the chair and resolutions were passed. These were subsequently drafted into a telegram. On 13 July, this was sent by Thuku from his desk at the treasury direct to the Prime Minister, the India Office and known sympathisers Wedgwood in the Commons and Islington in the Lords.

As well as being unprecedentedly direct, the petition went far beyond the appeals of the KA, including a call for money raised from Africans to be spent on national schools and for educated Africans to be given the franchise and represented in the municipal and legislative councils.

But sending the cable from the treasury address brought down the ire of the government. 'Mr Kemp, the Treasurer, was instructed to tell me that I must choose between politics and government service,' Thuku wrote. 'I choose politics,' Thuku immediately responded. 'Mr Kemp was a very kind employer, and when he heard my answer he laughed.' Kemp then suggested that Thuku take the three months' leave due to him and 'find out if your people will support you in politics – because I know you think the Government is doing many injuries to your people. If they are behind you,' he went on, he could resign in two months. Otherwise he could return to his job.[29]

It was very soon apparent that 'his people' were behind him.

Hundreds of Africans in paid employment, many of them non-Kikuyu, contributed a shilling a month to the new organisation and took an oath of loyalty. Many supporters were the missionary-educated who had rejected traditional tribal society, its customs and its leaders. He had a particularly good response from the Fort Hall district, where the Church Missionary Society (CMS) had established two of their earliest stations.* Thuku and his lieutenants addressed meetings, had leaflets and a tabloid newspaper, *Tangazo,* printed, hired motor cars and toured the reserves. Interviewed many years later, Thuku described his organisation as wishing to 'speak for Africans with a united voice', and to 'present their views in a constitutional way'. A gifted orator, Thuku was soon addressing crowds of thousands. He went by train to Kisumu and addressed a huge meeting of up to 25,000 Kavirondo. A few years before, a Kikuyu venturing into their territory would have been clubbed to death, Ross wrote. 'A polygot *nation* was beginning to emerge,' he reported (his emphasis), 'and it was a hostile nation.'[30]

Thuku was now attracting international attention. On one occasion in Nairobi he was introduced to C. F. Andrews, friend of Gandhi and campaigner against colonial injustice. He was asked if he had a message he wanted taken to Britain. Thuku kept it short: 'Ask the King of England to stop the European settlers using the *kiboko* [rhino whip] on their Africans.'[31]

As his support swelled, what Ross called his 'anti-Government bias' grew, and the speeches became more 'violent'. At one meeting he suggested that all the registration certificates and their tin containers be dumped outside Government House, Nairobi. At a rally at Fort Hall on 26 February 1922 he told his audience to pay only 3s in tax. The next day at Weithaga, where he addressed a crowd of 25,000, he forbade work on government projects. On 11 March he told a crowd that 'the government officers were nobody. The chiefs were nobody. If I send a letter to the Governor a chief would be dismissed at once.'[32]

* In his autobiography, Thuku would quote a French missionary from 1922: '"You British people, you have made a mistake. You sharpened the knife which is now cutting you." They meant the knife of education.'

He was showing signs of hubris. 'I, Harry Thuku, am greater than your Europeans,' he told one huge crowd. 'I am even greater than the Chiefs of this country.' He also took aim at the missionaries, who 'did not come here to preach the Word of God but of the devil only. I do not want them.' Printed prayers were circulated at meetings, casting Thuku as a David against Goliath, 'anointed by our God'.[33]

Even the most sympathetic Europeans started to worry. Native Commissioner George Maxwell, described by the Convention of Associations as 'anti-white', found Thuku's increasingly messianic style concerning. 'When the element of religion is introduced into native activities of this kind we are liable to get fanaticism,' he reported after attending a meeting, 'and that may lead to anything very suddenly.' In March 1922, a senior CMS missionary warned that 'a big element of the Christian community, the mystical section, are seeing in him a deliverer of the prophetic type and religious fervour is contributing to his popularity'. (They both might have had in mind the case of John Chilembwe, an American-trained Baptist pastor who returned to his native Nyasaland to lead a rebellion in 1915 that at one point had him preaching from a pulpit while holding the severed head of a white plantation owner. His face is now on the Malawian 50-kwacha note.)[34]

On 3 March, the Colonial Office received a dispatch from Charles Bowring, the Colonial Secretary in Kenya, enclosing a letter Thuku had written to a Mathew Njeroge, including the sentence 'The DC [District Commissioner] is nothing to us nor is any European what-ever anything to us because we know that all men are subjects of King George.' Bowring said it was 'illustrative of the growing difficulties of native administration in this colony caused by the activities of semi-educated natives'.

The Colonial Office was concerned. 'There is a distinct element of sedition about this,' commented one official. 'If these feelings are widespread there is all the more reason for early drastic action – before punishment means martyrdom.' The Permanent Secretary, Sir Herbert Read, agreed: 'I believe in nipping this sort of thing in the bud at any rate where primitive natives like those in Kenya are concerned.'[35]

Soon afterwards the DC for Fort Hall reported, 'He seems now to have assumed the attitude of a dictator, and a failure on our part to deport him will only be construed as weakness ... The Chiefs here are thoroughly upset and ask that immediate steps be taken to deport him.'[36]

Along with a handful of close associates, Thuku was arrested at 6 p.m. on 14 March 1922 and taken to Nairobi police station. The following evening, protesters gathered.

At 6.15 p.m., the Acting Commissioner of Police, J. C. Bentley, was informed by telephone that a large crowd had assembled at the police lines. He was there within fifteen minutes to find about 1,000 people demanding Thuku's release. He ordered them to disperse, but instead their number grew. He sent for the magistrate, who also ordered them to leave, but without success.[37]

By about 10 p.m., some had drifted away, though some 800 remained all night. The following morning, a large number of workers, mainly in offices and European houses, went on strike and by 9 a.m. a crowd of up to 4,000 had assembled. A guard of native police, who had been on duty all night, were retained under arms. The total force consisted of 140 rank and file, six officers and ten European constables. At this point, Bentley made the preparations for a baton charge. 'I consider that I would have been able to disperse the crowd with the men at my disposal at that time,' he later reported. (Other European witnesses disagreed, speculating that it would have caused even more casualties.) But he received a message from the Colonial Secretary Charles Bowring that he wanted to see the 'leaders of the mob', and no action should be taken until he had done so. 'I called on the crowd to select six of their men which they did'; among these were senior EAA lieutenants. Bentley took them to the Secretariat about a mile away and then at 10.45 returned on his own to the police lines, where he found that the crowd had considerably increased to between 7,000 and 8,000 Kikuyu including a large party of women.

McGregor Ross had earlier driven to the police lines to see what was going on. He saw 'A line of armed police with fixed bayonets standing outside the low wall of corrugated iron sheets. Inside the Lines other police were standing upon some hastily contrived platform so as to be able to look over the wall.' He considered this a 'panicky demonstration', as apart from a group of around 150 'gaudily dressed town prostitutes', the crowd was 'inactive and silent'.[38]

This was not what Bentley reported. He said that by 10.45 'the mob had been continually harangued by its leaders. The speeches were strongly seditious and inflammatory until the crowd, which was constantly increasing in numbers, became excited and almost beyond my control.' They were still, however, some 25 yards of open ground away from the corrugated iron fence. Thuku saw through his cell window that a large crowd had gathered, 'but I did not want to show myself and make them rush the police'. By now a group of white men had gathered on the balcony of the Norfolk Hotel opposite to watch proceedings.[39]

When the six 'leaders' arrived back at last at 12.15, they went among the crowd, urging them to disperse. At first it looked as if they would succeed, until the 'women present shouted to the men in aggravating tones which made them apparently change their mind, and they pressed up to the gate and corrugated iron walls round the lines', Bentley later wrote. According to Job Muchuchu, an eyewitness and senior figure in the EAA, 'Mary Muthoni Nyanjiru leapt to her feet, pulled her dress right over her shoulders and shouted to the men: "You take my dress and give me your trousers. You men are cowards. What are you waiting for? Our leader is in there. Let's get him." ... Mary and the others pushed on ...' They were now only a few feet from the fence. The armed police were ordered to bring their rifles to the 'engage position'. The mood then 'became ugly', Bentley reported, 'the demeanour of the mob having entirely changed, although they continued to hold a white flag in front of them'. Bentley then called to the KAR and asked for reinforcements. This was at 12.20.[40]

The six-man delegation returned to the Secretariat to report their failure. By this time McGregor Ross was there. Suddenly they heard a shot, then a volley, followed 'by a ragged burst of rifle-fire which lasted perhaps for twenty seconds, tailing off, during a bugle-call, into a few popping shots. The noise of a shouting crowd, police whistles – and then abrupt silence.'[41]

What had happened was, of course, disputed. Bentley himself didn't see but was told by his deputy that 'a very truculent agitator was encouraging the mob to close in on the police; Capt. Cary, who was in command of the particular section at that corner of the lines, went to arrest this agitator who seized him by the shoulder, then he was surrounded by the mob, the white flag had previously been dashed to the ground'. Cary stumbled and disappeared from view, at which point one of the policemen fired the first shot. It was 12.53. According to the deputy, 'at the same time' as this shot, stones were thrown at the police. (In the Governor's subsequent report, 'stones were already flying' before the shot.) This was immediately followed by rapid firing by about forty of the police at point-blank range into the massed crowd. Job Muchuchu reported that 'Mary Nyanjiru was one of the first to die.' The firing continued, according to the deputy, for 'between one and two minutes'.

Official reports condoned the shooting – 'the police had no option but to fire when they did: the mob was by then closely surrounding the building which they could have torn down in a few moments'. If the prisoner had been freed, 'a situation of grave peril might have arisen'. Also blamed was the fact that the police had been on duty for eighteen hours and 'the taunts of the women had by then roused the ugliest passions'. The implication being, of course, that less tired and provoked men would have made a different decision. So it was somehow necessary, but also a mistake.[42]

The Kikuyu view, as expressed by Thuku and Parmenas Githendu Mockerie, was that the demonstration was 'peaceful' and 'quite harmless, because anyone who knows that the weapons of Africans are such things as sticks, would not contemplate that the demonstration could stand up against the defence force of Kenya with machine-guns and rifles'. Mockerie wrote that the police 'were ordered to shoot down the demonstrators'. The British insisted that no order to fire had been given.[43]

Officially twenty-one people were killed on the spot, including four women, and twenty-eight wounded. The post-mortems reported death caused by 'shock and haemorrhage caused by wounds from bullets'. But amid accusations that the white settlers who had gathered on the balcony of the nearby Norfolk Hotel had opened fire on their own initiative into the back of the crowd and those fleeing, leaders of the demonstration, according to Mockerie, 'collected over two hundred names of persons who received bullets and died at their homes, and in addition there were many who, although they escaped death, suffered from permanent injury because they were afraid to go to hospitals to get bullets extracted; the only hospitals in Nairobi are controlled by the Government'. There was also 'talk of hundreds being killed by the police and being shot on the road back by civilian Europeans in cars and on horseback, and several white men I knew boasted about it'.[44]

The KAR had arrived five minutes after the shooting finished. They quickly sent heavily armed patrols across the town and to the villages to the north of Nairobi. Soon, they reported, all was quiet.

The EAA immediately called for a general strike, but the organisation was declared illegal and fifty of its leaders arrested. Thuku himself was carried off into internal exile in the extreme north of the country, though he was never charged with any offence.

According to Norman Leys, who would make it his life's work to campaign for the rights of black Africans in Kenya (he was accused of 'pro-native fanaticism' by the CO), the arrest of Thuku and its proscription saw the collapse of the EAA, and of the hope that the Africans could unilaterally and peacefully improve their situation. 'They have no constitutional ways of representing their grievances, far less any means of redressing them ... The least movement of protest would be far too dangerous to the protestors,' he wrote in his book, published in 1924.[45]

His key hope now was that domestic pressure and opinion would force reform in Kenya, as it had in Congo, where the exposing of atrocities by the likes of E. D. Morel and John Harris had brought sweeping changes. The introduction to the first edition of Leys' Kenya book was written by Gilbert Murray, brother of Papua Governor Hubert, leading light in the League of Nations Union and powerhouse of humanitarianism in Britain. In his introduction, Murray extolled the 'high principle of the League of Nations' – 'government in the interest of the governed' – and its acceptance by English people at home. The problem was that 'colonials regard it as pernicious rubbish'. 'There is at any rate', he continued, 'a real and dangerous opposition between average colonial opinion, based on knowledge of the facts and daily intercourse with black people, but exposed to perversion by prejudices of race and class, and very often by economic self-interest, and public opinion at home, sentimental, disinterested and genuinely anxious for justice, but grievously crippled by ignorance and lack of understanding.' This is what Leys, through his books and campaigning, aimed to change.[46]

William McGregor Ross, the other great 'creator of a crisis of imperial conscience' over Kenya, saw it in similar terms. Near the beginning of his book he reminded his British readers that 'the Government officials, whose actions and attitudes are described, are their servants. The British public, through their representatives in Parliament, have entire responsibility for the policies pursued in Kenya – policies which affect the happiness and welfare of millions of African men, women, and *children* [his emphasis].' He later added to this 'the old and crushing obligation which lies upon us as a nation, to reduce the debt which is due from us to Black Africa, for our participation in the Slave Trade'.[47]

Norman Leys laid out his manifesto for change: freeing the labour market, letting wages reach their natural level, direct taxation on the rich and reduction of it for the poor; spending in the reserves of taxes raised there, on education and organising native agriculture. He pointed out that the colony spent fourteen times as much on troops and police as on the education of Africans. 'If the authorities want to evoke loyalty from the common people they must spend what they receive from native taxation on books and slates and ploughs and ginneries', he wrote, 'rather than on machine-guns that can only ever be used for killing Africans.'

The alternative, the status quo, would see the colonial power 'wait five, ten or twenty years until we suddenly discover that Africans have become ungovernable, and we are compelled . . . to make a humiliating withdrawal'.[48]

Leys overestimated the 'collapse' of the EAA. Thuku, though physically removed, had not gone away. Even two years later, missionary John Arthur reported, all talk was of Thuku. A song had been written about him, performed by young women (and accompanied by 'disgraceful' dancing), which called him 'the chief or great one of the girls', because of his ultimately successful campaign against female forced labour. 'The Kikuyu cannot see what H.T. has done wrong and can only attribute his arrest by Government as a desire upon the part of the Government to bring them sorrow,' Arthur reported. 'They hold that in what H.T. did he defeated the Government. No chief and no missionary has done what he did.' In fact, Arthur continued, the conservative collaborationist chiefs were held in large part responsible for 'H.T.' being 'deported away'. 'Today they do not talk outwardly about H.T.,' Arthur wrote, 'but when alone especially the young men they are talking about him and thinking about him.'[49]

As well as securing albeit small concessions on labour recruitment of women and girls and a reduction in taxation from 16s to 12s per hut, the eight months of Thuku's campaigning laid the foundations upon which future generations of African politicians were to build. He had made contact with politically active Indians as well as other African groups; he pioneered the first political journalism, the first modern political use of a tribal oath; he spread urban political ideas into the rural areas. His East African Association constituted the first real political challenge to the government by any organised East African political body. While the EAA remained banned, 1924 would see the formation of the Kikuyu Central Association in which Jomo Kenyatta would cut his teeth.

29

India's America

Given a bit of common sense, the good government of
a purely native area is generally speaking, not a very
difficult matter. But in the case of a mixed population
whose interests must almost necessarily conflict,
problems of a vastly different nature are encountered.

HERBERT 'REGGIE' MCCLURE
on 'The Indian Question' in Kenya[1]

On 29 September 1923, the Standing Committee of the East
African Indian National Congress (EAINC) met at the
Harmony Club, near Jeevanjee Gardens in Nairobi. There was an
atmosphere of furious disappointment. Despite vigorous support from
India, the latest delegation to London demanding equal rights for
Indians in Kenya had just returned empty-handed. It was confirmation
that the promise made earlier that all subjects of the King-Emperor
were equal regardless of race was worthless.[2]

As far as the assembled Congress members were concerned, Kenya
was effectively an Indian colony. They had been there in numbers
long before the British (and even the Portuguese), and now there were

22,000 Indians (mainly Muslims) against only 8,000 'Europeans'. Indians controlled 85 per cent of the country's trade, and paid most of the taxes in Nairobi. But now confirmation had been given that they were second-class citizens.[3]

Alibhai Mulla Jeevanjee, founder of the EAINC, owner of the Harmony Club and donor to Nairobi of the eponymous gardens, was Kenya's richest man by some distance. He was born in Karachi in 1856 into a very large and very conservative family. His education focused on religion and exposure to the outside world was minimal. His father died when he was young and he was brought up by two tyrannical uncles, who set him to work in the family carting business. Fed up with maltreatment, at the age of thirty he ran away with some stolen rupees to set up a stevedore business in the Karachi docks, and then moved on to Australia, initially selling Indian linens and spices door to door. This then grew into a substantial import business. In Australia, he was befriended by British officials, one of whom wrote him a letter of introduction to the head of the Imperial British East Africa Company. So, in 1890, after a brief detour back to Karachi to marry Jenabai, a twenty-two-year-old woman from a well-to-do family, Jeevanjee arrived in Mombasa. Having rapidly established thriving businesses there, in 1895 he won the contract to supply and feed the labour for the building of the railway. This brought a large expansion of Kenya's Indian population. Some 38,000 were recruited, mainly from the Bombay area, not just 'coolies' but also masons, carpenters, blacksmiths, clerks, surveyors, accountants, draughtsmen and overseers. Nearly 2,500 died during the six-year construction period – at one point work ground to a halt after lions devoured twenty-eight Indians – and many returned home, but nearly 7,000 remained.[4]

Jeevanjee funnelled the profits of his railway enterprise into property, the import trade and soda and ice factories (Richard Meinertzhagen reported from Nairobi in 1902 that the KAR barracks were 'owned by Mr Jeevanjee, for which we pay him rent'). As early as 1900 Jeevanjee's assets were worth an astonishing £4 million. He had substantial residences in Mombasa and Nairobi and was the first to import racehorses into the colony. 'I may almost say I made the country,' he would declare in 1910. 'All the best property in Nairobi belongs to me. I built all the government buildings and leased them to the administration. I built all the hospitals and post-offices between Mombasa and Port Florence.' According to his granddaughter, Zarina Patel, for the greater part of his life he was 'an ardent admirer of British imperialism', which had given him the opportunity to escape his restrictive background and to prosper. In 1906, he presented a statue of Queen Victoria to Nairobi. But soon afterwards his views started to change.[5]

East Africa was, for sturdy historical reasons, envisaged at the beginning as an offshoot of the Indian Empire, what Churchill would call a 'grand-daughter colony'. The charter for the Imperial British East African Company, signed in 1888, included clauses, such as religious toleration, designed to be favourable to Indian settlement and enterprise. There were already successful Indian businesses in Mombasa. The directors of the Company envisaged these traders being augmented with 'Indian families of the agricultural class' for the 'colonisation of the vast unoccupied areas'. The Company adopted Indian currency, penal and civil codes and commercial laws.[6]

Pioneer administrator Harry H. Johnston declared in 1901 that 'East Africa is, and should be, from every point of view, the America of the Hindu'. Frederick Lugard, who secured Uganda in 1890–2, saw Indian immigration as useful for introducing cash, clothes and agricultural techniques of irrigation, manuring and well sinking. 'It is not as imported coolie labour that I advocate the introduction of the Indian,' he wrote, 'but as a colonist and settler.'[7]

As late as 1906, the government and the Mombasa Chamber of Commerce were still trying to attract Indian migrants, but by now the tide was turning. In the book he published after his visit to the colony in 1907, Winston Churchill reported white farmers expressing 'in strident tones' their ambition 'to make East Africa a white man's country'. But how could this be? Churchill asked. A 'white man's country' meant places, like the UK or Canada, 'inhabited wholly by white people and subsisting upon an economic basis of white unskilled labour'.

Nonetheless, he made the point that black and white were not at this point in competition: 'It is the brown man who is the rival.'

'The Indian was here long before the first British official,' Churchill wrote. 'Sikh soldiers conquered it and Indian businessmen developed it ... the Indian labourer built the railway, the Indian banker supplies most of the capital for business and enterprise.' The future belonged, he concluded, to the 'Asiatic ... his power of subsisting upon a few shillings a month, his industry, his thrift, his sharp business aptitudes give him the economic superiority'. The fact that Indians were being excluded from South Africa and Australia made it 'all the more desirable', he wrote, 'that the Imperial Government should afford in the tropical Protectorates outlet and scope to the enterprise and colonising capacity of Hindustan'.[8]

But the likes of Delamere and Grogan, now firmly established in the Highlands, had very different ideas as the growing white population secured for themselves, with the connivance of compliant officials such as Sir Charles Eliot, a raft of special privileges. In 1907, a Legislative Council met for the first time. It had three non-official European nominees (one of whom, inevitably, was Delamere) but no Indian representatives. There was also a Land Board, again with no Indians, that first met in September 1907. Here we see the mood shifting. The board reported that 'It is agreed as a general fact that the intrusion of the Indian agriculturalist meant the expulsion of the European element ... Indian immigration [should] be discouraged as much as possible.'[9]

'I felt very keenly the humiliating condition of my fellow-Countrymen,' Jeevanjee later said. 'I could not bear to see with philosophical calmness the unequal and unjustifiable treatment meted out to them by the white population of East Africa.' In 1909 Jeevanjee was nominated to join the Legislative Council as the solitary Indian member (the European unofficials were raised to five). He took up the position reluctantly and soon decided that, as a sole Indian member in a council otherwise entirely European and hostile, it was pointless and withdrew. He was not replaced until after the war.[10]

In the autumn of 1910, he visited England to lay out his community's grievances directly to the Colonial Office. Everywhere, he explained,

Indians were treated as second class. The growing town of Nairobi was a case in point. Restrictive covenants on leases had resulted in 2,000 Europeans living on nearly 3,000 acres of high ground, while more than 4,000 Indians were packed into 300 acres of swampy marshland, where sanitation was impossible due to standing water and malaria and enteric fever were rife. It was apartheid in all but name. Furthermore, the European-controlled Municipal Council saw that the white area was well supplied with roads, water, public lighting and sanitary services, while the opposite was the case outside their area. In Mombasa it was the same story, with the European quarter on the healthy side of the island beautifully laid out with tree-fringed roads and paths, a golf course and good sanitary and police services.[11]

Only Europeans could purchase land in the fertile Highlands, and this effective colour bar also applied to the civil service, police and military in which Indians were never appointed to higher posts. Indian degrees, especially in medicine and law, were not recognised, and Indians, along with Africans, were forced to use separate and inferior hospital, education, prison and transport facilities. Unlike the whites, they were denied trial by jury and the right to bear arms. They were also barred from first-class hotels, restaurants and resorts.[12]

'We have never claimed preferential treatment,' Jeevanjee declared. 'The most that we have asked and shall continue to ask is equal treatment and equal opportunities ... we have been taught to believe that the name of British Rule stands for justice and equality.' He went on to suggest that 'this African territory' should be 'annexed' to the Indian Empire and placed under the direct control of the Indian government under the Viceroy. His visit garnered much press attention in Britain, which was then picked up in India, where Jeevanjee began to look for support. In London, the India Office started to take an interest.[13]

In 1911, Delamere established the Convention of Associations, an umbrella body of white-farmer pressure groups. At their first meeting they repeated the demand for a restriction on Indian immigration. By now Jeevanjee had joined the Mombasa Indian Association, and in 1914 he founded the East African Indian National Congress, whose mission was to demand election of Indians on a common roll to both the legislative and municipal councils, and to end the widespread discrimination.

This alarmed the hardcore followers of Delamere, whose vision was now of Kenya becoming a white-minority-controlled country free of the restraining influence of the Colonial Office, along the lines of South Africa (or even in some sort of union with them), whose non-white populations had been abandoned by London in the treaty of 1909. (For their part, after the war, Indians would want Tanganyika as well as Kenya annexed by and run from India. The Ismaili leader the Aga Khan, in a book published in 1918, described East Africa as 'a free field for India's civilizing mission'.)[14]

In 1919, Delamere and a commission of his supporters produced an 'Economic Report' for the Governor in which a new line was taken: that Indian dominance of trade and the middling ranks of the police and civil service was holding back the 'development' of Kenya's African population.

'The Indian', according to the report, 'plays the part of clerk, artisan, carpenter, mechanic ... functions which the African is capable with training of performing ... the presence of the Indians, organised as they are to keep the African out of every position which an Indian could fill, deprives the African of all incentives to ambition and opportunities of advancement.' The report concluded with an extraordinary accusation. 'Physically, the Indian is not a wholesome influence, because of his incurable repugnance to sanitation and hygiene,' it argued. 'In this respect the African is more civilised than the Indian, being naturally cleanly in his ways; but he is prone to follow the example of those around him ... The moral depravity of the Indian is equally damaging to the African, who in his natural state is at least innocent of the worst vices of the East. The Indian is the inciter to crime as well as vice.' The then Colonial Secretary back in London summed up the attitude of both houses of Parliament, calling the report 'purely deplorable'.[15]

A similar commission in Uganda, which included Indian representation and witnesses, took the opposite view: 'The country owes much to the Indian trader ... He has shown energy and enterprise and has assisted in the opening up of the more remote districts ... and we consider that a broad policy of toleration should be adopted towards him.'[16]

According to Ewart Grogan, the 'Natives' hated Indians 'above all things in the world' thanks to the Indians' 'competition and unethical business practices'. Others outside the storm centre of the Convention of Associations reported that they had never met with 'any expression of dislike on the part of the negroes to the advent of the Indian ... Dealing with the Indians is preferred to dealing with the Europeans, on account of their greater suavity of manner.'[17]

In fact, common resentment against the growing emphasis on European settlement was drawing Africans and Indians together. A number of the fifteen Indians who appeared as witnesses in front of the Native Labour Commission of 1913 described the mistreatment of African workers by European employers.[18]

For Harry Thuku, Indians were Africans' 'best friends'. After all, outside missionary or official circles, he wrote, 'the only voice that has been consistently raised in favour of the equitable treatment of the native population is to be found in the Indian community'. Thuku had worked with Indians in his government and his newspaper jobs, and made many friends. After the inaugural meeting of the East African Association on 10 July 1921, he was among a number of EAA members who were invited to Jeevanjee's villa. (Jeevanjee's Masai chauffeur was an early member of the EAA.) Hearing of this tea party, later that night a group of Europeans vandalised Jeevanjee's house sign, daubing it in black and red paint. Jeevanjee had it taken down and sent to the CO to show them what they were up against.[19]

In Thuku's direct cable to London – which led to him losing his government job – he was careful to contradict the Convention of Associations' latest line of attack. The Indians were 'in no way prejudicial to natives' advancement', he wrote. Later he argued that 'The Natives by being in close contact with the Indians in their everyday life obtain the opportunity of learning from them all kinds of skilled work, such as masonry, carpentry, turning, fitting etc. and their experience both in the office where they work side by side with Indians and in workshops is that they are guided and shown every sympathy.'[20]

A particular Indian friend of Thuku's was Manilal A. Desai. He had arrived as a lawyer's clerk in Nairobi in 1915, aged thirty-six. A brilliant writer and organiser, he was part of a new generation of leaders of the Indian community in Kenya. After a short time in business and the law, he took up newspaper editorship – the Indian-supporting *East African Chronicle* – and politics. He was given free living quarters in Nairobi by Jeevanjee.[21]

It was Desai who had introduced Thuku to C. F. Andrews, the influential anti-colonial campaigner. He also helped with the production of leaflets, petitions and his tabloid, *Tangazo*. When Thuku was arrested, Desai worked tirelessly, though unsuccessfully, to secure his release. He also looked after Thuku's mother. In addition, Desai strengthened the EAINC links to the Indian National Congress and other sympathetic organisations and publications in India.[22]

Any sort of alliance between Kenyan Indians and Africans was most unwelcome to the politically active among the white minority. They hit back that the gullible 'mission boy' Thuku was merely a tool of Indian subversives; that the project was under Bolshevik or Khilafat influence. Both sides sent delegations to London to press the case for their particular communities. Delamere always travelled with two enormously tall and eye-catching Somali servants, guaranteeing him excited coverage in the newspapers, particularly the Dyer-supporting *Morning Post*. Another publicity stunt was to invite, on behalf of his Convention of Associations, the Prince of Wales to visit the colony – the justification being that Delamere's organisation represented the 'entire white population of the colony'. (When, on his seemingly never-ending imperial tour, the Prince got to Kenya, in 1928, he travelled out with Delamere's wife, and in a private letter to the King declared himself firmly on the side of the white settlers, against Africans, Indians and imperial officials alike.)[23]

Between 1920 and 1923, various formulas were suggested to

address the key issues of contention between the Indian and European populations, namely: the reservation of land in the Highlands for Europeans; urban and commercial segregation; the proportion of seats allocated in the Legislative Council and whether the franchise should be communal or on a common roll (all adult Europeans had been given the vote in 1919); and whether Indian immigration should be restricted, as vociferously demanded by Delamere's Convention of Associations. In 1920 the Colonial Secretary Lord Milner proposed a formula of keeping the Highlands restriction, condoning urban residential segregation, a communal franchise and eleven elected Europeans and just two Indians on the Legislative Council, but no restriction on immigration.

Having been part of a delegation to London and subsequently visited India and consulted with Gandhi, Jeevanjee returned to Kenya in November 1920 to preside over the annual EAINC meeting in Mombasa. Out in the street were Indian protests against the Milner scheme. At the meeting, Jeevanjee made a scathing denunciation of what he called 'unfair' British colonial policy in Kenya. How could two representatives look after the interests of 22,000 Indians, if it took eleven to look after 8,000 Europeans? he asked. (Meanwhile, of course, the 2.5 million Kenyan Africans had no representation at all.)

After that, he travelled to Nairobi where another energetic crowd gave him a hero's welcome, with a ceremonial horse-drawn carriage ride round the streets. Local Indians removed the horses and pulled the carriage themselves from the station to the lavish Jeevanjee villa. At the December opening of the EAINC, Jeevanjee declared, 'We do not mean to accept these proposals which constitute a denial of our rights.' Any elections, it was decided, would be boycotted by the Indian community.[24]

Meanwhile the Milner formula had caused an outcry among the Indians' friends in Britain and in India itself. The same month, Gandhi warned that 'If ever India becomes lost to Britain and the British Empire, it will not be so much on account of questions of internal administration ... but on this question of treatment of Indians in the Colonies.' Desai was still in India, garnering support. He called Milner's scheme 'disappointing, deplorable, unBritish all-round'.[25]

Desai would expand this theme the following year in an editorial in his newspaper the *East African Chronicle*. The British Empire promised so much, he wrote. It was a 'wonderful conglomeration of races and creeds and nations' which offered 'the only solution to the great problem of mankind – the problem of brotherhood. If the British Empire fails then all else fails. No more potent League of Nations was ever founded.' There followed, however, an enormous caveat: 'Either the British Empire must admit the equality of its different people ... irrespective of the colours of their skins and the place of their birth, or it must abandon its attempt to rule a mixture of people. There can be no half way.'[26]

The following year, with Churchill now Colonial Secretary, the Delamere faction were more optimistic. At a dinner in London given by the Convention of Associations, Churchill, having seemingly changed his mind since before the war, said that he saw Kenya becoming a 'distinctly British colony' and eventually achieving self-government. But, under pressure from the Indian government and the Anti-Slavery Society, he soon regretted his unscripted outburst of support for the Delamere agenda. Shortly afterwards he blocked a Public Health Ordinance passed by the Kenya Legislature that entrenched racial segregation in the towns, and his new formula on the key issues, while sticking to the exclusivity of the 'white highlands', included equal immigration restrictions for Indians and Europeans and a common electoral roll. This was tempered with property and educational conditions that gave only 10 per cent of the Indians the vote (against 100 per cent for Europeans), but it would clearly not take long for Indians to be the majority of the electorate, and thus have control of the colony.[27]

On top of the worrying proclamation at the 1921 Imperial Conference that all races should have equal rights in the empire, a new formula the next year was even worse for those who wanted to create a new South Africa in Kenya. The 'Wood-Winterton' formula of the end of 1922 not only went with the Indian demand for a common roll, but also for unrestricted immigration. It included, as well, an end to segregation.

Delamere's faction decided it was time for direct action.

In January 1923, Brigadier-General Philip Wheatley, a veteran of the South Africa Wars, was sent on a tour of the colony taking a census of rifles, ammunition, transport, petrol and horses, while calling mass meetings to stir the white settlers to action. Wheatley was to be the military leader of a potential coup against the colonial government. On 6 February, the Convention of Associations held a meeting in Nairobi at the Norfolk Hotel (from the balcony of which they had shot at the Thuku demonstration nearly a year earlier). Here it was resolved to resist the new scheme, 'armed force being employed if necessary'. A plan was hatched to seize control of the railway, postal and telegraph systems and to kidnap the Governor and remove him to a remote location under armed guard. Delamere was to be proclaimed president of a new independent country. If the local garrison, the King's African Rifles, put up resistance, they would be shot down, white officers included. The general assumption, though, was that officers of the police and KAR would not order black soldiers to fire on whites. An oath was drawn up, demanding obedience to the Directorate of the Convention of Associations. 'Practically everyone signed,' Wheatley reported in a letter home. 'They mean to fight if necessary, make no mistake about this. Our military preparations are practically complete.'[28]

There was nothing secret about any of this. Resolutions from the meetings were collected up and passed on to London. On 14 February, the Colonial Office responded to the overt threat with an analysis deciding that 'The introduction of a white force of sufficient strength to deal with a European community of 9,000 persons, the male portion of which, almost to a man, has experience of military service' would be 'costly', 'unedifying' and 'out of the question'. As anticipated, it was deemed that the use of black KAR troops against whites would be 'political suicide' for the Conservative government.[29]

From Kenya, acting Governor Charles Bowring reported to London his 'firm belief' that the sympathies of practically the whole of the civil service were now with the settlers and 'though they could be relied on to do all in their power to uphold the authority of Government they would be doing so in a half-hearted manner and solely from a sense of duty and loyalty to the Crown'. If 'rebels' attempted to take over government stations and were resisted, he said, they would sooner or later be overpowered by superior numbers after considerable loss of life. 'The effect on the native tribes cannot be foreseen but it would be far reaching and very grave.'[30]

Later the same month, Jeevanjee was requesting from the Indian government arms and an army contingent to protect the Kenyan Indians. The government in Delhi urged the white settlers to step back, and rushed a delegation to London, which included V. S. Srinivasa Sastri, C. F. Andrews and Muhammad Ali Jinnah. Yet another white delegation from Kenya followed soon after.

Meanwhile, the first months of 1923 saw a new low in Indian–European relations, much of which was played out in the colony's newspapers.

The English-language newspapers the *Observer* and the *Kenya and Uganda Critic*, both of which had often supported the Indian case and denounced the racism of the Highlands whites, now took the side of Delamere. 'Western civilisation must not be endangered by oriental ideals of human advancement,' wrote the editor of the *Critic*. 'The European must remain the dominant power in Kenya colony ... The Indian is not fit to take his place side by side with the Europeans in matters affecting either the Government of his own kind or the ruling of the subject race.'[31]

The Rev. Ryle Shaw, in a letter to the settler-supporting *East Africa Standard*, asked whether the British settlers should really be classed with 'Asiatics imported for pick and shovel work' who were 'alien in mind, colour, religion, morality and practically all the qualities Europeans regard as necessary for constitutional citizenship'.[32]

The Mombasa-based *Democrat* newspaper, which under the editorship of Sitaram Achariar had emerged as the key Indian voice in the press, argued that such an attitude was counter-productive for those who supported the empire as a multi-racial project. 'So supremely selfish are our Convention settlers that they care a brass button for the stability or good name of the British Empire, all care being for their ill-gotten acres in Kenya and their under-paid black slaves.'[33]

A female correspondent to the *East Africa Standard* then attacked the Indian community's treatment of women, in particular the customs of purdah and child marriage.

Rev. Shaw then compared the Prophet Muhammad to Belial, the Hebrew Devil.[34]

This provoked outrage and protests from Muslims around the empire. The Muslim Association of Nairobi cabled the Under-Secretary of State for the Colonies alleging that the Kenya European settlers had 'set on foot an anti-Indian agitation' thanks to coming 'in contact with the South African Boers and having unwittingly absorbed the complexion prejudice which was invented by the Boers many years back'.[35]

The *Democrat* hit back at the charges of immorality and mistreatment of women. 'We all know that sexual morality has reached such a lowest ebb in Europe, particularly in England,' the paper reported on 16 February. 'Incest is fairly common in England – a crime which is unheard-of in Oriental countries.' Furthermore, many English women had 'one or two abortions before someone comes along to conduct them to the holy altar', and orphanages 'are generously patronized by the well-to-do classes ... We say this in no vindictive spirit but only to show that marriage several years after puberty is just as bad as Indian child marriage.'

The in-rush of death threats against Achariar, who had been on the 1920 delegation to London with Jeevanjee and was a supporter of Thuku, saw him make preparations to flee Mombasa. But instead he was arrested, found guilty of breach of the peace and blasphemy, and remanded by the Mombasa court for deportation. In his support, 10,000 took to the streets in the city, and a hartal was observed, 'from Mombasa to the lake'. The Governor, Sir Robert Coryndon, ordered the editor's release.[36]

Achariar was soon back at his desk, writing on 23 February that it was essential for the government of India 'to make it unmistakably plain to the British Government . . . that these flagrant breaches of the Imperial Conference resolution regarding equal Indian status could not possibly be allowed any longer to go on unregarded'.[37]

In fact, the Indian government, and by extension the India Office in London, was firmly behind the Kenyan Indians. The Secretary of State, Viscount Peel, told a settler delegation in London in early 1923, 'I think the best solution of this trouble is to buy you all out.' One of the settlers replied, 'You can't do that, sir – it is our home.' Peel later said privately that he had never negotiated 'with a more stiff-necked or unreasonable set of people'.[38]

Around the empire, the deliberations in London were closely watched. In late May, Lugard weighed in, sending a memo to the CO warning that 'the greatest circumspection and vigilance' would need to be exercised 'to maintain the present position of the white races in the British Empire'. Although he conceded that the Delamere faction was 'only a powerful minority' 'which has dominated the majority and even a large section of official opinion', 'The clash of race at Kenya is bound to have serious repercussions elsewhere . . . Kenya is a move in a game which, if not checked, may yet wreck the British Empire.' It was, he wrote, a battleground for Mauritius, Fiji and elsewhere with very large minority – or even, in the case of Mauritius, majority – Indian populations.[39]

From Australia, in the form of the Adelaide *Chronicle*, came the opinion that the Kenya situation justified the 'White Australia' policy: 'No more solemn warning could be given of the danger of permitting the influx of coloured races into British Colonies, where, with their greater fecundity, it is only a matter of time when they outnumber the whites.'[40]

Amid this global interest, the Cabinet was faced with a choice: if they supported Indian demands for unrestricted immigration and a common electoral roll, either Kenya would become essentially an Indian colony, or the whites would stage their coup and make some sort of unilateral declaration of independence. Either way, the territory would be lost to London. If they went with Delamere, 'Indian Progressives', it was reported, 'would advocate secession from the Empire'.

What emerged was a masterly though, it has to be said, rather dishonest compromise. 'Primarily, Kenya is an African territory,' read the famous 'Devonshire Declaration' of July 1923 (now described in some quarters as 'One of the most famous and powerfully worded declarations of Imperial policy ever made'). 'The interests of the African natives must be paramount and that if, and when, those interests and the interests of the immigrant races should conflict, the former should prevail ... in the administration of Kenya His Majesty's Government regard themselves as exercising a trust on behalf of the African population, and they are unable to delegate or share this trust, the object of which may be defined as the protection and advancement of the native races.'[41]

This was 'trusteeship' in capital letters, the rickety new theory that now dominated imperial governance and justification, with its baked-in assumptions about racial hierarchy. In reality, the declaration was a compromise between Indian and European interests; there was no suggestion as to how 'African paramountcy' would be implemented – nothing much changed for Kenyan Africans. For the other interests, it was a setback. For Delamere, his vision of a new white supremacist South Africa was over. Nonetheless, it was a continuation of the status quo, in which the whites enjoyed political and economic dominance. For the Indians, who were still banned from buying acreage in the Highlands and were offered five Legislative Council seats elected by a communal roll against the eleven European ones, it did nothing to reassure them that promises of racial equality meant anything in the British Empire. For many years they would refuse to take up their allocated seats on the Council.

The decision prompted protests, boycotts, hartals and dismay in India and across the huge Indian diaspora. Benarsidas Chaturvedi, a prominent Indian from Malaya, wrote in the August 1923 edition of *Indian Review*: 'The cup of our humiliation and degradation is thus complete ... All our fond hopes of participating in a free Commonwealth of Nations have been shattered to pieces and we see instead, the waves of White-Race supremacy surging violently towards us as if to sweep us away altogether.' Tamil Christian activist George Joseph wrote in September: 'I welcome the decision because it is one based on reality. It has exhibited the truth of empire. It exploded the praxis on which Indian Liberalism, English Labour and Mr. Montagu built up a confusing heresy. The truth of the Empire is this: Englishmen went conquering.'[42]

'English Labour' in the form of Josiah Wedgwood, chair of the India Parliamentary Committee, condemned the decision in part because while the whites threatened force, the Indians relied on the merits of their case. The Labour *Herald* reported the regretful conclusion that 'the Government of the Empire has declared to the world that its Indian citizens are not worthy of the freedom of the Empire'. Instead they were to be 'subjected to exclusion from both the political and economic privileges of the white man'.[43]

On 29 September 1923, the *East African Standard* carried a report of a dinner held at the Hotel Cecil on the Strand in London. It was hosted by Sir Ali Iman, until now an arch-moderate, opponent of the Indian National Congress and constitutionalist. The star guest was V. S. Srinivasa Sastri.

Sir Ali made the first speech. The government, he said, 'has thrown the Moderate Party of India overboard'. Indians were prepared to accept, he went on, that the British Cabinet was now unable to impose its authority on the domestic arrangements of the self-governing Dominions of the empire. But in Kenya, as a Crown Colony, they had responsibility for direct internal administration. The decision was a gift to the 'extremists' in India at the expense of the constitutionalists.[44]

Sastri had been responsible for securing the pledge at the 1921 Imperial Conference that all subjects of the empire should enjoy equal rights, whatever their race. Since then he had travelled around the empire's Indian communities and made a big impression at the League of Nations, where he was described as its finest English-language

orator. As an arch-moderate, he had attracted the ire of Jawaharlal
Nehru. But the Kenya decision seems to have changed everything.[45]

He started with a joke. Welcoming the recognition of the interests of
the African and the idea of trusteeship, he said he hoped that the colonial authorities 'will take their trust more seriously and conscientiously
than they have done heretofore [laughter]'. 'Far be it for me to ignore
or even to underrate the enormous benefits of the British rule in India,'
he went on in a more serious tone. 'I have often spoken and written of
these and of the glorious mission of the British Commonwealth. And
I hope to live to do so again in better times, when British Imperialism
shall have shed its lower and assumed its higher character. But I am
sad to contemplate a people with a high destiny within their reach and
calling themselves a lesser League of Nations, setting up, after mature
deliberation, a colour bar firmer than the Boer pattern.' Indeed, the
Kenya settlement, by making Indians what he called 'unredeemed
helots in a Boer empire', was a 'grave national humiliation ... The
colour bar of South Africa is spreading over the British Empire, and it
is now infected with the poison of the Boer spirit.'

'How short is human memory!' he then exclaimed. 'It is not so long
ago that no words were good enough for the Indian for his services
during the war, his loyalty, his bravery on the battlefield, and the
rich compensations he had earned. Where are the pledges gone, and
the full rights of citizenship and absolute equality and partnership in
the Empire?'

He ended on a comment about 'the Indian', which sounded like a
self-examination of his politics until this point. Kenya had been 'the
acid test of empire', he said. 'The Indian has been cruelly betrayed.
Victim of many broken pledges, dupe of many solemn promises, his
faith in the character for justice and impartiality of the British seemed
almost incurable. He is at last undeceived.'[46]

30

'A Red-Letter Day'

Nigeria was once a land of great hope and progress, a
nation with immense resources at its disposal – natural
resources, yes, but even more so, human resources.

CHINUA ACHEBE, *There was a Country*[1]

On Saturday 29 September 1923, the streets of Lagos were still
heaving. An historic election had just taken place – the first of
its kind in West Africa – and the people were celebrating. The election,
according to the *Democrat* newspaper, had been 'a red-letter day ...
for it saw the ushering in of a new era when for the first time in West
Africa the people are in reality going to have a voice in the management
of their affairs'.[2]

Up for grabs had been four unofficial seats on the newly reorganised Legislative Council of Southern Nigeria. Previously there had
been nominated African unofficial members, mainly chiefs, on the
Council, but now four were to be elected. One was for Calabar, and
three for Lagos, and this is where the excitement was concentrated.
There were ten candidates standing, including two Europeans, long-
time Lagos residents. Three of the Africans were representing the new

Nigerian National Democratic Party (NNDP). Only founded in July that year, this was West Africa's first organised political party. The rest were essentially independents, though some, including one of the Europeans, associated with what was called the 'Nigerian Patriotic Party (under the banner of Moderation)'. It had no comparable organisation and was essentially made up of leaders of the People's Union. This had been formed in 1908 as a lobbying body to protest against the imposition of an unfair water rate on the city, but during the war, under intense pressure, it had backed down and supported the government, earning itself the reputation of 'selling the country to the whiteman'.[3]

There were 100,000 living in Lagos at this time, but only males with an annual income of £100 or more were eligible to register to vote. This produced an electorate of 2,083 Africans and 153 Europeans. Each voter could select three candidates.

As the day of the ballot neared, the NNDP campaigned vigorously, their slogans including 'Three Acres and a Cow' and 'Promised Land'. Newspapers noted 'a degree of animation beyond the most sanguine expectation'. The conservative press, in particular the *Nigerian Pioneer* – whose proprietor, Sir Kitoyi Ajasa, was a People's Union stalwart – warned that the NNDP had 'Bolshevist proclivities'. Others took a different line. The bilingual (English and Yoruba) *Eleti Ofe* urged voters to choose three African candidates, not out of 'hostility to Europeans' but – invoking 'Negro giants of the days that are gone: Sir Samuel Lewis, Dr. Edward Blyden, Bishop James Johnson' – to 'move forward in the path to national manhood'. This was followed, however, by a warning about some of the African candidates: 'No nation respects national aspiration, liberty and loyalty like the Englishmen although, like other men, they take care of their own interests by using anybody who offers himself as a willing tool, to be inwardly laughed at and spurned, of course, as traitors and fools must be.[4]

'Extraordinary excitement prevailed throughout the day' of the polling, the *Advocate* newspaper reported. As the vote-counts were about to be read out in Glover Hall, there was 'a look of grave anxiety and feverish concern on each individual face for it was a matter of life and death ... whether the wishes of the people shall prevail or not'.

Immediately after the declaration of the polls there followed 'what can only be described as pandemonium', reported the *Advocate*. It had been an extraordinary landslide victory for the NNDP. Each of their three candidates garnered more votes than all the other seven put together – 1,303, 1,298 and 1,281, with the next highest only receiving 271. 'The din of continual cheering reverberated with deafening intensity through the precincts of the Hall and the jubilations were carried on till the small hours of the morning in different quarters of the Town.'[5]

The three victorious candidates, denounced in some quarters as 'rabble-rousers', were all 'repatriates' – that is, they had been educated in Britain. J. E. Shyngle, who was president of the party, had studied at Christchurch, Oxford. He had been called to the Bar in 1882 and had been working as a barrister in Lagos since 1892. (His eldest son, Ladipo, had been killed fighting for the empire in East Africa.) Eric Moore had attended Combe College, Bath. He was also a barrister. The third, Dr Adenyi Jones, had trained at Durham University and in Dublin, London and Liverpool. He had established a 'first-rate' private hospital in Lagos in 1914.[6]

According to the *Advocate* newspaper, despite the 'extraordinary excitement' during polling day, 'no breach of the peace and no conflict with the Police occurred'. The conservative *Pioneer* told a different story under the headline 'Disgraceful Behaviour'. It reported that 'The unruly crowd proceeded to loot the stalls of market women and girls, and we are informed that in some cases assaults were committed on these poor and defenseless people.' There was also from the raucously dancing crowd abuse of the grandees of the People's Union – including *Pioneer* publisher Kitoyi Ajasa – 'using most offensive and disgusting language. Some day we fear the exuberant spirit of the party will lead to a clash and a jolly good fight.'[7]

The triumph of the NNDP and this rowdy behaviour, which was still occurring on the evening of 29 September, confirmed the *Pioneer* in its long-held opinion that 'the people of this Colony are not ready for the Franchise for some generations to come'. The *Messenger* agreed, having pointed out that the new Legislative Council still had an official majority and should not be seen as on the same level as the parliament of a self-governing Dominion. 'All those who really know the country and mean it good', the paper reported, have the opinion that 'Nigeria cannot yet altogether do without some form of strong autocratic Government'.[8]

Other papers celebrated the win. *Eleti Ofe*'s headline was 'The People's Sweeping Victory. National Honour Vindicated'. The *Advocate* congratulated the victorious candidates, and their highly competent campaigning. But it saved special praise for 'the "man behind the scenes" – the organising genius – the Sadi Carnot of the National Democratic Party, namely, Mr Herbert Macaulay'.[9]

Now considered by many the father of Nigerian nationalism, Herbert Macaulay, just short of sixty years old in 1923, had grown up in a 'rigidly Victorian' and highly Europeanised household. His father had been the founder and first headmaster of the Church Missionary Society school in Lagos. His mother Abigail was the daughter of Bishop Samuel Crowther, the first African to be appointed an Anglican bishop. Both Herbert Macaulay's paternal grandparents were Yoruba who had been captured by Portuguese slavers, then freed off the coast by the Royal Navy before settling in Freetown, Sierra Leone.[10]

Macaulay joined the civil service in the Public Works Department after attending his father's school, and then won a government scholarship to study civil engineering in Britain. While there, he was elected a Fellow of the Royal Geographical Society. He returned to Nigeria in 1893 to take up an appointment as Surveyor of Crown Lands for the colony of Lagos, thus becoming one of the first Nigerians to hold what was then known as a 'European Post'. Paid much less than a European of the same rank, he resigned in 1898 to set up in private practice.

Always immaculately dressed in a jacket and bow tie and sporting a square-cut moustache, he was a great entertainer, for African and

European alike, at his Lagos house, Kirsten Hall. An accomplished violinist, he also had the colony's only Bechstein Boudoir Grand. He was also the first African in Lagos to own a car.[11]

Increasingly, he became involved in journalism and politics, throwing himself into every controversy in Lagos. He had plenty of informants within the bureaucracy, and on several occasions embarrassed the colonial government. He also campaigned against segregation and economic inequality. On one occasion, in response to claims by the British that they were governing with 'the true interests of the natives at heart', he wrote: 'The dimensions of "the true interests of the natives at heart" are algebraically equal to the length, breadth and depth of the whiteman's pocket.'[12]

However, his ambitions for a political position came to an end when, in 1913, he was convicted of misappropriating funds from the will of a widow for whom he had been entrusted as an executor, and was sentenced to two years' imprisonment. Thereafter he was barred from standing for office, otherwise he would certainly have been one of the candidates for the NNDP in 1923, of which he was the principal founder. It was he who put together the coalition of support for the party which included chiefs, imams and market women leaders as well as the 'educated elite'.[13]

As the most consistent and effective West African critic of the administration of the colony of Nigeria, he was considered by the government an appalling nuisance and rabble-rouser. In 1921, a Gold Coast newspaper described him as 'a veritable Parnell in Yoruba affairs' as well as 'a veritable Cicero in debate'. In fact, Macaulay always drew a distinction between the actions of the local government in Lagos and what he saw as the high principles of fair play, justice and freedom of the British people at home and of the empire as a whole. Although he pushed for self-government, he never envisaged Nigeria leaving the empire, of which he was a fierce admirer. He remained grateful for the ending of slavery and of civil warfare in Yorubaland. He would later summarise his view of what he called 'Pax Britannica': 'for the Liberty of the subject; for the incalculable advantages of education; for

WEST AFRICA

GAMBIA *(British)*

PORTUGUESE GUINEA

FRENCH GUINEA

SIERRA LEONE *(British)*

Freetown

FRENCH WEST AFRICA

LIBERIA

Monrovia

IVORY COAST *(French)*

Niger

GHANA *(British)*

ASANTE

DAHOMEY *(French)*

TOGO *(British)*

YORUBALAND

Accra

Cape Coast

Sekondi

Axim

Tarkwa

Abeokuta

Oyo

Ikoyi

Lagos

Sokoto

Kano

Lake Chad

NIGERIA *(British)*

Benue

British Cameroon

Onitsha

IGBO

Calabar

Port Harcourt

CAMEROON

French Cameroon

SPANISH GUINEA

GABON *(French)*

FRENCH EQUATORIAL AFRICA

BELGIAN CONGO

Fernando Po

Príncipe

São Tomé

Atlantic Ocean

Under League of Nations mandate

500 km
500 miles

protection from Foreign powers; for free and lawful trade; for religious toleration; for our security of tenure; for the liberty of the press, for the establishment and maintenance of order and good government'.[14]

Herbert Macaulay, and others among the 'educated elite', have, as elsewhere, been accused of seeing the colonial structure as the best means to advance their own interests. Nigerian historian E. A. Ayandele described the pre-independence elite such as Macaulay as 'a cowardly set of irresponsible deserters of the unlettered chiefs and masses'. But this is a minority view. Macaulay is pictured on the one-naira coin, and Nigerian schoolchildren are taught to see him as the 'Gandhi of Nigeria'. Nigerian nationalism would change, of course, but would often acknowledge its debt to him. Obafemi Awolowo, a leading nationalist of the 1940s and 1950s (and now pictured on the 100-naira note), would remember as a teenager in 1923 seeing everywhere almanacs and calendars with Macaulay's picture and captions along the lines of 'The Champion and Defender of Native Rights and Liberty'. Awolowo wrote much later that the 'personality and the views of Herbert Macaulay' had an 'impact' and 'cast a spell' that was 'enchanting and profound'. There is, perhaps, in the lionisation a nostalgia for the time before Nigerian nationalism became destructively associated with ethnic affiliations.[15]

In the aftermath of the triumphant election, the *Eleti Ofe* newspaper praised Macaulay as 'The most courageous, most fearless and strongest Native African in the whole of Nigeria ... a man of indomitable courage and unlimited resourcefulness.' The weekly journal *West Africa* had been published in London since 1917, with the financial backing of large British West African commercial interests. Its manifesto was friendship towards 'every cause which holds out a prospect of advancing the position of West Africa as a prosperous and contented member of the Empire'. In its issue of 22 September 1923 it defended Macaulay against his European detractors: 'however much those in authority may hesitate to own it, he represents a section of public opinion – a loyal section, it is said, and a thoughtful one'. The next issue – 29

September – surveyed the election results. It commended the high turnout – with three quarters of those eligible voting – and reported that 'the candidates specially identified with the most adverse, and in some respects unfair, criticism of the Government ... have come out at the top of a poll'. Hope was expressed that the victory would not lead to 'catch-phrases' such as 'the government of the people by the people': the country 'is not, and cannot, for many years yet, be ready for self-government'.[16]

But then the magazine challenged what might be many of its readers' views of Macaulay and his party. 'Those who only read the official press would have thought the National Democratic Party ... at its best as a frothy agitation against the beneficent policies of the British Government, and at its worst as a movement by which a supposedly ignorant mass of electors has been organized to serve the selfish ends of a few unscrupulous leaders.' In fact, the journal continued, it was the only party 'to enunciate a clearly defined, if ambitious, programme'. This, 'although admittedly impossible of rapid realisation, is progressive, and cannot be regarded as anything but beneficial, save by the most biased class of anti-African Europeans or (dare it be said?) Europeanised Africans'.[17]

The NNDP manifesto, and indeed the fact that the elections took place at all, owed everything to the recently formed National Congress of British West Africa (NCBWA). Inspired by the Indian Congress, as well as by black groups elsewhere, particularly on the east coast of the US, it first convened in the Native Club, Accra, the Gold Coast, in March 1920. The aim was to create an organisation that could express the aspirations of educated West Africans across the four British territories. The forty-five delegates included representatives of educated groups in Nigeria, the Gold Coast, Sierra Leone and Gambia. The Nigerian delegation included J. E. Shyngle, who would later top the poll in the Lagos election.

The *Times of Nigeria* expressed concern about the 'powerful obstacles' presented by 'long standing inter-tribal dissensions, and inter-colonial antipathies', but another paper, the *African Times and Orient Review*, argued that 'it is unthinkable that a Native of Sierra Leone should be accounted a foreigner on the Gold Coast or in Nigeria, and vice versa ... All non-Europeans are labelled "n*****s" by Europeans ... it behoves the coloured people of the world to show a united front.' In fact, as Gambian historian J. Ayodele Langley points out, educated middle-class Africans had more in common and communicated more easily with their counterparts along the coastal towns than with their brethren in their own hinterland.[18]

The Congress's resolutions, subsequently embodied in a memorandum taken to London, included demands for legislative councils in all the colonies, with half of the members elected Africans; the expansion of education including the founding of a university; the separation of the judiciary from the legislature; the abolition of racial discrimination in the civil service; and regulation of the immigration of Syrians and other non-Africans. (There had been anti-Syrian riots the previous year. The Freetown-based *West African Mail and Trade Gazette* of 29 September 1923 reported that the current high price of rice was down to Syrian traders cornering the market.) With the exception of the 'Syrian' issue, this was pretty much the platform of Macaulay's NNDP.[19]

It also included, as was customary, a fervent declaration of loyalty to the King (also expressed by all the NNDP candidates before the Lagos election). This was repeated in the resolutions passed by a later Congress in early 1923, where it was pronounced that the 'strict and inviolate' policy was to maintain the British West African dependencies within the British Empire. 'The great ideal before us', reported a Sierra Leone newspaper, 'is the distant one of West Africa as a self-governing state in the British Commonwealth of nations.' By then, branches of the Congress had been established across the four territories.[20]

Inevitably, the Nigerian *Pioneer* newspaper attacked the first Congress for its 'reckless assumption of powers not granted'. The journal of the London-based African Society was far more supportive, writing that 'West Africa should no longer be regarded as composed of separate colonies ... but as one self-conscious and articulate community.' There was criticism, though, for the delegates' English names and dress, including top hats and 'Paris frocks'. 'At present,' the journal complained, 'the educated West African is too ready to Europeanise himself ... Now that West Africa is demanding a voice in its own affairs, might it not with advantage devise a culture of its own?'[21]

In fact, for the Congress delegates, most of whom had been educated at some point in Britain and were indebted to but frustrated by the colonial system, this was a hugely complex and challenging issue.

Perhaps the key figure behind the new Congress was Joseph Casely Hayford, a Gold Coast journalist, politician and Cambridge-trained barrister. The son of a reverend, he was educated at the Wesleyan boys' school in Cape Coast, undertook further study in Sierra Leone and then worked there as a teacher and a journalist, coming strongly under the influence of Edward Blyden. Originally from the Caribbean, Blyden had arrived in West Africa in the 1850s, where he taught and wrote prolifically, condemning the reduced state of black people internationally, and arguing for a celebration of indigenous African ingenuity, culture, art and political and social structures, including polygamy. Casely Hayford would call Blyden 'the foremost thinker of the race', and praise his ambition to 'lead the African back unto self-respect'.[22]

In 1903, Casely Hayford had published *Gold Coast Native Institutions*, in which he argued that 'before the British came into relations with our people, we were a developed people' with 'native institutions'. 'Authorities in Downing Street', he wrote, should allow the people 'to develop upon the national lines of their own institutions'. In 1911, he published an autobiographical novel, *Ethiopia Unbound*. The title page featured below his name, in brackets, his Fanti name, Ekra Agyiman. In the story, the main character Kwamankra bemoans the changes brought by 'the plague of modern civilisation' to the Gold Coast, 'thinking how much his people lost in passing from their ways to those of the white man'. In earlier days of 'healthy Fanti manhood', the young people 'joined hands together in the moonlight under the open sky' and sang the old songs – 'simple, natural, spontaneous'. Now they are crowded into church 'clad each in a few fathoms of Manchester home-spuns', with a schoolteacher in 'black morning coat and spotlessly bright patent leather shoes' looking 'a veritable fool', all listening to the 'wheezing sound of an old harmonium upon which a missionary boy was performing' dreary hymns. The white man, he goes on, with gin bottle in one hand and Bible in the other, was claiming 'a monopoly of culture, knowledge and civilisation'. This was 'a terrible scourge, a veritable canker, eating its way slowly, yet surely, into the very vitals of the life of the black people', now facing a 'national and racial death'.[23]

At the end, the hero resolves to return to Africa to 'devote the rest of his life in bringing back his people to their primitive simplicity and faith'. The model, as elsewhere, was the 'brave fellows of Japan' who had proved 'to the world that the Orient is capable of measuring swords with the Occident on any field of battle'. Their success was down to the fact that although they adopted and assimilated Western culture, they still respected the institutions and customs of their ancestors.[24]

The other of the pair whom cultural historian Kwadwo Osei-Nyame described as the 'two great figures of African nationalism and Pan-Africanism in the Gold Coast' is Kobina Sekyi, twenty-six years younger than Casely Hayford, and for a while his protégé.[25]

Like Hayford, he was from a wealthy, high-status family and was educated at the Wesleyan school in Cape Coast. Up until 1910, when he sailed to England for education, he was an 'Anglomaniac', he later confessed, brought up and indoctrinated to be ashamed of most things African and to believe that 'civilisation' and 'progress' came through Anglicisation and Christianisation.[26]

Within a short time of his arrival in London he underwent a transformation. He later wrote that he 'shed the chrysalis of European externals'. Lodging in a poor area of the city, he was appalled by the food, the lack of regular baths, and the general squalor. Furthermore, it did not take him long to 'find out he is regarded as a savage, even by the starving unemployable who ask him for alms'. Going to church, he was horrified to be in the company of 'housemaids and domestics', and found that, unlike in West Africa, 'religious enthusiasm is a form of low class emotion in England'. Questions he was asked, by both the working class he met and by his fellow students, betrayed a shocking and insulting ignorance 'respecting "Natives" in the "Colonies"'.[27]

His original intention was to study English literature at the University of London, but he switched to philosophy, graduating in 1913, and returned to the Gold Coast determined to reintegrate himself into Akan-Fanti culture. To this end he undertook a study of traditional institutions and found himself 'restored to my mental health'. At this time he wrote a play, *The Blinkards*, a merciless satire on the Gold Coast nouveaux riches' 'slavish' imitation of all things European. The central character, Mrs Borofosem, has been to England, and mistakes English working-class culture for *the* English culture – she insists her husband call her 'Duckie'. She is always on edge to prove her 'Europeanness', but constantly gets things wrong, wanting at one point to 'kill a bird with two stones'. The sympathetic characters avoid unsuitable European clothes, speak Fanti and reject the European cake and wine on offer in favour of local food.

Nonetheless, bowing to the wishes of his family, Sekyi returned to England in 1915 to study law. On the voyage out, his ship, the SS *Falaba*, was torpedoed by a German U-boat while in the Irish Sea. Quite a few of the passengers perished, but Sekyi made it to a lifeboat. As he clambered aboard, a European shouted at him that he should get out as a black man had no right to survive when whites were drowning. Needless to say, this had a profound effect on Sekyi.[28]

His second time in England confirmed his view that Africa was superior to English society in almost every respect. In 1917 he wrote an article for *West Africa* magazine comparing the 'Social Life in England and on the Gold Coast' in which he painted a picture of English families as lonely and dysfunctional compared to the multi-generational model in Africa. In England, even close neighbours were often strangers, while the African must 'greet everybody he meets or

passes ... no rigid ceremony of introduction is demanded as a preface
to intercourse ... Each man's joy is everybody else's joy; each man's
grief is everybody else's grief.'[29]

The following year, the same magazine serialised his autobiographical novel, *The Anglo-Fanti*. A Gold Coast boy is baptised and sent
to a school where he is taught to look down on his 'uneuropeanised
fellow-children' and to admire the 'greater sweetness of European con-
fectionery, the greater attractiveness of European manufactures ... the
superiority, in every aspect, of everything European over everything
African'. High school is conducted in English and demands European
clothing to be worn. He adopts an English name, and soon finds himself thinking in English rather than Fanti. When he travels to England
to further his education he goes sure in the knowledge that 'England is
a paradise on earth'.[30]

He is almost instantly disillusioned with the class system and
inequality, the dirt, the terrible weather and food, and what he sees
as the ugly, ill-clad women. He returns to the Gold Coast and to
the bafflement of his Westernised family rejects European food and
clothes and refuses to marry in the European fashion. Pulled in two
directions – his family and his desire to 'de-Europeanise' – he has a
breakdown and dies.

Sekyi left England in 1918, having secured a Masters in Philosophy
and qualified as a barrister. He returned to legal work in Cape Coast,
and was soon involved in journalism and nationalist politics. Despite
his unhappy time in England, he did not reject everything European.
He was a life-long admirer of European literature, philosophy and science and, according to his son, a connoisseur of fine wine and cigars.
He conceded that African institutions were in need of some modifications to bring them into step with modern times, but argued that the
change must be gradual, otherwise the social fabric, the 'organic structure', more advanced and more humane than the European, would be
destroyed.

His son, H. V. H. Sekyi, wrote in an introduction to a later edition
of his works that the 'European man on the spot' called him 'a Cape

Coast lawyer, able, intelligent and well educated, but with a most pronounced anti-European complex'. The 'European intellectual', he went on, 'called him the outstanding example of a tragic and unresolved conflict desiring at once to be pagan and Christian, aboriginal and European, Akan Traditionalist and Western Progressive'. His son rejected the idea of his father being tragic or unresolved, 'any more than modern Japan or the modern Japanese is tragic or unresolved'.[31]

Sekyi would strongly disapprove of his mentor Casely Hayford accepting an appointed position on the Legislative Council. He would also fall out with some fellow West African nationalists in his call for a complete rejection of Christianity, in favour of traditional African codes of ethics and duty, which he saw as more useful. Eventually, he would suggest that Africans have as little to do with Europeans as possible.[32]

On his return to the Gold Coast and the beginning of his legal career, he would become the first African lawyer to wear traditional dress in court. He also contributed in a large way to the establishment and organisation of the first National Congress of British West Africa in March 1920, where he was one of only three of the forty-five delegates to attend in native dress. There, he delivered a well-received paper on 'Education With Particular Reference to a West African University', which would become one of the manifesto demands.

However, the delegation to London, carrying the memorandum of their resolutions to present to the British government, experienced severe difficulties, in large part thanks to the extraordinarily vitriolic response of the man now the most powerful in West Africa, Sir Hugh Clifford.

In Trinidad, Clifford had been faced with a very un-Malaya-like situation of an articulate middle class demanding constitutional reform, and a white creole population very different from the tiny, prestige-obsessed and self-policing white community in Malaya. According to Clifford, the 'white man' in the West Indies 'has never maintained his position in relation to the coloured and black peoples in the way that has kept up the white man's reputation and authority in the East'. Also, there was no 'higher purpose' as in the Malaya mission to sustain the old indigenous hierarchy and culture; the West Indies colonies had never been about anything other than making money. (Clifford even suggested that Britain swap the West Indies for the Philippines, the US being good at dealing with ex-slaves, and the British good with Asians.)[33]

There was also a personal tragedy. His wife fell from a pony cart as it was taking a sharp corner. While recuperating from a nasty head wound, she caught pneumonia and then meningitis. On 14 January 1907, she died. The following month Clifford sailed for England with his infant daughter to spend a short time with his 'poor motherless bairns', ten-year-old son Hugh and nine-year-old Mary. Soon after that he sailed alone for a new position as Colonial Secretary in Ceylon. He was immediately acting Governor, a role he would fulfil for much of his time there.[34]

He soon made himself unpopular, attacking the educated elite who were pushing for political reform. They had, he told the CO, 'ceased to be in any sense typical Orientals and thereby forfeited their right to speak with authority on behalf of the typical Orientals who form the immense bulk of their fellow-countrymen'. He went so far as to call them 'the little core of rot'.[35]

Clifford clearly saw the future of empire as one of permanent administration and noblesse oblige by British officials who knew what was best for the colonised and would protect the weak against their stronger countrymen. Brown and black races would never be fit for self-government. Either they were insufficiently educated, or educated away from being representative.

Clifford continued to attack any mooted concessions, particularly around the elective principle. Such was the tone of his dispatches that a CO official minuted on one 'Astounding'. Another wrote, 'enough to make one despair of Sr. H. Clifford's sanity'. In fact, Clifford's commendable energy sometimes was beginning to look manic, and stories started circulating about his growing 'eccentricity', including one in which he supposedly greeted guests wearing nothing but his socks.[36]

After quitting Ceylon in 1912, Clifford, now knighted and remarried to a recently widowed novelist, Elizabeth de la Pasture, was posted as Governor to the Gold Coast. He would serve there until 1919, when he took over the governorship of Nigeria. In the Gold Coast, he expanded the appointed African unofficial presence on the Legislative Council – Casely Hayford was one of those who accepted a position in 1916 – but abolished as inefficient the largely elective Municipal Councils of Accra, Cape Coast and Sekondi. The elective principle, he declared, was out of the question in West Africa 'for a long time to come'.[37]

Nevertheless, he won praise for his expansion of the road network and port facilities to serve the local cocoa growers, and his stewardship of the fairly painless 1914 takeover of neighbouring German Togoland. He also negotiated the difficult, sometimes competing interests of the traditional 'chiefs' and the educated elite with tact and skill, which makes his later outbursts all the more surprising.

On a personal level, it was for Clifford an immensely difficult time. The new Lady Clifford had caught yellow fever in 1914, and thereafter her health remained bad, necessitating many voyages home. This presented severe danger due to frequent U-boat attacks. Elder Dempster, the leading shipping line of the coast, lost twenty-nine vessels during the war, a third of its fleet. When his wife was at sea, Clifford reported, 'I am unable to relax, and have agonies of anxieties on her behalf.' He only managed to sleep three hours a night.

His wife also contracted malaria, as did Clifford himself. Malaria, of course, can recur – as it did with Clifford – and can cause severe depression. Worse was to come in 1916. In the spring of that year, as soon as he was eligible, his son, Hugh, had applied for and received a commission from the Second Lincolnshire Regiment. On 1 July 1916, a few months after his eighteenth birthday, he was reported missing during the first day of the Battle of the Somme. His parents in Africa would have heard by the end of the month. Only in October did they learn through the 'finders' of the Red Cross that a Private Taylor, who had been wounded on the same day, had seen Lieutenant Clifford shot through the head by a machine-gun bullet. His body was never recovered. 'Of course the event was not in any away unexpected,' Clifford wrote to a friend about hearing the news, 'but he was my only son and I was very fond and proud of him and for a time it was as much as I could do to concentrate my mind fully upon my official work, which at this season of the year is always particularly heavy.' Clifford's younger brother, Henry, was a brigadier. Despite long periods apart, Hugh considered him his 'dearest friend in the world'. Shortly after news of his son, Clifford learned that Henry had, while reconnoitring a forward position, been shot dead by a German sniper.[38]

With the war over, Clifford moved to Nigeria and handed over the governorship of the Gold Coast to General Sir Gordon Guggisberg. A Canadian Army engineer, his appointment came about because of his wife's connection to the wife of the then Colonial Secretary, Lord Milner. Guggisberg had no experience of imperial governance or of West Africa, and as such was the antithesis of everything Clifford thought essential for colonial servants. Clifford would write to Leo Amery that Guggisberg's appointment was 'the most blatant public insult that has ever been offered to the Colonial Civil Service'. The two Governors quickly established mutual hatred. When, in mid-1923, they were both required to travel to London to consult ahead of the Imperial Conference and to lay foundation stones for the West Africa Pavilion in the Wembley exhibition, Clifford deliberately booked a passage on the steamship a week early to avoid spending the voyage with his enemy. But Guggisberg did the same thing for the same reason, and they ended up having to endure travelling together.[39]

Switching from the Gold Coast to Nigeria, Clifford faced a larger and more complex challenge. Interference in local politics, motivated by pressure from anti-slavery missionaries as well as commercial and mining interests, had led to direct British control of the Nigerian coastal states between 1861 and 1885, when the littoral was divided up by the European powers. Expansion inland, driven in large part as a means of foiling French and German ambitions, saw the defeat of two great African empires, the Asante in the Gold Coast and the Sokoto

Caliphate in Northern Nigeria. The latter was accomplished under the leadership of Sir Frederick Lugard, Clifford's precursor as Governor. The mud walls and goats'-hide gates of the ancient city of Kano proved no match for his modern artillery, and the defenders armed with spears and sharpened agricultural tools were powerless against the new Maxim machine-gun. Twelve hundred were killed for the loss of only one of Lugard's men. The defenders of Sokoto, the capital of the Fulani Federation, prudently ran away and the city was captured intact. Within a few years Lugard had subdued almost all the Fulani emirates and where necessary replaced the emirs with men willing to take advice from a British political agent.

There was a coda in 1906, when a self-styled Mahdi led a peasants' revolt in a village near Sokoto. Two British political agents and an officer were killed, along with nearly seventy black soldiers. Lugard, supported by the Emir of Sokoto, sent 500 men to take revenge. Some 2,000 were mown down by machine-gun fire, with no loss to the attackers, and the village razed to the ground. Prisoners were executed and their heads put on spikes. The new Liberal government was not impressed. 'The chronic bloodshed which stains the West African seasons is odious and disquieting,' minuted Churchill. 'Moreover the whole enterprise' of Lugard's conquering of the north 'is liable to be misinterpreted by persons unacquainted with imperial terminology as the murdering of natives and stealing of their lands'. Clifford privately described Lugard as 'blood-stained to the collar-stud'.[40]

Only in 1914 had the north and south of Nigeria been amalgamated. This produced a territory of 365,000 square miles, the same area as the British Isles, France and Belgium put together, with 18 to 19 million people (against 1.5 million in the Gold Coast), making it the empire's third most populous territory. These people consisted of some 250 ethnic groups and distinct languages, living under a bewilderingly disparate range of political structures. With only one Political Officer for 100,000 people in the north and 70,000 in the south, there were fewer officers per population than in any other colony. Furthermore, some borderlands remained 'unpacified'.[41]

One Fine Day

Lugard had left the northern emirates bedevilled by corruption and the general administration in chaos. Clifford applied himself to this with his customary energy and bureaucratic skill. He would stay in Nigeria until 1925. As early as 1922 he was being warned by a concerned friend not to 'burn the candle at both ends' and that he should take more rest. Stories started circulating about his erratic behaviour. On one occasion he turned up at the house of the wife of one of his officers with the news that a mistress who had committed suicide many years before had spoken to him in the middle of the night on the telephone. The wife made sure that this behaviour was reported to the Colonial Office. When the Prince of Wales visited towards the end of his tenure, he was moved to write privately to Leo Amery about Clifford: '*entre nous*, he's a very sick man – nerves all gone to pieces'.[42]

One of Clifford's first challenges, however, was that presented by the new National Congress of British West Africa. The delegates had assembled in London by October 1920. The Nigerian branch had been unable to raise the money to send men, but J. E. Shyngle and Chief Oluwa happened to be in London, so took on the role. (Shyngle was presenting an appeal to the Privy Council on behalf of the chief, who was accompanied as interpreter and secretary by Herbert Macaulay.) The delegates set about 'educating the British public'. They lobbied newspapers and magazines, contacted African groups such as the African Progress Union and the West African Students Union and recruited sympathisers such as Gilbert Murray, J. H. Harris and Sir Harry Johnston to help present their case to the Colonial Office.

But Colonial Secretary Milner then received 'gubernatorial thunderbolts' from West Africa. Guggisberg sent a telegram on 23 October warning that Congress's demands 'practically amount to self-government' (in fact they were only asking for half of each of the legislative councils to be elected), and that this would be 'fatal to the progress of the native race, and to the development of the colony, which is not ready for it'. Claiming erroneously that the 'chiefs' resented the attempts 'of the literates to govern them', he argued that the Gold Coast delegates represented only a fraction of the whole population.

A month later a far more vitriolic telegram arrived from Clifford. He ridiculed the idea that there could be a West African nation, or even a Nigerian nation. Nigeria, he explained, was a 'collection of self-contained and mutually independent Native States, separated from one another, as many of them are, by great distances, by differences of history and traditions, and by ethnological, racial, tribal, political, social and religious barriers'. The demands of Congress, he told the Colonial Office, were nothing more than 'loose and gaseous talk emanating from a group of self-appointed, self-selected educated gentlemen' entirely unrepresentative of the bulk of Nigerians. To agree to their programme 'would cause anarchy, wholesale discontent and probably sporadic insurrections'.[43]

The result was that the CO refused to grant the West African delegates an audience. 'There can be little doubt that a nominated man will provide better representation of the views of the people than any kind of election can produce,' the CO concluded. Under-Secretary of State Sir Herbert Read agreed with Clifford and Guggisberg that the delegates were unrepresentative except of the 'intellectual natives of the barrister and trader class', and referred to the Nigerian delegates as 'this precious pair of rascals'. Shyngle wasn't even a native Nigerian and Chief Oluwa was a 'ridiculous petty chief . . . masquerading as a Nigerian potentate with his ex-convict secretary Mr. Macaulay'. The CO even turned down the request of the delegates – now being referred to as 'Herbert Macaulay and his gang' – to lay a wreath on behalf of West African soldiers at the Armistice Day ceremony.[44]

In his address to the Nigerian Council at the end of the year, Clifford continued his attack on the 'self-selected and self-appointed congregation of educated African gentlemen who collectively style themselves the "West African National Congress"'. Their eyes were fixed, he said, 'upon political theories evolved by Europeans to fit a wholly different set of circumstances, arising out of a wholly different environment, for the government of peoples who have arrived at a wholly different stage of civilization'. Instead, they should concentrate on their 'tribal obligations' and 'their duties to their Natural Rulers'. The consistent policy of the government of Nigeria, he said, was 'to maintain and to support the local tribal institutions and the indigenous forms of Government ... which are regarded as the natural expressions of African political genius'.[45]

In public, Clifford would sing the praises of the system of indirect rule established in Northern Nigeria. Nowhere in the empire had the local system of native rule suffered so little disturbance, he said. To an extent, this was making a virtue out of a necessity – the British did not have the resources to directly run these vast areas – but it was also seen as an attempt to preserve existing cultural and political structures, and as such was admired by the likes of Wedgwood, E. D. Morel and Leonard Woolf. Wedgwood called Northern Nigeria 'the pearl of our crown colonies'. But, as with the Indian and Malay princes, the result was to ossify a system that previously was dynamic and flexible. Kobina Sekyi complained that it 'put us back in our social and political development to a stage lower than that at which our ancestors first came into contact with British administrators'. It was a 'perversion of chieftaincy' that 'threatened political evolution'. Lugard, the creator of the Northern Nigeria system, admitted, 'we are dealing in many cases with the identical rulers, who were responsible for the misrule and tyranny which we found in 1902'. In private, Clifford acknowledged that the policy of the preservation of archaic social forms was, by any criteria of development – health, industry, trade, education, political opportunities – failing, and tried unsuccessfully to make changes.[46]

In Southern Nigeria, existing chiefs were given subsidies and protection. A classic example of the downside of this was the Yoruba kingdom of Oyo. All decisions by the Alafin (king) of Oyo required the approval of his council of chiefs. In former times, a gift of parrot's eggs from the leader of the council was a sign to the Alafin that his death was desired by the chiefs and the people. Invariably the Alafin complied by taking poison, so the threat of a dread gift was a safeguard against tyrannical rule. The proscription of this custom by the British 'dislocated the checks and balances of the old constitution'.[47]

In the eastern Igbo provinces, so low was the British opinion of the level of civilisation there that they made no attempt to understand the people's indigenous government based not on chiefs but on assemblies of villages and village groups. But to streamline the administration, the British insisted on imposing chiefs. As Chinua Achebe would write, 'Igbo people would regard the absence of such a recognized leader as the very defining principle of their social and political identity.' (When asked to present their chiefs, villagers, thinking they were going to be killed or taken into slavery, often put forward their criminals, slaves or ne'er-do-wells.) The new system of 'warrant chiefs' was much resented for the corruption and oppression it produced, for undermining the democratic institutions and also for how it ignored the role of women in local politics (this was one of the causes of the 'Aba Women's Riot' in 1929). Clifford would confess that the British had 'swept away, intermixed with much that was evil, a medium that might with profit have been utilised for the more efficient management of local native affairs'. Unsurprisingly, one of the key demands of the West African Congress was that chiefs should, as before, be appointed and, where necessary, deposed by their own people.[48]

Torpedoed by Clifford and Guggisberg, the Congress delegation returned home in February 1921 empty-handed. But only two months later Clifford performed a surprising U-turn, suggesting to the CO the creation of a new Legislative Council of Southern Nigeria including four elected members. This was reluctantly agreed, leading to the historic election in September 1923. The reasons for Clifford's abandonment of his prior opposition to the elective principle were much debated at the time, and ever since.

Clifford's own reasoning, as expressed to the CO, was that 'the occupation of seats on a Legislative Council by local demagogues would tend to imbue them with a sense of responsibility which they do not feel so long as they are able to spread all manner of mischievous rumours among an ignorant population without incurring the risk of being publicly brought to account therefor'. Kobina Sekyi surmised that it was down to the efforts of Congress, 'the despised leaders of

African political thought'. 'There can be no doubt', he wrote, 'that the terror which this movement inspired in the heart of Sir Hugh Clifford led him to recommend a form of elective representation for West Africa.' It may have been that Clifford did not anticipate that he was establishing a precedent (once conceded in Nigeria, it was almost automatic elsewhere: limited franchises were introduced in urban areas in Sierra Leone in 1924 and the Gold Coast in 1925). Or he may have believed that the nationalists, who invariably won the elections, would not want more than just a chance to express their views. But they saw it as a path to real power. Clifford seems to have been confident that the British would continue to control the situation.[49]

As elsewhere, Nigeria experienced a sharp downturn in 1921; perhaps Clifford felt concessions were necessary to forestall serious protest. A Lagos newspaper suggested that it was down to Clifford's well-known antipathy to Guggisberg, that he had 'rushed through the Nigerian scheme' 'as a necessary expedient for taking the wind out of Sir Gordon's sails and forestalling the Gold Coast in the grant of the franchise'. It has also been suggested that this decision was down to Clifford's 'complex and unstable personality'. It remains puzzling, particularly as in June 1923, when making a speech in London to the Union of African Students, Clifford described democracy for Africa as 'an alien bacillus'. Self-government in the southern provinces, he declared, 'would mean a recrudescence of savage superstition, accompanied by universal lawlessness'. Shortly after this speech, Clifford experienced a severe breakdown, and was sent by his doctors for a complete rest in Cornwall. In theory, he made a 'full recovery' and returned to Nigeria in September.[50]

Whatever the reasons, this first recognition of the elective principle at this level of government was a historic change, even if it fell far short of what Congress had demanded.

Sekyi was something of a recluse, but Joseph Casely Hayford and others of the Congress now had an international profile, and were part of a pan-African movement that reached London, the United States and the West Indies. Hayford had participated in Booker T. Washington's International Conference on the Negro in 1912 in Alabama, and had given financial support to the *African Times and Orient Review*, the pan-Africanist newspaper published in London. He was also in regular correspondence with W. E. B. Du Bois, the leader of the US National Association for the Advancement of Colored People (NAACP). Du Bois played a leading role in Pan-African Congresses held in London in 1900, in Paris in 1919, and in London again in 1921 and 1923. By the early 1920s, however, there was a radical new voice in pan-Africanism: 'Provisional President of Africa' Marcus Garvey.

31

'Africa for the Africans'

I asked 'Where is the black man's Government? Where
is his President, his country, and his ambassador, his
army, his navy, his men of affairs?' I could not find
them, and then I declared, 'I will help to make them.'

MARCUS GARVEY, September 1923[1]

The September 1923 issue of *Current History* featured an article by
Marcus Garvey titled 'The Negro's Greatest Enemy'. Thirty-six-
year-old Garvey was by some distance the world's most famous black
man, adored, despised, feared and ridiculed. He was seen by London
as constituting the greatest single threat to the empire in Africa and
the Caribbean. But at the time of writing his article, subtitled 'a chapter of autobiography', he was in prison in New York and pretty much
everything he had worked for was in ruins.

Garvey was born and brought up in rural Jamaica. His father was a
stonemason; his mother worked in the fields and as a domestic servant
for the neighbouring family of a white Wesleyan minister. In his article, Garvey tells the story of how he used to play with the minister's
daughter – 'We were two innocent fools who never dreamed of a race

feeling and problem.' But when they were both fourteen, her parents decided 'the time had come to separate us and draw the color line'. The girl was sent away to school in Britain and told that 'she was never to write or try to get in touch with me, for I was a "n*****"'. In response, Garvey later wrote, 'I developed a strong and forceful character.'[2]

He left school the same year and was apprenticed to a local printer. In his free time he undertook elocution lessons and each day taught himself two or three new words from the dictionary he carried with him. He then worked as a printer in Kingston, where he became ever more conscious of 'racial injustice' and soon became involved with politics and trade unionism.

In 1910 he spent a year in Central America, working in various jobs and publishing newspapers attacking the treatment of the large West Indian expatriate communities employed by United Fruit Company and in the brutal US Panama Canal construction. Two years later, he was in England. He initially supported himself working in the docks of London, Cardiff and Liverpool, but then got himself a job as a runner and handyman on the *African Times and Orient Review*, the newspaper recently established with financial help from Joseph Casely Hayford. Edited by Egyptian-born Dusé Mohammed Ali, its ambition was to 'lay the aims, desires, and intentions of the Black, Brown and Yellow Races ... within and without the Empire – at the throne of Caesar'. The paper was a hub of black intellectual life, and soon Garvey was reading Casely Hayford, Edward Blyden and Booker T. Washington. Author of *Up from Slavery*, Washington was founder of the Tuskegee Institute in Alabama, which focused on technical education to improve the material well-being of American blacks in the South. Blyden preached black pride, but in addition argued that God had assigned a portion of the earth to each race; he abhorred miscegenation and was a supporter of the repatriation of the diaspora to Africa.[3]

As well as reading in the British Library (Dusé Mohammed Ali gave accreditation for his reader's pass), Garvey visited the House of Commons to see noted orator Lloyd George in action. He also undertook evening classes in law at Birkbeck College. In late 1913, after much badgering of the editor, Garvey had an article published in the *Orient Review* which fiercely criticised Britain's record of greed and violence in Jamaica, and predicted: 'there will soon be a turning point in the history of the West Indies; the people will be the instruments of uniting a scattered race who . . . will found an Empire on which the sun shall shine as ceaselessly as it shines on the Empire of the North today'.[4]

Mirroring the hero of Casely Hayford's *Ethiopia Unbound*, in August 1914, only five days after his return from London to Jamaica, Garvey founded the Universal Negro Improvement Association and African Communities (Imperial) League (UNIA). Initially a literary and debating society, its aim was 'to establish a brotherhood among the black race, to promote a spirit of race pride, to reclaim the fallen and to assist in civilising the backward tribes of Africa'. There were also plans for moral and material 'uplift' charitable programmes at home. There was little anti-imperialist about any of this, and the association secured the patronage of the Governor and the Colonial Secretary of Jamaica, as well as others of the white elite. Indeed, the new UNIA's manifesto included praise for 'the great protecting and civilising influence of the English nation and people'.[5]

It was less successful with non-white Jamaicans. Part of the problem was the inclusion of the word 'Negro'. Jamaica had a parallel class system based on what Garvey called 'the prejudice of our race in shade colour'. For many, the ambition for their children was to be lighter-skinned than themselves and thereby join the 'brown' elite. 'I was openly hated and persecuted by some of these colored men of the island who did not want to be classified as negroes, but as white,' Garvey later wrote. He would complain of his fellow Jamaicans in an early pamphlet: 'you have consistently been unfair to yourselves, because you hate and despise yourselves'. Part of the new UNIA manifesto declared, 'Negroes the world over must practice one faith, that of confidence in themselves.'[6]

There were also rumours of money raised for the UNIA's charitable programmes being diverted to cover Garvey's personal expenses. Garvey had an ambition to found a technical school in Jamaica along the lines of the Tuskegee Institute, and failing to make an impact in Jamaica, he decided to travel to the United States to raise money for the venture.[7]

Here, with a new urban black proletariat after mass migration from the South, a resurgent Ku Klux Klan, ongoing disenfranchisement, an overt colour bar and frequent atrocities being committed against black people across the country, it was an entirely different story. Garvey's forthright message and populist charisma would find millions of admirers, and Garvey himself would change from reformist to radical.

Having worked his passage to New York, Garvey headed for Harlem, home to many of New York's 150,000 black population. There, he joined the unofficial speaking circuit of step-ladders in streets, churches and halls and, learning quickly from Harlem revivalist preachers, black and white, his forceful oratory soon made an impression. Jamaican poet and radical Claude McKay, an early leader of the Harlem Renaissance, later wrote: 'Garvey shouted words, words spinning like bullets, words falling like bombs, sharp words like poisoned daggers, thundering words and phrases lit with all the hues of the rainbow to match the wild approving roar of his people.' Another listener 'heard a voice like thunder from Heaven'.[8]

An important early supporter was veteran journalist and influential campaigner John E. Bruce. He was far more radical than anyone Garvey had come across in Jamaica or London. After one particularly bad episode of racial violence he wrote: 'If they burn your house, burn theirs. If they kill your wives and children, kill theirs.' Bruce was hugely impressed with the 'little sawed-off, hammered-down black man, with determination written all over his face, and an engaging smile that caught you and compelled you to listen to his story'. In part, Bruce was converted by Garvey's enthusiasm for Africa. Bruce, who had been born in 1856 into slavery, was a collector of scholarly African books and texts and in 1911 had started the Negro Society for Historical Research. For most black people across the Americas, Africa, whose inhabitants were often popularly pictured as cannibals with bones through their noses, living in squalor, was an embarrassment. But Garvey spoke of Africa as 'the motherland' and celebrated its artistic, technical and cultural accomplishments. Here, Garvey declared, 'all the Negro peoples of the world' could unite into 'one great body to establish a country and Government absolutely their own'.[9]

Bruce introduced Garvey to the 'leading men' in New York and other cities who might help him. In early 1917, Garvey embarked on a year-long speaking tour over thirty-eight states, finding a constituency frustrated with the moderation and lack of success of the black leadership in the face of serial lynchings. Thirty-six were lynched in 1917, sixty in 1918, seventy-six in 1919, and in the region of fifty to sixty a year from 1920 to 1923. The Ku Klux Klan had strong links with the police and the courts, and very few were prosecuted.[10]

Stung into action, and sensing potential support, in January 1918 Garvey formed the New York branch of UNIA. Much later he would explain part of his motivation. Soon after arriving in New York, Garvey had paid a visit to the National Association for the Advancement of Colored People (NAACP) headquarters in the hope of meeting W. E. B. Du Bois.

Following the death of Booker T. Washington in 1915, Du Bois was now the acknowledged leader and voice of black America and was steering the cause in a different direction. In an argument mirrored across the British Empire, Du Bois had taken issue with Washington's emphasis on 'industrial education' such as agricultural and mechanical skills, arguing that black schools should focus more on the liberal arts and humanities required to develop a leadership elite. This 'talented ten per cent' would lead change towards a real enforcement of full legal and political rights. The NAACP was an inter-racial organisation that benefited from rich white philanthropists and enjoyed the support of sympathetic white liberals. The majority of the readers of its journal, *Crisis*, were white. Its aim was integration, or even assimilation, and its hope was that, in time, African-Americans could enjoy equal status with their white fellow Americans.

When Garvey visited the NAACP offices, Du Bois himself was

absent. But Garvey was very struck by the fact that in the offices 'the whole staff was either white or very near white'. For 'our "so-called leading men" (apes) to seek the shelter, leadership, protection and patronage of the "master" in their organization and so-called advancement work' (which he had done in Jamaica), he later wrote, demonstrated 'the slave spirit of dependence'.[11]

In his September 1923 autobiographical article, he wrote that he visited 'negro leaders' and discovered 'they had no program, but were mere opportunists'. This was the moment, he said, when he decided to stay in America, to found the UNIA there, and 'to teach du Bois and his group what real race pride meant'.[12]

Touring Harlem with a megaphone, he quickly recruited thousands of members in the district. Membership was open to anyone with 'Negro blood and African ancestry' who was able and willing to pay 25 cents a month. Branches were opened across the country and soon membership was growing by 25,000 a month. UNIA divisions were also established in the Caribbean, Central America and Sierra Leone. Garvey reckoned that by June 1919 there were 2 million members.

Just as the colonised differed in their attitudes to the coloniser and the 'West', so Garvey and Du Bois represented two different philosophies of change, and different ideas about how races should relate to each other. Du Bois was an integrationist, proudly mixed-race, and looked forward to a time when race no longer mattered. He considered 'black pride' simply racist. 'The day black men love black men simply because they are black', he wrote, 'is the day they will hate white men simply because they are white, and then, God help us all!' 'The race pride of Negroes is not the antidote to the race pride of white people,' he argued, 'it is simply the other side of a hateful thing.'[13]

But for Garvey, integration would lead to disaster. First, it would 'make a black man a Frenchman, or American citizen or British subject . . . they cannot be our ultimate aims . . . there would be no Negro, no African people'. Second, it was a 'race destroying doctrine' as social equality would inevitably see the creation of 'mongrel types' 'against the Creator's plan'. Like Blyden, he abhorred miscegenation, which

'would destroy the racial purity of both ... We believe that the white
race should protect itself against racial contamination,' he declared,
'and the Negro should do the same.' Third, such a goal was simply
an impossibility. Du Bois looked to a distant future when there could
be a black President of the United States; Garvey thought this a 'vain
assumption' as 'white men ... are not disposed to hand [power] over to
the negro or any other race'.[14]

Taking advantage of his experience in printing and journalism, in
August 1918 Garvey launched the UNIA weekly paper *Negro World*.
In time, this would have a huge global impact. Each edition of ten
to sixteen pages featured a statement from Garvey on the front page
addressed to the 'Fellowmen of the Negro Race'. It soon had a circulation of over 50,000. Unlike its many rivals, the paper refused to carry
adverts for skin-lightening or hair-straightening products. Garvey was
adamantly opposed to 'trying to bleach ourselves up, straightening out
our hair to make it look like the white man's'.[15]

Reflecting the continued influence of Booker T. Washington's
programme of material uplift, Garvey also formed what he called the
Negro Factories Corporation (NFC). Despite the make-up of the population, there were very few genuinely black-run businesses in Harlem.
Garvey changed this by establishing, under the banner of the NFC,
a restaurant, a steam laundry, a tailor shop and a chain of grocery
stores, employing over a thousand people. 'Wealth is strength,' he later
declared, 'wealth is power, wealth is influence, wealth is justice, is liberty, is real human rights.' The plan was to establish similarly black-run
businesses across the US, the Caribbean and in Africa itself.[16]

But the project that, as the *Negro World* put it, 'stunned the world'
was the launch of the Black Star Shipping Line. In April 1919, Garvey
announced a plan to raise money to establish an 'all-Negro steamship
company that would link the coloured peoples of the world in commercial and industrial intercourse'. The potential material, political
and social benefits were immediately apparent. Shareholders would
enjoy dividends, black businesses would profit from priority access to

cargo space, and passengers would pay less for their fares (and be free of the prevailing unequal treatment of black steamship customers). Furthermore, pan-Africanism would be boosted by hugely increased communication and interchange between the black populations of the Atlantic. To top it all, here was an easy passage for those from the Americas who wanted to return to Africa to build the great free republic.[17]

The project was greeted with tremendous enthusiasm, and with Garvey declaring that 'any Negro not a stock-holder in the BSL will be worse than a traitor to the cause', money flowed in for a share in the business. Joshua Cockburn, one of the few black men in America to hold a maritime master's certificate, was recruited as captain of the first ship and, in a new impressive Captain of the Black Star Line uniform, joined the fund-raising efforts.[18]

'To walk into these offices', wrote a journalist visiting the UNIA, 'is to enter a fantastic realm in which cash shares and the imminence of destiny strangely commingle ... At the centre of those dreams, spinning them like so many webs ... is Marcus Garvey.' In fact, the small office was completely overwhelmed, and amid the chaos, unopened mail was being shoved into cupboards. The five company directors almost immediately fell out, with some accusing Garvey of being too ambitious and overbearing, and also of using Black Star Line money to prop up the Harlem businesses, none of which were making any real profits. Garvey responded that the directors lacked self-belief. Then, auditors from the organisation panicked and took the chaotic books to the District Attorney, who took no action, but kept a watchful eye thereafter.[19]

Also taking a keen interest was the General Intelligence Division of the Bureau of Investigations (BOI), the forerunner of the FBI. Its chief, J. Edgar Hoover, recruited the agency's first-ever full-time black employee as part of his successful ambition to infiltrate Garvey's organisation, even to the very top level. In 1921, Hoover would become deputy head of the BOI. Garvey became something of an obsession for Hoover, and he was determined to bring him down.

By September 1919, Garvey had raised a staggering $50,000, easily enough for a deposit on the BSL's first vessel. None of the directors had any experience of the complicated maritime regulations and insurance issues involved, so responsibility for purchasing the ship was passed to Captain Joshua Cockburn.

With so much money sloshing about, and organisation lax, it was inevitable that Garvey's project would attract chancers and sharks. Cockburn was perhaps the worst. He succeeded in purchasing a ship, but it was a terrible deal. The SS *Yarmouth* was a thirty-three-year-old tramp steamer with a modest cargo capacity of just 1,400 tons. For this, he paid $165,000, with a 10 per cent deposit. It almost immediately required expensive repairs. It was later reckoned that the ship's true worth was about $25,000. Cockburn didn't mind: he took kickbacks from both the seller and the repairers.

But Garvey had his first ship, and at noon on 31 October, to the accompaniment of the UNIA band, thousands gathered to witness its launch from the 135th Street pier on the Hudson River. Somehow, the rickety vessel staggered to the Caribbean, where it was met by cheering crowds in Cuba, Costa Rica, Panama and Jamaica. It was clear that the shipping line had captured the imagination of blacks across the world. Even Du Bois was impressed by this 'definite plan to unite Negrodom'. In early 1920, two further vessels were purchased: a pleasure yacht for $60,000, which they hoped to convert to freight, and a paddle steamer for $35,000. Of profits, and therefore dividends, there was as yet no sign, although Cockburn was exposed and sacked in July.[20]

With his gaze now firmly set on the global scene, in August 1920 Garvey staged 'The International Convention of Negroes of the World' in New York. With 2,000 delegates from twenty-five countries, it was 'the most representative gathering of Blacks ever'. From this came 'The Declaration of the Rights of the Negro People of the World', which included attacks on education systems that taught black children that whites were 'superior to the Negro race', and on 'the exhibition of picture films showing the Negro as a cannibal'. There were plenty of plans for practical uplift on the Booker T.

Washington model, but also a political angle, namely, that 'the culmination of all efforts of the UNIA must end in a Negro independent nation on the continent of Africa'.[21]

The emphasis was on display and grand gestures. The convention had started with a silent march of delegates and members through the streets of Harlem. This was followed by a parade of UNIA units. Garvey had formed the 'Universal African Legion', 200-strong, young men with black uniforms with red and green stripes down the leg and ceremonial swords. Marching behind them to the music of the UNIA band were 200 'Black Cross Nurses' in matching uniforms, followed by the Black Eagle Flying Corps, also with uniforms and officers. The pageantry attracted thousands of onlookers.

After the march, 25,000 gathered in Madison Square Garden to hear Garvey speak. A BOI informant reported that 'As far as I can see, the movement has ceased to be simply a nationalist movement but among the followers it is like a religion.'[22]

As the convention drew to a close, representatives from Sierra Leone and Liberia were made 'Potentate Leaders of the Negro People of the World', with annual salaries, in theory, of up to $10,000. Other close supporters would be given titles such as Duke of Uganda, Baron of the Zambezi and Duke of the Nile. Garvey himself, 'arrayed in a flowing robe of crimson slashed with green', was elected 'Provisional President of Africa'. A flag (black, green and red) and anthem ('Ethiopia Arise!') for the new republic were unveiled.[23]

The convention had a massive international impact. UNIA divisions across the world increased from 95 to 418. Soon, Garvey was claiming that he had 4 million members.

Others, however, had found the whole populist business a severe embarrassment. Du Bois described the UNIA pageantry as like 'a dress-rehearsal of a new comic opera'. His view was shared by fellow university graduates among the Afro-American community, who saw autodidact Garvey as an unwelcome upstart. A. Philip Randolph, who had been one of Garvey's key early supporters when he arrived in Harlem, wrote that Garvey 'has succeeded in making the Negro the laughing stock of the world'. The conservative black paper *The New York Age* noted that the incessant demand for support for the Black Star Line throughout the proceedings had given 'the whole meeting the appearance of a gigantic stock jobbing scheme, put forth under the guise of racial improvement'.[24]

Du Bois also criticised the idea of an African republic, in part because of the 'natural fear which it threw into the colonial powers'. At his Pan-African Congresses, Du Bois did address specific colonial issues such as the exclusive right of white Kenyans to trial by jury, and did call for Africans to take part in governing their countries as fast as their development permitted, or more exactly when they had moved on from being 'uncivilized peoples'. At the 1923 Congress, though, he admitted that his organisation was 'primarily interested in the local American race problems ... [and] did not feel they could do anything further for the Pan-African movement except in a small way'.[25]

In contrast, Garvey's rhetoric presented a radical and immediate challenge to the British Empire, particularly in Africa and the Caribbean. 'Everybody knows that the British have built themselves up on the blood and wealth of the Negros, especially of Africa and the West Indies,' he declared. *The Times* reported from the celebrations at the launch of SS *Yarmouth* Garvey's announcement that '400 million black men are beginning to sharpen their swords for the war of races'. ('Words that have been making trouble for me ever since,' Garvey later wrote.) At the convention's Madison Square Garden speech, the reporter noted Garvey's resolve that 'Africa, not in patches but in entirety, should become a black republic, peopled, administered, and exploited by negroes.' In the same speech, Garvey demanded 'Africa for the Africans ... War is the only method by which men can obtain salvation.' After the lynching of a pregnant woman the year before, when her belly was slit open and her unborn child trampled underfoot, Garvey had furiously declared, 'when they lynch a Negro below the Mason-Dixon Line ... since it is not safe to lynch a white man in any part of America, we shall press the button and lynch him in the great continent of Africa'. 'We pledge our blood to the battlefields of Africa,'

Garvey said at the convention. 'We mean to retake every square inch of the twelve million square miles of African territory.'[26]

Garvey frequently intervened in imperial issues. He sent telegrams of support to Eamon de Valera in Ireland and to Gandhi after Amritsar, sending 'best wishes from 400,000,000 Negroes ... for the speedy emancipation of India from the thralldom of foreign oppression'. After the Thuku shootings in Nairobi, he sent a telegram to Lloyd George protesting against 'the brutal manner in which your government has treated the natives of Kenya East Africa'. He also organised a demonstration in New York.[27]

However, the greatest immediate impact, particularly in West Africa, came from the Black Star Line. Novelist Joyce Cary, who was a district officer in Nigeria at the time of the convention, remembered that in the white newspapers, Garvey 'cut a comic figure'. But he was amazed to be told by an illiterate man in the deepest north about 'Garvey's ship'. 'Garvey's manifesto went all through Africa,' Cary wrote. 'News spreads, above all, if it tells of a black victory.' To his Hausa political agent, Musa, 'the black steamship appeared like a startling triumph. He thought nothing of manifestos or the rights of peoples, but he was clever enough to set great value on economic power, and the control of expensive machinery. He had not expected to hear of black men owning and driving ocean-going ships, and he was deeply moved. He felt his colour.' From Liberia, the US military attaché reported to Washington: 'You would be surprised to find how Garvey has worked up an interest in his scheme all along the West coast ... any all black proposal, well-financed, cannot fail to succeed in Africa. Race consciousness is just that strong.'[28]

It wasn't all about 'race consciousness'. Because of the way the economies of West Africa had been structured, black business owners had a huge amount to gain from the potential success of the Black Star Line.

As elsewhere across the empire, West Africa's economy had been redirected towards external markets, making the colonial endeavour self-sustaining through customs revenues, and profitable for British and European business. Trade, dominated by Liverpool companies mostly headquartered in the Liver Building itself, was originally based on the export of groundnuts, cocoa, gold, palm oil and tin, in exchange for simple consumer goods like cloth, gin and lamps. In the 1860s and 1870s, European traders were based offshore on the island of Fernando Po to avoid tropical disease. They rarely traded with the final consumer, but passed on goods to African merchants and market women locally.

Medical advances in malaria treatment and other prophylaxis, hand in hand with colonial expansion, saw European merchants increase their networks along the rivers and then railway lines, displacing and undermining indigenous commercial elites, but there still remained prominent African trading companies.

Local industries suffered from competition from cheap imports. Kobina Sekyi would urge Africans not to use inessential imports, and to revive traditional industries of spinning, weaving, pottery making, carving and iron smelting. In fact, he wanted his country to have nothing to do with development along European lines in terms of industrialisation and international trade, because it would lead to the inequality and pronounced social classes he had seen and so disliked in England. Instead, West Africans should, he suggested, concentrate on internal trade and barter.[29]

But the volume and value of international trade, particularly from Nigeria and the Gold Coast, had increased dramatically in the first twenty years of the twentieth century, from £7.9 million to £79 million. It was one of the great imperial success stories. For Nigeria, the most important commodity was palm oil and kernels, needed to feed what Albert Demangeon called 'the great centre of oil and soap works' of Liverpool. For the Gold Coast, cocoa dominated. First sold on the international market in 1885, by 1911 the Gold Coast was exporting more than 40,000 tons a year (worth £1.5 million) and was the world's leading producer. This rose to between 165,000 and 213,000 tons in the 1920s, supplying half the world's consumption and making up 80 per cent of the country's exports by value.[30]

Almost all of this production was in the hands of small family operations established without the assistance of European capital. Many became wealthy (Sekyi satirises the nouveau riche cocoa farmer in *The Blinkards*). Unsurprisingly, in the years immediately preceding the war the success of the crop attracted European interests looking to establish plantations. But they came up against Governor Hugh Clifford. Stung by his earlier experience in Borneo, he was determined to ensure that the indigenous inhabitants were not sacrificed to big business. Rebuffing the large-scale capital interests, he argued that the large and reliable labour force on which plantations depended needed either compulsion or immigration – as he had seen with tea in Ceylon and on rubber estates in Malaya – as well as expensive European overseers. Furthermore, he wrote, 'A plantation system is not a society; it is an economic agglomeration erected for the pursuit of profit. It substitutes itself for those primitive societies which in sickness and in health sustain their members.'[31]

Similarly in Nigeria, palm oil production was largely in the hands of indigenous farmers. In sharp contrast to Kenya, where more than 40 per cent of adult males worked for some form of European enterprise, in Nigeria and the Gold Coast it was 2 and 6 per cent respectively (mostly in mining, which was European-dominated).

Strongly backed by the CO, Clifford in Nigeria would continue the policy of preserving 'native production'. This would bring him up against arguably the most powerful businessman in the empire, William Lever, Lord Leverhulme.

Alongside his earlier highly profitable investment in the Pacific Phosphate Company, Lever had substantial interests in copra across the Pacific. But he had long been eyeing up West Africa as a source of palm products for his giant soap and margarine works at Port Sunlight on the Wirral. He made his move in 1910, buying out three existing trading companies. Seeing the business as inefficient, he quickly established mills with modern machinery. But he soon encountered problems when local producers held back their stocks in efforts to raise the price, leaving the mills idle. What was needed was plantations and therefore control of the supply. 'The African native will be happier, produce the

best, and live under the larger conditions of prosperity', Lever wrote
in the early 1920s, 'when his labour is directed and organized by his
white brother who has had all these million years start of him.' When
Clifford refused to comply with his wishes, Lever launched a string of
personal attacks, calling him a 'bureaucratic and autocratic' official.
Clifford's administration, he alleged, 'refused to see the march of
progress'. Eventually, Lever gave up and concentrated instead on establishing vast palm concessions in Belgian Congo, where production
increased nine-fold.[32]

Protection of 'native production' and local land ownership was welcomed by organisations such as the National Congress of British West
Africa, but there were still complaints about European dominance of
other areas. Local businesses struggled to be given credit by the banks,
all of which were foreign-owned and distrusted Africans, while liberal
credit was given to European, Syrian and Lebanese concerns. Some
producers felt they were being ripped off by European buyers. In the
Gold Coast, rivals Cadbury-Fry and Rowntree's, riding the wave of a
hugely increasing demand for chocolate in the UK, were accused of
combining to reduce the price of cocoa.

The end of the 're-stocking boom' and the great slump of mid-1920
to 1922 hit Nigeria particularly hard. The value of trade halved from
1920 to 1921. Everyone suffered, but the African producers and traders
most of all. The European businesses responded with a wave of amal-
gamations, sheltering under the wings of big international combines.
This, of course, increased their purchasing power. Before the war competition between the numerous European firms meant that producers
were paid a fair price, in fact a greater proportion of the prevailing
market price than they were ever consistently to receive again. When
the slump came, many African merchant houses, unable to secure
credit or access international protection, went to the wall. Wealthy
independent businessmen of 1919–20 were back at their desks in 1921
working as clerks and agents for the now completely predominating
European survivors. So, by 1923, trade in goods for import or export
were firmly in European hands.

No more completely was this the case than in the issue of shipping. European firms were operating what was essentially a closed-shop agreement between themselves to exclude everyone else. African farmers or middlemen who tried to undertake the shipping of their produce got nowhere.

Kobina Sekyi summed it up. Garvey's Black Star Line should be welcomed, he said, as a chance to take on the 'gigantic combinations that are being formed in England for the undisguisable purpose of establishing a sort of legal or legalised monopoly of trade'.[33]

When he heard Garvey's plan for the Black Star Line, Herbert Macaulay sat down to write the Jamaican a long letter. A hand-written draft, with numerous corrections, is to be found at the National Archives in Ibadan. His enthusiasm for the scheme and his desire for it to succeed is evidenced by the time and effort he took to provide practical details of ports, lighthouses, infrastructure, imports and exports, and what Garvey would need locally in terms of staff, warehousing and other shipping facilities. 'It is the duty of every Negro', Macaulay explained, 'to do all he can towards the consummation of so noble and laudable an object.'[34]

'Negro enterprise', he wrote, had been seriously handicapped thanks to the Europeans' 'sweet monopoly of the whole of the Ocean Carrying trade of the west Coast of Africa'. This was 'prone to strengthen the position of the European merchants at the expense of the entire negro trading population'.

He made it clear that this monopoly would not be surrendered lightly. Although Macaulay praised the local representative of the mighty Elder Dempster shipping line as a man who treated everyone from any race equally, he warned Garvey that he should expect to face 'unrelenting competition on the West Coast of Africa ... founded upon commonplace commercial jealousy intermixed occasionally with intolerable "racial prejudice"'. Furthermore, English firms involved in trade were aggressive enough to overpay for produce and undersell imports in order to see off newcomers. He alerted Garvey, as well, that the Black Star Line would struggle to obtain a supply of coal, as the one productive mine was firmly in the hands of the government. There were many different languages in Nigeria, Macaulay warned, but he went on to say that, happily, English was fast becoming a lingua franca.

On the political side of Garvey's project, Macaulay was a little less forthcoming. 'European greed ruthlessly tore your ancestors and ours away from Africa, their hearth and home ... throughout four hundred years of Slavery and suffering,' he wrote. So, how could the empire object to repatriation of 'the descendants of those negroes'? But Macaulay's vision, although of 'solidarity of the race', was in the framework of 'sound national organizations', not quite the same thing as Garvey's all-Africa republic. Furthermore, he expressed pride that the '17 million of your countrymen of unmixed blood ... form an important position of the vast British Empire over which the glorious sun never sets'. At the top of the letter, perhaps with one eye on the potential censor, he declared that the Union Jack, flying over Government House in Lagos, 'forms an unblemished emblem of Justice and Fairplay, or Truth, Equity, and Unity, the unmistakable ensign of British national philanthropy'. German 'methods of colonization', in contrast, had been 'brutal'.

But, if reluctant to endorse Garvey's anti-imperialism, he ended on a positive note for the Black Star Line, declaring that 'There is sufficient Produce and raw material in Nigeria to supply the Markets of the whole world.' He was confident, he said, of Garvey's success and looking forward to a time when 'Black people' scattered across the world could 'combine their economic and racial interests' and thereby 'consign "Racial Prejudice", that European cankerworm, which preys with vast delight upon the manhood of the Negro Race ... to linger in a morbid condition until the end of time'. Sending 'heart-felt prayers for the success of the Black Star Line', he signed off as 'Your Fellowman of the Negro Race'.

Other West African voices embraced the idea of taking on the European cartels and providing for the black traders who faced shortage of space on British ships. For the Sierra Leone *West African Mail and Trade Gazette*, the project 'fills us all with the contagious and unkindling power of rapturous enthusiasm'. Joseph Casely Hayford, writing in the *Gold Coast Leader*, pointed out that throughout the African colonies, 'European enterprise of every description is encouraged and welcomed'. Why should obstacles any longer be placed in the way 'of the enterprise of the African abroad?' His West African Congress resolved that the Black Star Line should be supported, 'it being a Negro undertaking and its object being solely for the purpose of giving us more and brighter prospects as Africans in our commercial transactions'.[35]

But the West African university-educated elite, like Macaulay, were less keen on the idea of the upstart, low-class Garvey leading an African republic outside the empire. Unsurprisingly, the most vitriolic opponent was the conservative *Nigerian Pioneer*. For them, Garvey was the 'self-styled president of the moon' and with his gaudy uniforms would make a 'splendid prospect' for a Gilbert and Sullivan comic opera. His idea of an African republic was a 'pipe-dream ... "Africa for the Africans" like other beautiful and hysterical cries will end in smoke. West Africa has inseparably and indissolubly woven her destiny with that of Empire.' Furthermore, with his talk of black pride, the paper echoed Du Bois that this was unforgivably adding 'fuel to the fire of racial hostility'.[36]

African Messenger pointed out 'that while numbers of sensible people were in sympathy with many of Garvey's ideas, it was impossible for them to accept his absurd claims to the Presidency of Africa, or to approve of his disposal of high-sounding titles, or other dubious methods of raising funds'. The *Times of Nigeria* supported the Black Star Line – 'a great and even sublime conception for which everybody of African origin will bless the name of Marcus Garvey'. But 'the inclusion, however, of such a tremendous political plan, as the founding of a Pan-African Empire, is too obviously ridiculous to do aught else than alienate sympathy from the whole movement'. Furthermore, the future seemed to belong not to a huge African state, but to the European-created nation states, however randomly they had been put together.

Kobina Sekyi wrote that they had much to learn from Garvey's 'industrial or economic organisation', but argued that the diaspora in the
West Indies and the US had 'inherited Anglo-Saxon prejudices against
Africa' – to the extent of being 'black white men' – and so were disqual-
ified for leadership there. This was the attitude picked up by a police
intelligence report on Congress: 'They recognise they are much better
off under British Rule and have no desire to change ... for American
Negro rule.' The Gold Coast press had long expressed reservations
about the efficacy of black Americans in solving Africa's problems.[37]

Nonetheless, in the wake of the eye-catching August 1920 International
Convention in New York, UNIA groups sprang up in a number of
African colonies. The first in West Africa was in Sierra Leone, which
had actually sent a delegate – George Marke, a Methodist minister –
to the Convention, but the largest and longest-lasting was in Lagos. It
announced its formation in the *Lagos Weekly Record* in late September.
Ignoring Garvey's political programme, and carefully laying out its
loyalty to the Crown, it spelled out its aims: the 'establishment of technical and industrial schools for boys and girls and the organization of
local and commercial economic enterprises on co-operative lines'.[38]

    Even this was too much for the *Nigerian Pioneer*, who advised 'the
Police to keep an eye on the Garveyites in Nigeria'. The *Lagos Weekly
Record* countered that although they disliked Garvey's 'aggressive and
militaristic tendencies', they supported 'his doctrine of worldwide cooperation among Negroes for their economic and industrial upliftment' and
stressed that the Lagos branch was 'neither traitorous nor revolutionary'.[39]

    In August 1922, the Colonial Office received a confidential report
from the British Consul in Senegal. Five men from Sierra Leone,
who had arrived there speechifying and looking to establish a UNIA
branch, had been swiftly and ruthlessly deported. The *Negro World* had
been banned across the French colonies with stiff penalties for anyone
found with a copy – five years' imprisonment in Senegal, the death
sentence in Dahomey. The Consul asked whether the British should
take the same firm line.[40]

Clifford was asked his opinion. He reported that a very few 'mal-content Africans living in Nigeria' had contributed to the Black Star Line, but said he was confident that 'from what I know of the West African negro, I feel certain that his notorious ability to take care of himself where money is concerned will operate as an effectual check upon any extensive exploitation of the people of Nigeria by Garvey'. The Lagos UNIA, he said, was harmless.[41]

Nonetheless, the authorities put whatever obstacles they could in UNIA's way. For a long time, until they employed lawyer J. E. Shyngle to argue their case, they were refused a band permit (having a brass band was part of the UNIA's constitution). When they asked the government about supplies of coal for the Black Star Line, it was made clear that none would be forthcoming. Then the Church was pressured into refusing the group the use of any of its premises for their Saturday evening meetings.[42]

Alongside these meetings, the group, composed of some 300 members, mostly lawyers, journalists, teachers, clergymen, civil servants and merchants, held fund-raising and social functions, concerts, talks, dances and produce sales. The original leadership consisted of a Nigerian, newspaper journalist Ernest Ikoli, and two West Indians: John Ambleston, a successful builder and contractor, and Amos Shackleford. After only a couple of months, Ikoli resigned complaining that Garvey lacked the necessary 'statesmanship'; 'he should shed some of his dreams and come down to hard facts', he wrote. Leadership then fell, more than anyone else, to Amos Shackleford.

Shackleford was born in Buff Bay, Jamaica in 1887. His father was a saddle-maker. He attended elementary school, had some private tuition, and at sixteen joined the Jamaica railway, starting on 15s a week and working himself up by 1912 to the position of station agent on 45s. The same year, an appeal came from Nigeria Governor Lugard for skilled West Indian staff to work on the Nigerian railways. Shackleford jumped at the chance: it had been his childhood ambition, he later said, 'to return to West Africa to become one of the people of his ancestral home'.[43]

He spent three years managing a fairly large station before briefly returning to Jamaica. But he was back in Nigeria in January 1918. Most West Indians in Nigeria were employed on the railway and lived in separate quarters away from the local population, with whom there was little mixing and little sign of pan-African sentiment. They almost always returned home when their contract ended. The West Indians were accused of an attitude of 'overlordship' towards Nigerians. For their part, the West Indians disliked being lumped with 'natives' when it came to issues like rules on the consumption of spirits (banned for Africans, allowed for Europeans). Shackleford was different, making many Nigerian friends, including Herbert Macaulay. He was also a regular correspondent of John E. Bruce, the veteran American pan-Africanist.[44]

On his return to Nigeria, Shackleford secured a position as head clerk in S. Thomas and Company, a highly successful Nigerian-owned commercial firm in Lagos. Here, he received his apprenticeship in accountancy and saw at first hand the difficulties facing African firms against stiff European competition, particularly after the arrival of the slump. 'Trade is at present so stagnated out here that all the native firms and middlemen are gone to the wall,' he wrote to Bruce in November 1920.

A year later, now a leader in the UNIA, Shackleford decided to strike out on his own. With the import–export business in disarray, he opted to go into local manufacturing. Spotting a gap in the Lagos market, he imported state-of-the-art bread-making machinery, employed a chief baker from Sierra Leone, and launched what would be a highly successful business. Thanks to various innovations – a dough brake which accelerated the fermentation process, using hops as a raising agent rather than palm wine (yeast not being available), and a system of vendors paid on commission – he was soon known as the 'Bread King', selling up to 8,000 loaves a day. (In Lagos, non-English speakers started calling bread 'Shackleford'.) Now a rich man, he would go on to form other companies concentrating on inland transport.

Although a pan-Africanist, Shackleford never changed his name to an African one, nor wore 'native' dress. He was an organist and active member of the Christ Church in Lagos. He played cricket. Under his leadership the Lagos UNIA remained apolitical – his political energies were directed towards not racial or cultural nationalism, but the territorial nationalism of Macaulay's NNDP, of which he was a founding member and vice-president.[45]

But as a black man of the diaspora who had repatriated himself to 'Mother Africa' and at the same time, through his own efforts, become materially successful and independent, as much as anyone he lived the Garveyite dream.

Unlike the French, the British colonial authorities in Africa remained fairly relaxed about Garveyism. But then, at the beginning of 1923, news came in a dispatch from the British Consul-General in New York that 'so-called Provisional President of Africa' Marcus Garvey was now planning a grand world tour, taking in all the principal cities of the US and Canada, as well as the Caribbean and, for the first time, Africa.[46]

In the meantime, Garvey had been ratcheting up his anti-imperial rhetoric. 'Rome failed,' he declared, 'Great Britain is on the verge of collapsing. We have become alert to its subversive propaganda of "divide and rule" among the subject races.' 'Let us pray for the downfall of England,' he said on another occasion; 'as the Tsar lost his throne some years ago, so I fear that George of England may have to run for his life'. The attacks were increasingly directed towards Britain's African Empire, 'the biggest game in the hunt of nations and races'. The British Empire, he said, 'owes its present financial existence to the wealth which has been recruited from Africa, the wealth that we Negroes could have controlled'. It was time 'to make it warm for all aliens in Africa ... if England wants peace, if France wants peace,' he said, 'I suggest to them to pack up their bag and baggage and clear out of Africa.'[47]

As concerned correspondence flowed between the various British officials in Africa, Colonial Secretary the Duke of Devonshire was initially reluctant to see any overreaction, suggesting that there should

be as little interference as possible with Garvey's movements. To pro-
hibit his landing in African colonies 'would probably do more harm by
magnifying his importance than if he were treated as a person of little
consequence'. Under-Secretary of State William Ormsby-Gore agreed,
as did some colonial officers on the spot, who considered that Garvey's
'preposterous claims' meant that he was little threat.[48]

But Devonshire wanted a uniform policy across the colonies, and it
soon became clear that the weight of local opinion as well as some in
London were against any such complacency. 'Marcus Garvey may be
a wind-bag,' one Under-Secretary of State minuted to Ormsby-Gore,
'but his speeches are likely to be dangerous. If any lead is given, it
should be in favour of exclusion.' The Colonial Secretary of Nigeria
expressed concerns that the purpose of the visit would be to collect
money 'on false pretences from the most ignorant and gullible sections of the semi-educated African populace of the west Coast', and
reported that they were going to refuse him entry and had banned the
importation of *Negro World* as 'coming within the category of seditious, defamatory, scandalous or demoralizing literature'. The Colonial
Secretary of Gambia agreed.[49]

On 9 July 1923, Sir Herbert Read, Assistant Under-Secretary of
State, concluded that Garvey had a larger following in the West Indies
than he had in West Africa, but 'it is in Africa that he wants to institute his Negro State: consequently his object must be to stir up trouble
and to incite sedition in Africa ... if his movement is ever to achieve
anything he must also create a spirit of unrest in Africa. I agree that it
is undesirable that he should land in West Africa.'

By September 1923, everyone was in agreement: such was the threat
he posed, it was decided that Garvey should not set foot in Africa and
would be denied a visa to visit any of the British Empire territories.[50]

In fact, by this time the Garvey project was in serious trouble on a
number of fronts. Garvey's repatriation scheme had gone as far as the
UNIA buying a few hundred worthless acres in Liberia. The hope was
that here would be the germ of the great African republic. Garvey's

plan was to 'send our scientists, our mechanics and our artisans'. They would build railways, schools and factories, ready for the influx to be called 'home'. In Liberia, the UNIA negotiators found themselves faced with staggering levels of corruption as well as an Americo-Liberian elite unwilling to see their privileges challenged, and under pressure from the French and British colonies on either side opposed to the UNIA establishing itself in Africa. They were also being wooed by US tyre company Firestone, keen to establish rubber plantations to break the British semi-monopoly. For the UNIA, it had been an expensive failure.[51]

The story of the flagship programme, the Black Star Line, was far worse. Ever since its launch at the end of 1919 it had stumbled from one mishap to another. The second two vessels proved to be buys as poor as the first and were constantly needing repairs. The few contracts the organisation secured were often poorly negotiated and some even ended up costing the company money. It didn't help that the line had launched into the teeth of the global downturn.

'Our ships were damaged at sea, and there was a general riot of wreck and ruin,' Garvey wrote in his September 1923 'The Negro's Greatest Enemy' article. Furthermore, the line was suffering 'robberies from within and without . . . employees started to be openly dishonest'. In August 1921, a general secretary absconded with a large amount of money, and by the end of the year active business was suspended and the Black Star Line faced bankruptcy.[52]

Across the UNIA operations, lacking the procedures and structures to process incoming money, pay salaries and prevent theft, there was factionalism, disunity and corruption. In his *Crisis* newspaper, Du Bois wrote of Garvey: 'He has been charged with dishonesty and graft, but he seems to me essentially an honest and sincere man with a tremendous vision, great dynamic force and an unselfish desire to serve.' But he was also 'dictatorial, domineering, inordinately vain . . . he has absolutely no business sense'. Certainly one of Garvey's greatest strengths, his huge confidence in himself, was a weakness – his domination of the organisation robbed even the most able of his colleagues of initiative.

Garvey seems to have had a gift for falling out with pretty much everyone he worked with, and then took to appointing people for apparent loyalty and enthusiasm rather than competence or even honesty.[53]

At the end of 1921, with the SS *Yarmouth* sold for scrap, the yacht stranded in Cuba beyond repair and the pleasure boat banked and rusting on the Hudson River, Garvey launched a new fund-raising appeal – to purchase a larger steamer capable of crossing the Atlantic to 'Mother Africa'. A vessel was found – the *Orion* – which was to be renamed the *Phyllis Wheatley*, after the iconic eighteenth-century black poet. This would be his downfall.

The mailout to supporters included a photograph of the *Orion*. But someone had changed the name on the picture to the SS *Phyllis Wheatley*, implying incorrectly that it was already owned by the Black Star Line. This gave the authorities the chance they had long sought, and on 22 January 1922, Garvey was arrested for mail fraud.

He was released on a $2,500 bail and headed for his base, Liberty Hall, Harlem, where he told his supporters that he had been the victim of a conspiracy. Most agreed with this view, and, with the trial date repeatedly delayed, Garvey assumed that the prosecution was struggling to build a case. In fact it was receiving plenty of help from UNIA members who had not been paid the salaries they had been promised, or who were otherwise estranged from their leader.

Garvey pressed on, planning his huge world tour, including Africa. He also, in June 1922, took the extraordinary step of holding a meeting in Atlanta with Ku Klux Klan Acting Imperial Wizard Edward Young Clarke. 'He believes America to be a white man's country,' Garvey told his supporters afterwards, 'and also states that the Negro should have a country of his own in Africa.' Effectively, they agreed that America's black population should be 'repatriated' to Africa. The alternative, for Garvey, was 'a terrible clash that will end terribly for [the black man]. We desire to prevent such a clash by pointing the negro to a home of his own.' Garvey even added that 'Between the Ku Klux Klan and the . . . NAACP, give me the Klan for their honesty of purpose towards the Negro.' But for many of even Garvey's most loyal supporters, including

UNIA activists who had suffered at the hands of the Klan while campaigning in the South, it was a baffling betrayal.[54]

In May 1923, Garvey's trial began at last. When his lawyer recommended a guilty plea, Garvey – supremely confident in his abilities to the last – decided to defend himself. Having irritated everyone with his overblown oratory, he was convicted on 21 June and sentenced to five years' imprisonment. 'The interests of France and Britain', Garvey concluded, had secured the verdict. 'I was convicted because I talked about Africa and about its redemption for Negroes,' he wrote.[55]

Enough supporters still rallied around to raise the huge sum of $15,000 for him to be released on bail from Tombs prison on 10 September 1923 to prepare his appeal. He immediately announced plans for a new shipping line. But when his appeal failed in February 1925, he was imprisoned again and then deported to Jamaica in 1927. He would never return to the United States, and although he remained politically active, he would never again reach anywhere near the heights of the international support and enthusiasm of 1919–23.

In his September 1923 article, Garvey laid the blame for this fall firmly at the feet of 'jealous and wicked members of my own race'. His 'fame among negroes was too much for other race leaders and politicians to tolerate. My downfall was planned by my enemies. They laid all kinds of traps for me.' He referenced the famous Booker T. Washington analogy of black people being like crabs in a barrel – if any attempted to climb out, the others would pull him back in. 'Most of the trouble I have had in advancing the cause of the race has come from negroes,' he wrote. 'Having had the wrong education as a start in his racial career, the negro has become his own greatest enemy,' he concluded. The following year he would tell an audience, 'We are going to emancipate ourselves from mental slavery because while others might free the body, none but ourselves can free the mind.'[56]

Despite the enthusiastic support of Macaulay and others, no Black Star Line ship ever made it to Africa, nor did Garvey himself. But many believe that his ideas had a lasting impact. At the end of 1924, a Gold

Coast newspaper, while questioning the 'methods' of Marcus Garvey, declared that 'there isn't a sane African living who in his heart of hearts can say he disagrees with, or protests against, his ideal'. In 1929, another West African paper declared that 'Marcus Garvey's name will go down in history as the man of the Negro race who more than any other has contributed to the racial awakening which is proving such a disturbing factor to white autocrats all over the continent. By preaching "Redemption of Africa" and "Africa for the Africans" he has set people thinking and has fixed a definite goal for the race to attain.'[57]

For many, Garvey catalysed their first questioning of colonial racist assumptions and colonial rule itself. But it would be a later generation than that of late 1923 that would act on his radical ideas. Nationalists of the future, including Dr Nnamdi Azikiwe and Dr Kwame Nkrumah, first Presidents of independent Nigeria and Ghana, would speak of their debt to reading Garvey as young men or teenagers. Jomo Kenyatta remembered that in 1921, when he was in his early twenties, Kenyan nationalists unable to read would gather round a reader of Garvey's newspaper the *Negro World* and listen to an article two or three times. Then they would 'run various ways through the forest carefully to repeat the whole, which they had memorized, to Africans hungry for some doctrine which lifted them from the servile consciousness in which Africans lived'.[58]

Norman Manley, who would lead Jamaica to democracy and independence – a process he frequently described as a constant battle against black people's 'lethargy', 'culture of dependence' and 'self-contempt' – later paid tribute to 'the great work of those pioneers in America' who had helped 'Negroes inch forward'. But they had an 'assumption', he went on, that 'you had to maintain the good will and support of the white man by being nice to him and often by being subservient to him. And here was a man [Garvey] – and today we know he was a prophet – who dared in that world to get up and say: "Rise, you people, for you are God's children and you are the equal of any people in the world." And the man who did it, did it by such dramatic means that the whole world heard.'[59]

In November 1924, *Negro World* itself made a prediction: 'While Mr. Garvey might not live to see his dream come true, what he has said from the platform of Liberty Hall will be repeated in the years to come by unborn generations, and some day in the dark remote corners of Africa the Red, the Black and the Green will float.'[60]

32

Health and Education in West Africa

We are producing a type, puffed up with conceit and ridiculous imitation, which considered himself already to be the equal of the white man.

DOUGLAS FRASER, Nigeria, 1923[1]

L ike almost all nurses of the Overseas Nursing Association (ONA), Mary Lucas found arriving in West Africa exciting, surprising and somewhat overwhelming. The surroundings, climate, food and people were so different, she wrote home, 'one feels as though one has been dumped into a new world'.[2]

Mary Lucas's first job was at the Colonial Hospital in Lagos. 'It was a little strange at first,' she later wrote, 'dealing with native nurses who all looked really alike. It was a week or two before I could tell one from the other. Now I wonder how I ever failed to notice the difference.' But, she reported, 'I like it tremendously here and feel very well. I like everything and find the country most interesting . . . whatever happens I am ever so glad I came.'

The Colonial Nursing Association (renamed the Overseas Nursing Association in 1919) was founded in 1896 through the efforts of the wife of a colonial official in Mauritius, and funded by voluntary contributions. Its first two appointees were in the government hospital in Accra, where, according to the chief medical officer, they 'achieved a state of perfection' in the hospital and contributed to a 'marvellous reduction in the death rate'. The association recruited trained nurses, mostly middle-class daughters of engineers, professionals or businessmen. They had to be between the ages of twenty-five and forty – the average age was thirty – and unmarried. They were expected to be 'pleasant, capable women, with some tact, and of good private reputation', as a pre-war circular put it. Their behaviour should reflect the authority of the colonising power and do nothing to undermine it – 'A nurse's success is her own, but her failure is not her failure only.'[3]

They were contracted for three-year tours at £60 for the first year, then £5 extra each following year to a maximum of £80. There was an annual holiday of six weeks, and four months' leave with free passage after the completion of the three years.[4]

They were originally recruited to look after Europeans, but after the war increasingly were assigned to 'native' hospitals, where the training and supervision of African nurses became one of their main tasks.

Over the sixty or so years of its existence, the organisation sent some 8,000 women across the empire and further afield. In late 1923, there were ONA nurses in Iraq, Ceylon, Trinidad, Nevis, St Lucia, Siam, Shanghai, Fiji and elsewhere. Forty-two were in West Africa, and of these, twenty-six were in Nigeria.

The association gave single women a rare opportunity to travel, to have an adventure, as well as to fulfil professional ambitions. For some, it presented a chance to make a good marriage – a fifth of the first hundred recruits married while on their tour and therefore had to resign. The experiences of the nurses are presented in the large ONA archive of their letters back to Britain. They are mostly proud of their professional and personal achievements 'battling with primitive surroundings, conquering apathy and prejudice, learning a variety of languages and dialects, making important decisions without help or advice'. They saw themselves as 'women pioneers ... blazing civilisation's trail in the far corners of the world'. There were also a number who found the conditions and the frequent loneliness and isolation intolerable.[5]

After a few months, Mary Lucas was posted to Onitsha, a town on the Niger River, 400 miles east of Lagos, deep in the palm belt. She was the only nursing sister on the station, where about ten government officers lived on a hill overlooking the river.

Lucas described it as 'the most beautiful spot a human being could wish to live in although the living is a trifle primitive in parts'. It was 'a curious and rather happy life. Everyone working all day absorbed in their various shops, then soon after 5pm everyone gets equally busy playing tennis or golf, and then a much needed drink.' Several of the men – 'kindly and patient souls' – had taken it upon themselves to teach her golf on the hospital's course.[6]

There was great excitement when the post arrived, which would be announced by an approaching launch blowing three times on its siren. Then, 'the entire station retires into its fastnesses like rabbits and absorbs its mail'. Very occasionally, officials or businessmen would pass through the station, at which point there would be 'a spasm of gaiety, dinners and if there are one or two women someone seizes the opportunity to have a little dance, perhaps there will be about 6 ladies and 12 or more men. Then we have to do our duty nobly to the strains of the gramophone.'

'The warmth of the climate has suited me wonderfully,' she wrote after a few months, 'and the pleasure of the warm makes me feel contented like the cat in front of the fire. But for all that it is, underneath, a sinister country and you get glimpses at times of things that make you think.'

Eight months into her tour, she was posted to Calabar during the rainy season. 'Here it rains and rains and rains and sun seems to have forgotten how to function and the stars are lost to us.' There was a 'heavy, dull heat'. She found the city ugly and her clothes became covered with green mould. Here, she was working in the Native Hospital for six months. Although, she wrote, it was a 'credit to the doctors and sisters who have organised it', it was chaotic and filthy and she had never seen 'such a succession of horrible cases'. She started dreaming about them. 'And then the native staff! A doctor said to me "It is not the climate that kills, it is trying to teach the natives to work!"'[7]

At the Native Hospital, she wrote, 'endeavouring to care for my black brethren, or rather trying to teach them how to care for each other ... requires patience and again patience and then more patience for at least 8 good hours every day'. The proportion of good native nurses was very small, she said. 'You not only have to teach them how to do a thing by showing them how, but you have to watch them do it for days and weeks until it becomes a habit with them ... Some people say that the average African is a phenomenal liar and incapable of speaking the truth. I don't think that exactly. I think that their knowledge of English is so inaccurate that mostly they quite fail to understand you and just answer yes or no and trust to luck.' 'I shall be talking pigeon English when I get back,' she added. Transferring to the European hospital was 'the most blessed peace in comparison ... exquisite cleanliness and the comfortable well-furnished order of it ...'[8]

Some of the nurses, spread across the empire, did not wait to be moved back to the comparative serenity of the European hospitals. One nurse in Nigeria resigned, the secretary of the ONA reported, because 'she doesn't really care for nursing natives – finds the partly educated West African difficult and dishonest'. In Trinidad, two nurses resigned complaining about the appalling conditions in the Port of Spain Hospital. The acting Governor wrote to the ONA: 'these ladies accepted their appointments apparently under the impression that they would be treating European patients only; and as they entertained strong objections to nursing coloured patients under the supervision of medical officers, many of whom are of the coloured race, it was considered that their services would be of little use to this Government'.[9]

Across the wide range of letters in the ONA archive, there is a general pattern of many of the nurses moving from initial excitement in their far-flung posts to increasing frustration and exhaustion. In an early letter, Mary Lucas reported that lots of the British nurses in Nigeria, particularly those who had been out for more than a year, were counting the months and even days till the end of their tours. This she considered 'silly'. Later she wrote that 'perhaps one's views change after the first year, for you see people at the end of their tour get very used up, irritable, and generally tired out, and even now I realise I cannot do nearly so much as in England'.

Judith Godfrey, having worked in a European hospital in Nigeria where 'everybody was very nice', was posted to Sacred Heart Hospital in Abeokuta in south-west Nigeria, founded by a French Roman Catholic priest thirty years earlier. 'No doubt he has done wonderful work in a way but on the other hand of course it is not run anything like a European Governmental hospital and it is all very new and strange,' she wrote. Godfrey, in common with many of the ONA nurses, was working in maternity and female wards. She soon appreciated 'what a wide scope there is for improving the infant mortality of the country ... We very rarely get any normal midwifery cases, all abnormal and extraordinary ones at that.' Two women died in child-birth soon after her arrival. 'Really it is too awful to see what some of those poor creatures suffer,' she wrote, 'and a lot of it so unnecessary if they would only come in in time.' This presenting too late is a common theme across colonial medical accounts. Instead, Godfrey reported later, 'They usually go to their own doctors first ... with the most appalling results. We have had case after case come in dying from "ju-ju" ... Ante-natal classes and centres are very badly needed.' At the same time, she added, 'we are very badly equipped'.

Nearly a year later she was still at the missionary hospital. 'I have had very trying periods and occasionally felt it was almost too much for me but at least there's the consolation of knowing I did even a little for these poor creatures who suffer such agonies and mostly in such stoical silence.'[10]

During his campaign, Dr Adenyi Jones, one of the three victorious candidates in the Nigeria elections of September 1923, stressed that the first claim for his attention would be 'the Health of the masses and their sanitary condition'. As a visiting American Harvard researcher, Raymond Buell, noted of Nigeria, 'the situation with regard to public health is serious'. There had recently been an outbreak of plague in Lagos, and meningitis and relapsing fever in Northern Nigeria, with several hundred thousand deaths. Widespread malnutrition had contributed to what a medical report published the following year deemed an 'appalling' mortality rate. At the same time, infant mortality in West Africa was running at three times the rate in Britain, or in the case of the poor relation Gambia more than five times at a staggering 502 per 1,000.[11]

The Nigerian government estimates of 1923 called for 125 'medical officers'. But they had struggled to fill the quota, and there were thirty-five vacancies. Part of the problem was that European doctors were poorly paid compared to other officials. But even at full strength, this would only have meant one doctor per 160,000 people. A European member of the Legislative Council urged the government to do something to alleviate this 'appalling state of affairs', but was told that the government had gone to great lengths to recruit doctors, but 'no progress can be made until the people are induced to take preventative measures'. As noted elsewhere, unless it impacted on the efficiency of workers in the employ of Europeans, health was a low priority – in Nigeria in 1923 only 6 per cent of government expenditure was on health and sanitation (compared with 11 per cent in Belgian Congo). This translated to less than £2 a year per 100 people.[12]

An exception to this parsimony, Dr Adenyi Jones alleged, had been made for the new European cantonment, Ikoyi, just outside Lagos. In many quarters of Lagos there was 'squalor and misery existing ... owing to lack of proper drains and adequate sanitary arrangements'. This sharply contrasted, he went on, with 'the excellent conditions that are today obtaining at the "Garden City" at Ikoyi. One is tempted to presume that the sanitary progress of one section of the community (the European) is being considerably accelerated and highly maintained at the expense of the other section (the African); and that such inequitable and injudicious distribution of Colonial Revenue and Municipal Expenditure, calls for immediate redress.'[13]

Another key issue for the platform of the NNDP in the elections – and in the manifesto of the National Congress of British West Africa – was education, also a supposed blessing of imperial rule. Macaulay's party, reflecting public aspiration, called for compulsory primary education for all. Governor Clifford dismissed this ambition, pointing out that this would require 44,000 teachers and an annual expenditure of £2.5 million, nearly half the colony's revenue. At the time, education commanded less than 3 per cent of expenditure. Compared to the cost of government, the police, infrastructure projects and the cost of servicing debts raised in London, it was a low priority.[14]

Education spending was at a similar level for African children across the British colonies. (In Kenya in 1923, spending was reported as £22 per European child of school age, £2 5s per Indian and 1s per African child.) But they shared Nigerians' desire for what Chinua Achebe would call 'Education, the white man's knowledge . . . a collective aspiration of the entire community . . . the path to individual and family success.' The 1923 report from the Kenyan District of Machakos contained much that was discouraging. 'I doubt whether much progress has been made during the year,' wrote the district officer, W. F. G. Campbell. 'The apathy of the elders to all questions other than women, wine, and goats, is depressing.' But the one upside was that eight new schools had been constructed, and attendance had risen from 200 to 747. 'One of the brightest aspects of work amongst the Akamba', Campbell wrote, 'is the intelligence and keenness shown by the children once they begin to attend the schools . . . It is obvious that education is greatly desired by the children . . . I am convinced that once the children can be rescued from their drink-sodden fathers and be given an education, the tribe will go ahead more rapidly than in the past and take their part far more in the industrial life of the country where their natural mechanical instincts fit them in an exceptional manner to become firemen, artisans, carpenters, masons etc.' He urged 'most emphatically that nothing be done to curtail the vote for equipment for these out-schools ... it will be intensely discouraging if, when I have forced the children into school, equipment and teachers run short ... what is taking place is only what should have been occurring in past years'.[15]

In Nigeria, the 1923 report stated, 'the demand for schools is great throughout the country. Existing schools are overcrowded, and the supply by no means meets the demand.' Many of the schools, moreover, were 'of little or no value, being carried on by teachers who have no real qualification or competency to undertake such work'. Only a small number of schools had any government support; most were self-supported or run by the missions. The result was that there were only approximately 32,000 European-educated Nigerians, some 0.5 per cent of the population. Another 4 per cent had started but not finished primary education. There was only one government establishment – King's School in Lagos – dedicated to secondary education. Tertiary education abroad – to produce doctors, lawyers and engineers – was extremely rare. In 1921, Southern Nigeria had only seventy-three professionals of such training.[16]

In the Gold Coast, where education spending per hundred people (in a population only a tenth of Nigeria's) was much higher, 30,000 children were in elementary schools. There were 12,000 teachers, clerks and clergy, fifty lawyers and eleven doctors. This had allowed a programme, started during the war and enthusiastically promoted by Clifford as Governor, of replacing European officials with Africans. The motivation was largely financial: Africans doing the same job in the civil service would be paid only a sixth of the salary of a European, and would not be granted long periods of paid leave. The hope was that in twenty years, half of the European positions would be transferred to locals. 'No other colony in Africa has mapped out such an ambitious and such a liberal program,' reported Harvard researcher Raymond Buell, 'but no other colony in Africa has a class of Africans capable of taking advantage of such a program.'[17]

It was surprising, then, when Clifford's successor Gordon Guggisberg, in a speech on 9 June 1923 to the Manchester Chamber of

Commerce, sharply criticised the education system in the Gold Coast. 'The cry was all for education,' he said. 'They wanted universities, schools, technical schools, everything that was to be had in England. They wanted them right away, too. The trouble was to stop these demands and keep things going at a sound, safe and easy rate.'

There were three classes, Guggisberg said. A very small number of men had received their higher education in England, Scotland or Ireland. They were 'highly educated and intelligent', but their education was 'superficial ... The trouble was that in the great majority of these cases the Natives became denationalized ... They returned to the Gold Coast with ideas 200 or 300 years ahead of the rest of their race.' (An opinion, as we've seen, shared by his enemy Clifford.) The second class consisted, according to Guggisberg, of 70,000 to 80,000 'semi-educated boys who had been to primary schools, and a few girls who had a smattering of English and literary education generally'. They became the class of small traders and middlemen of the Gold Coast world. Some of them, he said, were extraordinary, good and very smart and intelligent, but most of them were 'not sufficiently educated to do their work thoroughly'. Part of the problem was they were 'without a vestige of character training'. This he defined as 'the kind of training which turned a boy into a decent fellow so that when kicked at school he learned to kick others about afterwards'. Instead this class 'knew just enough to be able to read and write and to absorb the literature of agitation, and to talk loudly about rights and other ridiculous things. As a class, they were prey to every agitator that cared to come along. In short, they were building up a pretty hornet's nest.' The third class were the 70 to 80 per cent of the population who were illiterate.[18]

This ambivalence about education, and dislike and distrust of the 'mission boys' or 'babus' that it created, was widespread. This was for a number of interconnected reasons. There was concern, as seen with Grimble in the Pacific, that the ambitions instilled by education would find no outlet in the particular environment and lead to frustration; or that, as in Malaya, it would deplete the manpower needed for agriculture. (The chief executive of an American company in India told an American journalist, 'If I were running this country I'd close every university tomorrow. It was a crime to teach them to be clerks, lawyers and politicians till they'd been taught to raise food.') This is linked to the idealisation of the peasant cultivator or pastoralist as the 'real' Indian or African, etc. A white settler in Kenya wrote of her admiration for the Masai – 'fierce, handsome and shrewd' in contrast to the almost comical Christian Africans, 'the parody of the white man'. The 'detribalised African', the concern went, had lost contact with the structures that sustained his society. Furnivall, writing about Burma, contended that Western education had caused 'alienation and estrangement'; the districts with the best records for education had the worst records for crime.[19]

Perhaps most importantly, European education, with its tradition of political thought that stressed the rights of the individual and the limits of state power, was creating, some thought, opponents to imperial rule. Australian Walter Crocker was a district officer in Nigeria. Beneath the tiny professional class, he wrote, was a large group who were 'quasi-literate, parasitic, litigious, showy, noisy, insolent, and as irresponsible as they are untrustworthy'. If the policy was for expanding education, he warned, 'the Government will find that it has, like Frankenstein, raised up a monster which will consume it'.[20]

Gordon Guggisberg's controversial speech in Manchester, reported in *West Africa* magazine, prompted a number of objections. The first, printed in the 18 August 1923 issue of the magazine, was from a European businessman resident in the Gold Coast. If the elementary schools were producing 'semi-educated' pupils, it was hardly their fault: 'Look at an average primary school, an African struggling with 40 or 50 boys, trying to teach them all sorts of things in a language he does not understand. It is the case of the blind leading the blind every time.' As for criticism of the 'intelligentsia', the vast majority were 'fine fellows' and, moreover, 'indispensable in all branches of business and service ... let us understand them better, so get to know who is who ... hand them a little much-needed sympathy, and Europeans will be surprised to find what hidden good qualities there are within them', he wrote.

The following week, the magazine printed a response from Kobina Sekyi to what he called Guggisberg's 'discouraging and depressing views'. School standards were low, Sekyi wrote, because poorly qualified Europeans were given all the most high-ranking positions. Taking issue with the claim that Africans educated in Europe – like, of course, Sekyi himself – were 200 or 300 years ahead, and seeing Guggisberg's comments as an attack on his West African Congress, he argued that it did not require a foreign education to put forward the doctrine 'that taxation should go with representation', or that 'it is bad for executive officers to try cases, or that it is unnatural to expect a judge to reverse his own judgment on appeal'. 'If he thinks the views of the Congress years in advance of the views of the man in the street, the Governor knows little indeed of the people over whom he rules,' Sekyi suggested.[21]

For Sekyi, Guggisberg's attack on education was an attempt 'to reduce the general level of our intelligence, and to prevent or retard the rise of any generation that will be able to defeat the aims of the Government'. But as well as the extent of education, there was also a keen debate about its content.

Sylvia Leith-Ross was the sister of the Lieutenant Governor of the southern provinces. She was appointed to the Education Department, becoming one of the minuscule number of women in any sort of position of authority in the empire in 1923. She lived in Lagos, in a gloomy and ramshackle bungalow. Nearby were slums of 'indescribable squalor'. However, this was 'infinitely preferable to exile in Ikoyi', she wrote, 'with its segregation from the smallest contact with the African life which it was the officials' duty and interest to know'. (There, Leith-Ross noted, 'wives were marooned all day ... with few household duties and little interest in the country'.)[22]

Leith-Ross reported that Nigerian children were being taught 'the height of the Chilterns, the Queens of England, and poems concerning primroses and Father Christmas' reindeer'. On one tour of inspection she came across 'the words "Eleanor of Aquitaine" written large on a blackboard in a primary school somewhere among the Yoruba ... stared at by twenty or thirty small and puzzled children'.[23]

It was a long-standing complaint that schools' curricula, what Blyden in 1908 would call 'training by aliens', 'either ignored or distorted African culture and emphasized European history and culture, thereby instilling the idea that the important developments of the past, even for Africans, occurred in Europe'. In *The Anglo-Fanti*, Sekyi's character by the age of twelve 'knows at least as much of English history and geography as the average English boy, [but] knows nothing about the great Ahuba festival'. An Indian journalist, writing in early 1923, drew a picture of an Indian school leaver as 'an emaciated being who could repeat like a machine the dates of births and deaths and of coronations of all the Kings and Queens of England'. (In Nigeria, Lugard had discouraged the teaching of the Stuarts as this might 'foster disrespect for authority'.) The Indian schoolchild, the journalist complained, 'is taught day after day to despise everything Indian and to admire everything British, with the result that he ends up being neither an Indian nor an Englishman, but a sorry ape'.[24]

Joseph Casely Hayford in his *Ethiopia Unbound* suggested the founding of a university in West Africa with a chair of history who would lay stress on 'Africa as the cradle of the world's systems and philosophies, and the nursing mother of its religions ... In short that Africa has nothing to be ashamed of [about] its place among the nations of the earth.' The suggested university – which became part of the Congress platform – should also promote the study of the Fanti, Hausa and Yoruba languages. The hope was that it would attract people from the United States and the West Indies as well as from Africa. 'Graduates that such a school will turn out', Casely Hayford wrote, 'will be *men* [his emphasis] – no effete, mongrel, product of foreign systems.'[25]

In fact, on 29 September 1923, Casely Hayford's estranged wife Adelaide was putting these ideas into direct action.

33

Freetown's Technical School for Girls

There is hardly any place on earth where the true
interests of women are neglected as in West Africa.

ADELAIDE CASELY HAYFORD[1]

O f the schoolchildren themselves, of course, there is precious little
record of how they felt and what they thought. One exception
is a book published in 1919 called *Our Days on the Gold Coast*. It was
put together by Lady Clifford to raise money for the Red Cross and
consists of a selection of responses to two essay competitions. The
first was to describe 'a typical day on the coast' (and includes an entry
from a nurse arriving for her first day at a hospital in Bathurst – 'I was
thunderstruck: the floor was clean, and that is all that could be said for
it'). The second was for schoolchildren under the age of sixteen. The
boys were asked to respond to 'What Work do I wish to do when I am
a Man and why?' The girls had 'Why Educated Girls ought to be able
to keep house clean and cook better than Uneducated Girls'. It goes
without saying that the responses should be read as from an untypical

group of children at the best European schools, and through the prism of the competition and the desire to please and to win, as well as the selection process of what was actually printed. Nonetheless, they are fascinating.[2]

Lady Clifford wrote a thoughtful introduction to the children's letters, noting how struck she was by what she calls 'filial piety' – the wish to provide for their parents and make them proud, and to repay the money spent on their education. She said this belonged to 'native tradition' – 'The strict recognition of family obligations'. She also commented on how many of the letters 'contain regretful or resigned allusions to the fact that the writer's parents, if themselves uneducated, regard European education with doubting or disapproving eyes, and believe that it is causing their children to become proud and undutiful, to lose their respect for the illiterate elders, and to despise native customs, native dress and native ideas.'[3]

The boys' letters are full of expressions of loyalty to Britain, made more urgent by the fact that the war was still going on at the time of writing. One respondent, wanting to become a soldier, hopes he can be 'as brave as Nelson'. The winner, chosen by Governor Clifford, was James Bannerman Thompson. You can see why Clifford appreciated his letter. His friends might laugh at him, Bannerman wrote, but despite being educated, it hadn't made him 'disregard manual labour'. He wanted to be a fisherman; after all, 'England, who we imitate doggedly to-day on the Gold Coast, has not shunned the fishing work.' He was awarded a cricket bat and ball and a certificate signed by the Governor. (Second prize was a football.)[4]

All the top-ranked girls' letters came from Catholic girls' schools. They all write a lot about cleanliness and hygiene and how the ability to read gives them access to recipes and other instruction books. The winner, who received a gold brooch, was Nellie Ampiah. She wrote, 'Uneducated girls think that they must be bold and answer roughly ... educated girls know they are bound to be subject to their husbands, and to do all they can to make him happy.' Theresia D. Grunitzky received a certificate of merit. She wrote, 'It would be nice if every girl here was educated as she would know how to do all things much better, she would be like the Europeans, who know how to do all things for themselves.' Another wrote that she 'would like to be like little girls at England'.[5]

Adelaide Casely Hayford wanted to do things very differently.

On 29 September 1923, Casely Hayford opened the doors of what would be the first of its kind – an African-run technical secondary school for girls in Freetown, Sierra Leone. Her school was determined to be different: in the place of celebrating everything European, the girls would be taught to be proud of being African; instead of simple preparation for marriage, they would be trained to be independent and self-sufficient. It was as unique and extraordinary as its founder.

She was born Adelaide Smith in Freetown in 1868, into a family that reflected Sierra Leone's unique history. A European trading station from the seventeenth century, by the end of the following century Freetown had found itself the destination of groups of black people from distinct backgrounds. It was supposed to be a place of new-found freedom and independence. First, under a scheme put together by British abolitionists led by Granville Sharp, destitute black people from Britain's cities had been rounded up and shipped there to make new lives for themselves. Soon after that, loyalist blacks from the United States who had sided with Britain during the Revolution started arriving. They were followed by some 500 Jamaican Maroons, who had been exiled from their island to Nova Scotia after the end of the Second Maroon War. Finally, between 1809 and 1863, when Freetown was the base of the Royal Navy's anti-slavery squadron, some 26,000 'recaptive' Africans who had been rescued from slave ships off the coast were deposited there, where many were taught English and Christianised. The descendants of these groups came to be known as 'Krios' and for a long time dominated the colony and its interior, where a number of African groups lived under a protectorate system. This made Freetown the most Christian and Westernised of all the coastal settlements. The richest Krios were soon sending their sons to be educated in Britain.[6]

All of these groups, and more, are represented in Adelaide's family tree. On her mother Anne's side, her great-grandfather was a 'recaptive' Bambara butcher who married one of the original settlers from Nova Scotia and they became rich property owners. Although both illiterate, they sent their children, including Adelaide's grandmother Hannah, to England to be educated. Returning to Freetown, Hannah married the son of a Maroon mother and an English former colonial surgeon. Adelaide's paternal grandfather, William Smith, was a Yorkshireman who had come to the Gold Coast in about 1820 to work for the African Company. He later moved to Sierra Leone and was appointed Commissary Judge for the Mixed Courts in Freetown, whose task was to prosecute slavers and attempt to reunite scattered families. Smith, who owned substantial properties in Freetown, married an English woman and had a son, but also had another son by a Fanti woman. This was William Jr – Adelaide's father.

William Jr worked in his father's court and rose quickly up the ranks. He was also recruited as a Wesleyan lay preacher. His first marriage was to the daughter of Governor Kenneth Macaulay and a recaptive woman. They had seven children before her death aged thirty-four. His second marriage was to Anne, who also had seven children, the second youngest being Adelaide. So there was inherited wealth on both sides of the family.[7]

When Adelaide was just short of four years old, the family took what she would later call 'a very unusual move'. Krios were used to sending their children to school in England, but on his retirement in 1872, William Jr moved his whole family there. Adelaide's earliest memory, she later wrote, was not of Africa but of the sea voyage and arriving in England. They lived first in Norwood, a suburb of London, and then moved to St Helier in Jersey. His wife Anne's health was almost certainly a factor in the decision. But she remained poorly and died just under three years later, shortly before Adelaide's seventh birthday.

In Jersey, where apparently they were the only black family, they lived in a 'big rambling old-fashioned house, with a large garden'. Apart from 'the one dark blot' of her mother's death, Adelaide's childhood there was, she wrote, 'glorious ... characterized by a spontaneous

happiness and joy'. A number of the offspring of the children of her
father's first marriage joined them there, so they often had enough 'to
form our own cricket eleven'. Her eldest sister took on the mothering
role, helped by a 'darling maid Annie', and later a governess, daughter
of an Anglo-Indian colonel.[8]

At the age of twelve, she and her younger sister Nettie started at
Jersey Ladies College, where they were the only black pupils. 'School
life still remains a gorgeous memory,' she later wrote. 'How happy we
were in spite of our colour, or perhaps because of it, since we were sin-
gled out for extra titbits of love, kindliness, and good will. What did
we know of racial prejudice, and an inferiority complex? Nothing! But
we knew a lot about the milk of human kindness.'

Their large, rambling house in Jersey became a stopping-off point
for West Africans visiting Britain, mostly for education. Several of her
elder sisters married visiting bachelors and returned to Sierra Leone and
elsewhere.

Several years later her father married again, to a Yorkshire woman
he had met through the Methodist Church. She seems to have taken
against Adelaide, who put it down to her dark skin. Her other sisters,
she explained, had inherited their father's light colouring, while she
was more like her mother Anne, who was 'very dark – a real Sambo'.
Then again, she went on, 'It was unreasonable to expect that a lady so
rigidly religious, and devoid of humour could put up with an impulsive
harum-scarum teenager who never thought before she spoke, and who
consequently was definitely lacking in tact.'

Perhaps in part because of this clash, at seventeen, Adelaide, a gifted
musician, travelled to Germany for three years to study at the Stuttgart
Conservatory. Here, she sometimes felt horribly homesick. 'Germany
had only just begun to acquire Colonies, so I was the first negress they
had seen and instantly became Curio No. 1. I suffered from acute self-
consciousness not so much because I was black but because I was so
conspicuous.' She later told the story of going into a shop, and all the
assistants fled. 'Fortunately my sense of humour came to the rescue,
and I was able to make a big joke over it, but it did hurt. Now I know

that God never makes any mistakes, and that my black skin was part of the equipment with which he endowed me to make good in life.'

Her career would start properly when she was in her late twenties. Following the sudden death of her mother-in-law, her father had 'aged greatly' and soon afterwards died of liver disease. By this stage only Adelaide and her elder sister Emma remained of the children in Jersey. Nettie had married and moved to the Gold Coast. Her father's dying wish was that they should return to Africa. They were loath to leave their friends in Jersey and, she wrote, Africa 'did not attract us, because we were more or less strangers'. Although she was grateful for her 'excellent European training for such a lengthy period, it turned us out as black white women', she later stated.[9]

'One Sunday morning, in November 1897,' Adelaide wrote, 'we two forlorn orphans landed in Freetown.' If leaving Jersey was a 'terrible wrench', arriving in Africa was worse. Becoming 'acclimatized to an African environment' was 'anything but a happy experience'. The 'educated Africans' of Freetown 'shunned us, snubbed us, ostracised us'. At one ball at Government House, Adelaide came across a man she had met in England. She asked to be introduced to his wife. 'He came back and told me that his wife did not wish to know me.' Adelaide later wrote that it was a great mistake to raise black children overseas as 'they lost touch with their home environment: they find they don't fit in, and are not happy. England, too, is not their home, so they become more or less homeless.'[10]

Furthermore, little of the family money was left by the time of their father's death, so the two women had to be self-supporting. Adelaide took on pupils for tuition and taught music. After six months, she wrote, they had overcome some of the hostility that greeted their arrival and had 'lived down all this black prejudice'. But she became ill with malaria and excruciating earache. Then, two years after their arrival, a family tragedy occurred when the husband of her sister Nettie died at the age of only forty-four, leaving behind two young children, Charlie and Kathleen. Nettie left the Gold Coast to live with them in Freetown. But the facilities, according to Adelaide, were very uninspiring, so the three sisters decided to return to England to have the children educated there.

Still short of money, they opened a boarding house for bachelors in Shepherd's Bush, London, near Charlie's new school. One of the friends Adelaide made during this time was the celebrated half-Sierra Leonean composer Samuel Coleridge-Taylor, with whom she shared a box at the Albert Hall for an early performance of his *Hiawatha* trilogy. She also received a letter from Joseph Casely Hayford, who was in London and was keen to meet her.[11]

Joseph had lost his first wife two years previously and had a five-year-old son, Archie. Adelaide herself said that she had recently fallen in love but that her beau had died of TB. 'From that experience', she later wrote, 'I knew I could only offer a second-best affection to any suitor who might come along.' But she invited Casely Hayford to tea, and was impressed with his 'quiet, unassuming, straightforward demeanour'. Casely Hayford himself 'told me quite plainly' that he had adored his first wife, and that 'he too had nothing but a second-best affection to offer me. I honoured him for this frank avowal, and accepted his offer in the right spirit.'[12]

They married on 10 September 1903. She was thirty-five, he was four years older. His son Archie, Adelaide wrote, 'needed mothering badly'. They honeymooned for a week at the Shakespeare Hotel in Stratford-upon-Avon, staying in the Antony and Cleopatra room. Then, shortly afterwards, they left for Axim on the Gold Coast, where Joseph had his successful legal practice.[13]

At first, 'everything seemed very strange, and the language loomed up as a formidable barrier', but his family gave Adelaide a warm welcome, and for three years the couple were happy, despite his frequent absences for work. And here came the first record of her undertaking public speaking, addressing the Axim Literary Club on the role women could play in the welfare of the country.[14]

In late 1904, she gave birth to a daughter, Gladys. It was not easy. 'Our baby came before her time,' she wrote, 'and as I was no longer young, her advent nearly killed me.' Gladys was born with malformation of the hip joint, so when she was nearly three they decided she needed specialist treatment in London. The hope was that Joseph would follow, but Adelaide, staying at her sisters' new boarding house in Ladbroke Grove, waited in vain. For the marriage, 'it was the beginning of the end'.[15]

By the time she and the infant child returned to Africa, Joseph Casely Hayford had moved to Tarkwa, in the heart of the gold-mining district. It was a dismal place. There was no doctor, and children with malnutrition everywhere. Their house was 'a wretched affair' with barbed wire in the windows to deter thieves, and rats running freely across the dinner table. 'Worst of all,' Adelaide wrote, 'there was no companionship whatsoever. One civilised woman came to spend a few days in the place, but otherwise I was entirely surrounded by illiterate peasants.' (Much later she would confess to a 'tremendous conceit . . . undoubtedly I am a bit of a snob. I have often looked down upon people of my own race who have been plentifully helped to an inferiority complex. Of this I am heartily ashamed.')[16]

Pregnant again and mindful of her previous difficulties, she decided she would have the baby in England. She was booked into a first-class berth on a German steamer, but once at sea the chief steward moved her to 'the worst second class cabin on the boat'. There, she had to share a small bunk with Gladys, who kicked her all night. She harangued the captain, who was astonished to be addressed in fluent German, and he moved her to a slightly better cabin, but while still at sea 'the baby arrived stillborn'. 'A black skin', she wrote much later, 'can prove a terrible handicap.'[17]

She stayed for a while with her sisters in England, but with Gladys suffering from bronchial problems, she returned, this time to Cape Coast, 'by far the best spot for an educated woman on the Gold Coast'. There, she formed a social club of like-minded women. Her husband, though, lived at Sekondi. Soon after, they agreed on a separation, and just before the beginning of the war, Adelaide, with her daughter, moved to Freetown.[18]

*

Her welcome this time, she wrote, was much more friendly. Her nephew, who had a government position, allowed her and Gladys to live in one of the extended family's houses in the centre of the town. They were soon joined from London by her beloved sister Nettie and her daughter Kathleen, who had recently become the first African graduate of the Royal College of Arts. Adelaide's estranged husband provided some money – she did take issue with the unequal amount he was prepared to spend on Gladys's education against Archie's (who was studying in England) – but she still needed to make a living. As before, she worked as a tutor and taught music. She also became involved in community affairs. At the end of her first year there she gave a public lecture entitled 'The Rights of Women and Christian Marriage'. Unlike Blyden, and other African cultural nationalists, she was firmly against polygamy. (There are hints that her husband's different view on this issue might have contributed to the failure of their marriage.) She became president of the Young Women's Christian Association, and later joined the Ladies Division of the Freetown UNIA, becoming its president in early 1920. By now she had started, on special occasions, wearing 'native' dress.[19]

In her capacity at the YWCA she had started offering young women lessons in singing, while Kathleen would teach handicraft and stencilling. This soon evolved into a bolder project. In early April 1920 a notice appeared in the *Sierra Leone Weekly News (SLWN)*, a paper strongly sympathetic to pan-Africanism and African cultural nationalism. Under the heading 'Our Girls' it announced a 'Great Public Meeting at the Wilberforce Memorial Hall – Tues. the 6th instant at 7 p.m. Come and hear about A Great Scheme for an Industrial and Technical School for Girls. All are invited.'[20]

The 'Great Scheme' for the school was inspired in part by Casely Hayford's own difficulties in supporting herself and her daughter and by what she had seen of local schools for girls. Women's education, she said, was 'a hundred years behind men's', with 'nothing to fit them for the battles of life'. Her school would produce girls 'fully trained for such professions as dress-making, millinery, market gardening, poultry-farming, so that they will be able to earn their own living'. Her younger sister Nettie would teach weaving, basket-making and other handicrafts. Her precept was that women had to be economically independent to retain their self-respect. She even expressed the ambition that the whole of the west coast 'will be supplied with fully trained stenographers etc. recruited from the ranks of the institution'.[21]

Addressing the 'appalling fact' that 'so many young girls lose their lives in their first confinement', she announced a course in which 'prospective brides' 'shall be trained in their duties not only to their husbands and their children, but to themselves ... with up to date scientific methods'.[22]

Perhaps most striking was her ambition, as she put it, to 'hear the young mothers teaching their sons the glory of black citizenship, rather than encouraging them to bewail the fact that they were not white'. Education as it stood, she said, 'either consciously or unconsciously, taught us to despise ourselves, and that our immediate need was an education which would instil into us a love of country, a pride of race, and enthusiasm for the black man's capabilities and a genuine admiration for Africa's wonderful art work'.[23]

Music and dancing would be encouraged rather than discouraged, as 'being splendid media for promoting a sense of social and communal values, which, after all, are the chief foundation of all African customs'. Higher literary education would not be neglected as 'no race can thrive without writers, poets, artists, musicians'.

She hoped, in due course, for a custom-built school, but in the meantime it would be housed in the top floors of her own residence in central Freetown. Every rich family in Freetown and in Gold Coast, she hoped, would make a financial contribution to the school's establishment.[24]

The reaction of the *SLWN* to what they called 'the first institution of its kind in West Africa' was enthusiastic, praising in particular the scheme 'to enable the female section of our country to get their livelihood by honourable means and *independently* [their emphasis]'. Furthermore, 'it is purely a native enterprise, which shows that they are endeavouring in a practical way to help themselves'. But the paper then added ominously that local people were 'only half awake to their own best interests'.[25]

In fact, the general response was lukewarm at best, and in some parts actively hostile. First, there was a row with the UNIA, under whose auspices the first fund-raising meeting had been held. They wanted control of the project, and the money raised for it, and insisted that only UNIA members should be on the school's executive committee. Casely Hayford resigned her position and left the organisation. Second, the National Congress of British West Africa also wanted to collect money for its own projects and actually forbade her from fund-raising in the Freetown area. Third, the colonial government initially promised financial support – all its most senior officers agreed to be patrons of the school – but this failed to materialise. More generally, the public were unenthusiastic. One correspondent to the *SLWN* asked why it was necessary to raise charitable funds for a fee-paying school, and suggested that the greater need was 'to bring the vast number of neglected women in the Protectorate up to standard'.[26]

In the reckoning against Casely Hayford was the fact that she had received none of her education in Freetown, did not have a formal college degree and possessed little experience of classroom teaching. Her forceful personality and status as an independent woman had ruffled feathers. Clearly, some of the hostility she had experienced when first arriving in Freetown as an outsider still remained.[27]

The failure of the government to provide financial support she later put down to 'dreadful racial discrimination on the part of the white race ... the majority of white people do not want to see well-educated black ones'. 'The utter lack of appreciation on the part of my own people', she wrote, was 'probably because they were not accustomed to native leadership'. 'Had I been starting a brothel,' she declared, 'the antagonism could not have been worse.'[28]

The upshot was that the school, if it was ever to see the light of day, would need funding from elsewhere. In July 1920, she and her niece

Kathleen gathered together what little money they had raised locally
and booked a steamer for the United States.

On the boat over, Casely Hayford, a seasoned traveller, was struck by
the differences with a British ship. For one thing, there were religious
services on Sundays, something she had never encountered before. In
addition, there was a lack of alcohol, unlike British steamers, where
'wine and spirits flow like water almost at all times of the day'.

They had, she wrote, 'boarded the ship in great trepidation, having
heard so much about the American treatment of coloured people'.
But they were agreeably surprised, receiving 'nothing but courtesy',
particularly once they had established they were 'African rather than
American negroes' by donning their 'native' dress.[29]

In New York, there were headlines in the press that two African
princesses had arrived. A film crew turned up to show off the 'African
exhibits' – leather and fur handbags and slippers – they had brought
with them to sell.

First off, they headed for Harlem where, Adelaide wrote, they were
'astonished' at the number and prosperity of 'coloured people', with
'plenty of successful lawyers, doctors, estate agents, merchants and
even politicians'. They also noted the progress of 'the coloured girl. In
every walk of life she takes her place beside the man.'[30]

They found New York extremely expensive, and were soon running short of funds. But, as would be the case across the country,
the black churches took them under their wings, providing money
and accommodation, as well as introductions and invitations. The
Casely Hayford name also opened doors. She would almost always be
described as the 'wife of the Hon. Casely Hayford OBE, member of the
Gold Coast Legislative Council'. Adelaide was surprised at how well
known and respected her husband was among black readers. 'I never
miss the opportunity of rubbing in who you are,' she wrote to him in
December. 'People out here think that we are a very united couple, and
I want them still to continue to think so,' she cautioned him. 'I act as if
everything is all right,' she wrote two months later.[31]

Adelaide and Kathleen stayed in the United States for over two years, visiting thirty-six cities and towns, some more than once. Adelaide gave public lectures. One was reported from the meeting of the National Council of Negro Women in Richmond: 'Madam Hayford, dressed in attractive native costume, held the audience spell bound, as she pleaded the cause of African womanhood. She stressed in a very forceful way that we should be proud of our ancestry – that we had nothing to be ashamed of.' The collection on this occasion raised $142.52. Meanwhile, her niece staged pageants of African scenes aimed at correcting the misguided American notions about Africa. 'Having expected to see two semi-civilized, illiterate uncouth women,' Adelaide wrote, 'the Negroes were overwhelmed with enthusiasm, especially after they had listened to an address portraying the good points of our downtrodden race, instead of the usual fetish barbaric practices, and devil worshipping rites to which they were accustomed.' She reported a young black girl of six saying about Kathleen, 'She ain't no African! She ain't got a ring in her nose.' At Indianapolis for the National Convention of Colored Women, Adelaide reported, 'in our picturesque native costumes, we arrived and saw and conquered'. In her performance, she had never felt more African.[32]

Along the way, the pair were introduced to some of the most out-standing African-Americans of the day, including scientists, artists and educators, all inspiring and valuable contacts. But the fund-raising itself was a disappointment for now. They had taken in £1,800, but all save about £400 had gone on expenses. She had, however, put together an impressive American committee for the school, which included Mrs Booker T. Washington, the educator, feminist and civil rights campaigner Nannie Burroughs ('undoubtedly the greatest Negro woman of the day' in Adelaide's opinion) and Dr R. Moton, the new principal of the Tuskegee Institute. The committee would secure the patronage of the immensely wealthy philanthropist Dorothy Payne Whitney to the tune of £200 a year, one of 'the lovely white people who gave us their unstinted support'.[33]

'Even if we did not succeed in raising the amount we desired, we have certainly succeeded in giving the American Negro a new vision of Africa and her people,' Adelaide argued. Furthermore, a big part of the purpose of the trip was that America 'understands more fully than any other country the racial side of teaching the coloured scholar'. It had been a 'most valuable educational asset because it has trained me in progressive methods which would otherwise have been a sealed book.'[34]

Back in Freetown, critics were still sniping. When the figures for the trip's expenses were published, a correspondent to the *West African Mail* in May 1923 asked 'whether that was a business trip or a holiday jaunt?' There were also suggestions that the money raised would go to nothing more than improvements on Adelaide's house. Casely Hayford's supporters came to her defence. In June, the *SLWN* wrote that it 'emphatically deplored the bunking rumours' that had been circulating, instead praising Adelaide's 'indomitable grit' and 'patriotic zeal'.[35]

A speaker at a 'fairly large' fund-raising meeting at the Wilberforce Hall at the end of July praised the two women's US trip as so 'heroic' that 'possibly some African poet will immortalize their deeds in an epic poem'. Veteran pan-Africanist and friend of Adelaide Professor Orishatukeh Faduma told a meeting in early September, 'I have noticed that we in West Africa are inclined to think that women are inferior to men, but this is because we have not given to women the opportunity to come into mental life with us.' Missionaries, he said, 'have done much for us. We thank them for it; it is time we begin to help ourselves ... I appeal to you. White men are looking at us and saying, "They are infants, they cannot do anything unaided." If we fail, this will make them feel sure, that we cannot do anything. Let us bind ourselves together and start this school, even if it is on a small scale.'[36]

It was indeed on a small scale when the school, with just enough money scraped together, opened at the end of September 1923. There were only fourteen pupils, all under the age of ten. The following year was better, with fifty, including twenty in the senior division and two boarders. The Casely Hayfords' daughter Gladys had arrived to teach

African folklore and literature. The school's income was £210 from fees, £325 from donations (the majority from Dorothy Payne Whitney in the US). Expenses, almost all on teachers' salaries, were £327. The 'school so pluckily started', reported *West Africa* magazine, 'is destined to continue its useful work'.[37]

As school principal, Adelaide Casely Hayford would have preferred the pupils 'instead of blindly copying European fashions' to be 'dressed in attractive native garments, which would enhance their personal charms'. However, this idea was firmly rejected by the Krio community. The compromise was her creation in her school of 'Mother Africa Day', held once a quarter, when the pupils dressed in African clothes and studied African history, folklore, songs and artwork, played African games and performed traditional dances.

One of her biggest clashes with the local community came about when the Prince of Wales, still on his endless empire tour, turned up in Sierra Leone in 1925. Casely Hayford, as she put it, 'begged' those women invited to meet him to wear traditional dress, 'to show we are proud of being Africans. They all turned me down.' In the end, causing something of a stir, she was the only one to attend the Prince's reception and ball in traditional *buba* and *lappa*. She subsequently wrote in her report of the visit for *West Africa* magazine (which included the comment that the Prince seemed 'bored to extinction by the ceremonial') that the Krio women had been in a frenzy trying to 'get, borrow or steal gloves for the grand reception'. This, with its implied slight on the ability of the guests to have the resources to own these things themselves, caused great offence. A local lawyer urged her to apologise for this 'libel'. More than the snobbish slur, with her African costume campaign it seems that local people thought she was simply trying too hard to be something she wasn't.[38]

Casely Hayford's sympathetic biographer, A. M. Cromwell, wrote that her subject 'would never have an African name, speak an African language or consider African dress other than a costume'. (It was, Adelaide wrote, 'eminently unsuitable for practical purposes'.) Historian Rina Okonkwo, who included Adelaide Casely Hayford in her book *Heroes of West African Nationalism*, concluded that 'Hayford was a cultural nationalist, but her understanding and integration into African society was limited'. She pointed out that Adelaide refused to consider illiterate protectorate women for the roles of teachers of native crafts (of which they were the masters) as they were 'too lazy', and resisted urgings to establish a vocational school for these women, who needed it far more than the Krio. During the research for the Adelaide chapter in her book, Okonkwo interviewed a woman, Foulabi Miller Lewis, who was the daughter of a teacher at Casely Hayford's school. She was 'an aristocrat . . . cut off from the rank and file', Miller told her. Furthermore, Casely Hayford was 'absolutely English, the African was superimposed'.[39]

After her retirement, Adelaide took to writing. Her best-known short story is 'Mister Courier', a satire, like Sekyi's *The Blinkards*, on Africans who want to be European. An African undertaker wears unsuitable European clothes and builds himself a house in Sierra Leone in the English style, with thick walls and narrow corridors, that is stuffy, uncomfortable and unsanitary for the African climate. It's hard not to wonder, however, whether local people in Freetown thought that she, after her twenty-five-year-long upbringing in Europe, remained, as she herself had put it, a 'black white woman'.[40]

Many of the original ambitions of the school, which remained in operation until Adelaide's retirement in 1940, were not fulfilled. It was not able, as hoped, to offer teacher training. Apart from instruction in traditional arts and crafts, its goal of providing an education that would enable women to earn their own living was never properly realised. Instead, to attract pupils, it became a kindergarten and junior school, a feeder for the Church Missionary Society Girls' Senior School in Freetown.[41]

Nonetheless, it, and its founder, had an impact. Adelaide Casely Hayford, who in 1924 had become the sole black female member of the colony's Education Board, continued to campaign for female education to be given equal status with male, for schools to instil 'some pride of race, love of country, and pride in their own colour', and for the employment of properly trained and paid African teachers, using African-produced textbooks in a locally run environment. 'A school entirely controlled by white people can never promote a national out-look in the mind of the African child,' she wrote for a speech delivered by her daughter in 1931 at an international conference in Geneva. Education aside, she was also one of the first African women to gain prominence in public life, and paved the way for others to follow.[42]

34

The Economic Conference

Both sides, victors and vanquished, were ruined.

WINSTON CHURCHILL on the First World War[1]

O pening the Imperial Economic Conference, the President of the
Board of Trade struck a gloomy note: 'Today our export trade is
still far below its pre-war volume,' he said, 'reflected in unemployment
of a duration and on a scale without precedent. It would be difficult to
exaggerate the gravity or the urgency of such a situation.'[2]

To blame, almost everyone agreed, was the war. One of its many
casualties was the world's financial system. During the latter half of
the previous century, a complicated machinery of international credit,
centred in London, had been built on the back of the gold standard.
This had created an impressive expansion of trade and prosperity across
the world. In 1919, that machinery, on which Britain depended more
than anyone else, lay in ruins.

Instead, there was now a huge, unsustainable edifice of inter-
government debts. During the war, the Allies had drastically outspent
the Central Powers by a factor of more than two. By far the largest
contribution was from Britain, which also handed out huge loans to

its allies in Europe. About a third of its expenditure was from revenue, but the rest was funded by borrowing. This saw Britain's national debt expand more than ten-fold from £700 million to £7.4 billion. Most was raised domestically, but not all.[3]

When the United States joined the war in 1917, London hoped that lending to the likes of France and Italy would be taken on by them, but the US preferred to lend to the more creditworthy British, who then continued to hand out equivalent sums to the Europeans. So by the end of the war, Britain owed the US some £900 million, while being owed more by European allies, even when the loans to Tsarist Russia were written off.[4]

To pay the Americans, Britain needed money from France, but this could only come from reparations from Germany, which was on its knees. The whole system was failing. Bankers and industrialists in the US were urging debt reduction for Europe; the alternative was 'wantonly destroying our best markets'. But any politician standing on that platform would be committing political suicide. Instead, the US adopted the disastrous policy of calling in its debts and retreating behind tariff walls. 'America watches and waits for her money with a hard face,' commented the 29 September 1923 edition of *Spectator* magazine. America was 'largely responsible' for the 'financial collapse of the exchanges', argued a Scottish university professor. 'America has gained the gold of the world. She controls the money markets . . . and has let loose the forces of disorder which', he warned, 'will destroy her after they have completed the destruction of Europe.'[5]

In the United States there was a new President. The previous incumbent, Warren Harding, had as a senator voted against the US joining the League of Nations, and at his inauguration in early 1921 had pledged that America would enter no permanent military alliance, nor assume 'economic obligations'. Harding died in office in August 1923, and his successor, Calvin Coolidge, suggested a commission of experts to look at the 'reparations tangle'. But, a spokesman was quoted in October's *Current History,* his administration 'has no specific proposal to make to the allies or to Germany at this time, but is ready to do anything within its power, *short of becoming involved in the situation* [my emphasis], to aid in dissipating the chaos that now prevails in Europe.'[6]

With no help forthcoming from the US and faced with huge debts, the European nations had a choice: whether to deflate – raise interest rates sharply and increase the cost of credit – or to devalue, setting a new currency conversion rate to gold. This was the central economic decision for every major economy after the war. Devaluation would hit savers. Deflation would cause dramatically tight credit and would hit workers, businesses and borrowers.

Both France and Germany devalued, but Britain, for whom 'sound money' was a matter of national prestige, took the other route, with the Bank of England reducing money supply and raising interest rates to 7 per cent. The British budget was balanced, as was deemed right and proper for her long-term credit rating and the status of the pound, but 2 million were thrown out of work.[7]

Currency devaluation in Europe hit British manufacturing hard, with every industry from steel to hosiery and textiles damaged by the import of low-priced foreign goods. Even more important was the ongoing political and financial chaos on the continent. Between 1917 and 1923, Europe experienced no fewer than twenty-seven violent transfers of political power, many accompanied by latent or open civil wars, revolutions and counter-revolutions, as well as border conflicts between the emerging new states. In January 1923 France had occupied the Rhineland to enforce reparation payments, further inflaming the situation. In the last three weeks, reported the 26 September 1923 edition of the *Australian Worker* newspaper, 'Three dictators have been appointed in three different countries; and there are two or three more virtual dictators in other States ... the present danger is that the dictator disease may spread.' Spain had just fallen to a military dictator. On 2 October, the *Daily Mail* interviewed Adolf Hitler and found him a ridiculous figure and his Munich headquarters 'a madhouse'. But days earlier Hitler had declared, 'We need a revolution, bloodshed and a dictatorship.' Chancellor Stresemann warned, 'If my Government fails, accomplishing nothing, then I shall perhaps be the last civilian

Chancellor of Germany.' British Prime Minister Stanley Baldwin was reported in the *Daily Herald* of 29 September saying that the great task of the British Empire might in the end be to 'preserve democracy'.[8]

This political instability, along with currency collapses and widespread impoverishment, destroyed the European market for British exports, almost always more important than distant colonies. Other factors due in part to the war also contributed to the dire economic situation. The end of the war had seen a 'restocking boom', but this had come to an end in 1921–2, with a commodity prices collapse causing severe difficulties across the empire. In Britain, trade unions had flourished during the war, achieving their highest-ever membership. This drove up labour costs and in September 1923 disputes and strikes involved 95,000 workers. The granting of the extended franchise in 1918 had focused politicians' minds on domestic priorities, and led to a huge increase in spending on housing ('homes fit for heroes'), health, education, pensions (including, of course, hundreds of thousands of war pensions for disabled soldiers and widows) and the inevitably attendant rise in taxation, which dampened domestic demand.

Wider afield, the war had caused Britain to lose touch with overseas agents and customers, thus giving up ground to its rivals in international trade. Japan had increased its merchant fleet's tonnage by 50 per cent; the United States' share of world exports rose from 13.5 per cent in 1913 to over 25 per cent in 1920.[9]

Some factors, though, had little to do with the war. British economic hegemony in the nineteenth century had been built on railways, steel, coal and textiles. But it had failed to modernise and largely missed out on the 'Second Industrial Revolution' based on chemicals, oil, electrical goods like refrigerators and radios and, above all, cars. In Burma, British exporters still provided steel and railway plant, but only 9 per cent of the imported cars, with 73 per cent coming from the US or US-based companies manufacturing in Canada. In Malaya, the empire's richest colony, buying an annual £100 million of imported goods, only a sixteenth came from Britain. All the beer advertisements in Malayan papers in September 1923 were for Japanese Asahi. Efforts were made to encourage the empire to 'buy British'; Arthur Grimble in Ocean Island, which had not a single car, received a circular urging the shunning of Ford in favour of British-made models. But American cars were hardier, better built and better value, despite the punishing import tariff. Only in the luxury market were British manufacturers still holding their own.[10]

Although accelerated by the war, this was part of a pattern that had seen Britain's share of trade with the empire steadily decline. In 1890, Britain had provided 75 per cent of India's imports. By 1923 it was only around half. All the time, American and Japanese shares had been creeping up.[11]

India is a special case for the sheer size of its potential market, particularly in cotton goods, which was the most important British export, making up in value a third of all goods shipped overseas. 'The fortunes of Lancashire are thus inseparable from those of the country,' one British newspaper pointed out on 1 October. Most raw cotton came from the United States (of the 58 million spindles in Lancashire, 42 million used American cotton), despite vigorous efforts to promote production of the crop within the empire. So, as was pointed out, 'Unfortunately for Lancashire, the raw materials of the cotton industry are purchased from the wealthiest nation in the world, while its products are sold to the poorest.' And in the US, not only was a domestic cotton manufacturing industry being quickly developed (35 million spindles, which by 1923 absorbed a quarter of the US crop), but a plant disease had severely reduced output of the raw cotton. The result was a rise in price of up to 150 per cent.[12]

To make matters worse for Britain's most important export industry, the Indian government had recently imposed import tariffs of 15 per cent on cotton goods. In 1922, the Indian government faced a severe deficit that threatened to force it to default on loan repayments to the City of London. It was politically impractical to introduce new direct taxation, so tariffs were imposed, not to protect or nourish domestic Indian industry, but to raise revenue. In effect, the Indian government had to choose between the City and the industry of Lancashire, and went for the former.[13]

In 1920, Leonard Woolf had published his *Empire and Commerce in Africa*, in which he looked at trade patterns across the continent. He came to the conclusion that the actual occupation of territories did nothing to help British trade. For instance, before the war, British exports had been growing faster to German-controlled East Africa than to any local British territory. Debates about the economic value of empire had been ongoing since the end of mercantilism and the embrace of free trade at the beginning of the nineteenth century. A long line of liberals, radicals and socialists – Cobden, Gladstone, J. A. Hobson – had argued that empire actively harmed the nation's growth prospects. It increased military spending and warfare, which meant higher taxes. The benefits, they suggested, which were enjoyed by only a few, were outweighed by the costs, which were borne by every taxpayer.[14]

On the other hand, supporters of empire, like Disraeli, Rosebery and Joseph Chamberlain, saw it as providing markets and openings for investment, justifying the defence costs. The alternative, they argued, would be large tracts of territory lost to the world economy, or occupied by Britain's rivals, who would erect tariffs against British trade.[15]

Lord Palmerston had famously declared, during a mooted takeover of Abyssinia, 'All we want is trade and land is not necessary for trade; we can carry on commerce very well on ground belonging to other people.' This was the nub of Woolf's argument. In the case of the early days of economic penetration of Nigeria, a key trader, J. R. Holt, campaigned against direct imperial control, while the conquistador George Goldie declared that 'it was hopeless to try to do business where they could not impose real law and order'. However, there was nothing to stop other nations – like the United States with their cars – taking advantage of this clement environment without picking up any of the costs.[16]

Colonial governments could, and did, tinker at the edges. Free trade was not sacrosanct. Efforts were made to make the empire pay. You were charged a little less export duty on tin from Malaya or palm oil from Nigeria if you were shipping it for processing in Britain. Land policy in Malaya benefited British rubber firms; in Kenya, the growing of coffee by Kenyans was effectively forbidden. But these were measures – ostensibly to prevent crop diseases – aimed at local rather than at European rivals. Certainly, members of the empire paid less than foreigners on their borrowings; confidence in standards of law, justice and security in the empire made it possible to raise money more cheaply. But this, again, was to an extent subsidised by the UK taxpayer picking up the huge bill for the Royal Navy.

At the Imperial Conference the Dominion leaders pleaded for preferential duties for their exports to the British market. They were joined by the colonies: West Indians, who supplied a mere 5 per cent of the British sugar market, Under-Secretary of State William Ormsby-Gore admitted in the House of Commons, were looking at 'what America is doing for Cuba and Porto Rico. They see the enormous preference which America gives to the products of those Colonies. They see the result. They see that the exports of Porto Rico have gone up not 100 per cent. or 200 per cent., but by 2,000 or 3,000 per cent. owing to the economic stimulus and encouragement which America has given to those places since she took them over. They say, if America can do this, why cannot Great Britain do it also?' In return, it was promised preferential duties on British imports would be increased.[17]

Reporting on the Economic Conference, the Labour Party *Daily Herald* struck a dismissive note: 'They have been telling us during the last few days that in closer trade ties within the Empire lies our best hope of repairing our damaged industrial machine. What "close trade ties" mean in plain English is Tariffs.' This would mean import duty on 'wheat and other foods sent us by "foreigners" ... There is not the slightest chance of this suggestion being put into effect.' The whole idea was 'an illusion ... it is futile to suppose that fewer than 20,000,000 people [in the Dominions], with growing manufactures of their own, could, even if they dealt with none of our competitors, take the place of the 100,000,000 in Central Europe with whom we did such valuable trade before the war.'[18]

British politics had been here before. Joseph Chamberlain had proposed an imperial customs union, with tariffs on imports from outside the empire. But no one was going to vote for more expensive food, and the proposal had contributed to the Liberal Party – standing on a platform of free trade – achieving a landslide victory in 1906. Nonetheless, Baldwin saw the Dominions' point of view – what was the point of empire if it gave no economic advantage to its members? – and the end of the Economic Conference saw an agreement for at least some increased imperial preference. As the Conservatives had promised not to introduce this in their manifesto, Baldwin called an election. The idea remained unpopular and the December 1923 election resulted in the first ever Labour government.

35

The Morbid Age

Under the brown fog of a winter dawn
A crowd flowed over London Bridge, so many
I had not thought death had undone so many

'The Waste Land', T. S. ELIOT

To rule requires a belief in one's own right to rule.

MAX WEBER

An inquest was held in Bristol on 29 September. The risible verdict was 'accident'. The man, forty-year-old Samuel Britton, had sat in his car in his garage until killed by the fumes. 'It was stated that Mr Britton had suffered from a nervous breakdown owing to war service,' a newspaper reported. The war, of course, had cost much more than just money.[1]

Across the combatant nations, there was an epidemic of 'shell-shock'. In September 1923, as many as 160,000 British ex-servicemen were receiving pensions for experiencing the symptoms of some sort of mental trauma. And this was the tip of the iceberg. 'Something was wrong,' wrote a war correspondent in 1923. 'They had not come back the same men. Something had altered in them.' 'The shadow of the Great War shows itself in nervous lines on many old-young faces,' commented the wife of a white farmer of new arrivals in Southern Rhodesia after the war. In London, it was reported, 'utterly unemployable human derelicts, some of them with Mons medals and decorations for valour, were begging on the streets'. In Australia, the *Worker* newspaper wrote about 'limbless soldiers begging in public thoroughfares ... there is much official talk of hunting them off the streets as a nuisance to the business people in whose interests they were mutilated'. There were 170,000 returned servicemen in Australia, 'coming back battered, broken, and some with shattered nerves ... coming back, many of them, to broken faiths, lost jobs and billets, and domestic troubles and miseries'. On Ocean Island, a lance-corporal in the police called Kaipati, aged twenty-two and 6ft 2in tall, had been 'longing to go to the war'. Edward Eliot had helped him achieve this, but when he returned in 1919 'His youthful high spirits had gone. He had grown into a silent man.'[2]

Damaged veterans were nothing new, but the scale of the problem after the First World War was unprecedented, reaching into almost every home across the empire. Lloyd George declared, 'The world is suffering from shell-shock.'

Almost every family in the empire, from the humblest to the grandest colonial Governor, had suffered loss, either from the war or from the devastating influenza pandemic that followed. Everywhere, memorials were being built, pilgrimages to graveyards undertaken, and expressions made of the deepest grief. The front page of *The Times* for 29 September 1923 was dominated by 'In Memoriams' from families for soldiers killed on that date (mainly in 1918, just before the end of the conflict during fierce fighting near Cambrai). The inside pages included an appeal for funds for a home for 'shattered heroes' and news of the opening of a new British Legion memorial hall in Birkenhead. The *Daily Chronicle* from the same date carried the story of a party of a thousand 'Pilgrim mourners', crossing the Channel to Boulogne.

There, the 'St. Barnabas Pilgrimage Association' had organised special trains to take them to the five great cemeteries at Arras, Albert, Bethune, Amiens and Etaples. Sections of All Hallows choir, Barking, accompanied each party and led the singing at the gravesides, where addresses were given by clergymen. 'Few of the pilgrims had visited France before,' the paper reported, 'and in several cases it was a journey made in the eventide of life ... When they saw the beautifully-kept cemeteries and realised how well their dead were cared for many broke down trembling and in tears.'

Just as the psychological effects of combat in the war were often delayed until a few years after – one veteran wrote that 'the most profound impressions came to me later, with some distance' – so the memorialisation swelled. When Remembrance Day was started in November 1921, 8 million poppies were sold. In November 1922, it was 30 million.[3]

In *The Decay and Restoration of Civilization*, published in 1923, Albert Schweitzer declared, 'We are living today under the sign of the collapse of civilization.' The disaster of the war had smashed up many of the certainties on which the empire was sustained. Anthropologist Bronisław Malinowski wrote that 'all the ideals, cherished and proclaimed as the highest achievements of civilisation, science and religion, have been thrown to the winds'. Orwell described 'official beliefs' 'dissolving like sand-castles'. E. M. Forster, returning from Egypt at the end of the war, found England 'like a person who has folded her hands and stands waiting. I do think that during the war something in this country got killed.' The lay religion of progress and 'civilisation' had given way to extreme doubt.[4]

This manifested itself in many ways. Regular church attendance fell to a new low. In politics, the left benefited from the bankruptcy of the old order, while there was a corresponding shift of conservatism to extreme positions on the right. At the end of the war, Orwell remembered, there was 'a general revolt against orthodoxy and authority'. Leonard Woolf wrote about 'the horrible urgency of politics after 1914'.

Orwell described how 'it was all the fashion to be a "Bolshie", as people then called it. England was full of half-baked antinomian opinions. Pacifism, internationalism, humanitarianism of all kinds, feminism, free love, divorce-reform, atheism, birth-control – things like these were getting a better hearing than they would get in normal times.' It was all a long way from the 'solid fellow' archetype of the British colonial officer. Now the imperial language of honour, patriotism and sacrifice was treated with suspicion or even derision. According to the *Daily Herald* of 29 September 1923, the war had 'made the word "patriotism" stink in the nostrils of thousands of decent men and women'.[5]

This destruction of the old certainties expressed itself in Dadaism in art and in a new, fractured, self-doubting modernism in literature. The twenty-ninth of September 1923 is the publication date of the first British book edition of T. S. Eliot's 'The Waste Land', typeset at the Hogarth Press by Virginia Woolf. Woolf herself was writing *Mrs Dalloway*, featuring the young shell-shocked and suicidal veteran Septimus Smith. In James Joyce's ground-breaking *Ulysses*, published the year before, Stephen Dedalus declares, 'history is a nightmare from which I am trying to wake'. The same year, the first volume of Marcel Proust's *À la recherche du temps perdu* had been published for the first time in English, a book described by E. M. Forster as the 'adventure of the disillusioned post-war world, when the whole man moves forward to encounter he does not know what: certainly not any good'.[6]

Gambling, alcoholism and suicide all had striking upsurges. With the social fixities of pre-war life in ruins, constraints fell away. There was a craving for newness among the 'bright young things' – treasure-hunt parties, nudism, body-building, a yo-yo craze, ever faster dances, cocaine and stronger cocktails. The fashion was to adopt an American accent and to obsess over sentimental Hollywood cinema. Stephen Spender famously wrote: 'The war had knocked the ball-room floor from under middle-class English life. People resembled dancers suspended in mid-air yet miraculously able to pretend they were still dancing.' John Sumner, leader of the New York Society for the Suppression of Vice, who unsuccessfully prosecuted D. H. Lawrence's US publisher for

Women in Love, warned in his 1922 report that 'an ebbtide of moral laxity, as a result of the great war, has revealed itself ominously'.[7]

Among others there was a heightened emphasis on mysticism, the occult, spirituality and the unconscious (evident in the public's fascination with Freudian psychology). On 29 September 1923 a huge meeting took place in St Matthew's church in Auckland, New Zealand, where 10,000 people had turned up to meet faith healer James Hickson. 'Marvellous cures were recorded at the hands of Mr. Hickson,' a newspaper had reported of an earlier meeting, 'deaf and dumb and blind being made to hear and speak and see, people with crutches walking away without them.' At the Albert Hall, 9,000 assembled to talk to the dead through Ouija boards. (A high-profile adherent of this practice, it later turned out, was Mackenzie King, the Prime Minister of Canada.) The New Zealand *Truth* newspaper of 29 September carried an advertisement for a 'spirit board' to receive messages from the dead.[8]

In February 1923, Fabians Sidney and Beatrice Webb published *The Decay of Capitalist Civilization*. Its first print run was 3,750, but by the end of the year sales had reached 15,000. The entire system, they wrote, was suffering from 'morbid growths and insidious diseases'. Capitalist civilisation had made the 'monstrous catastrophe of the Great War' 'an inevitable incident in the pursuit of outlandish markets' and the resultant imperial rivalry. The war had demonstrated that civilisation as understood in the West was doomed to self-destruction.[9]

This doubt in the 'civilizing mission' spread across the empire, undermining the certainty of purpose among colonial officials and their 'right to rule', and raised questions among those colonised who might earlier have accepted the superiority and 'prestige' of the imperial system. Leonard Woolf wrote in 1919 that 'men in Asia' were already talking of the war as 'the first act in the passing of the civilization of Europe'. 'Even in the eyes of simple men', reported Sylvia Leith-Ross from Nigeria, there were 'cracks in the façade of British prestige. After years of being told that intertribal wars were wrong ... it seemed strange the British themselves should have gone to war against fellow white men.' Walter Crocker in Nigeria, addressing the challenge of managing the 'African wish for assimilation', lamented that 'unfortunately the African meets with European culture at a period when it is in chaos, perhaps in decay, where all is doubted, divided, jaded, uprooted, and where religion, morality, and taste are falling before the advance of the vulgarian and the machine'.[10]

In East Africa, black soldiers and porters had seen white men shot down by each other and the Germans had staged organised humiliation for British prisoners by African guards – white men were harnessed like oxen to a cart and forced to drag it through a bazaar in front of jeering Africans.[11]

In another crucial way, the war had undermined the loyalty of the colonised. Indian sepoys who had served in Europe had returned politicised, as Gandhi had hoped. As an American white supremacist warned in his 1920-published *The Rising Tide of Color*, 'As colored men realised the significance of [the Great War], they looked into each other's eyes and there saw a light of un-dreamed hopes. White solidarity was riven and shattered [and] fear of white power and respect for white civilisations dropped away like garments outworn.' Perhaps even more important was the reaction of non-white soldiers to their treatment by the European authorities while on active duty. They were furious, and none more so than the West Indians.[12]

36

'The Empire's Darkest Slum'

As comrades of the war our efforts we'll unite
To sweep injustice from our land, our social
wrongs to right.

SERGEANT H. B. MONTIETH
of the West India Regiment[1]

On 29 September 1923, the sun rose over Jamaica at 5.52 a.m. In London, it was just before midday. On Ocean Island, it was ten minutes to midnight. The *Jamaica Gleaner*, very much *The Times* of the British West Indies, provides a snapshot from that day of the island and the wider region.

A lot of sport is happening in Jamaica. There's a gymnastic display at the Ward Theatre, put on by the YMCA. In Port Antonio, there's been a boxing contest between 'the best boys in Kingston'. Cricket in various forms – teams from clubs, companies, churches – dominates, though there's a lot of football too, which the paper reports is growing in popularity.[2]

Elsewhere in the *Gleaner* there is news of the Prince of Wales in Canada, eating a corn-on-the-cob 'in regular farmhand fashion', and of the exciting plans for an imperial airship route.

Advertisements for motor cars are exclusively for American models – Buick, Chevrolet, Dodge. Lombard Bicycles, though, sell themselves proudly as of 'British Manufacture Throughout'. There's a large photograph and enthusiastic caption of a recent visitor to Kingston harbour, the US Navy's new 'Streak of Lightning' scout cruiser *Omaha*, capable of 35 knots and with a cruising radius of 10,000 nautical miles.

The recent goings-on in the Legislative Council are dismissed as 'tedious minute discussion of trifles', but there's a story from London of Mr A. O. Crane, the deputy mayor of Georgetown, British Guiana, complaining about the lack of representation of the West Indies at the Imperial Conference. The 'only means of saving the sugar industry', he says, is increased preference from Britain. He's also calling for more to be done 'to develop the social and moral side of the life of his black fellow-subjects of the West Indian colonies'. It would help, he states, if there was 'greater association' of colonial officers 'with the native peoples, for whose benefit that government ostensibly exists'.

Marcus Garvey is covered in a sneering article which describes him as 'ex-president of Africa and all the kingdoms and principalities therein'. The paper notes that 'some of his Knights and Dukes have fallen away from him and given evidence against him'.

A new arrival from Britain as the head of the Jamaica Public Service Company is quoted saying that fare dodging on the trams is prevalent because 'One gathers the impression in Jamaica that in the past a great deal of money has been taken out and very little put in.' Meanwhile the Ladies Committee of the West St Mary Citizens' Association has reported after a meeting that illegitimacy 'is our national sin'. There is a pressing need to 'see that these wicked unprincipled young men who stalk the country and ruin our young girls are compelled to support their offspring and the unfortunate mothers as well'.

A letter to the paper deplores the new practice of people sending handkerchiefs to faith healers, then getting them back to place on ailment areas: 'I am asking you, sir, to do your best to put an end to an evil that, if not tackled in time, will put us fifty years backwards.'

There has been a good crop of breadfruit, though otherwise unusual drought has affected agriculture. In addition, producers are being badly hit by praedial larceny. Food is 'scarce in Bethel Town', in part due to land being given over to bananas grown for export. There are problems with water supply throughout the island. It's worst at Oracabessa, where ancient piping has become dilapidated. Now the only supply of drinking water is a small spring, whose flow is 'reduced to mere dripping. . . . the mobs which throng the spring day and night to obtain a little water, resort to force in order to get it . . . the police are kept busy. Innumerable fights occur daily, and even cases of wounding. All decent minds recoil from the horror that prevails.'

The patriotic women's Victoria League of Jamaica has, we learn, donated £5 to the Pedro Plains Starving Children Fund. One of their members has 'visited the district and been an eye witness to the misery and starvation that these people are facing'. At the same meeting they resolve to give £5 to the St Dunstan's fund. This is a charity helping the thousands of veterans from across the empire who have been blinded during the war, mainly from gas attack. St Dunstan's has established hostels where the men with this 'terrible affliction' are taught braille as well as typing, basket-making and vegetable and poultry farming. On 29 September, the charity is holding a fund-raising clay pigeon shoot in Wilson Park. The band of the West India Regiment, we are told, 'will render a fine programme of music which will add much life to the proceedings'.

At the beginning of the War, West Indians had been keen to fight. Writing in an editorial for the *Federalist and Granada People* in June 1915, black activist William Donovan lamented the British government's failure to recruit a West Indian contingent and black men more generally to fight in the war. The pre-existing West India Regiment (WIR), he complained, was only doing garrison duty in the islands and in Sierra Leone while 'Senegalese and West Coast blacks are fighting side by side with their white French comrades . . . Why has not England utilised in the same manner the services of her black warriors? Because of the nasty cowardly skin prejudice characteristic of the Empire. This war however will end that.'[3]

Norman Manley, future first Prime Minister of Jamaica, arrived in England just after the outbreak of the war. He had won a Rhodes scholarship to study law at Oxford. He found the university practically deserted as 75 per cent of the students had volunteered. In 1915, he and his younger brother decided to do the same. In fact, his brother Roy, who had been at school in England, had already put himself forward. But despite coming from a good public school and having spent three years in the school's cadet force, he was refused entry to the Officers' Training Corps because, Manley wrote, 'he was a coloured man'. 'I think he expected the army to be like that,' Manley wrote in his unpublished memoir. 'This is not to say that he was not hurt and angry. We both were hurt.'[4]

Instead, the brothers applied to the Royal Artillery and underwent three months' training in east London. It 'came naturally' to his Cockney fellow gunners to call him 'Darkie', but Manley made it clear he didn't like it and they stopped. When a new arrival 'automatically called me "Darkie"', Manley remembered, 'a real rough gang got hold of him and said "Don't call him that, he doesn't like it. We call him Bill and we like him."'

Manley showed great proficiency and by the end of training and the move to France he was a corporal. Here the troubles began. 'The rank and file disliked taking orders from a coloured NCO but their attitude was mild in comparison with that of my fellow NCOs.' Corporals and sergeants resented sharing status with him because of his colour and were 'rude, spiteful and later conspired to get me into trouble. It was only the officer class that I could expect to behave with ordinary decency,' Manley wrote.

When things came to a head, Manley had a long talk with his CO, a 'decent fellow'. Manley offered to give up his stripes if he and his brother could be transferred to another battery. The commanding officer agreed to the request, and with Manley many times refusing any sort of promotion for risk of inciting resentment, it was an easier situation.

Manley saw action at the Somme and Ypres and, despite a number of terrifying near-misses, survived the war unscathed, picking up a Military Medal along the way. His brother Roy, however, was killed by a shell splinter in 1917. He was twenty-one. Thereafter, Manley wrote, he became 'lonely and bitter'. He shared none of the euphoria at the end of the war. When he visited Edna, his cousin and later wife, she found him 'utterly worn out and Roy's death had done something quite terrible to him'. At the end of 1919, Manley had a breakdown. He recovered and was called to the Bar in 1921. The same year he married, and he and Edna spent part of their honeymoon visiting Roy's grave in France. In August the following year they returned to Jamaica, where he soon became the country's leading barrister, and later, of course, one of its political giants.[5]

For the British West India Regiment, it was a slightly different story. Towards the end of 1915, with the supply of volunteers from Britain exhausted, recruitment began in the West Indies. The hope among volunteers there, as elsewhere, was that serving with white British and Dominion soldiers would gain respect for West Indian men, break down racism, and put the empire in their debt. Not everyone agreed. Some argued that it was a 'white man's war' and that West Indians should avoid getting involved. Some volunteers were jeered as they marched through the streets. Nonetheless, eventually 15,600 West Indians would serve overseas, all volunteers, with two thirds from Jamaica. The first contingent arrived in Britain for training in October 1915. Most wanted to be sent to France where everyone knew the war would be decided. Private Elmo Sweetland wrote home in July 1916: 'We will soon be sent to the firing line. I am hoping it will be to France – then we can show what Jamaicans can do. Yes it will be a happy day when I return to Jamaica, if I live it out, but even if I do not I am quite contented to die for England. I am only too eager now to be sent to the firing line.'[6]

He and his comrades would be severely disappointed. The army command believed that, unlike the so-called 'martial races' of India, black West Indians would make poor combat troops. Furthermore, the idea of having black West Indians serving alongside white troops as equals or fighting against white Germans was considered a clear threat to the imperial order.

So instead, almost all of the men of the WIR saw out the war guarding railway junctions or prisoners of war, or working behind the lines loading shells on to trains. The majority were sent to Egypt – deemed a more suitable climate for black people – and later shipments of men from the West Indies sailed direct to Alexandria. From there, a contingent did see combat service in Palestine, against the safely non-white Turks. They earned a number of rewards for gallantry. Throughout the entire war the WIR had 185 killed in action, 697 wounded, and just over 1,000 dead from disease.[7]

Writing home from behind the lines in France, the men would stress the danger of shelling and air attack on their positions. But not being trusted for combat duty was a huge humiliation. With the heroic engagements described in recruiting campaigns failing to materialise, motivation and morale fell away.[8]

Throughout the war, the black West Indian soldiers were treated as second class. They had lower pay and allowances than British soldiers and officers' commissions were refused to men, however deserving, 'who are not of unmixed European blood'. The tone was set by the training camp for the first arrivals. They were housed in damp huts with insufficient sanitary facilities. Soon the local hospitals were full of men with pneumonia. In France, they were banned from the local *estaminets*, cafés which provided welcome relief from army rations for British soldiers. Elsewhere they were excluded from cinemas and YMCA clubs and consigned to the inferior 'native' hospitals. From Egypt, a Trinidadian wrote home: 'We are treated neither as Christians nor as British citizens, but as West Indian "n*****s" without anybody to be interested in or look after us.'[9]

It came to a head just after the end of the war at Taranto. The men had been forced to perform humiliating duties, washing linen and cleaning the latrines of the Italian labourers. Officers (who were all white) complained to the South African camp commandant, but were told that 'n*****s had no right to expect to be treated like British troops'.[10]

On 7 December 1918 the men of one battalion refused to take on any of these duties. They were swiftly disarmed, but unrest had spread. A Jamaican private, Samuel Pinnock, was shot dead by his sergeant; a battalion of British troops was quickly dispatched to Taranto. Although the protests fizzled out, the High Command was rattled. Forty-nine men were found guilty of mutiny and sentenced to between three and five years' imprisonment. The supposed ringleader, Private Sanches, received a death sentence, later commuted to twenty years. The authorities decided that they needed to return the West Indians home as quickly as possible. Lack of transport made this difficult, and there was further unrest while they waited for demobilisation.[11]

While in Paris the contribution of the Senegalese soldiers was publicly celebrated, West Indian troops were excluded from participation in the victory parade in London in July 1919. In September, around fifty West Indian servicemen recovering from lost limbs at Belmont Road Military Hospital in Liverpool came under attack from white South African soldiers who objected to unsegregated hospital facilities. There were also clashes elsewhere with white American soldiers, who were used to overt racial segregation. Meanwhile, West Indians gathered in London and elsewhere, nurturing their grievances. Radical Jamaican writer Claude McKay visited a club for black soldiers in London's Drury Lane, where he saw a number of black American newspapers being handed around. McKay was subsequently invited to the Repatriation Camp in Winchester, where he distributed what he called 'revolutionary newspapers and literature'. 'They had been disillusioned with the European war,' he wrote to Leon Trotsky; 'they kept on having frightful clashes with English and American soldiers, besides the fact the authorities treated them completely differently from the white soldiers.' For McKay, this offered the hope that the men would return to their countries and force radical change. 'We should rejoice that Germany blundered,' he wrote in the *Negro World*, 'so that Negroes from all parts of the world were drawn to England to see the Lion, afraid and trembling, hiding in cellars, and the British ruling class revealed in all its rottenness and hypocrisy.'[12]

Colonial officials in the West Indies, already under pressure from strikes and unrest, were nervous about the return of these in many cases radicalised, newly racially conscious and angry young men. The Governor of Jamaica urged the Colonial Office to ensure that pensions and other allowances were settled without delay, in the meantime making plans for the returning men to be quickly dispersed on arrival. A battalion of British infantry was sent to Jamaica to strengthen the garrison.[13]

The war had seen a sharp rise in prices, which led to demands for higher wages, and protests when these were refused. In Trinidad in 1917, a strike by oil and asphalt workers saw valuable property damaged. Troops were sent in and five ringleaders arrested and imprisoned under wartime defence regulations. In Jamaica in 1917 and 1918 there were strikes by the fire service, pier labourers, stevedores and others. During a strike at a sugar works in July 1918, police fired into a crowd, killing three and injuring twelve. The same month, Chinese and Syrian businesses, accused of profiteering, were attacked and looted.[14]

Just as the veterans were starting to return to their home islands in mid-1919, Colonial Secretary Milner sent a secret telegram to all the local Governors. He had heard alarming reports about a 'Caribbean League' made up of ex-servicemen, as he put it, proposing on their return to 'suddenly fall on and murder the whites'. He requested urgent information.[15]

The Caribbean League had been formed in the aftermath of the Taranto mutiny. Its aim was 'the Promotion of all matters conducive to the General Welfare of the islands constituting the British West Indies'. At a later gathering, an informer reported, one speaker, to great applause, declared that 'the black man should have freedom to govern himself in the West Indies and force must be used, and if necessary bloodshed, to attain that object'. It was planned that on return to the islands, the league should organise a general strike to secure higher wages for all workers.[16]

In fact, the Caribbean League was not only short-lived but also not as radical as Milner feared. It was made up of sergeants – the most senior rank to which black WIR men could aspire – while the Taranto mutineers had all been privates. The sergeants even shied away from involving men of lower ranks as 'they might not understand the objects and get excited'. In addition, they were also all Jamaican, which meant they had little chance of Caribbean-wide support.[17]

The Governors' response to the Milner telegram of July 1919, while all deny any knowledge of the Caribbean League, does give a picture of their views of returning soldiers. From Trinidad, the Governor reported that 'discontent among the soldiers at their treatment was acute, and agitators were taking advantage of that feeling to increase the general unrest in the Colony'. The answer, he suggested, was to 'make the men realise that the Government was grateful to them for the sacrifices they made' and that they should 'treat them with justice but also with generosity'. The Governor of Barbados started by saying that the behaviour of the returned soldiers 'had been quite correct' and that they had 'benefitted by the years under discipline', but then gave the view of his Chief of Police that 'there is a sullen feeling ... that has been augmented by the dissemination of pernicious newspapers of the character of the "Negro World" which incites hatred of the white race'. He concluded that 'the presence of a warship in these waters during the coming six months would be a comfort to all Governors'.

The Governor of British Honduras also requested a 'periodical visit by a ship of war'. A contingent of WIR men had returned on 8 July demonstrating 'a strong undercurrent of grievance on account of discrimination'. A week later the 'Union flag displayed at the Picture Show was hissed ... men will probably join agitation for political reform'. The Governor of British Guiana explained that the returned soldiers 'talk frequently about the colour question ... for during their four years' service they came in contact with troops from all parts of the Empire and the colour question frequently arose – in an aggravated form when in contact with South Africans ... They were frequently handled in a tactless manner by officers who did not understand them.'[18]

During the same month there was a scene of anarchy on a boat carrying repatriates from Barbados to Jamaica, and on 18 July servicemen were involved in fighting in Kingston with British sailors, several of whom were injured. The Jamaica Governor, reporting to the CO, called the attackers 'blacks of the hooligan class', and blamed an activist, F. E. M. Hercules, visiting from London, whose Garveyite language, 'not calculated to improve relations between white and black', had stirred them up. Hercules was subsequently banned from landing in Trinidad, 'in view of the excitement prevailing'. Across the region, the authorities now moved to tighten up sedition laws and ban the import of newspapers like the *Negro World*.[19]

In Trinidad also in the same month, British sailors were assaulted by demobilised veterans in the streets of Port of Spain. Amid concern in the white community that black policemen would not take action against rioters and strikers, vigilante forces were formed, including among the Americans based around the oil industry. In early 1920, 350 British troops arrived, and feeling more secure, the authorities clamped down with a hundred arrests of activists and trade union leaders.[20]

But the return of the politicised and radicalised soldiers had already acted as a shot in the arm for nascent nationalist and trade union movements across the region. 'There is a sentiment of solidarity among the blacks, and white supremacy is no longer uncontested,' wrote Albert Demangeon. If the war had sapped the energy and will of the British, the opposite was the case for the black inhabitants of the British West Indies. Veterans, forming groups demanding economic change and improvements in health, housing and education, were at the forefront of labour activism and demands for constitutional reform across the region.[21]

*

Constitutional reform campaigns, as elsewhere, had long been the preserve of the middle classes, but together with the soldiers, now a new
urban proletariat, particularly in Trinidad, had joined the campaigning. At the end of 1921 a commission under the leadership of Edward
Wood, then Under-Secretary of State at the Colonial Office, was sent
by Parliament to report.

They spent three months touring the islands and hearing depositions
from sometimes rival interests. On his return, Wood warned that 'We
shall be wise if we avoid the mistake of endeavouring to withhold a
concession ultimately inevitable until it has been robbed by delay of
most of its usefulness and of all its grace.' Nonetheless, there were few
concessions as a result of his report. In Trinidad, where Wood had
rejected communal voting for the large Indian population as 'perpet-
uating differences' rather than producing 'a homogenous community',
the franchise was only expanded in 1925 to 6 per cent of the population. To concede more, Wood warned, might deter foreign investors
in the oil and asphalt industry. Across the region, amid continuing
strikes, the miserly concessions merely stimulated the appetite for further reform.[22]

Wood's commission did, however, draw London's attention to
the impoverished state of the colonies. In a debate in the House of
Commons on 4 July 1922, Wood talked about the 'suffering' in the
West Indies due to economic woes. William Ormsby-Gore, then
another Under-Secretary of State who was on the Wood commission,
admitted that the West Indies 'has been neglected by this House'.
There was 'a tremendous amount to do on the question of public
health. The mortality rates are very high ... many of the doctors are
grossly underpaid ... the West Indian people feel that this country has
not done all it might do to help the British West Indies economically.'[23]

In the House of Lords in 1923, Viscount Burnham, chairman of the
West Indian Parliamentary Committee, spoke following a tour there.
He reckoned the region hadn't been mentioned in the House for a
quarter of a century. 'They counted for a great deal in the past', he said,
but 'I do not think we have had reason to be proud of the record of

this country during the last half century in regard to the West Indies. There are blank pages in British history which I think most of us would have liked to have seen filled with the account of how, through all these years, this country had done its best to develop West Indian resources.' Instead, communications were 'deplorable as to shipping, telegraph and news service. Nearly all the news in the West Indian papers was supplied from America.' The construction of the Panama Canal, he warned, had made it a 'necessity of American policy that the West Indian Colonies should pass under the Stars and Stripes'.[24]

At the end of the year he gave a paper about the West Indies to a royal society, entitled 'Our Neglected Empire'. He attacked what he called the 'starvation policy that Great Britain has pursued in her colonies'. In the same vein, in his 1923 essay 'Our Undeveloped Estate', former Colonial Secretary Lord Milner asked: 'Who can contemplate without some feeling of shame the economic decay of the British West Indies, the oldest overseas possessions of the British Crown?'[25]

Once, of course, the sugar islands had been Britain's richest and most valuable possessions. At the beginning of the eighteenth century, the Leeward Islands, Barbados and Jamaica each exported to the United Kingdom more than all the mainland colonies of North America put together. The sugar business, with its attendant racial slavery, led to Britain becoming the world's leading shipper, insurer and banker. It was the foundation stone of the British Empire and British prosperity. But now the West Indies was labelled 'the Empire's darkest slum'.

The key problem, as Wood told the House of Commons, was 'the collapse of the sugar industry'. In Jamaica there were the beginnings of the banana business with 13 million stems shipped in 1923 (though the marketing and transport were all in the hands of a giant US company), and there were hopes for tourism, if only it were possible 'to remedy the undesirable feature of diseased and filthy beggars in the main streets of Kingston'. Emigration was producing remittances from Panama, the United States and elsewhere which were now coming to something like a third of the value of exports. Sixty thousand had left Jamaica in the three years after the war to work in Cuba, but the Jamaica League, a local campaigning group, were unhappy about this. 'Emigration at this rate is ruinous to the best interests of the Colony,' they wrote in a petition to the Colonial Secretary. 'It tends to destroy initiative and to keep the country floundering in the mire of commercial inactivity. And this does not accord with the British spirit of enterprise.'[26]

The islands, for historical reasons hugely over-populated, still depended on sugar, whose price had been in steep decline since the early-nineteenth-century heyday. With free trade in the ascendancy over mercantilism, the West Indies had lost their monopoly of the British market in 1852, and consumers thereafter enjoyed sugar from cheaper rivals or from the huge expansion of beet production. There had been a brief spike in the price during the war, but in 1922 alone the price had fallen by a further 60 per cent.[27]

This meant pathetically low wages for plantation workers. Furthermore, sugar only provided intensive employment for the first half of the year, when the cane was cut and processed. Then, for the rest of the year, half of the field workers and two thirds of the factory workers would be laid off. Those remaining, engaged largely in weeding and manuring, tended to be the lowest paid. Coffee, fruit and tobacco workers were in largely the same situation.[28]

A typical worker would spend a staggering 70 per cent of his income just on food. Widespread malnutrition led to vulnerability to disease. An official report from Trinidad some years later described a situation where every adult over the age of twenty was afflicted by some sort of deficiency disease. This severely shortened lives and led to 'a condition of lethargy [which] pervaded the whole community ... only broken on festive occasions or in times of disorder'.[29]

A medical report from Guiana in 1918 which looked at 3,000 schoolchildren from eighteen schools found 51 per cent suffered from internal parasites, 41 per cent from skin diseases, 31 per cent from malnutrition and 25 per cent from filariasis – pretty much the same rates as in the Gilbert Islands. Infant mortality across the region was running at four times that of Britain.[30]

On 7 August 1923 there was a meeting in London of the Colonial

Advisory Medical and Sanitary Committee. Dr J. Hutson, a public health inspector, was interviewed after a recent visit to Barbados. 'No advance had been made in health or sanitation in the last ten years', Hutson reported, and there was 'little hope of any improvement in the next ten years'. Committee member Dr Prout drew his colleagues' attention to the fact that only 3 per cent of the population had the right to vote. The 'negro population was intelligent and responded very well to education'. Why then, Prout asked, was the franchise so restricted? A Mr Jackson suggested that 'one reason was the poverty of the population and another their lack of interest in politics'. The problem, he went on, was 'the apathy of the governing classes in Barbados, who did not seem to realise that Barbados was the most unhealthy of the West Indian colonies, whereas it should be the most healthy'.[31]

The Jamaica League was a multi-racial organisation which before the war had concentrated on cultural uplift, but which now took much more of an interest in economic issues. Under new leadership, it also became more racially exclusive, advocating 'patriotic sentiment' and Jamaican identity based on the majority African Jamaican population. It urged Jamaicans to buy from their black neighbours rather than the Chinese and Syrian traders who had a near-monopoly on the grocery trade, the bakery, laundry and restaurant businesses. It also wanted to end the island's ruinous dependence on imported food – huge quantities of tinned milk and salt fish, the salt for which actually came from one of Jamaica's island dependencies and was sent to Canada to cure the fish.[32]

In mid-May 1921, the Jamaica League petitioned the Colonial Secretary to do something about starvation on the island. To blame, in part, was the inefficiency of peasant cultivators in the hinterland who 'for want of facilities to transport their produce to market, are forced to eke out a miserable existence, their only recourse being to apply for pauper relief. And thereby each year brings about a larger increase in pauper doles.' In some parishes, they wrote, 'from 45 to 80 per cent of parochial revenue goes to maintain paupers'. They warned that 'even intelligent members of the community are being impregnated with the belief that Jamaica's progress under American domination would be phenomenal'.[33]

The Jamaica League also called for compulsory education for young people over the age of fourteen, so that 'the masses' could learn 'some useful industry that will fit them for life'. In fact, many children did not last to fourteen, and rates of illiteracy were high – 43 per cent in Trinidad, 45 per cent in Jamaica, 60 per cent in Guiana. And what education was given, wrote Trinidadian historian and politician Eric Williams, was done on the cheap (six times more was spent on a child in England) and 'ignored everything West Indian – West Indian history, geography, economics, community organisation and problems'. Children in the Virgin Islands, he wrote, were taught to sing a song about 'tripping through the snow to my grandfather's house'.[34]

A planter giving evidence to a committee of the Trinidad Legislative Council argued that if the 'whole mass' were educated beyond simple reading and writing, 'you will be deliberately ruining the country ... you will never get them to work in the fields'. 'As long as this is an agricultural country, of what use will education be to them if they had it?' another asked. Some improvements would be made, but effectively the interests of the planters were privileged over the rights of the child.[35]

With sugar still king, what was urgently needed, West Indians argued, was massive investment in development from Britain and, crucially, much greater preference for West Indian sugar on the British market, 'to preserve their hitherto undoubted Empire loyalty, and not to leave them adrift or drive them into the arms of the United States of America'. The contrast with the seemingly prosperous condition of the American Caribbean dependencies was stark. One American visitor reported from Kingston, 'there are not lacking Jamaicans who would welcome a change in allegiance to the United States'.[36]

The *Jamaica Gleaner* of 29 September 1923 summed up everyone's expectation, the 'widely prevalent sentiment that the manifest destiny of the British Islands ... is to fall within the sphere of the political influence of the United States'.

37

'Not Yet'

During the year 1900
there came on Ocean Island
the company, the BPC.
Face and look this way universe,
At these clever white skins
Confusing us with the price of phosphate,
And our ancestors of long ago!
How pity ... how pity ... oh!
They misunderstood the value of money!
Our ancestors! Of long, long ago.

Banaban song, recorded in the 1990s[1]

When, at the end of 1923, Colonial Secretary the Duke of Devonshire slapped down Fiji High Commissioner Rodwell's plan to force the Banabans off Ocean Island and hand it over to the British Phosphate Commission (BPC), the action had echoes of his declaration earlier in the year about 'native paramountcy' in Kenya. Devonshire had insisted that on Ocean Island 'Native interests cannot be sacrificed in order to secure any advantage financial or other'. So, it seemed, the Banabans could stay on their island and would not be forced to give up any more land for mining.[2]

But the following year, pressure resumed from the powerful BPC. At the end of November, the head of the business suggested that it would actually be 'to the advantage' of Banabans to vacate the island in order that the whole of the phosphate-bearing land could be mined, as they were now 'living in complete idleness' on Ocean Island. It would be better for them if they were undertaking 'congenial work' on another island. He then approached the CO direct to push again for the 150 new acres.[3]

The commission and the government authorities in Suva both agreed that 'Mr. Grimble would be most competent to deal with this matter ... details should be left to his discretion'. With his long experience and unrivalled knowledge of the language, customs and society of the islanders, indeed his 'kinship' with them through undertaking ceremonial rituals such as his tattooing, made him, they realised, the man the islanders trusted the most.[4]

Arthur Grimble, however, now had his own agenda. For all his later oft-expressed feelings of romantic affection for the islands and their people, he was desperate to leave. He had been serving in the Gilbert and Ellice Islands for thirteen years and had for a long time felt he was due a promotion to somewhere less remote, more prestigious and more family-friendly. He had worked out that in the last ten years, he had seen his children for only nine months. He was also ill with chronic dysentery and suffering from what he called 'mental and metaphysical starvation'. If he could pull off a deal with the Banabans, he hoped he might be rewarded with a better position. Furthermore, he knew what had happened to previous officials who had sided with the islanders against the phosphate business. He did not fancy the Falkland Islands. In short, he was not going to allow Banaban interests to jeopardise his career.[5]

Arriving as Resident Commissioner in late 1925, bearing an offer of £150 an acre with a royalty of 10½d per ton, he got to work cajoling and intriguing. He met Banabans individually and in small groups.

He exploited family rivalries and disputes over issues like fishing rights to try to build up a 'party', as he put it, in favour of selling. His initial approach at mass meetings to discuss the issue was designed to appeal to the islanders' long-held trust of their Resident Commissioner – he himself believed the deal to be fair, he said, and he knew what was best for them. He then appealed to their imperial loyalty: the empire, he said, was 'holding out its hands to them, asking to be fed'.[6]

He did make some converts, but the majority of the islanders resisted his efforts, pointing out that the designated 150 acres were the most fertile part of the island, essential for their continued occupation of their ancestral home, and that they had been promised by Eliot in 1913 that no more land would be taken and that they would not be forced to leave. If they wanted the phosphate so badly, Rotan Tito, the islanders' leader, said, they should pay £5,000 an acre. It was effectively a refusal to sell. (In fact, hearing of this price, Rodwell's successor as High Commissioner in Fiji, Sir Eyre Hutson, was not that taken aback. He worked out that the land that had been purchased at about £60 an acre had produced between £37,500 and £48,000 per acre.)[7]

Grimble decided that a more aggressive approach was needed. 'It remains only to work upon their fears a little more than I have done up to date,' he wrote in his diary. If they refused to sell, he told the Banabans, the BPC would leave the island, which would see the loss of their doctor, school, hospital and store. But the response was: 'We are willing to suffer all these things. All we want is to be in peace with our land.' Grimble then wrote an infamous letter. This came to light many years later, long after his death, when in the 1970s the Banabans unsuccessfully sued the British government and the BPC: the government for breach of trust, the BPC for failing to keep its promise to replant the land. 'You understand that the Resident Commissioner cannot again discuss with you at present as you have shamed his Important Chief [George V],' the letter begins, 'but I will put my views as from your longstanding friend Mr. Grimble who is truly your father.'

The choice was, he wrote, 'LIFE OR DEATH'. If they signed the agreement, 'POINTS FOR LIFE' included 'your offence in shaming the Important Chief will be forgiven and you will not be punished'. 'POINTS FOR DEATH': 'If you do not sign the agreement, do you think your lands will not go? Do not be blind. Your land will be compulsorily acquired for the Empire.' He ended with: 'because of my sympathy for you I ask you to consider what I have said now that the day has come when you must choose LIFE OR DEATH. There is nothing more to say. If you choose suicide then I am very sorry for you but what more can I do for you as I have done all I can. I am your loving friend and father, Arthur Grimble.'[8]

He added a P.S.: 'If everyone signs the agreement, the Banabans will not be punished for shaming the Important Chief and their serious misconduct will be forgiven. If the agreement is not signed consideration will be given to punishing the Banabans. And the destruction of Buakonikai village also [will be] considered to make room for mining if there is no agreement.'

The judge in the case in 1977, although finding in favour of the British government on the grounds that the original mining deal had been with a private company, was critical of breaches of governmental obligations, and of Grimble in particular, who 'had compromised himself with a disgracefully threatening letter about destroying the village and unspecified punishments if they did not agree to sell their land'. Grimble may have been ill and run-down at the time, the judge conceded, but 'even so, with every allowance, it is impossible to read that letter without a sense of outrage'.[9]

The letter was, of course, traumatic for the Banabans. They had long loathed the company, but, as a Banaban descendant wrote, 'the betrayal of one who they had considered "kin" was devastating'. They had trusted Grimble and, more widely, the empire. He betrayed that trust.

Meanwhile, pressure had been building on the Colonial Office from the BPC and from the New Zealand and Australian governments. In 1928 legislation was passed that allowed for compulsory land purchase if no agreement could be reached with its owners, 'provided the Resident Commissioner was satisfied as to the fairness of the deal'. Land rights on the island were reduced to surface, mineral rights now held by the Crown. Devonshire's promise of only five years earlier was in the bin. Rotan Tito sent Grimble a bag of gold for him to recruit and pay for a lawyer; Grimble turned him down and signed the compulsory purchase order.[10]

Shortly afterwards, in another attempt to be moved elsewhere, Grimble reported to his superiors that the 'General opinion of Banabans is that I am their enemy and have deliberately failed to represent their interests.' (Modern-day Banabans often still name their dogs Kirimbi (Grimble) – a severe insult.)[11]

Under the new arrangement, the Banabans got a worse deal than had previously been on offer, and the destruction of their island continued apace. Grimble finally left in 1933 to become Administrator in St Vincent, then Governor of the Seychelles three years later. He was knighted in 1938. From 1942 to his retirement in 1948 he was Governor of the Windward Islands. In 1956 a film, *Pacific Destiny*, was made from material from his highly successful romantic books about the Gilbert Islands, with Grimble played by Denholm Elliott. Arthur Grimble died the same year, his reputation as one of the 'nicest colonial administrators in history' still, for now, intact.

With Japan entering the Second World War, demolition gangs wrecked the key mining installations, and almost all of the Europeans departed. The Banabans were left there under the theory that as fellow 'Asiatics' they would be treated kindly by the Japanese. But under Japanese occupation a third of the islanders died of disease, starvation, or were simply murdered – 160 were shot or beheaded, five died from flogging. Others were shipped off as forced labourers elsewhere.[12]

At the end of the war, a thousand or so Banabans were rounded up from Tarawa and other islands and shipped to Rabi Island in the Fuji archipelago, 1,600 miles away from Ocean Island. It had been purchased three years before from Lever Brothers for £25,000 from the Banabans' fund. Nine times the size of Ocean Island, it was heavily forested and five times as wet – quite unlike their home. They hoped the move would be temporary. Rotan Tito told an interviewer: 'I did not want to stay. Our people wanted to return to Ocean Island. But they didn't agree to this.' The phosphate concern on Ocean Island now had what it had always wanted, free rein. In 1947 it took over another 600 acres, pretty much all that was left. The English adviser employed by the Banabans was told to keep away from the negotiations and they got a poor deal.[13]

In 1977 a documentary, *Go Tell it to the Judge*, was broadcast covering the story of the island and the recently completed legal action brought by the islanders. Rotan Tito is seen, aged seventy-six and in poor health, making the journey to London to present their case. They also filmed him returning on a visit to Ocean Island. Everywhere we see a desiccated moonscape of white dust and rock. It is a scene of extractive colonialism at its most literal. Tito stands in one area of wreckage showing where the Buakonikai village he was born in, and its children's playground, once stood.

There's an interview with a BPC worker, a white Australian. He points to an area of rocky, dusty wasteland and says that even in the 1950s it had been covered with vegetation, including coconuts, mangos and other tropical fruits. 'It's sad to see the destruction of trees, of course,' he tells the interviewer, 'but in this place there is a great benefit to Australia and New Zealand.'

Rotan Tito's grandson, Tomas Teai, secretary of the Banaban Council, is there too. He is asked why his people want to return to Ocean Island, where nearly all the workers have respiratory problems due to the clouds of white dust, and all water has to be imported. 'We lived here before the BPC, we had no problems,' the young man replies. 'If it goes up, we will revert to our old system. Our people thrived on the island ... All these ideas of difficulties are all English. You put a native on Ocean Island and he will survive.'

'I think the BPC are the greatest exploiters of Banaban people,' he

ends. 'We have been ill-treated by them since 1900 . . . we were uneducated then . . . It's just sheer exploitation . . . I can't understand how
people can do such a thing to another human being.'

After leaving Nigeria, with 'his nerves', according to the Prince of
Wales, 'all gone to pieces', Hugh Clifford had an extended leave of six
months in England before voyaging out to take over the governorship
of Ceylon. It was the eve of his sixtieth birthday and he had served
forty years in the tropics. After two years there, where he heartily
disliked the relatively advanced constitution, he was at last granted
his much-requested appointment. He was going back to Malaya after
twenty-three years away, returning to the people, he said, 'I love best
in the world'.[14]

On arrival, he toured the country 'and was welcomed as a hero, an
almost mythical figure from the dim past'. He made a huge impression
by replying to speeches of welcome in fluent, and often poetic Malay.
He looked up old friends from his youth. A senior Raja who had been
a friend when they were both young men greeted him warmly, pronouncing that Sir Hugh would 'soothe and cure all ills'. In Singapore,
he enlivened the King's Birthday Ball by organising an impromptu
beauty contest. Clifford returned to his old haunts, even visiting the
old wooden residency he had built in Kuala Lipis. As he sat there, he
wrote, 'Almost am I cheated into the belief that the intervening years
are an illusion and that I am once again the substantive Resident of
Pahang. Almost I wish that indeed were so.'[15]

Soon after, he wrote to the Secretary of State: 'My return to Malaya
has been, and still is, to me the most wonderful thing that has ever
befallen me in the course of a long life.' He was immediately struck by
the general prosperity – key exports rubber and tin were enjoying high
prices. But the standard of living of the government officers was, he
said, 'quite undesirably extravagant'. Furthermore, they were spending
too much time on 'sport and amusement' among themselves. Cadets
were arriving and being posted to the towns where they were acquiring
expensive habits and were denied the 'opportunity of mastering the

vernacular or of acquiring the sort of intimate knowledge of the people which is, in my opinion, essential for a Civil Servant in British Malaya'. One of his first acts was to post the cadets away to rural districts, so that they could learn 'something of the manners, customs and characteristics of the indigenous population'.[16]

Before his arrival there had been a tug-of-war between those who wanted a more centralised administration, and greater acknowledgement of the multi-racial make-up of most of the peninsula, and those who warned that this would reduce the independence, however nominal, of the rulers of the Malay States. Clifford made his position clear: the states must remain Malayo-Muslim monarchies. 'Britain had neither the mandate nor the desire to make them anything else,' he told the Federal Council. 'Democratic and socialist theories and doctrines were spreading like infection', but any form of 'democratic or popular government' was 'inapplicable to the circumstances of these States' and 'would lead to submersion of the indigenous population ... by folk of other races'. This would, he considered, be a betrayal of trust.[17]

In mid-1928 there were rumours that he was in line for a peerage. Unsurprisingly, he put it about that he wanted to be Lord Clifford of Malaya.

But around this time he started suffering, once more, from depression and poor mental health. A number of reasons for this have been suggested. It might have been syphilis or heatstroke, which can leave permanent neurological complications. There were the tragic losses in his family. The most obvious one, which had already been drawn to his attention, was a lifetime of workaholism and little sleep. There was also frustration in his job – as in Ceylon, he found his powers as Governor reduced. The days of noblesse oblige were over. Furthermore, as Governor, the intimate contacts with Malays were no longer possible. It was the world not of his early fiction but of Maugham's, where non-Europeans, if they appear at all, are only waiters or servants.

There's also a suggestion that his return to Malaya, after an initial period of euphoria, was a disturbing disappointment. It was not the Malaya of his youth; the ground had shifted under his feet. He spoke about the threat to Malays of 'absorption and denationalization' and the 'tremendous ordeal' to which they had been subjected by their material progress, and by the 'disturbing and disintegrating effect of close association with alien races'. Perhaps there was a return of the nagging doubts he had always had – and which he expressed in his fiction – that the imperial mission to which he had dedicated his life was destroying too much that was precious.[18]

A lot of the time he was fine. Then he would have attacks that led to bouts of impatience and irascibility, combined with sleep-walking. Stories started circulating about behaviour inappropriate for a man of his age and rank. When an aeroplane he was travelling in came down in Singapore harbour, he recklessly ran up and down the wings to keep it from capsizing. He would instruct his staff to segregate the better-looking young women from the others at Government House parties and then present them all with signed photographs of himself. There are stories of far more eccentric behaviour, some of which undoubtedly have a basis in fact. At times there were bouts of insanity that meant he had to be kept from public view. Later, his Colonial Secretary was reproached by the CO for not reporting Clifford's aberrations earlier.[19]

In mid-1929 he announced he was taking early leave. The reason given was his wife's health. In fact, she was fine. He was not.

Back in England, his doctors recommended complete rest. Again, some of the time he was in good health. He even learned to fly – quite an achievement for a man his age. But then he deteriorated. It was reported that he would sometimes put on Malay dress and sit on the steps of the Colonial Office, giving colleagues the benefit of his advice on the imperial issues of the day. His family transferred him to a private nursing home in west London.[20]

There he remained, not even reading, let alone writing. After a while it became too distressing for Lady Clifford to visit him. He died on 18 December 1941, at the very moment when his beloved yet fatally divided Malaya was being overrun by Japanese invaders.

*

E. M. Forster's *A Passage to India*, completed at the end of 1923, was published in mid-1924 to critical and commercial success. The *New York Times* called it 'one of the saddest, keenest, most beautifully written novels of the time'. It did particularly well in the United States, selling over 50,000 copies by the end of the year. Forster cynically put this down to the novel being about 'the difficulties of the English in India. Feeling that they would have had no difficulties in India themselves . . . the more they read it the better it made them feel.'[21]

In the novel, Anglo-Indians, with very few exceptions, are portrayed as narrow-minded bigots. (When he was criticised for being unfair, Forster conceded that they were based on pre-war types, but also responded, 'I loathe them and should have been more honest to say so. Honesty and fairness are so different.') Forster suggests that the Anglo-Indian culture corrupted even previously tolerant people. One of the central characters is the city magistrate. 'I am out here to work, mind, to hold this wretched country by force,' he declares. 'I'm not a missionary or a Labour member or a vague sentimental sympathetic literary man. I'm just a servant of the Government . . . We're not pleasant in India, and we don't intend to be pleasant. We've something more important to do.' His newly arrived mother, who notices he has changed much for the worse since being in India, thinks to herself: 'One touch of regret – not the canny substitute but the true regret from the heart – would have made him a different man, and the British Empire a different institution.'[22]

Forster had always been furious with British domestic ignorance about India, and indeed the empire as a whole. Even after two centuries of connection, he wrote, 'we in England know next to nothing about Indian cultures. Our ignorance is disgraceful and is indeed an indictment of our Empire.' In *A Passage to India*, British officials have no interest in getting to know Indians, or Indian art, literature or culture. In fact their ignorance is a badge of honour, 'and they lost no opportunity of proclaiming it to one another'. Furthermore, the Europeans live apart, their enclave sharing 'nothing with the city except the overarching sky'. They refuse to have Indians in their club, even as guests. The

one effort by officials at 'mixing' – a 'Bridge Party' – ends in offence
and misunderstandings.[23]

But there is something defensive and fearful about this ignorant
apartness. They realise, Forster wrote, that they are 'thousands of miles
away from any scenery that they understood'.[24]

Jawaharlal Nehru might have thought that 'the magic moment had
passed' after the collapse of non-cooperation, but it had had a massive
and lasting impact on the British in India. The Prince of Wales had
left after his often successfully boycotted tour with a deep feeling of
foreboding. He reported that having talked to British soldiers, civil
service and police, he had encountered everywhere a feeling of general
demoralisation. 'They one and all say the same thing,' he wrote, 'they
won't let their sons come out here to earn their living in the Indian
Army, Indian Civil Service ... The reason for this is that India is no
longer a place for a white man to live in.'[25]

Indeed, expatriate recruitment to the all-India services had become
very difficult. Of the eighty-six candidates for examinations in 1922
to join the Indian Civil Service, only twenty-six were British, of
whom three were taken on against thirteen Indians. At the same time,
between 1919 and 1923, one in six British ICS officials opted to take
early retirement on a reduced pension.[26]

To blame, in Mountbatten's opinion, was Montagu and his reforms,
which, he reported, had pleased 'neither the natives nor the British and
the only tangible result is an enormous loss of British prestige, which
grows worse with every succeeding day'. It was 'hardly safe to mention
Montagu's name to any of our officials ... as he has all but lost India for
us!' the Prince wrote to the Queen. 'Having once given in & pandered
to the natives as E.M. has done, they naturally want more which they
can't possibly have so long as we maintain the policy of governing &
running India! The result is a state of hopeless unrest & we are really
sitting on the top of a volcano.'[27]

During the House of Commons debate on 14 February 1922 attacking Montagu for his censure of General Dyer – which led indirectly
to Montagu's dismissal – another cause for the demoralisation was

expressed by a Conservative MP: 'the officials in India are suffering from the fact that they feel that their future is uncertain, and they do not believe that if they get into trouble the Government will stand behind them'. Racial unity was under threat.[28]

In the same debate, a Liberal MP, Joseph Kenworthy, turned this on its head: 'We Anglo-Saxons have a universal habit, very praiseworthy, of considering ourselves superior to all other races on the face of the earth. Such a feeling has its uses, but when we show that feeling to others it becomes very bad manners. I believe that in recent years the universal exposure of that feeling of superiority has worked us great ill in the East.' 'The War has quickened the self-respect of the Indian people,' he continued, 'and they object, not unnaturally, to this exhibition of race superiority on the part of ourselves, when it is too obvious and thrust into their faces.'[29]

Forster wrote about this when he was on his post-war trip to India. 'Here is the Sepoy, back from France, failing to see why the Tommy should have servants and punkahs when he has none. And here is the European chauffeur who drives through the streets shouting at the pedestrians and scattering them; the looks of hatred they cast back at him show how deep the trouble goes.'[30]

'We have to treat these races as fellow subjects of the King and with much greater courtesy and consideration in the future,' Kenworthy urged. 'I believe an example in that direction has been set from the top in India. It is urgently necessary that this matter should be taken in hand or we shall not have trouble in India alone, but in Egypt, Iraq, in our African Colonies, and everywhere else where there are so-called subject races.'[31]

Instructions 'from the top' had indeed gone out in India. On his second trip in 1921–2, Forster reported that 'English manners out here have improved wonderfully in the last eight years.' Most noteworthy was when he revisited Rupert Smith, now a collector in Agra, who, pre-war, had been so spectacularly impolite to, and about, Indians. Now Forster found him much less rude to his servants and subordinates, and Smith even had an Indian friend staying in his house. (On the publication of *A Passage to India*, Smith wrote Forster a 'violent letter' and broke off their friendship for thirty years.)[32]

In 1922, *Nation and Athenaeum* magazine published an article by Forster titled 'Too Late in India'. It began with a story he had been told by Masood. Ten years earlier, the Indian was sleeping in a railway compartment when an Englishman entered and ordered him out. Now, when Masood went into a compartment with an Englishman in occupation, the latter leapt up and offered him his berth, saying, 'Take it, man ... this is your country, not mine.' Masood, recounted Forster, remarked grimly, 'Don't do this sort of thing, please. We don't appreciate it any more than the old sort. We know you have been told you must do it.'

This 'hasty and ungraceful change of position' was, post-war, Forster said, 'something of a stampede'. It was not just down to orders, he argued. For one thing, post-Dyer, officials could not rely on their superiors to back them up if 'they are rude or overbearing'. Some, he suggested, were 'frightened'; others had undergone a genuine change of heart, in part because during the war 'the Indian has proved himself a man'.

It was also 'a recognition, though a muddle-headed one, of past mistakes'. 'The decent Anglo-Indian of to-day', Forster wrote, 'realizes that the great blunder of the past is neither political nor economic nor educational, but social; that he is associated with a system that supported rudeness in railway carriages, and is paying the penalty.'

He ended his article recalling the woman he had met on the boat out eight years before, who had told him: '"Never forget that you're superior to every native in India except the Rajas, and they're on an equality."' She 'is now a silent, if not an extinct, species', Forster wrote. 'But she has lived her life, and she has done her work ... never in history did ill-breeding contribute so much towards the dissolution of an Empire.' The damage had been done. It was too late to make amends.

In a letter to a friend while in India post-war, Forster remarked that the tone of Anglo-Indian voices was now one of 'tragic resignation'. In 'Too Late?', he described this new mood as 'wistful melancholy ...

"Yes, it's all up with us" is their attitude. "Sooner or later the Indians will tell us to go. I hope they'll tell us nicely. I expect they will."[33]

George Orwell's writings about the Burmese part of the Indian Empire, in *Burmese Days* and *The Road to Wigan Pier*, share some of Forster's 'end-of-days' feel, but with an interesting difference. Of course, Orwell had a very contrasting imperial role, not as an observer but as an active enforcer with the conflicting feelings that situation caused him. He is also a very different writer, political and polemical where Forster is literary and nuanced. In *Burmese Days*, the dreadful Mrs Lackersteen pronounces that 'Young men will not come out here any longer to work all their lives for insults and ingratitude. We shall just go ... And then, what a lesson that will teach them!' The policeman Westfield says, 'time we cleared out of it ... the best thing we can do is to shut up shop and let 'em stew in their own juice'.[34]

But alongside the spite, there is elsewhere a contrasting, somewhat Clifford-like ambivalence and regret. Even the thickest-skinned Anglo-Indian, Orwell wrote in *The Road to Wigan Pier*, was aware of what Orwell called the 'unjustifiable tyranny' of imperial rule. The majority were 'not nearly so complacent about their position as people in England believe. From the most unexpected people, from gin-pickled old scoundrels high up in Government service, I have heard some such remark as: "Of course we've no right to be in this blasted country at all" ... The truth is that no modern man, in his heart of hearts, believes that it is right to invade a foreign country and hold the population down by force.'[35]

After Amritsar, Forster wrote to his friend Malcolm Darling that 'it seems improbable that a rule which now rests avowedly upon force can endure'. Everyone knew it was a breaking point. In *A Passage to India* there are oblique references to Amritsar – mention of the 'crawling order'; the subsequent new-found but temporary unity between Hindus and Muslims and the way the Anglo-Indian community closes ranks and retreats into a bubble of racial mistrust after the supposed attack in the Marabar caves by an Indian, Aziz, on a British woman,

Adela. There are also echoes of the rhetoric of the Khilafat movement and of Gandhi's and Nehru's speeches on being imprisoned. But Forster's interest as ever is in the personal rather than the political, in particular in the possibility of true transcultural friendship and understanding. This is played out through the relationship of Dr Aziz and Fielding, an English teacher.[36]

Nehru in his autobiography quoted Forster on relations between the British and Indians: 'every Englishman in India feels and behaves, and rightly, as if he was a member of an army of occupation, and it is quite impossible for natural and unrestrained relations between the two races to grow under these circumstances'. Elsewhere Forster wrote that if the British, of all ranks, had 'taken their stand upon a common humanity instead of the pedestal of race – then foundations of a democratic Empire might have been well and truly laid'.[37]

'When I began the book,' Forster said of *A Passage to India*, 'I thought of it as a little bridge of sympathy between East and West ... this conception has had to go, my sense of truth forbids me anything so comfortable.' Indeed, the novel demonstrates that all the foundations of the empire – white supremacy, the platonic idea of a ruling elite, technical and military superiority, even 'trusteeship' – were based on an idea of British superiority that could not help but insult and irremediably divide. In mid-1922, Forster wrote that he hoped unrest in Egypt and elsewhere would soon mean that 'the whole bloody empire was over'.[38]

Initially, Aziz and Fielding become 'best friends', 'brothers'. When Aziz is wrongfully arrested, Fielding is the one European who takes his side, despite huge pressure from the Anglo-Indians. But Aziz's experience turns him from eager-to-please to deeply resentful. 'We wanted to know you ten years back,' Aziz tells Fielding, 'now it's too late.' There are small and large misunderstandings between them – 'a pause in the wrong place, an intonation misunderstood, and a whole conversation went awry'. When they disagreed, 'something racial intruded – not bitterly, but inevitably'. Soon Aziz feels a 'tragic coolness between himself and his English friend'.[39]

Fielding, for his part, originally loves India, and plans to live out his life there. But he returns to Europe for a break and visits Venice, where he finds a 'civilization that has escaped muddle', a place where, unlike India, everything stood in 'the right place ... He had forgotten the beauty of form among idol temples and lumpy hills.'[40]

Back in India, he visits Aziz and a major misunderstanding is cleared up. But Aziz tells him that 'My heart is for my own people hencefor-ward ... I wish no Englishman or woman to be my friend.' Aziz is adamant that the British will be forced to depart. 'Until England is in difficulties we keep silent,' he presciently tells Fielding, 'but in the next European war – aha, aha! Then is our time.'[41]

The novel ends with the two men on horseback, 'wrangling about politics'. Fielding tells Aziz that without the British, Indians would 'go to seed', and that religious divisions would overwhelm the country. 'We may hate one another,' Aziz replies, 'but we hate you most ... we shall get rid of you, yes, we shall drive every blasted Englishman into the sea, and then,' he says, 'half kissing him', 'and then you and I shall be friends.'

'Why can't we be friends now?' Fielding asks, holding him affection-ately. 'It's what I want. It's what you want.'

But, Forster writes, 'the horses didn't want it – they swerved apart; the earth didn't want it, sending up rocks through which the riders must pass single-file; the temples, the tank, the jail, the palace, the birds, the carrion ... they said in their hundred voices, "No, not yet."'

At the end of the second week of October 1923, the silk-hat and morning-coat-attired delegates to the Imperial Conference dispersed to their distant territories across the globe. Few can have felt reassured about the future of the empire. In the same month, a deal was done between Britain and Belgium that saw the Sultan of Rwanda's land handed over to the latter, reducing the British Empire by some 2,100 square miles. A few months later, in keeping with an earlier agreement with Italy to help persuade them to join the war on the Allied side,

Jubaland, a small, desolate strip of stone and scrub in the north of Kenya, became part of Italian Somaliland – Mussolini's first imperial bauble.

Very soon, of course, the trickle became a flood.

Acknowledgements

I am grateful, first and foremost, for all the hard work and expert local guidance provided by additional researchers around the world: Sarah Dunbar at Auckland University Archive, home of the papers of the Western Pacific High Commission; Lorraine Clarke in the Battye Library, Perth, in the archive on Group Settlement; Thomas Bouril in the library of Syracuse University, New York State; Nile Painter in the National Archives, London; Kareithi Kimani and Peterson Kithuka at the Kenya National Archives, Nairobi; Ayo Ojebode and the brilliant and very generous Dr David Olayinka Ajayi in the Nigerian National Archives, Ibadan.

Thanks also to all the archivists who have gone beyond the call of duty to offer assistance, in particular: Stephen Innes, Auckland University Library; Stewart Gillies, British Library; Trish Hayes, BBC Written Archive; Jeri Tatian, State Library of Western Australia; Alison Metcalfe, National Library of Scotland; Saw Nan New, director of the National Archives Department in Nay Pyi Taw, Myanmar; Janelle Duke, Trinidad National Archives; Nicola O'Toole and Sam Lindley, Bodleian Weston Library, Oxford; Sarah Walpole, Royal Anthropological Institute, London.

I also owe a debt of thanks to Ngayu Thairu and Aniz Damani for introductions in Kenya; Paul Swain for translating Chinese-language sources and much else; Zarina Patel for help with her grandfather Jeevanjee's story; Gus Casely-Hayford for support and encouragement with the writing about his family; Anna Livia Cullinan, Dr Nicholas Farrelly, Mish Khan, Alice Dawkins and Dr Nick Cheeseman for welcome help with Myanmar;

Mistica Young and her family in Sri Lanka; Sir Richard Lambert and Liam Halligan for expert help with the economics and Dr Katie Lloyd for checking the medical material. All mistakes remain, of course, my own.

As ever, huge thanks to Professor Barbara Bush, who has been a brilliant sounding board and source of expert guidance throughout the many years of this project. I would also like to acknowledge my debt to my friend the late Ben Shephard, who gave great assistance at the beginning, and is very much missed.

I'm grateful to other friends who have read and meticulously commented on earlier drafts, in particular Dan Hillman and Christy Swords.

I would also like to acknowledge my debt to the many scholars who have shown me the way to the most important primary sources while providing insight and interpretation.

I'm grateful to Joanne Paul and Shaun McGrath for help with their respective native countries, Canada and New Zealand. Thanks also to my mum, Sheila, sister Caroline and to Emilia Catlin, Upasna Mishra, Izzie Cartledge, Shaanvir Kaur Johal, Piers Brendon and Mark Painter for all their help and support; also to genius Mike Trow for his generous photos.

Thanks go to expert freelancers: copyeditor Dan Balado and proofreader Steve Gove. I've been lucky once more to have the services of excellent cartographer Martin Brown. It's been a pleasure to work with Nithya Rae, Nico Taylor, Jess Gulliver, Linda Silverman and all at Abacus Books in London as well as Clive Priddle, Kiyo Saso and all at PublicAffairs in New York. As ever, I'm hugely indebted to my brilliant agent Julian Alexander at The Soho Agency, and especially grateful to my editor Richard Beswick for his heroic patience and matchless expertise.

Many thanks and lots of love also to my treasured friendship group of fellow writers/historians, who have over many years provided a vital space for off-loading, moaning and mutual encouragement, debate, fun and gossip. You know who you are.

I'm hoping that one day my beloved immediate family – Hannah, Milly, Tom and Ollie – will forgive me for how extremely long this book has taken to research and write, and how all-consuming it's been. I don't deserve you.

Index